FOR REFERENCE
Do Not Take
From This Room

THE
ENCYCLOPEDIA OF
VIOLENCE

THE ENCYCLOPEDIA OF VIOLENCE

Origins, Attitudes, Consequences

Margaret DiCanio, Ph.D.

Facts On File 1993

The Encyclopedia of Violence:
Origins, Attitudes, Consequences

Facts On File, Inc.
460 Park Avenue South
New York NY 10016
USA

Library of Congress Cataloging-in-Publication Data
DiCanio, Margaret.
   The encyclopedia of violence : origins, attitudes, consequences /
by Margaret DiCanio.
        p.   cm.
   Includes bibliographical references and index.
   ISBN 0-8160-2332-8
   1. Violence—Encyclopedias.   I. Title.
HM291.D484   1993
303.6′03—dc20   92-39721
A British CIP catalogue record for this book is available from the British Library.

Facts On File books are available at special discounts when purchased in bulk quantities for businesses, associations, institutions or sales promotions. Please call our Special Sales Department in New York at 212/683-2244 or dial 800/322-8755.

Jacket design by Mark Safran
Composition by the Maple-Vail Book Manufacturing Group
Manufactured by R. R. Donnelley & Sons
Printed in the United States of America

10 9 8 7 6 5 4 3 2 1

This book is printed on acid-free paper.

CONTENTS

ACKNOWLEDGMENTS

Special thanks to Elizabeth Frost Knappman, my agent, for suggesting violence as a topic. My daughter Teddi DiCanio helped in numerous ways, not the least of which involved recovering files my computer discarded for mysterious reasons. She and the busy staff at Abbot Public Library are doubtless glad to see an end to helping me locate data on violence. The staffs at several libraries in Boston and on the North Shore were also a great help, as were staff members who answered questions on the 800 line of the Department of Justice Statistics.

Many organizations that are engaged in trying to ameliorate violence graciously sent huge quantities of information, only a fraction of which could be included in the resources section of the appendixes. Many thanks for moral support and technical advice from Lieutenant Richard Kelly of Interpol and the Massachusetts State Police and from Terri Landwehr, Administrator of the Division of Adult Institutions of the Wisconsin Department of Corrections, and her staff.

INTRODUCTION

There is no grand, unified theory of violence. This book, *The Encyclopedia of Violence,* is an album of snapshots of the places where violence enters everyday life in late 20th-century America as well as a taxonomy of some of the many varieties of violence.

Most kinds of violence are treated as if they were unrelated. But they all share three characteristics: They are committed mostly by males; they are all political at the most elemental level, since by definition violence involves the exercise of power by one person or group of people over another; and they are all personal, in that the victims are harmed in their persons, physically and psychologically.

Although not usually identified as such, violence is the world's most serious health problem. It maims and kills people daily; it interrupts and interferes with their everyday lives by robbing them of loved ones, homes, food, medical care, education or jobs, and too often the opportunity to grow up. The riots in Los Angeles and other cities during 1992 were dramatic examples of the fear and misery inflicted by violence on ordinary people who are just trying to live their lives as best they can.

In contrast to residents of some inner-city communities, many citizens in the United States live in communities where violence is uncommon. They do not face the chance of being caught in a drive-by shooting every time they leave home. Nevertheless, exposure to violence in the nightly news and in entertainment fare has routinized it and created a sense that violence can happen to anyone.

This fear has led to a narrowing of daily options. Burglar locks, window bars, car alarms, downtowns empty after dark and shops where customers are buzzed in only after being scrutinized from inside have become commonplace. Violence not only threatens everyday freedom of movement, it adds enormous expenditures of time and money for security measures to the ordinary expenses of daily living and doing business. Understanding violence is in everyone's best interest, yet it receives scant political and scholarly attention.

The Encyclopedia of Violence attempts to relate the various kinds of everyday violence, to reconceive them as a single, if complex, threat to the quality of everyday life and to life itself. As its subtitle suggests, it seeks to find the social and psychological origins or generators of violent behavior, the cultural and social attitudes that sustain it as a prominent feature of contemporary life, and the consequences it has on our persons, our thinking and our institutions.

Conventionally, wife abuse is treated separately from child abuse; the logistics of emergency rooms' "battle-zone medicine" is not discussed in relation to the logistics of prisons' struggle to cope with inmates who need psychotherapy, psychiatric treatment or medication rather than incarceration. Executives who commit corporate crime are seldom compared to street thugs who all together could not do as much damage as a few Wall Street insiders or corporate officers.

Much of the kind of everyday violence described in *The Encyclopedia of Violence* is common around the world, but the book focuses mostly on the United States and, to a lesser extent, Canada. The narrowed scope makes it possible to keep the book a reasonable length.

The United States is often depicted as one of the most violent societies in the world. There is no question that it is violent, but it has plenty of company. In part America's violent public image can be attributed to the existence of a free press and to official efforts to keep track of crime and violence. A high level of violence is recorded and reported in the United States, and official efforts are made to determine the level of unreported violence.

In many countries with apparently low rates of violence, there exists much unreported and unacknowledged violence, some of it government-sponsored. While a significant amount of political activity goes on behind closed doors in the United States, there is no hint that the nation has a secret police or officially sponsored death squads.

Violence is quick and dramatic, an attention-getter that is over in a few minutes, hours, or days. Recovery from violence, on the other hand, is slow, boring, and painful. It may take years or be impossible. For too many, the high of a violent encounter is perceived as heroic and the complaints of victims as whining.

A factor that contributes both to an escalation of America's violence and to its violent image is a constant stream of violent American-made television programs, movies, and videos that are distributed within the nation and throughout the world. Opinions differ about whether such media reflect the nation's taste or merely a small cadre of mostly male media executives' idea of the nation's taste. Foreign observers point to America's frontier past as evidence of a long and violent history.

CONFLICTING PERSPECTIVES

Some of the fragmentation in violence research is due to differences in ideology and world view. Franklin Zimring and Gordon Hawkins in their 1987 book *The Citizen's Guide to Gun Control* describe one distinct cleavage found among those who advise on policies dealing with crime. With some notable exceptions, the differences can be distinguished as conservative or liberal, that is, those who think of crime as sin or evil and those who think of it as social pathology.

The conservative "original sin" camp views criminals as a class apart, a different kind of human being. Criminologist James Q. Wilson separates "the wicked" and "the innocent." J. Edgar Hoover characterized the true criminal as "nearer to the beast than others of us."

Those who regard crime as a product of social conditions reject any division into the law-abiding and the lawless. They cite numerous studies of self-reported crime as evidence of criminal behavior throughout all strata of American society. Criminologists Edwin Sutherland and Donald Cressey in their 1974 textbook *Principles of Criminology* state that "almost all persons have at some time deliberately committed crimes, often of a serious nature." They argue that a combination of adverse social conditions and highly selective operations of law enforcement agencies creates an illusion that there is a "criminal class."

Conservatives speak of "wars against crime" and "fighting crime," while liberals speak of "a cure for crime." Crime, in the liberals' view, can be reduced only by public policies that address fundamental, structural social problems, which are manifested in deteriorated cities, broken families and inadequate education.

Conservatives argue against gun control by asserting that few if any lives would be saved, since the criminal would simply select other weapons. Liberals argue in favor of gun control by focusing on the circumstances surrounding homicide rather than on wickedness in the murderer.

Conservatives and liberals appear to switch position in connection with corporate, so-called white-collar, crime. Conservatives question whether white-collar crime is really crime and not just a venial violation of social norms. Liberals attack the concept of "white-collar" as trivializing conduct based on the status of the actor. They complain that white-collar offenders are accorded more benign treatment.

Unfortunately, the opposing sides confuse the public and make solutions difficult. Liberals find it hard to believe that there can be many people who think only in violent, criminal terms. They conceive of violence as a symptom of something else without understanding that, for some, violence is an end in itself. The conservatives' "us against them" stance makes it difficult for them to recognize that in deteriorating social circumstances, the violent (the truly evil, in their terms) may draw others into their orbit, out of socially generated anger or despair.

The conservative perspective, and a "war on crime"—mostly drugs—prevailed during the 1980s. In many states, prison construction became the largest budget item.

COUNTING HEADS AND BUILDING PRISONS

An area where opinions seem even more at odds than they are about the nature of violence involves the amount of crime that exists in the United States. While some criminologists express concern about a rising level of violence, others insist that fears are exaggerated and blame politicians and the media for the public's misperception. Some politicians use crime as a lever to get into office, but once there they tend to minimize crime to suggest that they have it under control.

Experts disagree about whether the incidence of crime is going up or down. No one really knows. During the 1980s, FBI tallies of violent crime arrests indicated a downturn until the mid-1980s, when violent crime arrests began to increase once again. The annual Victimization Survey of unreported crimes of the Bureau of the Census for the Department of Justice showed modest fluctuations during the decade. There is no disagreement that, nationally, violent crime has been on the increase since 1985.

The amount of unreported crime in the United States revealed by the Victimization Survey suggests a kind of stoic acceptance of crime by the public. For 1989 the percentage of all crimes reported was 36.8% and that unreported was 62.2%. Reporting for violent crimes was a little better: 44.9% reported and 54.2% unreported.

A key question in assessing the validity of official figures is the accuracy of local arrest data reported to the FBI. Some police departments take accuracy seriously; others guess.

Whether crime was going up or down in the 1980s, the public was willing to spend increasing amounts for security. By 1991 the United States was spending $60 billion annually on all aspects of law enforcement.

Mandated prison sentences, particularly for drug offenses, became a national norm. Overcrowding was one result, a result that casts further doubt on crime tallies because no one knows how much crime is being ignored by police and prosecutors to prevent prisons and jails from becoming even more overcrowded.

State spending on prison construction rose four times faster than spending on education. Despite the building boom, prison construction was unable to keep pace with the flood of new prisoners. Overcrowding regularly forced prison administrators into releasing criminals early to make room for another batch. If states continue to throw people into jail at the 1980s' rate, the national cost in the 1990s is expected to be $5 billion annually.

ZONES OF SAFETY SCARCER

Criminologists who perceive crime and violence as just a popular subject that people like to chat about and turn into a false crisis probably have had little exposure to neighborhoods suffering from what criminologist James Q. Wilson calls the "broken window syndrome." The syndrome arises when unfixed broken windows, uncleared graffiti, overgrown weeded lots and other signs of decay demoralize a neighborhood's residents. Petty disturbances, such as loud radios and voices, frighten ordinary citizens out of proportion to their seriousness, and fear makes them shun the streets. The absence of responsible adults on the streets encourages a cycle of deterioration, additional fear and more crime.

The broken window syndrome has spread beyond deteriorating neighborhoods and might be better characterized as the "abdication of responsibility through fear syndrome." Where once a youngster sitting on a bus picking the chocolate off his ice cream bar and dropping it on the floor would have been reprimanded by an adult, the behavior is now ignored because the child may well have a gun or a knife in his pocket. Violence has become commonplace. No one wants to die over slivers of chocolate underfoot.

The age at which the commission of violence begins is dropping precipitously. The age at which young people become victims of crimes also is dropping sharply. Murder, suicide and accidents are the leading causes of death among the young in the United States. Some neighborhoods are battlefields, complete with attack rifles, where a black male between 15 and 24 is more likely to die by gunfire than was a U.S. soldier in Vietnam.

The widespread availability of guns means that shooting sprees, although more common in poor neighborhoods, can break out anywhere. Moreover, easy acquisition of assault weapons means that any group of people on a street, in a restaurant or in a schoolyard can be killed in a single salvo.

LITTLE COORDINATION IN RESEARCH

In the spring 1989 issue of *Violence and Victims,* Roland Maiuro of the University of Washington School of Medicine and Jane Eberle of the Seattle School District published an article entitled "New Developments in Research on Aggression." This article summarized the work of the Eighth World Conference of the International Society for Research on Aggression (ISRA) in 1988.

Speakers at the conference presented papers on a variety of topics. Some had worked with animals developing variations of a "hawk-dove" model. Others described the "disinhibitory process" that follows unpenalized attacks, as well as cognitive acts that justify attacks by disparaging the victims. Still others had examined why so many people choose to be exposed to images of violence in the media and evaluated proposed mitigation strategies. Other areas covered included family relationships, social conditions that discourage or facilitate abuse of women and the relation between body chemistry and violent behavior.

Maiuro and Eberle concluded that despite some researchers having called for eclectic models of aggressive behavior, "true interdisciplinary exchange is a relatively rare phenomenon in the field of interpersonal violence." They characterized the situation as reminiscent of "the tale of the 'The Blind Men and the Elephant,' in which six investigators attempt to identify the nature of the beast by grasping a different part or appendage."

TIME FOR CHANGE

Violence as a vital area of study has not had a champion. President Richard Nixon asked Congress to fund a coordinated research effort to cure cancer. The National Cancer Institute leads that struggle; if it has not found a single cure for cancer, it has had many successes. Many voices asked Congress to fund a coordinated effort to stop AIDS. The National Institute of Allergies and Infectious Disease coordinates that race and has made strides in understanding basic cell biology. Similar attention to violence, which can do more social and physical damage than cancer or AIDS or a whole host of other life-threatening diseases, is long overdue. The Centers for Disease Control (CDC) has a little-known violence division (divided into "intentional" and "unintentional" sections). That is not enough.

New York University cell biologist and physician Gerald Weissman makes a case for a concentrated, united approach to violence in his 1985 book *The Woods Hole Cantata:*

> It is unlikely that our social problems can be traced to a single, clearly defined cause in the sense that a bacterial disease is "caused" by a microbe. But, I daresay, social science is about as advanced in the late twentieth century as bacteriological science was in the mid-nineteenth century. Our forefathers knew *something* about cholera; they sensed that its spread was associated with misdirected sewage, filth, and the influx of alien poor into crowded, urban tenements. And we know *something* about street crime; nowhere has it been reported that a member of the New York Stock Exchange has robbed a poor, black teenager at the point of a gun.

Social scientists would object in part to Weissmann's position by asserting that much of the research has already been done. However, they would have to concede that it is scattered through small-scale studies by individual social scientists around the world. (They might also add, to Weissmann's comment about the socioeconomics of class, that nowhere has it been reported that a poor black teenager was able to plea bargain to keep millions of dollars made in securities frauds that cost the American public billions.)

Medical school professors in the early 1970s were fond of saying "If we could only find it, the cure for cancer may have already been found and lie buried in the voluminous medical literature." Social scientists would probably agree that the "cures" for violence may lie buried in the voluminous social science literature, if they could only be found and brought together.

The Encyclopedia of Violence underlines the seriousness of the overall problem of violence by calling attention to many of the separate issues that need to be studied in concert, as a whole. The study of violence warrants its own institute among the several that make up the U.S. National Institutes of Health (NIH). Perhaps it might be called the National Institute of Violence Research.

ENTRIES

A–Z

A

---

accord and satisfaction To influence a judge to lessen a sentence, a defense counsel may encourage a defendant to pay the victim or victims an agreed-upon amount of money. Prosecutors may seek to block such agreements. One veteran prosecutor refers to them as "authorized payoffs."

(See also ASSEMBLY-LINE JUSTICE; PROSECUTORIAL DISCRETION IN THE DISPOSITION OF CASES; SENTENCING: A TREND TOWARD LONGER SENTENCES.)

acquaintance rape. See RAPE.

adolescent violence. See VIOLENCE RESEARCH: A LONGITUDINAL STUDY OF VIOLENCE AMONG THE YOUNG.

age and crime Ages 14 to 25 are the most crime-prone years all over the world, for a variety of possible reasons. After age 25 street criminals may become bored, lose their energy for crime, be in jail or dead or have concluded that the risks outweigh the gains of crime.

By the year 2000, more than three quarters of the U.S. population will be over 25. Some criminologists therefore believe that the chances of being a street-crime victim are getting smaller. However, Marvin Wolfgang, a leading criminologist, asserts that while the percentage of juvenile offenders as a segment of the overall population is getting smaller, age of entry into crime is dropping and the crimes being committed are increasing in number and degree of violence.

One factor that has changed the pattern since the mid-1980s has been the introduction into the streets of cocaine in the form of crack. Crack has shifted down-ward the age of entry into criminal activity. Children as young as nine or ten, chosen because punishment for children is far less severe than for adults, and because children do not fully understand the risks involved, are recruited to act as lookouts to warn drug dealers and their customers of the approach of the police. For this lookout activity, some youngsters can make as much as $200 or $300 a week—much more than they might make selling papers, bagging groceries or working at McDonald's.

An early introduction to crime might indicate a longer career in crime, hence an increased number of crimes per criminal. On the other hand, the earlier a child begins a life of crime, the less judgment he or she can be presumed to have and the greater the chances are that he or she will be caught or killed during the course of a career in crime.

At the other end of the age spectrum, the increase in criminal behavior among the elderly is far outstripping their rate of growth in the population. The Federal Bureau of Investigation (FBI) reports that arrests of those 55 or older doubled between 1970 and 1980. Sociologist Gary Feinberg, who specializes in studying old-age crime, likens the status of the elderly to that of juveniles. Like youngsters, the elderly are unlikely to be regularly employed and are exempt from family obligations. Although the percentage of the population 65 and over living in poverty dropped from 24.6% in 1970 to 12% in 1988, many old people share with the young a low position on the socioeconomic scale. The percentage of people below age 18 living in poverty has climbed from 14.9% in 1970 to 19% in 1988.

A nationwide survey of elderly state prison inmates revealed that compared with younger inmates, they were more likely to be in prison for violent crimes. On the other hand, they were less likely to have had a history of juvenile crime. Half had been jailed for the first time after the age of 55.

Old people never have been, and probably never will be, a major element in street crime. They account for the commission of only one out of every 22 homicides, and the distribution within that 1% is highly skewed. Elderly black males are ten times more likely than elderly white males to commit homicide and 175 times more likely than elderly white females. In her 1987 book *Crimewarps: The Future of Crime in America,* Georgette Bennett stated that race is not the factor prompting more elderly black males to kill than white. Fear is the factor. According to Bennett, "Male blacks are more often victimized by street crime. By the time they grow old, there has been plenty of time for healthy paranoia to set in. When they feel threatened, the aged may strike back—sometimes inappropriately."

Guns are used more often by older assailants than by younger ones, perhaps because firearms can make up for lack of physical strength.

Psychiatrist Stephen Hucker, in one of the few studies into the psychiatric characteristics of older sex offenders and violent criminals, found that three quarters of his sample suffered from either organic (deriving from physical damage to the brain) or functional psychiatric disorders. The study revealed a high incidence of paranoia.

Neal Shover, in his book *Aging Criminals* (1985), interviewed older male criminals, both incarcerated and those who had finished their time, and those whose criminal careers ranged from successful to unsuccessful. He asked them to reflect on their lives and, according to their responses categorized them as "despairing," "satisfied" or "ambivalent."

By despairing, he meant those who were depressed because they were dissatisfied with their present lives and felt helpless to change them. They expressed severe regrets over their past behavior and their present lives. Along with their awareness of the pettiness and unrewarding results of crime they had gained a sense that their misfortune had been their own fault.

The despairing are a significant part of the small group of older men who continue to commit crimes and go to prison well into middle or even old age. Some eventually commit suicide. Others, out of desperation, plan high-risk crimes to gain a stake. Some commit petty crimes just so they can go back to prison, where they will have regular meals, be in out of the cold and be with old friends.

The satisfied had achieved some measure of success, either legitimately or through crime. Those who internalized responsibility for their crime often saw incarceration as having been a positive experience, fearing that they would have committed far worse crimes had they not been caught.

The small ambivalent group consisted of men who were vaguely dissatisfied with their life circumstances and tended to blame their experience of crime and punishment as the source of their problems.

Older criminals have learned how to do time. They have learned how to "go along with the program." In prison they are cited for misconduct less often than younger prisoners. However, having become aware that life is finite, the older prisoner's perception that his life is getting shorter makes putting in time in prison more difficult.

Being confined with the young can also be a problem for older men. To men who no longer have to prove their masculinity, much of the younger convicts' conversation and activity seems affected or ridiculous. Moreover, many view contemporary prisons as violent and unpredictable, and fear that they may become victims.

alcohol dependence   The National Council on Alcoholism and Drug Dependence defines alcoholism as a primary chronic disease with genetic, psychosocial and environmental factors that influence the course and characteristics the disease takes. Despite a recent decline in per-capita consumption of alcohol, overall U.S. alcohol-related deaths have not declined.

An average of 300 Americans died each day in 1987 from alcohol-related causes—a total of 105,095 deaths. Each victim lost an average of 25.9 years of life that he or she could otherwise have expected to live.

In one survey of offenders convicted of violent crimes, 54% had used alcohol just before the offense. The breakdown for specific crimes was: 68% for manslaughter; 62% for assault; 52% for rape and other sexual assaults; and 49% for murder or attempted murder.

About 21% of all suicide victims are alcohol-dependent, and an average of 18% of deaths of alcoholics are due to suicide. About 25% of all hospitalized patients have alcohol-related problems. In the United States, the use of alcohol is closely connected with the four leading causes of accidental death: about half of all auto crash deaths are alcohol-related—23,352 in 1988; fires and burns account for an estimated 37% to 64%; falls account for an estimated 17% to 53%; and drownings account for 38%.

Operating a vehicle while under the influence of alcohol or other drugs is potentially lethal. Drunken driving is one of the leading causes of death among those age 15 to 24. An estimated 40,000 teenagers are injured each year in auto accidents. A Louis Harris poll conducted on behalf of *Prevention* magazine reported that 10 million Americans—8 million men and 2 million women—admitted that they sometimes or always drive after having four or more drinks.

Two out of every five Americans (40%) will be in an alcohol-related crash in their lifetimes. One out of every three truck drivers (33%) who dies in a highway accident has used alcohol or other drugs. The National Transportation Safety Board estimated that 32% to 64% of recreational boating deaths in 1983 were related to alcohol. Between 1975 and 1984, alcohol- or drug-impaired employees were implicated in 48 railroad accidents that resulted in 37 deaths, 80 nonfatal injuries and $34.2 million in damages.

Research into the risk effects of alcohol on flight crew performance found that alcohol intake sufficient to produce a BAC (blood alcohol content level) of .10 decreased precision and accuracy on all variables 14 hours after ingestion of the last drink. Federal rules prohibit flying within eight hours of the last drink and while having a BAC of .04 or higher.

Each year alcohol contributes to about 15,000 fatal and 6 million nonfatal injuries at home or in public places. An estimated 20% to 45% of approximately 3 million people who experience homelessness each year, either temporary or chronic, have alcohol problems.

Alcoholism and related problems cost the nation an estimated $85.8 billion—39% from reduced productivity and 33% from deaths—and illicit use of other drugs costs an additional $58.3 billion, not including the cost of law enforcement efforts to contain illegal drug traffic. An estimated 10.5 million Americans display symptoms of alcoholism or alcohol dependence, and another estimated 7.2 million display heavy drinking patterns associated with compromised health and/or social functioning.

Two-thirds of the American population drink; however, the 10% who drink most heavily drink half of all the alcohol consumed. Per-capita consumption of alcohol in 1987 was 2.54 gallons of *pure* alcohol, which is roughly the equivalent to 56 gallons of beer, or 20 gallons of wine, or six gallons of distilled spirits.

Alcohol users, particularly women and younger drinkers, frequently use other drugs. Of Alcoholics Anonymous (AA) members, 46% report addiction to other drugs in addition to alcohol.

Women are at a higher health risk from alcohol than men. They are more sensitive than men to the toxicity of alcohol because their bodies contain 5% to 10% less water and therefore provide less dilution. Moreover, they have a lesser amount of an enzyme that digests alcohol, and alcoholic women may lack it altogether.

The progress of the illness from early-stage problem drinking to late-stage alcoholism is much faster in women and children. An estimated 700,000 teenagers have serious alcohol problems, some as young as ten or 11. Organic damage to the central nervous system seems to be more extensive in youngsters. Even more damaging is multiple drug usage. Combinations of drugs shorten the time it takes to do irreversible physical damage.

One in six women in the peak childbearing ages, 18 to 34, may drink enough, either chronically or episodically, to present a hazard to her unborn infant. Fetal alcohol syndrome (FAS) is one of the top three known causes of birth defects and the only one that is preventable. FAS affects one in every 750 babies born, with an annual average of about 5,000 FAS births, and typically results in a cluster of birth defects, including mental retardation and lifelong physical problems. Fetal alcohol effects (FAE), a less severe version of FAS, result in low birthweight, mild physical malformations and subtle behavioral problems.

Although alcohol is a central nervous system depressant, the areas of the brain that inhibit behavior are affected first; therefore, instead of acting as a sedative, alcohol can release usually restrained behavior. Alcohol-influenced behavior patterns are not predictable. They vary among people or among different episodes in the same person—a quiet person may become boisterous or even violent and a happy person may become sad or even maudlin.

Despite alcohol's destructiveness, it has a long history as a symbol of hospitality and its use is therefore considered legitimate. Use of other drugs (abused prescribed drugs and street drugs) is considered illicit and dangerous and has mostly been outlawed.

Approximately 1.2 million of the estimated 17.7 million Americans with alcohol problems have entered treatment programs. More would like to enter such programs, but they are unevenly distributed across the country. For example, there are 11 times more specialty substance abuse treatment programs in Alaska than there are in West Virginia.. Successful treatment of alcoholics costs one tenth what it costs to cope with the problems caused by alcoholics (auto and industrial accidents, broken families, suicide, etc.)

Damage from alcohol can affect every organ in the body. The residual effects of alcohol, particularly on the brain, can persist long after detoxification. Full recovery from alcoholism takes two to three years.

The Surgeon General's Workshop on Drunk Driving recommended elimination of alcohol promotions and advertising on college campuses, where a high proportion of the audience is under the legal drinking age. A 1987 Gallup/Advertising Age poll found that 74% of adults favor warning labels on ads for alcoholic beverages, and 42% felt alcohol advertising should be banned altogether.

Consumers spent $88 billion on alcoholic beverages in 1988, 51% on beer, 35% on distilled spirits, and 14% on wine. The alcohol beverage industry spent $1.2 billion on consumer advertising in the same year. In a typical year, much of the advertising is done in connection with sports, via large billboards in baseball parks and sponsorship of sports events and broadcasts.

The problems of alcohol and sports were the subject of much discussion in May 1991, prompted by an alcohol-related auto accident involving two prominent major-league baseball players. The drinking had taken place at a bachelor party held in a tavern. One player was put on the injured list for a week, the other for 60 days.

Sports teams have policies on the use of illegal drugs, but little attention is paid to alcohol. To outside observers, team management inattention to alcohol misuse seems irrational, given the huge financial investment that owners have in their players. Some observers believe that alcohol abuse is ignored because it is common not only among those who play on the field but also among those who work in the front office.

Even if owners and managers were reluctant to dictate player behavior, it would seem reasonable to expect that they would take steps to protect their investments. For example, paying to have a limousine pick up the players at the tavern following the bachelor party would probably have been a lot cheaper than having two players on the disabled list.

Some athletes find retirement almost unbearable. Shortly after 59-year-old jockey Willie Shoemaker retired, following a long and illustrious career, he drove his car over an embankment. Before climbing into his car, he had consumed several drinks. The accident broke his neck, and he became a quadriplegic.

(See also CAMPUS VIOLENCE; DRUG ABUSE AND TRADE: PREVENTION AND EDUCATION; HOMELESSNESS AND VULNERABILITY TO VIOLENCE; POST-TRAUMATIC STRESS DISORDER (PTSD).)

alternative sentencing. See PRISON OVERCROWDING: COPING WITH THE COSTS.

anger The physical sensations of feelings such as anger—tingling, energy, excitement, arousal—are the effects of the chemicals adrenaline and noradrenaline. These adrenal hormones act on all organs of the body reached by the sympathetic nervous system. They stimulate the heart, dilate coronary vessels, constrict blood vessels in the intestines and shut down digestion. As levels of adrenaline and noradrenaline rise, memory, concentration and performance improve. Beyond a certain point—if the body is flooded with adrenaline—performance worsens.

The level of hormones explains the sensation of being overwhelmed by emotion—a feeling of being seized or flooded. Yet the presence of hormones does not necessarily mean being ruled by emotions. For some individuals, the physiological excitement is pleasant and associated with risk, fun, vibrancy, power. For others, the rush of adrenaline causes fear in anticipation of danger and powerlessness. The difference in perspective is related to attitudes and experiences, not to the presence of surging hormones.

W. I. Thomas, one of the founders of modern sociology, observed that ''if men define situations as real, they are real in their consequences.'' In her book *Anger: The Misunderstood Emotion* (1989), social psychologist Carol Tavris echoes Thomas by saying that as emotions are defined, so too are their consequences.

As an example of the social definitions of anger, Tavris uses a domestic wrangle over a messy bathroom. She says:

> If Jane believes that she is not really angry at Arnold for leaving the bathroom a mess, but ''really'' angry with her mother for teaching her to be angry with men who leave bathrooms in messes, her relationship with her mother is likely to be affected. If she attributes her anger to the day's stresses, *she* may be the one to apologize. If she thinks her anger with Arnold is legitimate, and if she convinces him that it is, she may get him to be more sensitive to her feelings. If she thinks her anger is really directed to sex-role

inequities of national magnitude, she may join the woman's movement and leave Arnold to do his own cleaning up.

To try to pin down a single explanation for anger is to court failure. Tavris argues that anger is not a disease with a single cause, it is a transaction, a process, a method of communicating. Most incidents of anger are social episodes—with the possible exception of anger brought on by organic abnormalities. Anger assumes meaning only in social terms, having to do with implicit or explicit agreements about relations among people. Beliefs held about anger and the interpretations made about the experience of anger are critical to understanding the expression of the emotion.

Tavris writes:

> I'm not saying that all explanations are created equal; rather that we have to be careful which explanation we choose, because then we have to live with it. There are, certainly, ways to determine why we feel angry and how we might then behave, but they have to do with what actions will ease the feeling and which will escalate it . . . No single remedy fits all. Sometimes suppressed hostility can aggravate stress and illness, but sometimes suppressed hostility is the best thing for you. It used to be called common courtesy.

In Tavris' view, contemporary ideas about anger have been fed by what she calls "the anger industry." By that she means psychotherapy, which is too often based on the belief that inside every apparently tranquil soul is an angry one raging to get out.

Yale psychiatrist Albert Rothberg shares Tavris' skepticism. He is uneasy with the claims of success heralded by psychotherapy because, in his view, its functioning is based on a series of assumptions none of which can be verified objectively. Moreover, although therapists devote considerable energy to helping clients deal with their anger, few distinguish anger from rage, hatred, chronic resentment or violence.

Tavris asserts that the anger business is based on several assumptions. She spells out a few:

- That emotional energy exists in a fixed quantity that can be dammed up or, conversely, that can flood the system.
- That anger and aggression are inextricably, biologically linked: that anger is the feeling and aggression its overt expression; that both are aspects of an aggressive instinct.
- That anger is an instinctive response to threat and to the frustration of goals or desires.

- That when blocked, the outward expression of anger "turns inward," where it is felt as depression, guilt, shame, anxiety or lethargy.

In her book, Tavris brings together studies from the social and biological sciences, together with 50 interviews she conducted with men and women about their own beliefs about and experiences with anger. Tavris believes that the careful study of anger matters because anger so strongly affects behavior; it has a potent capacity for good and evil. She explains her belief by saying

> I have watched people use anger, in the name of emotional liberation, to erode affection and trust, whittle away their spirits in bitterness and revenge, diminish their dignity in years of spiteful hatred. And I watch with admiration those who use anger to probe for truth, who challenge and change the complacent injustices of life, who take an unpopular position center stage while others say "shhhh" from the wings.

American culture is ambivalent about anger, not sure whether it is righteous or dangerous, whether it should be admired or feared. For much of Western history, reason was thought to give humans a device with which to control anger and other deadly sins. The healthy individual was thought to be someone who did not erupt in anger.

In the last two centuries widespread confidence in reason has given away to doubt, transformed, in Tavris' opinion, by the work of Charles Darwin and Sigmund Freud. Although the two men were not solely responsible for the change, their ideas fell on fertile ground.

Darwin took the position that the origins of human emotions could be found in lower animals. He argued that rage is a simple response to a threat that requires an animal to defend itself. He defined the rage response as the motivation to retaliate. Because of the many similarities between animal and human behavior, it seemed logical to Darwin to conclude that the rage response is programmed into humans as into other species. He concluded that anger was only watered-down rage. Anxious to emphasize the similarities, he overlooked the differences.

Unlike animals, humans can hide their emotional state and can be roused to anger by memories or can decide retroactively to get angry. Unlike humans, animals do not respond to insults about their intelligence, ancestry or religion.

Darwin's theory that emotions are instinctive suggested to modern theorists that emotions cannot be suppressed and therefore attempts to control them are useless. Theirs is a position with which Darwin would have disagreed. He believed that those who give way to violent gestures will increase their rage and experience fear in greater degree. The self-control Darwin advocates is a choice beyond the limitations of instinct, and such a choice opens Darwin's hypothesis to question.

Anger can be expressed in hundreds of ways, from housecleaning to protest marching. And aggression can be expressed without anger; for example, an assassin can kill someone he or she has never met, or an employer can fire a subordinate simply to trim the budget.

James Averill, a psychologist who has studied the social functions of emotions, believes that anger is solely a human emotion because only humans can judge actions they deem deserving of anger on the bases of intention, justifiability and negligence. Thus anger involves a conscious judgment that injustice, insult or foolishness has been committed.

An episode of anger contains a sequence of rapid decisions: Is the body language of the individual who inspires anger provocative or joking? Is the potential outcome of responding to the provocation safe? Does the provocation merit laughter, retaliation or rapid retreat? Human anger is more intricate and serves more purposes than Darwin's analogy to the rage reflex of lower animals would suggest.

To Freud is owed the widely accepted notion that the rational faculties know little about the seething cauldron of instincts that guides many emotions and behaviors. Freud regarded humans as being at the mercy of their instincts. While Darwin viewed aggression as adaptive and self-defending, Freud emphasized the destructive, violent aspects of aggression. Anger in both men's views was just a weaker expression of the basic aggressive drive. In Freud's model, everyone at every age is unwittingly furious with everyone else.

Freud described repression of anger as a pathological process that produces neurotic symptoms. His development of psychoanalysis as a method of treatment was intended to bring the repressed feelings into consciousness.

Freud never argued that suppression of instincts was not desirable. On the contrary, he viewed suppression and redirection of emotional energy into endeavors such as building a bridge, starting a business or painting a masterpiece as necessary to the survival of society. He was horrified at those who wanted to liberate mind and body by doing away with authority and guilt. He said the conflict between sensual and ascetic tendencies was not resolved by helping one side to win out over the other. Yet, in Tavris' opinion, that is what many of his successors have tried to do.

Freud believed that what he called the libido was a finite amount of energy that powered internal battles. Energy blocked in one place emerged in another. This concept is often called the hydraulic model.

In Freud's view, humans under the pressure of violent instinct did not attack each other more regularly than in fact they did because of what he called catharsis. By that he meant the emptying out of emotions in a whole range of voluntary and involuntary activities, such as driving too fast, kicking the cat, talking to a friend or having a headache or a heart attack.

Freud used the idea of catharsis sparingly, but many modern therapists seem to believe that all ways of "releasing" an emotion have equal value. For them catharsis means "letting it all hang out" emotionally.

The essential feature of anger in its various manifestations is the angry person's belief that he or she can influence the object of his or her anger. One assumption is that the other is responsible for his or her actions and ought to behave differently.

The "ought" characteristic of anger implies that anger serves as a policing or control function. Anger with its threat of retaliation helps to regulate everyday social relations, family disputes, neighborly quarrels and business agreements. Throughout most of Western history, individuals have had to ensure that their rights were respected and justice was done. Anger operated as a personal judiciary in the absence of a formal one.

Small groups rely on informal, highly effective methods to keep inappropriate anger in check: gossip, ridicule, witchcraft, public discussion, shame and ostracism. In many cultures, including Western cultures, everyday angers are not only determined by the culture's needs and values, the culture often allows for the fact that sometimes an individual may "go crazy" with rage.

In many cultures an enraged individual and an insane one are both regarded as being out of control, and thus unable to take responsibility for their actions. In others, such as the Inuit, two conditions of anger are distinguished. A person legitimately insane cannot be expected to control him- or herself, but one who is merely angry is expected to control his or her behavior.

In 1894 psychologist G. Stanley Hall conducted the first modern scientific effort to study anger. He collected 2,184 questionnaires from people willing to answer his complicated queries about their angriest episodes. One of the most startling results was the wide variation in people's physical experience of anger. Some it made sick, others more alive. The array of physical responses to anger was matched by the array of causes. One category of provocation might be called the "stupid inanimate object"—pens broken because they would not write, mirrors smashed, paper crushed, toys destroyed—things that do not behave as they "ought" to. A modern equivalent might be vending machines that swallow money without delivering. They arouse a moment of brief fury.

A more cerebral category of anger provokers cited in Hall's study is the special aversion that irritates—short hair on women, too much jewelry, flashy ties, hats worn to one side.

The greatest number of anger provokers were those that involved one person's treatment of another. This category may be subdivided into injustice, stupidity (of self or other), cheating, bootlicking, insults and condescension. The various categories seemed to combine both a wide variety of physical reactions and an equally wide variety of mental perceptions.

Modern scientists have gone beyond what people say they feel. Some explore neural connections in the brain to stimulate anger and violence or to locate aggression's master switch. Others attempt to reproduce real-life emotions in the laboratory and then measure blood pressure, heart rate, perspiration, skin temperature and accompanying attitudes.

Biological explanations of anger hold great appeal. Studies look at brain tumors, brain chemistry, allergies and genetics, to mention a few. An implicit assumption of many studies is that each of the various emotions is distinct, with its own genetic code and anatomical program apart from external events. An implicit goal is to pinpoint the connection for anger, which might help to prevent family quarrels, murder and war.

Research has found that various emotions produce physiologically similar physical states, which differ only in their circumstances and the interpretations given to them.

Evidence of brain abnormalities in children and adolescents who had committed unusually violent crimes was discovered in 1951, when a peculiarity was found in their electroencephalograms (EEGs, measurements of brain waves). More recent studies have also found that the majority of those who had committed violent antisocial crimes had an odd EEG pattern. However, not everyone who had the particular abnormality was found to be subject to rage attacks, nor was it clear whether the abnormality caused the violence or resulted from it.

A series of studies whose results were published by Dorothy Otnow Lewis in her 1981 book *Vulnerabilities to Delinquency* compared delinquent and nondelinquent boys. The former had more hospital visits, accidents and injuries than the latter. When imprisoned delinquents were compared with nonimprisoned delinquents (imprisonment being a measure of the greater seriousness of their crimes), their medical histories were similar in number of accidents and injuries, but not in kind. Among the youngsters in prison, 62.3% had sustained severe face or head injuries, many in the first two years of life, compared with 44% of those not in prison.

Lewis' team went on to compare two groups of imprisoned delinquents: more violent youngsters, who had committed murder, rape or very serious assaults; and less violent youngsters, who had threatened others with weapons or taken part in fistfights. Among the more violent, researchers found a much higher incidence of symptoms associated with temporal lobe seizures and neurological impairment, such as blackouts, stumbling and paranoid thinking. Among the more violent boys, 98.6% had at least one neurological impairment compared with 66.7% of the less violent boys. Almost 30% of the more violent delinquents had grossly abnormal EEGs, grand mal epilepsy or both, but none of the less violent delinquents had either.

More than three fourths of the more violent boys had suffered head injuries as children, had suffered serious and extensive medical problems, and had been beaten savagely by their parents; this was true of only one third of the less violent. While Lewis did not assert that a single factor would make a child violent or delinquent, she concluded that violent delinquency arises from a combination of child abuse, social deprivation, trauma to the nervous system and other factors. Lewis' studies do not offer the final word on understanding anger. Not all cases of explosive rage can be attributed to brain damage, nor do all cases of brain damage produce explosive rage. One operative assumption of some brain research is that an understanding of abnormal rage will lead to an understanding of normal anger.

Most kinds and intensities of everyday anger do not result from inflammation of a rage center or a disabled neuron. They occur in response to provocation in a social context—the phone ringing as something boils over on the stove. Rather than suffering from a biological allergy to caffeine, a woman given to frequent rages may be reacting to an abusive husband.

Tavris comments on biological explanations of anger this way:

> To say the limbic system contains mechanisms for anger, rage, and aggression does not imply that the limbic system is the *only* origin of such feelings and actions, or that all three are inevitably connected. The human capacity for cold, premeditated revenge, for violence for profit, for hatred at injustice, for anger at arrogance: these angers originate in the neocortex, the center for symbolic thought, logic, and reason . . . There is no such thing as a "rage circuit" that is unresponsive to, or independent of, environment and learning.

Leonore Tiefer, a physiological psychologist, supports Tavris' view: "The brain does not operate in an all-or-none, on-or-off, yes-no fashion; that's not nature's way. Social experience can affect our basic physiology."

Instead of regarding brain circuits as if they were on-off switches, researchers now talk about individual thresholds of responsiveness, from the low threshold of quick to anger to the high threshold of almost always placid.

In Tavris' opinion, researchers and therapists engage in heated debates over anger because they are talking about different phenomena. Some researchers are focused on the physiological side, the quick rage reflex engendered by "stupid" inanimate objects—automatic responses to danger, threat and pain. Others are looking at the social context. The latter may be using a Freudian model in which they interpret occasions of anger in terms that fit the model, or they may be using a phenomenological approach in which they record the separate occasions and try to put them together into a model.

Tavris proposes that, in contrast to many others, Judeo-Christian culture produces "active pessimists," people who assume that nature and other people are to be conquered, must be conquered, and that individual striving is essential to survival. The individualism of American life inspires anger and encourages its release, because when almost everything is possible, limitations are irksome. When the desires of the self are paramount, the needs of others are tedious. To one who feels deserving of all, getting only some can enrage.

If anger is not a biological reflex or an unconscious instinct, the question is raised of why it has survived. The answer is probably because, under certain circumstances, anger serves a purpose. Determination of the circumstances in which anger is useful creates much confusion in anger research because the meaning of anger is defined by the local culture. In Tavris' words, "Anger in America restores the sense of dignity and fair play."

But fair play, competitiveness and individualism are not universal values. In some highly cooperative African societies, the "instinctive" expressions of anger familiar to Americans are unknown. It is not that feelings of anger are unknown in those societies, but that the actions taken as a consequence of that anger are learned from and managed by the culture.

Confusion about the appropriateness of anger is particularly widespread in the United States, a highly violent society. Tavris says:

> We are ambivalent about anger not because of an "internal war" between reason and emotion; we are ambivalent about anger because sometimes it is effective and sometimes it is not, because sometimes it is necessary and sometimes it is destructive . . . Anger, therefore, is as much a political matter as it is a biological one. The decision to get angry has powerful consequences, whether the anger is directed toward one's spouse or one's government. Spouses and governments know this. They know that anger is ultimately an emphatic message.

Without boundaries to control anger, anger can produce emotional anarchy. Thus a basic principle of parliamentary law is courtesy.

(See also RAGE, EXPLOSIVE.)

Anti-Defamation League.   See HATE GROUPS.

anti-Semitism.   See HATE GROUPS.

Armed Career Criminal Act   Legislation passed in 1984, known as the Armed Career Criminal Act, was the inspiration of Senator Arlen Specter, (R, Pa.). As originally written, the law provided that anyone caught with a gun after three burglaries or robbery felonies would go to jail for a minimum of 15 years. The act was amended in 1986 to include anyone who had committed three violent or drug-related crimes.

An August 21, 1989 *U.S. News and World Report* article entitled "A Criminal Lack of Common Sense" described how the little-known law ended the career of a violent California criminal, Warren Bland. When Bland stuck a knife in a man's stomach in 1958, he got off with probation. In 1960 he plea-bargained a series of sexual assaults, one of which involved breaking a woman's jaw, down to one rape and one kidnapping, and under the state's "mentally disordered sex offender program" was sent to a state mental hospital.

The hospital warned that Bland was a sexual psychopath and if released would be assaultive and/or homicidal toward women. Nevertheless, after seven years of treatment, the same hospital declared that Bland had changed completely and set him free. Within months he was once again engaged in violent sexual attacks. He was convicted of two more rapes. A presentencing report declared him "a dangerous individual who warrants segregation from society for the longest possible time under existing laws." Bland served seven years.

Shortly after his release, he kidnapped an 11-year-old girl and her mother, molested the mother and sexually assaulted and tortured the child. Once again he plea-bargained and served only three years. Despite his continuing level of violence, his prison terms were getting shorter.

Eight months after his release, Bland was back in jail for sodomizing and torturing a small boy. He plea-bargained for a nine-year sentence and was out of prison in four and a half years.

Bland was released in early 1986. In December of 1986, a seven-year-old girl disappeared while walking to school in South Pasadena. Her body was found in a ditch, mutilated with the same kind of instruments Bland had favored in the past. An Orange County 14-year-old also died the same way, and Bland was implicated in the death of an 81-year-old San Diego woman who was discovered bound, nude and choked to death.

Three years after the police had linked Bland to the seven-year-old girl's death and charged him with murder, the county prosecutor had not even managed to hold a preliminary hearing. Larry Burns, a San Diego assistant U.S. attorney, ended the delay when he filed federal charges against Bland under the Armed Career Criminal Act. Under the act, it took Larry Burns 30 minutes in court to take Bland off the streets for life, a feat the state of California had failed to do over the course of three decades.

(See also ARREST: CONSTITUTIONAL RESTRICTIONS AND LEGAL PROCEDURES; ASSEMBLY-LINE JUSTICE; FELONY ARRESTS: SCREENING PROCEDURES; PROSECUTORIAL DISCRETION IN THE DISPOSITION OF CASES; SENTENCING: A TREND TOWARD LONGER SENTENCES.)

arrest: constitutional restrictions and legal procedures

Restrictions on Arrest, Search and Seizure.   The U.S. Constitution requires law enforcement officers to have reasonable or probable cause before arresting any person. This restriction is part of the Bill of Rights. The Fourth Amendment states: "The right of the people to be secure in their persons, houses, papers, and effects, against unreasonable searches and seizures, shall not be violated, and no warrants shall issue, but on reasonable cause, supported upon oath and affirmation, and particularly describing the place to be searched, and the persons or things to be seized."

Through a long history of court cases, the standard of probable cause has refined the conditions under which a police officer may make an arrest. In his book *Police Operations* (1976), Gwynne Peirson defined probable cause as "facts or apparent facts viewed through the eyes of an experienced police officer, which would generate a reasonable belief that a crime has been committed."

Police officers in most U.S. jurisdictions are taught to look for three conditions in determining probable cause: (1) whether a crime has occurred, is occurring or is about to occur; (2) whether seizable items are present; (3) whether seizable items are present in a specific place or on the persons the officer wishes to search.

For a search to hold up in court it must be legal. For it to be legal, police must: (1) have probable cause; (2) have a valid search warrant issued by a court following submission of a written affidavit specifying probable cause and describing in detail the premises to be searched and the items to be seized; (3) carry out the search only as directed by the warrant; (4) return the warrant within seven days. (Warrants must be used or returned; they cannot be held for some future search.)

To an ordinary citizen, the process of obtaining a warrant may seem unnecessarily bureaucratic, but the constitutional requirements are based on the experience of the framers of the Constitution with unreasonable searches and seizures by arbitrary authorities. On these constitutional grounds, courts have traditionally been reluctant to validate searches made without warrants.

There are several narrowly defined exceptions. Among them are:

• *Search in connection with an arrest.* In the conduct of a lawful arrest, a search may be carried out without reasonable suspicion or probable cause to believe that the arrestee is in possession of a weapon or evidence of a crime. In addition, an officer may search the area within an arrestee's reach, though not the adjacent or surrounding area. If the arrestee is driving at the time of the arrest, an officer may search the interior of the vehicle, but not the trunk. The reasoning behind this restriction is that although an officer may search the arrestee to protect his or her safety and that of those nearby, and to prevent the destruction of evidence, areas not within the reach of the person arrested present no such immediate danger and therefore remain subject to the requirement for a warrant.

- *Reasonable suspicion.* If an officer has a reasonable and articulable suspicion that a person is armed, the officer may frisk the person but only for weapons. If the person is in an automobile at the time, and the officer has a reasonable fear that weapons may be in the vehicle, he or she may ask the person to exit and search both the suspect and the interior of the vehicle—limited to the areas within the reach and control of the suspect.
- *Consent.* If a person who has control of and access to the premises to be searched "voluntarily and intelligently" consents, an officer may search without a warrant. There are many limitations on consent searches, and some courts are unwilling to accept consent as voluntary when given by someone in custody. Before obtaining consent, an officer must warn the person being asked that he or she is an officer, the search is for evidence of a specified crime, that the person being asked for consent has a right to refuse permission and refusal will not be construed as incriminating.

  Such a search must be limited to areas specified in the consent. Consent voluntarily given may be revoked at any time, and the search must cease immediately.
- *Abandoned property.* Since there would be no reasonable expectation of privacy, abandoned or discarded property may be searched and/or seized.
- *Open fields.* Open fields, woods and pastures that are not part of the curtilage of a dwelling may be searched. In law "curtilage" refers to a yard, garden, enclosure or field near or belonging to a dwelling.
- *Inventory.* In accordance with a standard written policy of the officer's department, which reflects state and local laws, an officer may conduct an inventory search of a defendant and his or her property at the time of arrest. If a car is inventoried, all containers and possessions in the vehicle may be searched. An inventory search is not a search for evidence. It is intended to protect both the officer and the defendant against possible loss of the defendant's property.

- *Exigent circumstance.* Under conditions where a delay of a search while a warrant is sought might jeopardize the seizure of evidence, an officer may search without a warrant. Moreover, an officer in "hot pursuit" of an armed fleeing suspect may conduct a search of a home if the suspect is thought to be there. Officers frequently invoke the exigent circumstance exception to justify warrantless searches; judges are most likely to view it with skepticism.
- *"Plain view."* If an officer is legitimately on the premises, carrying out a valid search supported by a warrant, and sees an item that he or she has probable cause to believe is evidence or contraband, he or she may seize that item.
- *Automobile.* In contrast to a vehicle search incident to an arrest, an entire automobile, not just the interior within reach of the driver, may be searched without a warrant provided that there is probable cause to believe that there is evidence of a crime within the automobile.
- *Arrest warrant.* If an officer has obtained a valid arrest warrant, he or she may search for the suspect in the suspect's home, provided that the officer has probable cause to believe the suspect is there at the time of the search. However, the arrest warrant is not sufficient to allow the officer to search another person's home, even if there is probable cause to believe that the suspect is there.

In order to make a legal arrest for a felony, typically an offense punishable by a year or more in prison, an officer is not required actually to witness the offense. However, for a misdemeanor, typically an offense punishable by less than a year in jail, the officer must have witnessed the crime. Misdemeanors include offenses sometimes referred to as victimless crimes, such as gambling, prostitution or vagrancy.

Until recently domestic violence was a misdemeanor in many states. As a consequence, although a battered woman might exhibit visible evidence of a beating, officers could not take her abuser into custody because they had not witnessed the crime.

Some criminal acts may be defined as felonies in one state and misdemeanors in another. For example, purse-snatching may be defined in some states as unarmed robbery, a felony, and in others as a theft—either as grand theft, a felony, or petty theft, a misdemeanor—depending on how much money was in the purse. Typically the cutoff point is $100.

An officer is justified in making an arrest—and even, in some circumstances, in killing a suspect—so long as any "reasonable and prudent person," supplied with the same information available to the officer, would have drawn the same conclusion of probable cause drawn by the officer.

An officer when acting lawfully is authorized to use all necessary force to accomplish an arrest, regardless of the seriousness of the crime or the ultimate disposition of the case. The reason is that if resistance to arrest on the grounds of innocence were permissible, then a guilty person would be encouraged to resist with deadly force to eliminate an officer who had witnessed the crime.

Necessary force is not deadly force. It is only the force needed to subdue a person who is resisting arrest but not attempting to kill or harm the arresting officer. Deadly force is a last resort and justified only under specific conditions.

Most jurisdictions permit a police officer to shoot to kill only when defending his or her own life or the life of another, or capturing a fleeing felon when all other efforts have failed. The threat presented must be immediate.

The Rights of a Person Accused. The Bill of Rights also specifies the rights of a person accused of a crime. The Fifth Amendment says:

> No person shall be held to answer for a capital, or otherwise infamous crime, unless on a presentment or indictment of a grand jury, except in cases arising in the land or naval forces, or in the Militia, when in actual service in time of War or public danger. Nor shall any person be subject for the same offense to be twice put in jeopardy of life or limb; nor shall be compelled in any criminal case to be a witness against himself, nor be deprived of life, liberty or property, without due process of law; nor shall private property be taken for public use, without just compensation.

For a police officer the import of the Fifth Amendment is that the person accused has a right to be silent and not be compelled to answer questions. The case of *Miranda v. Arizona,* decided by the Supreme Court in 1966, defined the breadth of this right. The Court ruled that the Fifth Amendment pertains outside criminal court proceedings and serves to protect persons whether or not they have been arrested. The Court held that persons suspected of crimes must be apprised adequately and effectively of their right to remain silent and that the exercise of that right must be honored.

The intent of the Miranda rule is that the accused must be made aware of the consequences of answering questions in order fully to understand his or her right to avoid self-incrimination. Once the accused has indicated that he or she is unwilling to answer questions, questioning must cease.

While many police officers gripe about legal restrictions and the amount of paperwork they must do, most accept the safeguards that surround the arrest process. A glance at countries such as Chile, where police torture has been routine, or Brazil, where rural violence escalates in direct relation to the failure of police to enforce the law, makes it clear that this legal and constitutional structure protects ordinary citizens as well as accused criminals, who are after all also citizens.

(See also ASSEMBLY-LINE JUSTICE; BILL OF RIGHTS: PROTECTION AGAINST GOVERNMENT TYRANNY; CHILDREN'S RIGHTS; FELONY ARRESTS: SCREENING PROCEDURES.)

arson A fire set for malicious or fraudulent purposes is called arson. Arson is not limited to residences; it includes commercial and public buildings and structures such as bridges, aircraft and motor vehicles. "Malicious," legally, implies that the fire was not accidental, but does not necessarily presume malice (ill will). Intention or outrageously reckless conduct is enough to impute maliciousness.

Between 1958 and 1978, the annual number of fires believed caused by arson rose to 100,000 a year, a 1,157% increase. In 1979, by congressional mandate, arson was added to the U.S. Justice Department's Uniform Crime Report, Part I Crime Index, which includes the violent crimes of murder, nonnegligent homicide, forcible rape, robbery and aggravated assault, and the property crimes of burglary, larceny/theft and motor vehicle theft. Until the change, arson had not been considered a major crime and had been cataloged as a Part II crime, along with drunken driving, gambling and other such crimes.

Arson comes in many forms. Fires are started for revenge, for profit, for excitement, for recognition, out of fear and to cover other crimes. Arsonists include grandmothers who are arson ring leaders, jilted lovers, Mafia members, preteenagers seeking revenge against school principals, teenage crack dealers, respected lawyers and businesspeople and volunteer firefighters hoping to demonstrate their skills. Arson is committed by lone individuals and by groups.

The Demographics of Arson. Annually, there are about a million structural fires in which about 6,000 people die. The number of fires attributable to arson is difficult to estimate because of the way arson is tabulated. To be counted by the Federal Bureau of Investigation (FBI) in the Uniform Crime Reports as arson, a fire must have been determined by investigation to have been maliciously or willfully set. Fires of suspect or unknown origin are not counted.

In 1989, 99,599 arson offenses were reported to the FBI by 12,759 agencies, whose reports covered from one to 12 months. The rates ranged from 103 per 100,000 inhabitants in cities with populations over a million to 21 per 100,000 in rural areas. Overall the rate was 49 per 100,000.

The largest and busiest arson investigation agency in the world is the New York City Fire Department's Bureau of Investigation. In his 1991 book *Heat: The Fire Investigators and Their War on Arson and Murder,* Peter Micheels described the work of the bureau. Of the city's 101,000 fires in 1989, 10,140 merited investigation by 239 fire marshals; 5,362 were deemed arson, leading to the arrest of 445 men and 132 women.

In 1988, of the 15,000 arrests in the United States for arson, 86.9% were of males. Their age breakdown was: 28.4% under age 15; 14.5% ages 15–17; 20.5% ages 18–24; 30.6% ages 25–44; 6% ages 45 and over. In other words, 63.4% were under the age of 25. Overwhelmingly, arson is the crime of young males.

The Motives for Arson. In his 1978 book *Arson,* Arnold Madison categorized some of the major motives for arson. Experts estimate that about 40% of unlawful fires are set for economic gain. An owner may determine that a property or a business is worth more in the form of an insurance payment than it is intact or functioning. Frequently such an owner will hire a "torch," a professional arsonist. One New York City landlord reportedly paid to have 26 of his own buildings burned down for the insurance money.

Sometimes financial gain is indirect: The owner of a business will have a competitor torched and put out of business.

Revenge is an increasingly common motive. Chicago police homicide squad commander Joseph DiLeonardi told Madison, "People are not burning buildings solely for money. They are doing it for revenge."

New York City Fire Marshal James McSwigin described a typical revenge fire. He characterized the arsonist as a man who is angry at his girlfriend for seeing—sometimes just for talking to—another man.

This type of fire setter is probably one of the most dangerous because he's usually enraged when he's starting the fire. But

he's usually the easiest to catch. In his rage, he'll try to burn her out, or burn the new boyfriend, with a Molotov cocktail [a bottle filled with gasoline that has a cloth protruding from the neck to serve as a fuse] or by squeezing flammable liquid under the door and he won't care who sees him or about anything else. Consequently his crime of arson isn't surreptitious. Revenge is probably the second most frequent cause of arson fires in the City of New York and in the nation today.

In McSwigin's opinion, juveniles start more fires than anyone else. He estimated that juveniles set 50% of the deliberately set fires in the United States. Other experts have estimated that 60% of all vacant building fires are set by juveniles.

Intimidation is also a common motive for arson. In an intimidation-for-profit arson, underworld gang members typically have threatened a store owner with fire-bombing if the owner refused to pay protection money. In a racially motivated intimidation arson, a minority family has usually moved into a single-race neighborhood; arson of their new home is intended to force them to move.

Another frequent motive is the concealment of a crime. Arson has been used to cover up every possible type of crime. It has been used to hide such crimes as the theft by a competitor of a secret formula or future plans. It also has been used to camouflage murder.

Fun is a frequent motive too. A Los Angeles fire set for fun in November 1977 in Topanga Canyon burned for two days and destroyed 1,100 acres of brush, oak and eucalyptus trees, as well as a few private homes.

In so-called vanity fires, the opportunity to be a hero is the motive. McSwigin says he always considers the possibility that a suspicious fire might be a vanity fire. "I often stand back and watch for the guy that helps the firefighters . . . One of the first questions a fire investigator asks is 'Who discovered the fire?' " Discovering the fire is part of the heroic role.

Convictions Are Not Easy to Obtain. Among the most difficult types of investigations fire marshals face are those fires set by wiseguys (people working for organized crime). McSwigin talked about a case he had against two men connected with organized crime.

The evidence that the men had blown up a gas station belonging to one of them was blatant. The fire marshals collected evidence from 18 witnesses. But the district attorney (DA) delayed trial for a year and a half. McSwigin was convinced that the DA was stalling to have the case come up before a particular judge.

After a jury found the two defendants not guilty, despite the witnesses and a 12-inch pile of documents in evidence, McSwigin learned that the acquittal of the two obviously guilty men stemmed not only from the delay and the presence of a particular judge but also from the public's attitude toward insurance companies. McSwigin and an assistant DA questioned a few of the jurors about what went wrong with their case.

The jurors agreed that the men were guilty. One explained the jury's attitude: "Oh, fire marshal, there was no doubt that he [the gas station owner] made the fire."

"Why wasn't he convicted?" asked McSwigin.

"Well, you did such a good job proving how he had spent so much money on cars and how he was so deeply in the hole, that we felt sorry for him." Another juror added, "Listen, really, the only one affected by this is the insurance company. Nobody was hurt."

McSwigin asked if the jury had thought about the firefighters who had risked their lives to put out the fire, or about the toxic fumes they had been forced to breathe, or about the potential rise in consumers' insurance premiums that would inevitably come from the payment of bogus claims.

There was one bright spot in the case of the two wiseguys. One sued his insurance company for payment of his $150,000 claim. Such a case is handled in civil court, where the rules of evidence are less stringent than they are in criminal court. Because the fire marshal would have been free to say many things in civil court that he could not say in criminal court, the defendant settled out of court for $18,000. For McSwigin, the defendant's loss of money was a source of great satisfaction.

Another seldom-prosecuted type of swindle that still goes on in various forms was common during the Johnson and Carter administrations, when low-interest and no-interest loans were made available to rehabilitate tenement buildings. Unscrupulous landlords and insurance agents collaborated. The landlord would take out insurance on a building and hire a torch.

Typically the fire was set on the top floor in the back of the building, in an apartment that had been allowed to go vacant. The top-floor rear had a number of advantages. It was out of sight of people in the building or on the street. Since insurance pays a maximum only when the roof of the building is removed, the selection of the top floor insured that the roof would be burned off. Moreover, the water pumped into the top floor maximized water damage on lower floors. When a landlord had tenants whose rents were limited under rent-control laws, the water damage would force them out when nothing else would.

With the building vacant, the landlord was in a position to apply for federal loans to rehabilitate the building. With the money in hand, the owner would put a roof back on and make a minor effort to fix up the building. Then the owner would insure it again.

Once again the building would have a fire. This time it would burn to the ground or to a point where it was no longer possible to rehabilitate it. Once again the owner would collect insurance. Moreover, on the grounds that he or she had no tenants, the landlord would not pay back the federal loan.

The owner would then walk away from the building site and refuse to pay taxes. When the city took over the property and cleared whatever was left of the building, they would auction off the site for back taxes, and the former landlord would, in all likelihood, buy it back.

The number of arson cases that result in prosecution is small. One expert estimated that fewer than 5% ever reach trial.

Arson Rings. Arson rings (two or more people who engage in arson) tend to be less structured than gangs of burglars. Members often do not know everyone involved. There is also an added element of risk: They have to seek out clients.

The arson ring leader can be anyone—including an attorney and or a public adjuster (a professional who legally represents clients pressing claims against insurance companies). The leader typically avoids contact with clients by using an intermediary.

One 13-member gang was made up entirely of relatives by blood or marriage. Two or three members of the gang would move into new town and rent a small house on the outskirts. They would buy new furniture on credit and obtain insurance on the house and furniture.

After a short while, other members of the ring would remove the furniture, replace it with junk, and set fire to the house. The isolated location of the house ensured that the local fire department would be delayed long enough so that the house would be completely destroyed. Once the insurance money was collected, the gang would move on to a new location.

An arson ring in Massachusetts was brought to a halt in October 1977, after detectives spent four months examining 150 suspicious fires in and around Boston. The investigators learned that the ring used a variation of the building rehabilitation approach. Some members would sell burned tenements to other members at a low price. The new buyer would notify an insurance company that he or she planned to rehabilitate the building. After a new policy was issued, a fire would break out.

Three people died as a result of the ring's blazes, and insurance companies paid $6 million in fraudulent claims. The gang had 33 members, including wealthy landlords, real estate operators, attorneys, a former captain of an arson squad and a former member of the state fire marshal's office.

Pyromaniacs. Pyromania literally means "fire-madness" and refers to people who are driven to start fires in the same way that alcoholics are driven to drink and drug addicts are driven to drugs. Such people generally have unhappy lives. Many adult male pyromaniacs live alone in shabby surroundings and have little social life. The sudden loss of a job will sometimes precipitate the behavior. Only occasionally does the behavior stop when the pyromaniac regains employment. The need to watch the fire he or she has set will often lead to the pyromaniac's detection, particularly when the pyromaniac plays the role of the helpful hero.

Most pyromaniacs use the same method of operation. Typically, they use public portions of buildings to start fires, favorite sites being hallways and cellars. They prefer buildings where the doors are unlocked; they tend to be reluctant to break in. To start the fires they almost always use matches with rags, papers or trash.

Individual pyromaniacs develop standard patterns. Some set fires during specific hours or on specific nights of the week. Once started on the pattern, the frequency escalates. An individual may set fires once a week, then two or three or seven nights a week, then several in one night. Most pyromaniacs work alone, although one Massachusetts group included nine people.

Teenage Arsonists. Few teenage arsonists are motivated by financial profit, a primary motive for adult arson-related fires. Occasionally a teenager will be hired as a torch. Some torches start their careers when relatives hire them.

A primary motive for teenagers is "fun" or relief from boredom. "Joke" fires tend to be more common in rural and suburban areas and are comparable to the turning in of false alarms common in urban areas. Usually such fires are set where there is little danger to buildings or people, and are sometimes viewed as harmless pranks. However, like all fires they carry the risk of death or injury to the fire fighters, and they can divert equipment from more serious fires.

The largest group of teenage arsonists usually exhibits behavior that fits a pattern of "character disorder" (irresponsible, antisocial behavior) begun in childhood. Like adult arsonists, they often have histories of unhappy homes, use of drugs or alcohol, poor attendance at school and evidence of great anger.

Madison describes the teenage firesetter's anger by saying "Whether hidden or broadcast, the fury causes these teenagers to set fires. If they are angry with their parents, their own home may be set afire. Anger at school officials results in school arson. Or the revenge may be directed at the 'establishment' or society in general."

An expression of anger at society was evident during the July 1977 New York City blackout, when more than 1,000 suspicious fires were set by teenagers and adults in a 36-hour period. The blazes killed three people and injured 59 firefighters.

There is no clear answer to why teenagers turn to arson rather than to some other kind of crime. Some experts suspect that they may have discovered the power of fire at an early age. Others believe that the tools needed to start a fire are easy to acquire. Moreover, fires create enormous havoc for only a small investment in time and energy. Some youngsters may be attracted to possible media attention.

Arson as a Weapon of War. Arson has been a traditional weapon of war. The Trojan War is said to have ended when the ancient Greeks burned the city of Troy. American troops burned down government buildings in what is now the city of Toronto during the War of 1812. British troops, in retaliation, invaded Washington, D.C., where they set fire to the White House, the Capitol and other public buildings. A 1933 arson fire in the Reichstag (parliament) building in Berlin was used by Adolf Hitler as evidence of an impending Communist reign of terror, which only he could successfully put down.

More recently, as the Persian Gulf War was coming to an end in February 1991, Iraq's leader Saddam Hussein ordered his retreating troops to set fire to 732 oil wells in Kuwait; it took until early November to extinguish them and cap the damaged wells. In the long run, the carcinogens in the smoke from the oil fires carried the potential to kill more people than were killed in the fighting.

Asian gangs in New York In search of a better life, waves of new Chinese and Southeast Asian immigrants have flooded New York and, to a lesser extent, other U.S. and Canadian cities. The crowded neighborhoods in which they live suffer from increasingly violent street gangs engaging in criminal activities reminiscent of the Mafia at its peak. New York's problems are typical of those elsewhere.

The problems in New York are expected to continue to escalate as three factors challenge the traditional order imposed by the tongs, the fraternal societies that have ruled Chinatown for generations. The first is the growth of street gangs competing for control of the expanding Asian communities in other areas of the city. The second is the effort of Hong Kong-based Triads (secret criminal societies) to set up a stronghold in New York in anticipation of the 1997 transfer of Hong Kong's sovereignty from Britain to China. The third factor is the emergence of a generation of violent, ruthless young Vietnamese gangsters.

The established criminal activities in New York's Chinatown are branching out from traditional rackets—protection, gambling and prostitution—into extortion, armed robbery, large-scale importation of heroin and smuggling of illegal aliens, who are held under conditions of near slavery until they pay for their passage.

An example of the illegal smuggling of aliens surfaced on New Year's Day in 1991, when the police had a call from a Chinese restaurant on Manhattan's Lower East Side. Three armed men had entered the restaurant and kidnapped one of the workers. The kidnappers demanded a $30,000 ransom payment for smuggling the restaurant's kitchen helper into the United States four months earlier.

To contact them about the ransom payment, the kidnappers gave the restaurant the telephone number of their beeper-page system. When the police traced the number to a four-room apartment in the Bronx, they found 23 illegal immigrants from the Fujian province of China living there.

During an interview for a January 6, 1991 *New York Times* article entitled "New Immigrant Wave from Asia Gives the Underworld New Faces," Ko-lin Chin, a sociologist and researcher with the New York City Criminal Justice Agency and the author of the 1990 book *Chinese Subculture and Criminality: Nontraditional Crime Groups in America,* described prevailing conditions in the Asian communities. "There are no norms anymore, no rules, no values; the code has broken down. That's why it is so violent."

Chinatown's traditional boundaries have expanded in every direction. New banks accommodate Hong Kong investments on Broadway and elsewhere; Division Street is the site of a cluster of new immigrants from Fukien province in southeast China; Centre Street is now home to Taiwanese; the Burmese are found on Henry Street; and Canal Street is the hangout of Vietnamese gangs. The Chinese also have moved out of Manhattan along the subway lines, with large numbers in Brooklyn and the neighborhoods of Jackson Heights, Elmhurst and Flushing, in the borough of Queens, several miles east of Manhattan.

At the end of a subway line in Flushing, east of Shea Stadium, is a rapidly growing Chinese community. In this area, the traditional tongs have not operated, and, youth gangs are fighting for control.

In an interview with the *New York Times,* Lloyd Hutchinson, a Shanghai-born police detective who has spent time undercover in Chinatown's gambling dens and now works for the Queens District Attorney's investigative squad, characterized the status of the new neighborhood: "It's not sanctioned territory like Chinatown. The question is who's going to be the first one to take over."

Asian communities in North America have traditionally been closed to law enforcement officials. The residents rarely cooperate with police or prosecutors or talk to outsiders. The only time the outside world becomes aware of the closed community is when the level of violence gets out of bounds. For example, in July 1990 a leader of the Vietnamese gang "Born to Kill" was slain. At his funeral in New Jersey, several purported mourners pulled weapons from behind funeral wreaths and sprayed the legitimate mourners with gunfire, wounding a dozen.

To abort a planned shootout with a rival gang, the White Tigers, a Federal Bureau of Investigation (FBI) task force, in December 1990, halted its investigation of youth gangs that were extracting protection money from Asian merchants in Queens in order to arrest seven leaders of a gang called the Green Dragons. The FBI seized 29 weapons, including two Uzi submachine guns and a Mac-10 machine pistol. Prior to the arrests, investigators believe, a half-dozen killings had already taken place.

The growth and expansion of New York's Chinese community are the result of an improvement in U.S. relations with China and the removal by the 1965 Federal Immigration Act of long-standing racial restrictions on Asian immigration.

In 1980 there were approximately 120,000 people from China in New York. By 1991 the city's Planning Commissions estimated that there were 300,000 in the area legally and an unknown number illegally, with a growth rate of about 11,000 each year. Arrests of illegal Chinese immigrants in the United States increased from 288 in 1988 to 1,353 in 1990.

Under the pre-1965 immigration policies, Chinatown residents were almost exclusively descendants of poor Cantonese farmers, who had been imported in the mid-19th century to work in the mines and on the railroads. The Cantonese farmers formed tongs (the word means "meeting hall") modeled on traditional organizations such as the Triads, which were formed in the 17th century to fight against Manchu invasions.

Tongs in the United States resembled the self-help organizations of other immigrant groups. However, in addition to self-help services the tongs offered basement gambling dens and houses of prostitution. The tongs continue to perform dual functions as legitimate merchants' associations and as major sources of illegal activities.

Within the traditional boundaries of Manhattan's Chinatown (a very small area), two tongs dominate. The tong On Leong controls the area of Mott Street. The tong Hip Sing controls the area of Pell Street.

Street gangs, made up in the main of alienated Hong Kong-born youths, emerged in the 1970s. Until the members were eventually absorbed into the tongs, the street gangs' illegal activities progressed from robbing parking meters, to muggings and store robberies. They were not absorbed into the tongs until after several gun battles between gangs.

In an interview with the *New York Times,* Nancy Ryan, chief prosecutor of the Manhattan District Attorney's "Jade Squad," which concentrates on Asian-community crime, said:

It's a symbiotic relationship; the gang gets protection, such as lawyers, under certain circumstances and vastly increased power in the community. It [the tong] integrates the gang into the community in a very unhealthy way. The tongs also get power in the form of visible muscle. Most of the people in the tongs could be perfectly respectable. They join to enhance their prestige. But they are perpetuating the gangs by giving them respectability. There have been periods when one gang or another got beyond the control of the mother tong.

Detective Hutchinson said of the tongs' decision to affiliate with the gangs, "They created a monster. The tongs don't want this level of violence, all this heat. But for them to get rid of these kids now, they'd literally have to kill them."

Typical gangs are headed by a Dai Lo (elder brother), usually in his 20s. Gang members are recruited as young as age 14 from high schools and junior high schools. Usually foreign-born, they are boys who tend to have trouble with English and in school. The gangs offer easy money, flashy cars, guns and women, who are available in communal apartments. Gang life is exciting in contrast to the lives of the members' parents, who are often each working in two or three low-paying jobs.

An additional lure for gang members may be the portrayal of gangsters in popular Chinese movies and videos. The shooting at the New Jersey funeral virtually replicated a scene in a film playing at the time at a theater on East Broadway.

The On Leong and its affiliated youth gang, the Ghost Shadows, were somewhat weakened by a series of federal indictments. The Hip Sing and its affiliate, the Green Dragons, remain powerful.

Ko-lin Chin described the effect of the growth of the Chinese communities outside Manhattan by saying "Queens is like the Wild West; it's a frontier . . . Coming to the United States for an illegal alien is like winning the lottery. That's the expectation. There's tremendous pressure to send money home."

For the police and prosecutors, the major problem remains the virtual impossibility of getting witnesses to crimes to testify. Either they fear reprisals or they fear that involvement with the government could mean deportation.

The kidnapping of the kitchen worker was just one episode among many causing growing concern about illegal Chinese aliens. The smuggling alarms officials because the process involves international gangs, kidnapping, extortion, drugs, torture and indentured servitude.

The immigrant-smuggling operations are run by Chinese Triads headquartered in Hong Kong. They charge $20,000 to $50,000 for each person's documentation and transportation. Those who cannot pay up front are required to work off their debts once they arrive. Some pay by becoming indentured servants; others by smuggling Asian heroin into the United States.

(See also APPENDIX 1D; THE CHINESE TRIADS; GANGS: PICKUP OR TEMPORARY; GANGS: STRUCTURED STREET; OUTLAW MOTORCYCLE GANGS; POSSES, JAMAICAN; VIETNAMESE GANGS WARS WITH OTHER ASIAN GANGS.)

assassin   Scholars define an assassin as a hired or delegated killer of some politically important person, who strikes suddenly and without warning. Although the term occasionally is used in connection with organized crime, such a killer is generally referred to as a hired killer or "hit man."

The origin of the word assassin can be traced to Hassan Ben Sabbah, an 11th-century Iranian (Persian). Ben Sabbah was a fervent member of the Ishmaili Islamic sect, which held sacred the Imams, religious leaders descended from Ali, the Prophet Mohammed's son-in-law. A zealous missionary propagating the Ishmaili interpretation of Islam, Ben Sabbah established himself during the middle of the 11th century as a political leader, and using hired killers, he carried out a campaign of terror against the Sunni sect.

Ben Sabbah's method for indoctrinating his political killers is described in Edgar O'Ballance's book, *Language of Violence: The Blood Politics of Terrorism.* Ben Sabbah constructed a secret garden, furnished with all the delights promised in the Koran, the sacred text of Islam, to those who reach paradise. Potential assassins selected by Ben Sabbah were drugged and taken at night, one or two at a time, to his hidden garden. The recruits awoke from their drugged sleep to find themselves surrounded by houris (nymphs, represented in the Koran as beautiful virgins endowed with unfading youth). The houris ministered to the chosen ones' every desire. After a day or two of pleasure in the constructed paradise, the potential assassins were again drugged and returned to their squalid homes.

Ben Sabbah subsequently sent for his selected assassins and began their indoctrination by describing, to their amazement, the events that had taken place in the garden. (Those picked by Ben Sabbah tended to have lower than normal intelligence.) In retrospect, the garden appeared to have been a dream of paradise. During their highly successful training, and while on a mission, the political killers were drugged with hashish. Thus they became known as hashishim or assassins, a word that ultimately became universally synonymous with political murderers.

Ben Sabbah's assassins were known as his faithful *fedai,* or Fedayeen (men of sacrifice), whom he sent on murder missions in the name of Allah (God), missions that were usually suicidal. The Fedayeen accomplished their tasks at all costs, knowing that as soon as they thrust a dagger into the intended victim they would be killed by the victim's bodyguards. Convinced that they would regain paradise, the Fedayeen welcomed death. Ben Sabbah frequently paid his Fedayeen in advance so they could turn the money over to their families.

By the time of Ben Sabbah's death in 1091, governors of cities, commanders of fortresses and religious dignitaries were likely to wear coats of chain mail as protection against daggers wielded by his killers.

assault weapons   In a March 27, 1989 *Newsweek* column entitled "Playing With Guns," author George Will asked the question "Why are they called assault rifles?" He answered his own question by saying

> The rifles are called that because they are made to hurl a hail of bullets in front of advancing troops. Hence they are useful for settling commercial disputes between drug dealers . . . Because of these rifles' volume of fire and muzzle velocity, emergency wards must use Vietnam War medical techniques on wounds of a sort once associated with battlefields.

Gun control advocates characterize assault weapons as the semiautomatic versions of military weapons. Gun lobbyists argue that a ban on semiautomatics would affect their hunting rifles, since a semiautomatic hunting rifle fires one shot per trigger pull, as does a semiautomatic assault rifle. However, semiautomatic hunting rifles hold only three to five rounds compared to semiautomatic assault rifles, which hold 20 or more. Moreover, many semiautomatic hunting rifles can be converted to assault weapons by changing the magazines.

All firearms, whether military assault rifles or civilian pistols, are classified into three broad categories: fully automatic, semiautomatic, and other (such as single shot, or revolver). The groupings are based on how the weapon fires and loads bullets into its chamber for the next firing.

Many firearms, including revolvers and breech-loaded and pump-action guns, fire a single bullet with each pull of the trigger. They use a variety of means to position up to eight rounds for firing before reloading is necessary.

Automatic weapons are designed for battlefield conditions. As long as an automatic weapon's trigger is depressed, it fires a continuous stream of bullets from an attached magazine or drum. The gas that escapes when one round is fired activates the mechanism that ejects the spent shell and automatically chambers and fires the next round. Often called machine guns, automatic weapons have been banned from civilian sale and ownership, with few exceptions, since the 1930s. Fully automatic weapons seized by authorities often are found to have been imported illegally, often along with illegal drugs.

A semiautomatic weapon differs from an automatic weapon only in that the trigger has to be depressed to fire each round; chambering the next round is automatic. Some weapons can fire in either mode, at the flick of a safety switch. The sale and use of semiautomatic weapons by civilians is legal in the United States, subject to state and local restrictions. Although such conversions are illegal, gun publications regularly advertise kits to convert semiautomatic weapons into automatic ones.

But even without conversion, automatic military-style assault weapons, such as the AKM (a version of the Soviet AK-47), the AR-15 (a version of the American M-16), and the Israeli Uzi-Carbin, lay down a devastating fire.

Assault weapons are the weapons of choice among criminals because they are concealed easily and because the semiautomatic action of the gun makes rapid fire possible. Moreover, unlike revolvers, which hold only five or six bullets, semiautomatic pistols are commonly equipped with 30- or 32-round magazines.

On the grounds that they were used in 10% of crimes involving firearms, the Treasury Department's Bureau of Alcohol, Tobacco, and Firearms (BATF) issued a ban on the importation of semiautomatic weapons. President Bush approved the ban on July 7, 1989. The ban had little impact on the presence of assault rifles in the United States, since nearly 75% of all assault weapons are manufactured domestically. Moreover, Bush did not propose to support tougher controls on U.S. semiautomatics. Instead he proposed building more prisons and passing harsher laws against the criminal use of firearms.

Although a day after the ban went into effect, Colt withdrew from the market its AR-15, the weapon that most resembled the imports, American manufacturers were expected to fill any void left by the ban. Estimates of the number of assault weapons owned by Americans vary from 500,000 to 3 million. The weapons include AK-47 and Uzi rifles as well as TEC-9, MAC-10 and MAC-11 handguns. MAC-10 and MAC-11 pistols can be converted easily to fire like machine guns.

An automated AK-47 fires up to 30 rounds with one trigger squeeze. A semiautomatic AK-47 looks just like an automated one. A MAC-11 can fire 20 rounds in less than five seconds and is made to accommodate a silencer. The MAC-10, designed by the military for close combat, is not much bigger than an old Army Colt .45. In full automatic mode, it delivers 15 rounds per second.

Prior to President Bush's signing of the import ban on semiautomatic weapons, a number of violent incidents had done much to turn public opinion against assault weapons. An AKS, a Chinese-made semiautomatic version of the AK-47, was used to kill five children and wound 29 others and a teacher in a Stockton, California schoolyard in January 1989. An AK-47 was used by a former worker who had been put on total disability by his employer in Louisville, Kentucky. In September 1989 he entered his former workplace and killed seven people, wounding 13 others, five critically.

In the 1980s semiautomatics were the weapons of choice not only of drug dealers but also of a neo-Nazi terrorist group called the Order, which converted them into automatic weapons. One such weapon was used to kill the Denver radio talk-show host Alan Berg, who was Jewish and a sharp-tongued critic of racism.

In 1981 U.S. gun manufacturers produced 1.6 million revolvers and 764,000 semiautomatic pistols. By 1989 the figures had almost reversed—the number of semiautomatic pistols had climbed to 1.4 million and the number of revolvers had dropped to 629,000.

Among the confiscated firearms that could be traced by the BATF in 1987, 6.5% were assault weapons. A scant two years later, the number of assault weapons traced had climbed to 10%.

An odd gap in the law allows semiautomatic weapons with the potential to become automatic weapons to reach the American public. The BATF, while responsible for regulating guns, lacks the authority to review new domestically produced gun models before they are marketed. At least three times during the 1980s, U.S. gun manufacturers introduced semiautomatic firearms that could be modified in minutes to fire automatically. In each case, the BATF eventually ruled the weapons to be machine guns, thereby restricting their future sales and distribution. However, by the time the BATF had issued its negative rulings, the weapons had been widely available for months, in some cases years. Moreover, guns made prior to the rulings could still be sold as semiautomatics.

Another gap in the law prevents the BATF from keeping track of secondhand guns. There are no federal regulations on gun sales that take place outside a licensed dealership, a fact that makes it difficult for police to trace secondhand guns used in crimes.

Without federal leadership, states that have stringent gun laws must cope with poor enforcement of their gun laws. For example, scarce prison space and proliferating plea bargains have diluted the impact of the Massachusetts gun control law, which requires a one-year prison term for carrying a gun without a license. Massachusetts is one of the few states that requires secondhand buyers and sellers to report transactions, but the short-staffed Massachusetts State Police are routinely behind in logging such sales.

In December 1989 Massachusetts governor Michael Dukakis signed into law a so-called home rule petition that instituted a wide-ranging ban on assault weapons in the city of Boston. The weapons banned included the AK-47, Uzi, FN-FL and FN-FNC, Steyr Aug and SKD; all shotguns with revolving cylinders, such as the Striker 12 and Street Sweeper; and semiautomatic rifles with fixed magazine capacities of more than 10 rounds.

For someone who has the money, acquiring an assault weapon is easy. Wayne King, the author of a December 9, 1990 *New York Times Magazine* article entitled "Sarah and Jim Brady Target the Gun Lobby," described how, in May 1985, he walked into a gun show in the convention center of Jackson, Mississippi and bought a semiautomatic MAC-10 for $600, at one of more than 100 tables and booths set up by gun traders and collectors. Because the sale was ostensibly between two private gun collectors, no buyer's identification was needed nor proof of residence, nor was a permanent record made of the transaction.

Ten feet away from his initial purchase, King bought a conversion kit for $29.95 that made it possible with a drill press and a little skill to turn the semiautomatic pistol into a fully automatic one. At still another booth, for $90 King bought the inner workings of a silencer. He passed up a metal sleeve on sale for $39.95 to house the silencer, since possession of a silencer without a federal tax stamp is punishable by up to ten years in jail.

Although the "open-bolt" semiautomatic version of the MAC with the conversion kit is classified as a machine gun, the unconverted gun has been available for about two decades. An estimated 33,000 have been purchased by individuals.

A March 27, 1989 *Newsweek* article entitled "The NRA Comes Under the Gun" pointed out that imports of the AK-47 jumped from 4,000 in 1986 to 44,000 in 1988. The ban on imports prevented the importation of 113,000 weapons in 1989.

In an interview with *Newsweek*, Stephen Higgins, the director of the BATF, asserted that federal assault weapon control is inevitable because of the "close tie between violence and guns and violence and drugs." Even faced with an import ban, the global arms industry has proven itself adept at sidestepping restrictions. The South African-made Striker offers evidence. In 1986 the BATF banned imports of the Striker, which can fire 12 rounds in three seconds. The same gun is now manufactured legally in the United States under the trade name "Street Sweeper."

The speed with which assault weapons can do great damage was made plain following the Stockton schoolyard massacre, when California Attorney General John Van de Kamp, in mid-February 1989, rose from his chair at a California legislative hearing brandishing an AKS. He announced to his startled listeners, "Ladies and gentlemen, take a look at your watches and start counting. You are lucky that I am the attorney general and not some nut. Because if I had the ammunition, I could shoot every member of the assembly by the time I finish this sentence—about 20 seconds." In the same week that the California attorney general made his dramatic gesture, a New York man told to leave a Sweet 16 party took his revenge by spraying a subway platform with a 9mm automatic handgun, wounding six.

The United States has 20,000 federal, state and local laws regulating guns. By and large, they have not had much impact on the proliferation of guns.

A landmark bill passed the Washington, D.C. City Council in December 1990. The bill would have held manufacturers of assault weapons liable for the death and injury caused by such weapons within the District of Columbia. If such laws became widespread, they might make assault weapons less attractive to manufacture. Congress, however, which oversees local government in the capital, has, under the leadership of anti-gun control congressmen, nullified this legislation.

(See also: CHILDREN AND YOUTHS WITH GUNS; EMERGENCY MEDICAL CARE: THE IMPACT OF VIOLENCE; GUN CONTROL: ADVOCATES; GUN CONTROL: OPPONENTS; GUN-FREE SCHOOL ZONE; GUN OWNERSHIP; WEAPONS OF CELEBRATION.)

assembly-line justice   Much of the criticism of the criminal justice system arises from the routine, assembly-line manner in which cases are handled. In his 1990 book *Rough Justice*, David Heilbroner described his experience as a rookie assistant district attorney (ADA) in the arraignment court in New York County (Manhattan), and in doing so provided a snapshot of the arraignment ("to set in order") process in many urban courts throughout the United States. The assembly-line approach is a consequence of the sheer volume of cases and the limited resources available.

The New York City Criminal Court, Arraignment Parts, operate around the clock. In Manhattan, during an eight-hour Night Court session, as many as 150 newly arrested defendants appear before the presiding judge.

Heilbroner described the bustle of the court: "Even at four A.M., the courtroom is alive with lawyers haggling over bail and plea bargains, white-shirted corrections officers escorting prisoners in and out of the pens, a judge drinking coffee at the bench, and a prosecutor standing behind a stack of cases fresh from the complaint room."

In broad outlines, the district attorney's complaint, based on the arresting officer's testimony, is placed in the context of the defendant's criminal history and his or her version of the current incident. Like most criminal court procedures, arraignment has been reduced to a rapid routine.

The defendant and his or her lawyer come before the judge, the clerk reads the charges and the defendant pleads either guilty or not guilty. If the defendant pleads guilty in a misdemeanor (minor offense) case, sentence is passed immediately. If the defendant pleads not guilty, the court decides whether to release the defendant outright or to require bail.

During the time Heilbroner worked in arraignment court, defendants' files were kept on a table in numerical order, with yellow covers for felonies (serious crimes) and blue for misdemeanors. The ADA had no way of knowing which case would come up until the clerk read the defendant's name, at which time he or she would snatch up the file and make a hasty argument to the court. Then came the defendant's version. The average time for the process was about three minutes per case.

Heilbroner described the pressure the haste put on the ADA: "At times, I became so involved trying to locate all the pertinent facts that I arraigned defendants without even looking up at their faces."

Unlike prosecutors (who initiate and carry on criminal proceedings in court), criminal court judges have virtually no power to dismiss or reduce charges, except on technicalities. Therefore the responsibility for fitting the punishment to the crime and the criminal initially rests on the prosecutors.

The vast majority of misdemeanors in Manhattan's arraignment court were handled through plea bargaining (reducing the seriousness of the charge in exchange for a guilty plea). In a typical plea bargain, a misdemeanor

was reduced to a charge of "disorderly conduct." With repeat offenders, deals involved recommending low sentences in exchange for the guilty plea.

Under New York law, which is typical, a sentence for a misdemeanor cannot exceed one year. Routinely, sentences of 60 or 90 days were given. A defendant with 20 convictions for punching a stranger in the face (a class A misdemeanor) confronted the same one-year maximum sentence as a first offender. Therefore, in cases involving such repeat offenders, it was the responsibility of the ADA in Manhattan to battle, when appropriate, for the maximum. In order to give the overburdened system a break, Heilbroner quickly learned to concentrate on the serious offenders and to give marginal ones scant attention.

Some defendants refused to plea-bargain. They presented a problem. Typically when a defendant refused a plea bargain that seemed fair to the judge and the prosecutor, the judge was apt to ask the prosecutor at what level he or she was requesting bail to be set. For the poor, even a $100 bail would be impossible. Unable to afford bail, the poor defendant who refused to plea-bargain would face having to wait for trial in Riker's Island, the main city jail.

Heilbroner defended the pressure put on prisoners by manipulating the level of bail. "Strong-arming defendants into a plea was rough justice, but it kept the number of dispositions up, the number of 'bodies' in the system down and sped cases along to conviction."

Despite the ADA's power, judges in the arraignment court kept the prosecutors tightly reined in, because they were aware that the DA's office had a built-in advantage over defense lawyers. ADAs had the opportunity to speak to witnesses, police officers and detectives in the privacy of the complaint room, where they could sort out the charges and develop at least a coherent theory of the case. Legal Aid lawyers, by contrast, interviewed their clients in a holding cell minutes before arraignment. Moreover, their clients often lied and guilt was often a foregone conclusion.

Heilbroner described the defense lawyers' disadvantages and their response by saying "Defenders therefore had to use any means at their disposal to help their clients and judges accordingly gave them latitude. It was a standing joke among ADAs that Legal Aid had three basic approaches to weak cases: whining, shouting, and crying."

Prostitutes came through the system by the dozens. Some had rap sheets (arrest records) so long that the computer operators had invented a shortened format to fit more convictions on each page. Constantly concerned about the shortage of jail space, judges never took such cases seriously. In answer to one defense attorney's question, a judge quipped that he sentenced on the basis of the weight of the defendant's rap sheets.

Rough justice is all in a day's work in a typical urban arraignment court. It is undoubtedly not what the founding fathers had in mind.

(See also CALIFORNIA CORRECTIONS SYSTEM; CORRECTIONAL EDUCATION; EARLY RELEASE: THE IMPACT OF PRISON OVER-CROWDING; JAILS; PRISON OVERCROWDING: COPING WITH THE COSTS; TREATMENT PROGRAMS IN PRISON.)

B

bail See BILL OF RIGHTS: PROTECTION AGAINST GOVERNMENT TYRANNY.

battered woman's defense In many states women being tried for killing husbands who have battered them are not allowed to introduce evidence of the battering in their own defense. Traditionally, a plea of self-defense has required proof of serious and imminent danger. It has required that the person who ultimately kills retreat until his or her back is figuratively to the wall, and that the force used to repel an attack not be greater than the force used in the attack.

Defense attorneys for women who kill husbands and lovers who batter them raise such questions as "If a woman flees and her partner pursues and threatens her again and again, has she retreated to a wall the law recognizes?" They also ask whether in combat a woman's fist is the equivalent in force of a man's.

In the 1989 Massachusetts trial of Therese Rogers, the defendant was acquitted of the 1987 stabbing death of her boyfriend who had abused her and her nine-year-old daughter. Rogers' attorney, Kevin Reddington, won the acquittal on a first-degree murder charge on grounds of temporary insanity, which he likened to post-traumatic stress disorder.

Women scholars who have studied the problem of battered women object to the insanity aspect of the plea. Sarah Buel, a prosecutor and founder and former director of the Battered Women's Advocacy Project at Harvard Law School, views a plea of insanity as insulting to battered women.

In her book *Justifiable Homicide,* Cynthia Gillespie characterizes the so-called battered woman syndrome as a "new and excusable form of female irrationality, not quite insanity but something close to it." Such a perspective echoes the law's historic view of women as irrational, helpless, or both.

During an interview for a December 17, 1989 *Boston Globe* article entitled "Murder Acquittal Is Advanced in Battered-Woman Defense," Buel, who in conjunction with the Massachusetts governor's office had been studying domestic abuse, said, "There's a trend toward recognizing the syndrome. But where it is recognized, it is very narrowly drawn . . . The woman literally has to be so debilitated there is nothing else she can do."

Scholars search for another formulation of self-defense. Gillespie explained why they were not happy with the current form the defense has taken. "Obviously, a different law for men and women is an unacceptable answer. What is needed is a law that is sufficiently flexible that the actions of each individual defendant, female or male, can be judged fairly in the light of his or her own actual ability to have defended against the attack in a non-lethal way."

Perhaps the best-known cases successfully using the battered women's defense are those of Roxanne Gay, who in 1976 killed her husband, Philadelphia Eagles lineman Blenda Gay, when repeated calls to the police failed to protect her, and Francine Hughes, whose story of years of abuse that ended when she set fire to her husband's bed formed the basis of a TV dramatization, *The Burning Bed.*

The courts have typically been less than understanding in their treatment of battered women who kill their abusers. In 1971 Roberta Shaffer of Sharon, Massachusetts shot her live-in boyfriend, who had repeatedly beaten her and threatened her with death, as he started down the stairs to the basement where she was hiding with her two children. The Supreme Judicial Court of Massachusetts upheld her conviction for manslaughter on the grounds that there was insufficient evidence of serious and imminent harm.

Lisa Becker Grimshaw of Springfield, Massachusetts had left her husband and had obtained numerous restraining orders against him, which had had no effect on his behavior. On one occasion he smashed through a boarded-up window to attack her with a hammer. On a night in 1985, while she was awaiting his inevitable return, two men offered to attack him on her behalf. They killed him. Her sentence was reduced from first-degree murder, but she was nevertheless sentenced to 15 years in prison.

At the beginning of the 1990s, a gradual shift in attitude toward the dilemma faced by battered women began to emerge. A February 26, 1991 CBS *Night Watch* program discussed the change. The guests in one segment of the program included two women who had been convicted of killing their husbands, Mytokia Friend, a former Baltimore police officer, and Joyce Steiner, a private investigator, each of whom had been sentenced to five years. A third guest was Maryland Congresswoman Connie Morrella, who arranged a prison meeting between Maryland Governor William Schaefer and six women whose sentences he had commuted that month.

Asked to describe domestic violence in the United States, Morrella said, "Every 15 seconds a woman is battered by her husband or her live-in friend and every year 3 to 4 million women are battered. In Maryland in 1990, there were 70 women and children who were battered to death. Multiply that by 50 states and you see it is a national disgrace."

Governor Schaffer was not alone in his concern for women who were in prison for killing husbands who battered them. Outgoing Ohio Governor Richard Celeste commuted 25 such sentences shortly before he left office in January 1991, including four death sentences.

The violence that Mytokia Friend experienced began with slaps and bear hugs. Joyce Steiner's husband became alcoholic and abusive shortly after marriage. Each woman's husband broke down her self-esteem, making her feel that she had somehow caused his behavior. Friend kept hoping her husband would change. Each was afraid that if she left, her husband would come after her. Each woman's husband not only threatened her, he threatened her family.

Asked why she stayed, Steiner said, "Basically out of fear. They threaten your parents. They threaten your children. You don't want to be the person to make those threats come true. You don't know whether he means the threats or not. Any man capable of shooting the family pet in front of someone and using his gun to say 'This is how I'm going to use my gun on you,' you really don't know."

Asked how she reached the decision to kill her husband, Friend answered, "It wasn't a decision. I had reached a breaking point. My emotions and everything were too much. I had reached a breaking point and unfortunately one day I shot and killed my husband."

Asked the same question, Steiner said, "I was in a violent heated argument at the time. The thing that was so strange was at the time he threatened to kill me he was sober. This was completely out of character for him. When someone who has for seven years threatened you when they're drunk and turns on you when they are sober and say 'I'm going to kill you,' you know. I believed in my heart that he would kill me that evening. We had a violent argument and I grabbed my gun and shot him."

When asked why she had a gun, Steiner explained that the gun was a part of the equipment she needed for her job as a private investigator. She had had a license for the gun for many years before she ever knew her husband.

Representative Morrella explained that in most states, the kinds of stories told by Friend and Steiner would not be permitted in court. "In most states, it is not even up to the jurisdiction of the judge whether it will be allowed. It is just not allowed. We are not saying that this means that someone should be exonerated. We are simply saying that in a court trial the proper administration of justice would allow all the evidence to come to the fore. And that's part of the evidence—the years of abuse, and the terror and the fear."

The two women described the shock they felt when they became part of a group in prison called "The Unity Group." In the group they learned that there were other women who had experienced the same kinds of conditions that they had lived under. Each abused woman had felt completely isolated.

Prosecutors fear that permission to introduce evidence of battering might be misused and that women might claim that they were battered to excuse a crime committed for other reasons. Representative Morrella characterized such fears as "poppycock." "All we are saying is not that anybody should be exonerated or that this is any license. Simply, let's bring it out. Let's bring out the evidence as we do in the case of a burglary, as we do in the case of a street crime, as our American justice system is geared to do. Why should it be left out in this area? These women feel embarrassed, humiliated. They never show their bruises. In fact they try to disguise them."

Steiner was asked what she thought battered women needed in the way of help. She answered that they need understanding and to know that the battering is not their fault—that it was not due to anything that they have done or have not done.

Steiner described the psychological battering that leads women to feel that they are at fault. "I think we go through a period of brainwashing. Because they tell you that you are no good. You're worthless. You can't do anything right. That you are lazy. All these things. And you begin to believe them about yourself. And you lose all your self-respect and self-esteem. and you feel that this man is probably the only man in the world that wants you because he says you are no good. If he says you are no good there must be a reason that you are no good and you get beat.'' Said Friend, ''It seems like you sink deeper, and deeper, and deeper. The more you allow him to control you the more of yourself is given up.''

Representative Morrella pointed out that many attitudes needed changing. She told a story about one woman who participated in The Unity Group in prison. She had told her mother that she feared for her safety and her children's and planned to leave. Her mother's response was ''I always knew that you didn't know how to get along with men.''

One man who has been a batterer and now counsels other male batterers says that most abusive men seek help only to avoid separation or legal action. Out of every ten men who ask for counseling, five actually come to a session, three attend a few sessions and only one or two continue. Battering, he points out, includes not only physical attack, but throwing things, ripping up credit cards, locking people in or out and any other action designed to control or dominate.

The battered woman's defense has a long way to go to gain acceptance. Many men view the idea as a license for women to kill.

(See also BATTERED WOMEN: CONGRESSIONAL TESTIMONY; MACHISMO; VIOLENT CRIMES AGAINST WOMEN: THEIR CONNECTION TO GENDER BIAS.)

battered women: congressional testimony The Senate Judiciary Committee, chaired by Senator Joseph Biden (D.-Delaware) heard testimony on December 11, 1990 from experts on domestic violence and from women who had been battered. The hearing was the third and last on a bill entitled the Violence Against Women Act of 1990, sponsored by Senator Biden in response to this growing problem. (The bill has not passed, but Biden expects to reintroduce it.)

Tracy Motuzick, seated in a wheelchair, described the events leading up to her paralysis. After years of being terrorized by her husband, she had separated from him and was living alone with her small son in a third-floor apartment.

When she saw her husband's car pull up, she called the police. She stalled her husband for 15 minutes, going downstairs to keep him occupied until the police arrived. When they finally came, her husband pulled a knife. She ran to the back of the house to escape him. He followed and stabbed her 13 times.

After the police got the knife away from him, they turned their backs on him and he stepped on her head and neck, permanently paralyzing her. He raced up to the apartment, grabbed the child and carried him downstairs, telling the boy that he had killed his mother.

Prior to this incident, Ms. Motuzick had repeatedly called the police and obtained restraining orders, only to have the police lose the records and her husband ignore the restrictions. She believes that if the police had taken her seriously, she might not now be paralyzed.

Among the experts invited to speak before the Judiciary Committee was Dr. Angela Browne, a social psychologist at the University of Massachusetts Medical School. Browne has studied extensively the impact of domestic violence on women and children and the connection between domestic violence and homicide. Another was Sarah Buel, a prosecutor in the Norfolk County, Massachusetts District Attorney's Office, who specializes in domestic violence cases and is herself a survivor of abuse. The third expert was Susan Kelly-Dreiss, director of the Pennsylvania Coalition Against Domestic Violence.

According to Browne, national surveys have determined that approximately one quarter of U.S. couples have reported at least one incident of physical aggression during their current relationship. Over one third of such assaults are serious acts such as punching, kicking, choking, beating or threatening with a knife or a gun. Such surveys underestimate the actual problem because they exclude people who don't have telephones, who don't speak English or who are in a hospital. The surveys also represent only those who are willing even anonymously to report such actions.

It is to be expected that women who have been assaulted by their domestic partners, fiancés or boyfriends would be fearful of mentioning the assaults to a stranger. Nevertheless, enough are willing to admit it to suggest that there is a minimum of at least 2 million women each year who experience serious assault. Many experts estimate that the actual number is more like 4 million.

Homicide figures for the United States show that in the 12 years from 1976 to 1987, there were 38,648 deaths in which one partner killed another. Of the victims, 61% were women. The couples included boy-friend-girlfriend, married, formerly married and unmar-ried-living together.

Other studies of homicides based on court records and investigations show that among those homicides in which a woman kills her male partner, a substantial proportion is in response to the partner's aggression or threats. While the overall rate of spousal homicide did not change significantly during the years between 1976 and 1987, an analysis of the data done by Browne and a colleague revealed that the rate at which women killed their husbands declined between 1979 and 1986.

The data correlated with societal changes that began in 1979, when some state laws made arrest of batterers more likely and shelters began to open, making it possible for some women to escape from their partners. The presence of shelters, not necessarily the use of them, made a difference in the rate at which women killed their husbands because they made alternatives plausible. There was no correlation between the rate at which men killed their partners and a state's laws or the existence of shelters.

Women in the United States are more at risk of assault and injury, rape, or murder from their male partners, current or ex, than from all other categories of persons combined. Over half the women who are murdered in the United States are killed by a male partner. The area of sharpest increase in murder by men of their partners is among nonmarried couples, dating or living together, but not considered common-law married. Recent changes in the laws of many states intended to protect wives against abusive husbands do not include protection for women living with men to whom they are not married.

Buel spent the night before testifying with a woman with whom she had worked for three years. The woman had done everything the criminal justice system had asked of her, yet still wound up in the hospital.

The woman's 12-year-old son told Buel that he planned to kill his father at the first opportunity. Nationwide, among young males between the ages of 11 and 20 who are serving time for murder, 63% have killed their mother's batterer.

Buel lauded the bill proposed by Biden on many grounds, not the least of which was the effect it would have for prosecutors like herself. She said, "It will give a message to prosecutors like my boss that I shouldn't have to take a vacation day to come here to testify and take a vacation day last week to participate in police chief's training. . . . I do think that it [wife battering] is not dealt with seriously. They still insist that a lot of my caseload is drugs and other kinds of crime, which are very serious and are extremely related to domestic violence, but the message has not hit home that domestic violence is serious violent crime, and until and unless we treat it as such we will continue to see its rates spiral."

In describing her own experience of domestic violence, Buel reported that she had been repeatedly told not to irritate her husband or that it was her job to hold the family together. She made an analogy between domestic violence and alcoholism. Ninety percent of the men who are married to alcoholics leave them. Eighty-eight percent of the women who are married to alcoholics stay with them. Women are taught that their job is to be caring, loving and nurturing.

The National Centers for Disease Control (CDC) Violence Epidemiology Unit statistics reveal that women are in nine times more danger in their own homes than they are on the streets. Buel described leaving her home state to move to New Hampshire, where she thought she would be safe, only to have her husband track her down.

Once settled in New Hampshire, feeling that it was at last safe to go out of the house, she took her two-year-old son to the laundry, where she was confronted by her husband. Bruises were still visible on the side of her face from her most recent beating. She begged bystanders to call the police. Her husband countered with the explanation "This is my wife. We just had a little fight. I've just come to pick her up." Nobody moved. She said, "No, this is the person who beat me up. You need to call the police." Her husband repeated his words and added, "I'm going to take her home and we're going to talk this out." Nobody moved.

Buel described her reaction to the event by saying to the Judiciary Committee "I thought as long as I live I am going to remember what it feels like to be terrified for my life and nobody will even pick up the phone and call the police. Nobody wants to hear another story about a battered woman. Nobody wants to deal with the issues or the issues of our children."

Buel believes that the action of bystanders depends on the standards of the community. In Seattle there is a mandatory arrest law. When the police have probable cause to believe that an assault has occurred, they must arrest whether or not a restraining order has been filed.

Where the community has identified domestic violence as a serious crime, the citizens are more likely to call the police when they hear a neighbor being assaulted. The citizens believe that the batterer will be held responsible and that the caller will not be called into the limelight.

In Buel's opinion, laws to protect battered women and their children must include a mechanism for child support. A major reason why women go back to their abusers is that they have no money or resources. For every two women accepted in a shelter, five women and eight children must be turned away for lack of space and resources.

Buel described for the committee an exercise that she does in training sessions with police, judges and district attorneys. She points out that a woman is not safe, even in a shelter, in the same city in which her partner resides. Therefore she must get out of town.

Buel asks those in the training session to put their wallets on the table. She asks them to imagine that they are a battered woman with only $20 and a bus ticket to get herself and her children out of town. When they get to the new city, they must find a battered women's shelter, where there is a good chance that there might not be enough room. When they turn to the homeless shelters, they find that 95% won't take children. Welfare can't help because they do not have a legitimate street address. Even if welfare could help, it might take 30 days to get a check. Landlords won't rent to her because she does not have a source of income.

By the time the woman has learned all the resources that are not available to her, the batterer may have found her. He threatens to kill her if she doesn't come home— or else he has a box of chocolates and a bunch of flowers and promises that it will never happen again.

The $20 has already been spent on bus fare, diapers, fast food and transportation to the various agencies. The woman sees no recourse except to return. If she chooses to live on the street with her children, the local Department of Social Services will take them away and charge her with failure to protect and provide for her children.

The third speaker before the Committee was Susan Kelly-Dreiss, the director of the Pennsylvania Coalition Against Domestic Violence. She described the growth of the coalition over a period of 14 years from nine programs to 57. In 1990 the 57 programs served more than 74,000 battered women and children.

Because the criminal justice system does not keep adequate statistics to document the incidence of domestic violence, the coalition began a newspaper clipping effort to track the number of homicides and nondeadly violence-related injuries. In a 12-month period, there were reports on the deaths of 72 women and 40 children in the state of Pennsylvania.

Pennsylvania's programs are among the best funded in the United States, and yet in 1989 the coalition had to turn away 9,000 women who applied to it for help. Twenty-five of the 67 counties in Pennsylvania have no shelter facilities. Most are rural counties, where women may have to travel over 100 miles to the nearest shelter. One woman spent two days hiding under her porch because she couldn't get to a shelter.

Because of a lack of staffing, most shelters don't have 24-hour coverage. Over 300,000 hours were volunteered in Pennsylvania in 1989, but it costs money to train volunteers. The shortage of funding means that most programs are forced to pay low salaries without benefits. The daily costs of Pennsylvania shelters are about $25 per resident. Other types of residential programs run over $200 daily.

Despite their low comparative costs, battered women's programs nationwide continue to be underfunded and continue to disappear in the wake of funding cuts that began in the 1980s. In 254 counties in Texas, services are available to battered women only in shelters. According to a survey done by the Pennsylvania Coalition, about $300 million would be needed annually to fund and maintain an adequate number of shelters nationally.

In response to a question by Senator Strom Thurmond (R.-South Carolina), Browne explained that research has shown consistently that the vast majority of those men who are batterers witnessed some kind of violence in their homes as they were growing up. They may have been abused themselves.

In Browne's view, the lessons a little boy might learn in his home as a child are that the big person who imposes his or her will is the safe person and to be violent means that your needs are attended to immediately and that your wishes are taken seriously. When he learns the instant effectiveness of violence, a little boy does not learn to express anger or insecurity in ways that are not violent.

Until recently one reason that batterers in the United States could beat their wives with impunity was that the law was on their side. Until the mid-1970s in most jurisdictions, wife battering was a minor crime, a misdemeanor. In those jurisdictions, police were not empowered to arrest. Moreover, in every state's rape laws marital rape was a specific exemption. For women who took the defense of themselves or their children into their own hands, the self-defense plea was not available until about 1974 when the first major case was heard in Washington, D.C.

Until the recent changes, under the prevailing norms, a woman had to have some major injury to show that some violence had actually happened—a requirement often referred to as the "stitch law." Of those cases that actually went to trial, only about 4% resulted in convictions and almost none resulted in jail or prison sentences. In other words, the criminal justice system offered protection to the offender and not to the victim.

In Browne's opinion American society continues to support some of those norms and to sanction the use of violence as a conflict-resolution method. Domestic violence is still seen as trivial—a fringe issue rather than a national problem of epidemic proportions. Sometimes it is seen as comical.

Thurmond asked Sarah Buel what the main obstacles were that law enforcement faces in trying to deal effectively with domestic violence. She replied that as a starting point, training was needed to provide understanding. Moreover, in Buel's opinion, police need to be trained to look for evidence not only of physical abuse but for other related acts such as malicious destruction of property and intimidation of witnesses. In other kinds of crimes, such as drug cases, witness tampering automatically calls for an arrest. But in domestic violence cases a defendant's going to a witness and threatening her is never charged as an added offense.

District attorneys also need training. If the police officer does not have charges such as witness tampering written on the fact sheet of the complaint, then the prosecutor must have the clerk add the charge.

Battered women need access to the court system, which they do not now have. Judges desperately need to be trained. Many times police make an arrest, the prosecutor does his or her job and then the judge does not take the crime seriously.

The police and the victims need to understand that a woman is twice as likely to be assaulted again if the batterer is not arrested. Integrated programs in Seattle, San Francisco and Quincy, Massachusetts order the offenders into treatment.

Biden asked whether some of the recent progress is due to women no longer being willing to adopt the philosophy of "stand[ing] by my man" that Sarah Buel was raised on. Browne responded that when abused, women still blame themselves initially but that there is now more opportunity for them to recognize that abuse is not their fault.

However, there has been little progress in what Browne calls "the so-damned-bad question." That is, "If it were so damned bad, why didn't she leave?" The

question shows that society's thinking is not very advanced on this topic. It suggests that leaving will end the violence, but about 50% of women who leave are subsequently assaulted again. Leave-taking is a time of great risk.

Biden grappled with the idea of how any legislation could make a difference. Buel responded that compared with other crimes, domestic violence assaults and homicides are the most easily preventable crimes. In Kansas City, police report that in 85% of domestic homicide cases they were called to a house at least five times before the homicide occurred. Duluth and Seattle, through coordination among police, courts and service agencies, have reduced by 50% the number of repeat incidents. That is much greater success than in most other crimes.

Buel suggested that one way to make states take domestic violence seriously is to tie federal highway money to action. She was pleased that highway money was tied to the states' taking action against drunken driving and felt that the domestic violence issue would benefit from a similar tie. She suggested it would be helpful to attach three conditions to highway money:

1. Access to the courts for women—as criminal defendants have a right to counsel, battered women need a similar right. In Massachusetts a gender-bias study found that 75% of the men who attempt to get custody of their children in divorce or separation cases are successful simply because of their greater access to counsel. Over half of those who win custody have records of abusing their wives or children. In Buel's words, they get custody because she doesn't know how to play the filing game and the notice game.
2. Provision for child support for women who have left their abuser and taken their children with them. A lack of money leaves women and their children vulnerable.
3. Provision for keeping secret the address of the victim of abuse. A woman who has left an abusive partner is in extraordinary danger when he knows where to find her.

Biden, who has held many congressional hearings on drug abuse, pointed out that the impetus for Prohibition was wife and child battering, which were attributed to alcohol. During Prohibition, the reported incidence of family violence in fact dropped precipitously.

Asked why extreme violence happens at the termination of a relationship or at times of jealousy, Browne replied, "men . . . see attempts at autonomy or independence by the woman as lessening their power and control . . . they cut her off from others, 'she is my woman and I will say what happens.' "

Buel said that the head of the Boston Police Community Disorders Unit told her that in every case where there was a violent juvenile defendant, he found that in the juvenile's home the mother either had a restraining order against a batterer or needed one.

(See also BATTERED WOMAN'S DEFENSE; MACHISMO; VIOLENCE AS FUN: THE CASE OF THE CENTRAL PARK JOGGER; VIOLENT CRIMES AGAINST WOMEN: THEIR CONNECTION TO GENDER BIAS.)

Bill of Rights: protection against government tyranny

Safeguards written into the Constitution and the Bill of Rights protect the rights of the innocent and the guilty alike. In the daily practice of criminal law and justice, equal protection creates tension. When someone perceived as guilty by the public and law enforcement officials goes free, there is resentment among some, particularly if the release was on grounds of a constitutional "technicality." Whenever there is an apparent rise in crime, real or imaginary, some citizens decry the protection afforded criminals by the law, although if they stood accused they would want those same protections.

Since the mid-1960s, fundamental differences have become evident among Americans about how the Bill of Rights and other provisions of the Constitution should be interpreted. Controversies have been intensified by an increasingly conservative Supreme Court, hotly debated issues such as abortion and the death penalty, and the effects of the illegal drug trade, with its accompanying violence.

A number of surveys have revealed that many Americans are not familiar with the Bill of Rights and the protections it affords ordinary citizens. Only a limited number is aware of how those protections came into being.

When the Philadelphia Convention drew up the Constitution no bill of rights was included. During debate, fears were expressed that enumerated rights might later be construed as restricting rights to no more than what had been specified, a position that is in fact held today by some extreme conservatives. As constitutional conventions in the states ratified the new document, most called for a Bill of Rights. The first Congress sifted through some 200 proposals, weeded out duplications and passed 12 amendments, ten of which were eventually ratified. These, collectively, have become known as the Bill of Rights.

The U.S. Constitution with its Bill of Rights reflects many of the frustrations colonists had in the countries from which they had emigrated and with the colonial governments they had lived under. Bill of Rights protections are related to the unrest that eventually led to the American Revolution.

For instance, British authorities used general "writs of assistance" against colonists. Once issued, such writs permitted daylight searches at will by authorities of the specified person's home, business or other property, on minimal suspicion. The writs remained in effect until six months after the death of the reigning king. Moreover, there was no judicial recourse against false accusations. Most searches were intended to find evidence of contraband smuggled in to avoid parliamentary duties on imports.

Many of the framers of the Constitution had firsthand experience with governments that used accusations of crime as a way of disposing of political dissidents. At stake in the prosecution of accused criminals, the framers recognized, are citizens' lives, liberty and property. Therefore, they established as a foundation of American criminal justice rights that must be respected for every person who may be accused. Foremost among them is the right to be treated as innocent until guilt is proven. In actual practice, however, respect for the rights of defendants has often been lacking in the American criminal justice system.

In modeling the Bill of Rights, the framers drew on some state constitutions, which themselves had incorporated some traditional English common law rights. Articles I and III of the Constitution and four of the ten articles of the Bill of Rights address the rights of those suspected, accused, or convicted of crime. The Fourth, Fifth, Sixth, and Eighth amendments include prohibitions against unreasonable searches and seizures (of evidence), double jeopardy (retrial on the same charge after being acquitted), and forced self-incrimination; guarantees of the rights to grand jury indictment, to trial by jury, to confront witnesses and to call defense witnesses; and the requirement of due process in criminal justice proceedings.

Until 1868 the prohibitions and protections of the Bill of Rights restrained only the federal government. Most of the state constitutions had bills of rights, but the federal courts could not enforce them if the state courts failed to do so.

The 14th Amendment, ratified in 1868 with the intent of protecting former slaves and their descendants, provided that all persons born in this country (or later naturalized) are citizens of the United States and of the state in which they live. Despite the 14th Amendment, the Supreme Court ruled in 1873 that most of the basic civil rights were not privileges or immunities of U.S. citizenship but resulted from state citizenship.

Over the last four decades, the Court has changed its position on the 14th Amendment and has held that the due process clause incorporates most of the rights listed in the first ten amendments and in the state constitutions. In effect the Court has said that "due process" summarizes fundamental ideas about justice and liberty, and the Constitution guarantees them in every jurisdiction.

A Brief Glimpse of the Protections.   Article I, Section 8, of the Constitution guarantees that the writ of *habeas corpus* shall not be suspended except in times of rebellion or invasion, and prohibits *bills of attainder* and *ex post facto* laws. The term *habeas corpus* can be traced back to an English common law writ that typically began with these Latin words, which mean "you have the body." In other words, law enforcement officials had to have evidence that a crime had been committed. In American practice, habeas corpus means that a person may not be kept in prison without being formally charged; a writ of habeas corpus issued by a court will force law enforcement authorities to bring a prisoner before a judge who will determine whether the imprisonment is legal. Authorities who do not make formal charges will be forced to release the prisoner.

Bills of attainder are legislative acts that make certain crimes, especially treason, punishable by forfeiture of all property and civil rights. Ex post facto provisions make punishable actions that took place before a law was enacted.

Almost every phrase in the Fourth Amendment has been challenged. The Fourth Amendment reads:

> The right of the people to be secure in their persons, houses, papers, and effects, against unreasonable searches and seizures, shall not be violated, and no Warrants shall issue, but upon probable cause, supported by Oath and affirmation, and particularly describing the place to be searched, and the persons or things to be seized.

According to a 1988 special report entitled *Criminal Justice: New Technologies and the Constitution* prepared by the Office of Technology Assessment (OTA) of the U.S. Congress, many of the challenges to the Fourth Amendment have been on technological grounds. The amendment drafters could not have anticipated automobiles, wiretapping, satellite remote sensing and biomedical advances.

The Fifth Amendment begins: "No person shall be held to answer for a capital or otherwise infamous crime unless on a presentment or indictment of a Grand Jury." The concept of a grand jury is also derived from English common law. Its purpose is to prevent the arbitrary and unjust exercise of state power by forcing prosecutors to convince a panel of ordinary citizens to indict or accuse formally one or more persons of crime, on presentation of sufficient evidence to warrant a trial.

The requirement of a grand jury indictment does not apply to state governments, an interpretation that has prevailed since 1884. Its use varies from state to state.

The Fifth Amendment also stipulates that no person may ". . . be subject for the same offense to be twice put in jeopardy of life and limb . . ." Nevertheless, a person may be subject to both criminal and civil penalties for the same act, a circumstance that victims increasingly are taking advantage of. A person also may be tried by both the federal and state governments for some actions.

The Fifth Amendment also provides that no person shall ". . . be compelled in any criminal case to be a witness against himself . . ." In English common law, this prohibition was meant to prevent the practice of torture and trial by ordeal. In the 20th century, it has generally been applied to the question of whether the accused is allowed his or her rights in the courtroom or during police questioning. Evidence supplied against him- or herself by a defendant or a confession elicited during questioning, without the defendant's awareness of and voluntary waiver of the right to avoid self-incrimination, would render this protection irrelevant. Such evidence or confession may be ruled inadmissible in a trial.

Until 1966 the Supreme Court relied on the due process clauses of the Fifth and 14th amendments to overturn convictions secured with evidence obtained by the police through coercion. In 1966 in *Miranda v. Arizona*, the Court extended the prohibition against self-incrimination to include police questioning. The Court held that no conviction would be upheld unless the suspect had been told his or her rights, even if there were independent evidence sufficient to prove guilt.

The Fifth Amendment's concept of due process, repeated in the 14th Amendment, is the broadest, most often cited and most often challenged protection. The Court has two concepts of due process. Procedural due process means that laws may not be arbitrary, vague or inconsistent in application, and legal standards and procedure must be regular, fair and ordered. Substantive due process examines the purpose and substance of a law or government procedure. Laws and policies must be rationally related to legitimate legislative objectives.

The Sixth Amendment guarantees the right to ". . . a speedy and public trial by an impartial jury . . ." in all criminal prosecutions. The purpose of this guarantee is to prevent unnecessary incarceration prior to trial, to minimize anxiety, and to limit delay that might make it difficult for a defendant to obtain evidence needed to defend him- or herself. It does not prevent long delays brought about by the defendant and counsel.

Article III of the Constitution requires trial by jury for all federal crimes. Repetition of the requirement in the Bill of Rights emphasizes its importance. In federal trials the jury must have no more or fewer than 12 people, and a unanimous vote is required for conviction, but the states are not prevented from having juries with fewer than 12, nor do they have to require a unanimous vote for convictions.

The Sixth Amendment also requires that an accused person ". . . be informed of the nature and cause of the accusation . . . be confronted with the witnesses against him . . . have compulsory process for obtaining witnesses in his favor and . . . have the Assistance of Counsel for his defense."

The Eighth Amendment forbids "excessive bail." Bail should not be set so high that it precludes any chance of release, but it should be high enough to ensure that the accused will appear for trial.

The Bail Reform Act of 1966 allowed magistrates to take into account that defendants might be released on their own recognizance because factors such as a job or ties in the community would prevent them from running away.

The Eighth Amendment also protects those who have been convicted by forbidding excessive fines and cruel and unusual punishments. To the 18th-century framers of the Constitution, cruel and unusual punishment meant such penalties as burning at the stake, crucifixion and the thumbscrew. They did not have in mind abolition of capital punishment. Although the Supreme Court has recognized that standards change over time, it has avoided labeling capital punishment cruel and unusual.

Current Tensions May Erode Hard-Won Gains. Many people are unaware or have forgotten that only through bitter struggles over the course of the last 50 years have the rights pertaining to free speech, religion, domestic privacy and a fair trial—all provided for in the first ten amendments—become available to some American citizens who previously had been excluded.

For the first century and a half of the nation's history, many states practiced their own forms of majority tyranny. A number of states practiced legal apartheid, and some had religious qualifications for public office.

Beginning in the 1930s, the meaning of rights—civil and personal—underwent a 180-degree turn, to become a weapon used by those without power against those who held power. Before then, rights had essentially meant property and economic rights.

In the early part of the 20th century, free speech was not always free. The Supreme Court upheld an injunction against labor union advocacy, and Eugene Debs, a socialist candidate for president, was convicted for opposing U.S. involvement in World War I. Before the 1960s, in the absence of a Miranda warning, defendants often were not aware that they had a right to remain silent, and the right to legal counsel was mostly dependent on the goodwill of local attorneys, who frequently were not paid for their services or expenses.

During the last half century, constitutional rights have improved the societal position of minorities, women, prisoners, indigents, illegitimate children, homosexuals and welfare recipients. However, some observers believe that the long haul to gain the individual rights of those on the political edges has diverted attention away from collective, communal responsibility and civic involvement. As barriers to voting have been removed, participation at the polls has dropped.

In 1990 the civil liberties organization People for the American Way asked young people to describe what makes America special. Sixty-three percent mentioned rights and freedoms. When asked what being a good citizen involved, only 12% mentioned voting. A survey of college graduates found that while 60% thought that the right to a jury trial was very important, only 15% wanted to serve on a jury.

Examples of how society's rights and individual rights have become pitted against each other were discussed by Joseph Kahn in the April 7, 1991 *Boston Globe Magazine* ("Testing Individual Rights: Two Cases"). One case scheduled to be heard by the Supreme Court involved a pivotal Fourth Amendment search-and-seizure case.

The central figure in the controversy was Nick Navarro, a Cuban-born Broward County, Florida sheriff. Navarro had been controversial ever since he assumed office in 1985 and authorized the use of a widely criticized search-and-seizure practice, which targeted drug couriers suspected of transporting contraband through his county. The procedure involved having plainclothes

Broward county deputies board buses and trains and randomly ask to see passengers' tickets and identification and then request permission to search their luggage.

In theory, any passenger could say no. In practice, virtually no one did. One deputy reported having searched 3,000 bags without once being refused.

Over a 13-month period, in just one Broward County community, officers confiscated 24 handguns, 800 pounds of marijuana and 300 pounds of cocaine. During a similar period, a five-person detail assigned to the Fort Lauderdale bus terminal seized 260 pounds of cocaine.

Civil rights watchdog groups, such as the American Civil Liberties Union (ACLU), were not alone in being alarmed by the search-and-seizure practice. Local and Florida Supreme Court judges were alarmed as well. During an interview with the *Boston Globe,* Broward County circuit judge Robert Andrews expressed his concern with Navarro's practice by saying

> You're sitting on a bus in a cramped space, when an officer with a gun sticking out of his belt asks if he can look through your luggage. Maybe you've got something to hide, maybe you don't. But do you really think the average person believes he can say no? Or get up and walk off that bus? Don't be ridiculous. It's a total violation of the basic right of any citizen to be left alone.

The random search-and-seizure practice scheduled to be tested before the Supreme Court in the case of *Florida v. Bostick* during the summer of 1991 involved Terrance Bostick, who was sleeping when the officers boarded the bus on which he was riding. He gave them permission to examine a red bag that did not belong to him on which he was resting his head. The searching officers claimed that they then asked for permission to search a blue bag in the rack above Bostick's head and that he agreed. Bostick claimed the officers did not ask permission, because knowing there was cocaine in it he would not have agreed.

Bostick was sentenced to five years in prison. He and his attorneys mounted a challenge to the search itself on Fourth Amendment grounds, the right to be secure against unlawful searches and seizures. After Bostick had served two years of his sentence, the Florida Supreme Court in 1989 overturned a lower court ruling upholding the conviction, commenting: "The intrusion upon privacy rights caused by the Broward County policy is too great for a democracy to sustain."

The Florida Supreme Court decision effectively put an end to Navarro's random bus boardings, pending a final judgment by the U.S. Supreme Court. The Su-

preme Court decision was expected to affect bus-search procedures far beyond the borders of Broward County. Similar tactics used in Georgia, Virginia and the District of Columbia had been upheld in federal appeals court.

The specific issue to be decided by the court was whether the deputies had "seized" Bostick in the constitutional sense, or whether Bostick had given up his right to be left alone by consenting to the search. One key question the justices had to decide was whether Bostick or any other reasonable person, whether carrying something illegal or not, would feel free to put an end to the encounter and proceed about his or her business.

In June 1991 the Supreme Court in a 6-to-3 vote overturned the Florida Supreme Court decision. Justice Sandra Day O'Connor sent the case back to the trial judge for review with the comment, "The officers did not point their guns at Bostick or otherwise threaten him . . . This court is not empowered to forbid law enforcement practices simply because it considers them distasteful."

Legal scholars differed in their views of the impact of the decision. During an interview for a June 21, 1991 *Washington Post* article entitled "Court Allows Bus Search by Police Seeking Drugs/'Consensual' Questioning of Passengers Permitted," conservative legal scholar Bruce Fein said, "It sends a message that police can cow people into docility simply by running these searches." University of Miami law professor Mary Irene Coombs, who filed a brief on behalf of Bostick, noted that the ruling "gives trial judges an enormous amount of discretion."

A second case that demonstrated the rights of an individual pitted against the rights of society was a Sixth Amendment case concerned with the right of the accused to be confronted by his or her accusers. The case involved the alleged sexual abuse of four children at Craig's Country Pre-School in Clarksville, Maryland. None of the children was older than six.

In 1987, one by one, the four children testified on closed-circuit television, in the company only of a prosecutor, a defense lawyer and a television technician. They testified that they were abused by the owner of the school, Sandra Craig. Although Craig could see and hear the children's testimony on a monitor, the children could not see her. On the basis of the children's testimony, Craig was convicted on 53 counts of child abuse, assault and perverted sexual practices and sentenced to 10 years in prison.

Four years later, still free and appealing her case, Craig insisted that the children were playing games and performing for the camera. In her view, had they looked her in the eye, they would never have been able to tell the stories they told. Moreover, she claimed a phone hookup that was supposed to allow her to talk with her attorney did not work properly and that the jury was witness to her frantic efforts to communicate.

The Howard County prosecutor, Kate O'Donnell, dismissed the criticism of the technology. She said, "The system worked just fine. It simulated an open-courtroom situation in every way. The defendant could see and hear everything that happened on that witness stand. She had ample time to consult with counsel both during and after the children's testimony. The only thing she *couldn't* do was eyeball the kids directly. But bear in mind that Sandra Craig was an extremely intimidating woman in that courtroom."

No issue confronting the criminal justice system today is more daunting than the so-called confrontation clause of the Sixth Amendment, as it relates to the prosecution of sexual abuse cases involving children. Child abuse experts point out that children six years old and younger have trouble separating fantasy from reality and are vulnerable to manipulation by adults. If forced to confront their abuser, or alleged abuser, in court, they may become too distressed to express the simplest accusation.

Because of children's vulnerability and out of concern for their welfare, 32 states permit some form of closed-circuit television system allowing a child to testify outside the defendant's presence. Thirty-seven states allow videotaped testimony, and some states have liberal hearsay rules.

The events leading up to Craig's arrest polarized the community, which remained deeply divided over the issue. Initially alerted by a staff member, a health department worker launched an investigation after hearing about a four-year-old girl who had earlier attended the school and suffered from symptoms associated with postabuse trauma.

In accordance with the Maryland Child Video Statute, the presiding judge must determine that a child will not merely be traumatized by giving testimony in the presence of the accused abuser but will be unable to testify competently. In Sandra Craig's case, the judge heard testimony from the doctors, therapists and social workers who had worked with the children. On the basis of their evaluations, he ruled that video testimony could be used.

Craig appealed her conviction and the appeal was denied. Once again her attorneys appealed. The second time Craig's attorneys decided to challenge the constitutionality of the Maryland statute. The defense attorneys based their arguments primarily on a 1988 Supreme Court decision in *Coy v. Iowa*. In that case, in a 5-to-4 decision, the high court ruled that the use of a courtroom screen in an Iowa child sex abuse case had violated the defendant's confrontation clause rights.

Justice Scalia wrote that there was no denying that there was potential trauma in facing a defendant. However, this was insufficient reason for denying a defendant the right to face his or her accuser. Such a face-to-face confrontation may "upset the truthful rape victim or abused child; but by the same token it may confound and undo the false accuser, or reveal the child coached by a malevolent adult. It is a truism that constitutional protections have costs."

Using Scalia's strict constructionist language, the Maryland Court of Appeals reversed Sandra Craig's conviction in 1989. The court ruled that the trial courts must observe that child's inability to testify in the presence of the defendant, not rely on the opinion of others.

The state of Maryland appealed the overturned Craig conviction. In June 1990 the Supreme Court handed down a verdict in the Craig case.

Once again the Court was sharply divided. Justice O'Connor, who had been with the majority in the Coy case, changed her position and thus became the swing vote. By a 5-to-4 vote, the high court said that it had never guaranteed an *absolute* right to a face-to-face meeting. Justice O'Connor wrote, "That a significant majority of States has enacted statutes to protect child witnesses from the trauma of giving testimony in child abuse cases attests to the widespread belief in the importance of such a public policy." Justice Scalia, joined by Justices William Brennan, Thurgood Marshall and John Paul Stevens, delivered a stinging dissent.

In overturning the Maryland Court of Appeals, the Supreme Court established general standards for the use of closed-circuit television in child abuse cases. The high court sent the case back to the Maryland Court of Appeals to determine whether the use of closed-circuit television was in keeping with the standards.

Right to Privacy. The Bill of Rights does not use the word privacy, nor is it mentioned explicitly anywhere else in the Constitution. However, the Bill of Rights as a whole is understood to define or indicate a "penumbra of privacy" where government should not intrude. Thirteen state constitutions have explicit guarantees of a right to privacy.

Congress and the courts in 1928 grappled with whether an electronic surveillance device constituted a search and more recently whether accessing a computerized data base equates with a seizure. Recent questions have also arisen about whether the collection of breath for analysis of alcohol or urine, semen, blood or other body fluids or tissues amounts to seizure.

Concerns about surveillance and privacy in the past generally centered on the rights of the accused. But as surveillance techniques become more common, there is increasing concern that monitoring techniques impinge on the privacy of the public and go beyond the traditional boundaries of democratic practices.

In a 1928 wiretapping case, Justice Louis Brandeis said the Fourth and Fifth amendments together recognized "a right to be left alone." In a 1958 civil liberties case, Justice John Marshall Harlan spoke of the "vital relationship between freedom to associate (First Amendment) and privacy in one's associations." In a 1969 pornography case, Justice Thurgood Marshall said that the government has no business to tell a man "sitting alone in his own house, what books he may read or what films he may watch."

The right to privacy was clarified in the 1965 case of *Griswold v. Connecticut,* which struck down a state law prohibiting contraceptives. Since that time it has been expanded to other issues related to marriage, reproduction and health.

Preventive Detention.   Once a person is arrested and indicted, a trial may not take place for a year or more. The defendant may spend the time in jail or be released on bail. In cases where a judge suspects that the defendant may be a danger to the community, he or she may set the bail excessively high, thus in effect practicing preventive detention.

In setting bail, a court has two concerns: making sure the defendant both appears for trial and does not endanger others while on bail. Except in capital cases, federal and state courts have assumed that there is a general right to bail.

In their 1969 report, published in 1983 in 16 volumes as *Violence in America,* the National Commission on the Causes and Prevention of Violence discussed at length the issue of preventive detention. For many of the poor, any bail may be too much. But excessive bail has not been limited to the poor. During the civil rights movement, it was used to discourage demonstrators. A

70-year-old minister spent seven months in a Georgia jail when bail was set at $20,000.

The Bail Reform Act of 1966 was the first overhaul of the federal bail law since 1789. It established two primary principles. The accused should be released unless good reason exists to believe that he or she would not return for trial; a defendant's ability to post money bond should be irrelevant to a pretrial release decision. In the 1966 act, the defendant's appearance at trial—not his or her possible danger to the community—was the only consideration.

Reliability, that is, probable appearance at trial, can generally be assessed based on whether the defendant has ties to the community—a job, family, friends—that will discourage him or her from fleeing. Judging whether a defendant is a danger to the community is less certain. Nevertheless, the 1966 law was replaced by the Bail Reform Act of 1984, which endorsed a "public safety orientation."

The 1984 act reflected widespread practice. In 1970 District of Columbia statutes made it possible for judges to consider a defendant's dangerousness in making a bail decision in a noncapital case. By 1985, 14 other jurisdictions had followed suit.

Social science data may be reliable for predicting the behavior of large groups (aggregates) of people, but they cannot predict the behavior of individuals. Despite this, many judges, prosecutors and law enforcement officials believe that their experience permits them to make effective judgments about future crimes a defendant might commit. Studies of such judgments have not found them accurate. The predictors tend to overpredict criminal behavior and hence preventively detain many more defendants than necessary.

When a defendant on bail commits a violent crime, the public becomes irate at the criminal justice system for not making better predictions. As a consequence, in the absence of accurate means of prediction, many defendants are preventively detained in violation of their constitutional rights.

Concerned about the recent gradual erosion of defendants' rights, political scientist Diana Gordon in her 1990 book *The Justice Juggernaut* summed up why the public should be alarmed:

> Although due process generally becomes a subject of public debate when criminal cases arouse our passions, its fundamental significance lies in the protection provided to all of us, innocent or guilty, when our interests do not coincide

with those of the majority. In that sense the rights of the defendants are also the rights of students, employees, tenants, and everyone else who is ever in a position to be coerced by the exercise of government power over individuals.

(See also ARREST: CONSTITUTIONAL RESTRICTIONS AND LEGAL PROCEDURES.)

Brady bill   See GUN CONTROL: ADVOCATES.

C

California corrections system   California has the largest and probably the most complex prison system in the United States. Its problems encompass and its procedures typify those found in all present-day American prison systems.

The California Department of Corrections, which takes charge of all prisoners once they have been sentenced in state courts, uses a systemwide approach to incarceration and parole. Each inmate is expected to be "accountable" for his or her crime, to be "productive" while in prison and to succeed as a nonoffender after leaving prison.

Inmates are made aware of the impact of their crimes on victims and their families, and they must pay restitution. Goals are set for inmate behavior and productivity. Stepped-up efforts are being made to control inmates' substance abuse while they are in prison, a problem that affects 60% to 90% of all offenders.

About two thirds of the corrections staff are sworn peace officers. They work in prisons, are parole agents in the community or act as special law enforcement liaisons. The department operates three hospitals with a full range of services, and each prison has its own infirmary and dental clinic. Mental health services are available in prison and during parole.

At every California state prison, security is the number-one priority. Each inmate is evaluated for security risk and classified into security rankings from minimum (Level I) through maximum (Level IV).

Level I inmates are nonviolent offenders with less than 30 months to serve. They are housed in open dormitories without a secure perimeter.

Level II inmates live in dormitories, but their facilities are surrounded by fenced perimeters and armed guards. The inmates may have prior offenses but little history of institutional violence or escapes.

Level III inmates live in individual cells and are surrounded by fenced perimeters and armed guards. Sentences are longer, and inmates have had several prior prison terms or significant behavior problems.

Level IV inmates not only live in cells surrounded by fenced or walled perimeters with armed guards, but the maximum security prisons in which they are housed include electronic security systems, larger staffs and more armed officers. Inmates at this level have a long history of crime and generally pose escape risks.

In California's newest maximum security prisons, access to cells is controlled electronically from booths overlooking the housing units. Centralized command centers control movement in and out of the prisons. Some institutions have motion detectors built into perimeter security. Any movement in such areas is relayed to mobile security vehicles for immediate response.

For emergencies or major disturbances, each prison has its own trained Special Emergency Response Team (SERT). Other available staff are trained in crisis management and negotiation. Trained dogs enhance prison security and help control drug trafficking.

Maximizing the Value of Time Spent in Prison. The corrections department aims to keep every eligible inmate working, studying or in training. Inmates manufacture all of the clothing, shoes, jackets, and other apparel they wear. They build their prison's furniture, harvest crops, bake bread, cook meals, clean the buildings and maintain the grounds.

Other California agencies benefit from prison labor. Inmates manufacture a variety of office furniture, supply eyeglasses to MediCal patients and restore and refurbish vehicles such as fire engines and trucks.

Communities in the neighborhood of a prison rely on inmates to maintain local parks and roadways, restore community buildings and make toys for needy children. In San Diego an inmate crew keeps the Tijuana Trolleys clean and polished. Crews from Jamestown prison designed, constructed and maintain a minipark. At Vacaville and Soledad, inmates built and maintain Little League facilities.

After the Bay Area earthquake in 1989, inmate kitchen crews fed thousands of victims and rescue workers. Corrections staffs helped local law enforcement agencies with crowd control and search and rescue operations.

Trained inmate fire-fighting crews play a large role in protecting California's forests and wildlands. Every year inmates spend 1 to 2 million hours on the fire lines. About another 4 million hours are spent on flood control, conservation projects and other community service work.

Except for those serving life sentences, inmates who work or study in prison can earn a day's credit toward their sentences for every day they work. However, if they cause problems, they lose work credits.

Inmates are paid for their work. The more skill and discipline the work calls for, the higher the pay, an approach that creates an incentive to improve performance.

More than 65 vocational programs are offered throughout the system. Among the available programs are automotive repair, electronics, woodworking, building and metal trades, machinery repair, masonry, meat-cutting and horse training. Corrections operates the largest primary/secondary adult education program in California. About 15,000 inmates participate in the program each year.

Controlled Release.   Reentry into the community is controlled and offers more than one option for each prisoner. Some inmates are ready for immediate release, others fare better with a gradual return to society, a so-called work-furlough program. Corrections' Parole and Community Services Division oversees community reentry facilities, but the day-to-day work is usually handled by a contractor—a city, county, private profit-making or nonprofit organization. Once in the program, inmates are expected to find work or training, reestablish family ties and plan for their ultimate release. The reentry facility, more informal than a prison, is locked at all times, but inmates leave for work or scheduled appointments.

Selected female inmates with young children can live with their children in small community-based facilities. During their stay, they may participate in parenting classes, vocational and educational training, drug and alcohol abuse counseling and work.

Certain nonviolent parole violators are held in Return to Custody (RTC) centers rather than being returned to prison. Except for those who participate in supervised work crews, RTC inmates are confined to facility grounds for the time remaining on their sentence. RTCs hold down prison overcrowding and are less costly to operate.

Selected parole violators with a drug and/or alcohol abuse problem may participate in a 90-day residential program at a specialized substance abuse center. The program includes intensive counseling, treatment, job development and work furlough.

A California Corrections system priority is to have felons repay their victims' financial losses. Toward that end, the system opened a community restitution center for nonviolent low-risk offenders, who are allowed to leave the facility to work. After work expenses are deducted, the inmates' paychecks are divided equally among the victims, the department and the inmate.

The corrections department has a prison conservation camp system whose primary goal is protection of California's wildlands. Most of the approximately 40 camps are located in the areas that they serve.

Assignment to a conservation camp is a privilege that must be earned. Inmates must be physically fit and have no history of violent crime, sex offenses, arson or escape. They must also complete a rigorous two-week training program.

The typical conservation camp has about ten buildings, including a military-type barracks. There are no gun towers or security fences. The inmates are restricted within well-defined, marked boundaries.

Although fire fighting is their primary function, conservation camp inmates are kept busy with projects that enhance the environment. These tasks include fire prevention; clearing brush; building fire breaks; flood control; cleaning drainage canals, creeks and streams of debris; public land improvement; landscaping; building ramps, tables, fences and firepits; planting new trees; and clearing debris from beaches and marshes.

The corrections system also meets some unique special needs. Inmates at Soledad, Vacaville and San Quentin prisons record and distribute books for the blind. Soledad and Vacaville inmates provide the only braille machine repair service west of the Mississippi. Every state prison and parole office participates in building and restoring toys for children.

Conditional release under the scrutiny of the parole staff for at least a year offers some control over an offender's behavior during the transition back into society. All sentences, except those for life without possibility of parole, have minimum terms after which prisoners become eligible for parole. For inmates serving life sentences, an independent agency, the Board of Prison Terms (BPT), is responsible for setting parole dates. The BPT annually denies parole to about 93% of those who have hearings. Inmates serving life sentences who are released are required to spend three to five years on parole.

All parolees are subject to search, for cause, without a warrant by parole agents or other peace officers. Some parolees wear electronic monitoring devices.

From 1980 to 1992, California's prison population increased from 25,000 to approximately 100,000 and was expected to double again by 1997. California's is among the most crowded prison systems in the country. Overcrowding increases the likelihood of prison violence. During the 1980s California committed about $3.2 billion to new prison construction.

Over the past few years, the corrections department has constructed facilities for 23,000 new prisoners. Unique multiphased planning, design and construction methods pioneered in California have saved a great deal of time and money (and become models for programs in other states), but construction still has fallen far behind current and projected needs. Additional planned projects, if built, will house only 18,000 more.

In 1989 female prisoners in state and federal institutions represented 5.8% of the total population. In October 1990 the corrections system opened the world's largest women's prison, the Central California Women's Facility (CCWF), six miles southeast of Chowchilla. The new institution was intended to be a model prison for women. Its capacity is 2,000.

Although the California Corrections System is larger, more complex and probably more innovative than systems in many other states, like other systems it is faced with a prison population that is growing faster than it can find approaches to manage it.

(See also CORRECTIONAL EDUCATION; JAILS; SENTENCING: A TREND TOWARD LONGER SENTENCES; PRISON OVERCROWDING: COPING WITH THE COSTS; PRISONERS: MANAGEMENT OF THE PERSISTENTLY VIOLENT.)

campus violence   College and university campuses are safer than the country at large. Crimes occur at a rate of 26 per 1,000 students—only half the 57-per-1,000-population rate for the nation. Nevertheless, campuses are not the bucolic havens often depicted in college and university brochures. They are small, sophisticated cities, where campus police must know how to deal not only with run-of-the mill thefts but also with crimes of violence, actions of hate groups, turf wars among gangs and firebombings.

The murder in the fall of 1990 of four University of Florida students, three female and one male, and the murder of one female student from the nearby Santa Fe Community College, prompted New York State Senator E. Arthur Gray to write (letter to the editor, *New York Times,* September 23, 1990):

> The problem of campus crime has been shoved under the rug for too long. A highly respected 1987 survey, for example, reported 285,000 campus crimes nationally, including 31 murders, 600 rapes, 1,800 robberies, 13,000 assaults, and 22,000 burglaries. It is estimated that only 10% to 22% of our colleges even report their crime rates to the Federal Bureau of Investigation.

Reports of campus crime spurred the passage of the federal Student Right to Know Act of 1990, which took effect in September 1991. The law requires colleges that receive federal aid to make crime data available to students and employees and to the U.S. Department of Education.

Until passage of the Right to Know Act only slightly more than 300 of the nation's 2,100 four-year colleges and universities reported data individually to the voluntary Uniform Crime Reports system of the Federal Bureau of Investigation (FBI). Crime figures for most institutions had been lumped in with local crime statistics—assuming that the campus reported the crimes at all. Many schools did not report crimes for fear that such information would damage their reputations and hurt their fund-raising efforts. They preferred to maintain images as safe academic havens. However, college administrations have been forced to deal with campus crime issues as a result of pressure from women over the widespread incidence of date rape, gang rape and sexual harassment, several widely publicized crimes, and a growth in the number of lawsuits claiming negligence in campus security.

In an interview for a November 29, 1990 *USA Today* article, "Campuses No Longer A Safe Haven," Edward Lee II, who teaches security in Washington, D.C., reported that 75 campus security suits had been filed between 1980 and 1990. Twice as many were filed in 1990 as had been filed in 1985.

The results of a survey of 2,000 randomly selected students, conducted by the Center for the Study and Prevention of Campus Violence, were reported in the February 4, 1990 *Boston Globe* article entitled "Use of Drugs, Alcohol Plays Role in Campus Crimes, Study Shows." The center, based at Towson State University in Maryland, found that one third of the students surveyed reported that they had been the victims of crime, and that alcohol and drugs had played a part in many of them. The more the students had used alcohol and drugs, the more likely they were to have been the victims of crimes or to have committed crimes.

Alcohol and drugs also create bad feeling between colleges and universities and their neighbors. For example, Northeastern University students live in apartment buildings in the vicinity of the campus in Boston. Often several hundred students spill out of apartments into the street, where they drink on the sidewalks or in cars and leave behind litter, beer bottles and cans. A Boston police officer described the large, noisy, drunken celebrations by saying, "These are not parties. These are major disturbances between midnight and 4 A.M."

The Towson survey found that about two thirds of the total number of crimes took place on campus. In descending order of frequency, the crimes were theft, vandalism, fights and physical assaults, rape by an acquaintance and sexual assault and rape by a stranger. Although men and women were about equally likely to be victims, only 29% of those who committed crimes were women. About 60% of those who committed violent crimes said they were "high" at the time. In the view of the director of the Towson survey, Assistant Vice President of Student Affairs Jan Sherrill, the survey results about substance abuse suggested that colleges and universities need to address the problems of irresponsible and abusive drinking.

Being high can be lethal—especially being high when high off the ground. A University of Vermont student, Brett Klein, fell from the roof of the Kappa Sigma fraternity house on July 4, 1990. According to witnesses, Klein was intoxicated.

In an interview for a November 4, 1990 *New York Times* article entitled "Campus Crime 101," Jan Sherrill pointed out that at least 80% of campus crime is committed by students. College students are in the age group most likely to produce both criminals and victims.

Not only are college students at a demographically crime-prone age, there seems to have been a change in the level of patience among current college students. David Stormer, the assistant vice president of safety and environmental mental health at Penn State University and the president of the International Association of Campus Law Enforcement Administrators, told the *New York Times,* "The students of the late '80s and early '90s want retribution and action much quicker than the systems are set up to do it. If someone says something that offends them, they want their pound of flesh much more quickly. They go outside the system."

Fraternity Involvement.   Fraternity members are responsible for a great deal of on-campus crime, often in connection with rituals such as initiation hazing or as expressions of fraternal solidarity achieved through verbal or physical attacks on women. A 1989 study initiated and conducted by the dean's office of the University of Illinois at Urbana-Champaign found that frat men, who represented one quarter of the male student population, perpetrated 63% of student sexual assaults, ranging from verbal abuse, to acquaintance rape, to gang rape. Experts believe that gang rape is more common on college campuses than in the society as a whole, is seldom reported and is almost never prosecuted.

The fall of 1990 was not a comfortable season for fraternities. In December four Northeastern University (Boston) students were arrested for trying to steal two flags from a building in New York City. The flags were two of 60 items the students had been sent to look for in a fraternity scavenger hunt.

In December 1990 the University of Vermont suspended a fraternity for seven years, after eight of its pledges were charged with second-degree burglary, third-degree larceny, criminal trespass and possession of burglary tools. The charges were filed by campus police at Yale University and at Southern Connecticut State University, both in New Haven. The Southern Connecticut campus police apprehended the students as they left dormitories with gym bags filled with stolen property. Several of the items had been taken from rooms in which people were sleeping. In the students' possession was a list of tasks they were expected to perform at different colleges.

Fraternity-related crimes were not confined to the Northeast. Following a succession of hazing incidents, in mid-November 1990 a Travis County grand jury issued subpoenas to 29 fraternities at the University of Texas to obtain names, photographs and other information about every member and every new pledge. The 29 fraternities included about 2,300 members out of the university's approximately 50,000 students.

On the day the Texas subpoenas were handed down, the mother of a Sigma Nu fraternity pledge told police in an affidavit that her son had been beaten with a broomstick, walked on by fraternity members in boots and led around by a cloth wrapped around his testicles. Someone called the mother to warn her that her son was in danger. She found him hiding in a fraternity house closet, his legs and buttocks a mass of bruises.

Despite declining college enrollments, crime rates do not appear to be dropping. An April 10, 1988 *New York Times* article entitled "The Reality of Crime on Campus," reported that a Towson State University survey of crime on 1,100 campuses for 1986 and 1987 had detected a rise in violence. Towson's Jan Sherrill said:

> What we've been finding is there has been some increase in acts of violence, physical and sexual assault, rape, and major vandalism in the last year. What we don't know, because this is all self-reported, is just how extensive it is. What we do know is that most of the facts that are given to us are considered by the people who are reporting them to us to be lower than what's actually happening.

Sherrill said assessments of violence varied widely, even on the same campus. For example, two thirds of the deans of students believed that violence on their campus was under control, but two thirds of the residence hall directors felt that it was out of control. An obstacle to arriving at an assessment of campus crime is that a substantial number of the crimes involving students, fraternities and other student organizations takes place off school property.

Sexual Assaults. There are two broad categories of campus crime: crime against students by outsiders and student-on-student crime. Urban campuses have long been faced with the problem of outsider crime. Outsider thieves are tempted by the large quantity of stereos, computers and bicycles. Outsider sex offenders are drawn by the concentration of young women. Serial killer Ted Bundy was attracted to college campuses for this reason.

Only recently have suburban and rural campuses had to recognize that they are no longer isolated and protected from crime. In 1986 Katherine Hawelka, a 19-year-old sophomore, was raped and murdered at Clarkson University in Potsdam, New York, a quiet town near the Canadian border.

About 3:30 one morning, two security guards drove by and saw Ms. Hawelka on the ground with a man. They assumed the couple were engaged in consensual sex, so did nothing. They returned later to find Ms. Hawelka beaten and unconscious. She died three days later. Her murderer, Brian McCarthy, was not an outsider—he was a fellow student. He was sentenced to 23 years to life, and her family sued Clarkson for $550 million on the grounds that the security guards were negligent.

The category of crimes committed by students against other students raises a whole range of questions about what crimes a college can actually prevent. In the late 1960s and early 1970s, most schools dropped rigid codes of conduct that had theretofore governed college life. One of the major changes was the institution of coed dorms and the adoption of relaxed standards about liquor on campus.

As a consequence of societal pressure after the drinking age in many states was returned to 21 in the 1980s, many colleges stopped serving liquor at campus events. In the mid- to late 1980s and early 1990s, female students subjected to sexual harassment urged colleges to take a more active role in student life. Often administration efforts were insufficient.

In 1986 Jeanne Ann Clery was raped and murdered in her Lehigh University dorm in Bethlehem, Pennsylvania. Although Clery's dormitory had locking doors, students often propped them open. Her parents sued the school for $25 million on grounds of negligence.

Although Lehigh denied the charge of negligence, it undertook major improvements in security. The administration increased the security force, established a foot patrol, installed better lighting, locked dorms around the clock (instead of only at night) and started a campus shuttle-bus service during evening hours.

Clery was killed by a Lehigh student who had been in trouble with the law earlier. In addition to suing the university, her parents launched a campaign for legislation to require all colleges to disclose to applicants their crime statistics for the previous three years, their policies on student drug and alcohol abuse and data on the admission of convicted felons. Their efforts led to the passage of the federal Student Right to Know Bill and prompted 12 states to require public reports of campus crime. They also launched an organization called Security on Campus, Inc., which sent out 200,000 "security questionnaires" to prospective students and their parents alerting them to the kind of information they needed to obtain from colleges and universities.

Although some schools took a lesson from Clery's death and installed dorm alarm systems that alert campus security when doors are kept open, some administrators viewed measures such as those the Clerys propose as misguided. Daniel Keller, the director of public safety for the 23,000-student University of Louisville in Kentucky, told the *New York Times,* "It's real difficult to lock up a university, so to speak. It's an atypical society. It's not like a K-Mart that you can lock up at 9 at night and not expect anyone to be in there til 9 in the morning. It's a very, very live and vibrant environment that's very difficult to put an umbrella over."

Sexual assaults by students on students are the most difficult for schools to come to grips with. They are also the crimes most often ignored or hushed up by college administrations. A 1985 survey of 7,000 American students by psychology professor Mary Koss of Kent State University in Ohio revealed that 12% of female students—one in eight—had been raped (the data included both stranger rape and acquaintance rape) and that 8% of male students—one in 12—admitted using physical coercion to force or try to force a woman to have intercourse.

A booklet entitled *Sexual Assault on Campus* by Aileen Adams and Gail Abarbanel, published by the Rape Treatment Center in Santa Monica, California, reported the findings from a survey of 6,000 students from 32 colleges across the country concerning their behavior in the previous year. The survey found that one out of every six female students (16%) reported being the victim of a rape or attempted rape and one out of every 15 male students (6%) reported committing rape or attempting to commit rape. The booklet refers to the crime as campus rape.

All crime is underreported, but rape is far more underreported than other crimes, particularly rape by an acquaintance. It is even more underreported if the rapist is a campus acquaintance. A study of eight of the nine campus rape prevention centers in the University of California system revealed that they annually saw about 240 rape victims who had failed to report the assaults to police.

While she was the executive director of the Association of the American Colleges (AAC) Project on the Status and Education of Women in Washington, Dr. Bernice Sandler, the author with Julie Ehrhart of *Campus Gang Rape: Party Games* (1985), collected data on 100 gang rapes over an eight-year period. Her office also received reports from several campuses of a practice called sharking, in which men publicly bite a woman on the breast or buttocks.

At the AAC, Sandler published a quarterly newsletter entitled "On Campus With Women" as well as some 70 books and manuals. In 1987 she published a report on campus date rape, with shocking data on the rise in fraternity party rapes.

The report did not go unnoticed; 10,000 copies were sold. Perhaps as a result of the unfavorable publicity, the AAC board in the spring of 1990 suddenly gave Sandler a year's notice of her termination. Although the future of the project remained uncertain, all signs suggested that it would deal with less controversial issues.

Women's Defensive Strategies. The fall of 1990 brought a major change in women's tactics to protect themselves and each other against sexual assaults. On the bathroom walls of the Brown University library in

Rhode Island, women made lists of the names of the male students who they said had raped them. Repeatedly scrubbed away by the janitors, the names reappeared, grew to as many as 30, and appeared in several other bathrooms on campus as well.

The lists served as a catalyst for a noisy debate. Some men named complained to the university. Since the compilers of the list remained anonymous, the university could not take action against them.

Prior to the appearance of the lists, the issue had been approaching a critical point at Brown and many other campuses as a growing number of women had pressed charges against their alleged assailants and had been met with indifference by the administration. Complaints against Brown's policies originated from four female students. They organized other women to demand changes. At a noisy forum on November 15, 1990, 350 students, mostly women, attacked university officials as insensitive and demanded the appointment of a dean for women's concerns. One woman said that in response to her rape complaint, university officials ordered the young man to write a letter of apology to her, and a dean had told her, "I think this can all be boiled down to a case of bad chemistry."

The idea of posting lists on bathroom walls spread to other campuses, and female students broadened their range of tactics. At a public forum at Hampshire College in Amherst, Massachusetts, women living in the school's two coed dormitories reported that a man had been entering the bathrooms of both dorms and pulling aside the shower curtains as they showered.

Dissatisfied with the university's response to this and other complaints, the women gathered 700 signatures on a petition and presented it to parents and administrators on the morning of Parents Weekend. Hampshire officials ordered additional campus lighting and had doors with locks installed for dormitory showers.

The installation of locks by university officials is not always met with universal student approval. In New Jersey when Princeton University officials installed a new $200,000 electronic card-key locking system—the first in the school's 244-year history—in the university's five freshman and sophomore residential halls, some students complained that routine events such as visiting friends in other dorms or throwing parties had become complicated. Other students complained that anyone could beat the system by slipping in behind card-carrying residents or by coming in with a pizza to deliver. Besides the new locking systems, "panic alarms" were installed in bathrooms of unlocked halls, hand-held alarms were distributed and 50 emergency telephones were installed throughout out the campus.

In an effort to increase responsiveness to crime, Carnegie-Mellon University in Pittsburgh installed a bicycle patrol. The officers wear street clothes and carry small radios. They can get around the small campus faster than officers on foot and can get into places a squad car cannot reach. During a trial period, crime on campus, particularly car theft, dropped.

While the lists on bathroom walls became catalysts for change, and the installation of protective devices offered some protection against future crime, lawsuits seemed to be the most effective leverage for change in universities. Such suits have included a landmark case in which $195,000 judgment was lodged against Pine Manor College in Boston for failure to protect a student who was raped; a $2 million suit won against George Washington University, Washington, D.C. following a sexual attack in a soundproof room; a suit reportedly settled for $700,000 by Catholic University after a freshman was raped and shot on a running track; and a $3 million judgment awarded to a Dade Community College student in Florida who was raped in a parking lot.

The threat of suits and the continuing pressure from female students have led many schools to make security audits. The schools typically follow such audits with increased training, increased patrols, improved lighting and the installation of electronic security systems in dorms. Harvard University, Cambridge, Massachusetts and the University of Colorado in Boulder distribute plastic whistles to incoming freshman women. A University of Colorado senior reports that when a whistle blows on her campus, a number of men, including security, faculty and students, respond. Brown University put into place a massive escort service.

Most administrative policy changes deal with sexual assaults by strangers. However, many experts believe that major changes have to come in approaches to acquaintance and gang rapes committed by fraternity and athletic team members. These crimes are an outgrowth of prejudices against women.

Murder Has Become Less Rare. Although murder is not common in universities, it seemed to become more so in the 1990s. In January 1990 Northeastern University in Boston was already the subject of severe criticism for lax security when a sophomore, Mark Belmore, was killed on a city street near the campus, after being chased down by a group of youths and stabbed 22 times. A second student was killed near his apartment a few miles from campus, apparently during a marijuana transaction.

While there may not have been much that the Northeastern campus police could have done to prevent the murders, students felt that a program to make students more aware should have been in place. They were pleased at the start-up of an escort service but thought it was long overdue.

The University of Florida, in Gainesville, was struck in 1990 by a serial killer. The first body was found on August 26, 1990. Within a span of about 40 hours five students, four women and one man, were murdered and mutilated. One victim had been decapitated. The man suspected of committing the crime had been severely abused as a child by his police officer father. At the time of the Gainesville murders, the alleged murderer was wanted for the attempted murder of his father.

At the University of Montreal, in December 1989, an armed man named Marc Lepine entered an engineering classroom, ordered all the men in the room to leave and shot and killed 14 female students before killing himself. In the three-page suicide note he carried on him, Lepine blamed "feminists" for ruining his life and for leading him to massacre the female students in revenge.

Montreal police described Lepine as very intelligent. He had aspired to attend the university's prestigious Ecole Polytechnique but had failed a course needed for admission to graduate-level studies. The number of women in the engineering school has increased significantly in recent years, to about 10% of the 5,000 students. Authorities speculated that Lepine may have become convinced that one of the female engineering students had taken his rightful place.

Minority Groups as Targets. The apparent growth in sexual bias on college campuses has been accompanied by evidence of increasing racial and ethnic prejudice. In Atlanta, a black Emory College freshman, Sabrina Collins, was terrorized by a bigot. In April 1990 she came home to find her teddy bear slashed, her clothes soaked in bleach and NIGGER HANG written in lipstick on the wall. When death threats began arriving in the mail, university officials supplied extra locks and an alarm system for her apartment. In May 1990, as she prepared to move out, she lifted the rug to find DIE NIGGER DIE written in nail polish on the floor. She collapsed and had to be hospitalized.

Since 1986, according to the Baltimore-based National Institute Against Prejudice and Violence, more than 250 colleges and universities, including many of the most prestigious schools, have reported racist incidents, ranging from swastikas painted on walls to violent attacks and death threats. A survey conducted by the institute indicated that one in four minority students had been the victim of a racial incident, which would mean 800,000 to a million victims nationwide.

Students were not the only ones committing hate crime offenses. A professor at California State University at San Bernardino was put on probation for three years for putting a note containing obscenities and racial slurs on a black student's car.

At the Chicago campus of the University of Illinois in mid-November 1990, students demonstrated after a series of incidents directed at black and Hispanic students, including one in which a penis severed from a medical school cadaver had been hung outside the door of a black female residence hall advisor.

A variety of on-campus violent incidents was described in a Carnegie Foundation for the Advancement of Teaching report, entitled *Campus Life: In Search of Community,* issued in May 1990. The report characterized the incidents, such as the terror inflicted on Sabrina Collins, as examples of a general "breakdown in civility" on U.S. campuses. The result of a year-long study of American colleges, the Carnegie Foundation report used muted and scholarly language, but it sketched a vision of campus life rife with racism, sexism, homophobia, anti-Semitism and anti-Asian feeling. Support for the report's analysis came in a May 7, 1990 *Times* article entitled "Bigots in the Ivory Tower," which chronicled a long list of violent campus incidents.

Virtually every minority group finds itself under siege on the nation's campuses. Whatever their individual backgrounds and achievements, black students are belittled as the beneficiaries of lowered standards. Asian students, on the other hand, are attacked for "curve-busting" on grading scales and for raising the level of competition for jobs in fields such as math, science and engineering.

Fear of AIDS has been used to escalate gay-bashing. At Pennsylvania State in University Park, Pennsylvania, a group calling itself the Committee for an AIDS-free America tacked up posters around campus carrying a skull and crossbones and a message that read: HOMICIDE HAS A DEFINITE PLACE AT PENN STATE.

A fraternity at Trinity University in San Antonio, Texas was put on probation after requiring a Jewish pledge to wear a Nazi uniform on campus. Jewish women are derided as Jewish-American Princesses (JAPs). Students at Cornell and elsewhere wear T-shirts

that read: SLAP-A-JAP and BACK OFF BITCH, I'M A JAP-BUSTER.

Rabbi Laura Geller, director of the Hillel Jewish Center at the University of Southern California, described such attitudes: "Anti-Semitism masked as sexism is more socially acceptable, because, unfortunately, sexism is still an accepted form of bigotry."

The current college generation came of age after the civil rights battles of the 1960s and 1970s. Their parents have apparently failed to transmit the message of those years. Daniel Levitas, executive director of the Atlanta-based Center for Democratic Renewal, told *Time,* "We have today a whole young society that has not been called to conscience."

Until they arrive on campus, the site of a grand-scale social experiment, many students have not had firsthand experience with different cultures. Over the past two decades, previously closed colleges have opened their doors to women, minorities, the poor and the disabled. Not only are campuses more diverse than they were 20 years ago, they are more heterogeneous than most high schools and most neighborhoods. The chemistry is volatile.

The effect of constant racial friction on nonwhite students creates a tremendous pressure to outperform the stereotypes. As a consequence, some drop out or move to more supportive schools. Those who remain often segregate themselves.

In the 1989–90 school year, Columbia University in New York organized a mandatory "multicultural sensitivity training" session for 1,880 new students. William Damon, chairman of the Education Department at Brown, said of such courses, "These things may seem kind of Mickey Mouse. But I'm in favor even of symbolic gestures because it does communicate to young people what the priorities are."

On other campuses, activism has made a difference. Toni Luckett, a spiked-haired lesbian African-American Studies major who quotes Malcolm X, built a minority coalition and was elected student-body president at the University of Texas. Luckett staged rallies that put the university on notice that students would take to the streets if officials failed to deal with racial incidents.

Another debate on campus is being waged around issues of free speech. Dozens of universities have introduced tough new codes prohibiting speech that leads to, among other things, a "demeaning atmosphere." Some schools have suspended students for using offensive epithets toward blacks, homosexuals or other minorities, not only in the classrooms but in intramural sports on and off campus. (Administration of such codes is apparently not always even-handed. The University of Wisconsin at Parkside suspended a student for addressing another as a ''Shaka Zulu,'' while the University of Wisconsin at Madison held that the term redneck was not discriminatory.)

A host of noncampus organizations decry the loss of free speech implied by such codes. Those forced to live with the passions the slurs stir up have a different view. In an interview for a April 1, 1991 *Time* article entitled ''Upside Down in the Groves of Academe,'' John Jeffries, a black associate dean of the Graduate School of Management and Urban Policy at the New School for Social Research in New York, said, ''Freedom of expression is no more sacred than freedom from intolerance and bigotry.''

Campus Police.   As universities have changed over recent decades, so too have campus police organizations. Once viewed as organizations of law enforcement washouts, campus police are now considered to be specialized security forces. Often trained by and working closely with local police, they have been recognized by the International Association of Chiefs of Police (IACP), which created a Campus Police section in 1990.

In an interview for an August 5, 1990 *New York Times* article entitled ''Social Security: Campus Police Carry New Power and Sometimes Guns,'' Derry Bowles, police chief at the University of California at Berkeley, described the change: ''In the old days, most of the campuses, if they had any crime at all, called the local police authority. Now we can take something as serious as a homicide or just shoplifting.''

Gang violence on or near campuses has led to the development of special training in those areas for campus police. Richard Young, director of public safety at the State University of New York at Stony Brook, told the *New York Times,* ''Campuses are no longer for the elite. You have all the problems of a regular community, with drugs and violence.''

Many campus police departments are being given full police powers, through state legislation or by local authority, that make it possible for them to execute search warrants, serve arrest warrants and pursue suspects off campus. Officers at the nine University of California campuses have the authority to perform police work anywhere in the state.

The University of Miami police have been granted police powers by Coral Gables, the small city in which the campus is located, southwest of Miami. In company with city police, the campus police of the University of

Tennessee at Knoxville patrol an area called ''the strip'' on weekends. Many other campuses foster joint efforts with local police.

Not all those who live and work on campuses view the notion of armed campus officers favorably. Robert Reichley, vice president for university relations at Brown University, told the *New York Times,* ''We feel the presence of guns in a community of undergraduates is not a good idea.''

Some states have considered the possibility of making campus police a part of the state police. Such a move could alter the special relationship campus police have with campus administrations. That relationship has been a source of criticism by female students, who complain that certain crimes, such as acquaintance rape, are minimized by police as reflections of administrative policy, thus leaving female students in jeopardy.

(See also CLASSROOM VIOLENCE; HATE CRIMES; HATE GROUPS; RAPE; SERIAL KILLERS; VIOLENCE RESEARCH: A LONGITUDINAL STUDY OF VIOLENCE AMONG THE YOUNG; VIOLENT CRIMES AGAINST WOMEN: THEIR CONNECTION TO GENDER BIAS.)

capital crime   An offense punishable by death or life imprisonment is a capital crime. Typically capital crimes include such offenses as treason and murder. Although the ''capital'' is often assumed to imply a crime that requires the death penalty, in states that have outlawed the death penalty, life imprisonment is the alternative.

(See also DEATH PENALTY; SENTENCING: A TREND TOWARD LONGER SENTENCES.

capital punishment   See DEATH PENALTY.

career criminals   See AGE AND CRIME; CRIMINAL THINKING: THEORIES AND TREATMENT MODELS; SENTENCES: TREND TOWARD LONGER SENTENCES.

case stripping   The common practice of dropping some charges to reduce the penalties faced by someone accused of a crime is known as case stripping. Concessions by law enforcement officials are generally made in exchange for something the person charged can offer, such as information or an agreement to testify against someone at a higher level in a criminal organization or someone who has committed more violent or a greater number of crimes.

(See also ASSEMBLY-LINE JUSTICE; INFORMANTS; PROSECUTORIAL DISCRETION IN THE DISPOSITION OF CASES; APPENDIX IB: THE SICILIAN MAFIA.

causation   See CRIMINAL LIABILITY.

Centers for Disease Control (CDC) Violence Divisions: An epidemiologic approach to research and prevention

A federal public health agency, the Centers for Disease Control (CDC) uses epidemiology (the study of the occurrence of disease in a population) as its conceptual framework. In 1981 Wllliam Foege, then director of the CDC, ordered a study to determine the most serious health problems in the United States. High on the list was violence.

The study's report inspired the formation of the violence epidemiology section within the CDC in 1983 to apply epidemiologic techniques to the problems of homicide, child abuse and suicide. It was followed by the creation of an injury epidemiology and control division in 1985. The two merged in 1986, the same year that Congress charged the CDC with establishing a national injury prevention research center. The CDC's Center for Environmental Health and Injury Control has responsibility for researching and monitoring the nation's "intentional" and "unintentional" injuries.

The methods of epidemiology were developed during the investigations of the great epidemics such as bubonic plague and smallpox. John Snow's studies of cholera outbreaks in London are a classic example of the development of an epidemiologic approach. Snow used residence and employment information to plot a "spot map," on which a dot indicated a specific number of cases. Since water was suspected of being implicated in cholera outbreaks, Snow identified public wells on his map in areas of high disease occurrence. Then he plotted identified cases and related them to the wells. He found clusters of cases associated with specific wells.

An epidemiologist examines three factors: the causative agent, the host and the environment. Causative agents may be biological (bacteria or viruses), chemical (pesticides, drugs, industrial chemicals) or physical (heat, noise, vibration), or speeding objects (bullets, moving cars).

Host factors may include age, sex, ethnic group, socioeconomic status, degree of exposure to risk, resistance or susceptibility. Environmental factors may include water, food, housing, weather or environmental pollutants. The agent, the host and the environment interact in complex combinations to put populations at risk of disease, injury or death.

The chief of the CDC's violence division compares research into the prevalence of violence in the United States with the medical model for grappling with disease. The death rates from tuberculosis began to fall long before there was a clear understanding of the disease because it was recognized that nutrition and sanitation were contributing factors. Before violence can be brought fully under control, researchers believe that such behavior will have to be understood at least as well as contagious diseases are now understood. But in the meantime because of the severity of the problem, some interventions will be necessary in the absence of full understanding.

A 1988 paper in *Violence and Victims* (vol. 3, no. 4), by Division of Injury Epidemiology and Control researchers James Mercy and Patrick O'Carroll reported some of the demographics of the problem. Homicide was the 11th leading cause of death among Americans, the third leading cause among those in the age range of 15 to 34 and the leading cause of death among African-American males 15 to 34. The lifetime risk of death from homicides for black males is 1 in 28; for white males it is 1 in 164. There are an estimated 4 to 12 million abused spouses and 60,000 to 1.5 million physically abused children each year.

Placing curbs on violence does not have a high national priority. Mercy and O'Carroll wrote:

> Although the toll of injuries and death due to violence is unacceptably high, our society has yet to develop cogent and effective policies to address this problem . . . an exclusive reliance on criminal justice response to violence is likely to fall substantially short of the goal of preventing injuries and death from violence. Applying public health perspectives and practices should help us move closer to achieving this goal.

There has been an increasing acceptance within the public health community of the importance of behavioral factors in the etiology and prevention of disease. Effective prevention efforts in heart disease, cancer and stroke have focused largely on exercise, diet and cessation of smoking. Such successes have convinced public health professionals that behavioral approaches can help in the reduction and prevention of violence. The 1979 U.S. Surgeon General's Report, *Healthy People,* emphasized that health professionals could not ignore the health of children, adolescents and young adults.

A Public Health Approach. Key elements in a public health approach include: prevention of disease or injury, a focus on those most at risk, ongoing evaluation of preventive interventions and a multidisciplinary perspective. Prediction is of central importance in targeting resources to develop prevention strategies.

Identifying those at risk, assessing factors that contribute to or reduce risk and evaluating strategies requires a continuing systematic collection, analysis and interpretation of health data. The CDC does not depend solely on its own monitoring systems but makes use of others already in place, such as the Bureau of Justice Statistics National Crime Survey, the National Center for Health Statistics' mortality studies, state and local vital statistics records and child abuse and trauma registries.

Risk group identification examines characteristic risk patterns by person, place and time. In the case of interpersonal violence, identification is expanded to include the risk of committing violence as well as the risk of being injured by it. Risk group identification allows statistical prediction even before underlying etiology is understood and permits the targeting of potentially productive areas of research. Sociologists and criminologists have long applied the basic techniques of risk group identification and, like the CDC, have identified young black males as at highest risk of homicide.

Studies by the CDC of the temporal patterns of homicide incidence rates have confirmed some expected correlations, such as that between alcohol and drug use and the risk of becoming a homicide victim. They also have revealed less obvious relationships. For example, children are at greatest risk of homicide below age 3 and above age 14. The leading cause of death for women on the job in Texas is homicide.

Although knowing which groups are at highest risk of disease or injury makes it possible to target resources, it does not explain why they are at risk. Epidemiologists have traditionally relied on three basic types of study to explore risk factors: cohort studies, case-control studies and cross-sectional studies.

Cohort studies involve two or more groups of people who do not suffer from the problem under study but who differ in their level of risk for it. They are followed over time to discover the incidence of the problem in each of the groups. For example, to examine the relationship between chronic use of alcohol and wife abuse, a cohort study might follow three groups of married

men, alcoholics, nonalcoholics who drink and nondrinkers.

Case-control studies compare individuals who have the particular condition or behavior under study with a control group representative of the population within which the condition or behavior arose. For example, within a geographic area the proportion of a group of abusive husbands who are alcohol and drug abusers could be compared to a randomly selected group of nonabusive husbands from the same geographic area.

Cross-sectional studies measure at a point in time or over a relatively short period of time exposure to the risk factor and the occurrence of the problem under study. For example, a comparison might be made from a self-report study of the prevalence of wife abuse among married men who are nondrinkers, who drink moderately or who abuse alcohol.

For a cluster of homicides of children in Atlanta from 1979 to 1981, the case-control method was used to obtain information from each victim's primary caregiver. The information was compared with similar information obtained from primary caregivers of control families with children who were the same age and sex as the victims and who lived in the same neighborhood. The investigators concluded that an increased risk of victimization was associated with less supervision, uncertainty of the caregiver about a child's whereabouts, a child's absence from home after 8:00 P.M. and a child's greater willingness to trust adults.

Although there are numerous examples of successful prevention strategies in combating a variety of public health threats such as influenza and cardiovascular disease, violence prevention is still in its infancy. Two high-priority areas are poverty and the accessibility of handguns.

To be effective, a public health approach to violence must give high priority to the development of monitoring systems for morbidity (the rate or proportion of disease or injury in a given locality). Such systems would need to include information on victim-offender relationships, circumstances such as drug or gang involvement and the types of weapon used.

At the national level, the only source of routinely collected morbidity data on interpersonal violence has been the National Crime Survey (NCS). The NCS data are complicated to use and are aggregated on a national level and hence not useful for state and local jurisdictions.

At those levels, such data are virtually absent. The logical sites for collection are hospital emergency rooms, schools and law enforcement agencies. Without such data it is difficult to assess the magnitude of the problem or plan intervention or prevention strategies.

Although homicide data are generally thought to be accurate, little research has been done to check their reliability and validity. One 1986 study done by C. Loftin in Baltimore found classification of robbery homicides on the Federal Bureau of Investigation's (FBI's) Uniform Crime Report forms to be very unreliable. Yet in the absence of morbidity data, such mortality data has to form the basis for policy decisions.

Research has determined that violence is not a unidimensional phenomenon. For example, homicides related to the commission of crimes may be very different from non-crime-related homicides. Risk factor exploration would be more fruitful if directed toward specific types of violence rather than broad categories such as homicides or all assaults.

Criminal justice risk factor research has determined that an individual has a greater likelihood of violently injuring another person if he or she was exposed to violence as a child, uses drugs or alcohol and has access to a lethal weapon such as a handgun.

Some of the known risk factors that have important implications for preventing homicide and assault need to be defined more explicitly. For example, although there is a clear relationship between poverty and homicide, unknown factors may worsen or lessen the effect of the link. The presence of lead in the environment may contribute to biological and psychological changes that lead to aggressive behavior. On the other hand, the presence of family members with conflict resolution skills may avoid aggression.

Despite the fact that much analytic investigation remains to be done, the health consequences of interpersonal violence are such that, at the very least, legal and social mandates already in place, such as reducing the exposure of adolescents to alcohol, should be enforced.

Moreover, the cost-effectiveness of programs already in place needs to be evaluated. Emergency-based efforts to detect, assess and treat victims of interpersonal violence; therapy for abusive men; and similar efforts should be strengthened if effective or replaced if not.

The CDC funds violence research programs. In 1992 a number of studies were under way. A Pennsylvania study was designed to study risk factors related to suicides among 7,000 patients at two psychiatric outpatient clinics, with a view to developing a profile of high-risk suicidal outpatients. A New York City study sought to improve the recognition of adolescents at risk of suicide and to secure appropriate care for them.

Two studies concerned firearms. A Maryland study was designed to examine the effects of gun laws. A Tennessee study examined three metropolitan counties to determine whether the presence of a firearm in a home increased or decreased the probability of a resident's becoming a homicide victim.

A Massachusetts study was designed to develop, implement and evaluate education intervention approaches to prevent violent behavior among inner-city high-risk young adolescents. A California historical cohort study proposed to test the hypothesis that the presence and severity of past criminal history serves as a predictor of future criminal activity. The research was designed to identify 10,000 California residents in 1977, 5,000 with a criminal record and 5,000 without, and determine their subsequent risk.

The CDC also conducts its own research on violence. Epidemiologic research in one geographic area revealed that almost half of all incidents of domestic assault occurred among couples who were estranged, living together unmarried or neither married nor living together, and that the violence was generally part of a repeated pattern. The finding suggested a need to link data collection efforts among criminal justice, health and social service agencies in order to identify repeat offenders and introduce prevention strategies.

Another in-house study found that adolescents at excessively high risk for so-called copycat suicide have a distinctive set of identifying characteristics. Based on the findings, the CDC developed and published guidelines under the title ''Recommendations for a Community Plan for Prevention and Containment of Suicide Clusters.''

(See also VIOLENCE PREVENTION: THE EVOLUTION OF A PILOT PROGRAM FOR ADOLESCENTS; VIOLENCE RESEARCH: A LONGITUDINAL STUDY OF VIOLENCE AMONG THE YOUNG.)

child abuse and neglect   The U.S. Child Abuse and Neglect Act defines child abuse and neglect as physical or mental injury, sexual abuse or exploitation, or maltreatment or negligent treatment of a child under 18 (or the age stipulated by the child protection laws of the child's home state). A charge of abuse can be lodged against any person responsible for the child's welfare, including employees who provide residential or out-of-home care. Family violence experts characterize the practice of abuse as an abuse of power carried out to overcome a perceived absence or loss of power.

The American Association for Protecting Children, a division of the American Humane Society, reported 2.2 million cases of child abuse in 1988. The average age of the victims was seven.

In 1988 there were more than 71 million children under the age of 19, 53 million of whom were under 15. Among this population, experts estimate, during the years of their childhood, 3.4 to 4 million will be kicked, bitten or punched by a parent; 1.4 to 2.3 million will be beaten up; and 900,000 to 1.8 million will be threatened with a knife or a gun by a parent. On the average, three to five children a day die from abuse. From abuse and neglect, approximately 4,000 children lose their lives each year.

Research involving 949 cases of reported child abuse has determined that in almost half the cases, the children had suffered two or more kinds of abuse. Among those who had been sexually assaulted, at least half had been subjected to some other kind of abuse.

The reported incidence of abuse is likely to be substantially lower than the actual incidence. Children are seldom in a position to speak for themselves. Even though public attitudes are shifting toward greater support of the welfare of children, the rare child who complains to authorities about a parent runs the risk not only of not being believed, but of even greater abuse as a consequence. Many children fear the possible impact on their families if abuse becomes known and therefore try to hide it.

Another factor that contributes to underestimation of child abuse is "health care-hopping" by abusing families, who take abused children to different medical facilities each time the abuse is severe enough to warrant medical care. Although an emergency room staff might find a child's broken bone an odd type of "accident," they would not be in a position to notice a pattern, since the child's next "accident" would be treated elsewhere.

Still another factor that contributes to underreporting is the reluctance of outsiders to get involved. A January 8, 1989 *New York Times* article entitled "Stopping Child Abuse Before It Happens," reported one such incident of bystander reluctance.

The screams began sometime after dinner: a teen-ager and his father were having an argument that could be heard through the wall of a neighbor's apartment in a luxury building on East 87th Street in Manhattan. Suddenly the neighbor heard a banging. Apparently the father was bashing the son's head against the bathroom wall.

"I hope you kill me!" the boy shouted. "I hope you end up in jail for the rest of your life!"

The neighbor listened. She glanced at the telephone. But in the end, once it was quiet, she did nothing.

The article goes on to say, "It is the kind of awful moment that happens countless times every day, not only in apartment buildings but across backyards and picket fences around the nation, as neighbors, friends, relatives and others wonder whether to get involved, whether to tell someone they think they have witnessed child abuse." The young man was not apparently hurt— at least not physically. The emotional scars of physical abuse are not readily visible.

In a major shift in emphasis, social workers, federal agencies and child welfare advocacy groups have begun to urge relatives, friends, neighbors and bystanders to become personally involved or at least to report their observations.

Until the 1960s there was a long-standing presumption throughout the nation that favored the maintenance of family privacy, a stance that effectively kept child abuse hidden. Then, in a groundswell of concern, several states passed laws to require professionals, most often physicians and teachers, to report suspected abuse. In New Jersey, failure to report is punishable by a fine up to $1,000 and six months in jail. About the same time, the courts and the federal government recognized that family violence was a public policy issue, and battering was newly defined as a crime.

Reporting statutes are difficult to enforce, but they do serve to encourage bystanders to report abuse. Most states provide immunity from prosecution for those who "in good faith" report suspicions of child abuse, even if the suspicions prove unfounded.

The new emphasis on bystander involvement is a reflection of the view held by a number of experts that child abuse often happens when parents are unable to cope with their responsibilities. The 87th Street case in which the neighbor listened without intervening involved a single father who had recently taken over custody of his son from his former wife. Child welfare advocates suggest that anything that can ease a parent's feelings of isolation and frustration, such as an offer to baby-sit or help in finding financial or mental health assistance, may ease the shame and anger that lead to violence.

In an interview with the *New York Times,* Margo Fritz, executive director of Parents Anonymous, a nationwide self-help group for parents who think they are at risk of being abusive, said, "Instead of thinking of punishing people, we should think of giving families the support they need to do an adequate job of parenting.''

The emphasis on involvement also comes at a time when calls to child abuse hotlines are increasing and the resources of many agencies for investigating complaints are stretched beyond their limits. A substantial number of experts believes that a long-term solution lies in helping parents to become better parents. Many mental health and child welfare agencies offer courses in parenting skills.

While greater involvement of outsiders and agencies is critical, not all problems can be solved by a helping hand or the intercession of an agency. A 1964 study by Leotine Young of child abuse in a small midwestern city, *Wednesday's Children,* examined 300 cases of child abuse and neglect. Young divided the cases into severe neglect, moderate neglect, severe abuse and moderate abuse.

Abuse was defined as severe when either or both parents beat the children violently or consistently, leaving visible results. A significant finding of Young's study was that among the severe abuse cases, there was no constructive change in behavior as long as the family members stayed together. Her finding is completely at odds with the goal of most treatment plans devised by mental health and child welfare agencies for abusive families, which is to keep the family together.

Despite the reluctance of relatives, friends, neighbors and bystanders to become involved, some critics claim that child abuse hotlines are getting too many calls that are unfounded or less than urgent from families involved in custody battles. The American Humane Association estimated that about 60% of the 2.1 million calls received in 1986 were ''unsubstantiated.''

The fact that 840,000 cases were substantiated provides a sad measure of the scope and severity of the problem. Moreover, given the shortage of workers, the enormous turnover in staff and the often scant staff training in many child welfare investigation agencies, there is no way to assess how adequately the 1.26 million ''unsubstantiated'' cases were examined.

The adequacy of the investigations of child abuse cases categorized as unsubstantiated was addressed by three professors of pediatrics at New York Hospital-Cornell Medical Center, in response to an article in the December 11, 1988 *New York Times* that had contained criticism of escalating child abuse reports on the basis of the increasing number of unfounded cases.

In a letter to the editor published in the *Times* December 27, they wrote:

Douglas J. Besharov of the American Enterprise Institute and other critics are in the habit of pointing to the increasing number of ''unfounded'' child-abuse cases reported to highlight what they believe to be society's inappropriate intrusion into the privacy of the family. The intended inference of this view is that these reports are merely nuisance reports or otherwise unjustified.

There may be more evidence that the increasing number of so-called unfounded reports is a reflection of inadequately supported child-protection services and undertrained child-protection staffs. Given the burden of caseloads, the lack of resources necessary for more adequate investigations and the inability of our systems to make use of multisystem contacts and to collaborate, caseworkers are hard pressed to assess adequately the allegations in a large number of cases.

It is also true, though misleading, that the majority of the case reports involve neglect rather than the more dramatic abuse. This also is of little comfort. Neglect, as Mr. Besharov must know if he is familiar with recent fatality studies in New York, is responsible for roughly half of the deaths involving children. Therefore neglect is as dangerous as abuse.

A surprising trigger for child abuse is report cards. A May 1, 1989 *Time* magazine article entitled ''Report Cards Can Hurt You,'' described a parent-teacher conference in Detroit during which a parent grabbed her 12-year-old son, hit him in the face until he bled, punched him in the ribs and walked out of the conference. Because of their report cards, an Atlanta mother beat her three children, ages 12, 10 and 8, with a rolling pin until they were covered with bruises.

In Cobb County, Georgia, police reviewed child abuse accounts for a two-year period and found that reports of child abuse doubled during the three days following the issuance of report cards. The problem intensified toward the end of the school year. Children's protective services in Seattle found that their referral rates rose dramatically from March to the end of June.

In an interview with *Time,* child psychologist David Elkind of Tufts University described the harsh reaction to poor grades by saying:

The cards may be an emotional lightning rod . . . grades are a concrete embodiment of many issues. Bad grades remind parents of their anxieties about their own social status and their child's prospects in the future. Poor parents envision school as a route to escape impoverished lives. Middle-class parents push their children to surpass their own accomplishments. Wealthy, well-educated parents routinely expect first-class performances from their children.

Many parents view bad grades as a personal affront, because they equate good grades with good parenting skills. Schools contribute to the problem by not warning parents earlier in the term that their child is at academic risk, so that bad marks come as a shock.

Unfortunately for parents who hope to improve their child's performance in school by violence, abuse at home is likely to affect adversely their school behavior. A January 12, 1991 *Science News* article entitled "Charting the Aftermath of Child Abuse," described a study done by Kenneth Dodge of Vanderbilt University in Nashville, John Bates of Indiana University in Bloomington, and Gregory Pettit of Auburn University in Alabama, who examined 309 kindergarteners, all age four when the study began.

The scientists found that children experiencing physical abuse at home showed an excess of aggressive and violent behavior by the time they entered kindergarten, regardless of whether they came from a well-to-do or a poor family, lived in a one-parent or two-parent household or regularly observed cooperative or physically violent behavior among adults.

Physical examinations and interviews with mothers identified 46 children, almost evenly divided among girls and boys, who were consistently experiencing physical abuse at home. More than one in three displayed unusually high levels of aggression and deficient social skills, compared with one in eight of the nonabused youngsters. The abused children also showed more signs of emotional withdrawal. The researchers hoped to be able to follow the entire group into adolescence to see if they would develop high rates of delinquency, depression, drug abuse and anxiety.

A March 2, 1991 letter to the editor of *Science News* written by C. E. Wright in response to the January 12 article raised a critical question about child abuse, seldom considered. According to Wright

Correlation does not prove causality. Thus in interpreting the observations described . . . one must also consider the possibility that children with naturally "high levels of aggression" and "deficient social skills" are capable of eliciting abuse responses from previously nonabusive caretakers. Further studies are called for to determine where the abuse cycle starts—particularly studies investigating why certain children experience abuse in consecutive foster homes even when other children in those same homes are not abused.

Substantial research suggests that some children in abusive families are better able to avoid abuse than others. An October 13, 1987 *New York Times* article entitled "Thriving Despite Hardship: Key Childhood Traits Identified," reported the results of three decades of research into the lives of impoverished Hawaiian children. One out of ten children overcame the hardships and fared well. These resilient children's easygoing natures kept them from becoming upset easily and may have protected them from the anger of their parents. Children with difficult dispositions tended to be scapegoated by their parents.

Prevention. The large numbers of abused and neglected children suggest that prevention strategies be found. The Houston Child Prevention Council mounted a public education campaign to prevent report card-related abuse that has been adopted by a number of other cities. The council used newspaper ads, TV and radio announcements and flyers and brochures mailed to parents, all containing the basic message that raised voices or fists do not help to raise grades.

Because of the hidden nature of child abuse, prevention requires careful analysis and sometimes unorthodox strategies. In a January 24, 1989 letter to the editor of the *New York Times*, physician Daryl Altman described the difficulties posed for physicians by parental health care-hopping. Altman pointed out that if an infant is brought to Hospital A's emergency room for treatment of a minor burn, the mother's explanation that a cigarette ash had dropped on the child's skin might be plausible. However, if the physician knew that the child had been treated for a similar burn at Hospital B a week before and at Hospital C the previous month, or if the physician was aware that three or four "unsubstantiated" allegations of child abuse had been made to the welfare department, then he or she would know that the burns were not an accident.

Records of previous treatment for accidental injuries are not available and those of unsubstantiated accusations of child abuse are sealed. Altman wrote:

There needs to be a state or national registry of suspicious or traumatic injuries of children. Similarly, records of child welfare agency reports need to be quickly available to treating physicians; the details are not necessary, just the evidence that reports exist.

This would allow rapid identification of high-risk cases and early intervention, before the need for removal from the home, criminal prosecution or the morgue.

In the absence of such legislation, several hundred hospitals have formed teams to investigate suspicious accidents. The teams vary in format and include any number of people.

Pediatrician and child abuse specialist Daniel Kessler of New York Hospital-Cornell Medical Center put together a three-person team consisting of himself, a fourth-year resident and a social worker. A June 7, 1988 *New York Times* article entitled "Doctor-Sleuth Teams Fight Child Abuse," described the efforts of Kessler's team.

Together with his colleagues, Kessler gathers evidence, orders tests and blends medical with detective work to assemble scenarios that are often grim. When appropriate, the team reports its findings to city authorities and members make themselves available to testify in court.

In New York City, hospitals on the average provide about 15% of the total child abuse reports. Kessler estimates that in 90% of the cases physical abuse can be detected and reported with certainty. Injuries due to neglect are more difficult to determine.

In the same edition of the *New York Times* that carried Altman's letter, psychiatrist Margaret Ruth Kind suggested that high schools could help to avoid child abuse by teaching parent education as a health education course. Dr. Kind devised a curriculum that is taught at Manhattan's High School for the Humanities to students who are neither pregnant nor already parents. Kind said, "If students can learn about oxygen, nitrogen and the War of 1812, they can learn about the infant's need for attachment, the difference between discipline and punishment, and the importance of self-esteem and its development in the child."

An ambitious effort to combat child abuse called "Healthy Start" began in Hawaii in 1989. By 1992 the state aimed to evaluate every new parent to identify those most likely to abuse their children. Those so assessed are offered five years of counseling and home visits intended to help troubled families cope with their economic and psychological problems.

In its first year of operation, the program screened about 60% of all new parents and offered home visits to the 20% of those screened who were deemed to be at risk. Only about 5% of the parents offered help refused it. About 75% of those at risk were mothers on welfare.

Critics of the program have suggested that it is an invasion of a family's privacy. Hawaii state officials responded by saying that great care is taken to avoid labeling families as potential abusers and to offer help without threats.

The program was initially expected to cost $6 million annually. However, it quickly became apparent that this was an underestimate. Because of the spread of drug abuse, the first year of the program uncovered a larger number of high-risk families than expected.

Research.   Child abuse has come under increasing scrutiny in recent years, but except for the resilient-child studies, relatively little is known about the mechanisms by which one child is able to grow up to relative normality and another grows emotionally crippled and may even become an abuser.

Dr. Leonard Shengold, a training analyst at the Psychoanalytic Institute of the New York University School of Medicine, has been writing about child abuse for several years. His 1989 book *Soul Murder*, a careful study of a small number of cases, examined how child abuse cripples its victims, permanently distorting their capacity for thought and joy.

The term *soul murder* was coined by the author of a 19th-century book about Kaspar Hauser, a German child who was chained in a dark cellar for 15 years with no human contacts. Shengold used the term to refer to the deliberate attempt to eradicate or compromise the separate identity of another person. Soul murder is not a diagnostic category; it refers to behavior that cuts across all categories of psychopathology and that results in sexual abuse, emotional deprivation and physical or mental torture.

In abusive households with two adults, one parent or other adult responsible for the child is typically a passive collaborator. The abused child is caught in a tyranny from which there is no escape. In a December 17, 1989 *New York Times* review of *Soul Murder,* psychoanalyst F. Robert Rodman said:

Trapped by dependence, the child can only merge and identify with the tormentor, to whom he or she clings in pathologically powerful idealization, hoping for a better outcome "the next time." Such children become estranged from their own feelings, lose hold of a life on their own, and sink into a deadened state in which their very existence becomes a role that is played, rather than a spontaneous expression of inner being. Indeed, after a while there is no inner being. These confusing and horrible experiences do not yield to logic, for the process deprives the child of the capacity to think. Moreover, such abuse generates profoundly masochistic needs, which tends to provoke a repetition of violence throughout life.

In his work with badly abused children, Dr. Shengold has found that they are filled with murderous fantasies and overwhelming anxiety—and they often yearn for some overpowering physical event to put an end to this state. Through the grownup child's need for something to happen, the violence is apt to be carried out on the next generations, with the victims often becoming soul murderers themselves.

But not all such children become soul murderers. Only about one third of those abused as children go on to become abusers themselves. A January 24, 1989 *New York Times* article entitled "Sad Legacy of Abuse: The Search for Remedies", by Daniel Goleman outlined some of the factors that worsen the long-term impact of abuse. The key factor that identifies children who urgently need treatment is abuse that started at an early age, went on for a long time, was perceived by the child as harmful, involved a perpetrator who had a close relationship with the child and occurred within a cold, unfeeling atmosphere in the family.

Many studies have found that victims of child abuse are disproportionately represented among prostitutes, violent criminals, alcoholics, drug abusers and patients in mental health clinics and psychiatric hospitals. Virtually all those who suffer from multiple personality have a history of abuse. The separate personalities are thought to result from the mind's effort to isolate the child from the abuse.

A 1985 study of all 15 adolescents in the United States who had been found guilty of murder in the previous year found that 13 of them had been victims of severe physical or sexual abuse. In nine cases the abuse, characterized by the researchers as murderous, was so severe that it resulted in neurological damage. A similar study of women imprisoned for fatal child abuse found that all of them had been subjected to severe harm themselves.

Abuse Predictors. A survey of child abuse studies done by Joan Kaufman and Edward Zigler, psychologists at Yale University, found that abuse in childhood was the strongest predictor of becoming an abusive parent and concluded that 30% is the best estimate of the rate at which the abuse of one generation will be passed on to abuse of the next. A study of 1,000 pregnant women, 95 of whom had been abused as children, published in 1986 in the journal *Child Abuse and Neglect,* found that the strongest predictor of becoming an abusive parent was having felt as a child that one was unloved and unwanted by one's parents.

The substantial number of men and women who were abused as children but who nevertheless did not grow up to become child abusers, drug abusers, criminals or mentally ill typically managed to overcome the trauma with the emotional support and nurturance of a friend,

neighbor, clergy member or relative, or through therapy that made them aware that they were not to blame.

In an interview for a January 24, 1989 *New York Times* article, "A Sad Legacy of Abuse: The Search for Remedies," Terry Hunt, a psychologist in Cambridge, Massachusetts who specializes in treating victims of childhood abuse, said that a common refrain from such patients is "it just wasn't that bad." Yet when asked to describe what happened if they broke a rule, they often answer that they were locked in a closet for a day and beaten with a belt. When asked if that constituted abuse, they are likely to say "No, I was a bad kid and my parent had to beat me to make me turn out okay." The most troubled among Hunt's patients are those who were told by adults other than their parents that the abuse was justified.

One of the crucial factors that distinguishes those who go on to abuse their own children from those who do not is whether they are able to recognize that what their parents did was wrong. If the abused child is able to think "They should not have done that to me," then he or she is able to love the parents but resolve not to repeat their mistakes.

When the abuse is committed by outsiders, the parents' reaction upon discovery is critical for the child. Children whose parents blame them for the abuse fare the worst.

A study done at the University of Minnesota of a group of children born to parents with a high probability of becoming abusers included some whose parents had not been abused as children. The criteria for inclusion were that the parents had to be poor, single, pregnant at an early age or living in a chaotic household. In addition to children subjected to physical and sexual abuse, the study examined those whose physical care was neglected, those who were subjected to emotional abuse through constant berating and criticism, and those whose parents were completely unresponsive to their emotional needs.

Early findings from the Minnesota study were published in the collection *Child Maltreatment* (1990). Psychologists Martha Erickson, Byron Egelund and Robert Pianti concluded that the earlier maltreatment occurs, the more severe the consequences. Many psychological effects that last a lifetime arise from a lack of nurturance, which the researchers believe lies behind all forms of mistreatment.

(See also EMOTIONAL ABUSE OF CHILDREN; MULTIPLE PERSONALITY DISORDER; PEDOPHILE; SEXUAL ABUSE OF CHILDREN; SOCIOPATHS.)

child emergency trauma: a model prevention program   Since the mid-1970s child emergency trauma cases resulting from violence, falls and other accidents had been increasing at Harlem Hospital in New York City. The chief of pediatric surgery, Dr. Barbara Barlow, felt that many of the injuries being treated in the emergency room could have been avoided, and she set out to find ways to prevent them.

Harlem Hospital's first safety program focused pediatricians' and parents' awareness on the importance of window guards. After the program began in 1979, the number of fall injuries treated at the hospital dropped from 12 per year to one or less.

Barlow and her Injury Prevention Program team next targeted local playgrounds. In an interview for the fall 1990 *Advances,* the newsletter of the Robert Wood Johnson Foundation (RWJF), Barlow said, "Many injuries were occurring because children were playing in the streets rather than in local playgrounds, which were dirty, littered with garbage, syringes and empty crack vials, and had broken or no equipment."

With an initial two-year grant from RWJF awarded in 1988, Barlow organized a team made up of a pediatric trauma coordinator and two community residents. The team surveyed and documented the safety hazards they found in outdoor playgrounds in central Harlem. At each site, they took photographs and compiled data that included the number of injuries at the site and made suggestions about how to fix the problems.

Barlow and her team presented the findings to school and city officials and to community groups, who responded by forming coalitions of government agencies and community groups. By the fall of 1990 all playgrounds had received some improvements. Metal swings had been replaced by rubber ones and had been moved away from concrete walls. Little League games were played for the first time in 20 years in one six-acre park.

Police endeavor to keep the playgrounds free of drug-related activities, and parents and school personnel monitor and help clean the playgrounds on a regular basis. The success of the program is obvious in the hospital's statistics. From the fall of 1988 to the fall of 1990, overall admission for major injuries among those children who live in central Harlem fell 16%, and major injury admissions to the pediatric trauma service dropped 14%.

A second RWJF grant for 1991 and 1992 enabled the expansion of the window and playground safety programs and the development of programs targeting adolescents, whose injury rates had escalated 18% in 1989 and 1990.

(See also EMERGENCY MEDICAL CARE: THE IMPACT OF VIOLENCE.)

children and youths with guns   Many disputes among American young people that once might have been settled with fists are now likely to be settled with guns. Louis Sullivan, U.S. Secretary of Health and Human Services, in an interview for an April 8, 1991 *U.S. News and World Report* article entitled "Kids Who Kill," said, "Every 100 hours [just over four days], more youths die on the streets of America than were killed in 100 hours of ground war in the Persian Gulf."

According to the records of the National Center for Health Statistics, from 1979 through 1987, 1,022 teenagers between the ages of 15 and 19 died from firearms, and another 519 died in 1988. Between 1984 and 1988, the firearms death rate for teens 15 to 19 rose 43%. The picture was particularly bleak for young black males 15 to 19, among whom firearms homicides more than doubled.

The firearms death rate for black teenagers 15 to 19 was 2.8 times the rate from natural causes and 11 times the rate for their white counterparts. Research by James Alan Fox of Northeastern University revealed that the number of black teenagers who have killed with guns also rose sharply, from 181 in 1984 to a record 555 in 1989.

Surveys done by the National School Safety Center, when extrapolated for the nation, suggested that 135 students carried guns to school daily in 1987. A 20-state survey of 11,000 adolescents found that 41% of the boys claimed that they could obtain a handgun if they wished to do so.

It is not even necessary to buy a gun to commit an act of violence. In 1990 a 16-year-old suburban Chicago boy rented a gun from a fellow student for $100 and used it to kill his parents.

The presence of a large number of guns and easy access to them are what make the current atmosphere so volatile. The National Crime Analysis Program at Northeastern University reported that arrests of young people under age 18 for weapon violations rose from 19,649 in 1976 to 31,577 in 1989.

Youngsters in cities with strong gun control laws, such as New York, Boston and Washington, D.C., have little difficulty obtaining firearms. The guns are transported from states with weak laws, such as Florida, Texas, Virginia, Georgia and Ohio, and sold at a significant profit. Before being arrested, two men operating out of a van in a park east of downtown Los Angeles are estimated to have sold more than 1,000 handguns over an eight-month period in 1990, mostly to street-gang members.

There are four major sources of guns for youngsters: street corners, friends, drug dealers and thefts either from parents or from residential burglaries. A Florida study found that 86% of the guns taken from students came from their own homes.

For a year and a half, one Winston-Salem, North Carolina youngster averaged a burglary a day. He selected homes to burglarize based on two criteria: the owners had guns and they were not at home. To determine which homes had guns, he probably used clues such as a gun rack in the back of the owner's truck, National Rifle Association decals, and conversations in bars. He traded many of the guns for marijuana and cocaine.

An April 11, 1991 ABC News program, "Peter Jennings Reporting: Guns," included an interview with a police official who said he had started to tabulate killings in a category he called "You Don't Have the Guts to Kill Me," in which the victim taunted the youngster holding the gun. *U.S. News and World Report* described a typical such incident.

A dispute between adolescents broke out because the windows of a car belonging to one had been broken. The owner pulled out a gun. The other said, "You ain't going to shoot me." The first youth later described his actions: "I just started shooting because he didn't think I would. It would have looked stupid if I pulled a gun and then didn't shoot him. I would have looked dumb."

Many adolescents secure the money needed to buy a gun by dealing in drugs. Although there appears to have been some progress in the war against drugs, mostly among casual users, between 1.7 million and 2.4 million Americans still use cocaine each week. Some authorities think the drug trade has become even more deadly precisely because the traffickers are fighting over a shrinking market.

The growth of gangs is a significant factor in the rising number of deaths among adolescents. Gangs not only absorb wayward youngsters, they provide a social and emotional haven for those who don't find security, acceptance or protection at home.

The major California gangs, the Crips and the Bloods, began in Southern California about 20 years ago and have spread, with affiliations in 32 states and 113 cities. The price of having gangs serve as surrogate parents is steep. In five years the number and size of the gangs in the Los Angeles area doubled, from 400 gangs with 45,000 members in 1985, to 800 gangs with 90,000 members in 1990. In 1990 there were 690 gang-related killings, 35% of the county's homicides.

In communities where gangs are a significant social factor, a gun is a status symbol and a rite of passage required for acquiring a reputation or joining a gang. A 14-year-old Los Angeles youngster who wanted to prove to his gang that he was worthy fired a semiautomatic weapon as he rode his bike past a school playground filled with children.

Youngsters do not fear the justice system, because they know their chances of being locked up are not great. Juvenile court justices have more flexibility in sentencing than most judges. Many are reluctant to lock up youngsters in overcrowded facilities that are no more than holding tanks. In Austin, Texas, older gang members call the younger ones "minutemen" because they will be in jail "only a minute." The lesser penalties encourage drug dealers to hire youngsters to distribute drugs.

It is estimated that 20 to 25% of adolescents who shoot people are high on drugs. Alcohol or drugs act as "disinhibitors" that make violence more likely. Moreover, the gang ethos lowers the threshold of violence and makes it respectable. For some youngsters guns, drugs and gangs are routes to satisfy a desire for power and respect, to gain a tough-guy reputation. The fastest path to money or material goods, such as jackets or sneakers, is the use of a gun.

The extreme narcissism (self-absorption; grandiose sense of self-importance), hypersensitivity to the evaluation of others and lack of empathy characteristic of adolescence and young adulthood makes young people overresponsive to any sign of disrespect. In the language of the streets, disrespect is called "dissin'." More than any other motive, teenage killers cite dissin' as the reason for their crimes. One teenager told *U.S. News and World Report*, "If someone disrespects you or your homeboys [neighborhood or gang members], you've got to do something about it. You can't have them doing that and hold your head up."

Accidental Deaths. Federal Centers for Disease Control (CDC) researchers reported in the December

1990 *Journal of the American Medical Association* the results of a survey they had done of 1,005 Texas homes. They found that 15% of the surveyed homes with firearms had "latchkey kids," elementary school children who were home alone after school. Extrapolating that finding to the entire nation, the researchers estimated that a million children might be left unsupervised in homes with firearms.

A National Rifle Association (NRA) spokesperson, in an interview for a November 7, 1990 *USA Today* article entitled "Latchkey Kids Along With Guns," dismissed the survey findings by saying, "The CDC automatically assumes that the children have access to those firearms." The spokesperson asserted that gun-related child deaths had dropped since the mid-1970s. To this, a Center to Prevent Handgun Violence spokesperson responded, "People are bringing these guns into their home to protect their family, but they're actually placing their family in greater danger."

In mid-June 1989, after five Florida children had been shot, two fatally, in accidents with their parents' guns during a two-week period, a special legislative session was called to consider a bill that would subject to imprisonment anyone whose gun is used by a child to kill or maim.

Proponents of gun control proposed that the problem of guns in Florida was broader than one of risks to children. They proposed that all Floridians were at risk because 60% of Florida households have at least one gun. Florida and Texas have the highest rate of gun ownership in the country.

One state representative asserted that the child-involved shootings were the result of the gun law that went into effect in 1987, which virtually eliminated waiting periods for gun purchase, banned local gun control ordinances and allowed most Floridians to carry concealed weapons. Others argued that even under a much stricter law, the owners of the guns used in the five child shootings would not have been denied permits. All five were purchased before the 1987 law went into effect.

Opponents of the bill argued that a family would be doubly punished. If the potential death of a child was not sufficient motive for them to keep a gun locked up, then no law would make a difference.

Supporters of the bill insisted that a similar argument could have been made about the state law requiring the use of seat belts in cars. The risk by itself had not been enough to make parents and others use seat belts. The

law had required it and thereby reduced injuries and deaths.

In a June 18, 1989, *New York Times* article entitled "Children Shooting Children: Move Is On for Gun Control," the Center to Prevent Handgun Violence reported that a study of 533 accidental handgun shootings involving children from 1986 through 1988 found that 66% of the incidents took place when the children were home alone. The American Academy of Pediatrics reported that children younger than 14 are annually involved in about 250 accidental shooting deaths each year.

Although it took a year, the Florida law was passed, despite opposition, in mid-1990.

(See also CHILDREN'S RIGHTS; CLASSROOM VIOLENCE; GANGS: PICKUP OR TEMPORARY; GANGS: STRUCTURED STREET; GUN-FREE SCHOOL ZONE.)

children's rights   After ten year of negotiations, the General Assembly of the United Nations adopted a Convention on the Rights of the Child on November 20, 1989. The United Nations Children's Fund (UNICEF) officials believed that the primary reason for the delay was a general lack of interest in children. James Grant, executive director of UNICEF, said, "I didn't expect to see it in my lifetime. Historically, frankly, governments tend to treat children on a very low national priority basis, even though they use nice words."

The convention was approved by consensus, and still had to be ratified by at least 20 countries before becoming effective. The 54-article draft, initiated by Poland, dealt with such matters as a child's rights to a name, survival, education, protection from exploitation and abuse and protection against separation from his or her parents.

During an interview for a November 21, 1989 *New York Times* article entitled "U.N. Assembly Adopts Doctrine Outlining Children's Basic Rights," Grant said, "To get one common doctrine is a near miracle in its own right. It creates a new international norm." According to the president of the General Assembly, Joseph Garba of Nigeria, the value of having the convention is that "the rights of the child have now gone from a declaratory statement of purpose into what will become a binding piece of legislation."

Negotiations on the convention were slowed by a number of contentious issues, in particular abortion, adoption and the minimum age for combat. Nordic countries wanted the minimum age for military combat set at 18. The United States argued in favor of age 15, in keeping with the Geneva Conventions. Several countries objected to particular articles that conflicted with their national laws; for example, adoption is forbidden under Islamic law.

A Committee on the Rights of the Child, composed of ten experts from different regions of the world, will be responsible for monitoring compliance around the world.

The idea that children have rights is a recent concept. For most of recorded history, children, in the eyes of the law, were no more than the legal chattels of their parents, sometimes only of their fathers, and could be killed or abandoned. Infanticide was widely, although not universally, practiced.

For centuries, the only rights children had under the law were the right not to be killed and orphan's rights, which often amounted to no more than being apprenticed to a trade. Even in the latter years of the 20th century, under the Constitution of the United States, the rights of a child accused of a crime are fewer that those of an adult.

For centuries, children, whose crimes might be no more than stealing food to keep themselves alive, shared prison cells with experienced criminals. In the closing years of the 19th century, Jane Addams, founder of Hull House in Chicago, proposed a separate juvenile justice system. Cook County (Chicago) set up the first American juvenile court in 1899. By 1920 the idea had spread to every state and to other countries.

In the matter of protection of rights, the concept of the juvenile court system was fatally flawed. The freedom juvenile court judges had to rehabilitate rather than punish amounted to total control. The child defendant had no due process rights, no right to counsel, no right to proof beyond a reasonable doubt, not even the right to remain silent. The adversarial system of the adult courts, which forces the state to prove its case, had no place in the juvenile system, where decisions rested on the benevolence of the judge, who had few laws to restrain him or her.

The U.S. juvenile courts became a dumping ground for all of society's "problem" children, and caseloads became staggering. Many who worked in the system and tried to make it work for children deplored it. In 1967 the first real change in the juvenile court came about as a consequence of a Supreme Court decision, *in re Gault,* that conceded to children some constitutional due process rights.

The decision deplored the lack of "substantive standards" in the juvenile courts. It also specified the rights of a child brought before the courts in any case that could result in the deprivation of a child's liberty. The rights spelled out by the Court are:

- The child and his or her family have a right to written notice of the charges brought and the proceeding to be undertaken.
- The child has a right to counsel, and the right to have the court provide counsel.
- Written records must be kept that can be examined in an appeal of the court's decision.
- The child has a right to remain silent. (Awareness of the right to remain silent is critical for many children, who are reluctant to offend adults and apt to say whatever they think the adult wants to hear.)
- The child has a right to confront his or her accusers and to cross-examine, typically through an attorney.
- Anyone making a charge against the child must appear in court to state the charge in the child's presence.

Following the *in re Gault* decision, Congress passed several laws pertaining to the rights of children and their welfare, ranging from enforcement of child support, through the education of handicapped children, to protection from sexual exploitation. An attorney is much more likely to be present during questioning and in court than formerly. Nevertheless, juvenile defendants remain much more vulnerable than adults to the whims of the system.

Children in the United States are also highly vulnerable when they are a part of a state's foster care system, usually as a consequence of parental abuse or neglect. Children are frequently neglected and abused, and sometimes even killed, in foster homes. Following the beating death of a Newark five-year-old, Dyneeka Johnson, in a state-approved foster home, New Jersey officials introduced legislation in May 1989 to create a bill of rights for abused and neglected children. The legislation established an independent agency to oversee the state's handling of child welfare cases.

One of the issues raised in the Dyneeka Johnson case was the use of so-called para-foster homes, the homes of friends or relatives of the child's biological family that have been chosen by the parents. Dyneeka was placed in the home of a childhood friend of her mother's.

The rationale agencies offer for using para-foster homes is that placing children with people who know them serves to balance the child's right to safety with the family's right to care for their own children without excessive intrusion by the state.

Children's rights advocates have no objections to the use of para-foster families. They object to the failure of state agencies, which, because of a shortage of staff and of foster homes, fail to check the criminal records of the adults in the para-foster homes before placements (which include monthly payments) are approved.

The New Jersey policy is to reject para-foster parents who have been convicted of child abuse or neglect, sexual abuse or violent crime. In the Dyneeka Johnson case, the investigation was obviously not thorough. After Dyneeka's severely beaten body was found on a garbage heap in an empty lot, police records showed that the foster mother, Stacy Smith, had been convicted of drug possession, and her boyfriend, Willie Grant, had a long criminal record, including convictions for assault and distribution of drugs.

Both New York and Connecticut ran into difficulties in their use of para-foster families when they found that rigorous screening and monthly visits were less likely to be made for para-foster families than they were with other types of foster homes.

Other evidence of a lack of interest in children is not hard to find in the United States. Approximately 800,000 to 1.3 million teenagers run away each year in the United States. An estimated 300,000 live permanently on the streets. Thirteen percent of teenagers are pregnant or already parents. Eighteen percent have attempted suicide. Twenty-six percent have turned to prostitution to support themselves.

Runaways in the United States are often doubly victimized, first by their parents through physical, sexual or emotional abuse, which prompts their flight, and then by pornographers and other kinds of criminals once they are living on the streets.

As indifferent as Americans may be to children's rights, they have not conducted a war against the nation's children as has been done in the cities of Brazil and in Guatemala City. An estimated 24 million children in Brazil live in the streets, victims of Brazil's fractured economy. Approximately 5,000 children live on the streets of Guatemala City. Such children survive in the streets by begging, shining shoes, selling chewing gum, dealing in drugs, stealing, hunting through garbage for food and sleeping on sidewalks. Beginning in the 1960s, death squads, generally composed of retired or off-duty police officers, unhappy with Brazil's impotent courts, engaged in killing criminals and opponents of the mil-

itary regime in power. In the 1980s the death squads turned their weapons on street children. In Guatemala City, the National Police executed children publicly.

Rodrigo Sousa Filho, coordinator of the National Street Children's Movement in Rio de Janeiro, was interviewed about the Brazilian massacres in the summer/fall 1990 issue of *War Child Monitor,* the newsletter of the Center on War and the Child. He said, "Kids are being gunned down without question, as if they were dogs." He added that Brazil's four-digit inflation and foreign debt of $114 billion had led to significant cuts in education and the child welfare system.

A study by Brazil's Health Ministry reported an increase in the killing of young people in Rio from 287 in 1983 to 630 in 1989, and in São Paulo from 280 in 1980 to 1,880 in 1989. Store owners paid bounties to rid their areas of criminals of all ages.

Race seemed to play a significant role in the choice of who would be killed. A study by the Brazilian Institute of Social and Economic Analysis found that black or mixed-race children constituted 82% of all the street children killed.

As of February 5, 1992, 109 nations had ratified the UN convention on the rights of children.

The United States was not one of them. The convention clashes with several U.S. policies and laws, including the laws of several states that permit the execution of those under 18. Moreover, if the convention were signed, then the federal government would have to devote attention to the large number of children living in the streets of the United States.

(See also CHILD ABUSE AND NEGLECT; JUVENILE JUSTICE: A SYSTEM OF CONTRADICTIONS; PARENT ACCOUNTABILITY LAWS; PEDOPHILE; SEXUAL ABUSE OF CHILDREN; STREET CHILDREN.)

citizen watch committees   See DRUG ABUSE AND TRADE: PREVENTION AND EDUCATION.

civil forfeiture   During the 1960s and 1970s, states faced with ever-increasing budget demands turned to lotteries to supply revenue. To those who objected to lotteries, legislators predicted that state-run lotteries would deprive organized crime of a substantial source of income.

State lotteries may have diverted some gambling money, but they have not wiped out illegal gambling. In an interview in a 1990 issue (vol. 5, no. 1) of *Criminal Organizations,* the newsletter of the International Association for the Study of Organized Crime, Sharon Sharp, director of the Illinois State Lottery, estimated that $2.8 billion is spent each year on illegal lotteries nationwide.

There are many reasons why an individual would choose to play an illegal lottery when a legal one is available. It pays more; it is possible to play on credit and there is no record that would require a winner to pay income tax.

In spite of the fact that illegal gambling is a major source of revenue for organized crime, many jurisdictions do not view gambling as a serious crime problem. But illegal gambling is not a victimless crime. The revenue derived from gambling is used to finance drug smuggling and the corruption of unions, among other things, and therefore is a contributor to violence.

Those convicted of serious gambling offenses at the local level seldom receive more than probation. Even on the federal level, prison sentences meted out are usually short. Therefore, there is not much deterrent built into legal sanctions.

The Organized Crime Control Act of 1970 makes deterrence possible. The act makes it a federal criminal offense to conduct, finance or manage an illegal gambling business. An "illegal gambling business" is one that is in violation of state or local law, involves five or more people, has been in operation more than 30 days or has a gross revenue of more than $2,000 in any single day. Title 18, Section 1955(d), of the United States Code states that "any property, including money, used in violation of the provisions of this section may be seized and forfeited to the United States."

Forfeiture enforces obedience to the law by transferring to the government property that has been used in violation of the law. The forfeiture does not depend on the guilt or innocence of the owner of the property but only on the fact that the property "transgressed."

Custody of the property seized by local and state officers can be transferred to a federal agent who can in effect "adopt" the seizure as if he or she had originally seized it. Forfeiture is based on the "relation back" doctrine, which vests title to property in the United States government as of the moment a criminal act is committed.

Civil forfeiture actions are "in rem" proceedings against property that are used to determine ownership. They are in contrast to criminal forfeitures, which are "in personam" and refer to actions against individuals to determine their obligations and liabilities. Unless a forfeiture statute specifically requires a conviction, it is considered a civil action against property, independent of any criminal action against anyone.

Once probable cause is established, the burden of proof shifts to the defendant. He or she must demonstrate to the court by a preponderance of the evidence that the property is not subject to forfeiture. The court must simply make a decision about whose position is likely to be true, the government's or the defendant's.

The shift in the burden of proof reduces the protection of the Fifth Amendment against self-incrimination. A defendant cannot pursue his or her claim to the seized property without explaining the details of ownership.

In a Chicago application of civil forfeiture, the Reuben/Linda Lottery investigation conducted by the Chicago Police and the United States Attorney's Office, seven homes, a condominium, an eight-story apartment building and a liquor store were seized. In one of the luxury homes, the investigators found gambling records, including daily sheets summarizing the day's activities, and a large paper shredder. While the search was in progress, a runner for one of the organizations arrived carrying a tape cassette of betting records.

Forfeiture is a powerful tool, to be used sparingly. Justice Department guidelines permit property to be seized only if it has been substantially used to facilitate a violation of the law. Facilitation means the property makes the violation easier or less difficult. Courts have interpreted facilitation to mean a significant connection between the property and an offense.

(See also APPENDIX 1A: THE AMERICAN MAFIA AND OTHER ETHNIC CRIME ORGANIZATIONS.)

civil liberties (See BILL OF RIGHTS: PROTECTION AGAINST GOVERNMENT TYRANNY.)

civil rights (See BILL OF RIGHTS: PROTECTION AGAINST GOVERNMENT TYRANNY.)

classroom violence In increasing numbers, weapons are being brought into schools and schoolyards throughout North America. A by-product of the proliferation of weapons in schools is that youngsters who are not otherwise involved in delinquency feel they must carry weapons to protect themselves. When a teacher in a Boston special program for youngsters caught with weapons asked a class, "Is there any way to exist without a weapon?" one teenager answered, "Stay in the house."

For a great many youngsters, violence inside the school is not nearly as harrowing as the route to and from school. In a interview for a November 14, 1989 *New York Times* article entitled "When Violence and Terror Strike Outside the Schools," one 15-year-old sophomore at Julia Richman High School on the Upper East Side of Manhattan described the formidable task of returning home. She said, "I just walk home and I don't look at nobody or talk to nobody. People are just waiting for people after school to jump on them."

Some students are reluctant to report incidents unless they are seriously injured. One youngster who had been robbed twice refrained from reporting the robberies for fear of upsetting his mother. Feeling that there was no way he could avoid confrontations, he was considering getting a knife to protect himself. He said, "It just that way. You got it, they take it."

Even when students manage to arrive unscathed, school often is not a haven. Frequently violence follows them inside. The New York City school system's executive director of school safety told the *New York Times* that the principals of 14 high schools and two middle schools felt it necessary to install metal detectors to prevent students from bringing weapons into the school.

Although urban areas share with their suburban and rural counterparts the problem of violence in the schools, their sheer size make the volume of violence they cope with enormous. Perhaps the worst school year in New York City was 1984–85, when there were 1,660 assaults and 1,074 robberies.

Joan Jarvis, principal of Bayard Rustin High School for the Humanities in the Chelsea section of Manhattan, said, "I'm sure we're all feeling the same way—we're under seige. The whole system is held hostage by a roving band of crazies who want to cause trouble. It breaks my heart to make this an armed camp for my children, who are very good."

The major problem in New York appeared to be gangs known as posses, which do not have a stable membership or steady turf, a factor that makes them unpredictable. Sergeant John Galea, commander of the New York City Police Department's youth gang intelligence unit, expressed gratitude that New York's gangs are not tightly organized like those of Los Angeles and Chicago.

At Jordan High School in Los Angeles, teachers say that they must make safety and order their first concern before trying to focus their students' attention on school work. During an interview for a November 16, 1989 *New York Times* article entitled "Near a Los Angeles School, Danger Is a Constant Lesson," Joseph Santana, Jordan's assistant principal, described the risks his students faced.

I tip my hat to any student who comes here and graduates from here. What they have to work with in this school— making it through shows me they have guts, they have pride, they have integrity. When these kids come to school, they have to be watching their backs all the way. You see the environment: it is not conducive to peace of mind. Over the past weekend, 8 people were killed and 12 were wounded in gang-related problems.

Wesley Mitchell, chief of the Los Angeles schools' police department, observed that the spread of crack cocaine had magnified violence immensely in the communities around the schools. "What we have seen, more than an increase in violence in the schools, is increased jeopardy to children trying to get to and from school." Because a number of children were not taking the risk of coming to school, the Los Angeles school department as a last resort was planning to hold some classes at a housing project.

About 8% of urban junior and senior high school students miss at least one day of school a month because they are afraid to go. More than a third of these students report that someone threatened to hurt them in school, and 13% report actually having been attacked on school premises or a school bus at least once during a school year. Nearly half of all students in New York City's public high schools stayed home from school on Halloween 1989 because of violence on that day in prior years.

During interviews for a November 18, 1989 *Boston Globe* article entitled "Weapons Are an Ominous Part of a School Day in Boston," several school police officers, who requested anonymity, charged the Boston school administration with intentionally downplaying the extent of weapons possession in the schools and the violence those weapons have sparked. The officers felt there was a war in the streets that was spilling over into the schools.

After rescuing a youngster from the threat of a knife, a Boston school police officer said, "We have gangs from all over the city coming to these schools and the contempt that some kids have for each other does not end at the school door." Boston school officials agreed that neighborhood disputes spilled over into fights in the school. The headmaster of the Jeremiah E. Burke High School in Dorchester said, "Somebody will say something to somebody on Sunday and then at lunchtime Monday we'll have a fight."

In 1990 three Boston high schools, Burke, Hyde Park and Madison Park, had the highest number of confiscated weapons. James Watson, headmaster at Madison Park, said, "I think schools are a microcosm of what you see in the greater community. There have been more than 100 homicides in the city. The kids aren't bringing the weapons to protect themselves at school. They are bringing the weapons to protect themselves to and from school."

Although the level of violence in the Boston public schools has not reached that of some other urban school systems, some school officials support the installation of metal detectors. But most Boston school officials, including the high schools' headmasters, oppose them on the grounds that they make a school feel like a prison.

Many schools across the United States do resemble prisons or military installations in a war zone. More and more schools in inner cities have barred windows, camera monitors and bolted doors. Some school systems require students to wear identification badges. And not only do schools look like prisons, school systems are adopting techniques common to correctional institutions. Although Boston school officials may resist metal detectors, hundreds of Detroit students pass through them and one Seattle high school uses a breathalyzer daily on students suspected of drinking. In addition to metal detectors and security forces patrolling the halls, many schools have dress codes to prevent arguments over coveted items of clothing and jewelry, such as gold chains, that can erupt in violence.

U.S. News and World Report described a strategy used by teachers at Fairfax Elementary School in Mentor, Ohio to protect their students when gunfire erupts. They yell "earthquake drill!" and everyone dives under his or her desk.

A knife brought Boston's first experience with death inside a school in December 1990. A fight that had been stopped by adults erupted again when one of the participants jeered the other. The mocked adolescent stabbed his taunter.

The Boston school system had developed a program to try to prevent this type of outcome. Boston public school students caught with weapons are sent to the Barron Assessment and Counseling Center (BACC) for

a five- to ten-day stay, during which they undergo detailed psychological and educational assessment. During the student's stay plans are developed for working with them once they are back either in their regular schools or in alternative settings. The Barron students participate in counseling, regular academic work, violence-prevention classes and trips to local detention facilities.

Between 1988 and 1991, the center served 1,000 students with a recidivism rate of 5%. Although staff members admits that it would be helpful to have youngsters for a longer period, they believe that the stay provides the youngsters with a timeout to think and reflect.

Following the stabbing death in December, Boston's Mayor Raymond Flynn publicly called for metal detectors. Initially, he expressed unwillingness to compromise on School Department budget cuts, which would have closed the BACC, the public school system's only violence-prevention program. (A compromise was ultimately reached, however, and the BACC remained open. At present there are no plans to close it.) The state's programs, established by former Public Health commissioner Dr. Deborah Prothrow-Stith, had already been reduced by budget cuts.

There seems to be little hope that school violence will stop any time soon. Charles Patrick Ewing, author of *When Children Kill* (1990), believes that several trends coming together are ominous. Among them are a continuing proliferation of guns, increases in the numbers of abused and neglected children, enormous numbers of children living in poverty and a projected 7.7% increase in the population of five- to 17-year-olds. Ewing predicted that the 1990s would be the bloodiest decade ever.

A November 1988 *Teen* article entitled "Campus Showdown: The School Battlefield" provided some graphic examples of the forms school violence takes. A junior at Iroquois Central High School in Buffalo, New York was seriously injured when a pipe bomb was placed in his locker, allegedly by another student who was angry about a run-in he had had with the victim's girlfriend. At Wade Hampton High in Taylors, South Carolina, a conflict among three different groups erupted into a schoolwide riot that resulted in the hospitalization of several students. At Garner Middle School in Lansing, Michigan, girls were afraid to wear their hair down at school because roaming groups of girls would grab the hair as a prelude to a fight. At St. Patricia

Junior High, an exclusive Catholic school in Hickory Hills, Illinois, an argument between two boys came to an abrupt end when one set the other on fire.

Some firm data to support the impression that large numbers of school children are at risk from violence was included in a June 1990 *Atlantic Monthly* article by Karl Zinsmeister, entitled "Growing Up Scared." The author reported a number of findings of the 1987 National Adolescent Student Health Survey, which queried 11,000 eighth- and tenth-grade students in 200 schools in 20 states. Two percent of the students (338,000 if extrapolated nationwide) had carried a handgun to school at least once that year. One third brought their gun daily. About eight times as many carried knives.

Among the findings of the survey:

	Boys	Girls
Were in at least one fight at school	49%	28%
Had access to a handgun	41%	24%
Took a knife to school at least once	23%	5%
Took a knife to school daily	7%	2%
Took a handgun to school at least once	3%	0.7%
Took a handgun to school daily	1%	0.4%
While at school or on a school bus:		
Were threatened with violence	39%	30%
Were robbed	16%	12%
Were attacked	17%	9%
While not at school:		
Were threatened with violence	35%	30%
Were robbed	15%	15%
Were attacked	21%	12%

A Bronx (New York City) schoolteacher discussing his violence-plagued junior high school described the dilemma faced by his students who wanted to avoid violence: "The kid who demonstrates fear is raw meat."

Most teachers and school administrators believe that children have a right to learn in a tranquil classroom in a violence-free school. California voters shared their feeling and in 1982 added a "'Victim's Bill of Rights" to the state constitution that reads in part: "All students and staff of public primary, elementary, junior high and senior high schools have an inalienable right to attend campuses which are safe, secure, and peaceful."

The existence of the right to a safe, secure campus does not guarantee its implementation. In a 1986 lawsuit, Constance Hosemann and her son Stephen, a student in Oakland who had been repeatedly bullied, beaten and robbed at school, charged that their school district had failed to protect Stephen's right to a safe classroom.

An Alameda County Superior Court judge ruled in the Hosemanns' favor, allowing them to sue for monetary damages, and he ordered the school district to develop a safe-schools plan. But in May 1989 the California First District Court of Appeals overturned the Superior Court's decision. The three-judge panel held that while the California constitution provided students with a "general right" to security, it imposed no express duty to make schools safe.

Students are not the only ones at risk in the classroom. In 1988 New York City schoolteachers suffered a rash of violence. An elementary teacher was stabbed more than a dozen times by a mugger in a school bathroom. Another teacher was beaten with a bat after confronting a playground intruder. A third was badly injured when a powerful firecracker was thrown into her classroom. And a fourth was slugged by a student who objected to being asked to put out a cigarette.

City and school authorities reacted with identification cards for students, metal detectors at building entrances and silent alarms in classrooms. Controversy flared over a provision to expel students who strike teachers, since state law guarantees an education until the age of 16.

Violence against teachers was not confined to New York City. In January 1988, after receiving a poor grade, a Seminole, Florida 13-year-old bragged that he would "torture and kill" his social studies teacher. When the school security guards heard of the threat, they searched the boy and found a 9mm pistol, a box of 9mm shells and a loaded .22-caliber pistol in his gym bag.

In the Miami-Dade County, Florida area alone, school officials recorded more than 100 incidents of guns found on school grounds in the fall of 1988. In January 1989 the Dade County school board began the nation's first mandatory "gun awareness" program tailored for all students, kindergarten through grade 12. In an interview for a December 5, 1988 *Newsweek* article entitled "Pencils, Papers and Guns," School Board Supervisor Bill Davis said, "Our message is very clear and very simple: to let students know that guns kill."

Violence in schools is not always caused by those who have a right to be there. The design of schools built three, four or five decades ago made it easier to keep out intruders. More recent open-plan-design schools make it more difficult.

A December 1989 *Education Digest* article entitled "Protecting Schools from Outside Violence," by Donna Harrington-Lueker, addressed the problem of intruders together with the need to avoid turning schools into prisons. She quoted Robert Rubel, director of the National Alliance for Safe Schools, who cited schools in Greenwood, South Carolina and Winnetka, Illinois as models that have developed total school security in the wake of major violent incidents.

Winnetka schools adopted several security measures. Among them:

- All doors except the front door are kept locked.
- Visitors are greeted at the front door by a PTA volunteer, who asks them to sign in and wear name tags.
- Windows installed to increase visibility enable office personnel to keep track of who is going in and out.
- The main office of each school is provided with an emergency connection to the police station.
- Intercoms are installed in all classrooms.
- Each elementary school has a full-time school nurse.
- The school system's recess program has been revised so that fewer students take recess at the same time and more adults are available to monitor them.

Greenwood schools have installed two-way communication systems to permit teachers to talk to the main office. Most outside doors are kept locked, and visitors enter through a single front door.

The Greenwood and Winnetka programs strike a balance between a pessimistic "You can't stop random violence, so why try?" attitude and a paranoid "Let's barricade the schoolyard" approach. At the same time, they recognize that the greatest threats come from day-to-day events in the schools rather from outside intruders.

The article in *Teen* discussed a source of conflict seldom mentioned in coverage of school violence, that is, confrontations between cliques. This is a problem middle schools and junior and senior highs have in common with college and university campuses, where fraternities are responsible for a major portion of on-campus violence.

At Minnechaug High in Wilbraham, Massachusetts, battles are mostly with fists. The battle lines are drawn between "jocks," (athletes, cheerleaders and popular people) and the "heavy-metal" crowd (who wear punk clothes and are known as "maggots"). In June 1988 a building that housed athletic equipment was burned down by an unknown culprit.

At Garner Middle School in Lansing, Michigan, there are three groups at war, the "preps" (the popular crowd), the "burnouts" (the smokers and heavy-metal

listeners) and the "skaters," (students who bring their skateboards to school).

At Wilson Middle School in Cedar Rapids, Iowa, the conflict is between the "snobs" and the "nerds," with the nerds taking most of the beating, while at St. Patricia Junior High in Hickory Hills, Illinois, it is the "nerds" who are behind most of the fighting and who bring knives to school to threaten others.

At Wade Hampton High School in Taylors, South Carolina, the skirmishes are between the "frats" and the "rednecks." In the summer of 1988, glue was dumped into the pool and the tennis courts were wrecked at an exclusive club where the frats hang out. Both groups target particular students to harass.

The transition from junior high to senior high is often marked by "hazing." At one high school, a senior is alleged to have stuck a freshman's head in a toilet.

Not only are many youngsters afraid to go to school, many are afraid to go into certain areas of their schools that have been claimed by some hostile clique, in particular specific bathrooms or study halls.

A favorite expression of hostility is called "chain snatching," in which one girl grabs another from behind, yanks off her gold chain and knocks her down. Some stalkers wait until their victim is near a stairway so they can push her down.

A new phenomenon is "tough girls." These are girls who would rather get into a fistfight than talk over their differences. Muscle and might have become symbols of cool.

(See also CAMPUS VIOLENCE; GANGS: PICKUP OR TEMPORARY; GANGS: STRUCTURED STREET; GUN-FREE SCHOOL ZONE; VIOLENCE PREVENTION: THE EVOLUTION OF A PILOT PROGRAM FOR ADOLESCENTS; VIOLENCE RESEARCH: A LONGITUDINAL STUDY OF VIOLENCE AMONG THE YOUNG.)

community police   See POLICE.

concurrence   See CRIMINAL LIABILITY.

corporate crime   The power of corporations, many of them multinational, makes it possible for them, alone or in combination, to rob, maim or kill on a scale that makes street crime and organized crime pale by comparison. Despite its potential impact, corporate crime has received much less attention from scholars than has street or organized crime. This may be because corporate, so-called white-collar, crime does not generate the level of fear in the public that street crime does. It also may be that corporations can hide their activities so effectively that few scholars have the time or funds to penetrate their intricacies.

Some scholars believe that corporate crime has an adverse impact on a society's moral climate. A *Fortune* magazine editor commented in 1975, "How much crime in the street is connected to the widespread judgement that the business economy is a gigantic rip-off?"

Besides the effect on the moral climate, the ramifications of decisions made by a few can have enormous consequence. Russell Mokhiber, a lawyer and the editor of the Washington, D.C. weekly newsletter *Corporate Crime Reporter,* in his 1988 *Corporate Crime and Violence: Big Business Power and the Abuse of Public Trust,* wrote: "a man in a three-piece suit atop a Manhattan office building has the potential to inflict more violence on society than all the street thugs in New York City combined."

Although the 1990 loss from burglaries in the United States amounted to $3.5 billion, it was not the work of a few, but the result of more than 3 million burglaries. In contrast, in 1979, just nine major oil companies were sued by the Department of Energy and the Department of Justice for illegal overcharges in excess of $1 billion. The largest single robbery in U.S. history occurred in 1978 and involved the theft of $4 million from the Lufthansa terminal at Kennedy Airport in New York City.

Corporate crime resembles organized crime much more than it does street crime because it involves many people, both inside and outside companies. Avoidance of legal and moral obligations to workers, customers and manufacturing plant neighbors requires complicity from people not employed by a company, such as government regulators, physicians, scientists and politicians on the local and national level.

Although many of the insiders and outsiders involved in corporate crime stand to profit, a substantial number are merely trying to keep their jobs. Whistle-blowing employees risk being laid off or fired. Whistle-blowing regulators risk being transferred or demoted. Whistle-blowing politicians risk loss of campaign contributions.

University of Wisconsin criminologist Marshall Clinard and Yale sociologist Peter Yeager in their 1980 book *Corporate Crime* cite a range of illegal practices. They include false advertising, price fixing, marketing of untested or unsafe products, pollution of the environment, political bribery, foreign payoffs, disregard of safety regulations, tax evasion and falsification of records to hide illicit practices.

Through mergers, acquisition of foreign subsidiaries and other modes of growth, multinational corporations represent the largest accumulation of wealth ever seen in the world. Directors of multinational corporation have the power to trade across the boundaries of nations as if they did not exist. Moreover, while obeying antitrust laws in their own country, they often violate with impunity the antitrust laws of other countries in which they do business.

Transnationals play a significant role in world politics. Some try to manipulate the political stability and economic goals of a country's government. Moreover, they are able to play one country's laws against another by shifting operations to subsidiaries in countries with lax pollution and worker safety standards.

The mammoth size of many corporations requires delegation of responsibility. But responsibility often is confined only to a small portion of the process. The combination of large size, delegation of responsibility and specialization produce an organizational climate that permits abdication of personal responsibility. Under such conditions, almost any type of corporate criminality becomes possible.

Occupational Health.   Aside from illegality and immorality, many corporate crimes do not make fiscal sense. In 1977 the South Carolina state office of the federal Occupational Safety and Health Administration (OSHA) cited the Riegel Textile Corporation for cotton dust violations in one of its mills, a condition that leads to brown lung disease. Instead of lobbying in Washington for regulatory relief to avoid compliance, an industrywide practice, the company spent $5 million to deal with the problem.

The company's chairman told the *Charlotte Observer* on February 3, 1980 that the money was well spent because it resulted in an attractive place to work and made it easier to recruit workers in a tight labor market. A 1983 American Cotton Textile Workers' Union study found the profitability between 1978 and 1981 of seven companies that had complied with health and safety standards had increased by 22% compared with the industry as a whole. Nevertheless, many companies resist compliance with regulations that would protect their employees.

The disastrous health effects of brown lung disease, or byssinosis (from the Greek *byssos,* meaning "cotton" or "flax") have been known for 250 years. During the first year of exposure, a worker may feel a tightness in the chest and breathlessness. Initially, tightness may be noticed after a weekend off. After a few years, "Monday fever" hits every Monday. After ten years, unremitting breathlessness is permanent and a cough becomes a worker's constant companion.

Another airborne threat to workers is coal dust. The United Mine Workers of America (UMW) estimates that 11 coal miners die every day of miner's asthma, better known as black lung. According to the March 1980 *Journal of Public Health Policy,* over the course of a quarter of a century black lung has been responsible for the deaths of at least 100,000 miners and has disabled another 265,000.

At work, coal miners are constantly covered with dust. It gets in their hair, their mouths and in between their teeth, and they swallow it. To varying degrees, all miners suffer from breathlessness, spit up phlegm and have prolonged coughing fits. Gradually they become short of breath when they walk up a hill. Finally just walking across a room becomes difficult.

One miners' advocate, a West Virginia heart specialist, has examined many miners who have been told they suffered heart attacks to cover up the fact that they actually suffered from black lung disease. At one rally he expressed his ire: "Most of this state is owned by ten giant corporations interested only in making money, whatever the human costs."

Coal companies vigorously lobbied against the Federal Coal Mine and Safety Act of 1969, which when passed set up a federal framework for compensating black lung victims and set coal dust standards for the mines. The companies opposed the standards but they did not oppose the compensation, presumably because miners receiving compensation would be less likely to go to court to sue for damages.

The law requiring a coal dust standard of no more than 2 milligrams per cubic meter is enforced only loosely. Violators do not risk criminal prosecution. The government levies only minor fines on offenders.

The UMW documented that for fiscal year 1986, 80 coal mines had an average annual coal dust concentration in excess of the federal standard and 18 mines had exceeded the statutory limit for each of the previous three years. One West Virginia mine that operated for 14 out of 20 months at dust levels sometimes triple the federal limit was fined $140 for the 20-month period.

The Tobacco Industry. Perhaps the greatest corporate contributors to breathing problems and premature deaths are American tobacco companies. In her 1963 book *Smoke Screen: Tobacco and the Public Welfare,* U.S. Senator Maurine Neuberger (D.-Oregon) wrote: "I believe that the moral and intellectual poverty that has characterized our approach to the smoking problem must no longer be shrouded by the press agentry of the tobacco industry, nor the fancy bureaucratic footwork of government agencies charged with responsibility for guarding the nation's health."

The man most responsible for the financial success of the tobacco industry was George Washington Hill, who took over the American Brands tobacco corporation in 1923. A glimpse of a fat woman chewing gum and a slim woman smoking a cigarette gave him an idea that made Lucky Strike cigarettes the number-one brand in the United States for two decades, beginning in 1932. His slogan was "Reach for a Lucky instead of a sweet." Industry cigarette sales soared from 120 billion in 1930 to 267 billion in 1945.

Much of the danger inherent in cigarette smoking was known to tobacco company executives as early as 1900, when health experts noted an increase in cancer of the lungs. The 1900 study was the first of what became a flood of more than 30,000 reports that linked cigarette smoking to heart disease, emphysema, chronic bronchitis and other respiratory ailments, and cancer of the lungs, mouth, esophagus, bladder, kidney, pancreas, stomach, uterus and cervix.

In response to a December 1941 *Reader's Digest* antismoking article that received little publicity, the tobacco companies took the offensive and launched a nationwide ad campaign to firmly convince American consumers that cigarettes were not harmful to health but were in fact helpful. The company slogans reflected their health-oriented stance: "Not a cough in a carload" (Old Gold). "More doctors smoke Camels than any other cigarette." "The Throat-Tested Cigarette" (Phillip Morris).

A broad examination of the relationship of smoking to health began in the early 1950s when Drs. E. Cuyler Hammond and Daniel Horn of the American Cancer Society used 22,000 trained volunteers to enroll 187,783 men between ages 50 and 69 in a study. In October 1953 the scientists took a preliminary look at the comparative death rates of smoker and nonsmokers. Of 11,870 men in the study group who had died, 7,316 had been smokers compared with 4,651 who had been nonsmokers.

In the late 1950s, combined antismoking forces from medical, public interest and fitness groups pressured federal officials to establish minimum standards of health and safety for the industry that had been treated thus far as if it were immune from the law. But the tobacco industry's control over Congress was too powerful.

Nearly one fourth of the Senate committees were chaired by men from six tobacco-growing states.

Tobacco companies exert control at both the local and federal level. In his 1982 book *Coffin Nails and Corporate Strategies,* Robert Miles pointed out that the industry bemoans state and municipal tax burdens placed on their cigarettes, but those payments serve them well by creating revenue dependencies in legislatures that might otherwise have harmed their interests.

The most powerful tool on the side of antismoking forces was the 1964 Surgeon General's report, which concluded that cigarette smoking is a hazard sufficient to warrant immediate action, that cigarette smoking is causally related to lung cancer in men (less extensive data on women pointed in the same direction), and that the effect of cigarette smoking far outweighs the impact of other factors. There was a sharp, but short-lived, drop in sales.

In January 1964 the Federal Trade Commission (FTC) announced that the failure of cigarette manufacturers to warn consumers of the health hazards of smoking constituted an unfair and deceptive practice. Henceforth, the FCC prohibited several kinds of deceptive ads.

In 1967, pushed by a citizen's interest group, the Federal Communications Commission (FCC) required equal air time for antismoking groups to counteract broadcast cigarette ads. Within two years, there was one antismoking ad for every 4.4 cigarette ads and per-capita cigarette consumption dropped sharply.

Enforcement agencies all over Washington and around the nation followed the FCC's lead by imposing controls on smoking. The most significant move was to ban cigarette advertising on TV. Some observers believe that the ban may have been counterproductive because the antismoking ads disappeared along with the cigarette ads. By the end of 1971, per-capita consumption began to climb again.

The $225 million the tobacco industry had spent on television and radio went into print media advertising. In 1979 *TV Guide* and *Playboy* each took in $20 million in tobacco revenue, and *Time* collected $15 million. By then Americans were smoking 595 billion cigarettes annually.

During the 1980s, cigarette smoking among middle-class adults dropped sharply. Antismoking forces accused the tobacco corporations, in their search for new markets, of targeting teenagers, minority communities and third-world countries. Efforts to curb federal subsidies for tobacco inevitably have been countered with the claim that poor U.S. tobacco farmers would be the ones who were hurt.

Lawsuits against tobacco companies by dying smokers have been unsuccessful. They are the butt of jokes that suggest it is ridiculous to blame a company for personal actions. What the comedians overlook is the impact motivational advertising has had in such ads as those that featured handsome, rugged cowboy-style Marlboro men in handsome, rugged Western settings and beautiful, active Virginia Slims women proud of having their very own cigarette. The comedians and other critics also overlook the addictiveness of cigarettes. A whole industry has grown up around helping smokers to quit smoking. Most smokers try and fail to stop one or more times.

Highway Deaths. American automotive industry executives are as adept as tobacco executives at ignoring consumer safety. General Motors (GM) sold 1,124,076 defective Corvairs. The number of people who were killed or injured at the wheel of that dangerous car is not known. What is known is that serious questions were raised at executive levels of the corporation long before the cars were marketed.

In J. Patrick Wright's 1979 *On a Clear Day You Can See General Motors: John Z. DeLorean's Look Inside the Automotive Giant,* DeLorean is quoted as saying, "The questionable safety of the car caused a massive internal fight among GM's engineers over whether the car should be built with another form of suspension." The fight was between the company's most effective salesperson and the vice president of engineering, who wanted to keep the car out of production or to change its swing-axle suspension system.

As early as 1953 Maurice Olley, a GM specialist in car handling characteristics, publicly denounced rear-engine vehicles as a poor bargain, difficult to handle in wind even at moderate speeds. In 1956, as the head of research and development for Chevrolet, he warned of the dangers inherent in swing-axle suspension. He wrote in a patent application that under lateral forces produced by cornering, the rear end of the vehicle tends to lift so that both wheels tilt inward to an extent that the vehicle not only oversteers but actually tends to roll over.

Secret internal GM proving-ground tests, made public ten years after the Corvair was first produced, showed that GM was aware of the car's instability. In one June 1959 test, a Corvair flipped over as the driver attempted to maneuver a J-turn at 30 miles per hour (mph).

Before a stabilizing bar was added in 1964, unsafe Corvairs were sold for four years. The consequences of the flaw were disastrous. Driving what was promoted as a sports car, young owners took curves at high speeds and killed themselves in great numbers. Some of the young Corvair owners who died were the sons and daughters of GM executives.

Instability was not the Corvair's only flaw. Carbon monoxide fumes from a leaking engine could enter the passenger compartment through the heater. GM executives defended the subcompact to the end, and no GM executive went to jail, nor was the company fined.

Like the tobacco industry, GM had friends in Washington. The National Highway Traffic Safety Administration (NHTSA) in 1972 found that the "handling and stability of the Corvair does not result in abnormal potential loss of control or rollover."

Another lethal car, the Pinto, was the brainchild of the Ford Motor Company's then-president Lee Iacocca, who believed strongly that safety doesn't sell. In response to a flood of foreign imports, particularly the Volkswagen Beetle, Iacocca wanted to develop a competitor. He set out to rush his idea through production in 25 months, rather than the normal 43 months, and have the car weigh no more than 2,000 pounds and cost no more than $2,000.

In his disdain for safety, Iacocca was carrying on a industry tradition. Alfred P. Sloan, president of GM, corresponded with the president of Dupont, in the late 1920s and early 1930s about putting safety glass in Chevrolets. Sloan said that safety glass would not improve sales and might even inhibit sales by increasing cost. The notion that safety does not sell has remained an industry belief until very recently. The constraints Iacocca set for the Pinto meant that any time, weight or dollar additions, no matter what their benefits, safety or otherwise, were vetoed.

The Pinto's fuel tank was placed between the rear bumper and the differential housing (the box that connects the rear axle to the driveshaft). When hit from the rear at even a speed as low as 30 mph, the impact smashed the Pinto's fuel tank into four sharp bolts projecting from the housing, ripping it open to spew out gasoline. If the rear car hit at a speed of about 40 mph, the Pinto's doors would jam, trapping passengers in the gasoline-drenched wreck that inevitably ignited in the postcrash sparks.

During 1971, 400,000 Pintos made their way onto American highways with this defect, which would cause hundreds of deaths and injuries. Yet internal company documents of tests that began as early as 1968 revealed that the Pinto had been crash-tested 40 times and every test over 25 mph resulted in a ruptured fuel tank. In only three tests did the Pinto tank fail to rupture: when an inexpensive plastic baffle was placed between the bolts and the gas tank, when a piece of metal was placed between the bumper and the gas tank, and when the inside of the gas tank was lined with a rubber bladder.

When the NHTSA was considering a requirement that all automobiles beginning in 1973 would have to be able to withstand a rear-end collision at 30 mph, Ford engineers concluded that to meet the contemplated standard they would have to line the fuel tank, at a cost of $100 million over three years. Rather than meet the standard, Ford put its effort into lobbying to defeat the requirement.

For eight years, Ford harassed NHTSA officials with memos, requests for studies and paperwork. One of the documents from Ford's director of automotive safety to the administrator of the NHTSA reflected company thinking. Using government statistics, Ford estimated that the cost of a human death was $200,000, a burn injury $67,000 and an incinerated car $700.

In a given year, without making changes in the Pinto, Ford could expect to pay for 180 deaths at a cost of $36 million, 180 burns at a cost of $12.06 million and 2,100 cars at a cost of $1.47 million, for a total of $49.53 million. But if Ford fixed each Pinto so it would not explode when rear-ended at 30 mph, it would cost $11 for 12.5 million vehicles for a total of $137.5 million. By keeping the defect, Ford could save $87.97 million annually.

In 1978 three teenagers on their way to a church volleyball game in a 1973 Pinto were rear-ended by a van near Elkhart, Indiana. The car exploded and the three girls burned to death. An Elkhart County prosecutor brought murder charges against Ford Motor Company. It was the first time a major American corporation had been placed on trial for murder.

Ford's defense attorney made two shrewd moves. He had the trial location changed and hired as co-counsel a local attorney who for 22 years had shared an office with the only circuit court judge to serve the area. The judge's pro-Ford rulings prevented the jury from hearing key evidence. The verdict was not guilty.

The Equity Funding Corporation Charade. Raymond Dirks, a skeptical journalist with a reputation for tenacity, received a tip from Ronald Secrist, a fired executive of Equity Funding Corporation, an investment firm, that set him on a trail of a monumental hoax involving fraud, forgery, intimidation and conspiracy. In their 1974 book *The Great Wall Street Scandal,* Dirks and journalist Leonard Gross observe that the Equity Funding scandal would not have happened had securities analysts done their job.

The function of securities analysts is to determine the real worth of a company so that investors will pay a fair price for the company's securities. After the Great Depression stock analysts paid close attention to corporate balance sheets, a reflection of a company's net worth. With the passage of years, they became preoccupied with potential corporate earnings, which can change quickly, and grew less interested in net worth.

Using a measure known as "performance," analysts try to determine what the normal true growth rate of a company is in terms of its earnings per share and then determine the degree of confidence they have in that growth rate. The key to the confidence factor is the consistency and growth of reported earnings. Analysts ask how many straight quarters have earnings risen and at what percent. If earnings have followed a consistent pattern of growth, analysts assume they will continue to grow. On paper, Equity Funding was an analyst's dream of consistent growth, a factor that perhaps should have made many suspicious.

Analysts rely on the reports of other analysts, which are often monitored, managed and even partially written by the companies being judged. After a few perfunctory checks of a written report, an analyst may churn out another report based on the reading for his or her brokerage firm. Thus a company-managed report can have escalating impact.

Most analysts, in the view of Dirks and Gross, are not really analysts. They are salespeople motivated by the need to generate commissions, who must deal with a Wall Street axiom that negative stories don't sell. Analysts who write negatively about companies find that eventually companies won't cooperate sufficiently to permit an analysis.

Equity Funding executives were immensely cooperative with analysts. One brokerage firm noted uneasily that Equity's management was so available to analysts that they didn't seem to do anything else. Its report noted that there had long been negative rumors floating around about Equity Funding, but the brokerage firm had not been able to substantiate them. Despite its reservations, the firm recommended purchase of the stock.

The Equity Fund put together four different ingredients, insurance, savings, a mutual fund and a loan, which the customer paid for with one check. The company's insurance fraud began in 1969, when the public began to sense that attempts to combine life insurance and investment might not be a good idea. The company had borrowed heavily to run its business, but it could not convince enough customers to do the same.

To make up for its lack of customers, the company created 64,000 fictitious life insurance policies with a face value in excess of $2 billion. To acquire cash, using a practice known as reinsurance, the company sold the fraudulent policies to other insurance companies. To provide an appearance of sustained growth, the company faked assets of more than $100 million, counterfeited bonds and forged death certificates.

Equity Funding issued nearly 8 million shares of stock that traded for anywhere from $12 to $80 a share. At a representative price of $40 a share, the stock's market value would have been $300 million, but in fact it was worthless.

Besides the inadequate scrutiny of individual stock analysts, there were plenty of other culprits. The Securities and Exchange Commission (SEC), the agency of the federal government charged with monitoring those corporations that trade through the exchange, failed to take proper action, despite rumors about Equity Funding that reached stock exchange officials as early as 1968, five years before the story broke. The various state insurance audit agencies charged with policing insurance operations in their states conducted only superficial examinations and did not penetrate the corporate facade.

Dirks and Gross laid much of the blame at the feet of the insurance industry. They commented that as lax as the monitoring of the investment industry might be, it is highly regulated compared to the insurance industry, which involves an estimated 1,800 companies with policies worth approximately $1.5 trillion at face value. The insurance industry has consistently battled against regulations by the federal government, characterizing such regulation as unnecessary and intrusive.

The revelations about Equity Funding had a devastating ripple effect on Wall Street. The April 14, 1973 issue of *Business Week* reported that many investors apparently had concluded that independent auditors, state examiners and the SEC were not reliable protection against fraud and knocked down the value of the whole group of insurance stocks by 10% to 25%. In the week following April 2, 1973, the day the *Wall Street Journal* broke the story, the value of shares on the New York Stock Exchange dropped by $15 billion.

The fraud also had an effect on the nation as a whole. Dirks and Gross wrote:

Had the Equity Funding scandal occurred in a time of prosperity and serene national confidence, it might have been absorbed. It did not. The scandal unfolded during a period of self-doubt unparalleled in our history . . . a newspaper cartoonist pictured five vultures perched on Wall Street. They represented higher gold prices, inflations, devaluation of the dollar, Watergate—and Equity Funding.

Political Interference and Bank Examiners.   A bigger and more complex financial fraud was to follow in the 1980s among American savings and loan institutions (S&Ls). Originally called building and loan associations, S&Ls, also known as thrifts, were largely organized as mutual societies in which depositors became shareholders and provided loans to home buyers and small businesses.

The title of Wall Street Journal reporter James Ring Adams' 1990 book, *The Big Fix: Inside the S&L Scandal, How an Unholy Alliance of Politics and Money Destroyed America's Banking System,* sums up the scope of the crime. Conservative estimates placed the cost of paying for the behavior of America's savings and loan institutions (S&Ls) at about $285 billion. (The figure has since risen.)

Bank runs are the nightmare of American bank regulators, who envision a line of angry depositors clamoring for their money at the door of a closed savings institution. In the view of Adams, that image is linked to an overriding concern with shoring up depositor confidence, even if it means ignoring the prevention and punishment of bank fraud.

A simple run is a rational form of behavior. Depositors receive information that makes them question the safety of their bank. Knowing that the bank cannot pay everyone, they rush to get their money before the bank runs out. Depositors' behavior sometimes gets out of hand and the bank property may be damaged.

Bank failures by themselves do not trigger a panic. During the 1920s, 4,400 savings institutions closed. Their failures were masked by the general prosperity of the times. A high proportion of the failures could be traced to fraud.

The first of the depression-era banking crises began in October 1930. It engulfed more than 600 banks, and reached its peak with the failure of the Bank of United States in New York City on December 11. More than 440,000 New Yorkers, many of them hard-pressed Jewish immigrants, had placed their savings in the bank's 57 branches thinking that it was government-owned. Two more waves of bank panics followed in the next two years.

The first thing Franklin D. Roosevelt did upon taking office as president in March 1933 was to order all banks closed. The Treasury Department then divided them into three classes. Banks that were solvent reopened. Insolvent banks that were savable reopened gradually. Hopeless banks stayed closed. In one year 1,005 state and national banks were liquidated.

The banking system was purged of its weakest members. At that point, in the opinion of Adams, the cleaned-up system with new built-in safeguards had no need for the federal deposit insurance that was put into place. The new system required all banks to contribute a premium equal to a small sum of their deposits to an insurance fund. The fund was to pay off depositors should a bank fail. The rationale behind the insurance was that there would be no need for depositors to make runs on banks.

Before passage of the measure, critics pointed out that only a few failures could wipe out the fund. Strong northeastern banks with large deposits objected that they would pay the highest premium for insurance they did not need, thereby subsidizing smaller and more poorly run banks in the rest of the country. President Roosevelt, who was at first opposed to the idea of deposit insurance changed his mind in response to a flood of letters from victimized depositors of the previously closed banks.

Once banks had been given the support of the Federal Deposit Insurance Corporation (FDIC), which insured deposits up to $10,000, S&Ls soon asked for it. The Federal Savings and Loan Insurance Corporation (FSLIC) came into being and insured S&L accounts up to $5,000.

From the outset, federal deposit insurance was a subsidy, not an insurance policy. There was no effort to match premiums to risk. There was no equivalent of auto insurance premiums that penalize high-risk drivers. Premiums increased across the board, with healthy institutions carrying the weight of sick ones.

For a time, depositors with banked amounts beyond the limits kept institutions in line. Over the years, the amount of coverage inched up to $40,000.

In the 1980s the implications of the subsidy became apparent after the chairman of the House Banking Committee, Fernand St. Germain, alleged to have spent many of his evenings in the company of lobbyists for the United States League of Savings Institution, proposed in 1980 that the limit be raised to $100,000.

The steep rise dramatically changed the nature of the guarantee, which had in the 1930s been aimed at protecting the small saver. The change took away the monitoring function played by those who had funds above the guaranteed limit.

In addition to individual accounts, the FDIC and FSLIC cover trust and joint accounts. Bankers quickly figured out how to market the new $100,000 subsidy. For example, Citibank mailed a brochure to its customers showing how to stretch the FDIC to cover up to $1.4 million by various permutations of individual and joint accounts—husband and wife, husband and child, wife and child, and child and child, each insured up to $100,000.

Brokerage firms created an even greater potential drain in the form of jumbo "certificates of deposit" (CDs). They packaged funds in amounts just under the federal guarantee and searched for S&Ls with the highest interest rates, usually the weakest in the system, as a federally guaranteed investment. Many of the depositors taking advantage of the jumbo CDs were themselves federally insured banks, S&Ls and credit unions.

By the mid-1980s the S&L industry defied elemental laws of business. Thrifts losing more than they were making remained in business. According to one study, sick thrifts in 1986 held $315 billion in liabilities (deposits and loans), about 40% of the amount held by healthy thrifts. By mid-1988 they held 50%.

From the depression until 1980, banks and thrifts had been permitted to offer depositors only a fixed rate of interest. The legislation that increased the deposit ceiling to $100,000 also did away with the fixed interest rate. Deregulation meant that S&Ls could hold on to depositors by offering higher interest rates, but they could not change the rates of earning on mortgages already issued. Thus more was going out than was coming in.

As profits vanished, S&Ls began dipping into their capital, the money put up by investors when each thrift was formed. By 1982 most capital industrywide had been exhausted.

St. Germain came to the rescue again. The Garn-St. Germain Act of 1982 sought to rebuild S&L capital by expanding the type of investments S&Ls could make beyond the traditional mortgages. A new breed of owner was sought, an aggressive risk-taker, who presumably could help the thrifts earn their way out of debt. At the same time, capital requirements were drastically lowered.

A horde of risk-takers was thus set loose on the S&Ls without actually being subjected to any risk. One regulator described the setup as "Heads they win. Tails FSLIC loses." Insurance professionals called it a "moral hazard," a policy that offered too much temptation to cheat.

One Brooklyn Federal Court judge dismissed a criminal case against a thrift president on the grounds that the government had encouraged his high-risk lending. S&Ls also had become a target for those who were tempted by scams.

Efforts to rein in the S&Ls' high-risk ventures were constantly thwarted by interference from Congress and the White House. The heroes in the whole S&L debacle, in the opinion of Adams, were the regulators and Ed Gray, the S&L Bank Board chairman. The national thrift lobby had pushed for Gray to be chairman because they had counted on him to be a pliable free-market Reaganite.

Although Gray had worked for Reagan on and off for several years, once he understood the scope of the S&L problem, he set out to correct it. During a lunch at the White House mess, a budget official told Gray that he didn't understand the purpose of the administration. The official said, "We want to get government off the back of business. We ought to be reducing the number of examiners, not increasing them." At that point, Gray told Adams, he concluded that they were loony, blinded by ideology.

Gray took a stronger stand on principle than anyone, including himself, had reason to expect. His reward was vilification from the thrift industry, Congress, much of his own administration and a good part of the press. In the end, he was vindicated.

Constant political interference took an enormous toll on regulators, state and federal examiners and law enforcement officials. Despite their best efforts, there was a flood of S&L failures. Many regulators and law enforcement officials resigned and their suicide rate has been extraordinarily high.

A participant in bank failures in Tennessee claims there are eight signs of potential disaster. They are: a change of ownership between 1982 and 1985; extremely rapid growth since 1982; a risky asset portfolio; a weak structure of loans; impressive architecture and art collections; opulent means of transportation; luxurious lifestyle of management; and political contributions.

Wall Street Revisited. The high-risk adventurers and outright crooks of the S&Ls had their counterparts in Wall Street during the 1980s and were often connected to them. In his 1991 book *Den of Thieves,* James Stewart, the *Wall Street Journal*'s front-page editor, describes the intersecting activities of many corporate criminals on Wall Street. The most prominent were Michael Milken, Ivan Boesky, Martin Siegel and Dennis Levine, whose inside trading and junk bond-financed corporate takeover deals had the potential to destroy

Wall Street and did in fact destroy or severely damage a great number of American corporations.

On May 12, 1986 Levine, an investment banker with the brokerage firm of Drexel Burnham Lambert, was charged by the SEC with insider trading. The arrest signaled the end of a four-year money-making boom in Wall Street, the end of a takeover craze (buyouts of other companies, many of them hostile) and exposure of the biggest criminal conspiracy the financial world had ever known.

Financial crime was commonplace on Wall Street in the 1980s. Many defendants who were charged claimed that it was unfair to single out one individual when so many others were guilty of the same practices. A Wall Street code of silence allowed crime to flourish to an extent that overwhelmed the resources of the Manhattan U.S. attorney's office and that of Gary Lynch, head of enforcement at the SEC.

Many household-name corporations disappeared in takeovers, often artificially stimulated by arbitrageurs, who specialized in mergers and takeovers. Other companies survived attempts to take them over but were left crippled by debt. Debt payments consumed profits and thousands of workers lost their jobs. Many companies were forced into restructuring or bankruptcy. Bondholders and shareholders lost millions.

Historically, arbitrageurs had traded to take advantage of price discrepancies on different markets, such as those of London and New York, a conservative, virtually risk-free form of trading with small profits. Arbitrageurs like Boesky became progressively more daring. At first they bought heavily stocks that were the subjects of announced takeover bids, taking the risk that the deals would go through. Eventually they began to buy stocks of corporations only suspected of being targets of takeover bids or set up conditions so that takeover seemed inevitable. Illegally obtained inside information vastly improved their odds.

Although each of the four, Levine, Siegel, Milken and Boesky, operated independently, they eventually found one another increasingly helpful in furthering their inside trading. One of the ways they and others like them got together was attendance at a lavish yearly affair put on by Drexel Burnham Lambert, a junk bond conference known as the Predators' Ball.

Although there were sometimes large payments for services rendered among co-conspirators, more often the payments came in the form of information. Dennis Levine was the weak link in the chain. Although just

as greedy as the others, he overestimated his own abilities. His insider information made him appear more knowledgeable than he actually was.

During Levine's first week with Smith, Barney, Harris Upham & Co., he passed on inside information to a friend. Highly persuasive, he built a network of friends from whom he gathered insider information. He coaxed one into admitting him into his company at night, where Levine prowled through desks and files looking for information he could use.

The intricate world of the four began to unravel when an anonymous letter arrived at Merrill Lynch, a brokerage firm more serious than most about compliance with trading regulations. The letter complained about the use of insider information by two account executives. The investigation was turned over to the Securities and Exchange Commission (SEC), where the investigation broadened to include many other people.

Prior to this investigation, most earlier examples of insider trading had involved only a few stocks. Yet the SEC staff had been aware that isolated cases could not account for what seemed to be an epidemic of insider trading. They suspected there had to be a network with access to the most confidential information.

Levine was arrested on May 9, 1986. He told the investigators that he had been bored as an investment banker and that insider trading was exciting. He doubted that he would have ever stopped, no matter how much money he made.

Levine pleaded guilty to four felony charges, paid an $11.6 million fine to the SEC, plus an additional $362,000 levied by the court, and was sentenced to two years in prison. He implicated others, including Boesky, who had opened his own arbitrage firm in 1975.

Lynch of the SEC had always thought that arbitrageurs would be hard to convict on insider trading because their business was built on rumor and the gathering of market intelligence. Boesky could legitimately be expected to have large amounts of stocks in most takeovers and thus could claim that legitimate information had triggered his purchases. Nevertheless, Lynch crafted a subpoena that called for testimony and voluminous documents designed to let Boesky know that Levine had implicated him.

Before he made a decision about what he would do, Boesky spent two weeks painstakingly taking his defense attorneys through his activities. One of his attorneys, Harvey Pitt, was stunned, in part by Boesky's seeming fear of Milken and in part because he seemed to have no sense of the magnitude of what he had done. Besides insider trading, Milken and Boesky were involved in a wide array of violations, including a "broad conspiracy to interfere with the control of corporations."

When his attorneys went to the SEC to negotiate a deal, which included the payment of $100 million to the SEC, Pitt told the officials that a deal with Boesky would give them a glimpse into Wall Street practices comparable to the hearings that led to the passage of the securities laws. Boesky, he said, "would be a window on Wall Street."

Among those Boesky agreed to testify about were some of the most prominent names in the world of finance: Michael Milken, the junk bond king; Martin Siegel, Drexel's star investment banker; Boyd Jefferies, a prominent West Coast broker; and Carl Icahn, a famous corporate raider.

The SEC was worried about how the stock market would react to rumors of Boesky's end as an arbitrageur. The market of the 1980s had been fueled by arbitrageurs like him. The SEC delayed the announcement for two weeks so that Boesky could sell his stock in an orderly manner. They also wanted to protect the SEC's $100 million, which in part depended on the value of Boesky's portfolio.

When the news broke at 4:00 P.M. on November 14, 1986, a storm of criticism was launched against the SEC for the delay. A flurry of untrue rumors made it appear as if Boesky had made great profits from the delay.

Martin Siegel was next. In a series of moves to make him believe they were about to close in on him, the government nudged an already apprehensive Siegel into admitting his wrongdoing in exchange for a plea bargain. The agreement was reached on November 15, 1986. Stung by the criticism that they had been soft on Boesky, the SEC was unbending with Siegel. Although he had received only $700,000 from Boesky, the SEC confiscated all his assets, except his pension contribution and two houses. They even made him forgo $10 million in stock and a guaranteed bonus owed to him by Drexel.

Siegel made no attempt to excuse his behavior. To the prosecutors, the sorrow Levine and Boesky expressed had seemed to be about being caught. Siegel's remorse was about the wrong he had done and his desire to make amends.

Siegel had begun working on Wall Street in 1971 for Kidder, Peabody & Company. Because no one else was interested, he quickly became an arbitrageur, the firm's expert on merger-and-acquisition transactions (known as A&Ms). Hostile takeovers bore a taint and often generated bad feelings toward those who represented the attackers, which bothered others in the firm but did not seem to bother Siegel. In 1974 he wrote a textbook for the firm on A&Ms and two years later was made a vice president.

The year 1977 was eventful for Siegel. He was made a director of the firm, he met Ivan Boesky, who had already made a name in the small world of arbitrage, and he invented the golden parachute, an employment contract that provided exorbitant severance payments for top officers in the event of a takeover—a tactic that endeared him to scores of corporate managers. Parachutes were supposed to deter takeovers by making them expensive. In practice, they made senior corporate officers rich. Siegel also developed the "PacMan defense," a strategy that calls for a corporation threatened by a takeover to counterattack.

Although the government tried to use Siegel undercover, he was not particularly successful. Although he begged to be sentenced in order to get out from under the suspense of waiting, the government held him in reserve from February 1987 until June 1990 as a potential witness. Government officials felt they had entered into a deal too soon with Boesky and were determined not to do it again.

During the years of waiting, Siegel spent countless hours explaining the workings of the market and guiding the government investigators through reams of complex trading records. Because of his cooperation, in addition to the loss of his assets, Siegel was given only a two-month sentence, plus five years probation working in a computer camp for children he had set up in Jacksonville, Florida.

Milken never considered pleading guilty. Unlike Boesky and Levine, he had no one more important to turn in and little to offer the government in return for leniency. And unlike Siegel, he felt no remorse.

Hired in 1973 by Drexel Burnham & Co., Michael Milken began with $2 million in capital and by 1974 was generating 100% rates of return in an area called high-yield, unrated bonds. The rating or lack of rating of a bond is an assessment of the value of an investment, which depends on the issuer's ability to make promised interest payments until the bond matures and then to pay the principal.

American bond rating is dominated by two giant agencies, Moody's and Standard & Poor's (S&P). Top-rated companies are rated Triple A by S&P. Companies with weaker positions are rated lower, and some companies are deemed too risky for a rating. For such companies, interest rates on their corporate debt fluctuates with the rates of U.S. Treasury notes and the perceived risk of the issuer. The lower the rating, the more the company must pay to attract investors. The trading of low-rated bonds (commonly referred to as junk bonds) became Milken's specialty.

While in college, Milken had read an analysis of the average performance of low-grade bonds for the years 1900 to 1943. In this study, author W. Braddock Hickman had found that low-rated bonds yielded a high rate of return with no more risk than top-rated bonds.

At the time Milken began to specialize, no one else was doing research on the companies that issued low-grade bonds. A superb salesman, Milken did meticulous research, and with it he began to make headway convincing reluctant investors to buy junk bonds.

In 1975 Drexel allowed Milken to set up his own semiautonomous bond trading unit, with an unusually generous bonus arrangement. By 1977 his operation controlled 25% of the market in high-yield securities.

Milken created the only market-making operation with the purpose of increasing the market's liquidity (ready conversion into cash). A market-maker assures a holder of a security that the maker will buy it whenever the holder wants to convert it to cash. The market-maker, in turn, resells the security, keeping as profit any difference between the cost of buying the security from the holder and selling it to someone else. If there is no profit, the market-maker absorbs the loss.

Milken thrived because his market was almost entirely unregulated. The world of junk bonds was the rough equivalent of the American frontier. The weak lost out to the strong. Few ever got the better of Milken because he had a phenomenal memory. When someone did best him, he tried to hire him or her.

In 1978, still under the Drexel umbrella, Milken moved the operation to California. There he assembled a network of junk bond customers much larger than his New York array. Among them was Thomas Spiegel, head of Columbia S&L, Charles Keating, head of Lincoln S&L, and Fred Carr, head of Executive Life Insurance. When necessary, Milken kept junk bonds moving into and out of portfolios to maintain their apparent value.

Not content with his lucrative business in junk bonds, Milken recognized that there was big money in leveraged buyouts. In a leveraged buyout, the buyer borrows money to purchase the stock of a corporation to be taken over. After the takeover, the buyer uses the purchased corporation's earnings or sells off its assets to pay back the borrowed money.

Milken once told an employee that there was no deal he could not do, no company so big it need not fear his power. He said, "We're going to tee up GM, Ford, and IBM, and make them cringe."

Until almost the end, Fred Joseph and a large segment of Drexel maintained their faith in Milken and would not consider separating themselves from him. Many companies insist on getting to the bottom of an employee's alleged misconduct and if the employee does not cooperate, he or she is fired. Milken's lawyers effectively sealed him off from Joseph and other Drexel officers.

Milken's expensive lawyers, as well as an expensive public relations firm to polish his image, were paid for by Drexel. At one point, the average bills for lawyers and public relations were $3 million a month.

Although it was common knowledge that Drexel might be charged by the SEC at any moment, in the spring of 1986 the firm completed an impressive array of massive junk bond deals. Thus the government could not depend on clients to encourage Drexel to cooperate in their investigations against Milken. Clients were as defiant as Milken, and given his power over their futures, many had little option.

In December 1988 Drexel agreed to plead guilty to six felonies. SEC anger at the firm's perceived shielding of Milken resulted in a record $650 million fine. A minicrash in October 1989 was a harbinger of the demise of the junk bond market. A number of companies and S&Ls toppled. Drexel's new business dwindled and its ability to get credit disappeared. In the end, Drexel's faith in Milken destroyed the firm, which was forced into bankruptcy on February 13, 1990.

An analysis of the 1989 financial data confirmed a growing suspicion that Milken's oft-repeated premise that investors obtained better returns on low-grade issues than high was false. Over the decade of the 1980s, money invested in the average junk bond fund grew by 145%, in U.S. Treasury bonds by 177%, in investment-grade corporate bonds by 202%, and in stocks by 207%. In junk bonds, only the criminals earned astronomical returns. Milken's real genius was in making so many people believe him.

To indict Milken, the government needed more than just Boesky's word. During the long probe, one investigator was struck by the similarity between insider-trading investigations and Mafia cases he had worked on. The Wall Street suspects prized silence and loyalty, there were numerous interlocking cases and there were not enough investigators.

The investigator wrote down the names of the suspects, drew boxes around them and connected them based on interlocking relationships. He had almost 20 boxes roughly in a circle with Milken at the top and Drexel near the center.

When government investigators went looking for one of those under suspicion, William Hale, an employee of an obscure New Jersey firm called Princeton-Newport, they found that he had been fired. When asked why he had been fired, Hale said, "I couldn't stand all the crime they were committing."

According to Hale, Princeton-Newport routinely "parked" securities with Drexel as well as with Merrill Lynch, creating phony losses with which to cheat the Internal Revenue Service. Hale led investigators to a recording system that routinely recorded the firm's trades, a system common to many firms intended to resolve disputes with customers about orders. The tapes revealed that not only were Princeton-Newport top officials involved, their co-conspirator was Drexel's California operation, Milken's division.

By the spring of 1990, Milken had outlasted them all; Levine, Siegel, Boesky and even Drexel were gone from Wall Street. The two top government officials in the Milken case were also gone, but their case against Milken was finally ready.

While the Milken public relations campaign continued full tilt, his lawyers sought a plea bargain, evidently having realized that a trial no longer depended heavily on Boesky's testimony. Prosecutors had picked up more witnesses in 1990, and they threatened to add a new indictment, one that would have focused on Milken's alleged manipulation of the S&Ls, bribing of fund managers and cheating of Drexel.

In 1989 prosecutors had been willing to offer Milken just two felony counts. In 1990 they wanted six and the SEC wanted a payment of over $600 million. The fine was later criticized as too low. In 1986 alone Milken earned $550 million in salary and bonus.

Milken finally agreed to the terms. On April 24, 1990 he read a confession of the six felonies in court, inserting a comment that the junk bond market had enabled hundreds of companies to survive, expand and flourish. He was sentenced to 10 years, with a recommendation that he serve at least 36 to 40 months.

Once in prison, Milken changed his mind and hired the celebrity defense lawyer Alan Dershowitz to look for strategies to undo his guilty plea.

correctional education   Although the term correctional implies an intention to rehabilitate, many institutions do nothing more than warehouse prisoners, for a variety of reasons: overcrowding, poor management, lack of money or an attitude on the part of the prison administration that prisoners deserve no more.

There are four major reasons for locking a criminal up: punishment for crimes already committed; deterrence of future crimes through fear of punishment; protection of society from those likely to commit crimes; and reform or rehabilitation of prisoners while they are in prison. The first three reasons are often characterized as the "lock 'em up and throw away the key" position. The fourth reason may be characterized as the "they are going to get out some day, so you'd better do something while you've got them" position. Public attitudes in the United States have swung back and forth between the two positions, but there have always been substantial numbers of people taking each.

Closely tied to the notions of punishment/deterrence/protection versus rehabilitation are beliefs about whether prisoners can be reformed. To those who believe in the "once a criminal, always a criminal" concept, the best alternative seems to be to throw criminals in jail for as long as possible. With an emphasis on punishment, deterrence and protection, correctional institutions fill up and become overcrowded until conditions become so inhumane that a movement rises to reform them and the emphasis shifts to rehabilitation and alternatives to prison.

Public attitudes toward rehabilitation began to lose ground in the 1950s and punishment, deterrence and protection became paramount. The attitude seemed to be peaking by 1991, when the federal system was so crowded it was 55% above capacity and state governors saw corrections budgets draining off money that was desperately needed in areas such as health care and road building.

The attitude that prevailed during the 1980s had by early 1991 resulted in the United States having more people in prisons and jails than any other nation in the world. Out of every 100,000 people in the population, 426 people were in prison or being held in pretrial detention.

The Georgia Department of Corrections jokingly became known as the "Department of Construction" because a burgeoning prison population forced the state to undertake a frantic prison building program. In a November 6, 1989 *Christian Science Monitor* article entitled "Drug Crisis Burdens Prison System," political analyst Horace Busby was quoted as saying "In the

1950s and '60s, everybody was busy building public schools. But the biggest boom area of public contracting in the '90s will be prisons.''

The General Accounting Office, the research arm of the Congress, reported in 1989 that a record 673,565 Americans were in state and federal prisons. Princeton professor John DiIulio, author of *No Escape—The Future of the American Correctional System* (1991), estimates that an additional 2,250,000 people are on probation or parole and thus under some kind of criminal justice supervision.

For those who believe in rehabilitation, keeping people locked up without taking the opportunity to try to change at least some of the conditions that contributed to their criminal behavior makes no practical sense. If a prisoner serves time without changing his or her way of thinking or without gaining the ability to make a living, the chances are extremely high that he or she will repeat the behavior that resulted in a prison term.

An inability to read almost guarantees that a prisoner will not become involved with ideas outside the self with which to examine his or her past behavior. Moreover, jobs available in the 1990s require good reading skills.

At the outset of one reform wave to improve prison conditions and rehabilitate prisoners, the American Correctional Education Movement came into being. In 1789 clergyman William Rogers offered instruction at Philadelphia's Walnut Street Jail. The warden, anxious that a riot might ensue from such a revolutionary act, required the Reverend Rogers to be accompanied by two jail officers, equipped with a loaded cannon trained on the convict students. No riot ensued and prison education was under way.

Almost 100 years later, in another wave of reform, Zebulon Brockway, superintendent of Elmira Reformatory in New York, launched educational programs for every known type of handicapped learner. Brockway had drafted the New York State law that established Elmira Reformatory. The law required that school records be maintained on each individual student.

The special education staff Brockway brought together for his new reformatory included physicians, craftspeople, professors and teachers. Even by late 20th-century standards, Brockway's staff members were innovative and sophisticated. Some of their goals parallel the goals of current correctional educators.

Correctional education (CE) is based on the principle that attitudes, ideas and behavior can be corrected; CE and prison reform have been linked historically. Prison reformers advocated individual assessment and planning for each prisoner to make it possible to design appropriate treatment programs aimed at the criminal's reformation.

Brockway's staff tried to link academic learning with the inmate's physical health and with social and work experience. The institutional physician prescribed individual diets and exercise. Special hot and cold baths were provided, together with ''new Scientific Swedish massage techniques,'' performed by Swedish masseurs hired for the purpose.

Individually tutored remedial instruction was given in the early morning, since it was believed that the students were more receptive in the early hours of the day. Individual student files were established and included 53 separate measurements of the inmate's body that were recorded once a month.

Prison education programs have not been just pale examples of public education. They have often led the way. During the two decades immediately preceding World War I, as they struggled to develop local public school districts, urban school reformers examined CE practices to find models that could be reproduced in other school settings. In his 1907 book *Administration and Educational Work in American Juvenile Reform Schools,* the most prominent and influential reformer, David Snedden, described pioneer CE models in trade and industrial, physical and military education programs.

Snedden and other reformers, who hoped to put into place compulsory education for children throughout the nation, viewed reformatories and training schools as laboratories in which compulsory education had proved to be possible. They assumed that programs that could succeed in the most restrictive environment, the prison, ought to flourish in ordinary classrooms.

Modern public school teachers and administrators faced with daily frustrations in their classrooms continue to recognize the value of lessons learned from CE educators. CE teachers regularly work with students who have dropped out or been pushed out of public schools or have experienced repeated failure. Such students are likely to be embittered and/or apathetic learners, and many have learning, emotional or drug-related problems or combinations of all three.

Aside from the problems students bring with them, the physical environments of training schools, reformatories and prisons are typically bleak places to learn. Despite the unpromising conditions of the learners and the settings, most CE programs demonstrate substantial success, as assessed by accepted, traditional measurements of learning.

The original American prison reformers generally shared strong religious convictions and hence were committed to teaching inmates literacy skills that would enable them to read the Bible. Many were part-time volunteer chaplains, who organized the first CE programs as Sabbath schools. The most famous among the chaplains was Jared Curtis, whose work between 1825 and 1845 included founding prototype Sabbath schools in New York and Massachusetts.

Elmira superintendent Brockway was able to build on the CE improvements that reformers such as Curtis and early prison societies had introduced throughout the Northeast. For 50 years Brockway had prison-reform advocates and tough-minded prison managers working together, a feat most observers would consider virtually impossible today.

Brockway encouraged Thomas Mott Osborne, a millionaire industrialist and politician, to pursue a career in corrections. In 1913 Osborne disguised himself as a prisoner to learn firsthand about conditions in the prison in his hometown of Auburn, New York. Within weeks he had organized an inmate-run organization called the Mutual Welfare League that, with the warden's permission, managed all facets of the prison. Disciplinary problems at Auburn were virtually eliminated and prison shop production boomed.

Osborne later became the warden at Sing Sing in Ossining, New York, where the inmates established a model school, the Mutual Welfare Institute. For a half a century Osborne headed up the Osborne Association, one of the most active prison reform organizations in the country.

Austin MacCormick, trained by Osborne, based his CE theories on those of Brockway and Osborne. In turn, a book written by MacCormick provided a foundation for a reawakened CE movement in the 1930s and 1940s. MacCormick became the first assistant director of the Federal Bureau of Prisons, and he traveled throughout the country establishing and expanding CE schools and libraries.

Correctional educators have come from all walks of life. They have been clergy, sociologists, psychologists, novelists, businesspeople, community volunteers and advocates of law and reason.

Prison overcrowding makes CE difficult. Some prisons are so crowded that classrooms and recreation rooms—sometimes even hallways—where classes might be held are being used to house prisoners.

Perhaps the most serious consequences of overcrowding is that prisoners do not stay in prison long enough for CE to have an effect. In an interview with the *Christian Science Monitor*, Georgia's attorney general Michael Bowers complained that because of overcrowding, many criminals sentenced to five years serve as little as four months. A bitter blow for law enforcement officials came when a lengthy investigation of a father and his three sons for operating a multimillion-dollar motel-theft ring led to eight-year sentences, which because of overcrowding resulted in the three men being released in four months.

Forty-four percent of new inmates in federal prisons have moderate to serious drug abuse problems. The Los Angeles County Sheriff's office estimated in 1989 that 70% to 80% of the county's inmates were being held on drug-related charges.

Not much in the way of drug treatment, rehabilitation or individualized CE is likely to be accomplished in four months. Overcrowding has made it impossible to achieve any of the four goals for imprisonment: punishment, deterrence, protection of society or rehabilitation. The time for reform appears to be at hand.

(See also CALIFORNIA CORRECTIONS SYSTEM; ILLITERACY IN PRISONS; PRISON OVERCROWDING: COPING WITH THE COSTS.)

counsel   See DEFENSE COUNSEL FOR INDIGENTS: DEVELOPMENT OF THE CONCEPT.

crime statistics   By many accounts, violence is spinning out of control in the United States, imposing a huge, growing social and economic burden. The American prison population rose to 673,559 in state and federal systems by the end of 1989, double the number of ten years earlier. The cost for correctional systems has escalated even faster. Estimates vary from $13.9 billion to $22 billion, depending on whether jails and probation and parole transition facilities are included. Nevertheless, Christopher Jencks, a Northwestern University sociologist, contends that fears of an ever-escalating wave of violence are exaggerated. Jencks believes that a methodological distortion in crime statistics has fanned public fear.

The violent crime rate at least doubled between 1963 and 1974. During that period, Federal Bureau of Investigation (FBI) estimates of violent crime (mainly murder, robbery and aggravated assault) continued to climb at the same time that data of the U.S. Bureau of Justice Statistics (BJS) almost consistently showed a decline in the crime rate. FBI statistics are based on crimes reported by police departments to the agency. BJS statistics are based on national surveys of the public.

When the first victimization surveys of the public were conducted in the early 1970s, it was clear that police records reflected only a small proportion of reported violent crimes. As a consequence, the U.S. Justice Department began working with local police departments to improve their record keeping.

In response to these efforts, reports from local police now include crimes that often went unreported in the past, resulting in an upward trend in FBI data. The BJS data, on the other hand, between 1973 and 1981 showed no clear trend, declined during most of the 1980s and rose again in the late 1980s and early 1990s—but with violence levels still well below the rates of the 1970s.

Although murder rates rose in New York, Detroit and Washington, D.C. in the 1980s, they declined in Chicago, Los Angeles and Houston. Murder rates among blacks fell and then rose slightly in the 1980s but remained lower than they had been in the 1970s. The rates of aggravated assault and robbery committed by blacks dropped by 25% to 30% from 1973 to 1987 and declined less sharply for whites during the same period.

Jencks pointed out that demographic predictors of violent crime based on the percentage of males in the population between the ages of 15 to 24 were not borne out. The level of violent crime should have risen about 8% from 1960 to 1975 and then fallen by 7% from 1976 to 1988. In actuality it doubled in the first period and dropped by 15% in the second. Apparently the data available are not adequate to predict a continuing upward spiral.

A significant drawback to any assessment of crime data is that most experts estimate that at least half of all crime goes unreported. While it may be possible to say that crime appears to be going up or down based on reported crime in a specific community, with so many unreported crimes it is impossible to say whether crime on the whole is increasing. If more crimes are being reported, there may be fewer unreported crimes, or they may be increasing at the same rate or faster than the reported crimes.

Murder and auto theft are the most accurately reported crimes, but even they have their unreported incidents. A stolen auto that is restolen is not likely to be reported. Vulnerable people, such as those who live in the streets, often have no ties to others who might report them missing. For such reasons, prostitutes are frequent targets of serial killers.

(See also FEAR OF CRIME; INCIDENT-BASED CRIME DATA REPORTING SYSTEM; MURDER: U.S. PROFILE; NATIONAL CRIME INFORMATION CENTER [NCIC] OPERATION.)

criminal liability   The legal principle of criminal liability has four essential components: mental state, an act, concurrence between the mental state and the act, and causation.

Mental State.   In their book *Criminal Law: Understanding Basic Principles* (1987), Charles Thomas and Donna Bishop wrote, ''In general it can be said that the reach of the criminal law does not extend to those who act without mental fault,'' that is, without criminal intent.

Criminal liability is attached only when intent is present. This prerequisite for criminal liability is deeply rooted in Anglo-American legal history. By the 1600s judges defined all crimes at common law to include an element of intent, an idea expressed in the Latin phrase *''Non facit reum nisi mens sit rea,''* which means an act does not make a person guilty unless the mind is guilty. This principle is referred to as *mens rea.*

Mens rea connotes the actor's state of mind at the time the forbidden act was committed—as distinct from the act itself. A conscious awareness or recognition of the conduct in which an actor is engaged may be sufficient to fulfill the mens rea requirement. Mens rea is sometimes interpreted as synonymous with intent, but intent should be understood simply to mean the resolve to commit an act, and not necessarily to imply advance planning.

All offenses do not call for the same type of criminal liability. For some crimes, it must be shown that the offender acted ''with malice aforethought.'' For others, the prosecution must prove that the act was committed ''knowingly,'' ''willfully,'' ''negligently,'' ''wantonly'' or ''recklessly.'' Moreover, some crimes require only an intent to commit a forbidden act, such as arson or rape. Others require an intent to produce a forbidden result, such a murder or manslaughter.

Motive is also not the same as mens rea. Motive refers to the reasons for the act. Generally, the law is unconcerned with why the actor committed the forbidden act. Whether a murder was done for evil reasons or was a mercy killing, the law recognizes an intent to kill.

The law does distinguish between several distinct levels of mens rea. Aiming an automobile at someone for the purpose of killing him or her is held to be more culpable than driving recklessly at a high rate of speed, with the foreseeable result that someone may be killed.

States use a variety of terms to refer to levels of culpability. Thomas and Bishop discuss the four levels of intent, from highest to lowest, recognized by the

American Law Institute's influential Model Penal Code: purposive, knowing, reckless and negligent.

The first level of culpability, purposive, refers to a conscious goal to engage in forbidden conduct or produce a forbidden result, for example, conscious deliberation to set fire to a dwelling.

The second level, knowing, refers to the actor's awareness that actions taken are of a forbidden nature or will cause a forbidden result. For example, if an individual plants a bomb in the office of an employer who fired him, although he may have no desire to kill other employees who share the office, he knows that the death of others is an almost certain consequence of the action.

The third level, reckless, refers to action in which the actor "consciously disregards a substantial and unjustifiable risk of harm to persons or property." To act recklessly, the actor must be aware that his or her conduct creates a substantial risk of harm and nonetheless proceeds to act with a lack of concern regarding the danger.

The lowest level, negligent, refers to conduct that creates a risk of harm, when (1) the conduct represents a gross deviation from the standard of care that a reasonable person would observe, and (2) the actor is unaware but should be aware of substantial and unjustifiable risk.

Critics of negligence statutes object on the grounds that they dispense with the element of mental fault that lies at the core of criminal law theory. Supporters claim that the mental fault lies in the fact that the actor ought to have been aware of the risk.

In addition to different levels of intent, some crimes are related to different forms of intent, a factor that has implications for the kinds and amounts of proof of the defendant's mental state that the prosecution must show. For some kinds of crime, the prosecution need only show general intent, which means that the defendant's mental state can be presumed from the commission of the crime itself. On the other hand, specific intent crimes require that the prosecution prove beyond a reasonable doubt the defendant's intent with respect to a particular element of the offense. For example, the commission of a burglary commonly includes two elements, entry into a building and intent to commit a felony within the building. Proof of entry into the building is not sufficient for a burglary conviction; the prosecution must show that the defendant entered with the specific intent to commit burglary.

Another special mental element that must be established in connection with certain crimes is called scienter, which refers to the element of knowledge rather than intent or purpose. For example, the crime of receiving stolen property usually requires the defendant's having known that the property was stolen.

Conduct.   All crimes require action or conduct, referred to as *actus reus*. Evil thoughts are not punishable; something must have taken place. Words, however, may be considered acts. It is a federal offense to threaten the president, make terrorist threats, commit perjury or hire another to commit a crime. Illegal possession of statutorily controlled items is dealt with as a special kind of actus reus.

The actus reus may be either an overt act or a failure to act by one who has a legal duty to act, for example to pay income tax.

To be the basis for criminal liability, the action must be voluntary. A crime committed while sleepwalking would be involuntary. A killing resulting from a driver's having a convulsion while at the wheel would be deemed voluntary only if the driver knew that he or she were at risk of having a convulsion while driving.

A failure to act meets the actus reus requirement if the person failing to act has a legal duty to act. Some categories of persons have a special relationship that imposes a legal obligation to act. Parents are obligated to act on their children's behalf. Special relationships can be established by contractual agreements. Physicians, nurses, lifeguards and baby-sitters are among the many who have willingly accepted a responsibility to act.

Many European countries impose a legal duty to act upon everyone who is physically capable of aiding another who is in danger, as long as the provision of assistance does not imperil the life of the one assisting. The law in the United States has long taken the view that "the need of one and the opportunity of another to be of assistance" are not alone sufficient to give rise to a legal duty to take positive action. U.S. criminal law takes a very restrictive view of legal liability for omissions.

Concurrence.   A criminal offense will not be said to have been committed unless there is concurrence of the mens rea and the actus reus, which means that a mental fault must precede the forbidden act. If the mental fault follows the forbidden act, there is no crime. If a person buys a television, later learns the television was stolen and decides to keep it, there is no concurrence. To be held liable for receiving stolen property, the buyer would have to have known before the purchase.

If a person acts with intent to hurt or kill one person, but hurts or kills another instead, concurrence is still assumed, a principle sometimes called the doctrine of transferred intent. The doctrine has important limitations. With significant exceptions, if an individual has mens rea for one type of crime but the behavior engaged in requires a different type of mens rea, the defendant will not be held liable. Thomas and Bishop use the example of a sailor who descends into the hold of a ship intent on stealing some rum, lights a match to see and sets the ship on fire. The sailor would not be liable for arson.

The significant exceptions to the rule of nonliability for a mens rea for one type of crime together with a type of crime requiring a different mens rea are the felony-murder rule and the misdemeanor-manslaughter rule. The felony-murder rule holds that a killing that occurs during the perpetration of a felony constitutes a murder. The misdemeanor-manslaughter rule holds that a killing that occurs during the perpetration of a misdemeanor constitutes manslaughter.

The significance of these rules is that they hold offenders liable for killings that might have been completely unintentional. For example, a victim has a heart attack and dies while being held up; the robber is held for first-degree murder. During a robbery by seven men, one of the robbers becomes angry with one of his accomplices and shoots him; the six survivors are all convicted of murder. As long as the killing is causally related to the perpetration of the crime, the felony-murder or the misdemeanor manslaughter rule can be invoked.

Causation. A crime will not be said to have been committed unless there is a legally recognized causal connection between the offender's actions and the proscribed (forbidden) harm.

Often causation is easily determined. Alex aims a gun at Oliver, fires and Oliver dies instantly. The causation is clear. But Oliver may be hospitalized, appear to be recovering, have a relapse, become delirious, pull his tubes out and die—or he may be treated by an incompetent physician. Alex is still liable.

In order for a causal connection to be established between conduct and result, the conduct must be the actual cause and the proximate cause, the factors resulting in the death. The concept of actual causation is often expressed in terms of the "but for" tests. The actions of Alex are the "but for" cause of Oliver's death. But for Alex, Oliver would not have been in the hospital.

It is necessary, but not sufficient, that an individual's action be an actual cause of the proscribed harm. One clear standard of proximate causation is the "year and a day rule," which holds that a person cannot be held to have caused the death of another if the death occurs more than a year and a day after the harm was inflicted. This ancient rule arose prior to modern medicine when it was difficult to determine the precise cause of death. Because people can be kept alive for indefinite periods and because cause of death can be determined precisely, the rule now makes little sense; nevertheless, many jurisdictions retain it.

When an unforeseeable force intervenes to cause the ultimate result, the initial act of harm will not be perceived as the proximate cause of the result. For example, if an assailant leaves his victim unconscious on a roadway at night and the victim is subsequently killed by a car, the original assailant is responsible because passage of a car was foreseeable. However, if an individual knocks a victim down and a third party kicks the victim in the head causing death, the first assailant would not be liable for the death, because the conduct of the third party was not foreseeable.

(See also ARREST: CONSTITUTIONAL RESTRICTIONS AND LEGAL PROCEDURES; DNA "FINGERPRINTS"; JURISDICTION IN CRIMINAL CASES; PROSECUTORIAL DISCRETION IN THE DISPOSITION OF CASES.)

criminal thinking: theories and treatment models

One of the more controversial explanations of the psychopathology of chronic criminals, together with a treatment model to change such behavior, is found in the three-volume work by psychiatrist Samuel Yochelson and psychologist Stanton Samenow entitled *The Criminal Personality* (1975, 1977, 1986). A later volume, *Inside the Criminal Mind* (1984), by Samenow elaborates on the authors' 15 years of clinical research with chronic, often violent criminals.

Yochelson was trained in classical psychoanalytic theory, but found it unsuited to working with patients at St. Elizabeth's Hospital in Washington, D.C., an immense federal psychiatric facility. Many of St. Elizabeth's patients had been sent there by the courts after successfully mounting insanity defenses against incarceration for vicious crimes.

Carrying on the late Yochelson's work in private practice and training seminars around the country, Samenow uses a cognitive and phenomenological approach to treatment. Cognition is the process of knowing or becoming aware. Phenomenology is the classification and description of phenomena, in any branch of science, without reference to a preexisting explanatory supposition or theory.

The volumes written by the two men have been reviewed extensively by their peers. Along with grudging respect for the authors' point of view and for their detailed clinical examples of criminal offenders' thought processes, most reviewers express contempt for the zeal with which Yochelson and Samenow reject psychological and criminological theories of criminal behavior and the popular ideas that have been derived from them.

Among the ideas Samenow rejects are what he calls myths: Criminals don't know right from wrong. Criminals are hapless victims of oppressive social conditions. Crime is contagious. Crimes of passion are cases of temporary insanity. People turn criminal because they are rejected by society. Watching violent television programs brings out violent behavior in children.

In Samenow's opinion, the search to pin down the causes of criminal behavior has been futile. Programs, laws, policies and decisions based on current theories have wasted resources. A significant flaw in these theories, according to Samenow, is that they fail to explain why most people, despite troubled families, or impoverished neighborhoods, or physical or mental illnesses, manage to grow up and refrain from crime. If current theories were correct in their cause-effect analyses of crime, there would be many more criminals than there are.

In Samenow's view, criminal behavior is largely a product of thinking. To abstain from crime, criminals must learn to identify and then abandon patterns of thinking that have guided their actions for years.

The vast majority of criminals are men. For example, the 1990 *Uniform Crime Reports* cited 9,181,930 arrests of males in the United States and 2,068,153 arrests of females.

Criminals come from many geographical, religious, racial, ethnic and cultural backgrounds. They may grow up in orphanages, broken homes or closely knit families. They may be college graduates or grade-school dropouts, corporate executives or unemployed drifters.

Despite their differences, they are alike in the way they think. They consider themselves special and superior people and assume that others will do their bidding. Criminals look on law-abiding people as contemptible and their world of responsibility as a barren wasteland.

In 1930 the renowned psychologist Alfred Adler expressed a judgment similar to Yochelson and Samenow's when he said, "With criminals, it is different: they have a private logic, a private intelligence. They are suffering from a wrong outlook upon the world, a wrong estimate of their own importance and the importance of other people." Adler proposed that his or her crimes fit a criminal's general conception of life.

A firmly held view among social scientists, according to Samenow, is that criminals are basically like everyone else but have become antisocial because their aspirations have been blocked. This stance ignores the fact that responsible people work toward goals, while criminals behave as if what they want were owed them. Regardless of who might be hurt in the process, they take their desires by whatever means possible. Yet even when criminals get what they want, it is never enough; they always want more.

The crime for which a criminal is arrested is likely to be only one in a series. Contrary to the popular notion that criminals specialize, the average criminal rarely sticks to one kind of crime. Opportunity is the key factor: criminals engage in whatever type of criminal opportunity is available at the time. Even though they willingly commit many kinds of crimes, some criminals often reject those that they view as beneath them, or that are physically too risky or that they find personally repugnant.

The criminal's connection to other people is based on their utility. In Samenow's words, "The criminal values people only insofar as they bend to his will or can be coerced or manipulated into doing what he wants. . . . He visualizes people and property as opportunities for conquest."

Violence and the Criminals' Thinking.   A need for excitement and a low tolerance for boredom or frustration are hallmarks of career criminals. A number of researchers categorize such behavior as "risk-taking." Some propose that certain people are biologically predisposed to sensation-seeking. To measure such behavior, Martin Zuckerman, a psychologist at the University of Delaware in Newark, devised a four-part sensation-seeking scale: "thrill and adventure seeking" (activities with physical risk), "experience seeking" (nonconforming lifestyle and travel), "disinhibition" (drinking, partying, sexual variety) and "boredom susceptibility."

Other researchers relate risk-taking to issues of gaining or losing control. Loss of control is often attributable to "modular cognitive separation," that is, relegation of selected bits of information about risks to a mental Siberia because they contradict prior experience or because they thwart unrecognized wishes.

According to John Bush, the director of the Mentally and Emotionally Disturbed Unit, Correctional Treatment Programs at Oregon State Hospital in Salem, a striking characteristic of many people with personality disorders, both criminal and noncriminal, is a pervasive subjectivity in their overall experience of life. Their subjectivity makes them especially vulnerable to emotional injury, since any and all events are perceived as related to them personally.

Such people come to interpret social barriers to their immediate gratification as a personal injustice and react with anger. The state of anger becomes a permanent feature of their experience, and antisocial behavior is a natural outcome. They use all means possible, including physical force, intimidation and guile, to control their world.

Efforts to intimidate others by starting fights may be connected to criminals' need for constant stimulation and their low tolerance for frustration. So too may be the common habit of reckless driving, which generally begins early. "Teenagers terrify . . . motorists by cutting in, tailgating, screaming obscenities, and hurling objects out windows" (Samenow).

For many criminals, a sense of perfect control over their world accompanies the commission of a successful crime. Criminals commonly report that the elation and excitement that come with a successful crime are more important to them than any prospect of financial gain. Seemingly senseless crimes are done for kicks—the thrill of the forbidden. Excitement is generated by thinking about the crime, bragging about the crime, executing the crime, getting away after the crime and celebrating the crime. Even being caught brings the excitement of dealing with the police, publicity in the media and the trial.

The excitement of crime is present in the so-called crime of passion, usually committed by someone with no previous criminal record. In Samenow's opinion, although such killers may have a good reputation in their community, their family is usually aware of a rather different person behind the public facade.

Crime-of-passion murderers, when examined closely, have much in common with calculating cold-blooded murderers in their thinking processes, outlook on the world and attitude toward self and others. They are likely to be impatient, quick to fly into a fury and intent on getting even. While fantasizing revenge, thoughts of destroying the person thwarting them enter their minds. Before an actual murder, a crime-of-passion murderer is likely to have killed the victim many times in fantasy. Moreover, a homicide is often preceded by a long series of threats and assaults kept hidden within the family. To murderers who kill in a crime of passion, violence is no stranger.

Some criminals yearn for a constant diet of violence. Their superiority must be demonstrated regularly by overpowering other human beings. Others are merely willing for violence to happen; for example, some burglars carry guns with them in case something goes wrong. If they are subsequently held accountable for violence committed during a burglary, they blame the victims for interfering. As one 17-year-old said of his victim, "He should have had his house locked better and the alarm on."

The most common so-called impulse disorder crimes are kleptomania (compulsive stealing) and pyromania (compulsive setting of fires). Samenow objects to the psychoanalytic notion that one who commits such crimes is compelled by a deep-seated need to relieve sexual tension. From his clinical observations, he has concluded that kleptomaniacs and pyromaniacs are simply people who enjoy stealing or setting fires. He wrote:

Any criminal activity, repetitive or not, could be considered abnormal in that it is socially proscribed and most people do not engage in it. But this does not automatically make it a sign of illness or thereby exonerate the offender from responsibility. For behind such acts is a person who deliberates and acts with knowledge of possible consequences.

Like kleptomania and pyromania, substance abuse is considered a "disorder of the impulse control" by the American Psychiatric Association. Samenow finds the designation unhelpful. He wrote:

When held accountable, the criminal does his best to convince others that he is a victim of drugs . . . In every case that I have encountered, the criminal was immersed in crime *before* he ever smoked his first reefer, popped his first pill, or first shot heroin . . . Drugs knock out both fears of getting caught and consideration of conscience, and as a result, the criminal is prepared to *do* what previously he had only contemplated."

A by-product of criminals' fondness for violence is that many crimes go unreported because victims fear reprisals, since offenders may get off with probation or short sentences and soon be back on the streets, ready to take revenge. Due to criminals' skill at intimidation, many crimes that are reported are never cleared, a fact that contributes to criminals' sense of invincibility. (Clearing a crime means identifying offenders, charging them and taking them into custody). Of crimes brought to their attention in 1990, law enforcement agencies cleared only 46% of violent crimes and 22% of overall crime index offenses.

Criminals as a Part of Their Childhood Family.
A child's antisocial behavior can begin as early as pre-school. Samenow counters the explanation given frequently by criminals that they were rejected by parents, neighbors, schools and employers by asking why they were rejected. He answers his own question:

Even as a young child, he was sneaky and defiant and the older he grew, the more he lied to his parents, stole and destroyed their property, and threatened them. He made life at home unbearable as he turned even innocuous requests into a battleground. He conned his parents to get whatever he wanted, or else he wore them down with endless arguments . . . Not only did he reject his family, but he rejected the kids in the neighborhood who acted responsibly. He considered them uninteresting, their lives boring. He gravitated to more adventurous youngsters, many of whom were older than he.

In their 1987 book *High Risk: Children Without a Conscience*, psychologist Ken Magid and journalist Carole McKelvey present a picture of children who closely resemble those described by Samenow. They informally call such children ''trust-bandits'' and formally designate them as ''character-disturbed.'' When they reach adulthood, they are said to be suffering from Antisocial Personality Disorder (ADP); they are better known as sociopaths or psychopaths.

In Magid and McKelvey's opinion, such children are ''unattached,'' that is, either they never bonded with a primary caregiver or something interrupted their bond. Therefore they never learned to trust people. When the proper bonding—usually between the infant and the mother—does not take place during infancy or is disrupted, the child develops mistrust, has a deep-seated rage and becomes a child without a conscience. The authors believe that for a variety of reasons, particularly inadequate day care, the number of such children is growing.

Dr. Foster Cline, who practices at a mental health clinic in Evergreen, Colorado, is an authority on unattached children. He has developed a profile of the character-disturbed child: inability to give or receive affection; self-destructiveness; cruelty; phoniness; severe problems with stealing, hoarding and gorging on food; speech pathology; marked problems of control; lacking in long-term friends; abnormal eye contact; parents appear angry and hostile; preoccupation with fire, blood or gore; superficial attractiveness and friendliness with strangers; various types of learning disorders; pathological lying.

Cline's profile corresponds closely with a checklist developed by Hervey Cleckley of the characteristics of psychopaths. It is impossible to estimate how many psychopaths there are in the American population, but Cleckley, who in 1941 wrote the landmark work on them, *The Mask of Sanity*, said, ''It does not seem an exaggeration to estimate the number of people seriously disabled by the disorder . . . as greater than the number disabled by any recognized psychosis except schizophrenia.'' (Schizophrenia strikes one out of every 100 people under the age of 55.)

All unattached children do not turn out to be psychopaths, and not all psychopaths commit crimes that put them in jail. Nevertheless, trust bandits are likely to have lives strewn with broken promises and disrupted relationships.

Psychopaths who are criminals differ from ordinary criminals in a number of ways. Their criminal activity begins at a young age and pervades their social and personal behavior. They do great harm to people and indulge in antisocial acts that are incomprehensible. Unlike ordinary criminals who have attachments to friends and family, they have no loyalties.

Distressing for parents of a character-disturbed child is their youngster's vagueness. The parents know little about the details of their child's daily life, not from lack of interest but because of the child's ingenuity at concealing activities.

One factor that keeps parents trying to find a solution is that occasionally among these youngsters there emerges a sunny side, sensitive and gentle; but the phase never lasts. Throughout their lives, there are periods when psychopaths resolve to change. They settle down in school or work and cooperate at home. The change may last hours, days or weeks. But even the relatively calm periods are punctuated by restlessness, irritability and explosions of temper.

No matter what the family's social or economic circumstances, character-disturbed children have only contempt for their parents' lives, which they see as plodding and barren. To such children, having a good time is what life is all about, and they do not equate a good time with work or obligations. When there are other children in the family, they are likely to be victimized by their delinquent siblings.

Alcohol use begins early in delinquent children, often before adolescence. Drug use is more variable. Whether or not delinquents use drugs, their crimes over time become more daring, serious and frequent. Some youngsters who are fascinated with weapons have in their fantasies shot, clubbed and bludgeoned many people. They are likely eventually to transform their fantasies into reality.

As the personality of criminally inclined children emerges, parents learn to dread answering the telephone for fear that something awful has happened. Despite the parents' attempts to cope, their marriage and their relations with their other children and with other people deteriorate.

Some parents are afraid to push their criminal children out of the household for fear they will do something drastic. One parent told Samenow, "We've been through one flaky suicide attempt." Another said, "I'm afraid of my own son. I'm afraid I'll go to bed some night and never wake up in the morning."

The Influence of Peers and School.   Peer pressure is frequently cited as a source of criminal behavior among children. To this position, Samenow replies that criminals choose their friends, as all children do. They choose to associate with risk-taking youngsters who do what is forbidden. Activities that provide most children with fun and growth leave delinquent children restless and bored.

Even though delinquents may spend a great deal of time with others, they do not know how to be a friend. Trust, loyalty and sharing are incompatible with their view of life.

Often delinquents make trouble in the classroom as an antidote to boredom. In the same way that they reject whatever their parents try to teach them, delinquent children refuse to absorb academic material. In reality, the children are convinced that they are smarter than anyone else. They believe that they could get all As if they wanted to, but are not interested.

Many delinquents confine the turmoil they create to their classrooms, while others stake out various areas of their schools as their special territory. According to one study, fear made 4.6 million secondary school students avoid certain bathrooms in their schools.

If a high number of character-disturbed youngsters are congregated in the same school, the school becomes like a place under siege. In a climate of fear that paralyzes the learning process, students, teachers and administrators become hostages. The National Institute of Education has reported that an average of 5,200 secondary school teachers are attacked each month.

Relationships.   Criminals do not view themselves as obligated to anyone. Rarely do they justify their actions to themselves, except when they are forced by circumstances to defend their actions to others. Their greatest weapon is their constant striving to gain the upper hand. They assume they must be constantly vigilant because everyone else plots and conspires as they do. Their other great weapon is intimidation and violence.

Criminals are not against authority. They prefer an orderly world. They expect teachers to teach, parents to restrain and police to arrest. They object to authorities only when they get in their way.

Criminals' attitudes toward people are like quicksilver. Today's friend may become tomorrow's enemy. Depending on their mothers' readiness to do their bidding, their opinion of her vacillates from saintly to satanic.

Criminals rarely speak of love. They view people solely in terms of their use to themselves, as if they were property. If a spouse grows tired of the turmoil in the marriage and decides to leave, the criminal is surprised, indignant and angry. Using threats and force, some will not allow their spouses to leave. Criminals' treatment of their children is similar to their treatment of their spouses. Their attitude toward them is apt to fluctuate wildly from pampering to neglect or abuse.

Criminals do not think of themselves as bad people. Although criminals may not accept the moral standards of others, they claim to have their own set of principles. Even while in prison, inmates are not likely to see themselves as real criminals, although they consider the other inmates to be real criminals.

Criminals are apt to find little satisfaction in consenting sexual relationships. No matter who the partner is, the process of winning him or her over is far more exciting than the sexual act. One criminal has observed that if society legalized rape, he would no longer be interested in it.

The rapist does not rape because he believes that a nice woman would not have sex with him. On the contrary, he believes that he is irresistible to all women. At stake is affirmation of his image of himself as powerful and desirable. He believes that his victim already wants him. In a search for more excitement, his sex crimes are likely to become more and more bizarre. Even rape can become routine.

Samenow objects to the idea that criminals grow out of crime, the so-called burnout theory, which assumes that a criminal career ends at about age 40. The theory implies that criminals somehow achieve a level of maturity or responsibility. Samenow believes that aging criminals stop appearing in arrest statistics simply because they have lost their physical agility for street crimes and have turned to crimes with fewer risks. Their personalities remain unchanged and they continue to hurt people.

A Treatment Example.   Few criminals walk in off the street asking for therapeutic help. When they do appear, they may be momentarily depressed, or want to get a spouse or parents to stop berating them, but most are not interested in profound change. Samenow described Yochelson's technique in *Inside the Criminal Mind* throughout the course of therapy with an armed housebreaker named Leroy, who initially was not interested in profound change.

Leroy abandoned his wife and children for sex, heroin, guns and other excitement in the streets of Washington, D.C. He escaped a charge of bank robbery by faking insanity and was committed to St. Elizabeth's Hospital, where Yochelson was on the staff.

In quiet tones, Yochelson began by telling Leroy that he was a menace to society. Yochelson asked Leroy to listen to statements about himself and then tell him if he agreed. For close to three hours, Yochelson told Leroy about himself. Leroy did not like what he heard but found it hard to deny. Yochelson did not treat Leroy with anything less than respect while presenting him with an image of himself. He told Leroy that he had three options: He could continue in his present course and suffer the consequences; he could commit suicide and protect society from his influence; or he could learn to live like a civilized human being. Leroy returned for further interviews.

At the core of Yochelson's program is the premise that a criminal can choose between good and evil. No aspect of Leroy's life escaped scrutiny. Since behavior follows thought, the elimination of criminal behavior requires a change in the way a criminal thinks. Therefore criminals have to learn and put into practice patterns of thinking that are routine to others but new to them. After Leroy had been dissected in the course of several individual meetings, he was allowed to join a group.

Leroy had to be taught to stop and recollect what he had thought and then make notes on paper to bring to the group for discussion. The reason for the emphasis on thinking is that one day's thoughts become another day's crime.

When Leroy relayed that he was outraged about being unjustly accused by a nursing assistant and the thought flashed through his mind that he would break open the assistant's head, the thought was treated as seriously as if he had committed an actual assault. What seemed trivial to Leroy became a morning-long discussion.

Because criminals habitually lie, the leader of a group (with the criminal's knowledge and consent) has access to a responsible person who knows the criminal well— a parent, spouse or employer—to verify the criminal's accounts.

At the beginning of therapy, thinking of the consequences of behavior helps to deter it. Later the criminal learns new concepts that offer greater assurance against falling into old patterns, such as long-range thinking, teamwork and putting him or herself in someone else's place. The criminal has to learn to abort anger and to cut off criminal thinking before it has a chance to grow into criminal activity. A deterrent process that Yochelson emphasized requires that each criminal learn to hold up a mirror to his or her own behavior in order to take stock.

Inculcation of fear and guilt are essential to promote thinking about others and making responsible decisions. Because daily life demands endurance, the Yochelson-Samenow program requires tenacity, a quality that criminals tend to be short on.

In the Yochelson-Samenow program, the theme of the criminal's injury to others looms large. Learning what constitutes injury is critical to criminals' learning about themselves. Through the course of the program, Leroy faced tides of awareness followed by disgust at the scope of the damage that he had wrought on others for almost three decades.

Because money has no meaning for criminals, they must learn to account for every cent. And because criminals lie all their lives, they must maintain total integrity and avoid even the smallest lie.

Critics of the Yochelson-Samenow Approach.   Despite the fact that Yochelson conducted therapy with criminals and Samenow continues to do so, many critics believe their portrait of criminals rules out rehabilitation. One of the harshest critics is Oliver Keller, the former head of the American Correctional Association. In a March 1980 *Federal Probation* article entitled "The Criminal Personality or Lombroso Revisited," Keller said:

Both of them have, through their respective works, done real harm to corrections . . . the thrust of the book *[Inside the Criminal Mind]* is to indicate the criminal is indeed a different breed . . . One hunts in vain to discover how long they worked with particular individuals, in what way, and to what degree individual offenders were treated by individual psychotherapy or through groups. We do know that the total sample, over 14 years, consisted of 240 individuals. All were males. Despite this, the authors imply that their findings can be applied to females.

Another critic, University of Arizona sociologist Jerry Patnoe, in a 1985 review of *Inside the Criminal Mind* in the *Journal of Criminal Law and Criminology,* criticized Samenow's disdain for theories that attribute criminality to economic adversity, role models, broken homes or mental illness. About Samenow's treatment approach called "habilitation," Patnoe said, "This sounds suspiciously like Alcoholics Anonymous. The author says it does. It may well work, but it is difficult to see it as a breakthrough towards eliminating the crime problem."

Despite the criticism and Yochelson and Samenow's disavowal of sociological and psychological theories, several authors have demonstrated that their clinical descriptions can be fitted easily within mainstream diagnostic criteria in wide use. They compared Yochelson and Samenow's criminal personality with diagnostic criteria laid out in the American Psychiatric Association's *Diagnostic and Statistical Manual of Mental Disorders, 3rd Edition, Revised (DSM-III-R).*

DSM-III-R lists typical characteristics that are found for a diagnostic category and specifies how many of the characteristics are necessary to qualify, for example, four out of seven or ten out of 12. James Wulach, a psychologist at the John Jay College of Criminal Justice in New York, compared four separate personality disorders: antisocial, narcissistic, borderline and histrinic. On all four categories, the details chronicled by Yochelson and Samenow for the criminal personality exceeded the number of required criteria.

The Yochelson-Samenow model also fits the older, more traditional view of the classic psychopath described by Hervey Cleckley and detailed in an earlier version of the *Diagnostic and Statistical Manual, DSM-II* (In addition to *Mask of Sanity,* Cleckley was also co-author of *Three Faces of Eve*). Many of Yochelson and Samenow's "thinking errors" are also analogous to defense mechanisms discussed by psychoanalyst Otto Kernberg of the Albert Einstein College of Medicine in *Borderline Conditions and Pathological Narcissism* (1975).

Wulach concluded:

> Though Yochelson and Samenow were unconcerned about diagnostic criteria in their work while insistent upon the uniqueness of their typology, their detailed clinical description of a prototypical criminal, who meets both classical and

contemporary definitions of a psychopath and quadruple-diagnosis antisocial personality, provides a modest degree of validity for their Criminal Personality construct.

Front-line Workers Embrace the Ideas.   Despite the views of critics, professionals in the United States and Canada working in corrections, mental health, education, drug and alcohol counseling and probation and parole, who work with chronic offenders with long histories of violent offenses, have adopted and elaborated on the Yochelson and Samenow perspective because it offers them tools to work with.

Terri Landwehr, the administrator of Adult Institutions in the Wisconsin Department of Corrections, explained why the thinking errors technique is useful. She said:

> We can't treat the environment of the inmate. The chances are great that he will go back to his same old neighborhood— or one like it—when he is released. We can't change the parents he had. The only thing we can change is the way he thinks about himself and about crime. The best opportunity to do that is while he is locked up. It is not a pessimistic model. It is the most hopeful approach we can take. We owe it to him and to the public to give it our best shot.

One advantage in treatment by the phenomenological approach (observation without a theoretical explanation) is that it quickly establishes credibility with clients as they recognize the therapist's accurate description of how they experience the world. As clients learn to identify their patterns of irresponsible behavior, the act of identification interrupts their habit of indulging in narcissistic emotional excess and running wild with a sense of injury and rage.

Working with chronic criminals is not easy. Traditional therapeutic treatment models fail because the criminals lack the attributes that make them effective: an interest in changing, stable employment, a permanent residence, a stake in society, ties to family and friends. A newsletter called *E.D.I.T.* (Errors Defined in Thinking), published by Rick Bussard of the Colorado Department of Corrections Substance Involvement Program, enables those working with the Yochelson-Samenow model to keep in touch with one another and share their thoughts.

Eighty to 90% of all crime is committed by men; therefore most of the research on crime, including Samenow's, has been done on men. Nevertheless, his approach has been used with female offenders in several settings, including correctional halfway houses operated by the Wisconsin Resource Center in Winnebago.

Moreover, new officers in the Wisconsin Department of Corrections receive training in the model before they begin work to help them cope with the inmates who will try to take advantage of their lack of experience.

In the view of Professor George Beto, an internationally known figure in corrections, "Corrections is 150 years of undocumented fads." Perhaps Yochelson and Samenow's approach will turn out to be another, but to people working in corrections the approach seems intuitively sound. In the past the return of a criminal to jail was deemed a failure on the part of the criminal justice and correction systems. Using Yochelson and Samenow's philosophy, a return to prison can now be perceived as another chance for the corrections system and the criminal to work on the criminal's thinking patterns.

(See also ASSEMBLY-LINE JUSTICE; CLASSROOM VIOLENCE; SO-CIOPATHS.)

cults   A cult, formally, is a body of religious beliefs and practices, and its adherents. In modern-day America and elsewhere the term has come to mean an unorthodox kind of religion, distinguished from other, more traditional organized religious groups by certain common characteristics. A cult generally is new and has a living leader (often the founder) who claims to have been given the word of God and the responsibility to pass it on. Followers are led to believe that they will be rewarded by God for sacrifices. Those who refuse to accept the leader's dictates are viewed as damned.

Within the cult, the value of the individual is minimized and debate and critical thinking are discouraged. A principal mission of most cults appears to be the accumulation of new followers, wealth, and power. The annual number of recruits is unknown, but thought to be high.

In her 1984 book *The Cult Movement*, Joan Johnson reported that the major targets for recruitment are young people between the ages of 19 and 26. This is an age when individuals are beyond childhood but some have not yet learned to cope with adulthood. Rejection of childhood values has left a void, which the cult seems to fill. So long as the recruit is submissive and obedient, the cult will function as substitute parents, full of praise and acceptance. Recruiters typically seek out the newly arrived and the troubled, often outside bus stations and counseling centers.

Typically, indoctrination begins immediately. The recruit is never left alone, even in the bathroom. During a days-long workshop, the recruit is overwhelmed with new people and activities and never given a moment to reflect. The flood of attention, which Johnson calls a "contact high," overrides critical judgment.

The cult indoctrination technique closely resembles the brainwashing technique experienced by prisoners of war in Korea, without the violence. Cults deny the charge of brainwashing and point to the high turnover in their ranks as evidence of members' freedom to leave. Still, many former cult members insist that they were subjected to brainwashing and that the effects are often irreversible. Some former members are left with an impaired ability to make decisions.

Although recruits may be predisposed to entering cults, few understand to what they are agreeing. Many cults are communal, and the families of recruits are viewed as the enemy; every effort is made to keep the recruits away from them. Marriage, when permitted, is subordinate to the needs of the cult, and in most cults women are viewed as inferior, although possibly useful for sexual exploitation.

Daily life in the cult is filled with fund raising, witnessing (proclaiming the value of the cult in one's life), working, recruiting and attendance at prayer-lectures. Although some cult members are able to leave on their own, many cannot. Among those who escape, most are rescued or kidnapped by parents. Some are then "deprogrammed" to overcome the effects of the brainwashing.

The most bizarre known violent cult behavior involved the People's Temple, led by Jim Jones. When it pleased him to do so, Jones broke up families and had parents assign custody of their children to him. This technique became a tool for keeping the parents in line. Jones physically and sexually abused children and assigned them to hard labor. He used family members to spy and report on one another.

In November 1978 an investigating team led by California Democratic Congressman Leo Ryan visited the People's Temple in Guyana. As the team members were getting ready to board their airplane to depart, an executioner dispatched by Jones killed them.

In the meantime, Jones put into operation plans for a mass suicide that had been rehearsed 42 times before. More than 900 adults and children died from cyanide.

A variety of support groups such as the Cult Awareness Network (CAN) exists to help the loved ones of cult members.

D

date rape See RAPE.

deadly force See ARREST: CONSTITUTIONAL RE-STRICTIONS AND LEGAL PROCEDURES; POLICE USE OF DEADLY FORCE.

death penalty In the United States, methods for handling violent criminals have become a pressing public concern as the high rate of crime leaves citizens feeling beleaguered. In the 1988 presidential race, anticrime rhetoric was a major factor. The public seemed to want whichever candidate would be the most unforgiving of criminals. In the elections of 1990, politicians' positions on the death penalty became a significant issue in many political jurisdictions. For example, in her race for governor of California, former San Francisco Mayor Dianne Feinstein's support of the death penalty gained her 29 points in polls taken over a two-month period. Florida's governor, Bob Martinez, reminded voters in a television commercial that he had signed 90 death warrants, including that of serial killer Ted Bundy. (The reminder was not enough to reelect him, however.)

According to nationwide polls, a majority of the American public seems to believe that criminals should not be "pampered" and that penal policies such as parole, furlough and probation should cease. The majority believes that those who inflict pain must be made to suffer and that those who bring about the death of another human being should forfeit their own lives. Retributive justice, they think, will deter other criminals from preying on innocent citizens.

While Americans claim to be in favor of retribution, when they serve on juries or in some judicial capacity, they are far more lenient. Despite the rising number of death sentences meted out, American juries on the whole shun the responsibility for putting convicted killers to death. Moreover, while the number of condemned waiting in death rows in the United States is substantial and continues to grow, the number of actual executions remains small.

In their book *Death in the Balance: The Debate over Capital Punishment,* (1989) Donald Hook and Lothar Kahn describe the zigzag course of American opinion on the death penalty. Feelings about capital punishment can change depending on publicity about a flurry of murders or hijackings or a large number of well-publicized executions.

The death penalty has a long history. In some early societies, a father could put a member of his family to death if he concluded that that person had incurred the wrath of the gods. Under early Roman law, vestal virgins could be burned alive for violating their vows of chastity. A variety of other offenses were punishable by death, including starting fires, bearing false witness and disturbing the peace at night. The number of crimes that called for the death penalty waxed and waned throughout the history of the Roman Empire (27 B.C.–A.D. 395). During the thousand years that followed, attitudes to the death penalty remained essentially unchanged.

The criminal code of the Holy Roman Empire (1532), the *Constitutio Criminalis Carolina,* contained a catalog of crimes punishable by burning at the stake, including sorcery, arson, counterfeiting and various sex crimes. Serious offenses called for dismemberment. Ordinary crimes, including brawling, called for beheading. If a woman committed a major crime, she was drowned; if her crime was repetitive child-killing, she was buried alive.

The Holy Roman Empire's code remained in effect in Austria, Prussia and other Germanic states until the late 18th century. In England, as late as the early years of the 18th century, 700 to 800 criminals were annually put to death, for over 50 different crimes.

In the United States, there was some variation. Among 55 crimes punishable by death in Puritan Massachusetts were heresy, vagrancy and witchcraft. Quaker-influenced South Jersey's Royal Charter of 1646 allowed no capital punishment, and William Penn's Frame of Government of 1682 restricted capital punishment in Pennsylvania to treason and murder.

Opposition to the Death Penalty. The work of Cesare Beccaria, an 18th-century Italian criminologist, economist, jurist and ardent opponent of the death penalty, was made famous in France by François Voltaire, when he championed the cause of three men put to death because of religious intolerance. Beccaria called for the abolition of the death penalty, except when the imprisonment of a criminal could endanger the security of a nation. Ironically, one of the fervent followers of Beccaria's doctrines was Maximilien Robespierre, the man who signed his name to hundreds of death sentences during the French Revolution's Reign of Terror.

Early opposition to the death penalty in the United States is linked to physician Benjamin Rush, a signer of the Declaration of Independence. Rush advocated penal reform, individualized treatment and the establishment of a House of Reform. Rush's efforts spawned societies in opposition to the death penalty in several states and territories. However, states that were inspired to abolish capital punishment quickly reinstated it, apparently in response to the voting public's insecurity in its absence. Vacillation between the two perspectives on the death penalty has continued in the United States. Maine has changed its mind three times, finally abolishing the death penalty in 1887. In New York by 1992, the last two governors, Hugh Carey and Mario Cuomo, had been locked into an almost-annual stalemate on the subject for 17 years with the state legislature. Nearly every year the legislature passes a bill to restore the death penalty (by a narrow margin), and each time the governor vetoes it.

The Supreme Court's Continuing Role in Death Penalty Policy.   By 1967 the debate about capital punishment in the United States had shifted from philosophical and moral grounds to essentially legal ones. Swept up in the social changes of the 1960s, death penalty abolition groups, on constitutional grounds, sued Florida and California, the states with the most criminals on death row. The U.S. Supreme Court was asked to decide whether the death penalty violated the "cruel and unusual punishment" provision of the Eighth Amendment. The Supreme Court delayed all executions until it could rule.

In a landmark decision in 1972, the Supreme Court by a 5-to-4 decision in *Furman v. Georgia* held that the death penalty did constitute cruel and unusual punishment and that it often had been arbitrarily imposed. The decision was issued with nine separate opinions, reflecting a lack of consensus among the justices.

Although the Eighth Amendment had originally been addressed to the issue of torture, the liberal members of the Court in the *Furman* case held that the death penalty was invalid, regardless of the severity of the crime. The conservative justices held that the Fifth and Fourteenth amendments clearly allowed the death penalty. A third group of justices avoided broader interpretations and addressed the cases before them, finding that sentences and executions often had been arbitrary and capricious and therefore unconstitutional.

The Court's ruling in the *Furman* case essentially dealt with standards used to select those who would be executed. Although the death penalty was prevented in that case, the Court's ruling did not provide a final decision about the validity of capital punishment. In

response, states tightened up their laws to conform with the decision, and until death row inmate Gary Gilmore virtually demanded to be executed in 1976, there were no executions in the United States.

In 1968, four years before the *Furman* decision, the Supreme Court had ruled against the death penalty in a case involving William Witherspoon, who had killed a policeman. The Court held that a state could not impose the death penalty if jurors who opposed or had scruples against capital punishment were excluded from serving. The *Witherspoon* case was a rare Court intervention in the procedures used in a matter involving the death penalty. In the two decades that followed, the Court would intervene repeatedly, but never with a strong consensus for or against. The Court declared in 1977 that kidnapping did not merit the death penalty, leaving murder and possibly treason as the only offenses serious enough to call for it.

In cases that followed *Furman,* while retaining the death penalty, the Supreme Court made every effort to make it fair. Opponents claimed that there was no way to make the death penalty fair.

Outside of the United States, the historical trend toward eliminating the death penalty continued in other industrialized nations. On the whole, cultural evolution has everywhere tended to reduce the severity of penalties for crimes, but the conservative trend of the U.S. Supreme Court has made it unlikely that the death penalty will be abolished in the United States in the near future.

Rising crime rates in the 1970s generated public support for capital punishment. Several states restored the death penalty to their criminal codes. In 1981 Supreme Court Justice William Rehnquist asked the Court to change its procedures in order that states might impose the death penalty more quickly. Although nothing happened immediately, in the 1980s the Supreme Court made an evident effort to make speedier progress in cases involving executions. Defense lawyers involved with capital cases complained about a "rush to execute." The dearth of lawyers qualified to handle the low-paying and thankless job of defending murderers in states with a high death-cell occupancy rate prompted the American Bar Association to set up special programs to provide legal representation on appeal for convicted murderers.

In 1990 a special commission appointed by Chief Justice Rehnquist and headed by former Justice Lewis Powell set up to study the long delays in executions urged Congress to limit federal reviews of the death penalty. The commission advised the states to appoint qualified defense counsel at the original trial level to avoid the kinds of errors that made continuous appeals possible. Critics of the proposal agreed with the need for qualified attorneys at the original trial level, but pointed out the difficulty in defining the criteria that establish an attorney as qualified. Many stays of execution are based on the discovery of errors made by attorneys at each level.

Arguments Pro and Con. The paramount argument offered by proponents of capital punishment is that execution for a crime deters others from committing that crime. Opponents deny that there is valid evidence that capital punishment, or any other punishment, prevents people from committing crimes.

Proponents point to a near doubling of murders during the years 1968 to 1976 when no executions took place. Social scientists respond that many other societal changes also took place during those same years, including a sharp increase in drug use accompanied by commission of crimes by users to pay for drugs and a substantial increase in the number and firepower of guns available.

Hook and Kahn say about the death penalty debate:

The arguments have not essentially changed—nor have their bases in nearly two hundred years. In 1810, a chief justice in Britain is reported as arguing against a bill to abolish the death penalty for shoplifting. According to the justice, "Were the terror of death to be removed, it is my learned opinion that shops would be liable to unavoidable losses from depredations, and in many cases bankruptcy and ruin must become the lot of honest and laborious tradesmen."

They go on to say:

With scientific evidence inconclusive, we may well be reduced to using hunches, as the Supreme Court itself has been in recent years. The normal person's hunch is based on identifying his or her own reactions to the prospect of execution as the same as the reactions of potential murderers. But reliance on nothing firmer than probabilities and possibilities and hunches is terrifying, considering the irrevocability of death.

Research on the Effect of the Death Penalty. Studies of the death penalty by social scientists have taken several forms. One type compares homicide rates for states that have different stances on capital punishment. A second type analyzes homicide rates just before and just after an execution has taken place. A third compares homicide rates before and after the abolition or reintroduction of the death penalty.

A well-known study was done by a British Royal Commission in response to the fears of British police that abolition of the death penalty would threaten their safety. The commission found no evidence to support these fears in countries that had abolished the death penalty. In fact, the Austrian police claimed that the presence of the death penalty, in their opinion, had added to police risk because the fear of it prompted at-risk offenders to go to extremes to avoid capture.

The most highly regarded studies of the death penalty were done by Thorsten Sellin of the University of Pennsylvania. Sellin examined homicide statistics in clusters of adjacent states that shared ethnic, religious and economic characteristics; some had abolished capital punishment and others had not. Sellin found that the death penalty had no discernible effect on the incidence of homicides.

The arguments of death penalty proponents were made difficult by the absence of studies supporting a relationship between the death penalty and deterrence. A 1975 study helped somewhat to fill the void. The author, economist Isaac Ehrlich, concluded that during the period 1933 to 1967, on the average, the tradeoff between the execution of an offender and the lives of potential victims saved was on the order of 1 to 8. Death penalty proponents often interpreted the relationship to mean that each execution deterred as many as eight murders.

The two U.S. researchers, Ehrlich and Sellin, used fundamentally different research methods. Sellin compared data from different sources, selected pairs of states. Ehrlich worked out an analysis of a time series (a statistical process examining data taken from a single source at intervals) using data gathered from the whole United States. Neither approach is ideal for dealing with a multitude of social, geographic, cultural and demographic variables. Adding to the complexity, temporal variables change from generation to generation, year to year, week to week and day to day. In the absence of a study clearly establishing a relationship between deterrence and the death penalty, proponents have attempted to use Ehrlich's work to cancel out research that supports the idea that there is no deterrence. Ehrlich has never claimed that his study established that capital punishment has a deterrent effect, but he insisted that his work was as valid as other studies of the death penalty.

A study done by Hugo Bedau and Michael Radelet entitled "Miscarriage of Justice in Potentially Capital Cases," published in 1987, spanned the years 1900 to

1980. The study addressed cases that actually ended in execution or that would have done so, except for fortuitous circumstances. The study cataloged 350 cases of possible miscarriage of justice. Of the total, Bedau and Radelet claimed to have discovered 139 cases of innocent persons who were sentenced to death. Of these, 23 were actually executed. Ten executions took place between 1900 and 1922; the rest between 1922 and 1943.

Death penalty proponents believe the figures are small and are offset by the number of deaths deterred by the death penalty. Opponents perceive 116 near murders and 23 actual murders sponsored by the state.

Execution as a Public Spectacle. Since executions are intended to deter crime, some proponents of the death penalty (with a degree of seriousness) and some opponents (with a measure of satire) have suggested that executions should be made public. At this time only a handful of people actually see executions. One veteran journalist who witnessed some 200 executions has observed that the only one deterred by an execution is the person executed.

Since a 1937 Texas hanging, there have been no public executions in the United States. In 1936, 20,000 spectators gathered to watch a public hanging in Kentucky. Before his May 1984 execution, convicted Texas murderer James Autry asked that the event be televised so that the public could in his words "find out what they have done." One television camera operator's legal request to show the Autry execution was turned down.

Unlike law enforcement officials, wardens in death-house prisons have generally tended not to support capital punishment. The reason, in Hook and Kahn's opinion, may be that police officers, prosecutors and judges are mostly occupied with the crime committed by the person. They see the person in relation to a horrendous crime. The warden, on the other hand, sees the person in his or her last days and may glimpse a spark of humanity. Moreover, the warden is responsible for keeping the prisoner informed about the status of appeals and must worry about the possibility of a reprieve arriving a minute too late.

Unlike the warden, the average citizen is unlikely to attribute humanity to the criminal. The public sees a ruthless killer, like Willie Horton, whose crime while on furlough from prison was made into an issue in the 1988 presidential campaign. The average citizen is also unlikely to be dismayed about the feelings of inmates within prisons following an execution of one of their numbers.

Inequalities in Administration of the Death Penalty. An apparent inequity in the administration of capital punishment in the United States involves racial discrimination. Blacks constitute about 13% of the population but more than 40% of the inhabitants of death row. A 1975 study done by William Bowers and Glen Pierce concluded that systematic discrimination based on race in the criminal justice system often leads to the death penalty. The Bowers-Pierce study examined new sentencing statutes that were applied during the Supreme Court's moratorium. The researchers looked at Ohio, which has a death penalty but seldom uses it, and at three states that use the death penalty frequently, Florida, Georgia and Texas. The study found that all four states tended to sentence more harshly when the murderer was black and the victim was white. For example:

- In 173 cases of blacks killing whites, 44 death sentences were handed down, approximately 25% of the cases.
- In 803 cases of whites killing whites, 37 death sentences were handed down, approximately 5% of the cases.
- In 1,170 cases of blacks killing blacks, 20 death sentences were handed down, less than one fifth of 1% of the cases.
- In 47 cases of whites killing blacks, no death sentences were handed down.

In *Gregg v. Georgia,* the most significant post-*Furman* death penalty case heard by the Supreme Court, the Court dealt with the adequacy of guidelines for judges and juries, but failed to address the role of prosecutors who decide which cases call for the death penalty. Prosecutors, who are judged on the basis of their conviction records, may believe that convictions that call for the death penalty are easier to obtain for blacks than for whites.

The Continuing Controversy. There remain in the United States deeply held opposing views on whether the death penalty cheapens human life. In Hook and Kahn's words:

Death penalty advocates have been emphatic: since people need and crave justice; since, moreover, people have created systems based on justice—it follows that someone who has murdered must be punished in relation to the seriousness of that crime. Since murder is a final, irremediable, irrevocable act, the punishment accorded the murder can and must be also final and irremediable, and irrevocable. Failure to make it so would cheapen life. Death penalty opponents follow a different argument. The sacredness of life is violated if society deprives anyone of life, even one who previously deprived another of life. The initial act was a brutal, often heinous, murder, and the penalty for it must be permanent incapacitation of the murderer, but killing the killer would be to inflict the same cruelty and brutality on the killer. Killing is brutal, cruel, execrable, whether it is done criminally by the murderer or legally by the state. In either case, life is cheapened in the post-Auschwitz, post-Hiroshima age that has witnessed enough cheapening of life.

Many Americans remain uneasy about the imposition of the death penalty, despite the fact that a majority supports it. They want murderers punished in an appropriate manner. Yet when they sit on juries and hear the details of heinous crimes discussed for days or weeks, they nevertheless hesitate to impose the death penalty. Few would be eager to be present at an execution.

Former U.S. Attorney General Ramsey Clark, an outspoken adversary of capital punishment, has written that "capital punishment harms everything it touches." Among the elements of harm he had in mind are the long waits in death row, which add cruelly to the sentences, and the heavy burden of responsibility for their clients' lives that keeps attorneys trying to find technicalities, sometimes distorting the law, to stay the executions.

Despite the seeming widespread support for the death penalty, it was used relatively infrequently. From 1976, when the U.S. Supreme Court declared that the death penalty was not cruel and unusual, to mid-May 1990, there were 127 executions in 13 states, with a high of 34 in Texas and a low of 2 in Indiana. In 25 states the death penalty remained legal but unused, and 12 states continued to have no capital punishment.

As use of the death penalty has waned, states have moved toward adoption of life prison terms with no chance for parole for certain crimes. Given the level of violence in prisons and the overcrowding—many prisons have inmates sleeping on floors—some prisoners might find the death penalty more attractive.

(See also ARMED CAREER CRIMINAL ACT; EARLY RELEASE: THE IMPACT OF PRISON OVERCROWDING; SENTENCING: A TREND TOWARD LONGER SENTENCES; VICTIM IMPACT STATEMENTS: THEIR EFFECT ON DEATH SENTENCES.)

death penalty, juvenile See JUVENILE JUSTICE: A SYSTEM OF CONTRADICTIONS.

defense counsel for indigents: development of the concept Antilawyer sentiment has been a recurring theme in Western societies. Professional lawyers began as the servants of nobility, but, as individual lawyers' wealth and power grew, they increasingly worked for, married into or aligned themselves against the old aristocracy.

Out of the great constitutional struggles of the 17th century emerged the concept of a bill of rights, which eventually was incorporated into the U.S. Constitution. In line with the new thinking, criminal procedures were restructured. The charging and guilt-finding processes were institutionalized and the modes of proof were rationalized. Most important, there emerged the principle of the rule of law, the cornerstone of constitutional liberty, which supported the doctrine that where there is no law, there is no transgression and no punishment may be imposed.

Humanitarian concern for the common criminal was not the impetus for restricting governmental authority and making the criminal process more rational. On the contrary, it was the middle class that gained the most from the changes. The principle that there shall be no punishment in the absence of specific laws is of little use to the petty criminal whose crimes of theft, burglary and drunkenness need little interpretation.

As important to the legal profession as was the principle of the rule of law, the principle of the rule of lawyers as essential to an ordered existence was even more important. Although the seeds of such a principle had been sown in the 16th and 17th centuries, the primary means by which this idea came to be established was the right to counsel in a criminal case.

In spite of strong antilawyer sentiments in the American colonies, in some communities counsel was appointed for the needy long before required by law. The right to assistance of counsel was provided for in the Judiciary Act of 1789 and in the Sixth Amendment of the Bill of Rights, drafted in the same year. This right to counsel went beyond the English common law of the time.

Before the American Revolution, the English bar had stratified into two divisions, elite barristers, who could aspire to high office and who held a monopoly on pleading cases in court, and solicitors, who served as middlemen between barristers and clients. Efforts to reproduce the English two-tier system in the United States were squelched following the Revolution, when the old republican hatred of lawyers, and distrust of "professions" in general, reawakened.

But following the Civil War, stratification within the legal profession reemerged. Specialist lawyers began to do more advising of clients outside of courts than advocacy in them. By the end of the 19th century, with the growth of corporate law and the power and riches it provided, corporate lawyers held a high social rank. Others had to be content with criminal law, debt-collection work and small private practices. This division continues to this day.

William McDonald, in *The Defense Counsel* (1983), pointed out that the legal profession often defends its privileged status with "gratuitous praise of its professional altruism and concern for the legally disadvantaged." But in his opinion, "the profession's record in supplying counsel for the legally disadvantaged is better characterized as one of obstructionism, exploitation, and creative self-protection, than one of crusading vigilance for equal justice."

Between the Civil War and World War I, the United States experienced massive immigration, urbanization and severe class struggle between industrialists and workers. Industrial violence, strikes and riots became routine. New political movements—unionism, socialism, communism and anarchism—emerged to compete for the allegiance of the mass of working-class Americans and immigrants.

Although free legal services for indigents were available in theory in the majority of states by 1900, they were mostly discretionary. Fees for appointed counsel were inadequate or nonexistent. Lawyers who lived off such assignments tended to extract fees from clients in devious ways.

Many American leaders viewed the degradation of the justice system as an important source of converts to radical political groups. R.H. Smith, in his 1919 book *Justice and the Poor,* said that "To withhold the equal protection of the laws, or to fail to carry out their intent by reason of inadequate machinery, is to undermine the entire structure . . . It is not enough for the law to intend justice. It must be . . . actually attained."

Not only was the system of justice under attack, the legal profession itself was beleaguered. By the time of the 1932 *Powell v. Alabama* decision (the Scottsboro case), the legal profession was desperately seeking to convince the American public once again that lawyers were not just luxuries for the rich but essential for the entire society.

The Scottsboro case was one of the most significant decisions establishing a right to counsel in criminal cases. It involved the alleged rape of two white girls in 1931 by nine young black men in an open car of a freight train traveling through Alabama. The defendants, who were poor, ignorant and illiterate, and from out of town with no friends or relatives in Alabama, were seized by a sheriff's posse. Local hostility toward them was great.

The defendants were not asked if they had counsel, or offered it, and what counsel was attempted was only a token effort. Doctors who examined the women said there was no medical evidence of rape. After one-day trials, eight of the nine defendants were convicted and sentenced to death. In the case of the youngest, a 12-year-old, a mistrial was declared when the jury refused to impose the death penalty.

The case was ultimately brought before the Supreme Court. In 1932 the Court decided that even the educated layperson has small or no skill in the practice of law. He or she might have a perfect defense but be unable to prepare it. Without the guiding hand of counsel at every step of the proceedings, in the majority's opinion, the innocent defendant risked conviction because he or she did not know how to establish his or her innocence.

The case was sent back to the state court. A second trial resulted in a guilty verdict, accompanied by the death penalty. Another appeal was made to the Supreme Court, and in 1935 the Court held that the absence of black jurors in Alabama deprived the defendants of "equal protection of laws" under the 14th Amendment. The last of the nine men was not released until 1950.

Since the Scottsboro case, indigents have gained the right to appointed counsel at all stages of the judicial process, for offenses serious enough to warrant incarceration. In 1963, in *Gideon v. Wainwright,* the Supreme Court decided that not only ignorant, illiterate and feeble-minded defendants needed counsel, but intelligent defendants charged with noncapital felonies did also. Using language reminiscent of the Declaration of Independence, the Court asserted that it is self-evident that lawyers are "not luxuries but necessities." The American legal profession eventually did support reforms, and the American Bar Association has even expressed dissatisfaction with the inadequate funding of existing indigent defense programs.

McDonald is unimpressed by the legal profession's support of counsel for the indigent. He says:

The practice of criminal law has been vastly improved for the sake of the legal profession at least as much for the ideal of equal justice . . . The publicly financed criminal defense attorney not only prevents new challenges to the privileges of lawyers but also frees the elite lawyers from pro bonum work in the polluting atmosphere of the criminal courts.

And many judges are critical of the competence of criminal defense attorneys, attributing their weakness to the failure of law schools to teach practical litigation skills and blaming poor trial preparation on the economic pressure to handle too many cases at the same time.

The first public defender's office in the United States began in Los Angeles County, California in 1913, followed shortly by appointments in Portland, Oregon, Columbus, Ohio and the Connecticut Superior Court. The early programs were designed to be less expensive than the conventional practice, in which private attorneys received full compensation for defending indigents. Some early programs were severely criticized for cooperating unduly with prosecuting attorneys to the detriment of their clients, a criticism that is still heard in some jurisdictions.

At the beginning of the 1960s, more than 97% of the nation's counties relied on court appointments of counsel in criminal cases. In 38% of those counties, appointed counsel received no compensation. In the remaining counties, some compensation was provided but the lawyers donated a portion of their time on the theory that it was an obligation of the bar.

A survey published in 1973 reported that approximately 65% of the nation's felony defendants and 47% of misdemeanor defendants could not afford to retain counsel. Applying the indigency rates to Federal Bureau of Investigation (FBI) arrest statistics suggested that annually over 4 million cases each year required the appointment of counsel.

In 1964 the Ford Foundation donated $6 million to the National Legal Aid and Defender Association to provide the funds and technical assistance necessary to establish and upgrade organized defense systems in over 60 communities. The grant gave the impetus to the improvement and expansion of defender services in the United States.

In 1968 the Law Enforcement Assistance Administration (LEAA) was created by Congress as an agency of the U.S. Justice Department. LEAA funds established the National College of Criminal Defense Lawyers and Public Defenders, which provided national and regional training for lawyers representing the poor in criminal cases.

A second LEAA-funded institution was the American University Criminal Courts Technical Assistance Project. In conjunction with the National Legal Aid and Defender Association, the project assisted a number of jurisdictions in establishing new defender systems or in upgrading existing programs.

Given the growth in recent decades of procedural requirements imposed on state courts, the defender programs have grown in a haphazard fashion, with modifications made to existing programs and little time devoted to long-range planning and system design. However, there are some excellent programs around the country, which compare favorably with the private bar. Many defender systems are staffed by attorneys who have taken up criminal law as a specialty.

While the profession as a whole may continue to hold criminal defense lawyers in low esteem, their self-image has improved considerably. Many belong to the National Association of Criminal Defense Lawyers (NACDL), which serves as a conduit for information, education and support to attorneys around the country.

(See also ASSEMBLY-LINE JUSTICE; FELONY ARRESTS: SCREENING PROCEDURES; FELONY CONVICTION RATES; PROSECUTORIAL DISCRETION IN THE DISPOSITION OF CASES.)

delinquency   See JUVENILE JUSTICE: A SYSTEM OF CONTRADICTIONS.

DNA "fingerprints"   DNA (deoxyribonucleic acid) is found in every cell of the human body. It provides chemical instructions for life processes. An individual's DNA, like his or her fingerprints, is unique. Mapping the DNA patterns in samples of blood, semen and other body tissues has, since its invention in 1985, rapidly become a major forensic means of identification of humans and animals.

Geneticist Alec Jeffreys developed the technique at the University of Leicester in England after he observed that a number of DNA segments contain particular sequences of bases, the DNA building blocks, and that the sequences are repeated many times. Most important, he noted that the number of repeat sequences in each region—and therefore the length of the region—varied from one person to the next.

Jeffreys' technique involves cutting DNA into fragments, then arranging the fragments according to length. The ones that contain repeat sequences are tagged with radioactive probes and then spread out arranged by size on a sheet of special paper. The pattern that results is always the same for the individual. When the sheet of paper containing the pattern with the probes is sealed in a cassette with X-ray film, the radioactivity exposes the film, leaving behind an image of the fragments.

When the fragments from two separate samples match—for example, a sample from a suspect's blood and a second sample from blood or semen found at a crime scene—probability tables are used to compute the odds of such a match's occurring by chance. By combining the odds for different probes, scientists can sharply limit the possibility of a false match.

Given the current state of the art, scientists are willing to say that a particular pattern occurs in perhaps one out of a million people. With continuing development, they expect to be able to say with absolute certainty that a pattern belongs to a specific individual.

Two years after Jeffreys developed the technique, he established that a man suspected of murder and rape was innocent. DNA from the suspect's blood did not match semen samples found on the victims, two 15-year-old girls.

One of the first uses to which Jeffrey's new technique was put was described in a March 31, 1991 *Parade Magazine* article entitled "Whodunit? Quick, Check the Genes!" In 1985 the son of a family originally from Ghana, whose members lived in Britain and held British citizenship, went to Ghana for a visit. When he returned to Britain, authorities found fault with his passport and held him in custody. The family's lawyer, having read about the DNA technique, asked to have the mother and son tested. DNA fingerprinting established their relationship beyond a doubt and the boy was released.

British police used the method to track down a rapist-murderer by asking 5,512 men who lived in the neighborhood where the murder took place to submit blood samples. One man called attention to himself by asking a friend to give blood in his stead. His blood sample's DNA pattern matched that of a semen stain found at the scene of the crime.

Despite its high discriminatory power, Jeffreys' original approach requires relatively fresh samples of blood or semen and relatively large amounts of DNA. However, an April 23, 1988 *Science News* article entitled "Fingerprinting from a Single Hair," reported that Jeffreys and researchers at Cellmark Diagnostics—the company that licenses his DNA fingerprinting patent, had developed a modified, more sensitive technique. Instead of using the original repeat-sequence probes, which are relatively short molecules, the researcher made new "locus-specific" probes out of selected DNA fingerprint fragments.

Typical analysis of DNA requires several millionths of a gram. The larger probes are able to carry more

radioactivity, enabling researchers to detect DNA at levels as low as 20 nanograms. The new technique allows the group to use the technique on a single hair root, which typically yields less than 10 billionths of a gram of DNA.

An even more sensitive technique devised by scientists at Cetus Corporation in Emeryville, California and at the University of California, Berkeley can analyze even very old, degraded samples of DNA. To cope with the scarcity of DNA in hair and in the size of samples found at the typical crime scene, the researchers developed a technique called the polymerase chain reaction to make millions of copies of a DNA fragment. The copy making, known as gene amplification, makes enough DNA available from the fragment to permit analysis.

In the April 7, 1988 issue of *Nature* the Cetus and Berkeley scientists reported that they had applied the technique to both fresh and shed hair and succeeded in making enough copies of one small DNA region to perform three kinds of typing on it. By looking at the differences in the length and/or base sequence of that gene, they could classify individuals into 21 different types.

Unlike the Cellmark technique, the Cetus method can copy and type DNA that has been degraded by long exposure to light and enzymes. While the method does not permit absolute identification of the source of a sample of DNA, it makes it possible to determine which of several suspects the sample might have come from and which can be ruled out.

In a landmark case, DNA evidence was presented in Orlando, Florida in the first of two separate trials against a serial rapist. The trial began on October 20, 1987. Not only was the defendant on trial; so was the new technique.

When a new scientific test is used as evidence in a trial, it must meet the so-called Frye standard: the judge must be convinced that the technology is "sufficiently established to have gained general acceptance in the particular field in which it belongs." This usually requires a pretrial hearing with no jury present in which lawyers from both sides argue the reliability and reputation of the new technique.

The judge permitted the use of the DNA evidence, but the trial ended in a mistrial. One juror, an engineer, was quite forceful in his objections to the new technology.

By the second trial, in which the DNA evidence was also permitted, the attorneys had learned how to present the statistical evidence. Their expert witness, Michael Baird, director of forensic and paternity testing for

Lifecodes of Elmsford, New York, a DNA testing service, summarized his presentation by pointing out that the frequency of the defendant's pattern was one in 10 billion. He said, "In a world population of just over five billion, he's the only guy who could have left his semen there."

Once DNA typing becomes widespread, so too will data banks of individual patterns. One immediate concern that arises is where such data would be kept. One frequently offered suggestion is the Federal Bureau of Investigation's National Crime Information Center. The possibility of such data banks raises many questions about whose patterns should be included and how such data might be used.

Although members of the U.S. Armed Services and employees of the federal government are routinely fingerprinted for identification and their fingerprints become part of the government's data banks, DNA contains information not formerly available about parentage and genetic predisposition to disease, information that could be used to discriminate against individuals.

Routine forensic use of DNA typing will likely change the nature of defenses used in cases where identity is an issue. Plea bargaining is likely to become more common.

DNA can exonerate as well as incriminate a suspect. Among three companies that have been involved in forensic cases, Cellmark Diagnostics of Germantown, Maryland, Forensic Science Associates of Richmond, California, and Lifecodes all have had cases in which their analyses have exonerated suspects.

After being used in 80 cases of rape and murder, DNA testing received its first setback in August of 1989. An August 15, 1989 *New York Times* article entitled "Reliability of DNA Testing Challenged by Judge's Ruling," described a court ruling that came after 12 weeks of pretrial hearing and 5,000 pages of testimony.

The case involved a 38-year-old Bronx man, Joseph Castro, who was accused of murdering a pregnant neighbor and her infant daughter. Lifecodes testified that bloodstains found on Castro's wristwatch had been subjected to DNA testing and that the odds were a million to one that they belonged to the mother.

Defense witness experts challenged the test and said it was ambiguous. The judge ruled that the evidence demonstrated that additional experiments and controls may be necessary to ensure reliable results. Experts differed sharply about whether the Bronx case would set a precedent that might require opening previous cases.

During an interview for an October 31, 1988 *U.S. News and World Report* article entitled "Convicted by Their Own Genes," forensic expert Joseph Peterson of the University of Illinois claimed that DNA testing, though spectacular, will not affect most cases. He noted that fewer than a third of felony investigations produce crime-scene evidence testable for DNA. Moreover, in cases of rape, the test could not settle the frequently made defense claim that the victim had consented. Moreover, the cost of the test, averaging $1,000 per case, would limit its use.

(See also CRIMINAL LIABILITY; JURISDICTION IN CRIMINAL CASES.)

double jeopardy See BILL OF RIGHTS: PROTECTION AGAINST GOVERNMENT TYRANNY.

drive-by shootings Since the early 1980s, drive-by shootings have become increasingly popular among street gangs and others engaged in drug-trade turf battles. Taking aim from a moving vehicle is difficult. The likelihood is great that more than one person will be hit. Bystanders are frequently wounded or killed along with or instead of the intended victim. Unfortunately, the drama of the technique appeals to others as well. With guns, rifles and automatic weapons easier to obtain, some juveniles have added shooting to joyriding.

Shooting as a means of dealing with anger or frustration also appealed to motorists on congested highways. A wave of shootings took place on Los Angeles highways in 1987. On July 26, 1987 the driver of a sports car on the Pacific Coast Highway, angered after a confrontation with the driver of a pickup truck, pulled out a handgun and fired on the truck's three occupants, who miraculously escaped with minor injuries. Southern California law enforcement officials reported that the incident was the ninth in a rash of similar incidents over the period of a few weeks.

In another California highway incident, two days earlier, a teenager driver was shot and killed after he exited the Pomona Freeway onto another highway and pulled in front of a pickup truck. One of the passengers in the truck shot him in the head. Police later learned that the driver's male passenger and a female suspected of doing the shooting had had an earlier altercation.

Between June 18 and August 18 of 1987, there were 87 highway shooting incidents statewide, 78 of them on the freeways, mostly in southern California. At a legislative hearing on proposals to crack down on the highway incidents, California Highway Patrol Commissioner J.E. Smith testified that law enforcement officials had not been able to arrive at any particular pattern or profile that would help them to combat the problem.

From June 1989 to May 1990, Chicago had 334 drive-by shootings. On June 8, 1990 a young mechanic left his girlfriend's house at 2:40 A.M. He was shot and killed by two men driving past in a car because he wore a baseball cap cocked to the right side of his head. His killers belonged to a gang who wore their hats tilted to the left.

A six-hour stretch of violence in southeast Washington, D.C. in 1990, during which four people were killed, was capped by a drive-by shooting aimed at a group of children, leaving five of them wounded. In an interview for a December 21, 1990 *Washington Post* article entitled "5 Children Wounded in NW Attack," the director of the Children's Hospital emergency trauma services said, "There are five kids, and there are a lot of holes. When they all came in, it was a challenge to even learn which of the youngsters were in the most serious condition."

Drive-by shooting remains a problem in the 1990s. On the first weekend in February 1992, there were two California freeway shootings. A Tarzana man driving in his Jaguar was shot by a gunman in a passing van. The other shooting was aimed at a California Highway Patrol officer.

(See also APPENDIX IC: THE MEDELLIN CARTEL; GANGS: PICKUP OR TEMPORARY; GANGS: STRUCTURED STREET; OUTLAW MOTORCYCLE GANGS.)

drug abuse and trade: prevention and education   Drug abuse in the United States has followed cycles, according to Yale professor of psychiatry and the history of medicine David Musto, author of *The American Disease* (1988). In the past, drugs have risen in popularity for about two decades and then declined for another two decades.

During the 19th century, the United States was the only major Western nation with no national laws restricting narcotics. As a consequence, opium, morphine and cocaine use was widespread.

In the mid-1880s, when cocaine became readily available, Americans bought it to sniff, smoke, inject, rub in, eat or drink. Experts assured the public that it was safe and nonaddictive and had no aftereffects. Gradually, however, its risks became obvious, and in 1914 a federal law was enacted restricting it. Demand declined over the next 15 years, but in the 1960s it once again became popular.

Concern about drug traffic in the United States became acute in the 1980s. By then public anxiety about drugs had become so pervasive that a majority of Americans ranked it as the nation's number-one social problem. In response, President Bush declared a "war on drugs" (as had his four predecessors).

The president's major emphasis was to continue the government's ongoing campaign of interdiction, attempting to cut the supply of illegal drugs entering the country. In the 1980s the federal government created the South Florida Task Force, 12 Organized Crime/Drug Enforcement task forces around the country and the National Narcotics Border Interdiction System as well as a program of crop eradication in Latin America, carried on with the cooperation of the local governments.

There also were efforts to involve the military in law enforcement efforts to interrupt the flow of drugs. Neither the military nor the Drug Enforcement Administration (DEA) favored the idea, however, and President Reagan vetoed a military bill that included such a provision.

As a strategy, interdiction has some formidable problems. Latin American governments are ambivalent about American intrusions into their countries. Policing a 12,000-mile international boundary spreads forces too thin. Constitutional safeguards that protect the rights of American citizens limit police authority to search, detain, arrest, eavesdrop and maintain intelligence files.

By and large, interdiction together with traditional drug law enforcement methods, which have emphasized street-level arrests and investigation of distribution networks, have had little impact. Every year federal, state and local authorities seize an increasing quantity of drugs, and every year the total quantity of drugs coming into the country increases.

Evidence of yearly increase is easy to find. In 1982, when cocaine's price was $60,000 per kilo (2.2046 pounds), U.S. Customs, only one of the many agencies involved, seized 5.2 metric tons of cocaine (a metric ton is 1,000 kilos, or 2,204 pounds). In 1986, when the price per kilo had dropped to $9,000, the agency seized 24 metric tons. The steep fall in price indicated that the supply had increased substantially, despite the increasing amounts confiscated.

President Bush proposed that his war on drugs should have a cabinet-level leader, and Congress agreed. William Bennett, the first drug "czar," took office in the spring of 1989. Bennett's plans reinforced the longtime trend of putting most available antidrug funds into interdiction and law enforcement efforts. Bennett left his post in the fall of 1990 claiming that he had made great strides; it is more likely that he became discouraged by the intractability of the problem.

One effect of cocaine's lower price was to make the drug, formerly restricted to the wealthy, available to more people. The decline in price coincided with the introduction in the mid-1980s of crack, a smokable and more addictive form of cocaine. The use of cocaine mushroomed in poor neighborhoods.

A significant amount of crime occurs simply because users have no means except crime to support their expensive habits. The money to be made in drug distribution is high and the level of skill necessary is minimal. Therefore, much of the violence associated with drugs occurs during turf battles among distributors or street sellers. The risk of violence is high for everyone involved with drugs, users, distributors and law enforcement personnel.

Local law enforcement officials often feel that they are in a no-win war because even when they do occasionally succeed in ridding an area of drugs and dealers, the price of the drug rises and more dealers are attracted by the potential profit. During an interview for a November 9, 1986 *Boston Globe Magazine* article entitled "A Frustrating Battle Against Massive Odds, Huge Profits, and Inadequate Remedies," a Boston police officer who had participated in a drug raid the night before said, "I risked my life for what? To take off another coke dealer? . . . it doesn't seem like we're making any headway. We're shoveling against the tide."

By the 1990s older addicts, mostly heroin users, who began their drug use in the 1960s and 1970s, presented a new problem for society. Many had been exposed to the HIV virus, responsible for the life-threatening syndrome known as AIDS, via the practice of sharing needles.

The damage caused by the use of drugs is never confined to the user. Data from the Minnesota Adolescent Survey, presented at the Troubled Adolescent Conference held at the University of Wisconsin, Milwaukee, April 9–11, 1991, revealed that teenagers who have alcohol-abusing parents have significantly higher rates of chemical abuse, including alcohol, marijuana, hallucinogens, cocaine/crack, acid and tobacco. They also have higher rates of pregnancy, poor school performance, suicidal behavior and eating disorders.

Single-parent families become no-parent families when single parents develop a drug habit, as has become commonplace in poor neighborhoods. Their children seek refuge wherever they can find it, often with grandparents or elderly neighbors barely able to care for themselves.

A Questionable Drop in Demand, Little Impact on Traffic. The U.S. National Institute on Drug Abuse conducted research in 1974 and 1988 and found a decline in abuse of all drugs except alcohol in all age groups. A drawback to surveys about an illicit activity like drug use is that a large number of respondents may have lied or minimized their use. Moreover, such surveys are unlikely to tap heavy users.

Despite these drawbacks, the findings suggested an overall downward trend. Among those who had used marijuana in the month prior to the survey, 12- to 17-year-olds had reduced their percentage from 12.0 in 1974 to 6.4 in 1988; 18- to 25-year-olds from 25.2 to 15.5; but those over 26 had increased from 2.0 to 3.9.

Among those who had used cocaine in the month prior to the survey, 12- to 17-year-olds had remained about the same, 1.0 in 1974 and 1.1 in 1988; 18- to 25-year-olds had increased from 3.1 to 4.5; for those over 26, data were not available on current use for 1974, but their 1988 use amounted to 0.9.

While the overall use of illegal drugs in the United States appeared to be in decline, some observers questioned the applicability of such estimates for particular groups. Support for their skepticism came from an annual survey of high school seniors and another study of American households that those turning away from drug use were the most educated and the most affluent. Such surveys do not include high school dropouts, homeless people or younger children on drugs.

Some experts also questioned the validity of estimates of a decline in drug use among the middle class. Their doubts arose from many causes. City police regularly seize the cars of suburban drug buyers during transactions in inner cities. Between mid-1986 and October 1989, the New York City Police and the Federal Drug Enforcement Administration confiscated 3,234 cars from drug buyers, and more than half belonged to out-of-towners. Moreover, data compiled by the National Association of Perinatal Addiction Research and Education revealed that 11% of the women studied in hospitals located in a variety of socioeconomic and geographic areas had used illegal drugs during pregnancy.

The movement of drugs to rural areas increased in the 1980s with the "branch-office" spread of street gangs, particularly those based in Los Angeles. The armed gangs set up weekend operations in smaller cities and towns, where they could get a higher price than in the larger cities.

Few observers expect any solution to America's drug problems in the near future. Europeans have criticized the United States for its emphasis on interdiction and law enforcement, instead of drug abuse prevention and treatment. At a European and North American Conference on Urban Safety and Crime Prevention, a British delegate ridiculed the American approach by saying "As if you enterprising Americans would not be smart enough to produce drugs inside the United States if the imports were stopped." Americans are major growers of marijuana.

Many experts predicted that the Europeans would not have long to wait until they shared the U.S. drug problem. The planned elimination of all barriers to the movement of goods, people and capital in the European Economic Community in 1993 may well prove them right.

By 1990 South American drug barons had already targeted Spain as the gateway to Europe. In the first quarter of 1990, European cocaine seizures reached 3.3 metric tons, almost half the amount seized during the whole of 1989.

Legalization.   An approach to crime prevention that gained attention for a brief period in 1988 was legalization of illicit drugs. A major proponent of legalization was Mayor Kurt Schmoke of Baltimore. The idea was discussed in a September 13, 1988 ABC broadcast entitled "A National Town Meeting: The Legalization of Drugs."

Schmoke took the position that a major crime industry was created by the impact of Prohibition. From 1920 to 1933 the manufacture, sale, transportation, importation and exportation of intoxicating beverages was made illegal by the 18th Amendment to the U.S. Constitution. In Schmoke's opinion, drug addiction would be better treated as a national health problem. He pointed out that Maryland's prison system, designed to hold 9,500 prisoners, was actually holding 14,000, a significant portion of whom had been convicted of drug-related crimes.

Some historians would argue with Schmoke about the link between Prohibition and the crime wave in the 1920s and 1930s; it might have taken place regardless, since criminals were already beginning to dabble in drug traffic when they were detoured by the ban against alcohol. Moreover, Prohibition did have a positive impact on drinking. Between 1900 and 1910 the average

American drank 2 gallons of alcohol a year. When Prohibition was ended by passage of the 21st Amendment, American consumption had been cut in half. Following repeal, consumption began to once again rise, and by 1988 it had risen to 2.6 gallons per capita.

During his introduction to the ABC broadcast, the moderator, Ted Koppel, raised a potential flaw in the idea of legalization. He pointed out that alcohol and cigarettes, America's most popular and most addictive drugs, are both legal, and they are more lethal than all the other drugs combined. Alcohol is responsible for an estimated 100,000 deaths every year in the United States, and cigarettes approximately 350,000. By contrast, illegal drugs kill an estimated 5,000 to 6,000 each year.

The United States spends about $8 billion a year to fight drug-related crime and another $2 billion to imprison those who are caught. Advocates of legalization assert that a government-run drug distribution program would cut enforcement costs by 75%. Moreover, it would permit police and courts to deal with violent offenders and free funds to be used for drug abuse treatment.

William von Raab, commissioner of the U.S. Customs Service and the author of the government's "Zero Tolerance" policy, which is aimed at penalizing everyone caught with even small amounts of illegal drugs, found fault with the alcohol-drug comparison. He pointed out that only about 10% of the people who use alcohol become addicted, while 90% of those who use cocaine become addicted.

The Reverend Jesse Jackson expressed vehement opposition to legalization. He said, "If cocaine, crack, and heroin were as available as Scotch, bourbon, and cigarettes, you would have a fair comparison. The fact is that coke, crack, and heroin are much more deadly . . . and what you're doing, you're going to shift the drug flow from street hoods to corporate hoods."

A member of the audience, who had himself used drugs for 24 years before giving up both drugs and alcohol, raised a management problem of legalization. The typical addict may initially have a $30-a-day habit, but it soon grows. He asked where the government-sponsored clinics would draw the line on the size of an addict's habit. If the clinic set a cutoff point, then the addict probably would turn to crime to gain additional drugs.

After the brief flurry of attention in 1988, interest in legalization dwindled.

Alternative Crops for Coca Farmers.   In July 1990 President Bush announced a new program of trade concessions, expanded agricultural assistance and other measures to help Ecuador, Colombia, Bolivia and Peru develop alternative exports to replace coca (a major crop grown for export in those countries) and processed cocaine. The program was a response to continuing Latin American criticism that U.S. drug policy had been too law enforcement-oriented and had failed to take into consideration the economic and social repercussions for Latin American farmers of the policy.

During an interview for a July 24, 1990 *New York Times* article entitled "Bush Presents Plan to Help Andean Nations Grow Non-Coca Crops," Rensselaer Lee, head of Global Advisory Services, a consulting firm in Alexandria, Virginia, said, "When you wipe out a peasant's coca field and leave him with no reasonable economic alternative, he's faced with some rather stark choices—emigration out of the region or joining a revolutionary movement."

The centerpiece of the new U.S. program, which became effective on August 1, 1990, was the abolition of import duties on 67 different products, ranging from fresh strawberries to expensive bicycles, sold to the United States by the four countries. Lower duties were expected to help stimulate sales by giving the countries an edge over competitors such as Mexico, the principal exporter of strawberries to the United States. The competitors would still have to pay the 1.5% tariff.

Another part of the new program was an expansion of agricultural assistance to the Andean region. The goal of the assistance was to encourage alternatives to narcotics by identifying other products with export potential. Experts suggested oranges, avocadoes, tea, coffee, macadamia nuts and spices. Unfortunately, all would bring in less money, take longer to grow and face formidable transportation problems.

More complications were added when Alberto Fujimori, an agronomist, took office as Peru's president on July 28, 1990. The new president proposed a gradual approach to the eradication of coca cultivation and dismissed Peru's top police officers. Moreover, he declined to accept $36 million in American military aid that was to have been used to intercept small planes that travel daily from dirt airstrips in Uchiza, carrying coca paste to cocaine refining facilities in neighboring Colombia.

Uchiza is in Peru's Upper Huallaga Valley, source of half of the world's supply of coca. About 80% of Uchiza's economy revolves around coca. The coca growers of the region are mostly refugees who fled from the violence of the revolutionary terrorist group Shining Path, which plagues the nations of the Andes.

The Peruvian government estimates that 1 million of Peru's 22 million people depend on the coca harvest for their livelihood. Probably the nation's largest export, coca brings in annually $1 billion to $1.5 billion.

Justo Silva Vallon, the manager of the 1,400-member Upper Huallaga Agricultural Cooperative, was quoted by the *New York Times* as saying "The peasants want to change—if it's profitable." In a more militant tone, Mario Campo Roldon, a board member of the Defense Front Against Coca Eradication in the Upper Huallaga, said, "We are tired of studies, speeches and promises. We want to substitute, but we want concrete facts— better roads, agricultural extension services."

Without a higher level of cooperation on both sides, alternative crops do not appear to hold out much promise of making serious inroads into coca agriculture.

Civil Penalties for Drug Dealers.   On a smaller scale, states are adopting strategies to make life more difficult for drug traffickers. Reminiscent of a technique used to combat bootlegging during Prohibition, a number of states are using the tax codes to penalize drug traffickers and divert some of their vast income. Failure to pay the tax when caught possessing or selling drugs results in the imposition of enormous fines payable within hours of arrest. Fines are frequently obtained through confiscation of property.

When such taxes were imposed initially, some of those arrested challenged the confiscation of their property, citing the Fifth Amendment right against self-incrimination. They claimed that buying a tax stamp amounts to an implicit admission of being a drug dealer. Except in South Dakota, the highest courts in several states have rejected these claims. In South Dakota, however, the highest court overturned the law. Subsequently other states modified their laws to take into account the objections raised by the South Dakota Supreme Court.

In an interview for a December 23, 1990, *New York Times* article entitled "21 States Imposing Drug Tax and Then Fining the Evaders," Robert Ebel, an official of the United States Advisory Commission on Intergovernmental Relations, said,

"The drug tax is one of the best pieces of anti-narcotics legislation to have come along in years . . . This basic commercial aspect of the business creates a weak spot in the dealer's defenses against the law. There is absolutely no justification to giving drug dealers tax breaks just because their business is illegal.''

The key to the effectiveness of drug taxes lies in distinctions between civil and criminal penalties. Under criminal law requirements, the prosecution must establish guilt beyond a reasonable doubt, and assets can be seized only after a court is satisfied that the defendant's constitutional rights have been observed. Under civil codes like the tax laws, the burden of proof falls to the accused to establish that the penalty is unfounded or unfair.

Thus someone arrested with drugs in his or her possession could be fined for a civil violation of the tax code, provided the state could show that he or she had not paid any tax on the drugs. Ken Kincade, a collection officer for the Minnesota Department of Revenue, told the *New York Times,* "All we need to establish is knowledge and control. While the police have to establish ownership, we go after anyone who knows about the drugs and could do something to them." For example, a man who sold his house and helped the new owner move in his possessions, including some marijuana plants, was taxed and fined as well as the owner of the plants, who also faced criminal charges.

Not all states with such laws on their books have used them extensively, but Minnesota and several others have, effectively. The approach offers law enforcement several advantages. It can tie up a dealer's assets and be used in plea bargaining, and it permits a greater range of property forfeiture than is possible under criminal statutes, where a direct link has to be shown between the drugs and the property.

While many of the early reservations about the constitutionality of such laws appear to have been resolved, critics remain unconvinced about their effectiveness. They point out that trying to collect taxes on legal items is difficult enough and view taxes on illegal items as a gimmick.

Supporters of such taxes argue that the U.S. Supreme Court has repeatedly upheld the taxation of illegal gains, including a 1961 ruling in *James v. United States,* which involved embezzled funds. The Court held that there "has been a widespread and settled administrative and judicial recognition of the taxability of unlawful gains of many kinds."

The taxes on illegal drugs are typically high; in Minnesota they are $1,590 for a pound of marijuana and $90,800 for a pound of cocaine. Dealers are re-

quired to buy tax stamps to attach to the drugs in the same way that tax stamps are attached to liquor and cigarettes. Dealers are allowed to buy the tax stamps anonymously, thus meeting objections that it violates Fifth Amendment rights against self-incrimination.

To supporters, such tax laws are not only a constitutionally sound measure to discourage the illegal drug business, they represent a measure of economic justice as well.

Neighborhood Strategies. Tax codes do not help residents beleaguered by drug dealers in their neighborhoods. In the Allerton area of the northeast Bronx, in New York City, a neighborhood of well-kept row houses and small apartment buildings next to the New York Botanical Garden, residents had grown tired of sidewalks so thick with drug dealers that ordinary people were unable to use them. They asked for help from the Citizens Committee for New York, a nonprofit organization, which assisted them in developing a battle plan. The strategy the residents used was reported in a February 12, 1991 *New York Times* article entitled "Trench Battle Routs Drugs in the Bronx."

A neighborhood resident, Diane Simmons, a home-care nurse, recalled how the Allerton Neighborhood Anti-Crime Committee was launched. Sally Dunsford, a principal strategist with the committee, put charts on the wall and gave the group scenarios. She said, " 'What do you feel your alternatives are? If you go to the police, what are you going to tell them? How would you approach them for help?' Then we would start brainstorming. It started with these little meetings, and all of a sudden we had a full-blown committee."

Among the things the group did was to have sidewalk pay phones taken out to deprive drug dealers of their means of communication. They nagged the owner of a vacant lot used by addicts as a shooting gallery to clean it up. Merchants chipped in and hired private guards with attack dogs to patrol the main avenue.

The committee's approach to helping a neighborhood help itself is to avoid starting at the worst areas, where there is a high risk of discouragement. The committee advises residents not to confront drug dealers personally, but to take notes and relay the information to the police.

If, as in many neighborhoods, the police and the community do not get along, the committee's staff meets separately with residents and with the police and asks each group what the two sides should be doing about drugs and why they are not doing it. Typically, most responses are similar on both sides, which are then brought together to start talking to each other.

In the Allerton neighborhood, much of the drug dealing was being done out of apartments. The residents, with the help of the committee and the city's Neighborhood Initiatives Development Corporation, looked into eviction as a weapon. In a two-year period, they succeeded in driving about a dozen dealers out of neighborhood apartments.

Whether eviction as an approach would work in other states would depend on state and local laws governing the rights of tenants. In some jurisdictions, tenants' rights are so closely guarded that evictions might be impractical.

But there are other possible strategies. An Allerton grocery store whose manager had been indicted for selling cocaine to an undercover police officer was the target of a letter-writing campaign to persuade the store's suppliers to stop providing the store with merchandise. The neighborhood group had already tried to get the grocery evicted and had urged the fire and housing departments to send in inspectors. Before the letter-writing campaign was even under way, the grocery store manager told the *New York Times* that he planned to move out of the neighborhood. "There's too much trouble around here. People bothering you all the time."

Drug Prevention.   The best prevention strategy is education that helps people to avoid involvement with drugs. Perhaps the best-known effort was Nancy Reagan's "Just Say No" campaign. Most educators, however, viewed the idea of just saying no as simplistic and lacking in awareness of the pressures on teenagers, particularly inner-city teenagers.

Many local education programs use a group counseling strategy, bringing youngsters together to talk. The major criticism of such programs is that the members bring to the groups such a diversity of problems that the groups are rendered ineffectual. Moreover, such groups may create the illusion of progress even where there is none.

One approach that gained some favor in the 1980s was drug testing. On September 15, 1986 President Reagan signed an executive order calling for drug testing of a broad range of the government's 2.8 million civilian employees.

The notion of drug testing created storms of controversy in many arenas, among them boarding schools, businesses and sports teams. Those opposed claimed drug testing violated civil liberties and destroyed trust between those being tested and those doing the testing. Moreover, they questioned the reliability of the tests. Those in favor claimed that testing acts as a deterrent

and makes possible early identification of those in need of treatment.

Drug testing has not gone unchallenged in the courts. On March 29, 1991 the U.S. Court of Appeals upheld the testing of Justice Department job applicants in a split decision. The court noted that some of the nation's largest employers, including American Telephone and Telegraph, Exxon and Federal Express, require job applicants to submit to drug tests.

Drug testing is expensive. A survey of 38 federal agencies by the Civil Service Subcommittee of the House of Representatives found that only 160 of 24,559 applicants screened between March 1989 and March 1990 had tested positive for illegal drug use. Of 28,872 federal employees, only 153 showed evidence of drug use. The cost to the agencies was $11.7 million.

Treatment.   Other than prevention, treatment offers the best hope of doing away with the market for drugs. Nevertheless, funding for programs remains limited. The 1987 National Drug and Alcoholism Treatment Unit Survey's census of alcohol and drug treatment facilities revealed 5,015, with a capacity to treat 328,838 patients; actually in treatment were 260,151. The 1989 Survey census found there were 6,170 facilities, with a capacity of 433,647 patients; 344,529 were in treatment.

Over the course of two years, the number of facilities had grown by 1,155 and capacity had grown by 104,809, but the number in treatment had grown by only 84,378. Those convinced that there is a national drop in drug abuse would interpret the smaller number in treatment as reflecting a decline in need.

Those convinced that the number of addicts is growing would not only point out that there was still an increase of 84,378 in treatment over the previous year, they would add that a declining rate of increase might simply mean an increase in the barriers to getting into treatment. Long waiting lists are commonplace around the country for people who want to obtain treatment.

Many mental health professionals believe the most effective approach is "treatment on demand," that is, treatment immediately available when an addict requests it. Frequently addicts are told to come back in several weeks or months; many never return.

If there is any drop in drug use, it is not reflected in arrests, which rose from 256 per 100,000 in 1980 to 423 per 100,000 in 1988. The Federal Bureau of Investigation's Uniform Crime Report calculated there were 1.6 million drug-related arrests in 1989.

Most correctional officials maintain that 40% of their prisoners are in prison for drug offenses. If their estimate is accurate, their yearly head count does not reflect a drop in U.S. drug use. The 1990 U.S. Statistical Abstract reported that in 1988, state and federal prisoners totaled 603,928, and 1987 jail inmates totaled 295,873, for a grand total of 899,801. Of the total, 359,920 prisoners, or 40%, were incarcerated for drug-related activity.

The 1991 U.S. Statistical Abstract reported that in 1988, there were 343,569 jail prisoners and in 1989 there were 675,441 federal and state prisoners. Together they amounted to 1.02 million prisoners. Forty percent of 1.02 million amounts to 407,604. In one year there had been an increase of 47,684. If the down side of the drug cycle has begun, there are few signs of it.

(See also ALCOHOL DEPENDENCE; APPENDIX 1: ORGANIZED CRIME; APPENDIX 3: RESOURCES; CAMPUS VIOLENCE; GANGS: STRUCTURED STREET: OUTLAW MOTORCYCLE GANGS.)

due process See ARREST: CONSTITUTIONAL RESTRICTIONS AND LEGAL PROCEDURES; BILL OF RIGHTS: PROTECTION AGAINST GOVERNMENT TYRANNY.

E

early release: the impact of prison overcrowding In 1950, there were 166,123 prisoners in all federal and state prisons. By 1975, a quarter of a century later there were 240,593 prisoners. And by 1987, just 12 years later, there were 555,256 prisoners. Many jails could not transfer their inmates to prison following conviction because there was no room. The 1987 U.S. jail population of 158,394 had almost doubled by 1987, to 295,873.

In response to suits filed by prisoners, many of whom were sleeping on mattresses on the floors of crowded cells or corridors, federal and state courts around the country ordered prisons and jails to release prisoners when they exceeded capacity. A number of states passed laws requiring the release of prisoners when a prison or jail exceeded its capacity for a specified period of time, typically 30, 45 or 60 days.

On two occasions in 1982 Michigan Governor William Milliken, by mandate of a 1980 law, was forced to release 900 prisoners. Between 1981 and 1991 nearly 7,400 jail prisoners in four Massachusetts counties were

released due to overcrowding. Almost half of them, 3,490, were released between 1988 and 1991, when several court orders went into effect. Hampden County Jail, a facility legally approved by the Massachusetts Department of Corrections to hold a maximum of 256 inmates—with an absolute cap at 450—at one point in the late 1980s housed 724.

The kinds of crimes committed by inmates of Hampden County Jail are typically breaking and entering, robbery, drug use and assault and battery. Before the jail became so crowded, the typical length of stay was about a year. Because of the crowding, early releases have shortened the typical stay to 60 days—two months instead of 12.

During an interview for the January 6, 1991 broadcast of the Boston TV program *Chronicle*, Michael Ash, sheriff of Hampden County, reflected on the practice of early release to reduce crowding. "It's scary. Every day, we just count our blessings that something tragic hasn't happened—in terms of going out and committing some kind of heinous crime. We live with that every day."

Following a lawsuit by one of Ash's inmates, he was constrained to stay within the cap on the number of inmates housed. In 1990, when the jail population soared over 450, Sheriff Ash took drastic action. He took over the National Guard Armory in Springfield. The state administration vetoed his action—perhaps fearful that other sheriffs might make similar moves—and promised to find money to house the additional prisoners. A year later money had not yet been found, and state budget deficits suggested that none would be found.

Ash was able to stay below his cap because a court order enabled him to release inmates who had served a third or even less of their sentence in order to free space as needed. Early releases have become the norm at Hampden County Jail.

Two inmates who expected to get early releases told *Chronicle* host Mike Barnicle that some inmates preferred not to be released early. Particularly for those who are substance abusers, early release comes at a time when they have not yet fully recovered.

Criminal justice experts differ in their opinions about whether early release poses a hazard to the public. Some believe that it makes little difference; others feel that it carries risk because, unlike parole, early release does not require supervision. They also worry about the psychological effect early release has on the public. The frail old lady who was mugged on the street believes that her attacker deserves to be in jail just as much as someone else's Public Enemy Number One.

One expert summed up the case for early release by saying

> No one thinks that early release, per se, is a good idea, but it is infinitely preferable to maintaining unsafe, unconstitutional, unlawful prisons. And the Constitution says no cruel and unusual punishment and that means no matter that you've committed a crime you have a right to a safe prison . . . which means that you don't put 25 guys in the boiler room at Norfolk full of cockroaches and rats, because those guys are going to get out. If you put them there, they are going to come out angry.

At a time when budget constraints have slowed prison building programs to a virtual standstill, jails and prisons at the local, state and federal level are overcrowded all over the United States. Since overcrowding in the corrections system is not likely to end any time soon, early release is likely to continue as a widespread practice.

(See also JAILS; PRISON OVERCROWDING; COPING WITH THE COSTS.)

education in correctional facilities See CORRECTIONAL EDUCATION; ILLITERACY IN PRISONS; TREATMENT PROGRAMS IN PRISON.

emergency medical care: the impact of violence
Shortly after the killing of five children and wounding of 30 other people in a Stockton, California schoolyard in January 1989 by a man with a military rifle, a hearing was held in the California State Assembly, where legislation banning assault rifles was under consideration. Among the witnesses was Dr. Garen Wintemut, an assistant professor of medicine at the University of California at Davis and the former director of a refugee camp in Cambodia.

During an interview for a February 21, 1989 *New York Times* article entitled "Epidemic in Urban Hospitals: Wounds from Assault Rifles," Dr. Wintemut said, "The medical techniques used in the Vietnam War are now being used in civilian life. There's no difference. And that wasn't the case before the assault weapons."

Wintemut's views were echoed by dozens of doctors and paramedics across the United States. They described exploded organs, pulverized bones and abdomens filled with blood in bodies riddled with bullets from high-velocity, rapid-fire assault rifles. The cost of treating such patients, the majority of whom have no health insurance, further strains the nation's trauma and emergency medical care, a system already under severe financial stress.

In 1987 and 1988 Highland Hospital in Oakland, California treated 700 gunshot victims at a cost of $10.5 million, doing what Dr. Eric Stirling, director of the emergency room, called "trench medicine." The director of the trauma unit of Kings County Hospital in Brooklyn, New York said, "The colloquialism that there's a war in the streets is exactly right." The medical director of the Martin Luther King-Charles Drew Medical Center in Los Angeles, Dr. Tom Scalea, reported that he had offered his emergency room to the army for training surgeons in battlefield conditions.

Military-style assault weapons do more damage per bullet, and fire many more bullets before reloading, than the long-familiar small pistols. The muzzle velocity of an assault weapon exceeds 2,500 feet per second; a pistol's is about 800 feet per second. Moreover, bullets used by assault weapons are designed to tumble on impact, thereby shredding bones, organs and blood vessels in their path.

Stirling described in the *New York Times* the case of a man shot in the right side. Had he been shot with an ordinary pistol, he would have had minor damage to his liver. Because he had been shot with an assault rifle, his kidney, aorta, pancreas, diaphragm and one lung were destroyed. In the 24 hours before he died, he received 25 units of blood during surgery and 40 units of blood products subsequently.

Even when vital areas are not directly hit, the shock waves generated by the high velocity of an assault rifle's bullet can shatter a bone or explode an organ. Stirling told of one man who suffered a grazing head wound that caused no apparent brain injury. Had he been shot with a .22 or .38, he could have gone home the next day; since the bullet had been fired from an assault rifle, he died of brain swelling within 12 hours.

Injuries inflicted by assault rifles require the use of wartime techniques. Ambulances are equipped with inflatable trousers, invented in World War I and widely used in Vietnam, to maintain blood pressure. Another technique involves the use of two large-bore intravenous lines hooked up to the patient simultaneously to replace rapidly large volumes of blood.

Speed is vital. The initial work is done by a paramedic on the way to the hospital; often the victim is on an operating table within 20 minutes of the ambulance call. (By comparison, the wounded of World War II were usually operated on within six hours; during the Korean

War, 2.4 hours. In Vietnam, it was less than an hour, with a major improvement in survival rates.)

Many of the operations that are performed once the patient arrives at the hospital were developed in military field hospitals in Southeast Asia. Among such procedures are grafting and rerouting of shredded vessels (instead of attempting to suture them end to end), paring of dead tissue and clothing fragments along the route of the bullet, formation of colostomies (rerouting to an external pouch) when intestines have been ripped apart and, as a last resort, opening the chest to siphon off blood collected in the body cavity, a technique that also makes it possible to see where the holes are.

Estimates of the cost of treating assault-rifle victims vary widely. Initial trauma repair at Highland Hospital costs about $15,000. A two-month stay in an intensive-care unit can raise the price to $150,000. Following hospitalization, a patient is likely to need long and intensive rehabilitation, possibly followed by a lifetime of at least partial disability.

A study reported in the November 15, 1988 issue of the *Journal of the American Medical Association* estimated the annual cost of gunshot wound treatment in the United States to be $1 billion. The study, done by three researchers at the University of California, San Francisco, was based on the experience of 131 patients admitted to San Francisco General Hospital in 1985 with firearm injuries. Because all San Francisco gunshot victims are taken to San Francisco General, the researchers were able to extrapolate the San Francisco figures to make estimates for the nation as a whole. They estimated that 62,075 people had been hospitalized in the United States for gunshot wounds in 1984; hospital costs per victim ranged from $559 to $64,470, with the average cost $6,915 and the average length of stay 6.2 days. Because the use of assault weapons has escalated since 1984, the average cost per patient and the average length of stay of patients who survive have increased significantly.

The individual patient in the San Francisco study paid an average of only 1.4% of the cost. Various government sources together paid an average of 85.6% and the remaining costs were picked up by private sources such as insurance companies and health maintenance organizations. In an interview for a November 29, 1988 *New York Times* article entitled "Gunshots Cost Hospitals $429 Million, Study Says," Dr. Michael Martin stated:

"Firearm injuries are an important public health and economic problem . . . we should have some say over the public policy on firearms. If you compare us to other countries like Japan or even Canada, it's crazy and wrong how many firearms and firearm injuries our society tolerates. . . . If you look at who gets shot, it's generally indigent, inner-city people who don't have insurance. I think that explains why the government ends up paying 85% of the cost of firearm injury hospitalizations, but only 53% of the costs of all hospitalizations in the United States."

(See also ASSAULT WEAPONS; CHILD EMERGENCY TRAUMA: A MODEL PREVENTION PROGRAM; GUN CONTROL: ADVOCATES; GUN CONTROL: OPPONENTS; GUN-FREE SCHOOL ZONE.)

emotional abuse of children   Emotional abuse can be as lasting and damaging as physical or sexual abuse. Some experts estimate that physical abuse takes place in one in every ten American families and sexual abuse takes place in one of every five. There are no estimates on emotional abuse, but most mental health and education professionals believe that its incidence is considerably higher than the incidence of either physical or sexual abuse and often accompanies the other two.

During an interview for a April 17, 1989 *Boston Globe* article entitled "Abuse of Another Kind," Jetta Bernier, a psychologist and executive director of the Massachusetts Committee for Youth and Children, was asked, "Does an occasional outburst in the normal ebb and flow of parental emotions make you a child abuser?" She answered:

No. Does it mean you engaged in abusive behavior? Yes. That it doesn't happen frequently isn't the issue. It shouldn't happen at all. Every parent has to take a hard look.

It doesn't take much to cause emotional damage to a child. Any child—even a 2-year-old—who is consistently told that he can't do anything right, that he is a bad boy, he's stupid, he's a jerk, that child stops trying to do anything right. It becomes a self-fulfilling prophecy.

The author of the *Psychologically Battered Child* (1986), James Garbarino, believes there are degrees of psychological maltreatment, a term he prefers to emotional abuse. In his opinion, all parents cross the line at some time and reject, frighten, ignore, isolate or corrupt their child.

Some parents do it without realizing it. Garbarino is most concerned with those who recognize the impact such tactics have on their children and use them frequently. A parent might say "I'm going to sell you to the circus,'' see that the child is frightened by the idea and subsequently repeat it.

A parent who apologizes for a rare outburst is probably not likely to hurt an emotionally stable child, but even healthy children can be hurt by a pattern of derogatory remarks.

Professionals propose that parents get into destructive patterns because they are under stress; they assume a child understands something better than he or she does; they attribute an adult motive to a child's behavior; or their own parents behaved that way. Experts advise a few simple rules to avoid emotional abuse:

1. Tell a child that his or her behavior is unacceptable, not that the child is.
2. Use a firm, authoritative tone and direct eye contact to indicate the seriousness of a topic.
3. Talk softly when in a roomful of noisy children, to quiet them down.
4. Avoid taking frustration out on a child.
5. Have a plan to deal with the temptation of verbal abuse. Step outside for fresh air. Recite the alphabet.
6. Make a list of words that should never be used to a child.
7. Let a small child's temper tantrum run its course. If the noise proves too much, remove the child to a safe place—a crib, playpen or another room—and leave the room to regain control.
8. Avoid a shouting match with a teenager. Wait the youngster out until he or she calms down.

(See also CHILD ABUSE AND NEGLECT; CHILDREN'S RIGHTS; PARENT ACCOUNTABILITY LAWS.)

F

fear of crime For its February 1990 issue, *Boston Magazine* sponsored a survey of 349 Boston residents about the fear of crime in their lives.

About 70% of those polled thought their chances of being attacked or robbed had gone up, with 92% of Hispanics, 82% of those ages 35 to 49 and 76% of blacks feeling more at risk. The 1990 perception of risk by blacks represented a 27% increase over their perception in a similar survey in 1979.

Forty-six percent of respondents said that they had limited their activities because of fear of crime. More than 87% were more afraid of being attacked by a stranger than by an acquaintance, a response that is unrealistic, given national crime data. Those figures imply that murders are almost four times as likely to be committed by acquaintances as by strangers.

However, there are questions about this conclusion. In a Uniform Crime Statistics table entitled "Murder Circumstances by Relationship, 1989," the category "Unknown Relationship" amounted to 33.1%. Some of those unknowns might have been strangers, some acquaintances. Chances are that more of them were strangers, since clearing a homicide committed by a stranger is generally more difficult.

Homicide is not the only crime in which friends and relatives play a part. A 1989 U.S. Department of Justice Survey found that 23.9% of robberies and 23.3% of assaults were committed by relatives, friends or acquaintances.

Most respondents thought crime was more serious than reported by the media. (More nonwhites than whites believe that to be true. The breakdown was 89% Asians, 81% Hispanics, 67% blacks and 53% whites.)

Random violence and bizarre crimes engender fear and a sense of anxiety that social rules are becoming irrelevant and no longer provide for predictable social behavior. This increasing social instability in turn makes it likely that criminals will not be bound even by the loosest rules.

The disorder and decay of neighborhoods also increases the level of public anxiety. Research done by criminologist James Q. Wilson of the University of California at Los Angeles developed the concept of the "broken window syndrome." Wilson proposed that residents react with fear to disorder and neglect in their neighborhoods—beggars, the homeless, abandoned buildings, trash, graffiti and other manifestations of social crisis—out of proportion to the actual crime rate, which most of them are unlikely to know.

According to Northeastern University criminologist George Kelling, a collaborator of Wilson's, "The feeling is that if the government can't take care of minor things like graffiti, then how can they protect me in the streets?"

Rising fear of crime in the United States has coincided with curtailment of services and reduced enforcement of vagrancy laws resulting from pinched local government revenues. As signs of neglect and disorder increase in a neighborhood, residents tend to stay behind locked doors. The more they withdraw from the streets, the more hostile the streets become, and the more hospitable to criminals. Signs of disorder and decay increase in tandem with criminal activity. Those who retreat see evidence of their worst fears every day on television.

In the same issue of *Boston Magazine,* Kevin Convey wrote:

> Just as fear of crime eats away at us and our communities, so it eats away at our society. It makes us eager to relinquish our rights in exchange for an imaginary promise of security. It widens the emotional gap between rich and poor, providing more space for crime and fear to flourish. . . . [Fear] robs us—individually and collectively—of our ability to act. . . . fear of crime poses a greater threat to us than crime itself.

(See also CRIME STATISTICS; FELONY CONVICTION RATES; GRIEF: EXPRESSIONS IN THE AFTERMATH OF VIOLENCE; INCIDENT-BASED CRIME DATA REPORTING SYSTEM; MODEL MUGGING; MURDER: U.S. PROFILE; NATIONAL CRIME INFORMATION CENTER (NCIC); STREET CRIMES.)

felony arrests: screening procedures

A screening or filtering process serves to weed out weaker cases and thus reduces the number of arrestees who ultimately are convicted of felonies and imprisoned. To make a felony arrest, police need only probable cause to believe a suspect has committed a felony. To achieve a conviction requires proof beyond a reasonable doubt. Between arrest and ultimate disposition, each case goes through a series of procedural steps in which the seriousness of the alleged behavior and the strength of the evidence are evaluated. The charge is based on this evaluation.

The first cut is made by the police when they decide whether to seek a formal complaint from the prosecutor. In some cases no complaint is sought, typically because investigation fails to support the charge. In these cases, the suspect is released.

The next cut is made by the prosecutor, who weighs the seriousness of the crime and the quality of the evidence in deciding what can be proven in court. The complaint may be rejected, reduced to a misdemeanor or pursued as a felony charge. At this point, the prosecutor will take into consideration additional factors that may add to the eventual sentence, such as the defendant's prior record, the use of a weapon or additional charges.

The next cut takes place at an arraignment in court, where the prosecutor presents evidence before a judge. If the judge finds the evidence sufficient to support the felony alleged, the defendant is held to answer. Bail may be set at this time.

In some jurisdictions and in federal cases, the prosecutor must present the case before a grand jury, a group made up of 12 to 23 people drawn from the same pool of citizens used in ordinary juries. The grand jury hears the evidence gathered by the prosecutor and decides whether a crime has been committed. If it brings a verdict of guilty, then an indictment, a written accusation made by the grand jury, is filed.

In New York the prosecutor has 144 hours from the time the judge sets bail to obtain an indictment. If the deadline is missed, the defendant must be released.

Most states do not convene grand juries. In those jurisdictions, the accused is prosecuted through the use of an "information," a written statement of charges filed by the prosecutor.

The charges against a number of those held to answer will be dismissed. Dismissals may come as a consequence of the defense's efforts to exclude evidence because of improper police procedure.

Although the percentages of cases eliminated vary at each of the steps, the results are remarkably similar for different types of crime. In describing the winnowing process in four southern California counties in 1973, Peter Greenwood, in "The Violent Offender in the Criminal Justice System" (included in *Criminal Violence,* 1982, edited by Marvin Wolfgang and Neil Alan Weiner), remarked on the uniformity.

Greenwood wrote:

> The percentage of filed cases that result in conviction is remarkably consistent across crimes, varying from a low of 72% for robbery and rape to a high of 75% for homicide. This consistency in conviction rates across crime types clearly reflects the effects of prior screening by the police and the prosecutor, aimed at weeding out the weaker cases. The lower attrition rate for homicide cases suggest that the police have conducted a more thorough investigation prior to making an arrest.

The filtering process does not stop with conviction. The judges in one jurisdiction, or a particular judge in a jurisdiction, may view a particular type of offense as less serious than other judges might. Moreover, a prosecutor may be more willing to grant sentencing concessions in return for guilty pleas.

A study of sentencing practices in the Los Angeles Superior Court found that the percentage of convicted defendants who were sentenced to state prisons varied by more than a factor of two across different branches of the court. The difference was explained in one branch by the stricter plea-bargaining custom of the prosecutor, combined with the tougher sentencing practice of the judges.

(See also ARREST: CONSTITUTIONAL RESTRICTIONS AND LEGAL PROCEDURES; ASSEMBLY-LINE JUSTICE; FELONY CONVICTION RATES; JURISDICTION IN CRIMINAL CASES; PROSECUTORIAL DISCRETION IN THE DISPOSITION OF CASES; SENTENCING: A TREND TOWARD LONGER SENTENCES.)

felony conviction rates   Among those arrested for felonies, the number who reach trial is limited by screening procedures. According to Peter Greenwood, author of "Violent Offenders in the Criminal Justice System" (included in *Criminal Violence, 1982,* edited by Marvin Wolfgang and Neil Alan Weiner), only about half the arrests for violent felonies result in conviction. Of those convicted, fewer than half are sentenced to prison. The small number actually sent to prison raises several questions. Do a defendant's personal characteristics affect the probability of conviction? Are defendants in more serious cases sentenced to prison? Is sentencing affected by the relative strength of the prosecution's case, which affects the possibility of plea bargaining?

There are only a few studies, providing only limited answers to such questions. After examining the available data, Greenwood hypothesized that there might be two different patterns of convictions, dependent upon prosecutors' allocation of resources. If resources are allocated equally to all types of cases, there presumably will be no systematic variation rates among them. Where resources are concentrated on more serious crimes, chances are that lower conviction rates will result among less serious crimes.

A study published in 1977 by the Vera Institute, a nonprofit criminal justice research organization, examined a sample of adult felony arrests in New York for the year 1971. The study found that a prior relationship between the victim and the offender had a very strong effect on conviction rates in robbery and assault cases: The 88% rate in robbery cases among strangers was more than twice the 37% rate in nonstranger cases.

Such an effect is not surprising, since there is a larger chance among family, friends, and acquaintances that the crime actually will involve a personal dispute rather than an unprovoked attack. And there is a greater chance that the victims will refuse to cooperate with the prosecutor, because the defendant and the victim(s) might have become reconciled or the victim(s) might fear retribution. Other studies also have found that crimes among nonstrangers were less likely to result in incarceration.

A study done by K. M. Williams and J. Lucianovic, reported in *PROMIS Research Publications 6 and 7 INSLAW* in 1978 and 1979, which examined a number of prosecuted cases of robberies and assault, found that prior relationship did not have an effect. Williams found that the principal factor affecting conviction was the quality of evidence. Cases in which physical evidence or property were recovered and those involving multiple witnesses were more likely to result in conviction. Other studies have found that some police officers are more successful than others at securing physical evidence and multiple witnesses, which suggests that training and departmental policies make a difference.

In analyzing sentence severity, five factors are generally considered: prior record, victim-offender relationship, use of a weapon, victim injury and age. A number of studies have found that a prior record has an effect on the likelihood of incarceration. A California study found that only 5% of defendants with minor records were sentenced to prison in contrast to 22% of those imprisoned before.

A study by P. Cook and D. Nagin, "Does the Weapon Matter?" published in 1979 in *PROMIS Research Publication 8,* looked at the issue of firearms. The researchers found that those armed with guns were more likely to receive prison commitments than those who were not. The presence of other types of weapons did not have a consistent effect on sentence severity.

A surprising finding of the Cook and Nagin research was that the degree of injury to the victim did not have an effect on sentence severity. One possible explanation is that unarmed robbers are more likely to injure their victims than armed robbers—unless of course the armed robber uses the gun.

Given that sentence severity increases with prior record and a prior record takes time to accumulate, severity of sentence increases with the age of the defendant.

A frequent explanation for low conviction rates and strong reliance on plea bargaining typically found in criminal courts is that the system is overloaded. The explanation presumes that if there were more prosecutors, who had more time to devote to each case, conviction and incarceration rates would go up.

A special program to explore the relationship between the number of prosecutors and the number of convictions was sponsored by the federal Law Enforcement Assistance Administration (LEAA) in 1975. The premise of the program was that a small number of recidivists (career criminals) accounted for a disproportionate share of crime, and that a concentrated effort to get the career criminals convicted and confined to prison would lead to a drop in street crime.

Under the LEAA program, a number of prosecutors received federal grants for efforts to increase conviction rates and win longer sentences for career criminals. Efforts were made to strengthen cases and increase conviction rates, and to decrease pretrial processing time.

Prosecutors were given discretion to determine what type of criminals their programs would handle. Many handled robbers exclusively, while others included a mixture of street crimes. The Career Criminal Prosecution (CCP) programs involved several departures from normal procedures. Typically, a special unit within the prosecutor's office was developed to handle career criminals. This unit generally became involved with cases sooner than normal, in order to help the police with arrest and investigation procedures.

A special investigator might be assigned to the CCP unit to help speed up case preparation. A single prosecutor assumed responsibility for a case from start to finish. And plea bargaining was stringently limited if permitted at all.

As a consequence, career criminal cases cost three times as much to prosecute as comparable routine cases.

Aside from cost, evaluations of local programs found conflicting results. In two of four initially funded programs, there was an increase in the likelihood of conviction on the most serious charges. In none was there an increase in the conviction rate or in percentage of convicted defendants incarcerated. In one there was an increase in sentence length and in another a reduction in processing time.

A later evaluation of 12 CCP programs in California found markedly different results. This study found a small, though significant, increase in conviction rates, an increase in average sentence length, increases in incarceration rates and a large increase in the number of defendants convicted on the most serious charges.

Possible explanations for the discrepancies between the earlier and the later evaluations are that the early evaluations looked at programs only in their first year; that early evaluation sites were selected because they were thought to have a progressive management approach, which left less room for improvement; and most likely, that California prosecutors have more control over the disposition of their cases than do prosecutors in other states. In contrast with many other states, California prosecutors control plea bargaining with little interference from judges. Moreover, in California the seriousness of the charge is directly related to the severity of the sentence.)

The California results suggest that increased resources devoted to specific types of cases can make a difference, provided that the prosecutors play a dominant role in determining sentence severity.

(See also ASSEMBLY-LINE JUSTICE; EARLY RELEASE; THE IMPACT OF PRISON OVERCROWDING; FELONY ARRESTS: SCREENING PROCEDURE; JURISDICTION IN CRIMINAL CASES; PROSECUTORIAL DISCRETION IN THE DISPOSITION OF CASES.)

frotteur   A person who has sexual urges and sexually arousing fantasies that involve rubbing or touching a nonconsenting person is called a frotteur; the behavior is called frottage. Some experts distinguish frotteurism (rubbing) from toucherism (fondling), but the *Diagnostic and Statistical Manual of Mental Disorder, Third Edition, Revised, (DSM-III-R),* one of the most widely used diagnostic manuals, groups both behaviors under frotteurism. The *DSM-III-R* reports that most instances of frottage occur when the frotteur is between 15 and 25 years of age, and that there is generally a decline in frequency thereafter. The behavior is extremely rare in females.

The frotteur is most likely to engage in frottage in crowded locations such as marketplaces, busy sidewalks or public transportation platforms or vehicles. The victim usually has a body type attractive to the frotteur and is likely to be wearing snug clothing. While the frotteur rubs his genitals against the victim's thighs or buttocks or fondles her genitals or breasts with his hands, he imagines an exclusive, caring relationship with her. However, he remains aware that he must escape detection to prevent retaliation or prosecution.

Sometimes the victim does not immediately protest because she presumes the contact is accidental. She finds it difficult to imagine that such behavior would be committed in so public a place. While the frotteur is not physically violent, his act is a kind of assault, and has similar psychological effects on the victim.

(See also SEX CRIMES RESEARCH.)

G

gang prevention programs   See VIOLENCE PREVENTION: THE EVOLUTION OF A PILOT PROGRAM FOR ADOLESCENTS.

gang rape   See RAPE.

gangs: pickup or temporary   A hearing was held by the New York City Council's Youth Services Committee in mid-December 1990 about the then highly publicized phenomenon of informal groups of young people who joined together to rob, rape or kill for fun or money. Lieutenant Arthur Doyle, commander of the Police Department's Youth Services Division, told the hearing that youth violence seems to rise and fall in 20-year cycles. In his opinion, the city was in the grip of a new upswing.

In the early 1970s, there were about 400 structured gangs in New York, with close to 20,000 members. Violent youngsters who acted together in gangs in the 1990s were different. They went from one group to another, none with an identifiable name, gang colors, leadership, turf or reason to exist. Doyle said, "The kids are like chameleons." One such gang attacked a jogger in Central Park on April 19, 1989, leaving her near death. A 1990 outbreak involved a series of violent incidents by roving groups throughout the year.

A tourist from Utah was slain on a subway platform as he tried to protect his mother from a gang that wanted money to go dancing. Two Canadian students were set upon by ten or 12 bat-wielding youths when they stopped to assist an elderly woman who had fallen. On Halloween night, a rampaging group of as many as 18 youths left a homeless man with his throat slashed. In the fall, there was a rash of incidents in which young people were killed or injured by pickup gangs for the expensive coats or jackets they were wearing. Similar incidents occurred in other cities.

Sergeant Warren Glover, supervisor of the Police Department's gang intelligence unit, testified that the number of gangs with an identifiable structure, leadership and hierarchy was not growing. Rather, he said, an increasing number of youths were simply coming together to commit crimes in temporary groups. Some members of the committee were angered by Glover's distinction. One councilman responded, "How can there be all these groups? If they're groups, they're gangs."

The counsel to the chief of the city's Transit Police, Dean Esserman, was of the opinion that youth crime was growing. He pointed out that half of all subway robberies were committed by people under 17, and half of the robbers were under 15. "It seems that kids commit crime in groups. I don't think it makes a tremendous difference to the person victimized if they're identified as a gang or not."

The Transit Police instituted several measures to reduce the violence. These included using Asian-Americans as decoys, since many of the young robbers see Asian-Americans as easy targets. Michael O'Connor, chief of operations of the Transit Police's Field Services Bureau, provided a profile of the gang members he encountered. The typical member was a young man from a Brooklyn housing project, who carried as a weapon a knife designed for opening boxes.

O'Connor supported Lieutenant Doyle's assertion of the looseness of gang organization by saying that the only tie a group might have to one another was that they might have cut school together.

(See also ASIAN GANGS IN NEW YORK; CHILDREN AND YOUTHS WITH GUNS; GANGS: STRUCTURED STREET; OUTLAW MOTORCYCLE GANGS; VIOLENCE AS FUN: THE CASE OF THE CENTRAL PARK JOGGER.)

gangs: structured street   The term gang is used to refer to either an organized group of criminals or a group of children or youth from the same neighborhood, who gather together and who may or may not participate in criminal activities. Because a relatively small number of gang members wreak substantial violence and inspire widespread fear, the American public has become suspicious of young people in groups, an attitude that unfortunately penalizes adolescents who congregate just to socialize.

Although gang membership is relatively small, it has been growing. A 1990 University of Chicago study of 45 cities reported the presence of 1,439 gangs with an estimated 120,635 members. In 1987 Boston had six known gangs; by 1990, there were 25, with an estimated 650 members. Between 1984 and 1988, Miami's four gangs grew to 60, with more than 3,000 members. The Seattle area's 50 gangs were mostly new. The 2,000 gang members in Phoenix and 3,000 in Denver modeled themselves after Los Angeles gangs, whose membership had grown 100% in five years. The average age of gang members in 1984 was 15. By 1990 it had dropped to 13½. Most gang members are male.

The major difference between gangs of the 1980s and 1990s and gangs of the 1950s and 1960s, in the view of Sergeant John Galea of the New York City Police gang unit, is the newer gangs' mobility and disregard for human life. He attributed the change to easily available semiautomatic weapons with which gang members can terrorize entire neighborhoods.

Experts have determined that criminal youth gangs share certain characteristics. Gang members live in the same neighborhood, regularly spend time together, wear similar articles of clothing, often share symbolic behavior such as ceremonial rituals and participate in criminal activities. Each gang develops its own set of symbolic behaviors, such as initiation rites, secret handshakes and hand signals.

Public Misinformation about Gangs.   Law officials feel that a number of myths about gangs need to be corrected. For example:

- Gangs do not solely peddle drugs. Among 52 law enforcement officials polled for a U.S. Justice Department survey of 45 cities, 22 said that selling drugs is not the primary activity of gang members in their cities. Drugs are more likely to be found among black gangs than among Hispanic ones. Gangs that are not heavily involved in drugs make do with robbery, burglary and minor drug dealing. Sometimes violence by gang members is unrelated to the gang's crime business. Sergeant Kathy Johnston of the Boston Police Intelligence Unit said, "Sometimes, shootings are over girl friends, sneakers, or a dirty look."
- Gang members are not all black. Blacks comprise about half of the gang membership nationwide. Another 35% are Hispanic, about half of whom are Mexican. The other 15% are white or Asian. From city to city, racial and ethnic configurations differ significantly.
- Gang members are not all young. Gang membership may begin in the preteen years, but increasingly large proportions of gangs are made up of adults, especially those that are involved in drugs. Almost half of gang incidents involve adult members.

Gang Identifiers.   A March 26,1989 *Boston Globe* article entitled "Gang Rivalry on the Rise in Boston," by Sally Jacobs and Kevin Cullen, described how some Boston youth gangs use clothing to stake out their territory and identify themselves. A dozen pairs of sneakers dangling from a tree in a vacant lot referred to as Adidas Park mark the territory of the Intervale gang. Adidas sneakers hanging from electrical cables delineate the turf of the Greenwood Street gang. The Intervale gang wears blue sports caps with their street name embroidered in white on the crown. The Castlegate gang wears black sweatsuits and blue and gold Miami Heat caps. Other gangs identify themselves with the caps of their favorite professional sports teams. One gang wears medallions. All the Boston gangs wear Adidas sneakers and easily recognize New York gang members who come into the city to deal drugs, because they wear Nikes.

The emblems and colors to which gang members attribute great significance are displayed on a variety of clothing, such as sweaters, shoes, shoelaces and hats. The symbolic adornment is worn for various occasions from parties to gang fights to funerals. Gang "prayers" are often said before members engage in battle with rivals or, if there is time, chanted before a wounded member dies.

During the 1970s and early 1980s, gang members in the Chicago area could be easily recognized by the colorful, custom-made fraternity-style sweaters they wore. In the fall of 1981, the Chicago Police Department cracked down on people wearing gang sweaters, charging them with disorderly conduct and then usually dropping the charges within a few hours. A suit filed by the American Civil Liberties Union brought an end to the practice.

Some gang members resumed wearing their sweaters, but there were many fewer wearers. The sweaters had made the gang members easy targets for rivals. Moreover, because of robberies and break-ins, some knitting mills had stopped making the sweaters.

Corrections officers need to know about gang membership identifiers because gangs, both adult and juvenile, continue their affiliations in prison. For many gangs, there is a strong likelihood that more than one member will be in a prison at the same time.

A flyer shared among midwestern correctional officers in 1989 provided a list of 16 gang membership identifiers. Whether the identifier was worn left or right varied by gang. Among the identifiers were earrings, hats, gloves (one hand only), pant legs rolled up on one leg, belt buckles, bandannas, stars, crowns, rabbit heads, sneakers, laces, haircuts, friendship beads and Irish claddagh rings.

Many gang members pride themselves on wearing elaborate tattoos. The Marielitos, 25,000 criminals emptied out of Cuban prisons, were sent to the United States by Fidel Castro, along with a wave of Cuban refugees he allowed to emigrate in 1980. The Marielito gang members are recognizable by bluish-green tattoos and by the tattoo placed on their hands by the Cuban prison system. The Marielitos pride themselves on their code of machismo and violence.

Marielito gang members tend to prefer old-fashioned painful methods of tattooing to demonstrate their ability to withstand pain. The more elaborate and extensive their tattoos, the more courage implied, a view shared for centuries by the yakuza, Japan's organized gangs.

Gangs in Prisons. Many gangs are formed while their members are in prison. One of the most violent white gangs, the Aryan Brotherhood, was started in San Quentin, a state prison in California, in 1967. The transfer of gang members to various federal institutions enabled the gang to spread throughout the country. The Camorra of Naples, Italy was created by convicts in the 18th century. From inside prison, the Camorra's secret brotherhood robbed, blackmailed and killed. They terrorized Naples and dictated to its imperial rulers. Resurrected in the late 1950s by Raffaele Cutolo, the deadly Camorra was again directed from prison for the next 30 years.

Some gangs seem to be confined to prisons. An Illinois gang called the Northsiders, not seen in the streets, was founded in Illinois corrections institutions. The Northsiders is composed largely of white inmates from the Chicago area. A racist group, the Northsiders claim white supremacy, adopt Nazi symbolism and use a Christian crucifix with crossed shotguns as one of their emblems.

Corrections institutions, which by their nature bring together antisocial people, constantly have to cope with the emergence of cliques and gangs. Such groups form to gain control over other inmates. The reason usually given for gang formation is for protection, but in practice prison gangs are generally formed or maintained to engage in illicit activities.

Street gangs bring into the institutions a belief system and degree of organization that adds significant pressure to institutional dynamics. They harass, intimidate and terrorize inmates and sometimes staff. Moreover, in order to bring additional members under their power, they control sex, provide drugs and traffic in contraband. Institutional gangs look for opportunities to corrupt institutional employees.

Los Angeles Gangs: Their Franchises and Imitators. Los Angeles is the gang capital of the United States. During 1989, gang-related violence claimed an average of one life every day. The two most notorious Los Angeles gangs, the Bloods and the Crips, are confederations of hundreds of subgroups, or "sets." Sets are formed along neighborhood lines. On the average, a set has 20 to 30 members, but some have as many as 100, known as bangers or gangbangers.

Gang membership in Los Angeles is estimated to involve about 900 gangs with a membership between 70,000 and 100,000. The gangs are increasingly well armed, violent and adept at evading the law. Cocaine imports have transformed street gangs such as the Bloods and the Crips into ghetto-based, increasingly violent, large-scale drug-trafficking organizations that stretch limited local law enforcement resources to the breaking point.

Although most gang activity tends to be home-based, in 1987 Los Angeles gangs appeared to have broadened their base to other big cities, among them Denver, Colorado, Portland, Oregon and Seattle, Washington. By early 1990 smaller communities such as Tyler, Texas and Lexington, Kentucky were reporting the presence of Los Angeles gangs.

In Hope, Arkansas, street gangs from Los Angeles invaded in 1988 bringing rivalries, drugs and weapons. In Omaha, Nebraska, drug-dealing gangs began in 1987 to spread terror. In a one-day period of violence, the city experienced nine drive-by shootings. The Omaha police chief interviewed for a March 26, 1990 *Boston Globe* article entitled "Gang Woes Afflict Cities Nationwide," asserted that "Bloods and Crips are in 49 cities in 48 states."

Gang graffiti often carries coded messages warning others, usually other gangs, to stay away or risk death. Rival gangs no longer fight turf wars over the neighborhoods where they live. Instead they fight over the territories in which they sell drugs. Crip gangs are therefore as likely to fight each other as they are Bloods. Conflicts between members of a single gang or between rival gangs has became a form of urban guerrilla warfare sparked by drug trafficking. Informers, defaulters and competitors are viciously maimed or murdered.

Experts on gangs believe that the cocaine trade, which involves 75 to 100 gangs, is controlled in south-central Los Angeles by 15 to 20 gang veterans, many of whom are still in their teens and twenties. Some of the veteran leaders, known as "O.G.s" (old gangsters) or rollers (high rollers), have direct connections to top-level Colombian cocaine smugglers. Some gang leaders have established sufficient trust with the Colombians to be given their drugs on a consignment basis; that is, they do not have to pay on delivery. Some gangs have sales of as much as $1 million a week.

Gangs such as the Bloods and the Crips are able to move their organizations into smaller cities because of their capacity to buy top-quality cocaine at wholesale prices. They can buy a kilo (2.2046 pounds) of cocaine for as little $10,000 and sell it for as much as $240,000.

The profits make it possible for the gangs to support a multicity operation. They are better armed and far more violent than the gangs or drug rings already established in these cities. If the price and quality of their cocaine do not give the big-city gangs a business advantage in a new locale, they resort to assault and murder.

Law enforcement officers differ in their views of the meaning of the presence of Los Angeles gangs in other cities. Some see them as chapters of the Los Angeles gangs, and therefore a major threat. Others believe that any local hoodlum is free to adopt the symbols of the Los Angeles gangs and claim that he is a member, on the assumption that he can then inspire fear without having to expend much effort.

Degree of Structure.   Many midwestern gangs have become increasingly sophisticated and have made efforts to develop political bases in their communities. A large number have applied for and obtained charters as non-profit organizations. By claiming status as religious organizations or voters' leagues, gangs hope to obtain federal grants and to influence politics by organizing voters.

Unlike California and midwestern gangs, Boston gangs, according to police, are short-lived. Most members who manage to stay out of prison drift away from their gangs when they reach 18 or 19. While a few of the Boston gangs appear to be well established and growing in size, most come and go. The loose structure of Boston gangs contrasts sharply with the well-defined structure of the tightly organized midwestern gangs whose members retain their affiliation into adulthood.

An example of a long-lived midwestern gang is the El Rukns, formerly known as the Black Stone Rangers, which is now legally chartered as the Grass Roots Voters of Illinois. The El Rukns have a structure comparable to that of an organized crime family. Many members are ex-convicts who range in age from 20 to 40. El Rukn leaders, called generals, all have been booked for or convicted of murder. A younger, more physically violent version of the El Rukns emerged under the name the Cobra Stones.

The El Rukns claim that religion is the core of their organization, but their real business is extortion, gambling, narcotics, prostitution and real estate holdings. Paramount among gang values is loyalty, whether inspired by blind faith or by fear of reprisal.

Gang Prevention.   In a March 24, 1991 *Parade Magazine* article entitled "What Can Be Done About Teen Gangs," Al Santoli described several community programs aimed at keeping youngsters out of gangs. Unfortunately, in economically depressed cities many recreation programs have disappeared. Nevertheless, small determined groups have tried to make a difference.

A small group of neighborhood organizers and former gang members in the Los Angeles County communities of Carson, Harbor City, Lomita and Wilmington led a campaign that resulted in a reduction in gang violence.

The Community Reclamation Project (CRP), set up to bring together state and local recreation and job programs, organized workshops for parents and assisted troubled youth. CRP staff held meetings in the roughest housing projects and brought in leaders of service agencies to create long-term plans. They also formed Neighborhood Watch groups and activities to paint out graffiti and enabled community residents to work more closely with the police.

The life of one 14-year-old former gang member, Ta'a Ryan, changed when he heard Wally Rank, a former professional basketball player and a CRP staff member, speak to a school assembly. After the assembly, Ryan asked for help. Rank persuaded the boy's family to transfer him to a private school, where his grades climbed and he was able to participate in sports. Ryan explained his escape from the gang influence by saying "What made a difference is that whenever I had a problem—with my parents, at school, peer pressure about drugs—Wally has been there for me. There are hard-core gangbangers no one can reach. But many kids like me can go either way. Without someone to talk to, I'd be gone."

In Columbus, Ohio a black probation officer named Harvey Halliburton, in 1985, created the Youth Leadership Program, in a housing project where the average household income was less than $5,000 per year, crack-cocaine dealers openly controlled the streets and the local gang threatened everyone. Halliburton recognized that he could not succeed through confrontation. He opted to win the youngsters over with activities such as a basketball team, a dance group and talent shows.

In March 1989 Halliburton was joined by county and state health officials to form New Directions, the first local program in Ohio to take a hands-on approach within an embattled community. The male educators and counselors on Halliburton's team encourage youngsters to help each other succeed. One youngster, now in college, who was helped by the program, reflected: "Now kids realize they have a choice. They take pride in doing something educational. We have the power to change ourselves."

Franchise gangs have no scruples about the tactics they employ. Many have their recruiters enroll in schools in order to sell drugs. They sometimes move into the housing project apartments of those they have hooked on drugs.

In Miami, where out-of-state gang members began appearing in the mid-1980s, Barbara Wade, a mother of four and a social worker with 20 years' experience in the streets of Chicago, resigned her job with the city to start Positive, Inc., a program to redirect gang allegiances. Initially, working out of her old compact car with the support of the mayor and private donations, Wade has managed to stop gang wars by winning over the leaders.

Wade's meetings are like group-therapy sessions. Youngsters are given an opportunity to sit in a circle of their peers and vent their anger, enabling them to deal with what is on their minds. Wade tells them, "You started the gang problem. You can stop it."

The only nationwide antigang program is offered by the Boys and Girls Clubs of America, a network of 1,100 recreation and youth-service groups. One Boys and Girls Club in the South Bronx area of New York City serves as a haven for 4,500 children against the violence they confront in the blighted buildings that surround the club.

To prevent crime, residents from all segments of the community have to be willing to invest time, imagination and money on the youngsters who are the most vulnerable. When asked why he belonged to a gang, one Boston gang member said, "It's security—so if you're in a fight you aren't out there by yourself. It's like a family environment."

For many members, in the absence of adults who care about them, gangs have become family substitutes. Gang alliances are often so strong they lead to hard feelings against those who don't belong. A grudge, a threat to teenage love, desire for someone else's jacket or sneakers or a gang member "dissing" (showing disrespect to) a member of another gang can lead to violence and death.

In an interview with Santoli, Robert Sweet, the administrator of the Federal Office of Juvenile Justice and Delinquency Prevention, said, "Police can't solve the problem alone. We need a balance between punishment for serious offenders and recreational programs for those children who can be rescued."

Gangs and the Future.   There is nothing to suggest that structured street gangs are likely to disappear any time in the near future. In a May 14, 1989 *Boston Globe*

Magazine article, "The New Mobsters," Alan Lupo described the present and probable future of the gang scene in the United States:

> Today, the streets are up for grabs—and the drug commodity is more lucrative and potent than booze . . . It was a fight for control that produced so much violence during Prohibition and prompted the smarter hoodlums like Meyer Lansky and Lucky Luciano to organize . . . they started out as young punks—and that is precisely what's on the streets today. Jamaican posses engage in Wild West shootouts. Young black American hoods lay waste to their own communities. Chinese, Vietnamese, and Russian-Jewish thugs strong-arm their own people. From the ranks of these people will come tomorrow's Lanskys and Lucianos."

(See also APPENDIX 1: ORGANIZED CRIME; CHILDREN AND YOUTHS WITH GUNS; EMERGENCY MEDICAL CARE: THE IMPACT OF VIOLENCE; GANGS: PICKUP OR TEMPORARY; VIOLENCE RESEARCH: A LONGITUDINAL STUDY OF VIOLENCE AMONG THE YOUNG.)

grand jury   See BILL OF RIGHTS: PROTECTION AGAINST GOVERNMENT TYRANNY.

grief: expressions in the aftermath of violence
Social scientists who have studied bereavement and grief have found that reactions to the loss of a loved one follow a somewhat predictable course. There are a number of physical symptoms: a feeling of being weighted down, restlessness, listlessness, lack of appetite and a frequent urge to sigh.

Commonly there is a sense of unreality, denial that such a thing could have happened. Frequently there are instances of seeing or hearing someone who sounds or looks like the loved one and forgetting for a moment that the person is dead. Depression and severe fatigue accompany an effort to gain distance from the loss. Regret and guilt for perceived flaws in the relationship make survivors frustrated by opportunities missed. Anger at being abandoned by the person who died is frequent, together with guilt for being angry. Wistfulness for a return to those aspects of the relationship that were comforting is common. Because it is sudden and because horror is attached to it, violent death exaggerates the normal grief reaction.

The death of a neighbor or an acquaintance evokes a response similar to that experienced for a close family member or friend, but the process is not as intense. Of course, any death is a reminder of one's own vulnerability.

Rituals involving laying the dead to rest are common in most societies. In the United States, depending on customs and the tenets of a dead person's religion, the rituals performed by survivors may include choosing a casket, holding a wake, having a funeral (which may include a religious ceremony and prayers at graveside) and gathering for food and drink when the ceremonies are over. Such rituals help adults to move through the grief process. Children are frequently excluded from some or all of the ceremonies, often in a misguided effort to shield them from the truth.

Inner-city children are exposed to violent death much more frequently than children who live in more sheltered neighborhoods. The deaths are often in their own families. The children are not only excluded from the ceremonies; frequently the adults in their lives are too stressed emotionally and financially to provide the comfort and reassurance the children need.

The faculty of some inner-city schools have come to recognize that they are the only ones available to help their students cope with grief. When Dr. Melba Coleman took over as principal of the 102d Street Elementary School in the Watts section of Los Angeles in 1986, she quickly learned that about 10% of her students were "high risk." They suffered from learning difficulties and they disrupted classes.

In time, Coleman discovered that these "troublemakers" had something in common. Someone in their family had died and they had been given no opportunity to express their grief. She organized a grief class.

In an interview for a November 13, 1989 *Newsweek* article entitled "Teaching Kids to Grieve: In L.A., It Is Never Too Early to Learn," Brown University education professor Theodore Sizer said, "These children are living in a war zone. How can you teach a kid whose mind is jangled by the murder he saw?"

The Los Angeles school system has 32 psychiatric social workers for 610,000 students. Deborah Johnson, the psychiatric social worker who conducts the 102d Street School's grief class, spends most of her time handling emergencies.

In the grief class, students are taught to express their needs. They play a game called Feelings by mimicking emotions while staring into a mirror and talking about them. Often the children draw their feelings.

Sometimes they take field trips. When the children were asked where they would like to go, one little boy said, "The cemetery." He had never seen his mother's grave.

The mother of 10-year-old Brendon went to the grocery store and never came back. She was found wrapped in a rug in a closet. She had been strangled and her tongue had been cut out. During one class, Brendon drew a horizontal green line. Above the line he drew a white rectangle. Inside the rectangle he wrote "Linda Ross, October 11, 1986. Inglewood Cemetery." Below the tombstone he drew two arrows to a red heart, and inside the heart, he wrote, "The happiest day of my life was when you gave birth to me." He stared at his drawing for some time and then walked away smiling to himself. At an earlier grief class, he had said, "I be crying inside."

In an interview for a June 10, 1991 *Newsweek* article entitled "Growing Up Under Fire," James Garbarino, president of the Erikson Institute for Advanced Study in Child Development in Chicago, explained that occasions that call for grief in the lives of inner-city children are so frequent that the children must turn off their feelings in order to survive. "Very few children can afford to be open and emotionally engaged. It's too exhausting and too threatening."

Adult Suppression of Grief. A curtailment of grief similar to that of inner-city children came to light in the mid-1980s when ophthalmologists at the Doheny Eye Institute noticed that an extraordinary number of Cambodian refugee women living in an area of Los Angeles County called Little Phnom Penh suffered from psychosomatic blindness. There was nothing physically wrong with the women's eyes, but they could not see. About 150 cases came to light, the largest known group of such victims anywhere in the world.

The researchers saw no men who became blind. Most did not live long enough to develop the disorder. The Khmer Rouge is estimated to have killed 1.5 million people, 80% of them men.

In an interview for a June 23, 1991 *New York Times* article entitled "They Cried Until They Could Not See," Gretchen Van Boemel, Doheny's associate director of electrophysiology, said, "I tested a few of them and found nothing wrong with them. Then I began asking them about their pasts. The answers were nearly identical: starvation, 20-hours-a-day forced labor, killing, Pol Pot [brutal Communist dictator]." In the medical literature there were no clear answers as to why the symptom that struck the Cambodian women would be blindness.

The most likely place to begin the search for an explanation is in a state of altered consciousness that psychologists call dissociation. Eve Carlson, a Beloit College researcher who has studied emotional stress in a small Cambodian community in Greensboro, North Carolina, described dissociation in the *New York Times:*

Suppose you're driving down the freeway, sort of daydreaming. Suddenly you come out of it and think to yourself: "Did I already pass my exit?" Your eyes are open but you don't really experience things; it's not normal awareness. Dissociation is that lack of integration with what's happening. In an extremely traumatic state you eventually begin to depersonalize things around you and detach from the world. Reality is distorted as though you're watching yourself in a movie.

Although there were no cases of psychosomatic blindness among Greensboro's Cambodians, Carlson found an exceptionally high level of dissociation even among those who had been in the United States for years. Carlson said, "We didn't even necessarily test the people who had been through the most gruesome experiences. Ours was a random sample of the community and still their dissociation was way out of proportion with any normal group of people."

Freud in 1910 called the psychological escape from trauma into a physical ailment "conversion disorder." The classic example of conversion disorder is when an employee wants to hit the boss so much that his or her arm becomes paralyzed.

No one is certain why one area of the body is sacrificed rather than another. Memory loss and dissociation were common among survivors of the Holocaust. Loss of hearing and speech have also been observed.

The last clear scene one woman refugee remembers was a brutal killing. She told the *New York Times,* "I started crying hard for a long time. It felt like there was a big needle pushing into my head." Days later when she finally stopped crying, her sight was gone.

All of the women afflicted with blindness also suffer from post-traumatic stress disorder (nightmares, flashbacks, avoidance of reminders) and "survivor guilt" (remorse that they escaped and others did not). The women have much in common: They are all between 50 and 70; each spent from one to five years in forced labor in Cambodia; each spent from three months to six years in oppressive refugee camps in Thailand; 90% lost family members—some as many as ten—and many actually witnessed the executions. Fear prevents at least half of them from venturing outside their homes.

Inner-city children caught in the crossfire of drug wars have much in common with the women who escaped from Pol Pot's brutal regime. The horror lingers on even after the shooting has stopped.

(See also CLASSROOM VIOLENCE; POST-TRAUMATIC STRESS DIS-ORDER (PTSD).)

gun control: advocates The effort to control guns on a state and local level began before the American Revolution, when the Colony of Massachusetts prohibited the carrying of defensive arms in public. In 1813 Kentucky passed a law forbidding the carrying of concealed weapons, and Indiana, Arkansas and Georgia quickly followed suit. New York State's stringent gun control law went into effect in 1911. New York requires a license for the possession of a handgun in the home, a different license for possession in a place of business and still a different license to carry a handgun concealed on one's person.

Altogether there are more than 20,000 federal, state and local laws in the United States concerned with the control of guns. In their 1987 book *The Citizen's Guide to Gun Control,* Franklin Zimring and Gordon Hawkins distinguish "place and manner" laws from laws that attempt to restrict the availability of some or all types of guns. Many states and most cities have place and manner laws that regulate where and how firearms may be carried. These laws make up the majority of U.S. laws related to firearms, and most came into being between 1880 and 1915. On the whole, they were not carefully drafted; many are so ambiguous they are difficult to interpret, let alone enforce.

Most states prohibit the carrying of concealable firearms without a special permit and the discharge of guns within city limits, and many regulate the transportation of firearms by motor vehicle. Most state and local licensing laws provide for screening applicants, but in general, they are so permissive that individuals can be excluded from owning guns only if authorities can provide a reason why permission should be denied. The diverse provisions of the various laws range from severe restrictions on gun ownership in New York and Washington, D.C. to a virtual welcome mat in states such as Florida, Texas and Georgia.

Jurisdictions also differ widely in their definitions of assault weapons. Such state and local differences not only encourage Latin American criminals to travel north to purchase their weapons, they also encourage American criminals who live in northern states to travel south to purchase theirs.

The U.S. Bureau of Alcohol, Tobacco, and Firearms (BATF) conducted a study of guns recovered by the police in drug wars in Colombia. Police were able to track 158 guns used between January 1988 and September 1989; 85 of them came from Florida.

The gun business in Georgia is brisk. Except in Atlanta, there is no waiting period for purchasing guns in the state. The only requirements are that a buyer be an adult and show a Georgia license or state ID card. Gunrunning used to be "a crime of opportunity"—that is, someone on vacation in the south would purchase a few guns to take home to sell to friends. But given the demand on the streets for semiautomatic pistols such as the TEC-9 and the MAC-11, Boston street gang members regularly make round-trip bus trips to Georgia to pick up weapons.

Federal Control.   Gun control has never had a high priority as a federal legislative topic. Urban crime and handgun use in the post-World War I years provided the impetus for the passage in 1927 of a law prohibiting the mailing of concealable firearms to private individuals, an approach that had been used to circumvent state regulations on handgun transactions. The federal law had little impact because private express companies could still legally deliver firearms.

Additional federal legislation was sparked in the 1930s by machine gun-toting interstate bank robbers such as John Dillinger. The National Firearms Act was passed in 1934, followed by the Federal Firearms Act in 1938. The laws were largely ineffective and were not vigorously enforced.

President John F. Kennedy was assassinated in 1963, but it took five years of debate and the assassinations of Robert Kennedy and Martin Luther King, Jr., to convince Congress to pass the Gun Control Act of 1968. The law's primary intent was to help states and localities that sought to help themselves. There were five major areas of federal control: a prohibition against the owning of firearms by minors, felons and other designated high-risk groups; a ban against private ownership of bazookas, submachine guns and other destructive devices; curtailment of "Saturday night specials" (cheap handguns); a prohibition against sale of firearms to persons who resided outside the state of purchase (to prevent a flow of firearms from states with minimal control to states with restrictive policies); and a requirement that persons who sold more than a few guns must apply for a federal license and submit to controls and recordkeeping requirements.

The resources devoted to enforcement of the 1968 act were modest; nevertheless, the law became a target for lobbying by the major opponent of gun control, the National Rifle Association (NRA). In 1986, as a result of the organization's efforts, the McClure-Volkmer Bill, aimed at overturning the provisions of the 1968 law, was passed.

The NRA had spent millions to roll back the 1968 act, but the concessions it gained were less than it had worked for. The 1986 law did not do away with the ban on ownership by high-risk groups, or the prohibition against Saturday night specials or the ban on ownership of destructive devices. Gun sellers gained the right to sell certain guns to out-of-staters over the counter, as long as the sale was legal in the state of the buyer and the seller. Dealers could not sell firearms by mail, but they could sell ammunition. A last-minute addition to the bill banned the further manufacture of machine guns for private sale and made more difficult the conversion of semiautomatic weapons to automatic.

In the opinion of Zimring and Hawkins, the 1986 law was a symbolic victory for the NRA, but it might ultimately lead to a more focused federal role in gun control.

Citizen Advocates of Gun Control.   The assassinations of John F. Kennedy, Martin Luther King, Jr. and Robert Kennedy in the 1960s aroused a feeling that the widespread presence of firearms in American society was a threat. The most vocal advocate for gun control in the United States is the organization called Handgun Control, Inc., founded in 1974 by Peter Shields of Delaware after his 23-year-old son was murdered in California with a handgun. The organization has 250,000 active members, a million additional supporters who have signed petitions and contributed money and a $6.5 million operating budget. The organization is the strongest foe of the NRA, which has 3 million members and an operating budget of $86 million.

The nation's best-known and most vocal individual gun control advocate is Sarah Brady, the wife of James Brady, President Reagan's former press secretary, who was shot during an assassination attempt on the president in March 1981. Although the bullets that hit the president, a police officer and a Secret Service agent did not explode, the one that entered Jim Brady's brain did, with effects that will keep him disabled and in pain for the rest of his life.

A December 9, 1990 *New York Times* article entitled "Sarah and James Brady Target: The Gun Lobby," reported that Sarah Brady's championship of gun control did not begin with her husband's injuries in 1981. Her advocacy began four years later, in her husband's peaceful hometown of Centralia, Illinois, when her five-year-old son Scott crawled into a family friend's pickup truck, where he spied a plaything on the seat and pointed it at his mother. The toy turned out to be a loaded .22

pistol, which the family friend kept in his truck because he had been involved in a bitter labor dispute and feared he might need it.

The incident upset Sarah Brady for weeks afterward. Once back in Washington, she noticed that the Senate was getting ready to vote on the McClure-Volkmer bill, legislation intended to neutralize the Gun Control Act of 1968. After reading about the bill, Sarah Brady called Handgun Control, Inc. to offer her help. She was put to work immediately in what was to become a long-term commitment.

As long as James Brady's name remained on President Reagan's staff roster as White House press secretary, he refrained from participation in his wife's gun control battle, since Reagan was opposed to gun control legislation. However, once Reagan left office in January 1989, Brady joined in the effort, despite his severe handicaps. On November 21, 1989 he testified before the Senate Judiciary Committee on behalf of Senate Bill 1236—the so-called Brady Bill—which in various forms has been around since 1987. The bill requires a seven-day waiting period to purchase a gun to allow a background check of the purchaser to be made.

In the early months of 1990, the first Handgun Control print advertisement featuring Jim Brady appeared. In the ad, Brady cited polls showing that 91% of Americans—and 87% of American handgun owners—supported the bill, as did every major law enforcement organization in the country. His message commented: "It seems the only people against the Brady bill are psychopaths, criminals, drug dealers and the gun lobby."

Despite the ads, the Brady bill was bottled up in the House in 1990 and never reached the floor. Undeterred, advocates introduced the bill once again in the new Congress in 1991. That time, in response to a request from Sarah Brady, the bill got an unexpected endorsement by former President Reagan, a staunch NRA supporter. In subsequent weeks, former Presidents Gerald Ford and Jimmy Carter also endorsed the Brady Bill. Despite this support, the bill still had not become law by late 1992.

Not everyone was impressed by what could be accomplished by a seven-day waiting period. In an August 15, 1988, *Newsweek* article entitled "New Support for Gun Control," author Julia Trotman said,

"Critics dispute the value of requiring a waiting period at all. The N.R.A., for example, is probably right in arguing that criminals will have little difficulty in evading background checks by buying through middlemen. Lax laws in the so-called soft states—particularly Florida, Georgia, Virginia, Texas, and Ohio—have already created a booming interstate gun-smuggling business catering to criminal buyers. The explosive growth of handgun ownership nationwide suggests that the Brady amendment may be at least 10 years too late.

Whether or not the Brady Bill ever passes, the advocates remain undaunted because they have had other successes. Handgun Control, Inc. claims credit for the continuance by Congress of the ban on the interstate sale of guns; the ban by Congress against armor-piercing "cop killer" bullets, new machine guns and undetectable plastic guns; the passage in Virginia of a law requiring gun dealers to check with police for felony records of purchasers of handguns and assault weapons; and the prevention of the overturning of a Maryland law banning Saturday night specials.

Plans call for efforts to gain a series of new laws to curtail drug-related violence involving handguns and assault pistols. The gun control advocates' cause has been helped considerably by the endorsement of police chiefs around the country. The chiefs are alarmed at the firepower their officers face in the streets. The police chiefs have credibility with the public because they represent a sector of the society that cannot be accused of being soft on crime.

In his *New York Times* column "Politics" on March 28, 1989, E.J. Dionne, Jr. analyzed why gun control advocates were at last having some success against the gun lobby. He repeated the words of Linda DiVall, a Republican polltaker, who said, "The N.R.A. was successful when it could frame this as a simple constitutional rights argument. Now people are seeing a first-hand demonstration of what the right to bear arms means as they're watching shootouts in their neighborhoods and live on the evening news."

Public Attitudes and the Future of Gun Control. The most important reason given for handgun ownership, according to public opinion polls, is self-defense. If owning loaded handguns continues to be seen as a respectable way to defend households, then opposition to restrictive policies will continue. If, like smoking, having loaded handguns in the home falls out of favor with the public and comes to be viewed as part of the gun problem, then prospects for new restrictions will improve.

A factor that will influence attitudes toward handguns is the perceived efficiency of alternative self-defense measures such as burglar alarms, silent alarms to trigger security forces, and the presence of dogs in the home. In the opinion of Zimring and Hawkins, women and the elderly may play a key part in whether restrictions are increased or decreased in the future.

Women have played a dual role in public opinion about handguns. Historically, few women have owned guns. However, women's vulnerability to violent crime has been one of the most persuasive arguments used as a justification for having household handguns. President Reagan justified having a gun in his dresser drawer by citing the amount of time he spent away from his ranch.

But recently the social status of women has changed dramatically. Hence it may have a substantial impact on the presence of handguns in the home. In the 1960s, when 7% of gun owners were women, only 18.2% of American households were headed by females. Zimring and Hawkins point out that one Harris poll found gun ownership in female-headed households to be less than half that of households that included an adult male.

In contrast to men who, it is claimed, typically experience burglary as simply a loss of property, women experience it as a gross violation of their personal privacy. Moreover, women are the primary targets of sexual violence. Those two facts could prompt women living alone or as the only adult in a family either to buy handguns in unprecedented numbers or to turn as an alternative toward other antiburglary options.

The choice of women living in homes without men could have a wider impact. If single women continue their persistently low handgun ownership, then married women who object to the presence of a gun in the home, particularly homes that include children, are more likely to argue that they do not need protection while their husbands are away.

Another group that could have great impact on gun control is the elderly, whose numbers and influence have increased substantially. In 1970 those over 65 were 19% of the population; in 1989 they were 29%. During the same years, the number living below the poverty line fell from 64.9% to 30.7%. Taken together, these statistics indicate that their political clout as a group rose.

As a group, the elderly have often been depicted as living in constant fear of crime. But a survey by the American Association of Retired People (AARP) indicated that for the majority of the elderly, this was not the case. If this group, which is 58% female, many of whom live alone, is not afraid, and if women continue a pattern of low gun ownership, they could have

a significant impact on the fate of gun control legislation.

(See also ASSAULT WEAPONS; EMERGENCY MEDICAL CARE: THE IMPACT OF VIOLENCE; GUN CONTROL: OPPONENTS; GUN OWNERSHIP; RIGHT TO BEAR ARMS: THE SECOND AMENDMENT.)

gun control: opponents   The NRA (National Rifle Association), with a membership of 3 million, represents gun owners. Its wealth, political clout and activist membership make it the leading voice of those opposed to restrictions on gun sales, ownership and use. The organization is so strong that some observers believe that Congress will never pass sweeping gun control laws.

The NRA embodies the American attachment to guns. Many Americans assert that the wide distribution of guns in the United States was not only essential to establishing the republic but has been critical to maintaining it. NRA Executive Vice President J. Warren Cassidy reflected members' fierce veneration of guns when he said, "You would get a far better understanding if you approached us as one of the great religions of the world."

Cultural folklore also helps to maintain the NRA's advocacy of the widespread possession of guns. As historian Richard Hofstadter said in a 1970 essay, "Every Walter Mitty has had his moments when he is Gary Cooper, stalking the streets in 'High Noon' with his gun at the ready."

The NRA was founded in 1871 by a group of former U.S. Army officers who had been dismayed to find that many Union soldiers in the Civil War were so poorly trained that they were barely capable of using their weapons. For decades, the organization concentrated mostly on marksmanship and gun safety. Gun control became an issue in 1934, when Congress passed the National Firearms Act restricting ownership of machine guns, sawed-off shotguns, silencers and other "gangster"-type weapons.

Three decades later came the Gun Control Act of 1968. Although the NRA opposed the act, the organization did not become militant until the mid-1970s, when a hard-line faction was formed. At the 1977 NRA national convention, this faction staged a revolt and installed Harlon Carter, former head of the U.S. Border Patrol, as executive vice president and Neal Knox as head of lobbying activities. A decade of dedicated recruiting followed, tripling the membership to 3 million. The typical member is a white suburban man, above average in income and education.

The NRA became bellicose during the Reagan administration, particularly during the period preceding passage of the Gun Control Act of 1986. However, a turnaround in the organization began in 1985 when Carter retired and Knox stalked off to form a yet more militant splinter group. Knox was replaced by J. Warren Cassidy, a Dartmouth graduate, retired marine lieutenant colonel, and former mayor of Lynn, Massachusetts, who four years later became the organization's executive vice president. Unlike Carter and Knox, Cassidy is considered by many members to be too smooth, too comfortable in Washington and not a real gun enthusiast.

The NRA's legislative activity has shifted attention and drained a substantial amount of funding away from traditional sport-shooting and training activities. The organization continues to offer hunter safety programs and 64 firearms courses for police around the country.

Setbacks. After years of uninterrupted success blocking efforts at gun control, the NRA in recent years has experienced some legislative and political reversals. Besides achieving some limits on assault weapons, gun control advocates have pushed through other reforms in several states. Alarmed by murders of police officers and alienated by the NRA's initial opposition to a ban on "cop-killer" bullets designed to pierce bulletproof vests, several police departments threw their weight behind gun control efforts.

The backing of Maryland police chiefs in conjunction with that of Governor William Schaefer was a key factor in a November 1988 referendum in which Maryland voters upheld a state law banning the sale of cheap handguns known as "Saturday night specials." The NRA ran a $6 million campaign to repeal the law and suffered its first defeat ever in a statewide referendum.

Support for retention of the ban came from black Baltimore neighborhoods and from predominantly white suburbs, while support for repeal of the law came from rural voters. Peter Marudas, an aide to Baltimore Mayor Kurt Schmoke, explained the urban and suburban support for the retention of the law: "There is a perception in the urban and suburban areas that being against gun control is being soft on crime. Being pro-N.R.A. is being permissive. If that holds true elsewhere, you may have the beginning of a movement."

Undismayed by the shift in public opinion and the high volume of gun traffic in the United States, NRA president Joe Foss—highly decorated World War II fighter pilot, retired brigadier general, former governor of South Dakota and first commissioner of the American Football League—stated in an interview for a January 29, 1990 *Time* article entitled "Under Fire," by Richard Lacayo, "I say all guns are good guns. There are no bad guns. I say the whole nation should be an armed nation. Period."

Foss's attitude appeared to be at odds with that of many other Americans who were concerned that firearms are involved in approximately 30,000 deaths each year and that some drug gangs have arsenals that would be the envy of a small army. An archenemy of the NRA, former White House press secretary James Brady, who was wounded during John Hinckley's attempted assassination of President Reagan, described the NRA as an "evil empire," while testifying before Congress in 1989.

In response to Brady's characterization, Richard Lacayo wrote:

> That kind of hyperbole too often characterizes the gun debate on both sides. For one thing, Brady's description hardly does justice to a complex association that is partly a lobby, partly a sporting group and largely a gathering of the faithful. It also won't do because the N.R.A. is not just another special-interest group. It is the pivotal player in the evolving national concern about guns. What the N.R.A. is, and what it becomes, will do much to determine the outcome of the debate.

As in many organizations with an intense ideology, NRA members are split into factions. Some members complain that the organization is in the grip of extremists, who have turned the public against them. Others complain that the leadership in Washington has grown soft and too accommodating.

The NRA for many years enjoyed a reputation for being invincible. In 1986 the organization won a big victory when the Congress diluted the 1968 Gun Control Act, which had been passed shortly after the Robert Kennedy and Martin Luther King, Jr. assassinations. The 1986 law NRA helped pass, the Firearms Owners' Protection Act, repealed a ban on interstate sale of rifles and shotguns and restricted government agents to only one unannounced inspection of a gun dealer's premises each year.

Despite its years of success, in the closing years of the 1980s, the NRA found itself repeatedly at odds with police organizations, who saw themselves as outgunned by gangs and drug dealers. Ultimately, the NRA was forced to accept some legislation that it had at first resisted, such as a ban on "cop-killer" handgun bullets that pierce protective vests and a ban on plastic guns that can elude metal detectors. Opposition by the NRA to such measures made it easy for gun control advocates to paint the NRA as wantonly indifferent to public safety.

Exercising Political Clout. Getting out the anti-gun control vote has been a potent tool of the NRA, but recently the organization has not found it as easy to deliver the vote as it once was. The association's political action committee spent $4.7 million to back candidates in the 1988 elections and failed to unseat any of its targeted incumbents.

Nevertheless, the organization retains much of its power. The NRA spent $1.5 million to defeat Michael Dukakis in the 1988 presidential election and is credited with turning a portion of the vote against him. Moreover, after the passage of a handgun ban in Morton Grove, Illinois, the NRA persuaded 38 states to pass laws prohibiting similar actions by local communities.

With a membership less than a tenth that of the American Association of Retired Persons (AARP), the NRA continues to beat back its opponents, despite widespread opposition to its agenda. During an interview for a May 8, 1989 *U.S. News and World Report* article entitled "Secrets Behind the Gun Lobby's Staying Power," Executive Vice President Cassidy asserted that most mainstream American voters are untouched by the "Eastern media's" focus on gun control during traumatic incidents involving firearms. Cassidy claimed that pro-gun voters account for up to 5% of the electorate in states such as Texas, Pennsylvania and California, enough to swing close races.

Another source of the NRA's strength is its $70 million budget and its organization, which includes a staff of 350, affiliates in every state and 13,746 local gun clubs. To its opponents, the NRA's power lies not in its funds, organization or arguments but in its bullying tactics. Sarah Brady, wife of James Brady and a leading gun control advocate, contended that the NRA resorted to "out-and-out lies" in its 1988 campaign to defeat the Brady Bill, which called for a seven-day waiting period for gun buyers. Some police chiefs who had split with the NRA over the issue of cop-killer bullets claimed that the NRA tried to force them out of office.

Many political opponents of the NRA believe that it is now possible to be in favor of gun control and still win votes. Some urban Democrats in particular, with the help of local police chiefs, have looked for ways to take on the NRA.

Semiautomatic Weapons   The Stockton schoolyard massacre of January 1989 (five children killed and 29 children and one teacher wounded) by a man with a legal AKS Chinese-made semiautomatic assault weapon was a serious setback for the NRA. By the first anniversary of the massacre, the state of California and five cities elsewhere had passed laws restricting or prohibiting assault rifles.

Despite widespread citizen support for the California law, which prohibits the sale, manufacture or unlicensed possession of 56 military-style weapons, the NRA fought its passage. The NRA's position was that such guns are technically identical to semiautomatic hunting guns.

Although actions taken in California are often viewed as atypical and not representative of the rest of the nation, even gun owners themselves seemed willing to accept restrictions to which the NRA leadership objected. In a poll done for *Time*/CNN by Yankelovich Clancy Shulman, 56% of those polled described themselves as supporters of the NRA, yet 73% approved mandatory registration of semiautomatic weapons and 87% said that they would approve a federal law requiring a seven-day waiting period and a background check to purchase a gun.

No matter what the public attitude toward them might be, the NRA is not willing to support a ban on semiautomatic assault rifles. This unswerving stance opened it to some ridicule. In an April 3, 1989 essay entitled *Time* "The N.R.A. in a Hunter's Sight," Robert Hughes wrote:

> The N.R.A. never saw a weapon it didn't love . . . Now the pressure is on to restrict semiautomatic assault weapons, we hear the same threadbare rhetoric about the rights of hunters. No serious hunter goes after deer with an Uzi or an AK-46; those weapons are not made for picking off an animal in the woods but for blowing people into chopped meat at close-to-medium range, and anyone who needs a banana clip with 30 shells in it to hit a buck should not be hunting at all."

Although the NRA may receive no financial support from arms manufacturers, in the opinion of Hughes the organization serves their interests. "The stand the N.R.A. takes is only nominally on behalf of recreational hunters. The people it really serves are the gun manufacturers, whose sole interest is to sell as many deadly weapons of as many kinds to as many Americans as possible."

But ridicule seems to bounce right off the NRA; it remains a formidable organization. Columnist E.J. Dionne, in a March 28, 1989 *New York Times*, "Politics'' column entitled "Has the Gun Lobby Become One of the Unexpected Casualties of the President's War Against Drugs?" examined the continuing success of the NRA.

> John Buckley, the communications director of the National Republican Congressional Committee, said the N.R.A.'s well-tended mailing lists were gold mines for candidates who support the right to bear arms because they permitted pro-gun candidates to hammer home a pro-gun message to the one constituency sure to agree with it. Those who might not agree never see the message. And the Association does not leave matters to its favored candidates. Last year it sent out five million pieces of mail.

(See also ASSAULT WEAPONS; GUN CONTROL: ADVOCATES; GUN OWNERSHIP; RIGHT TO BEAR ARMS: THE SECOND AMENDMENT.)

gun-free school zones bill
In November 1990, as a part of the Omnibus Crime Bill, President Bush signed into law "gun-free school zone" legislation, which went into effect in February 1991. The new law followed a four-year period during which guns had been used in or near schools to kill more than 70 people, 65 of them students, severely injure 200 and hold hostage almost 250. Sponsored by Senator Herbert Kohl (D.-Wisconsin) and Representative Edward Feighan (D.-Ohio), the legislation prohibits possession and discharge of a firearm on school grounds or within 1,000 feet of a public or private school.

gun lobby
See GUN CONTROL: OPPONENTS.

gun ownership
There are an estimated 70 million gun owners in the United States. This estimate is based on such sources as data collected by the National Rifle Association (NRA), the memberships of gun clubs around the country and registrations and permits in the states that require them.

The estimate of 70 million gun owners may be low, because many owners do not belong to the NRA or a local gun club, and states and local governments differ enormously in their requirements for registration and the stringency of their penalties for noncompliance. Even assuming it to be accurate, however, based on the 1990 census one of every three adults in the United States owns a gun; there is likely to be a gun in more than half the nation's 93 million households.

Two seemingly contradictory pieces of data are often quoted about gun owners. They are supposed to own an estimated 140 million firearms, and the typical gun store patron is said to have three handguns, two rifles and a shotgun for a total of seven. If gun store patrons do own an average of seven firearms each, then the total of 140 million is too low, or gun store patrons make up only a portion of the gun-buying public.

Both conclusions are likely to be true. Firearms are virtually indestructible and therefore remain in condition to be bought and sold almost indefinitely with minimum care. Only a few states, such as Massachusetts, require buyers and sellers to report their transactions. A Harris poll conducted for the National Commission on the Causes and Prevention of Violence found that almost half of all rifles and shotguns and slightly more than half of all handguns are acquired secondhand.

There is no shortage of firearms for people to buy. In 1989 U.S. manufacturers made 4 million nonmilitary firearms (down from a peak of 5.8 million in 1974). The year's production included 1.99 million handguns, (50%); 1.382 million rifles (34%); and 688,000 shotguns (17%).

Handguns, mostly semiautomatic pistols and revolvers, are popular because they are small enough to hold and fire with one hand. Until 1985 the favorite weapon for consumers, law enforcement officers and criminals alike was the Smith and Wesson .38 revolver. But in 1985 the U.S. Department of Defense adopted as its standard sidearm a 9mm semiautomatic pistol made by the U.S. subsidiary of the Italian firearms manufacturer Beretta. Civilian sales followed the lead.

Compared with revolvers, semiautomatic pistols hold more ammunition (up to 16 rounds compared to a revolver's six). The 9mm size is compact and easier to conceal, and fits more easily into a small hand.

Because 9mms have been standard-issue military weapons in Europe since before World War II, European manufacturers picked up an enormous share of the American domestic market, so much that they were able eventually to buy up all but one of the major American firearms companies, Sturm Ruger and Company of Southport, Connecticut.

Americans not only own a greater number and variety of firearms than the citizens of any other modern state, they also use their guns more to assault, injure and kill one another. The United States also has more firearms legislation than any other country in the world, approximately 20,000 federal, state and local gun laws, which apparently have had little effect.

The Task Force on Firearms of the National Commission on the Causes and Prevention of Violence examined the ways in which other countries attempt to control the misuse of firearms in two surveys of foreign firearms laws made during 1968. These revealed that foreign countries, with few exceptions, have comprehensive systems of firearms control.

The U.S. State Department asked 102 of its diplomatic posts for information on local firearms laws and the Library of Congress analyzed the laws of 30 countries, 29 in Europe. The European countries all required either a license to carry a firearm or registration of the ownership or sale of each privately owned firearm, or both. At least five European countries totally prohibited the private possession of handguns.

In North and South America, 15 of 19 countries canvassed required a license to possess or carry a firearm or registration of all firearms or both. In Asia and Australia all 21 countries canvassed required a license to possess or carry, or registration of, firearms or both.

In Africa, 25 of 33 nations canvassed required registration of the ownership or sale of firearms. The remaining eight had licensing systems related to ownership or carrying a firearm.

The National Commission asked officials of 20 foreign governments to estimate the extent of handgun ownership per 100,000 population. Franklin Zimring and Gordon Hawkins in their 1987 book *The Citizen's Guide to Gun Control* provided a table ranking ten of the responding countries and the United States.

Swiss officials rated handgun ownership among their citizens as insignificant. Five countries, Ireland, Finland, the Netherlands, Greece and Great Britain, estimated gun ownership to be fewer than 500 per 100,000 population. Yugoslavia estimated 500 to 1,000 per 100,000; Israel, 1,000; Austria, 3,000; and Canada, 3,000. The U.S. rate was 13,500.

Zimring and Hawkins asked themselves why there is such indifference to high levels of violence in the United States. They concluded: ''The principal reason why so many citizens can retain their composure in the face of levels of violence that would topple European governments is that so many of those killed are ghetto dwellers. Most of the urban body count in the United States involves the faceless young black male 'noncitizens' who live and die without conspicuous outpourings of social concern.''

The Death Toll from Guns. The Statistical Abstract of the United States, 1991 offers support for Zimring and Hawkins' assertion that guns present a major threat to blacks. In 1988, per 100,000 population, there were 7.9 white homicides and 58.0 black homicides. Data on the weapons used in homicides in 1989 reveal that guns were involved in 62.4%. After shooting the next most common method (18%) was cutting and stabbing. The

most common motive for murder—in 35.2% of the cases—was an argument. In 23.7% of the cases the motive was unknown; the commission of a felony provided the circumstances for 21.4% of the murders.

Guns threaten the lives of those who live in white communities in a different way. In 1988 there were 30,407 suicides in the United States. Males accounted for 24,078 of them. Per 100,000 population, 21.7 white males committed suicide, while 11.5 black males took their own lives. Males used firearms in 65% of suicides, while females used them in 39.7%.

For at least three decades, suicides have generally accounted for more than half of the nation's annual firearms fatalities. In 1970 there were 11,772 suicides by firearms. In 1988 there were 18,166 suicides by firearms, a rise from 58% of the deaths to 65%. A recent trend has been a sharp increase in suicides among those under age 24.

Some researchers see American suicides as being more heavily influenced by drugs and alcohol than they are by guns. However, the presence of guns for those under the influence of alcohol or drugs makes spur-of-the-moment suicide more likely. The United States leads the world in use of guns for self-inflicted deaths.

Some experts point out that if a gun is not handy, someone determined to commit suicide will find another method. However, a deep depression, particularly in a teenager, might lighten by the time another method is found.

Shooting also is a more efficient method of committing suicide. One study found that 92% of those who use guns in suicide attempts succeed. Thus guns seldom permit a second chance, yet psychologists find that most people who attempt to kill themselves do not really wish to die.

Those who die by gunfire were personalized in a cover story entitled ''7 Deadly Days'' in the July 17, 1989 issue of *Time,* which chronicled the deaths of 464 ordinary Americans by gunfire during the week of May 1 through May 7.

The *Time* story opened by saying

They are the commonplace tragedies that occur every day in communities across the U.S. The smoldering anger between a husband and wife ignites and ends in a pistol shot. The suffocating weight of depression vanishes, with gun fire, into the imagined peace of death. A hunting trip turns tragic, and a family is destroyed. The stupidity of playing with a loaded weapon leaves a young boy dead. The momentary incivility of a pair of barroom brawlers results in a bloody death. Events like these happen so often that Americans' sense of horror and outrage has been numbed . . .

while the country is numb, the families and friends the dead leave behind are surely not . . . If the U.S. were losing this many people to a killer virus or to a war, there would be a public outcry.

Writing in the November 10, 1989 issue of the *New England Journal of Medicine,* Federal Centers for Disease Control (CDC) researchers James Mercy and Vernon Houk pointed out that the 62,897 people who died of injuries from firearms in the United States during 1984 and 1985 were more than the number of Americans who died during the entire Vietnam conflict. Mercy and Houk were of the opinion that "injury from firearms is a public health problem whose toll is unacceptable."

Opinions Differ About Homeowner Protection. A sense of who is most likely to get killed when someone keeps a gun in the house comes from a 1986 study called "Protection or Peril?" conducted by Dr. Arthur Kellerman, a professor of medicine at the University of Tennessee School of Medicine in Memphis, and Dr. Donald Reay, chief medical examiner of King County, Washington. The researchers concluded that for each defensive, justifiable (self-protection) homicide, there were 43 murders, suicides or accidental deaths. Out of 389 gunshot fatalities in private homes in King County between 1978 and 1983, only nine were motivated by self-defense.

Time's one-week survey had a similar finding. Out of the 464 deaths, only 14 resulted from defensive firing. An alarming 216 suicides—nine of whom first killed someone else—accounted for almost half of the total. Another 22 were preventable accidents, mostly the result of playing with a supposedly unloaded firearm. In many instances, the presence of a gun at a critical moment produced what Karole Avila, a psychiatrist at Detroit Receiving Hospital, has called a permanent solution to a temporary problem.

Such statistics do not refute the assertion that a gun, even if not fired, can save a life. However, sociologist James Wright at Tulane University in New Orleans points out that 90% of crimes in homes occur when the resident is not there. Wright told *Time,* "The vast majority of the population lives in low-crime neighborhoods and has virtually no need for a gun for defensive reasons. A tiny fraction has a great deal of reason to get anything it can get that might help reduce its victimization."

Many people do not come to grips with the fact that owning a handgun means being prepared to live with the aftermath of killing another human being, nor do they wonder whether they will actually be able to pull the trigger if confronted with a criminal. In a May 8,

1989 *U.S. News and World Report* article entitled "Should You Own a Gun for Protection?" George Napper, Atlanta public safety commissioner, said "If you don't actually shoot and a criminal fires at you, it is more dangerous to own a weapon than not to have one at all."

Gun Theft from Private Homes. Police estimate that if a household gun is ever used at all, it is six times more likely to be fired at a member of the family or a friend than at an intruder. Dr. Carl Bell, a Chicago psychiatrist who has conducted research into crime and victimization, claims that a gun is even more likely to be stolen than it is to be used by its owner. Guns are prime targets for burglars because they are easy to sell and profitable. In the rare shootout between a householder and a burglar, the burglar is likely to be more skillful with a gun than the householder.

James Wright collaborated in a study with sociologist Peter Rossi, in which they conducted in-depth interviews over a three-year period, starting in 1982, with 1,874 imprisoned felons. They learned from the inmates that the best source of stolen guns for criminals is home burglaries. More than 80% of the burglars' gun thefts were from private homes. Three out of four gun thieves said that they had come across the guns by chance rather than having set out to steal them. About 70% said they stole the guns to sell or trade rather than for personal use.

Fifty-six percent of inmates agreed that "a criminal is not going to mess around with a victim he knows is armed with a gun," and 57% believed that "most criminals are more worried about meeting an armed victim than they are about running into the police." More than 74% thought that "one reason burglars avoid houses when people are at home is that they fear being shot."

Despite Wright and Rossi's findings that suggest a gun may deter a criminal, most experts believe that owning a gun undermines rather than enhances safety.

Federal Bureau of Alcohol, Tobacco, and Firearms (BATF) officials estimate that only 10% to 20% of guns stolen in the United States are officially recorded as having been stolen. The underrecording is attributed to two major factors. First, many owners feel that they might have somehow done something wrong, and would rather sustain the loss than call attention to themselves. Second, most people in legal possession of a gun have not recorded the gun's serial number, without which authorities cannot enter a record into the national computer register. Nevertheless, as of April 1, 1990, the computer at the National Crime Information Center of the Federal Bureau of Investigation (FBI) contained information on 2.1 million stolen guns.

In states with strict gun control laws, the street resale value of guns is high. A semiautomatic pistol originally sold for $600 in Georgia, which has lenient gun control laws, might sell for as much as $1,500 in Massachusetts, a state with strict gun control laws.

Some gun thieves specialize in what police call "smash-and-grab" robberies. They smash open a gun store's front door and display cases and scoop up as much as they can quickly. Before police arrive in response to the burglar alarm, the thieves have collected a cache of guns and left. In one 1988 New Hampshire robbery, thieves got away with 105 guns, including 45 semiautomatic pistols, 53 revolvers (mostly .357-caliber Magnums) and seven long guns, including an AR-15 assault rifle. By April 1990 only seven guns had been recovered, in separate, unrelated arrests.

Many authorities believe that tighter gun controls might just create a more lucrative black market. They propose that a better approach would be to make the penalties for illegal possession of a gun more severe.

During an interview for an April 29, 1990 *Boston Globe* article entitled "Glut of Guns a Menacing Sign," Glenn Pierce, a Northeastern University professor who conducted a study of the effectiveness of Massachusetts' gun control law, contended that blaming guns for the violence in American cities is simplistic. He told the *Boston Globe* that

> Guns are not the cause, but they are an aggravating factor. The violence we commit and visit on ourselves will be more damaging, given the number of guns out there.
>
> We have to work on what's going on in underclass neighborhoods. The criminal justice system and law enforcement are a small part of the solution. They are dealing with a symptom of a much broader problem in the country: our failure to compete economically and our failure to educate. We have to invest in these areas. We pay now, or we pay later.

(See also ASSAULT WEAPONS; CLASSROOM VIOLENCE; GUN CONTROL: ADVOCATES; GUN CONTROL: OPPONENTS; RIGHT TO BEAR ARMS: THE SECOND AMENDMENT.)

H

habeas corpus   See BILL OF RIGHTS: PROTECTION AGAINST GOVERNMENT TYRANNY.

habitual offenders   See AGE AND CRIME.

handgun control   See GUN CONTROL: ADVOCATES.

hate crimes   Sometimes referred to as "aggressive bigotry," hate crimes victimize people because of some characteristic such as race, religion, ethnicity or lifestyle, or even simply because they are newcomers to an area. Feminists believe that actions motivated by hostility toward women as women should also be considered hate crimes.

Hate crimes are typically small-scale crimes of harassment, assault or vandalism against small groups or individuals by other small groups or individuals. More infrequently they are the results of planned activities by organized hate groups such as the White Aryan Resistance (WAR) or the National Association for the Advancement of White People (NAAWP).

Despite a shortage of consistent hard data, it is generally understood that hate crimes are increasing. Evidence of incidents appears daily in the nation's newspapers.

Typical hate crimes include threats, face-to-face, written and telephoned; assaults, verbal and physical or attacks with weapons; and defacement or destruction of property, from minor vandalism to arson or bombing.

There are few firm statistics on the extent of hate crimes in the United States, but this is expected to change. On April 23, 1990 President Bush signed into law the Hate Crimes Statistics Act, which requires the Justice Department to collect data for the calendar years 1990 through 1994 about certain crimes motivated by race, religion, ethnicity or sexual orientation. Crimes include murder, nonnegligent manslaughter, forcible rape, aggravated assault, simple assault, intimidation, arson and destruction or vandalism of property. The U.S. Attorney General will release annual reports that summarize the data.

The National Organization for Women (NOW) lobbied unsuccessfully to have gender included in the bill. Its exclusion means that murders, physical assaults and attacks on abortion clinics generated by gender bias will be excluded from federal tallies.

The origins of hate crimes are complex. Increases in incidence are generally associated with periods of significant social and economic upheaval. In times of trouble, people have a propensity to look for scapegoats for their anger and fear.

Ervin Staub, a psychologist at the University of Massachusetts at Amherst and author of *The Roots of Evil,*

(1989) explains "In times of great economic insecurity and political turmoil, people need to affirm a sense of their own value. These things shake your identity. You need to recreate a positive view of yourself and the group you are rooted in. But the very definition of yourself as a member of one group includes enmity towards another group."

Xenophobia in the United States. Hostility toward outsiders has a long history in the United States. From the very outset, Native Americans have been the targets of hostility and unequal treatment. In some American cities that have large Native American populations, it is not uncommon today to hear slurs in everyday conversation.

Political radicalism has been the focus of a great deal of officially encouraged hatred throughout the 20th century. During the post-World War I "red scare," the federal government under the direction of Attorney General A. Mitchell Palmer made nationwide mass arrests (the "Palmer raids") of political and labor agitators, among them thousands of immigrants. These people were held for long periods on groundless charges and ultimately given mock trials. Hundreds were deported. In December 1919 the transport ship *Buford* alone carried 249 aliens from New York to Russia, including well-known anarchists Emma Goldman and Alexander Berkman.

African-Americans have long been targets of hatred. When African-Americans were slaves there was little need for formalized segregation, although the treatment of the few hundred thousand African-Americans who were free or quasi-free foreshadowed what happened once slavery was ended. Free African-Americans were denied full rights and privileges of citizenship, deprived of equality in the courts and restricted in their freedom of assembly and movement.

Segregation, backed by legal codes and extralegal customs, began in the North and permeated all aspects of free African-American life by 1860. Segregation laws became increasingly harsh as they spread to the West. After the post-Civil War Reconstruction period ended, the elaborate pattern of legally codified segregation, that body of law and custom that later came to be known as Jim Crow, grew quickly in the South, where it remained in force until successful challenges began in the 1950s.

One State's Experience. Even before the Hate Crimes Statistics Act went into effect in 1990, police departments of some cities around the nation already had units devoted to the investigation of hate crimes. In 1990 the Boston Police Department's Community Disorders Unit

investigated 273 such cases, substantiated 243 and made arrests or sought injunctions that barred an individual from approaching the victim again in 20% of the cases. The total reflected a rise in hate crimes for the third year in a row.

In January 1991 the Massachusetts Executive Office of Public Safety, Crime Reporting Unit, issued *Hate Crime in Massachusetts: Preliminary Annual Report, January–December 1990*. Hate crime is defined by Massachusetts General Laws as

> any criminal act coupled with overt actions motivated by bigotry and bias including, but not limited to, a threatened, attempted or completed overt act motivated at least in part by racial, religious, ethnic, handicap, or sexual orientation prejudice, or which otherwise deprives another person of his constitutional rights by threats, intimidation or coercion, or which seeks to interfere with or disrupt a person's exercise of constitutional rights through harassment or intimidation.

The statewide hate crime data contained in the yearly report cover the period from January to August 1990. In 27% of the crimes, the victims suffered personal injury. In those incidents that involved simple or aggravated assault, 43% of the victims were injured. Treatments ranged from a bandage on a cut lip to hospital admission.

The Massachusetts report analyzed 266 crimes inspired by race, religion, ethnicity, sexual preference or the presence of a handicap. Approximately 67% were reported by the Boston Police Community Disorders Unit; the remaining 33% came from the rest of the state. The order of "bias motivations" was antiblack (29.3), antiwhite (19.3), anti-Semitic (14.6), antigay (male) (12.1%), anti-Hispanic (11.1), anti-Asian (11.1%) antiother race, Pakistani, Arab and unspecified (1.7%), antihandicap (0.3%) and antilesbian (.03%).

The most frequent victim groups in the study were white (42%), black (31%), Asian (14%) and Hispanic (8.7%). Victims ranged in age from 6 to 68, with an average age of just under 29. Seventy-five percent of the victims were male.

Offenders ranged in age from 11 through 56, with an average age of 22. Eighty-nine percent of the attackers were male. The races of the offenders were white (58%), black (30%), Hispanic (4%) and Asian (1.1%), and the race of the remaining 6.9% was unknown. In 175 cases (65.8%), the target of the hate crime was a person; in 60 cases (22.6%), private property; in 11 cases (4.1%), public property; and in 2 cases (0.8%), religious property.

The most frequent form of hate crime (143 incidents, or 54%) was verbal harassment or slurs, followed by spray-painted graffiti (35 cases or 13.3%), property damage (21 cases or 8%) and threatening mail (6 cases or 2.3%). In 10% of the cases, a previous incident had been reported against the victim. In only seven cases (less than 3% of all incidents) were there any signs of involvement by an organized hate group.

The report emphasized that hate crimes were likely to be underreported, for various reasons. In many cases, victims fail to report the crimes, either from fear or unwillingness to acknowledge that they have been targets of bigotry. Among victims who do report hate crimes, some also cannot or will not admit that the motive was bias or bigotry. Among police and prosecutors who receive reports of such crimes, a lack of trained awareness can result in a failure to record them as hate crimes.

Hate Crimes Aimed at Women. Hate crimes are those directed at individuals solely because they are members of a particular group. Attacks against specific women may or may not qualify as hate crimes. However, crimes directed against women because they are women are on the rise.

Women as a group make an easy target for hate crimes because around the world they are held in low esteem. Just how bleak their status is was evident in a February 3, 1992 *Boston Globe* article entitled "The Grim Mystery of the World's Missing Women." Demographers reported that in some parts of the world, particularly in Asia, the preference for males is so strong that females have a significantly lower chance of surviving to adulthood. Some studies have found that girls receive less food than boys. Others have found that parents are more likely to seek medical care for boys.

In a January/February *Bostonia* article entitled "Hate Crimes Against Women: Being As Nasty As They Want to Be," sociologist Jack Levin of Northeastern University in Boston wrote, "No one needs statistics to be aware that bigotry is making a comeback. Americans now tolerate forms of prejudice and discrimination that a decade ago would have been unthinkable."

Hate as Entertainment. An obvious example of exploitation of hate as entertainment is the routines of comedian Andrew Dice Clay, who has made slurring women a specialty. He was characterized by women who refused to appear with him in a 1990 television show as a "hate monger."

Clay was not alone in reaping benefit from his use of hate as humor. Ellen Goodman described the attraction of hate humor in a May 17, 1990 *Boston Globe* column: "Live from New York, It's the Bigot in the Comic Mask," She wrote: "Their fans praise them for the frankness of their racial slurs, the 'honesty' of their sexual hatred, for telling it like it is . . . It is avantgarde in America to be reactionary. Pop culture is rife with reverse discrimination in favor of discrimination, shattering the taboo against hatred."

University of Syracuse sociologist Gary Spencer has noted the growth of JAP (Jewish American Princess) jokes on campuses around the country. Such jokes contain elements of both anti-Semitism and sex bias. At one end of the spectrum, JAP jokes suggest that Jewish women, as Jewish women, are materialistic. At the more sinister end, they suggest that "When Jewish women go to have their nose jobs their tubes should be tied as well."

Professional comedians are not the only ones who make such jokes. In 1989 the National Institute Against Prejudice and Violence reported the testimony of a former employee of the San Francisco Board of Public Utilities in federal court about a joke made by a onetime president and current member of the board. When discussing a proposal to give employees Martin Luther King, Jr.'s birthday as a holiday, the board member had said, "Shoot four more of them and give them a week off."

The most grotesque expressions of hate against women are in films ostensibly for adults, whose largest audiences are actually among teenagers. Such R-rated "slasher" films depict the torture, assault and murder of women. For example, in *Tool Box Murders,* a glassy-eyed assailant is shown nailing a naked woman to a wall while romantic music plays in the background.

Hate Crimes on the Increase. Increases in hate crimes were revealed in a July 29, 1990 *Boston Globe* article entitled, "Hate Crimes on the Rise in US," by Larry Tye, who reported the results of a 20-city survey of hate crimes. The survey found that hate crimes were up substantially in New York City, Chicago, Denver and Boston.

The last steep rise in hate crimes in the United States was during the recession of the late 1970s. Since widespread tracking of hate crimes did not begin until the mid-1980s, it is not possible to compare current figures with periods in the past when hate crimes have escalated.

In an interview for a May 29, 1990 *New York Times* article entitled "As Bias Crime Seems to Rise, Scientists Study the Roots of Racism," Howard Ehrlich of the

National Institute Against Prejudice and Violence in Baltimore said, "Everyone who collects data reports a steady increase in hate crimes in the last year or two."

Attacks on homosexuals, generally referred to as "gay bashing," had a marked increase. Beginning in 1985, the National Gay and Lesbian Task Force began collecting reports of antilesbian and antigay violence, victimization and defamation. The number of incidents rose from 2,042 in 1985 to 7,031 in 1989.

In April 1990 Vermont's governor and some legislators, in response to the savage beating of a gay man that resulted in massive head injuries, mounted a campaign to pass a bill that would stiffen the penalties for crimes motivated by hate, based on religion, race, sexual orientation or other bias.

In Europe a steep rise in the number of hate crimes mirrored the rise in the United States. In response to a rise in attacks on gays, gay rights advocates in Great Britain began a campaign for equal rights in August 1990. According to their estimates, over a three-year period as many as 50 gay men had been killed.

The Gay London Policing Group, which collates data, estimated that there is an average of 1,000 attacks against homosexuals in London each year. Most incidents are not reported because the victims fear that the incidents will be trivialized or fear that they themselves will come under police scrutiny.

After the fall of the East German Communist Party, right-wing radical organizations gathered strength. A common factor in all the East German reports was the presence of young men identifiable as skinheads—most of them young factory workers—whose hostility was directed against anyone they deemed un-German, including political leftists, blacks, foreigners, Jews and homosexuals. Skinheads are easily recognized by their shaven heads, neo-Nazi tattoos, steel-toed work boots, outspoken racism, and generally menacing and violent behavior.

Beginning in March 1990, rallies have taken place almost every week in East Germany, with Nazi slogans and salutes in evidence. Some participants have openly echoed Hitler's anti-Semitic slogans. Reports have increased of violent physical attacks on foreign workers and of swastikas and anti-Jewish epithets on walls and tombstones. Gypsies have also been the subject of a number of attacks.

On April 20, 1990 right-wing radicals gathered to celebrate Hitler's 101st birthday. A month later they assembled to form a human swastika in front of the East German Parliament. In May 1990, in the coal mining town of Hoyerswerda, skinheads assaulted a group of workers from Mozambique, beating some so severely they had to be hospitalized. In August 1990 skinheads boarded an elevated train in East Berlin, surrounded a lone worker, beat him and stabbed him in the lung. The city of Rostock has become a center of far-right, racist, antiforeign activities.

Some skinheads admitted that their fathers had served in the Communist secret police, suggesting that joining the far right was a way of challenging their parents. While they might have been defying parental political ideology, they appeared to accept their fathers' views on repressiveness.

Ervin Staub in his book *The Roots of Evil* (1989) suggested a psychological rather than a political explanation for such behavior. "Who you are implies, at an emotional level, who you are not, and stress makes you cling all the more stubbornly to your ethnic identity."

Staub, who was born in Hungary, added:

> In Romania it was the Romanians against the Hungarians, in Czechoslovakia it was the Czechs against the Slovaks, and everyone was against the Jews. These enmities are ancient, but they surface whenever life is in turmoil. Devaluing the other elevates the self: this feeling that I am good is all the more important when your world is out of control.

Characteristics of Hate Crimes. As hate crimes have erupted around the world, social scientists have striven to understand the impetus for such acts, particularly when they are done by groups. Among other things, they have found that:

- The victims are usually alone.
- Most of the perpetrators are in their teens or 20s. Nevertheless, the crimes are not expressions of youthful rebellion. The acts express feelings shared by their family and friends.
- The majority of the crimes are committed by groups of four or more. The more people in the group, the more vicious the crime.
- The acts reflect deep feelings of group identity. Such feelings are common in times of economic and political uncertainty and among people who suffered from emotional neglect as children.
- The injury rate is high and lethal. The national average for injuries to an "ordinary crime" assault victim is 29%. In hate crime assaults, the average is 74%. Typically, at least one victim in a hate-based assault requires hospitalization. Victims are four times more likely to need hospitalization than in other types of assaults.

Northeastern University sociologist Jack McDevitt analyzed the events surrounding hate crimes that occurred in Boston from 1983 to 1987. He found that 57% involved issues of turf: They were attacks on someone walking or driving through or working in a neighborhood, or on a family moving into an area where it was not wanted.

A common pattern McDevitt found was that someone wandered into a neighborhood not realizing that he or she was "out of place." For example, a 12-year-old black girl took a shortcut to a convenience store from her school. A group of white youths drove alongside her and asked what she was doing in "their neighborhood." After taunting her, they got out of the car, pushed her down and kicked her, breaking a rib.

Another common tactic used by neighborhood groups on people who venture uninvited into their neighborhood is the so-called pincer movement. A group splits up and some members circle in front of the intended victim, cutting off any possible escape route, while the rest stay behind. Then they narrow down the circle until the group members are close enough to immobilize the victim and inflict a beating without much risk of getting hurt themselves.

Sheer numbers encourage viciousness, probably because a crowd diffuses responsibility and offers anonymity. Syracuse University psychologist Brian Mullen analyzed newspaper accounts of 60 lynchings in the United States earlier in the century. The larger the mob, the more likely the lynching would include burning or mutilation of the victim.

Crowds encouraged a series of sporadic racist acts of violence on June 3, 1943 in Los Angeles known as the "Zoot-Suit Riots." These began between U.S. Navy personnel and members of the Hispanic community clad in zoot suits.

Zoot suits were a fashion fad in the Los Angeles Hispanic community and elsewhere during the 1940s. The distinctive style featured a very long jacket and pants that were full around the knees and tightly pegged at the cuff. The zoot suit wearer wore long, well-greased hair and twirled a lengthy pocket watch chain.

Accompanied by civilian mobs, groups of sailors roamed through downtown streets or traveled in taxicab cavalcades through the east side districts of Los Angeles in search of zoot suit wearers. "Zooters" found on the streets or on streetcars or buses were assaulted and forced to disrobe amid the jibes of the crowd.

Gangs of adolescents retaliated with similar attacks on navy personnel. When public outcries ended the

riots, the claim of both sides was that the other side was "molesting our girls."

The public is prone to dismiss hate crimes as aberrations of the ignorant and undereducated. A May 1989 reprint of a *USA Today* article entitled "Prejudice, Conflict and Ethnoviolence," provided by the National Institute Against Prejudice and Violence, suggests that that view is limited. The institute collected reports of incidents of campus ethnoviolence that appeared in the print media. Between September 1986 and May 1988, occurrences at 155 different institutions of higher education were documented.

Joan Weiss, the institute's executive director, pointed out that it is easy to become disheartened in the face of relentless repetitions of hate crimes. Rather than be discouraged, her organization has developed a multifaceted approach to dealing with violence motivated by bigotry. The institute maintains a clearinghouse of information, publishes a newsletter and educational materials, provides consultation on prevention and handling incidents and conducts research on the causes and nature of incidents and their impact on victims. It also assesses the effectiveness of various methods of response.

Development of prevention strategies by the institute and other organizations such as the Anti-Defamation League and the Center for Democratic Renewal is slow, in part because not enough is known about how to intervene to prevent violent behavior. Experts are in general agreement that intervention to prevent prejudice must begin as early as kindergarten.

A growing interest in prevention is evident from the joining of state and local agencies with community groups to form coalitions and task forces. In response to such efforts several states have passed laws that forbid hate crimes and stipulate penalties for them. Moreover, a few criminal justice systems have used alternative punishments that require reparations in the form of service to the victims or money to repair damage, particularly in cases of vandalism.

(See also HATE GROUPS; PRISON OVERCROWDING: COPING WITH THE COSTS; SKINHEADS.)

hate groups   The secret society commonly known as the Ku Klux Klan, KKK or simply the Klan is estimated to number about 5,000 members. The membership is scattered throughout the United States in small groups, which vie with one another to recruit members. Among an estimated 67 hate groups in the United States with combined memberships of up to 200,000, the Ku Klux Klan (KKK) is the oldest.

Founded in the southern states in the wake of the Civil War to defend the southern way of life against northern efforts to change it, the Klan was devoted to keeping the African-American population from attaining equality and adopted terrorist intimidation, including lynching, shooting and beating, as means to that end. The organization was outlawed by Congress in 1871.

Reorganized in Atlanta, Georgia in 1915 as the Invisible Empire, Knights of the Ku Klux Klan, the Klan continued its well-established practice of intimidating African-Americans. During its brutal history, the Klan has also waged war on other people of color and against Jews.

Klansmen wear white robes with hoods. Their classic tactic of burning a cross in front of a black home is a sign of their presence and a signal of harassment to follow. The various Klans differ, but they all seek to perpetuate the dominance of the white race. Some believe in eliminating Jews and people of color.

Not all white people are deemed acceptable. Reflecting its roots in 19th-century nativism, the Klan includes Catholics among those they choose to hate. Although their literature and speeches are not openly misogynistic, Klan rhetoric does insist that the proper status of women is to be under the domination of men. Those who join the Klan take an oath to "uphold the principles of White Supremacy and the purity of White Womanhood." The Klan, like other white supremacist groups, is rabidly antifeminist; it characterizes feminism as the "Jew-dyke conspiracy against the white race."

In a March/April 1991 *Ms.* magazine article entitled "Women in Hate Groups: Who Are They? Why Are They There?," Helen Zia examined the role of women in hate groups. Although a few Klans had auxiliaries, women could not join Klans before the 1970s. David Duke, Grand Wizard of the Knights of the KKK from 1975 to 1980, opened the ranks of the KKK to women in an aggressive recruitment drive. Rival Klans followed suit.

Darlene Carver is Grand Secretary and wife of the Grand Dragon of the Georgia KKK. Her high rank is exceptional. She acquired the position when her husband was barred by court orders from representing the Klan. One of Darlene's happiest moments was when her granddaughter said her first word: "Nigger."

One of Carver's first acts as Grand Secretary was to put a recorded message on the Klan hotline asking women to take up the cause of teenagers and drugs. In an article entitled "Wake Up White Women" in the publication *Klansman,* she tells women that it is their place to stand up for their children's futures just as their husbands do. In contrast to the "enlightened" view of Carver's position, the same issue of the *Klansman* carried a tirade about the 19th Amendment, blaming women's suffrage for threatening what was left of the "lawful sovereign body, the white male common law citizen."

Doug Seymour, a police officer who infiltrated the California KKK, told Zia that Carver can never realistically aspire to become a Grand Dragon. He likened the KKK's structure to another male bastion—organized crime. Each den of seven to 14 members is expected to produce money for the Grand Dragon's coffers. If more affluent members do not produce funds, the poor members may be forced into burglary or drug trafficking. "There are some functions you bring your wife to, but the criminal activity is conducted like a men's club," Seymour said. "Women are seen as the downfall—the women will betray you."

The woman's job is to indoctrinate the family, but the family can be used to keep her in line. "It is easy to intimidate the women because they fear for their children," according to Seymour.

The husband of a woman who is under suspicion is checked for loyalty and then told to "take care of the problem." Domestic violence is viewed as an acceptable method of bringing her into conformity. As long as she goes along, the Klan offers a woman the security of an extended family.

A white woman who "race-mixes" with a man of color, especially if she has a child, deserves death. If she has an affair, she will be banished. However, her husband's womanizing is taken for granted.

While the Klan offers the lure of the "traditional family" to keep its members involved, the Christian Identity movement focuses on religion as a justification of white supremacy and anti-Semitism. The movement's message essentially says that white Anglo-Saxon Christians are the true chosen people of the Bible. Jesus was a northern European and Jews are the children of Satan. The U.S. Government, referred to as the Zionist Occupation Government (ZOG), controls not only the banks but also the media and most other major institutions, and must be overthrown before the Second Coming. Southern and eastern Europeans and all people of color are "mud people" and have no souls. Homosexuality is a perversion, and a woman is a weaker vessel who must serve the "one man God has given to rule over her."

The Center for Democratic Renewal estimates that there must be up to 30,000 followers belonging to over 100 Christian Identity churches. Many of the churches are associated with paramilitary white supremacist groups, such as the Aryan Nations, and some KKK and neo-Nazi factions. The teachings of such groups includes guerrilla warfare techniques, curricula for teaching children at home and information from groups such as Posse Comitatus, which objects to taxes on the grounds that they go to the illegitimate ZOG.

The Aryan Women's League (AWL), an offshoot of the White Aryan Resistance (WAR), rejects the hominess of the Klan and the religiosity of the Identity groups. A 21-year-old told Zia, "My religion is the white race." WAR, the parent group, is one of the most active recruiters among white supremacy groups. WAR was founded by Tom Metzger, who for a time was the Grand Dragon of the California KKK. Metzger hosts a broadcast called "Race and Reason" on cable TV and records for phone message lines around the country. Called "hatelines" by many, several phone message lines have been shut down. The shutdowns, in the view of WAR, were engineered by ZOG.

WAR, like other male supremacist groups, believes that men have become "demasculinized" by "Jew-dyke" feminists. An Aryan woman is the "seed bearer and life giver" who must give birth to 2.5 babies to maintain the race. According to Metzger, "The feminist movement was started by a Jewish woman to get women into the I-hate-men era."

In Zia's opinion, *The Turner Diaries* (1985), a novel by William Pierce, is taken by many white supremacists as a blueprint for revolution. The book is filled with murders of women and mass lynchings of white women who "race-mix." Two active women, partners of male commandos, die as the makers of history.

Skinheads.   An import from Great Britain, the skinhead style first attracted attention in the United States when a shaven-headed group from Chicago that called itself "Romantic Violence" took part in a national conference of white supremacists in Michigan. The group members displayed the now-familiar shaven heads, neo-Nazi tattoos, Doc Martens boots and outspoken support of racism and violence.

Not everyone with a shaven head (a baldy) or partially shaven head (a two-tone) is a racist. Part of their point is to shock society by their appearance and actions. The color of their shoelaces is one signal of their stance on race. In the Northeast, white shoelaces denote a white-power skinhead; yellow laces signify Asian bashers; pink laces signal gay bashers; however, black laces mean that the wearer is antiracist.

In the opinion of ADL, nonracist skinheads considerably outnumber racist ones, but an ADL survey found that as of the fall of 1990, racist skinheads were active in 31 states, compared with 21 in the fall of 1989. Moreover, their numbers had grown to 3,000 over an eight-month period. Between an ADL report in October 1988 and one in 1990, three murders were attributed to skinheads, as well as scores of assaults on minority group members and vandalism of religious institutions, particularly synagogues. The most troubling trend was a growing pattern of recruitment in high schools and the acquisition of deadly weapons.

Skinheads have tried with varying levels of success to recruits students directly on school campuses. In Waco, Texas they sent a mass mailing to parents of students at Waco High School. The letter addressed to "proud parents" warned of the dangers posed by "minority gangs and drug pushers" and proposed that "it is time that the common White Americans stand up and demand that their children attend schools not polluted with drugs, gangs, and anti-Christian immorality." The letter offered to send additional information on request.

The favorite weapons of skinheads tend to be crude and simple: knives, bats, chains and steel-toed Doc Martens boots. However, considerable evidence has come to light that they now possess more deadly weapons, including semiautomatic weapons, gunpowder and detonators. Skinheads have been helped in the acquisition of this weaponry by other organized hate groups.

Eric Andrew Anderson, whose master's thesis at Washington State University focused on the skinheads of Great Britain and San Francisco, has pointed out that violence and machismo are the core ideas of the skinhead culture. The record of skinhead activity throughout the nation confirms Anderson's assessment. Skinheads have beaten, stomped and stabbed other skinheads, punk rockers, long-haired hippies, gays and, in the case of racist skinhead groups, members of despised racial and religious groups. Such battles have often taken place in clubs, with the result that owners have either been forced to bar skinheads or had authorities close down the club.

Each April around Hitler's birthday, a festival of youth is sponsored by the Church of Jesus Christ Christian Aryan Nations in Hayden Lake, Idaho. The festival, begun by the Reverend Richard Butler, hosts gatherings for neo-Nazis from around the world. The influence of the older white supremacists who come can be significant. Following the 1990 festival, racist skinheads launched a series of attacks throughout Portland and Seattle. (See SKINHEADS).

Mainstreaming Hate. While WAR and the skinheads may represent the most blatant expressions of white supremacy, David Duke reflects the movement's efforts to insinuate itself into mainstream America. Duke has had a much publicized lifelong association with white supremacist groups, including the American Nazi party. With that background, he won a seat in the Louisiana state legislature in 1989. He lost races for the U.S. Senate in 1990 and governor in 1991, but in doing so he collected more than half of the white vote.

Duke's popularity appears to be based on his racist stance. When an outspoken critic of Duke's, GOP state committeewoman Beth Rickey, spoke at a Women's Republican Club function, she was booed. One person in the audience said, "I don't care if David is a Nazi as long as he tells the niggers where to go."

Duke is well known for his skillful handling of the media. To questions about his Nazi past, he says, "I was an angry young man. I wanted to make the world a better place." He compares his youthful radicalism to Jesse Jackson's.

He has rearranged his racist arguments into less abrasive language. He now talks about the "welfare underclass" that must be eliminated by getting rid of "shirkers and the lazy." Many women think that he is attractive, but the base of his support is men who feel victimized.

Three women worked on his campaign staff. One of them told Zia that she joined David because he had a "better message" for her. She said, "I want white grandchildren. I want white great-grandchildren. We have a right to want white blood. I don't believe that is racist. I believe in White."

Duke's publishing history is bizarre. Under a pseudonym, he wrote a sex manual, *Finderskeepers,* in which he enumerated the advantages of loving a married man and advised "women's libbers" on how to use their careers to find men. Under another pseudonym (Mohammed X) he wrote *African Atto,* a street-fighting manual for blacks. The style is comparable to a WAR newsletter and is filled with deliberate misspellings and advice such as the avoidance of fatty, weakening white milk. Duke claims it was a satire.

Duke's rapid movement into the mainstream may serve as an incentive for other white supremacists. A Klan hateline message boasted that a Duke victory would be one for "the entire racist movement."

Besides running for office, hate groups have found another way to tweak the noses of those who don't share their views, and to hit them in their pocketbooks. After having been denied a parade permit and having gone to court as a consequence, 30 Klan members and Aryan youth groups marched in Palm Beach, Florida on July 28, 1990 before about 1,000 spectators, journalists and police officers.

The Klan's leader, Richard Ford, has honed a strategy that enables a group of about a dozen people to reach hundreds of thousands of viewers, listeners and readers. The first step calls for the Klan to ask a high profile (well-known, wealthy) town such as Palm Beach for a parade permit. When the town refuses, the second step is to call the American Civil Liberties Union (ACLU) to defend the Klan's First Amendment rights (the right to assemble) and to get a federal judge to rule that the town's parade ordinance is unconstitutional. The third step is to demand legal fees and damages from the town. The fourth step is to hold a news conference before the parade/rally. The final step is to invite reporters to a "cross lighting."

When the Federal District Court judge ruled that the Palm Beach parade ordinance under which the Klan had been denied a permit was unconstitutional, the parade was scheduled. Eager to avoid violence, the Palm Beach Police Department brought in reinforcements from four neighboring cities and from the county sheriff's office, at a cost of thousands of dollars.

The high expense that the Klan can force on a community despite its small membership can be seen from a White Supremacist Rally on January 6, 1990 in Atlanta, at the Georgia Capitol. About 90 Klan members, surrounded by 1,600 National Guard troops and 800 police officers, rallied on January 15 to protest the observance of Martin Luther King, Jr. Day. The 2,400 troops and police officers were there to restrain about 50 counterdemonstrators.

The Anti-Defamation League, the Center for Democratic Renewal and the ACLU, organizations that monitor Klan activity, claim that the Klan's level of activity continues to increase. One monitoring group said that during every summer there is a Klan marching somewhere every weekend.

Instead of recruiting new members, some Klans were actually engaged in a quest for respectability. Local Klans in Lakeland, Florida began a "Krush Krack Kocaine" campaign in the spring of 1989, patrolling the streets against suspected drug dealers. Local blacks were angered when Klan members posed as police officers and detained two black women, one of whom turned out to be a police officer impersonating a prostitute.

The southern regional director of the NAACP (National Association for the Advancement of Colored People), Earl Shinhoster, expressed African-Americans' opinion of the Klan efforts to change its image when he said, ''Any way you look at it, it still spells K.K.K.''

In 1987 the Southern Poverty Law Center won a civil suit against Robert Shelton and the United Klans of America (UKA). The jury awarded $7 million in the death of a young black man, Michael Donald, who, after he had been killed, had been hanged in a public street ''to get the message out to, not just the state of Alabama, but the whole United States that the Klan didn't want black people on juries.''

The judgment effectively bankrupted the UKA, but by the early 1990s the Klans seemed to be making a comeback.

(See also HATE CRIMES; REVENGE; SKINHEADS; VIOLENT CRIMES AGAINST WOMEN: THEIR CONNECTION TO GENDER BIAS.)

Hell's Angels   See OUTLAW MOTORCYCLE GANGS.

homelessness and vulnerability to violence
Homelessness not only threatens biological survival, it severely damages self-esteem. It makes it impossible to create any zone of order or privacy. Boundaries of private life are rendered fluid and open to penetration by any outsider.

University of Maryland social work professors John Belcher and Frederick DiBlasio, in their 1990 book *Helping the Homeless: Where Do We Go From Here?*, assert that the public is ambivalent about the homeless because much homelessness is a direct result of economic dislocation. ''The homeless are viewed with disdain because they raise doubts about the ability of our economic system to create prosperity. On the other hand, society is curious about their plight because they are, in the end, human beings, like us.''

During the Great Depression, there was widespread recognition that many people were homeless because of economic factors. Following World War II until the 1970s, when anyone thought about them, the homeless were assumed to be largely made up of ''skid row'' alcoholics. Such assumptions ignored much of the rural poor living in shanties that barely qualified as housing.

The ranks of the urban homeless began to swell in the late 1950s when new drugs made it possible to

control the psychoses of many mentally ill people so that they could live outside of mental hospitals. Politicians seized on the opportunity to cut the budgets of large institutions but failed to fund mental health centers and support services to aid the newly released.

Populations of mental hospitals were cut to a tenth of their former size, and many former mental patients found themselves with no place to live. With no home and no way of obtaining medication, many became psychotic once again but were no longer eligible for hospital care because new legislation required them to be a danger to themselves or others in order to be admitted.

Other changes increased the population of the urban homeless. In the 1970s and 1980s, several factors came together to reduce drastically the amount of housing stock available to the poor and near poor. The Reagan administration virtually eliminated federally supported low-cost housing programs for working-class and poor families, and the building of such homes ground to a halt. Among middle- and upper-income families, divorces, delayed marriages and the setting up of separate homes by adult unmarried baby boomers had the effect of making the number of separate households grow faster than they had in earlier decades.

Thus, as the total amount of available housing declined, many more people began bidding for scarce shelter, which not only drove up the cost for the poor but increased the percentage of income paid for housing among all economic classes. Where once households had spent 20% or 30% of their income on housing, 40%, 50% and more became the norm.

Another phenomenon called the gentrification movement further exacerbated the housing shortage in many industrial countries. Movement out of the city by middle- and upper-income families that had been going on since the end of World War II reversed itself. Young, upwardly mobile professionals and businesspeople, tired of the suburbs, began to purchase rundown low-rent housing in borderline or poor neighborhoods to refurbish and make into middle-class homes. In doing so, they created a whole new lucrative real estate market, a boom that inflated the cost of all housing and drastically reduced the available stock of low-cost rental housing. In the process, low-income families and many of the elderly were often forced out of their homes and into the streets.

People who have no homes have few options. Some double up with family or friends, an arrangement that tends not to last because overcrowding frays tempers.

Others live under bridges and in abandoned buildings, jails, hospitals or shelters. Many simply live in the streets huddled in doorways or cardboard boxes. Estimates of the number of homeless people in the United States vary from a low of 300,000 to a high of 3 million.

The ranks of the homeless include those who have lost their homes because of social factors: children and teenagers who have run away from or been thrown out of their homes, people who have a mental illness, substance abusers, victims of family violence and handicapped people who are unemployable. The homeless also include those who have lost their housing because of economic factors: a rise in rent, a calamity such as an apartment fire, the loss of a job or a divorce that leaves a parent without child support and the grim choice of choosing between food and shelter.

Poor people who lose their housing for whatever reason are unlikely to have the money needed to move into a new place. Before moving in, a new tenant generally must pay the first and last months' rent (insurance against moving out without paying the final month's rent) and a security deposit to repair any damage that might be done during the tenant's occupancy.

Two or three decades ago, a landlord typically asked for only one month's rent and a small deposit. Deposits now may be as much as a half or a full month's rent. Where once it might have cost a few hundred dollars to move into new housing, today it might cost a few thousand. Having utilities turned on also can be expensive because they too require deposits.

Having no home complicates the most ordinary acts of daily living: cooking a meal, taking a bath, going to the bathroom, attending school, being safe from the weather and most important being safe from the intrusions of other people. Temporary housing such as shelters and welfare hotels may get the homeless in out of the weather and provide toilets, but most of the other aspects of daily living remain difficult and sometimes impossible, and risks of assault are often worsened.

Because of violence in shelters, many homeless people would rather take their chances in the streets. Children living in welfare hotels are often surrounded by violence. Not only are they at risk of being preyed upon, they are also at risk of being socialized to violence. In his 1988 book *Rachel and Her Children,* Jonathan Kozol quoted one of the mothers he interviewed in a welfare hotel, who said, "My kids ain't no killers. But if they don't learn to kill they know they're goin' to die."

The ranks of the newly poor homeless keep growing in the United States and in other industrialized nations around the world. A loss of manufacturing jobs and a shift to a lower-paid service economy in the United States has left many people underemployed or unemployed, and for many of them the specter of homelessness looms. Ambivalence about whether the homeless are "us" or "them" continues to grow.

homicide   Homicide is the killing of one human being by another. The term is often preceded by some qualification; the word is often used alone to mean unlawful homicide.

Unlawful homicide refers to the crimes of murder and manslaughter. A victim must be an independent person, that is, not still in the womb as would be the case in an abortion. The act itself must cause the death, which must occur within one year and a day after the act.

Lawful homicide occurs when someone uses reasonable force to prevent a crime or arrest an offender, in self-defense or defense of others and sometimes in defense of his or her property.

Excusable homicide involves a killing that took place in lawful self-defense or by misadventure (an accident not involving gross negligence).

(See also ASSASSIN; CAPITAL CRIME; MANSLAUGHTER; MASS MURDERERS; MURDER: U.S. PROFILE; SERIAL KILLERS.)

homosexual rape   See RAPE.

I

illiteracy in prisons   In a speech about PLUS (Project Literacy, U.S.) presented to the Correctional Education Association (CEA) on July 27, 1987, James Duffy, president of communications at Capital Cities/ABC, Inc., said:

I know I don't have to convince you of the urgency of the illiteracy problem in this country. The facts speak for themselves: across America more than 20 million adults 17 and older cannot read or write beyond 4th-grade level; another 30 to 35 million are semiliterate, with basic skills at the 5th to 8th grade levels. . . . three-quarters of the people in prison are functionally illiterate. Eighty percent lack a high school diploma. Add to that the fact that most lack significant employment history, and that most come from a poverty-level background. Combined with the hopelessness bred by illiteracy, is it any wonder that the prison recidivism rate is as high as 60 percent?

I am not about to suggest that illiteracy is the cause of all crime in this country—although research suggests a strong causal relationship between illiteracy and one's chances of ending up in the correctional system . . . Illiteracy may be the single greatest obstacle you face in providing a rehabilitative structure within the correctional environment. Illiteracy in prison creates a subculture of frustration and despair. It creates tremendous difficulties in developing successful vocational and academic skills programs for the incarcerated. In general, illiteracy renders a prisoner unable to move directly from the correction institution into the mainstream of society, and into a productive and independent life.

PLUS was a joint project begun in January 1986 by Capital Cities/ABC and the Public Broadcasting Service (PBS). Duffy told his audience, "The illiteracy cost to the United States is estimated at more than $225 billion annually in unemployment, poor job productivity, welfare, crime, and poor self-help health care. Among industrialized nations, America has the lowest level of literacy."

During a year of planning and research for the project, Duffy and the staffs of PBS and ABC learned about a variety of criminal justice literacy programs, such as one sponsored by Virginia's then-Governor Gerald Baliles called "No read, no release" and a literacy alternative sentencing program sponsored by the late District Attorney Mario Merola of the Bronx, New York. They discovered that an array of voluntary organizations across the nation labored to alleviate illiteracy. The biggest obstacle faced by both publicly financed and voluntary programs was that illiteracy remains a hidden problem, despite its massive proportions.

The unique contribution PLUS could offer to the national literacy effort was its capacity to inform huge audiences. Out of the networks' participation a number of programs resulted, including news programs, documentaries, local programming, after-school specials, serial segments and public service announcements.

As a consequence of the favorable response to their efforts and because the problem is long term, the two networks extended their original commitment and decided to focus their attention on three tasks:

1. Support for the widespread attainment of an 11th-grade reading level, sufficient to read and understand the Constitution, to participate in civic affairs and to vote.

2. Improvement of work force literacy needed to upgrade basic skills and to regain America's competitive edge in the global marketplace.

3. Reversal of the continuing growth of an "underclass" by approximately 700,000 school dropouts each year.

During the extended phase of PLUS, several major projects were offered to a national audience.

The largest teleconference that had ever been held took place on June 23, 1987, put on by the American Association of Community and Junior Colleges and sponsored by IBM and PLUS. The theme was "literacy, your community, and its work force."

A prime-time special on ABC entitled "A Star-Spangled Celebration of Literacy and Liberty" on July 4, 1987 delivered a message that illiteracy was widespread but literacy was attainable.

ABC aired a made-for-television movie on September 13, 1987, entitled *Bluffing It,* in which actor Dennis Weaver played an illiterate man who had built a successful career in a steel plant, but whose self-esteem was threatened when he was promoted into a job that required reading and writing.

PBS aired a documentary "A Job to Be Done," on October 21, 1987 about work force issues.

Many other local programs and public service announcements were done as a consequence of the push from PLUS.

Not everyone was impressed by this effort to address illiteracy. At a conference called the National Forum for Youth at Risk in Washington, D.C. during December 1987, a report released by the Education Commission of the States attacked what it called the "popular wisdom" about adult literacy. The report criticized the popular perception that volunteer coalitions, commercial media and corporate America can solve the problem of illiteracy. This assertion was based on the fact that the two largest volunteer tutoring programs in the United States reach only 127,000 clients each year, a little more than half of 1% of those in need. Moreover, the report said that contrary to popular opinion, the majority of adults in need of help to gain literacy are white Americans, not minorities.

Illiteracy is a risk for the society at large as well as for the individual who is illiterate because being unable to read and write limits job choices or prevents a person from getting a job at all, which may ultimately lead to crime. Illiteracy also poses a physical risk for an individual and his or her family because warning signs regarding public hazards are often written, as are directions on medicine labels and household appliances.

Illiteracy also carries an emotional burden of a lifetime of being assessed as dumb and of wondering if the assessment is accurate. Low self-esteem can also lead to crime. If inmates are not taught anything else useful in prison, at the very least they ought to be taught to read.

(See also CALIFORNIA CORRECTIONS SYSTEM; CORRECTIONAL EDUCATION; JAILS; JUVENILE JUSTICE: A SYSTEM OF CONTRADICTIONS; PRISON OVERCROWDING: COPING WITH THE COSTS; TREATMENT PROGRAMS IN PRISON.)

in re Gault   See CHILDREN'S RIGHTS; JUVENILE JUSTICE: A SYSTEM OF CONTRADICTIONS.

incest   See SEXUAL ABUSE OF CHILDREN.

incident-based crime data reporting system

Encouraged by federal action, new systems of reporting crime are being phased in across the country. The systems known as incident-based crime data reporting (IBR) systems are designed to provide data not available in the traditional Justice Department-sponsored, Federal Bureau of Investigation (FBI)-administered Uniform Crime Reporting (UCR) program.

The UCR was established in the 1920s by the International Association of Chiefs of Police (IACP). The program's goal was to standardize data collected by law enforcement agencies on a state and local level, despite the variability of state criminal codes, law enforcement practices and data collection systems. Participation in the UCR has remained voluntary since the beginning, although some state legislatures have mandated it.

Since the 1970s, increased use of UCR data to make policy decisions and award federal support have encouraged participation in the program. A Comprehensive Data System sponsored from 1972 to 1980 by the Law Enforcement Assistance Agency (LEAA) created state UCR programs that dramatically increased the quantity and quality of available data.

The UCR has retained the same format since its inception. Its major flaws are a lack of detail on offense and arrest data, particularly for less serious crimes; limited information about the victims of crime and lack

of correlation among data on offenses, arrests and victims. UCR analyses are usually restricted to eight "crime index" offenses: murder and nonnegligent homicide, forcible rape, robbery, aggravated assault, burglary, larceny-theft, motor vehicle theft and arson.

During the 1980s, the FBI and the Bureau of Justice Statistics (BJS) joined in a effort to promote the development of a national incident-based crime data reporting system (NIBRS). Many state and local law enforcement agencies adopted incident-based systems, and the U.S. Congress directed all federal agencies to adopt the approach.

The NIBRS approach improves on the UCR program in two significant ways: It collects information on many aspects of crime incidents not covered by the UCR, and it records multiple offenses committed during single crimes, making it possible to link resulting arrests with the various offenses.

In multiple-offense incidents, the UCR format collects information from police reports on only the most serious offense. A report to the FBI of an incident that included both a burglary and a forcible rape would mention only the rape.

The UCR program collects data in summary (aggregate or sum total) fashion, and the characteristics and circumstances of each offense or incident are therefore lost. The NIBRS not only aggregates data but also can maintain each discrete unit. Because of the nature and format of the computerized NIBRS databases, researchers can ask specific crime and offense-related questions.

The richness of NIBRS detail can be used to examine characteristics of crimes, such as the use of weapons, involvement of drugs or alcohol, location or time of day. For example, one analysis of the age relationship between sexual assault victims and offenders found that 56% of victims were assaulted by offenders within their own age range and 36% were assaulted by someone younger. Only 8% were assaulted by someone older.

An analysis of where simple assaults and simple batteries took place revealed that 54% occurred in residences and 33% in open areas or streets. A breakdown of simple assaults and batteries that occurred in public businesses found that 38% happened in places where liquor was sold, which seems unsurprising, but 37% happened in other kinds of businesses, which does not seem so obvious.

The summary UCR program collects information on the use of weapons only in connection with homicides, robberies and aggravated assaults (distinguished from simple assaults by greater use of violence and perhaps intent to do bodily harm or to rob). Given the frequency of simple assaults, information about the use of weapons in connection with them would be useful to law enforcement officials. One analysis of simple assaults and simple batteries found that weapons were used in 41%, typically whatever was handy.

If done well, IBR systems will vastly improve the quality of crime data; however, a high level of coordination and cooperation is required to ensure accuracy.

(See also CRIME STATISTICS; FEAR OF CRIME; NATIONAL CRIME INFORMATION CENTER OPERATION [NCIC].)

indefinite detention   See BILL OF RIGHTS PROTECTION: AGAINST GOVERNMENT TYRANNY.

informants   Many state, local and federal law enforcement agents admit that much, if not most, of their success in criminal investigations comes as the result of information supplied by informants, better known as "snitches." In recognition of the need for such information, in 1989 Congress passed a law to encourage such cooperation by allowing snitches to be rewarded with up to 25% of the proceeds seized in a successful criminal prosecution.

Such rewards come in addition to sums already routinely paid to informants, and the lighter sentences they typically receive in their own cases. Critics of the practice point out that the rewards serve as an incentive to lie. Even when the information is truthful, the dangers of relying on informants, their hidden costs and the potential for abuse often exceed the advantages.

A brief biography of a "career informant" was described in a March 1991 *Boston Magazine* article entitled "Snitch." The author, John Strahinich, told the story of the high-stakes deals cut by longtime narcotics addict and career criminal David Nagle.

The prison sentences Nagle received over his years in crime totaled 165 years. Nevertheless, before his current sentence in the Hampshire House of Corrections in Massachusetts, he had spent fewer than eight years behind bars.

By Massachusetts law, the uncorroborated testimony of an immunized witness (a witness who has been given immunity from prosecution for his or her own participation in a crime) is not enough to convict a defendant. However, a prisoner now serving at the Massachusetts Correctional Institution at Gardner, James Rodwell, was convicted of homicide on the evidence of two infor-

mants. One, Francis Holmes, in return for immunity, claimed that he saw Rodwell kill the victim. The other informant was Nagle. There were no gun, no fingerprints, no other eyewitnesses—no other evidence linking Rodwell to the murder.

Rodwell had been arrested and jailed for the then three-year-old murder in the summer of 1981 where Nagle was awaiting trial on five charges of armed robbery and one count of kidnapping, among other things. In July Nagle contacted investigators and told them that Rodwell had boasted to him about the murder. In return for his testimony, Nagle received a lighter sentence in his own case. The jurors at Rodwell's trial did not know that Nagle had been a police and government informant at least since 1974, and possibly as early as 1972.

Court records and similar documents indicate, and law enforcement officers as well as criminals attest, that Nagle has provided information, or worked as a paid informant for, the Federal Drug Enforcement Agency (DEA), the Federal Bureau of Investigation (FBI), the U.S. Department of the Treasury, the Massachusetts State Police, the Boston Police and the police of smaller cities in the Greater Boston metropolitan area. In some cases Nagle was paid money in sums ranging from a regular $25 to $50 from a Boston police detective in the early 1970s to $2,000 from a DEA agent in the early 1980s. In total, Nagle believes that he has received as much as $20,000 from the DEA alone. Other observers believe the sum is much higher.

In several cases, Nagle received substantially lighter sentences than he would have gotten otherwise, and many suspended sentences, for his own crimes. By his own estimates, before his current incarceration in 1985, Nagle committed more than 100 armed robberies. Law enforcement officials estimate the total to be about 200. Over a 13-year period prior to 1985, he was brought into court on a total of 116 serious felony charges, including 56 counts of armed robbery, 21 counts of larceny, eight counts of receiving stolen goods, four counts of assault with a dangerous weapon, four firearms violations and three counts of kidnapping. Nevertheless, he has never spent time in the state's maximum security prison at Walpole, the usual site for repeat offenders of serious crimes.

In a number of cases in which Nagle served as an informant, other evidence suggests that the people he informed on were guilty as charged. However, according to Strahinich, there is documented evidence that in at least one case he lied.

Law enforcement agents who know Nagle well, including his half brother, who is a federal agent, describe him as a "habitual, pathological and calculating" liar. A retired Boston police officer who used Nagle during the 1970s and 1980s described him as "a con man from the word go." He said, "Whatever he told me, I wouldn't believe until I checked it out."

Despite the fact that they did not trust him, whenever they thought his information was useful, law enforcement agents continued to use Nagle. Defense attorneys and other inmates claim that when he had no information to give, he fabricated it in hopes of making a deal.

Even while in prison, Nagle continues to keep in touch with his law enforcement contacts. According to other inmates, he regularly reads and clips news articles of criminal cases and tries to wheedle information out of inmates on cases against them. He has also used the mother of another inmate to research newspaper libraries for him.

Several law enforcement officials likened David Nagle to Leslie Vernon White, a California inmate who was profiled on the CBS TV program *60 Minutes*. White admitted fabricating the confessions of other inmates, sometimes without ever having talked to them, and then testifying in court against them. White demonstrated on television how he could phone a police station from jail and pose as a detective to learn details about a criminal investigation. A subsequent *Los Angeles Times* story revealed that some imprisoned informants kept newspaper clipping files on cases in which they were testifying against other inmates.

Following White's admissions, a special prosecutor was assigned to investigate several cases in which informants had been used. Moreover, the California state legislature passed a law restricting the use by prosecutors of informants, the only such law in the nation.

The author of the "snitch law," Gigi Gordon, a defense attorney, believes that the growing dependence on informants results in lazy law enforcement and passive investigations, in which the police wait for the informants to come to them.

David Nagle's career illustrates the changing mores of the criminal subculture. Not too long ago, informants in prison had to fear for their lives and be kept in protective custody. Their current safety appears to be related to their numbers. Nagle estimates that as many as 50% to 60% of his fellow inmates at Northhampton have acted as informants at some time.

Nagle views himself as a pioneer. He said, "I was one of the first ones to see how the system worked. It's a new game now. It's who gets there first."

Despite their new status, some informants do run a risk. In their book *Mass Murder* (1985), Jack Levin and James Alan Fox described the use of informants in a mass murder case against the Johnston brothers, the leaders of a family-operated burglary business in southeastern Pennsylvania. When several members of the gang were called before a grand jury in 1978, the brothers decided to eliminate the informants.

When the Johnstons were brought to trial for the murders, successful prosecution depended on gaining the cooperation of several gang members and other criminals willing to testify. Giving testimony was particularly rewarding for one informant who had admitted participating in the beating and drowning of one of the victims. He was allowed to plead guilty to a charge of voluntary manslaughter with a sentence of one to three years concurrent with the term he was already serving for transportation of stolen goods. In other words, he served no time for the murder.

Levin and Fox do not necessarily object to the use of informants, but they point out that the police use of informants in this case precipitated the murders, to eliminate them as witnesses. They write, "There is . . . an obligation on the part of such investigators to see that their witnesses are protected from the defendants against whom they testify."

(See also PROSECUTORIAL DISCRETION IN THE DISPOSITION OF CASES.)

inmate violence See PRISONERS: MANAGEMENT OF THE PERSISTENTLY VIOLENT; PRISON OFFICERS' CODE OF SOLIDARITY: A SHIELD AGAINST VIOLENCE.

insurance fraud See ARSON.

J

jails Over the course of 900 years of Anglo-American criminal justice, since the reign of King Henry II, the jail has been used primarily for temporary incarceration of those awaiting further judicial action. Although some jails, such as those in Rhode Island and Delaware, are administered by the state, the American jail, like its

English forebear, is typically a local responsibility. Run by local administrations, jails are often poorly financed.

There is a clear distinction between the ''lockup'' (sometimes referred to as the police lockup) and the jail. Those held in lockups are usually confined for less than 48 hours and typically are charged with offenses to be heard in lower courts.

Lockups as a rule are found in larger cities and generally serve specific areas of a city; a large city is likely to have several, one in each of its police districts or precincts.

In general, jails are administered by police departments, county sheriffs' offices or correctional authorities. Although distinctions often blur, a jail is typically a place of temporary and pretrial confinement, while a prison is a place of more permanent postsentencing confinement. The jail is intended to hold individuals while they await trial, are held for another jurisdiction, serve sentences of less than a year or await transportation to another facility such as a prison, mental hospital or work farm. Jails are run differently from prisons. The differences are reflected in the penal codes, sentencing, conditions for the serving of sentences and jail's relationship with the court system.

Most individuals who are processed through the criminal justice system following arrest are received initially through a facility such as a jail or a holding area, where they remain confined until released on bail or via some other device, or through trial to sentencing or acquittal.

In their 1980 book, *The American Jail*, James M. Moynahan and Earle K. Stewart estimated that between 1.5 and 5.5 million Americans enter, spend time in and leave jail each year. Despite the large numbers involved, in their opinion the jail is the least studied and most poorly understood element of the criminal justice system.

Despite religious and social reform movements of the 19th century that led to the construction of a few state prisons, most 19th- and early 20th-century American jails served the dual purpose of jail and prison. Conditions in jails remained poor, with overcrowding; poor housing, food and sanitation; a lack of medical care; no segregation by age, sex or mental condition; and indifferent, often cruel treatment, until the middle third of the 20th century, when serious efforts at reform began.

Some improvements in jail conditions in the 20th century were made because jail officers began to take an interest in their working conditions and the conditions of their jails. The National Jailers Association was formed in the early 20th century and the Jail Managers Association in 1974. Training programs during the 1960s

and 1970s, often supported by the federal government, helped spur the move toward professionalism.

Despite the positive changes, jails continue to grapple with the same handicaps they have always had. Funding is seldom adequate. Jails are understaffed and employees are low-paid and overworked. Funds for treatment programs for substance abusers and sex offenders are virtually nonexistent. Politically, jails often become pawns in jurisdictional struggles; cities and counties fight over the dubious honor of controlling inadequate jail facilities. Jails suffer from a lack of public concern for the facilities, the officers and the inmates.

(See also CALIFORNIA CORRECTIONS SYSTEM; ILLITERACY IN PRISONS; MENTAL ILLNESS: THE IMPACT OF DEINSTITUTIONALIZATION ON STREETS AND JAILS; PRISON OVERCROWDING: COPING WITH THE COSTS; TREATMENT PROGRAMS IN PRISON.)

jurisdiction in criminal cases Jurisdiction refers to the extent and limits of legal authority to hear and decide cases. Jurisdictional problems arise in the United States as a consequence of the existence of many political jurisdictions, each with its own body of criminal law. Each state has the power to enact its own laws. The federal government has a similar power. A Uniform Code of Military Justice applies to members of the armed forces. And federal legislation grants a limited degree of independence to Native American tribal governments and courts.

Clear-cut, unambiguous criminal jurisdiction would be established when a citizen of a state violated a criminal law of that state and no other jurisdiction. For example, Charles, a Californian, stabbed Kevin, his wife Victoria's lover, in a Los Angeles bar.

Jurisdictional complications would arise if Charles chose another method to hurt his wife's lover. He might wait until Kevin, a Floridian, returned home and mail him a bomb. Aside from federal jurisdiction over unlawful use of the mail, a question would arise about whether California, the state where the bomb originated, or Florida, the state where the bomb arrived, had jurisdiction. Charles might complicate the question of jurisdictions in another way. He might force Kevin into a car, head for Florida and along the way stab him, perhaps in Alabama, adding a third possible jurisdiction.

The examples illustrate three legal concepts: *situs*, the location where a criminal act took place; *venue*, the locality within which prosecution may be initiated; and *jurisdiction*, the specific body of criminal law whose provisions have been violated.

Charles Thomas and Donna Bishop, in their book *Criminal Law: Understanding Basic Principles* (1987), note that there are several jurisdictional theories, but the one that American courts have relied on by and large is a *territorial theory,* augmented by an *in whole* or *in part* extension.

A territorial theory, pure or augmented, holds that if a criminal act is completed—though not necessarily initiated—within the territorial limits of a jurisdiction, then the courts established by that jurisdiction may consider evidence in the case.

When the territorial theory, a position that grew out of common law, has been extended by legislation to include an "in whole or in part" addition, then if any "essential element" of the crime takes place within the territorial limits of the jurisdiction, that jurisdiction's courts may consider evidence, even if the "ultimate harm" took place elsewhere. Typically "essential element" means that evidence is sufficient to establish a criminal attempt.

Some limitations are placed on the jurisdictional reach of criminal law by statutes of limitations. Defendants have a constitutional right to a speedy trial, but they do not have a guaranteed right to be protected by statutes of limitations, which are benefits conferred by the individual states.

State statutes of limitations routinely permit prosecution of particularly serious crimes to be initiated at any time. Murder has no statute of limitations. Prosecution for other serious crimes, in many states, must be initiated within four years after the offense was committed, less serious felonies within three years, serious misdemeanors within two years and less serious misdemeanors within one year. The rationale behind statutes of limitation is to protect defendants from having to defend themselves when the basic facts have been obscured by the passage of time and to minimize the danger of being punished for acts in the far-distant past.

In addition to establishing that it has jurisdiction to initiate prosecution, the state must also show that it has jurisdiction over the alleged offender(s). Four types of offenders complicate the burden of establishing jurisdiction over the offender: juveniles, those protected by diplomatic immunity, those granted legislative immunity and those granted witness immunity.

The vast majority of juveniles, typically defined as those under age 18, charged with unlawful acts are not by custom or cannot be by law prosecuted in any criminal court. Over the past century and a half in the United States, there has arisen a juvenile justice system separate from the criminal justice system.

The juvenile justice system has its roots in assumptions about the nature of children. One is reflected in English common law, which presumed that persons below age seven lacked the capacity to form the intent to commit a criminal act and therefore should be immune from prosecution. Persons between age seven and 14 were "rebuttably presumed," which meant that the prosecution could introduce evidence that the presumption of incapacity did not apply.

The other assumptions are those associated with late 19th- and early 20th-century progressive social thought, which had evolved over the century and led not only to separate juvenile courts but to such reforms as child labor laws. The movement to establish separate courts for child offenders may be said to have begun with the establishment of the House of Refuge in New York City in 1825. The first juvenile jurisdiction legislation was enacted in Illinois in 1899, and by 1945 every jurisdiction in the United States had formed some type of separate juvenile system. Such courts claim jurisdiction over virtually all cases involving those defined as children.

For example, if a 13-year-old stole a car, his or her offense, grand theft auto (a felony), would clearly fall within the jurisdiction of a criminal court, but his or her age would put the case into juvenile court. A petition would be filed alleging that the 13-year-old was a delinquent child; evidence of the auto theft would be used to establish his delinquency.

An offender who is exempt from the criminal court's jurisdiction by reason of diplomatic immunity gains his or her status from a long-standing provision of international law. Full immunity applies to foreign diplomats, members of their families and many of their employees. More limited immunity is accorded to lower-ranking consular officials.

The rationale behind diplomatic immunity is that equal privileges are accorded U.S. diplomats working in other nations; diplomatic immunity is a tool whereby national interests are protected; those who violate a host country's laws are not likely to go unchastised by their own governments; and the net benefits of diplomatic immunity are greater than the harm created by individual offenders.

Critics in the United States of the rationale for diplomatic immunity point out that the victims of those who are free from prosecution have no remedies. Moreover, some modern nations are not model international citizens and are unlikely to chastise the culprits.

Legislative immunity is similar to diplomatic immunity, but a good deal more limited in scope and time span. Those in the executive branch of government, including law enforcement representatives, are prohibited from interfering with the representatives of the legislative branch as they go about their duties. This prohibition is written into the U.S. Constitution to protect members of Congress, and into the constitutions of most states to protect members of the state legislatures.

Witness immunity applies to persons called by state or federal prosecutors to testify in criminal cases. The impetus to grant witness immunity typically arises in cases where a sound case cannot be made against two or more culprits. Once witness immunity is granted, the person receiving the grant must answer questions, since self-incrimination is no longer an issue. To refuse amounts to contempt of court. To lie is to invite prosecution for perjury.

There are two categories of witness immunity statutes. Under the provisions of *transactional immunity,* there is an absolute bar against any further prosecution of a witness for any offenses concerning which he or she is asked to testify. The witness has less protection under *derivative immunity.* If law enforcement officials subsequently locate persuasive evidence regarding the witness's criminality in a way that is entirely independent of the witness's testimony, that is, in no way derived from the witness's testimony, then the witness can be prosecuted.

(See also ARREST: CONSTITUTIONAL RESTRICTIONS AND LEGAL PROCEDURES; FELONY ARRESTS: SCREENING PROCEDURES; PROSECUTORIAL DISCRETION IN THE DISPOSITION OF CASES.)

juvenile delinquency   See CLASSROOM VIOLENCE; JUVENILE JUSTICE: A SYSTEM OF CONTRADICTIONS.

juvenile justice: a system of contradictions   For

most of recorded history, children have had few legal rights. Children who did nothing worse than steal food to stay alive were for centuries thrown into prison cells with career criminals. Even small children were on occasion hanged. In some countries not much has changed.

At the close of the 19th century, Jane Addams, the founder of Hull House in Chicago and America's best-known social worker, proposed the idea of a juvenile court separate from adult court. In 1899 Cook County, Illinois set up America's first juvenile court. By 1920 every state in the nation had some semblance of a juvenile court and the idea had spread to other countries.

The settlement house workers and members of Chicago's elite women's clubs who had helped secure

passage of the juvenile court law did so because they viewed the intolerable home conditions of many children they had seen firsthand as factors contributing to delinquency.

There developed among reformers two strong opinions: that the young, with proper guidance and discipline, could be changed; and that America's cities were morally dangerous places to raise children. Based on the beliefs that children's lives could be redirected, that children could be saved from the dangers of urban life and that a juvenile court would act in the best interests of the child, the juvenile courts were given power to take jurisdiction not only over children who had committed illegal acts but also over those who appeared ready to succumb to the temptations of urban life.

Under Illinois law, for example, a juvenile could be declared delinquent if he

> is growing up in idleness or crime; or knowingly frequents a house of ill repute; . . . or frequents any saloon or dram shop where intoxicating liquors are sold; or patronizes or visits any public pool room or bucket shop [gambling establishment]; or wanders about the street in the night time without being on any lawful business; . . . or uses vile, obscene, vulgar, profane, or indecent language in any public place or about a schoolhouse.

The Illinois reformers shared a conviction that there was expert knowledge that could be used to understand and treat juvenile youths. In keeping with that conviction, in 1909 the reformers brought about the creation of the Juvenile Psychopathic Institute attached to the juvenile court in Illinois. The institute, under the leadership of Dr. William Healy, had the dual purpose of providing advice to the court on individual delinquents and studying the causes of juvenile delinquency. Similar institutions were developed in other cities.

Philosophical Models.   The thinking behind the formation of juvenile courts was based on a rehabilitative model. On the premise that the juvenile courts were there to rehabilitate, not to punish, and with experts to guide them, the normal protections available to defendants were deemed unnecessary.

Juvenile court judges acquired almost total control over the fate of child offenders, who had no "due process" rights, no right to counsel, no right to proof beyond a reasonable doubt, not even the right to remain silent. Moreover, the broad scope of the juvenile courts made it possible to make the courts the repository of the society's problem children, in addition to those caught breaking a law. Schools sent truants. Social workers turned over children who ran away from bad foster homes. Parents got rid of children they could not control or did not like, using what was called in some states a "Stubborn Child" statute. The courts' caseloads became enormous.

Ironically, while the juvenile court was being constructed on the rehabilitation model, there developed between 1905 and 1920 a biological theory of delinquency, which asserted that delinquency stemmed from hereditary feeblemindedness (mental deficiency), a term and a theory eventually discarded.

The most important factor leading to the biological interpretation of delinquency was the introduction of the Binet intelligence test into the United States in 1908. When large samples of delinquents were tested for intelligence, from 40% to 90% appeared to test at the "feebleminded" level.

The conditions of testing and the attitude of the tester have a substantial impact on the outcomes of intelligence tests. Moreover, the capacity to understand the material in such tests is heavily dependent on cultural background. Therefore, those creating and administering the tests early in the century—white, middle-class, native-born Americans—found what they expected to find in populations of rural and urban poor, immigrants, laborers and Jim Crow-era nonwhites.

In keeping with the widespread belief that delinquency often reflected feeblemindedness, the clinics attached to juvenile courts frequently conceived as their main function the administration of IQ (intelligent quotient) tests to diagnose feeblemindedness. As a consequence, clinics and diagnostic centers became a prominent source of the idea that most juvenile delinquents were "incurable."

Professionals working in the juvenile court system throughout the 20th century have deplored these conditions but, in the absence of other alternatives, have tried to make the overloaded, often high-handed system work. In her 1969 book *Throwaway Children,* Lisa Aversa Richette, a former prosecutor in Philadelphia who subsequently became a judge, wondered about the wisdom of this. "Maybe they should have herded these children into public view," she wrote, "screamed more loudly, even marched them into the halls of the legislatures and the city councils, into the offices of governors and mayors throughout the land. Activist protest, however, is not the lifestyle of either lawyers or social workers."

Efforts to Reform the Juvenile Courts. The first real change came to juvenile courts in 1967. The U.S. Supreme Court handed down a decision, *in re Gault,* that conceded to children some constitutional due-process rights—not as many as adults have, but some. In the years that followed, Congress passed a number of laws concerning children's rights and welfare. Legal representation expanded beyond delinquency cases.

Despite the expansion of rights, the overcrowding of juvenile courts is so acute that the idea of rehabilitation is mostly given lip service. Nevertheless, many courts still depend on the advice of professional psychologists and social workers and volunteer advocates to guide their decisions about whether to try to work out a rehabilitation plan or commit a youngster to a correctional facility.

One of the most successful rehabilitation programs for juveniles involves volunteers. In 1959 a newly elected judge in Royal Oak, Michigan, unhappy with the resources available to him, convinced a circle of friends to become volunteers in probation to enable him to be more flexible with the youngsters coming before him. A National Institute of Mental Health study documented that the Royal Oak volunteer program is 11 times more effective with misdemeanant offenders than ordinary probation. In courts that used volunteers, over a five-year period, only 23 out of every 100 probationers were convicted of a second offense.

In 1961 the Juvenile Court of Boulder, Colorado added volunteers to a system that already included professional probation officers. The Royal Oak and Boulder programs evolved into three national organizations: the National Information Center on Volunteers in Court (NICOVIC), Volunteers in Prevention, Probation and Prisons (VIP) and the National Association of Volunteers in Criminal Justice (NAVCJ).

A 1979 VIP survey identified an estimated 500,000 volunteers in about 5,000 courts around the country. A 1990 update estimated that 5,657,000 citizen volunteers were involved in juvenile and criminal justice rehabilitative programs throughout the United States.

Volunteers essentially work in four ways: one-to-one with offenders; as administrative volunteers providing services to victims (for example, restitution programs); as presentence investigators; and as professional volunteers.

Professional volunteers include psychiatrists, psychologists, optometrists, dentists, physicians, employment counselors and marriage counselors who volunteer a portion of their time to work in their specialty assisting probationers.

One reason for the success of volunteers is obvious. Volunteers can provide six to 12 hours a month of rehabilitative services. A probation officer working alone can give perhaps three minutes a month to a client.

VIP in Royal Oak, Michigan is set up to help volunteers start programs. In the view of VIP, even as war is too important to leave to the generals, so too is crime too important to leave to probation officers, judges and other professionals.

Extent of the Problem. Because of the veil of confidentiality that hides the proceedings of juvenile courts, information about their operations and the size of their caseloads is scarce. From 15 states, the National Center for Juvenile Justice of the U.S. Department of Justice, Office of Juvenile Justice and Prevention, collected data developed by the courts to meet their own 1987 information and reporting needs. Tables based on the data appear in the U.S. Department of Justice *Sourcebook of Criminal Justice, 1990.*

The 1987 populations of the 15 states, about 91 million people, represented about 36% of the nation's total population. The data revealed that the juvenile courts of those states handled 470,978 cases. If those states are representative of the nation as a whole, then there may have been as many as 1.3 million cases in 1987.

About 16% of the delinquency offenses (acts for which an adult could be prosecuted in a criminal court) were crimes against persons; about 57% were crimes against property; about 8% were drug law violations; and about 19% were public order offenses.

Crimes against persons include such acts as criminal homicide, forcible rape, robbery and assault. Crimes against property include such acts as burglary, larceny, motor vehicle theft, arson, vandalism and trespassing. Drug offenses include such acts as unlawful sale, purchase, distribution, manufacture, cultivation, transport, possession or use of a controlled or prohibited substance, or an attempt to commit such acts. Offenses against public order include weapons offenses, nonviolent sex offenses, disorderly conduct, obstruction of justice and liquor law violations unrelated to status offenses (acts that are offenses only when committed by juveniles).

Maryland, one of the 15 states, had a 1987 population of 4.7 million and thus would have represented about 5% of the total. One of Maryland's courts, the Baltimore Juvenile Court, permitted *Time* reporters to witness the court's operations. The information they gathered appeared in a January 27, 1992 article entitled "Corridors of Agony."

Baltimore juvenile court hearings in 1991 represented 61% of all hearings in the Eighth Circuit. In 1991 about 14,000 new cases were filed, about 20% more than in 1986. During the five years between 1986 and 1991, delinquency cases rose 15% and abuse and neglect cases climbed 40%. The court holds an average of 1,070 hearings a week. Almost 80% of the court's work is with young offenders. The remainder is with abused and neglected children.

The court spends much of its time trying to salvage children's lives. However, the court's efforts are hampered by the pressure of the caseload. Each case can be allotted only a limited amount of time. Moreover, the Baltimore city social services department has woefully inadequate means to care for children who are removed from their homes. One bright spot is a volunteer program called Choice that enlists college graduates to keep track of youngsters and ensure that help is available to them.

From 1989 to 1992, the rate at which children were placed in foster care doubled to 180 cases a month, and about 13 emergency-shelter cases entered the system daily. Nearly 10,000 reports of child abuse or neglect are investigated each year in Baltimore.

The Maryland Department of Juvenile Services spends $60,000 a year per child to incarcerate juvenile offenders at the Charles H. Hickey School, a gloomy correctional facility, and only $200 a year on preventive services. The Maryland Department of Social Services is under a court-ordered consent decree to improve its services, but additional budget cuts threaten the department's efforts to improve. Nationwide, almost 40% of the 340,000 children in foster care, nearly half of whom are under the age of six, spend more than two years in temporary homes.

Roxbury Juvenile Court in Boston, Massachusetts grapples with conditions similar to those in Baltimore. Overcrowding is so acute that the court's part-time psychologist is forced to conduct psychological tests (which are standardized and intended to be administered under conditions of quiet and privacy) for court-ordered assessments in space that houses several other youngsters.

Juveniles Tried as Adults and the Death Penalty. Throughout the United States, the issue of trying juveniles in adult courts for capital crimes (punishable by death or life imprisonment) is hotly contested. The

United States is only one of a handful of nations that permit the death penalty for offenders under 18. In some states minors charged with a capital crime are automatically tried in adult court. In others, there must be a juvenile court hearing in which a decision is made whether to transfer the case to the jurisdiction of the criminal court.

In a study done by Amnesty International U.S.A., entitled *United States of America: The Death Penalty and Juvenile Offenders* (1991), an examination was made of the criteria used to transfer cases to adult court. While the crime, record and age of the defendant were taken into account, the defendant's individual maturity seemed to play no part in the decisions taken. The most common ground for waiving juvenile court jurisdictions was a lack of facilities within the juvenile justice system to provide long-term custody, rather than a finding about whether the defendant could be rehabilitated.

Of the 36 states that have a death penalty, 24 allow death sentences to be imposed on juveniles. Between January 1974 and May 1991, 92 juvenile offenders were sentenced to death in the United States. Of the 92 inmates, 57 had had their death sentences reversed on appeal. Most were resentenced to life imprisonment, although several awaited new sentencing hearings, at which they could again be sentenced to death. Four of the 92 had been executed. As of May 1, 1991, 31 juvenile offenders were under sentence of death.

During 1986 and 1987 a team headed by psychiatrist Dorothy Otnow Lewis of the New York University College of Medicine and neurologist Jonathan Pincus of the Georgetown University Medical Center studied 14 juveniles on death row in four states. The 14 constituted 40% of the total juvenile death row population at the time. The prisoners were chosen solely on the basis of their youth and with no prior knowledge of their background.

In nearly every case, the researchers found evidence of psychiatric illness or brain damage. Twelve of the 14 had suffered serious physical abuse and five had been sodomized by an older male relative.

Only two of the 14 had IQ scores above 90 ("normal" intelligence ranges from 90 to 110, with 90 being referred to as dull-normal). Only three had average reading ability. Three had learned to read on death row. Alcoholism, drug abuse and psychiatric illness were also prevalent in the inmates' histories. Despite their deprived backgrounds, few such mitigating factors were brought to light during their trials.

During the 1980s the U.S. Supreme Court was asked to rule whether the execution of juveniles was permissible under the Constitution. Three key cases have addressed the issue. In each case lawyers for the petitioners argued that "evolving standards of decency" made execution of juvenile offenders cruel and unusual punishment, in violation of the Eighth and 14th amendments to the Constitution.

In *Eddings v. Oklahoma* (1982), the Court was asked to rule on "whether the infliction of the death penalty on a child who was 16 at the time of the offense constituted cruel and unusual punishment." This was the first time the Court agreed to hear an appeal based solely on the defendant's age.

In one of the clearest rulings against the imposition of the death penalty on an emotionally disturbed and socially deprived juvenile offender, the Court in a 5–4 decision vacated Eddings' death sentence. They based the ruling on the ground that at the sentencing hearing, the trial judge had refused to consider evidence of the prisoner's "turbulent family history, of beatings by a harsh father and of severe emotional disturbance." However, the Court failed to rule on the question of whether the death penalty per se was cruel and unusual when imposed on a 16-year-old. The principles set out in *Eddings* appear not to have been followed in a number of cases where juveniles have been sentenced to death.

In *Thompson v. Oklahoma* (1988) the Court addressed the question of whether the death penalty was cruel and unusual when imposed on a 15-year-old. In a 5–4 decision the Court vacated Thompson's death sentence. However, only four of the judges found that the execution of a 15-year-old defendant would be cruel and unusual in all circumstances. A fifth judge concurred with the decision to vacate based on the narrow ground that Oklahoma's death penalty statute set no minimum age at which the death penalty could be imposed; she found that the sentencing of a 15-year-old under this type of statute failed to meet the standard for special care and deliberation required in capital cases.

Subsequent to the Thompson ruling, a trial court in Alabama sentenced a 15-year-old to death under a capital punishment statute that, like Oklahoma's, set no minimum age. Moreover, a 15-year-old offender remained on death row in Louisiana. Both were sentenced under statutes that appeared to violate *Thompson*.

In *Stanford v. Kentucky* and *Wilkins v. Missouri* (1989), the Court held in a 5–4 decision about both cases that the execution of offenders aged 16 and 17 was permissible under the Constitution. Writing for the majority, Justice Antonin Scalia said that society had not formed a consensus that such executions constitute cruel and unusual punishment. He rejected evidence that suggested that the death penalty was no deterrent for young people because they had a less developed fear of death.

Writing for the dissent, Justice William Brennan objected that the majority had not taken into account the fact that, in addition to the 12 U.S. states which had imposed an age limit of 18 in their death penalty statutes, an additional 15 states and the District of Columbia did not authorize executions under any circumstances. Justice Brennan considered it relevant that "within the world community, the imposition of the death penalty for juvenile crimes appears to be overwhelmingly disapproved."

(See also DEATH PENALTY.)

K

Ku Klux Klan   See HATE GROUPS.

L

legalization of drugs   See DRUG ABUSE AND TRADE: PREVENTION AND EDUCATION.

M

machismo   Derived from the Spanish word *macho,* meaning a "strong man," the term machismo refers to a quality of ostentatious, assertive, self-conscious masculinity, characterized by virility, courage, aggressiveness and contempt for weakness. Machismo may be said to be the sum total of the qualities associated with the social role of "man," qualities attributed solely to

biological maleness by many men and women who do not realize that such roles have a learned, constructed—that is, cultural—character. (The female equivalent is called "femininity.")

Every culture has constructed such social roles. They determine how people behave in daily life. The rules are transmitted culturally and therefore implicitly understood by adults and are passed down from adults to children. Individuals are encouraged, sometimes forced, by social sanctions to perform these roles. Sanctions for nonperformance vary in form and severity; among them are ridicule, scorn, shame, guilt, punishment and ostracism.

Some social roles are more rigidly structured than others. Gender roles tend to be among the most structured. Typical male roles are: lover, hero, husband, father and provider. Appropriate performance of the various roles can serve the needs of the individual and of the larger society.

However, in some societies and by some individuals certain male sex roles may be neglected or exaggerated to the detriment of others. The lover may be a Don Juan, obsessed by seduction. The hero may be an athlete or soldier interested solely in winning or a scientist competing to be first to make a discovery. The husband may take the opportunity afforded by marriage to become a tyrant in his small domain. Although some societies encourage fathers to be nurturers of their children, in many fathers do little else except pass along their genes and possibly introduce their sons at the appropriate time to the world of adults. The role of provider, especially among the poor, and in many developed countries among the upper middle class, may demand a concentration of attention and energy that eclipses all other roles.

The more rigid the requirements of the various roles and the more insistent the expectation that they be performed simultaneously, the more tension they create and the more they can be thought of as a single overall role of "supermale," characterized by the quality often referred to as "hypermasculinity," or machismo.

Since the resurgence of the feminist movement in the early 1960s, machismo has acquired a negative image, among other reasons because it conceives of the role of women as one of servants providing maintenance services to macho males. Analysis has revealed that machismo is not only detrimental to women but is also destructive of men and plays a significant role in creating a climate of violence. This perspective on machismo sees its "maleness" in terms of posturing, swaggering and self-indulgence. Machismo requires men to treat women as inferiors, engage in personal violence when male honor is imagined to be at stake (assaults, fist-fights, domestic violence) and, at some times and in some places, participate in crime and even, for some men, to promote wars.

Violence is perceived by many analysts, particularly by Freud and his followers, as inevitable because they view it as the expression of an instinct or drive rather than as a requirement of a social role. In her analysis of violence, *Boys Will Be Boys: Breaking the Link Between Masculinity and Violence* (1991), Columbia University philosopher Myriam Miedzian rejects the Freudian notion of a drive and characterizes machismo as a cultural construct, with possible biological under-pinnings, that emphasizes violence. If violence is a cultural construct, then it is not inevitable.

There is almost universal agreement that from a very young age males act more aggressively than females, but it is not clear that aggressivity is preordained. In 1973 psychologists Eleanor Maccoby and Carol Jacklin published *The Psychology of Sex Differences* in which they analyzed 94 studies of male-female comparisons. While studies of American children represented the bulk of their data, Maccoby and Jacklin also reviewed cross-cultural data, animal studies and hormonal research. They found that in the United States and other cultures, boys from a very young age hit and insult each other more frequently, respond faster and more strongly when insulted or hit and engage in more rough-and-tumble play.

Although it would appear that boys are more aggressive, Maccoby and Jacklin emphasized that the differences were tendencies and not a dichotomy. In 52 studies boys were more aggressive, in 37 studies there was no difference, and in 5 studies girls were more aggressive. Such findings can be interpreted to mean that males as a group are more aggressive, but many males are no more aggressive than many females.

The difference in aggressiveness between males and females is often attributed to the presence of the hormone testosterone and linked to a biological explanation of violence. The male hormone testosterone leads to the formation in utero of male sexual characteristics. If for some reason testosterone is not present, a genetically male embryo develops into a female.

A study of such males, who looked like girls at birth and were raised as girls, was reported by John Money

and Anke Ehrhardt in *Man and Woman, Boy and Girl* (1972). The researchers found that testosterone-deprived males raised as girls exhibited to a marked degree traits thought of as "feminine" in American culture.

Another study looked at a group of girls who received high levels of testosterone in utero and who were born with ambiguous genital organs, usually surgically corrected shortly after birth. The girls tended to engage in more rough-and-tumble play, participate more in physical activities and compete more for dominance, yet they did not engage in fights, suggesting that the testosterone had an impact on activity levels but socialization restrained violent behavior.

Predispositions to Violence.   Some analysts suspect that testosterone may be linked to precursors (prior conditions) rather than to violence itself. Boys with higher testosterone levels tend to be more easily frustrated, more impatient and more irritable than boys with lower levels, which may increase the probability that they will engage in violent behavior.

Miedzian suggests that several physical conditions increase boys' risks of violence. Among these are attention deficit disorder with hyperactivity (ADDH), which is characterized by unresponsiveness to affection, short attention span, low frustration tolerance, restless physical energy and outbursts of temper. ADDH is often a predisposing factor in puberty to acts of physical violence and in adulthood to antisocial personality disorder (psychopathic personality). The disorder is six to nine times more common in boys than in girls.

Another physical risk factor for violence is learning disabilities (LD). An estimated 32% to 40% of the inmate population in the United States suffers from LD. Although recent research has determined that dyslexia, the most common of the learning disabilities, may be as common in girls as it is in boys, boys are at least twice as likely to be identified as learning-disabled by teachers as are girls. Such identification may reflect the greater tendency of boys to have less patience and to act out. The number of American males with LD is estimated to be about 6 to 12 million.

Another physical risk factor for violence is mental retardation. Mentally retarded children are three to four times as likely to suffer from ADDH as the general population, and an estimated 30% of prison inmates are mentally retarded.

Harvard sociobiologist Edward O. Wilson, the author of *Sociobiology: the New Synthesis* (1975) and *Human Nature* (1982), argues that aggression was advantageous for humans in early hunting and gathering societies that competed for limited resources (a view of prehistory that has been recently questioned). Warriors did the hunting and fishing and thus the competing, while females tended to food gathering and child raising, presumably solitary or cooperative ventures.

Unlike Freud's hydraulic or catharsis view of violence, which theorizes that violence builds up and must be discharged, Wilson insists that violent aggression does not grow out of an instinct or a drive. He believes that violence is innate in the sense that there is a probability that the trait will develop under specific environmental circumstances, but there is no certainty that the trait will develop in all environments.

Wilson supports his notion that the emergence of aggression is not inevitable by pointing to cultures that have gone from nonviolence to violence and vice versa. The Semai of Malay had no concept of violent aggression until the British colonial government recruited Semai men to fight Communist guerrillas in the early 1950s. After some kinsmen were killed by Communist terrorists, the previously peaceful Semai men became extremely violent.

The Maori of New Zealand followed a different course. The introduction of European firearms into the already violent Maori culture was catastrophic. Approximately one quarter of the population died during 20 years of war. By 1830 the custom of fighting for revenge was being questioned, and by the early 1840s warfare between tribes had ended.

Social Learning. While biological factors may set the parameters of aggressive responses (size, weight, agility), and individual genetic endowment may influence inclination to learn, social learning theorist and Stanford psychologist emeritus Albert Bandura proposes three main sources of aggression: the modeling and reinforcement provided by the family, the subculture in which a boy grows up and the impact of mass media.

Numerous studies have found that parental modeling of aggression and parental permissiveness toward aggressive behavior encourage aggression in boys. Research has determined that boys whose fathers are criminals are more apt to become criminals, particularly if their fathers are neglectful or cruel. Research has also found that abused children are more likely to abuse their own children.

Bandura and many others have emphasized that subcultures are critical in learning violent behavior. There is a greater emphasis on dominance, hierarchy and prestige in boys' play groups than in girls'. Eleanor Maccoby is convinced that peer groups are a more important influence on the behavior of boys than families, but she believes that family pathology predisposes a boy to greater aggression.

The Impact of Sports. The subculture of playing sports as well as the experience of being a spectator at a game or on television provide constant reinforcement of the acceptability of violence. American athletes get a high level of social approval, particularly from fathers. Many American fathers think that to have a son uninterested in sports is tragic.

In his book *Violence and Sport* (1983), Michael Smith of York University, Toronto, divides sports violence into four types: brutal body contact (tackles, blocks, body checks and all legal blows); borderline violence (assaults that while prohibited by the formal rules occur routinely, such as hockey fistfights, baseball brushback pitches, and late hits after a play is over in football; quasi-criminal violence (assaults that lead to severe injury, which may result in a suspension, a lifetime ban, and civil or criminal suits); and criminal violence (violent behavior among fans). When the Detroit Pistons won the National Basketball Association Championship in June 1990, eight people were killed during the "celebration," and 124 were treated at a hospital.

Brutal body contact and borderline violence loom large in the development of young boys' attitudes in Western societies about violent behavior. In October 1985 Professor Brenda Jo Bredemeir of the University of California at Berkeley reported in *Psychology Today* that a male college basketball player told her, "In sports you can do what you want. In life it's more restricted." A football player told her that the football field was the wrong place to think about ethics.

Many boys and men watching the many fights on the ice among hockey players are unaware that many of them want to abolish violence. But club owners refuse to take action because they believe the fans come to see "red ice."

In his autobiography *Out of Their League* (1970), former professional football player Dave Meggessey characterized as nonsense the justification of football as a character builder and described it as a body destroyer. In his opinion, most football players would like to see unnecessary football violence curbed but fear losing their jobs if they restrain themselves.

Proponents of contact sports claim that they teach youngsters not only how to play the sports but also how to play the game of life. Michael Oriard in his 1982 book *The End of Autumn* provided vignettes of coaches whose views of games and life were not worthy of transmission. For example, following a game one coach rewarded his players for the most vicious play he could find in the films taken of the game.

Many players who succeed in repressing empathy on the football field separate themselves into a "personal self" and a "football self." This is a psychological process called "doubling," a technique probably also used by generals and crime bosses.

Since life is filled with danger and suffering, proponents of contact sports wonder what could be wrong with teaching boys and men to overcome their fears, to be courageous and to withstand pain. If that were what was being done, there would be nothing wrong with it. But when, in order to win, a high school player is injected with novocaine so he can play with injuries that if aggravated could result in permanent damage, then he is learning to take unnecessary risks with his body and to hide feelings of fear, however valid they may be. Many coaches also teach that it is also proper to sacrifice others in order to win.

Such lessons can lead to reckless endangerment of self and others. In the United States in 1988, white males died from accidents and violence at a rate per 100,000 of 113.4, black males at a rate of 162, white females at a rate of 33.3, and black females at a rate of 35.0. Eighty percent of all spinal cord injuries in the United States occur to men.

Sports language and analogies are frequently carried over into military and foreign policy. In both arenas, anything that hints of empathy, concern with moral issues or aversion to violence is rejected as "feminine" or "soft."

Perspectives on Real and Imaginary Violence. Regardless of whether they have a biological risk of becoming violent or acquire one through exposure to sports, children participate in the society they live in and adopt its heroes. Violence in the abstract in books, videos, TV and movies is glamorized. Among American fictional heroes, John Wayne in the Battle of Iwo Jima and the lone cowboy riding into a frontier town where he will kill or be killed hold great appeal. When author Marc Gerzon interviewed Vietnam veterans for his book *A Choice of Heroes: The Changing Faces of American Manhood* (1982), many of them cited John Wayne movies as a reason why they volunteered for Vietnam.

Unlike videos, TV or movies, violence in real life is messy and painful. In his 1974 book *The Male Machine,* attorney Marc Feigen Fasteau described the dilemma of adult men—who are not counterspies, marines or football players—when confronted by violence in real life. He wrote:

Although most men think that physical strength is a necessary attribute of manliness, they generally avoid trying to settle things with their fists. Most of them have too much to lose from getting into a brawl and are afraid—sensibly, it seems to me—of getting hurt. Furthermore, they spend most of their time with other men who, like themselves, don't want to be put to this kind of test. But the fact that they don't actually lead lives filled with physical risk and violence doesn't mean that they have escaped the feeling that they are less masculine as a result.

Glenn Gray, who served in Europe and North Africa during World War II and wrote *Warriors* (1970), proposed that the attraction of war comes from the intense excitement and sense of power and a relish in destruction, which are often reactions to the boredom and emptiness of many men's daily lives. Many feminists believe that daily boredom is a result of men being cut off from their feelings and therefore estranged from their families.

Little boys in many cultures are taught to be brave and strong and not to reveal their feelings, particularly not the urge to cry or show fear. This suppression eventually prevents them from nurturing their children or being close to their wives. War not only provides an apparent release from boredom for men, it provides a camaraderie with other men otherwise missing in their lives.

In her quest to find ways to reduce violence, Miedzian interviewed many educators across the country who are determined at least to change the aspect of machismo that glamorizes war. They have developed curricula that describe real people on both sides of war. A New Jersey social studies teacher, who is a former Vietnam veteran, teaches a course entitled "The Vietnam Generation." He includes a picture of two dead soldiers, one American, the other Vietnamese. Laying next to the Vietnamese soldier is a photograph of a girl. The picture serves as a springboard for a discussion of such themes as that war involves killing real people and war involves risking one's own life.

Frances FitzGerald's 1979 book *America Revised* pointed out that part of U.S. college students' anger during the 1960s stemmed from their realization that teachers and textbooks, as well as government officials, had presented a distorted picture of U.S. history and policies. Essentially history texts have been and many continue to be nationalistic, painting American foreign policy simplistically as inevitably good. For example, one text described one of the most significant events in human history by saying "American planes dropped two A-bombs and destroyed two Japanese cities. Japan surrendered and the Second World War came to an end."

Moorehead Kennedy, one of the hostages taken by the Iranians in 1978, during his 444 days in captivity gained a sense of the need for Americans to understand how the world looks from the perspective of other countries and cultures. He and educator Martha Keys developed a series of simulation curricula to be used in the 9th grade through college. The students play the various roles of terrorists, hostages, government officials and others.

The Influence of Fathers.   An American boy with a father who displays empathy and tenderness can identify with his father without having to cut himself off from "feminine" emotions. But he is likely to experience a sharp contradiction between the way his father behaves and the behavior of his peers and may have to learn to appear tough in order to avoid being a prey for bullies.

Research has determined that traditional fathers are much more concerned with their son's masculinity than are mothers. Ironically, traditional fathers' rejection of sons who prefer reading to baseball or art to tinkering with a car may discourage their sons from identifying with them and increase the chances of the sons identifying with their mothers.

For most American boys, manhood is achieved by meeting certain criteria: by being strong, tough, good at sports and willing to fight, and by not associating with girls or with girls' activities such as cooking or housekeeping. Studies of families in which both parents share child care have found that boys' negative attitudes toward girls do not appear.

There are cultural obstacles in Western societies to men's becoming involved in child care. Men are responsible for almost all sexual child abuse, and the frequency with which they batter children suggests that given equal time with their children, they would batter more. Men and women are now about equally responsible for child battering; however, women spend a great deal more time with children. Such evidence fosters the notion that at best the care men might give would be inferior and at worst it would include child battering or child molesting.

However, some experts believe that if coparenting became more common, empathy and concern for others would become accepted as masculine qualities. As a consequence, battering of wives and children would diminish, and men would feel less compelled to treat their sons roughly to make them "real men." Such a change could have a profound effect even on men who did not fully share in parenting or who never become fathers.

Psychiatrist Kyle Pruett reported in his book *The Nurturing Father* (1987) that children raised by fathers performed better than children from traditional families on the Yale Developmental Schedule, which rates motor functions, language and social skills and ability to solve problems. The positive finding held true even when the father's initial commitment to the role of primary nurturer was dictated by practical rather than philosophical considerations.

Inner-City Black Males.   For boys without fathers, the mass media and their peer groups serve as sources of their concept of what it is to be a man. Nationally, about 50% of black families are headed by females, but the percentage rises to about 90% among families in housing projects.

Sociologist Walter Miller proposed in Marvin Wolfgang and coauthors' *The Sociology of Crime and Delinquency* (1962) that an extreme concern with male toughness found in cultures of poverty can be traced to the absence of a consistent male figure in the lives of many boys. The absence leads such fatherless boys to become obsessed by a "hypermasculinity."

Whatever it is called, supermaleness, machismo or hypermasculinity is contributing to the destruction of black males, particularly inner-city males. The leading cause of death among young black males is homicide. Accidents are second, and suicide is third. A 1991 report of the National Center for Health Statistics indicated that 49% of black males between 15 and 19 who died were shot, compared to 18% of white males. Black males 15 to 29 die at a higher rate than any other age group except those 85 and older.

An April 21, 1992 *New York Times* article entitled "Black Scientists Study the 'Pose' of the Inner City" reported that two academic research centers and a national group of social scientists and policymakers had recently been founded to focus on the predicament of black men. Dr. Richard Majors, a psychologist at the University of Wisconsin at Eau Claire, is at the forefront of a movement to understand black males better and to mobilize the black middle class to help.

In his book, *Cool Pose: The Dilemmas of Black Manhood in America* (1992), coauthored by Janet Mancini Billson, an executive officer of the American Sociological Society, Majors wrote about the posturing of young black males. To insulate themselves from an overwhelming negative reality, they adopt a "cool pose" of studied unflappability, accompanied by an aloof swagger.

The cool pose includes stylized language, mannerisms, gestures and movements that "exaggerate or ritualize masculinity." The cool pose also includes distinctive haircuts, flashy or provocative clothes, expensive sneakers, gold chains and unbuckled belts. All are designed to show others, especially the dominant society, that the young male is strong and proud.

Like most other forms of machismo, while it may help in the struggle to feel manly, the cool pose can be dysfunctional. It is often misread by teachers, principals and police officers as an attitude of defiance. It may also lock the young male into ritual behavior so that he cannot back down from a fight or say that he is sorry to his girl friend when he has done something hurtful.

Some black social scientists object to focusing on the problems of urban youth and point out that if one out of four young black males is involved with the criminal justice system, then three out of four are not. More needs to be understood about how they succeed, despite an absence of positive role models.

More also needs to be understood about how many men of all groups manage to avoid involvement in violence despite cultural encouragement to indulge.

The Contribution of Television. Mentally retarded, learning-disabled and emotionally disturbed children watch even more television than nonhandicapped children, according to a study by Joyce Sprafkin and Kenneth Gadow that appeared in the January-March 1986 *Journal of Applied Developmental Psychology*. Thus they see even more violence. In response to criticism of television violence, broadcasters typically defend violent fare on the grounds that it serves as a catharsis or a safety valve for pent-up aggression.

George Comstock, professor of public communications at Syracuse University, reviewed more than 235 studies on the effects of television violence, which have been analyzed in more than 2,500 articles, books and reports, and concluded that viewing television violence does not help children get rid of antisocial inclinations. On the contrary, at all ages it increases aggressive behavior.

Comstock's finding echoed those of the 1982 report of the National Institute of Mental Health (NIMH) entitled *Television and Behavior: Ten Years of Scientific Progress and Implications for the Eighties*. The NIMH study concluded that television emphasizes machismo stereotypes that perpetuate violence and commonly links sex with violence. "In magnitude, television violence is as strongly correlated with aggressive behavior as any other behavioral variable that has been measured. The research question has moved from asking whether or not there is an effect to seeking an explanation for the effect."

In 1950, when television was new, according to Neil Postman in his 1982 book *The Disappearance of Childhood*, there were only 170 persons under age 15 arrested for serious crimes. Those 18 and under arrested for violent crime, according to the U.S. Department of Justice Statistics *Sourcebook of Criminal Justice Statistics, 1990*, had climbed to 92,346 in 1989.

manslaughter The killing of one human being by another that does not legally amount to the crime of murder but nevertheless is neither lawful nor accidental is classified as manslaughter. Manslaughter may be committed in several ways. A killing may be considered voluntary manslaughter if the accused had malice aforethought (mens rea) but diminished responsibility (an abnormal state of mind that substantially reduced his or her self-control or ability to reason) or provocation (acts or words of the victim that made the accused lose self-control).

Voluntary manslaughter also may be charged if the accused committed an act of gross negligence or if the act, although not negligent, was illegal and also involved an element of danger to the victim.

The absence of the element of intent is the essential difference between voluntary and involuntary manslaughter. Additionally in most states, involuntary manslaughter does not result from the heat of passion but from failure to use reasonable care or skill in the commission of a lawful act, or the commission of an unlawful act that is less than a felony.

A person also may be guilty of manslaughter if he or she kills someone when drunk, although most cases of reckless driving that cause death are charged not as manslaughter but as other offenses usually less serious than involuntary manslaughter. The highly successful lobbying group Mothers Against Drunk Driving (MADD) has called attention to the fact that the average drunken driver who kills someone has a string of prior drunken driving offenses. MADD is working to change the lenient judicial attitude toward drunk drivers.

(See also CRIMINAL LIABILITY; HOMICIDE; MURDER: U.S. PRO-
FILE; POST-TRAUMATIC STRESS DISORDER [PTSD].)

mass murderers   On the average, there are about
22,000 murders annually in the United States. Because
the Uniform Crime Report of the Federal Bureau of
Investigation (FBI) is an aggregation of data from police
departments around the nation, it is difficult to tell how
many of those fall under the heading of mass murders.
Northeastern University professors Jack Levin and James
Alan Fox, co-authors of *Mass Murder: America's
Growing Menace* (1985), believe that the incidence of
mass murder is growing and is significantly underestimated.

Under the umbrella term mass murder, Levin and
Fox analyze both those who kill their victims all at once
or within a brief period, who are typically referred to
as mass murderers, and those who kill their victims
over days, weeks, months or years, who are typically
referred to as serial killers. Although each kills large
numbers of people, the two types are quite different in
their behavior and motivation.

Simultaneous slayings, in which victims are slaughtered in one ferocious attack, are often far bloodier and
more immediately shocking than a series of killings.
However, the latter can keep a community suspended
in terror for indefinite periods of time until the killer is
caught—if he or she ever is—and thus they can create
lingering damage to a community's psychic well-being.

In the opinion of Levin and Fox, there are three types
of mass murder: family slayings, mass murder for profit
or expediency and killings for sex or sadism. There may
be some overlap in particular cases, and mass murders
inspired by racial hatred do not fit easily into these
categories; nevertheless they help to understand the
phenomenon. Many mass murderers are law-abiding
citizens who generally obey the rules of society, but
they are able to adopt a set of justifications that permits
them temporarily or periodically to commit a heinous
crime and still participate in everyday life.

Research Strategy and Sample Characteristics.   Four
major studies formed the basis of Levin and Fox's book:
a statistical profile of 42 mass killers developed by the
authors; a large FBI homicide data set provided by
Northeastern University's Center for Applied Social
Research; questionnaires completed by dozens of attorneys general concerning their states' laws; and hundreds
of telephone interviews conducted by graduate students.

Besides the difficulties posed by data collected into
an aggregate that omits details about individual murders,

there are several other difficulties that arise in tabulating
mass murders. Typically, murderers are not always
charged with all the crimes they are suspected of committing. Ted Bundy, who killed in several states, was
charged with only three murders. A few hours before
his execution, he provided police with the names of 19
others that he had killed.

Self-reports like Bundy's offer clues to the extent that
mass murder may be underestimated. Some murderers,
after imprisonment or prior to execution, claim to have
killed large numbers of people, but authorities are not
always able to validate their claims, due to a lack of
resources or to a lack of sufficient information.

Because of the notoriety of mass murderers, Levin
and Fox were able to make use of newspaper indexes
in order to compile a diverse and representative collection of mass killers to study. They confined their study
to the years 1974 to 1979 to insure that most of the
cases had reached a final judicial disposition.

Their final sample included 33 cases and 42 offenders.
Each case represented at least four victims and one or
more offenders. Thirty-one of the offenders were convicted of murder, four were found not guilty by reason
of insanity, five committed suicide, one was killed by
a relative of one of his victims and one died in an
automobile accident.

The researchers set out to compare their 42 killers
with FBI information available on all homicides in the
United States for the years 1976 to 1980, a total of
96,263 cases. The data permitted the isolation of mass
murders in which four or more people had been killed
in the same incident. Obvious cases of arson were
eliminated, leaving 156 cases involving 675 victims.
Further cases were eliminated because certain information about the killers' characteristics had not been available to the police.

The final sample was 107 cases with 137 offenders.
Thus Levin and Fox were able to compare the FBI's
107 cases of simultaneous homicides with their compiled information on 42 mass killers, both simultaneous
and serial. (Serial murders are recorded as separate
single homicides in the FBI's annual data.) Based on
the comparative data, they were able to create a com-
posite profile of a mass murderer, distinguishing those
who killed all at once from those who killed in serial
fashion.

Profile of a Mass Murderer.   Typically, the mass
murderer is a white male, in his late 20s or 30s. In a
simultaneous crime, he kills people he knows with a
handgun or a rifle. In serial crimes, he murders strangers

by beating or strangulation. His specific motivation depends on the circumstances leading to the crime, but it generally has to do with expediency, money, jealousy or lust. Rarely is he a "hardened criminal" with a long record, although a history of sporadic property crime is common.

The murder often follows a spell of frustration when a particular event triggers sudden rage, although in some cases the killer is coolly pursuing some goal not otherwise attainable. Although the mass killer may appear cold, show no remorse and even deny responsibility, rarely does he suffer from a classic psychosis. In background, personality and appearance, he is extremely ordinary.

Levin and Fox point out that, despite the amount of racial conflict and violence in the United States, murders precipitated by racial hatred are statistically rare. Moreover, single-victim murders that cross racial lines in the United States amount to less than 10%. Although African-Americans commit about half of all homicides, only one in five mass killers is black.

Few are women. In single-victim murders, only 15% are committed by women, but among mass murders the percentage is much less.

To move beyond the simple explanation of "male aggressiveness," Levin and Fox focused on the weapon that facilitates the crime and the situation that precipitates it. Firearms are far more efficient at killing than knives or clubs, especially for killing a number of people at once. Men are more likely both to own and have access to guns and to be trained in their use.

Certain types of mass killing and serial rape followed by murder are the sole province of men, due, in the opinion of Levin and Fox, to their perceived need to dominate. Society permits women to feel weak and to be submissive. A man who feels weak or passive may experience societal pressure to live up to a powerful male image.

Although family murders, which are almost half of all mass murders, could be committed just as easily by a mother or daughter as by a father or son, they rarely are, even though mothers are statistically more responsible than fathers for child abuse (which may be a reflection of the greater amount of time mothers spend with children).

Simultaneous murderers tend to be older than other killers. The FBI's age distribution for homicides peaks at 25. Only 15% of simultaneous killers are under 25. In family mass murders, the father tends to be the oldest member of the household.

Advanced age is even more typical of serial killers. In Levin and Fox's view, many serial killers find it difficult to accept their diminishing sexual desirability— and possibly their diminished capacity. The novelty of intercourse is no longer enough. Arousal may take whips, chains and leather. For some it may mean crossing the line from consensual sex, no matter how bizarre, to the lust murder of partners.

Dean Corll, the homosexual murderer of 27 boys in Houston, was 33. John Wayne Gacy, the homosexual murderer of 33 boys in Chicago, was 37. Christopher Wilder, the suspected murderer of eight young women from coast to coast, was 39. And Angelo Buono, who raped and murdered ten girls and young women in Los Angeles, was 44. Many males in America's youth-oriented culture feel "over the hill" upon reaching their 30s and 40s. Homosexual lifestyles put a particular emphasis on a youthful appearance, making middle age a trauma.

The need for control and power is often evident in serial killers. Some dream of careers in law enforcement and collect police and military uniforms, guns and instruments of torture.

While most people choose socially acceptable ways to satisfy their need to control, serial killers find that overpowering a victim enhances their feelings of dominance. Those who go to such extremes have not internalized a moral code that forbids brutal treatment of others. In other words, they lack any conscience or sense of guilt. They have what is called a sociopathic or psychopathic personality, a disorder much more common in males than in females.

A sociopath lacks a sense of responsibility, guilt or morality and is unable to have a meaningful or lasting relationship. He or she is immature, finds it difficult to postpone impulsive behavior and is impervious to rewards and punishments that ordinarily inhibit immoral action. A sociopath's immoral behavior may range from lying and cheating to rape and murder.

Domination untempered by guilt is a dominant theme in serial crimes with a sexual character. Sadistic sex, consensual or forced, manifests power over another, a power that is further enhanced by murder. The so-called Sunset Strip Killer graded his victims on their power to please him sexually. He killed those who failed. He claimed to have killed 50 women and hoped to kill 100.

The Influence of Notoriety.   Not only has the actual incidence of mass murders increased, media coverage has escalated. Killings for sex or sadism arouse the most widespread public fear and interest. During the Los

Angeles Hillside Stranglers' spree of increasingly vicious murders from October 1977 to February 1978, citizens changed their routines significantly. When a physical education professor announced a six-hour course in self-defense designed for a maximum of 67 students, as many as 1,000 people called with inquiries.

After reading in the papers that the stranglers posed as police officers, citizens refused to stop for traffic violations. Police had to be satisfied with ignoring violations or with following motorists to the police station before the motorist would talk to them.

In the opinion of Levin and Fox, the extensive coverage of mass murder may have had the unintended consequence of encouraging others to commit murder. For example, in a well-publicized case, a Providence, Rhode Island physician who had gained control of a widow's assets gave her a New Year's Eve gift of a bottle of whiskey laced with arsenic. A short time later, a jilted San Francisco mistress sent a box of arsenic-enhanced chocolates to her lover's wife. The San Francisco chocolates may have inspired a poisoner to leave a bottle of cyanide-laced Bromo Seltzer in the mailbox of the director of the Knickerbocker Athletic Club in New York City. His wife took some and died an hour later.

The Bromo Seltzer murder was a forerunner to the 1982 "Tylenol scare" in Chicago. The Tylenol killer, either as a screen for a specific murder or as an impersonal method for getting even with society in general, laced Tylenol capsules with lethal doses of cyanide. The killer apparently went to several retail stores, bought bottles of Tylenol, filled some of the capsules with the poison and returned the bottles to the store shelves to be purchased by unsuspecting customers.

Subsequently, in more than a dozen states, copycat poisoners introduced lethal substances into pies, candy, mixed nuts, eyedrops, mouthwash and over-the-counter medication. In many cities Halloween celebrations were canceled because of the risk.

Theories. Levin and Fox quarrel with a variety of theories about mass murder based on uncommonly bizarre or hideous murders. Theorists have examined everything from family configuration to brain structures, from biography to biology, but the validity of the theories for more than a few cases is questionable.

One influential but questionable theory involves a set of childhood behaviors called the "Macdonald triad," named for the psychiatrist John Macdonald, who proposed them. The Macdonald triad is thought by some to predict adult violent behavior. The behaviors are bedwetting, fire setting and the torture of small animals. Supporters claim that the behaviors are reactions to parental abandonment, neglect or brutality.

Another theory holds that brutal childhood experience creates "homicidal prone-ness." Other theories propose biological causes. During the 1960s some researchers purported to demonstrate that inmates in institutions for the criminally insane were more likely to possess the "XYY syndrome," that is, to be born with an extra "Y" or male sex chromosome. Others have suggested a link between diet and violence.

Brain disorders are a frequently proposed explanation. Clinical studies do suggest that brain disorder or injury can sometimes result in outbursts of anger and less frequently in violent behavior. However, at least 14 million people in the United States are victims of some form of brain dysfunction, which may have been present at birth or be the result of injury or disease, including epilepsy, mental retardation, minimal brain disorders and dysfunctions resulting from strokes, brain tumors, head injuries or malnutrition.

A widely accepted theory is one proposed by psychiatrist Dr. Donald Lunde, who suggested that two kinds of mental states account for most mass murders: paranoid schizophrenia, characterized by aggressiveness and suspicion, together with hallucinations and delusions of grandeur or persecution; and sexual sadism, characterized by torturing, mutilating and killing for sexual gratification.

Although the various theories offer insights, they are usually based on only a few cases, most of which tend to be unusual or particularly bizarre. Missing from such illustrations are the more typical cases of mass killings to silence informants, eliminate witnesses and collect inheritances. Also underrepresented are multiple murders by those who kill family, friends, neighbors and coworkers.

The major difficulty in generalizing from unrepresentative cases is that they constitute a highly biased sample of all who commit criminal acts. They overpredict the incidence of the behavior because they fail to take into account false positives—those who have the observed characteristics but who do not grow up to be murderers. Childhood frustrations may lead to heinous crime, but they can also lead to striving and succeeding.

Although his triad was viewed with enthusiasm by others, even Macdonald himself rejected it after further research. Some who accepted the triad proposed that detection and early management of children with the behavior might prevent future violent crime. Such a policy would label and manipulate so-called murder-prone children, in effect treating them or incarcerating them for something they might never do.

Levin and Fox sum up their assessment of many prevailing theories by saying "Though the theories proposed to explain mass murder have been extremely varied, they share one feature in common: a narrow-minded focus on the killer. It has been the mistake of psychiatrists and other scientists to focus exclusively on individual characteristics."

Victim Vulnerability and Environmental and Social Influences. The susceptibility of victims is a factor seldom examined in theories that focus mainly on the psychological or psychiatric aspects of serial murders. Almost without exception serial killers choose vulnerable victims. Prostitutes are a frequent target. So are hitchhikers, stranded motorists, and children.

Prostitutes are at risk because of their willingness to enter areas controlled by their customers. Hitchhikers get into the cars of strangers. Children and teenagers are not only naive, they are likely to be smaller than their attacker. Stranded motorists may accept help from the wrong person.

The homeless and the aged are also vulnerable. Skid Row Slasher Vaughn Greenwood killed at least nine homeless men who were drunk or asleep in doorways or alleys. Several serial killers, including the Boston Strangler and the Stocking Strangler of Columbus, Georgia, killed frail and defenseless elderly women.

In the opinion of Levin and Fox, not only have psychological theories underplayed the role of victim vulnerability, they have overlooked situations and settings that could encourage a sense of domination through murder. Therefore, analytic attention has been focused on control through violence without regard to the relationship of the killer to the social environment.

The complete dependence of hospital and nursing home patients on their caregivers can create the perfect circumstances for the administration of lethal medications or poisons. In 1976 two Veteran's Administration Hospital nurses in Ann Arbor, Michigan were indicted on ten counts of poisoning, five counts of murder, and one count of conspiracy to commit murder. A pediatric nurse in Kerrville, Texas created life-and-death situations so she could rescue patients with cardiopulmonary resuscitation. A nursing home administrator in Orkdale, Norway admitted poisoning 17 patients and may have

been responsible for another 138 deaths. In the 1978 Jonestown, Guyana massacre, the cult dictator Jim Jones exercised such control over his followers that 913 voluntarily died from intake of cyanide.

An additional problem with explaining mass murder strictly in terms of individual psychopathology is that it overlooks the many instances in which murder is a collective activity. In a chapter called "Mass Murder As a Way of Life," Levin and Fox describe the process by which ordinary citizens become conditioned to mass murder. In wartime, combat soldiers who have been trained to kill routinely commit acts of "murder" on enemy forces and even on civilians.

British psychiatrist Henry Dicks, who interviewed several Nazi SS killers, noted that under ordinary conditions they would not have become "common murderers," let alone mass murderers. According to Dicks, the SS were conditioned to murder in a lengthy process of group pressure and indoctrination designed to instill absolute loyalty and dependence on the group. Moreover, everyone had a specialized job, so no one felt responsible for overall consequences.

On a smaller scale, mass slayings have been carried out by two or more persons. In 1973 and 1974, 14 execution-style murders and eight assaults took place in San Francisco. The investigation was called "Zebra," after the police radio band assigned to it. All 22 crimes during a six-month period involved white victims and black suspects.

The Zebra killers belonged to a Black Muslim cult called the Death Angels, which taught that whites were evil and had to be destroyed. In revenge for centuries of oppression, the Zebras declared war against the whites. The cult developed rules for killing that became a part of the shared culture. Those who complied with the rules were rewarded, those who ignored them were deemed traitors.

Most mass murders are premeditated purposeful acts to accomplish some goal. The goal may be dictated by an imaginary cause or leader. Between October 1972 and February 1973, Herbert William Mullin murdered 13 people to ward off earthquakes in southern California. In his mind he was successful, since there were no earthquakes.

Charles Manson was a charismatic leader, whose followers believed he was Jesus Christ. The motives of the murders committed by the Manson "family," mostly white, middle-class followers of Manson, can be likened to those of an attacking army. The movie actress Sharon

Tate's residence was their Pearl Harbor, the place they chose to begin their war on society.

Family Murders. Of the three types of mass murder, family slayings, mass murder for profit or expediency and killings for sex or sadism, family slayings are the most common. They make up almost half of all mass murders.

One family theme stems from conflict that may force a man to leave the security and emotional support of his family. Whether or not he deserves to be thrown out, he relies on that support. He may return to get even with his wife by killing all "her" children, as if they were solely his wife's. Psychiatrist Shervert Frazier calls this act of revenge against the wife "murder by proxy."

Despite the efforts of the women's movement to change images of sexual roles, most men perceive of themselves as the "breadwinners" in their families. When a man loses his job, he loses an important source of self-esteem and self-control. An unemployed breadwinner may elect to spare his wife and children the humiliation and hardship of unemployment by executing them in their sleep. Frazier calls this "suicide by proxy." To kill his children, an extension of himself, is for the family murderer to commit suicide.

Some families have a member that family therapists call by various names, all of which essentially mean the family "scapegoat" or "misfit." He or she is viewed by other family members as the source of all family dissatisfaction. Sometimes the misfit leaves and cuts his or her ties with the family. Sometimes the misfit retaliates and wipes out the family in one murderous barrage.

Investigative Obstacles. One of the most obvious distinctions between simultaneous and serial mass murder is the relative difficulty in solving the two types of murder. Simultaneous killings are solved with comparative ease; serial murders are much more difficult.

Because he or she murders repeatedly without getting caught, the serial killer must be viewed as a skilled or lucky practitioner, otherwise he or she would have been stopped before the numbers mounted. Even if the murderer leaves a signature, for example marks on the bodies or the position in which the bodies are placed, the pattern may go unnoticed in the sheer volume of unsolved crimes, particularly in large cities.

Even an unmistakable pattern does not guarantee a quick solution. Serial killer John Gacy would have remained at large if the mother of one of his victims had not succeeded in convincing a police lieutenant to investigate the contractor her son had gone to see when

he disappeared. Gacy had been killing for at least three years. Early in his string of killings and burials, missing persons reports in two separate areas cited Gacy as someone with whom the boys had associated, but the decentralized structure of the Chicago Police Department prevented a link being made between the cases.

Seeing a common element in several reports of missing or murdered persons in one city is difficult enough. Seeing it across jurisdictional lines is that much more difficult. Some mobile killers stay in an area for a while, but when the police begin to get close, they move on.

Ted Bundy killed at least nine women in the Seattle, Washington area before moving on to Utah. After Bundy's arrest in Utah, he was extradited to Colorado to face a murder charge, but he escaped and fled to Florida.

To shed some light on such cases, the FBI developed the VICAP, the Violent Criminal Apprehension Program, designed to collect, collate and analyze all aspects of the investigation of similar-patterned multiple murders on a nationwide basis, regardless of location or number of police agencies involved. The advantage of VICAP is that if the killer moves on and maintains his or her pattern, the investigation is able to move with him in a multijurisdictional effort.

The program requires a police agency that has an unsolved murder involving mutilation or torture of victims or the disappearance of children to submit to the FBI a thorough description of the case, using a 27-page questionnaire. The FBI computers can help only to the extent that the police encode the key items of data and to the extent that offenders exhibit patterns strong enough to detect.

(See also CAMPUS VIOLENCE; MENTAL ILLNESS: BEHAVIORS THAT ATTRACT NEGATIVE ATTENTION; SERIAL KILLERS; SOCIOPATHS; VIOLENCE AS FUN: THE CASE OF THE CENTRAL PARK JOGGER; VIOLENT CRIMES AGAINST WOMEN: THEIR CONNECTION TO GENDER BIAS.)

mean-world syndrome   The fear of crime, at least in some cities, appears to be growing faster than the crime rate.

George Gerbner, a professor at the University of Pennsylvania's Annenberg School of Communication, has found that frequent viewers of violence on television are oversensitized by their viewing habits. They develop what Gerbner calls a "mean-world syndrome."

According to Gerbner, "Heavy television viewing is the single largest contribution to the feeling of rampant criminality and the threat of violence lurking around every corner." His studies revealed that the more television viewers watch, the greater their distrust of strangers and the higher their estimates of crime and danger to themselves.

Criminal violence is shown in television dramas at a rate many times higher than it occurs in real life. TV drama shifts the focus away from the bulk of everyday crime. The vast majority of all crimes are simple larcenies; only about 10% are violent. Local TV news also focuses on crime and violence, thereby reinforcing the mean-world syndrome.

Oversensitization to TV violence may not mean that the heavy viewer shrinks into passivity as a consequence of fear. The sense that others are not trustworthy could just as easily result in conflict with strangers over trivial incidents. Moreover, the constant exposure may make violent behavior appear normal or behavior to be emulated.

The mean-world syndrome may also be related to one's perceived risk of being the victim of a crime. Kenneth Ferraro, associate professor of sociology at Purdue University, oversaw a 1990 telephone survey of 1,100 subjects 18 and older in 830 communities. The survey was sponsored by the American Association of Retired Persons' Andrus Foundation.

Respondents were asked to rate on a scale of one to ten their fear of ten different crimes, how afraid they were of becoming a victim of crime, and how much risk they thought they faced. The crimes included rape, murder, assault, burglary while at home or while away, vandalism, car theft, fraud, robbery and illegal solicitation by a beggar or panhandler.

The survey contradicted the common belief that elderly Americans are more frightened of crime than younger people. Ferraro found that people of all ages rated their fear of each crime at a level consistent with their own estimated risk.

The highest fear rates were among the 18- to 24-year-olds. They rated themselves at a high risk of being victimized, so their high rate of fear made sense.

Age probably determines which programs viewers watch on TV. Older Americans may avoid viewing crime and violence.

One area where some otherwise fearful people express violence is behind the wheel of a car. In a May/June 1991 *Bostonia* article entitled "Highway to Hell?: Fear and Loathing on the Road," the author Northeastern University professor Jack Levin wrote, "Even the most timid and passive individuals (or, perhaps, *especially* the most timid and passive individuals) may become fearless bullies and criminals just as soon as they get behind 3,000 pounds of steel which separates them from humanity."

The freeways of California were particularly violent during the 1980s and early 1990s. In Sacramento, a passenger enraged by another car's lane change took a rifle from the rack of his pickup truck and shot the driver of the offending vehicle. In another incident, after a minor sideswipe, a passenger was shot in the head. A driver who blocked the entry of a tow truck onto the Golden State Freeway fired on the tow truck operator. A police officer preparing to write a ticket was fired on.

The mean-world syndrome tends to drive out civility and become a self-fulfilling prophecy.

(See also ANGER; DRIVE-BY-SHOOTINGS; GRIEF: EXPRESSIONS OF IN THE AFTERMATH OF VIOLENCE; POST-TRAUMATIC STRESS DISORDER [PSTD]; RAGE, EXPLOSIVE.)

mental illness: behaviors that attract negative attention

The mental illness known as schizophrenia afflicts an estimated 1% of the American population. On any given day, 100,000 schizophrenics fill hospital beds and thousands more wander the streets among the homeless.

Schizophrenia is characterized by seven common symptoms, none of which is present invariably or peculiar to schizophrenia. The schizophrenic's thinking involves delusions that are often multiple, fragmented or bizarre. Particular bizarre delusions are common, for example that thoughts are being broadcast from one's head to the external world; that thoughts are being inserted or withdrawn, or that one's thoughts, feelings or actions are being controlled by an external force.

The schizophrenic's form of thought often involves a loosening of associations, in which ideas shift from one to another completely unrelated or only obliquely related idea. The content of schizophrenic speech may be impoverished, or speech may convey little.

The schizophrenic's perception is disturbed; particularly common are various forms of hallucinations. Although they occur in a variety of forms, the most common hallucinations are auditory, frequently involving voices that the schizophrenic perceives as coming from outside his or her head. The voices may be familiar, single or multiple, speak directly to the person or talk about him or her. They often make insulting remarks.

Sometimes the voices command that certain actions be taken. Occasionally these can create danger for the schizophrenic or for others. Tactile hallucinations typically involve electrical, tingling or burning sensations.

Affect (emotional expression) in schizophrenics is often flat or inappropriate. The schizophrenic's voice is apt to be monotonous and his or her face immobile. Schizophrenics often complain that they have no feelings.

When a schizophrenic's affect is inappropriate, the manner of his or her speech or thinking may be clearly at odds with the content. For example, while discussing being tortured by electric shocks, the schizophrenic may laugh or smile.

The sense of self, a feeling of uniqueness and self-direction, is frequently disturbed in a schizophrenic. The person may be perplexed about his or her own identity and the meaning of life.

A schizophrenic's volition is impaired. Inadequate interest, drive or ability may prevent following a course of action to its conclusion. Severe ambivalence about alternative courses of action can result in a near cessation of goal-directed activity.

Interpersonal functioning and relationships in the outside world are almost invariably impaired, often in the form of social withdrawal and emotional detachment. Sometimes the detachment is so severe that it excludes the outside world.

A schizophrenic's psychomotor functions (ability to perform voluntary physical movement) are disturbed in acute or chronically severe cases. A schizophrenic may maintain a rigid posture and resist being moved or exhibit odd mannerisms, such as grimacing.

Onset of schizophrenia is usually during adolescence or early adulthood, but the disorder may begin in middle or late adult life. Many studies indicate an earlier onset in males than in females. Although violent acts performed by people with this disorder often attract public attention, it is not clear that their frequency is any greater than in the general population.

The *Diagnostic and Statistical Manual of Mental Disorders, 3rd Edition, Revised (DSM-III-R)* distinguishes subtypes of schizophrenia. The subtype most likely to be associated with violence is the paranoid type. The essential feature of the paranoid type is a preoccupation with one or more systematized delusions related to a single theme. Paranoid schizophrenics are often characterized by unfocused anxiety, anger, argumentativeness and violence. The quality of their interactions are often intense, stilted and formal. However, they are often more able than those with other types of schizophrenia to function in an occupation and to live independently.

Paranoid schizophrenics are distinguished from those suffering from delusional (paranoid) disorder and paranoid personality disorder. Although those with delusional disorder have delusions, they do not have the schizophrenic's prominent hallucinations and bizarre delusions (thought broadcasts, thought withdrawal or insertion). Their nonbizarre delusions involve situations in real life, such as being followed, poisoned, infected, loved at a distance, deceived by one's spouse or lover, or having a disease.

Delusional disorders are categorized by the type of theme prominent in their delusions. Two types are most likely to come to the attention of the public.

The person with delusional disorder, erotomanic type, has a delusion that a person, usually of a higher social status such as a celebrity or his or her superior at work, is in love with him or her. Efforts to contact the object of the delusion through telephone calls, letters, gifts, visits and even surveillance and stalking are common. Males, in particular, are likely to come into conflict with the law in this way. Such erotic delusions are a significant source of harassment to public figures.

The person with delusional disorder, jealous type, is convinced without cause that his or her spouse or lover is unfaithful. Small bits of evidence such as disarrayed clothing or spots on bedsheets are used to justify the delusion. Almost invariably the person with the delusion will confront the spouse or lover and take such extraordinary steps to intervene in the imagined infidelity as trying to restrict the autonomy of the spouse or lover. The person with the delusion may even attack the spouse or lover, and occasionally may attack the suspected lover.

The person with paranoid personality disorder does not have delusions, but he or she interprets the actions of others as deliberately demeaning or threatening in at least four of the following ways:

- He or she expects, without sufficient evidence, to be exploited or harmed by others.
- He or she questions, without justification, the loyalty or trustworthiness of friends or associates.
- He or she reads hidden demeaning or threatening significance into benign remarks or events.
- He or she bears grudges or is unforgiving of insults or slights.
- He or she is reluctant to confide in others because of an unwarranted fear that the information will be used against him or her.
- He or she is easily slighted and quick to anger or to counterattack.

- He or she questions, without justification, the fidelity of his or her spouse or sexual partner.

People with paranoid personality disorder are often argumentative and exaggerate difficulties. They have a tendency to counterattack when they perceive any threat.

Mood Disorders. Mood disorders are another category of mental disorder with the potential for getting those who suffer from them into conflict with the public or the law. Mood disorders are defined by the *DSM-III-R* as having as an essential feature a disturbance of mood, accompanied by a full or partial manic or depressive syndrome, that is not attributable to any other mental or physical disorder. Mood disorders are divided into bipolar and depressive disorders.

Bipolar disorders are distinguished by the occurrence of manic episodes, usually including one or more major depressive episodes. The essential feature of a manic episode is a distinct period during which one extreme mood, either elevated or irritable, is predominant. The disturbance is usually severe enough to cause marked impairment in occupational or social functioning and may necessitate hospitalization to prevent harm to self or others.

Associated manic symptoms include inflated self-esteem, increased goal-directed activity, decreased need for sleep, rapid speech, distractibility, hyperactivity and excessive pursuit of pleasurable activities that, unrecognized by the person with the symptoms, have a high potential to end in painful consequences.

An elevated, euphoric mood often has an infectious quality for an uninvolved observer, but is recognized as excessive by those who know the person well. Although the typical mood is elevated, it may be irritable, which becomes most apparent if the person is thwarted.

Inflated self-esteem can range from uncritical self-confidence to delusional grandiosity. The person, despite a lack of knowledge or talent, may offer advice on running the United Nations, may start a novel or compose music, or, if delusional, may claim a special relationship to God.

A sleep disturbance may involve waking several hours early, full of energy. When it is severe, the person may go days without sleep and not feel tired.

Manic speech is loud, rapid and difficult to interrupt, and is often filled with puns, jokes and plays on words. Flights of ideas involve abrupt changes from topic to topic.

A manic episode's increased goal-directed activity often involves planning of and participation in an excessive number of activities. There is almost always increased sociability, which is likely to include efforts to renew old acquaintances and call friends at all hours of the night. The activities often have a bizarre quality, such as dressing in strange garments, wearing poorly applied makeup, or distributing candy, money or advice to passing strangers.

Frequently the person does not recognize that he or she is ill and resists all efforts at treatment. A common feature is lability of mood, that is, rapid shifts from elevation to anger or depression.

Manic episodes typically begin suddenly, with a rapid escalation of symptoms over a few days. Episodes usually last from a few days to months. They are usually briefer and end more abruptly than depressive episodes. Onset is on the average in the early 20s, but some studies have indicated that a substantial number of new cases appear after age 50.

The essential features of a depressive episode are either a depressed mood (or an irritable mood in children or adolescents) or a loss of pleasure in all, or almost all, activities, and associated symptoms, for a period of at least two weeks. Symptoms occur for most of the day, nearly every day. Associated symptoms include an increase or decrease in appetite, with an associated change in weight, insomnia or hypersomnia (daytime sleepiness or excessive naps).

Agitation takes the form of pacing, hand-wringing, pulling or rubbing hair, skin, clothing or objects. Speech may be slowed, with increased pauses before answering, a soft or monotonous tone, a marked decrease in the amount of speech or muteness.

In the midst of a depressive episode, the afflicted person may be filled with a sense of worthlessness that may range from feelings of inadequacy to grotesquely unrealistic evaluations of one's worth. Guilt may be expressed as an excessive reaction to current or past failings or as an assumed or exaggerated responsibility for some event. Difficulty in concentrating, slowed thinking, problems with memory, distractibility and indecisiveness are frequent.

Thoughts of death, not just fear of dying, and a belief that one would be better off dead are common. With or without a plan, there may be suicidal thoughts or attempts. The potential for suicide is the most serious consequence of a major depressive episode.

The average age at onset is in the late 20s, but the disorder may begin at any age, including infancy. Onset may take days or weeks to develop or may be sudden. Duration is variable. Untreated, an episode may last six months or longer.

Degree of impairment varies, but always creates some difficulty with social and occupational functioning. When impairment is severe, the person may not be even able to feed and clothe him- or herself.

Depending on the clinical features of the current or most recent episode, bipolar disorders are classified by *DSM-III-R* as Bipolar Disorder, Mixed; Bipolar Disorder, Manic; Bipolar Disorder, Depressed. There is evidence that cases of bipolar disorder with mixed or rapid-cycling episodes have a much more chronic course than those that do not.

It is estimated that 0.4 to 1.2% of the adult population of the United States has had bipolar disorder. Epidemiological studies in the United States indicate that the disorder is equally common in males and females, unlike major depression, which is more common in females.

Depressive disorders are mood disorders distinguished by the occurrence of one or more major depressive episodes without the occurrence of a manic episode or an unequivocal hypomanic episode (similar to a manic episode but with less severe symptoms).

Some people have only a single episode, with a full return to their former functions, but it is estimated that more than 50% of those suffering a single episode will eventually have another. The course of recurrent major depression is variable. Some people have episodes separated by many years of normal functions; others have clusters of episodes; still others have increasingly frequent episodes as they grow older. Functioning usually returns to the prior level between episodes, although in 20% to 35% of cases, there continue to be symptoms and social impairment.

Studies of major depression in the United States and Europe report a wide range of estimates of the proportion of the adult population that has at some time had the disorder. The range for females is 9% to 26% and for males from 5% to 12%. Estimates of the proportion of the adult population that currently has the disorder range from 4.5% to 9.3% for females and 2.3% to 3.2% for males. There is some evidence that the prevalence of the disorder has increased in those who reached adulthood in the years after World War II.

Almost all studies of major depression in adults living in industrialized countries have estimated the disorder to be twice as common in females as in males, as distinguished from bipolar disorder, which is equally common in both sexes.

(See also MENTAL ILLNESS: THE IMPACT OF DEINSTITUTIONALIZATION ON STREETS AND JAILS.)

mental illness: the impact of deinstitutionalization on streets and jails   From before the turn of the century until the early 1960s, large state hospitals for the mentally ill and retarded were the major providers in the United States of mental health services. In the years from 1955 to 1975, the population of such hospitals nationwide dropped from 550,000 to less than 200,000. Many hospitals reduced their average caseload from to 2,000 to 200 in just a few years.

Several factors made the change possible. The most significant was the development of a large variety of new drugs in the 1950s, loosely referred to as tranquilizers. The newly available drugs made it possible to tailor medication to a patient's specific needs.

Other contributing factors included a report in 1955 by a federal Joint Commission on Mental Illness and Mental Health, which called for a reduction in the size and number of large state hospitals and the development of local community services to take their place; federal investment in mental health professional training and federal financing of mental health services; and a joint commission on children's mental health, which directed attention to the lack of services for adolescents and children.

These elements coincided with the rise of the civil rights and consumer movements, whose advocates were appalled by the antitherapeutic living conditions in large mental hospitals. They joined with many professionals in the field who had protested these conditions for decades.

Because the idea of deinstitutionalization was so quickly seized on, it swept patients out of the hospitals into communities unprepared to receive them. The appeal to authorities of the movement to return patients to the community was not based simply on the restoration of civil rights to the mentally ill. Economics was the major impetus. Large mental institutions, however shabby and austere, had become too expensive to run.

Legislators envisioned themselves slashing a large budget item at the same time that they draped themselves heroically in the mantle of restorers of patients to the bosoms of their families. They did not, however, envision themselves transferring the funds saved into mental health services in the communities. They apparently did not seriously consider the possibility that adequate community care (''support services'') might cost even more than hospital care, as proved to be the case when courts mandated a full range of community programs.

The idealized view of the patients' futures held by advocates and accepted by legislators centered on a warm and generous family, understanding friends and a loving community. Implicit in this view was the assumption that public expenditures would be reduced by having patients live at home. But while some families did welcome patients home, many patients had no family, or had a family ill equipped to care for someone with a long-term psychosis, or had a family who had contributed to their illness originally. Moreover, in many cases family ties and friendships had been eroded by the illness.

Whether or not a patient who was returning to the community after a long hospital stay had a family, he or she needed more than just assistance in finding a place to live. He or she needed help in making new friends and in reconnecting to community organizations, such as the church. Former patients also needed opportunities for recreation and work. Nonprofit halfway houses and group living arrangements were created for some newly released patients, but they were not enough by themselves.

Federal grants were awarded to newly formed non-profit mental health centers. Many were given eight-year grants, with funds diminishing each year. The grants were predicated on the assumption that, once started, the centers would be able to find state, local and private funding, a very uncertain prospect. Many financially strapped states and local governments were intent on cutting back social service expenditures. A number of centers that were started up with federal funds closed at the end of eight years. Others struggled on with greatly diminished capacity.

In some areas, patients were released from hospitals under the mandate of a federal court. They at least had some chance of receiving court-mandated adequate services; patients who left the hospitals before court intervention were not protected. Moreover, patients who became ill after the hospitals had drastically reduced their size had nowhere to turn.

Once hospital size was reduced, most state statutes stipulated that patients could be admitted to mental hospitals only if they posed a danger to themselves or others. Most patients are not dangerous to others, and many are not likely to commit suicide. However, their psychosis is apt to keep them out of touch with the world around them, so that they often cannot take care of themselves or avoid getting into life-threatening situations.

Lost in the public rhetoric about the economics of care and patients' civil rights were the rights of people who did not want to leave the hospitals. Some had learned to live "in the cracks" of the institutions and had made homes and friends among patients and staffs. Their right to continue living in the hospitals was summarily overridden. Some former patients chose suicide attempts as the only method available to force authorities to return them to their state hospital homes.

During the 1980s, as homeless people became a more and more familiar sight in American streets, it became clear to most observers that a number of the homeless were mentally ill. Among the more obviously ill were former patients seen having auditory or visual hallucinations on city streets. Typically they were conversing with or warding off blows from imaginary people. Another common sight was former patients who stared unseeing into space for hours without moving, regardless of the weather or events around them.

During the 1980s funds for social services continued to be cut and low-income housing became increasingly scarce; by the early 1990s many areas of the country were in a recession and funds became even more scarce. By this time the mentally ill homeless had become, by default, the responsibility of the police, who often had no choice but to put them in jail. Moreover, because treatment alternatives are meager, large numbers of substance abusers (those who consume alcohol, drugs or both, to excess) also are vulnerable to arrest.

Since the mid-1970s, without much in the way of unambiguous research data, many mental health professionals have claimed that the nation's jails have taken in ever-larger numbers of people with mental disorders. One estimate placed the national total of mentally ill and retarded jail inmates at 600,000.

Their contention was given some support by a controlled study conducted by psychologist Linda Teplin of Northwestern University Medical School in Chicago, reported in the June 1990 issue of the *American Journal of Public Health*. A group of 627 men sent to the Cook County, Illinois jail between November 1983 and November 1984 was randomly recruited into Teplin's study. She found that more than 6% of all the men arrested for misdemeanors or felonies—about one in 16—suffered from a severe mental impairment upon arrival in jail. Clinical psychologists interviewed the men in a soundproof booth placed within the intake area, using a standardized psychiatric interview developed at the National Institute of Mental Health (NIMH) in Bethesda, Maryland.

Three serious mental disorders—schizophrenia, severe depression and mania—were found to be three times more common among the men interviewed than among men in the U.S. population as a whole. At a given time, less than 2% of the general population is likely to be suffering from any of these three illnesses, while among the men interviewed the rate surpassed 6%. At some time during their lives, almost 4.5% of the U.S. population has suffered from one of the three illnesses; among the inmates the rate was 9.5%.

Because the study was of randomly selected subjects and well controlled, it is probably safe to assume that it reflects the incidence of those three illnesses to be found in the nation's urban jails in the early 1990s. Jails are ill equipped to deal with large numbers of severely disturbed individuals.

An April 19, 1991 ABC *20/20* broadcast entitled "Jail for the Mentally Ill. Why Are They Here?" illustrated the situation.

In California, *20/20* found more mentally ill in the Los Angeles County Jail than in any mental health institution in the nation. So numerous are mentally ill inmates in this jail that they are issued pale yellow uniforms to distinguish them. The other inmates call them "dings," short for ding-a-lings.

The Dade County Jail in Miami, one of the nation's largest detention centers, has a separate cellblock where a nurse makes rounds twice a day with a sophisticated array of psychoactive medications. However, drugs don't work if patients don't take them. During the *20/20* crew's visit, a patient who had stopped taking his medication made a suicide attempt by trying to run into a wall.

The issue of medication is one of the factors that makes it difficult for some of the mentally ill to get along in unstructured settings. Many do not like taking their medication because they do not like the idea of being controlled by it. Moreover, even the best drugs can have disagreeable side effects. Patients stop taking their medication in the hope that their psychosis will not come back and they will finally be like other people.

The Dade County Jail is too crowded to accommodate all the psychotic patients. Jail personnel have to put mattresses on the floor for the overload. Although a patient might be put in an isolated cell when necessary, the jail does not have a padded cell. Dr. E. Fuller Torrey, a renowned psychiatrist who directed a study for the Washington-based Public Citizen's Health Research Group, met with the *20/20* staff at the Dade County Jail. "There's only one psychiatrist in this jail for 6,000 inmates," he said. "Six to nine hundred of them are seriously mentally ill." Most suffer from schizophrenia.

Asked to characterize the typical jailed psychotic patient, he said, "They are hearing voices. They may have delusional thinking. They may have illogical thinking, so that when you talk to them they don't make very good sense. That's the disease called schizophrenia. Then because of their confusion or because they were hungry or whatever, they committed some kind of minor crime." On each minor offense, a patient might be in jail for four or five weeks. By the end of the year he or she might have spent as much as nine months in jail.

The ironic fact is that the worse a patient behaves, the more chance he or she has to get appropriate care. One young woman had been jailed several times, but only after she slapped some children on a playground did she become eligible for hospital care, because she had then met the criterion of being a danger to others. Prior to the playground incidents, her mother had tried repeatedly to get her into a hospital.

The *20/20* moderator asked Torrey, "Isn't the jail more humane than having these people roaming around disoriented and victimized on the streets?"

Torrey answered, "Yes, but that's a hell of a choice to have to make. Leave someone on the streets or take him to jail. If that's where we are in the 1990s, we're not in very good shape."

(See also ALCOHOL DEPENDENCE; MENTAL ILLNESS: BEHAVIORS THAT ATTRACT NEGATIVE ATTENTION.)

Miranda ruling   See ARREST: CONSTITUTIONAL RESTRICTIONS AND LEGAL PROCEDURES; BILL OF RIGHTS: GOVERNMENT PROTECTION AGAINST TYRANNY.

model mugging   Model mugging refers to martial arts training designed specifically for women's self-protection. It was originated in 1974 by Matt Thomas, a martial arts instructor, following a brutal rape suffered by one of his students, a woman who already had a black belt in karate. Thomas realized that men attack women differently than they do men. Instead of striking directly, an attacker is more likely to grab a woman in an enveloping motion. Based on his analysis, Thomas developed a short, effective self-defense course for women.

The technique emphasizes fighting from the ground up, since the ground is where a rape victim is likely to find herself. This position gives her an advantage because it allows her to use her lower body, where her strength is greater. When using the force of her grounded hips and legs, a woman can overpower even a large man.

Instructors, encased in 40 pounds of protective padding, serve as model muggers. Based on years of experience, the instructor can determine when the woman has delivered a knockout and will continue to fight with her until she delivers one.

The training teaches women to break out of rape-specific holds, use full-force blows, aim for "taboo" areas such as the groin and eyes and deal with moving targets. At the same time, they are desensitized to verbal abuse, which rapists typically use to stun their victims. A major premise of the training is that if the woman chooses to fight off a rapist, she must commit 100% to the effort.

The intent of the course is not to hate men or to bait them. One instructor emphasized the goal by saying, "The art of fighting is to not have to fight."

money laundering The practice of hiding the source or ownership of large sums of money by moving them through national and international financial networks is referred to as money laundering. Laundered money can be separated into two categories, gray money and black money.

Gray money enters the financial stream for laundering from a variety of sources. The source may be legitimate; for example, a citizen of a country with strict currency-control laws might dodge them by moving his or her savings out of the country; a multinational corporation might reduce its tax burden by funneling profits into tax-free havens; and national intelligence agencies might divert funds used to finance covert or espionage activities. On the other hand, the source of gray money may be illegitimate. For example, a dictator might siphon funds from the national treasury to a personal account in another country.

Black or dirty money, the profits from criminal activities, travels through the world's financial institutions as part of the larger flow of gray money and is handled in similar fashion. An enormous amount of dirty money originates in the drug trade.

A December 18, 1989 *Time* article entitled "A Torrent of Dirty Dollars" pointed out that in the drug trade the money-laundering process usually begins with U.S. dollars. Cash may be carried out of the United States in the luggage of departing travelers, since outgoing luggage is seldom searched. Other methods involve large shipments of cash in private airplanes or in seagoing freight containers that are seldom inspected. U.S.

officials are unable to locate at least 80% of all the bills printed by the Treasury. Once out of the country, the cash is funneled into black markets, where the U.S. dollar is the favored currency.

A drawback to transporting cash out of the country for the owner of the cash is that interest revenue cannot be accrued while the money is in transit. Therefore many drug traffickers, who view the United States as a profitable haven for their money, prefer to launder and invest their cash in America. Perhaps the most difficult step in the process is depositing the cash in a U.S. financial institution because the Internal Revenue Service (IRS) requires all banks to file Currency Transaction Reports (CTRs) for deposits of $10,000 or more. During the early 1980s money launderers avoided CTRs by employing couriers (called "Smurfs" after the cartoon characters) who would make many deposits of less than $10,000 each in many banks.

Once the government required that financial institutions be on the lookout for Smurfs, launderers developed new methods to get around the $10,000 rule. The launderers established or bought retail businesses that collect large amounts of cash, many of which are exempt from the $10,000 rule. As fronts, some money launderers have created companies, such as restaurants, that accept no checks or credit cards. Other launderers have entered into agreements with employees of businesses such as convenience and computer supply stores. The volume of cash to be laundered is usually so great that many money launderers probably use several methods. Since the government must handle 7 million CTRs each year, even a business without an exemption can be used as a front, since it is unlikely to attract attention.

Once the money is introduced into a financial institution, it can be moved around the world rapidly. The volume of global money movement is so great that it cannot really be monitored. On an average day, the Clearing House for Interbank Payments System handles 145,500 transactions worth in excess of $700 billion.

The *Time* article provided several examples of laundering. One was the "Dutch sandwich." Using this approach, a Paris bank might set up a corporation in Rotterdam for an American customer with cash, which he or she would deposit in the bank's local branch. The American would control the newly created Dutch corporation through a trust company in the Netherlands Antilles in the Caribbean. The identity of the American owner would be protected by the island group's secrecy laws. The Caribbean branch of the bank would then "lend" the American his or her own money held in

Rotterdam. If questioned by the IRS about the source of the income, the American could point to the loan from a respectable international bank. According to Antilles bank officers, many American movie stars and corporations use the Dutch sandwich.

Because the world's economy seems to depend on a fluid and unencumbered financial system, politicians and bank officials have been reluctant to institute controls. The IRS estimates that as much as $50 billion annually is siphoned off by tax evaders from legitimate cash-generating business and laundered to avoid detection.

Much of the global electronic money passes through Switzerland. Money laundering is not a crime in Switzerland, unless it can be shown that the cash flows from criminal activity. Switzerland has been a magnet for money laundering because of its legitimate multibillion-dollar trade in foreign banknotes and because of the legally protected secrecy of its banking system. As much as 1.5 tons of foreign currency arrives in Zurich daily.

The drug trade brought about a change of attitude about banking in Switzerland, according to an April 10, 1989 *Newsweek* article entitled "A Drug Crackdown in the Alps." In the wake of billions of dollars of drug money flowing through anonymous accounts, narcotics themselves began moving through the country in large quantities and the drug trade reached the streets of Swiss cities, where it could not be ignored by ordinary citizens. The Swiss have one of the highest heroin-addiction rates in Europe and the incidence of AIDS related to addicts' sharing needles is accelerating. The Swiss made launderers less welcome as a consequence.

The launderers are moving to other countries, such as Luxembourg, where the total bank deposits grew from $40 billion in 1984 to $100 billion in 1988. Dozens of islands, ranging from Britain's Isle of Man to Vanuatu in the South Pacific, have bolstered their economies by becoming havens for money.

In the United States, money laundering has not remained the preserve of druglords, corporations and movie stars. IRS agents have been working overtime to contain an explosion of small-time cases involving car salespeople, real estate agents and other entrepreneurs who have been paid in cash and decided not to share the money with the government.

U.S. statutes governing money laundering began to tighten in 1986 when money laundering per se became a crime. Later it was made illegal to avoid the $10,000 currency deposit reporting requirement by making smaller deposits. A series of investigations in the mid-1980s that resulted in such venerable institutions as Bank of America and Bank of Boston being forced to pay substantial fines prodded banks to increase supervision. Nevertheless, many major banks continue to be participants, wittingly or not, in increasingly sophisticated laundering transactions.

Money laundering is not an issue of concern only to financial and law enforcement officials. It plays a role in the stability of world monetary systems. In his 1987 book *Hot Money and the Politics of Debt,* Robin Naylor described "hot and homeless money" as money that is ready to leave its present abode for more hospitable climes whenever a tiny interest rate spread, exchange rate change or shift in the political environment beckons.

The Bank of Credit and Commerce International Scandal. Hot money also plays a role in influence peddling. The Bank of Credit and Commerce International (BCCI), controlled by the ruling family of Abu Dhabi, largest of the United Arab Emirates, had $20 billion in assets in 350 branches in 70 countries and wielded a great deal of power in Washington, D.C. In 1988 Robert Gates, then deputy Central Intelligence Agency (CIA) director, reportedly dubbed the BCCI "the Bank of Crooks and Criminals."

On August 4, 1991 Deputy CIA Director Richard Kerr revealed that the CIA had used the BCCI to make deposits for covert operations beginning in the early 1980s. While those operations were ongoing, the CIA informed other U.S. government agencies that the BCCI was engaged in money laundering, drug trafficking and funding terrorists.

On October 11, 1988 the bank and its two top officers were indicted in Tampa, Florida on money-laundering charges. The bank pleaded guilty on January 16, 1990 and was fined $15 million. The BCCI was found to have provided money-laundering services to Colombian drug dealers and Panama's ousted dictator (and former CIA asset) General Manuel Antonio Noriega.

Despite the Florida indictments, the bank continued to do business as usual. In July 1991, after auditors found evidence of widespread fraud and losses of $5 billion or more, bank regulators around the world closed many of the BCCI's branches. Manhattan District Attorney Robert Morgenthau filed indictments in New York alleging that the BCCI and its top officials schemed to defraud depositors. Further indictments were expected to follow alleging that the BCCI schemed against federal and state bank regulators in Washington, D.C., Maryland, Tennessee, Florida, Virginia, Georgia and California.

According to a year-old audit report made public in the summer of 1991, BCCI directors used the funds invested by small investors to cover loans given to friends of the bank, including a dozen Arab sheikhs, that had not been repaid. The bank also took deposits that were never recorded from drug and arms traffickers in a desperate effort to cover mounting losses.

In August 1991 two Washington power brokers, Clark Clifford, a former U.S. defense secretary, and his protégé, Robert Altman, resigned as the two highest ranking officers of First American Bankshares, Washington, D.C.'s largest bank holding company, which investigators discovered was secretly controlled by the BCCI, which had illegally acquired it a decade earlier. An investigation by the Federal Reserve Board alleged that Clifford and Altman made millions of dollars in a 1988 stock deal involving a Caribbean company that the BCCI also illegally controlled and that they bought stock in the company with a BCCI loan.

By the fall of 1991, U.S. Senator John Kerry of Massachusetts had conducted ten separate hearings into the BCCI's activities. In an interview for an August 16, 1991 *Christian Science Monitor* article, "Unraveling of BCCI's Secret Tapestry Begins," Kerry described the BCCI's network as "this enormous undergovernment that's out there—a mixture of nefarious types of people."

Testifying before Kerry's committee, William von Raab, who was U.S. customs commissioner during the 1988 BCCI Tampa case, said that strong evidence he had collected indicated that the BCCI was the center of an underworld network, but the evidence was ignored by federal authorities.

Asked why federal authorities would fail to prosecute BCCI officials aggressively, von Raab replied:

A general softening of resolve in the senior U.S. officials by the incredible pounding they were taking by the influence peddlers in Washington . . . The result is that the senior U.S. policy-level officials were constantly under the impression that BCCI was probably not that bad because all these good guys that they play golf with all the time were representing them.

In addition to the impact of influence peddlers, von Raab said that he suspected that the Justice Department refrained from pursuing criminal charges against the BCCI because it wanted to use BCCI officials to build its case against former Panama dictator Noriega. Von Raab was pulled off the BCCI case for being too zealous.

A lawyer for Lloyds of London, James Dougherty, also reported that he had provided the Justice Department with evidence that the BCCI was involved in a criminal conspiracy, including money laundering, kickbacks, extortion attempts and obstruction of justice. His evidence and his offer to cooperate were ignored.

According to Kerry, the web of the BCCI's activities included financing parts of Pakistan's nuclear buildup and supporting Afghan rebels. Kerry planned to investigate allegations that in exchange for payoffs some U.S. officials made it possible for the BCCI to gain control of First American Bankshares.

Along with sheikhs and captains of industry affected by the collapse of the BCCI's worldwide operation, several small relief and development organizations were hard hit. The Sabah Project, which serves hundreds of homeless children in the Sudan, had all of its funds frozen—possibly lost forever—when bank regulators closed down the London and Khartoum branches of the BCCI. Oxfam lost a third of its annual budget for dozens of small agricultural projects in Senegal. The main victims will be thousands of individual depositors who will lose their savings if the BCCI's worldwide branches are liquidated.

(See also APPENDIX IC: THE MEDELLIN CARTEL.)

multiple personality disorder   According to the American Psychiatric Association's *Diagnostic and Statistical Manual of Mental Disorders, 3rd Edition, Revised (DSM-III-R)*, the essential characteristic of multiple personality disorder is the existence within an individual of two or more distinct personalities or personality states. Personality is defined as a relatively enduring pattern of perceiving, relating to and thinking about the environment and one's self, which is exhibited in a wide range of significant social and personal contexts. Personality states differ in that the range of contexts is narrower.

In classic cases of multiple personality disorder, there are at least two fully developed personalities who recurrently take full control of the person's behavior. The personalities and personality states each have unique memories, behavior patterns and social relationships. In other cases, there may be only one distinct personality and one or more personality states.

In children and adolescents, classic cases with two or more fully developed personalities are not as common as they are in adults. In adults the number of personalities ranges from two to over 100, with 50% having ten or fewer and 50% having more than ten.

The transition from one personality to another usually takes seconds or minutes, but in rare cases may take hours or days. The transition is likely to be triggered by psychosocial stress or social or environmental cues that are meaningful for the individual. Transitions also may occur when there are conflicts among the personalities.

Often personalities are aware of some or all of the others to varying degrees and may experience them as friends, companions or adversaries. They may or may not interact with them. The personality that presents itself for treatment often has little or no knowledge of the existence of the other personalities. At any given moment, only one interacts with the environment. Some of the other personalities may "listen in" or influence what is taking place.

The individual personalities may be quite different in attitude, behavior and self-image. A shy, retiring person may alternate with one who frequents bars and is promiscuous or gets into fights.

The major factor that individuals with multiple personality disorder have in common is a history of severe, sustained child abuse. In one large study, 97% of the patients had been abused as children.

In the 1950s, a popular book and movie called *The Three Faces of Eve* was believed to be a report of the only living case of a multiple personality. In spite of the book and although cases were reported in the 19th century, some professionals did not believe the disorder even existed. It did not become an official psychiatric diagnosis until 1980, when it was listed in an earlier version of the *DSM-III-R*.

Professionals now believe that multiple personality disorder may be as pervasive as schizophrenia, which afflicts one out of every 100 people. The assessment of the disorder's prevalence came from an ongoing study in Winnipeg, Manitoba of 1,055 people randomly selected from a much larger population. Results were presented at the sixth annual conference held on multiple personality disorder in Chicago in October 1989 and reported in a November 6, 1989 *Boston Globe* article entitled "A Mind Divided: Experts Probe Split Identities." The study found that between one in 100 and one in 1,000 suffered from the disorder. In several studies the disorder has been diagnosed three to nine times more often in females than males.

In an interview with the *Boston Globe*, Dr. Cornelia Wilbur, who diagnosed the case of Sybil, whose story became the basis for a best-selling book and film, said, "When you are abused like that, you either go crazy, die or become a multiple personality. Becoming a multiple personality is actually the healthiest way to deal with this kind of abuse."

In an effort to cope with their unbearable ordeals, some victims withdraw from reality, creating alter egos (other selves) to experience the abuse and absorb the pain. Psychiatrists do not fully understand how very young children develop other selves.

Children typically learn to keep separate their "school selves" from their "home selves," and their "in-class selves" separate from their "playground selves." In the children who develop multiple personalities, the normal integration of selves does not occur.

To protect themselves, the children acquire the ability to keep awareness of painful experiences confined to one self, thereby preventing the others from being flooded with painful memories. Researchers suspect that when some children are repeatedly abused they begin to imagine that someone else—perhaps an imaginary playmate—is being victimized rather than themselves. The children thus enter into an altered state, a trance, in which the "core personality" disappears.

As the abuse continues, the altered states become distinct personalities with their own memories, traits and behaviors. Because the abuse usually begins at an early age, many victims have personalities that remain childlike, frozen in terror from an experience or experiences that may have happened at that stage of their lives.

Dr. Frank Putnam, a psychiatrist at the National Institute of Mental Health, compares those with multiple personalities to war veterans who repeatedly relive the trauma of combat later on. In individuals with multiple personalities, alter egos are created to absorb and relive particular moments of trauma. The main personalities do not remember them because the memories are held in the other personalities that came into being when the abuse occurred.

Many of the separate personalities have specific roles and responsibilities. There are usually:

- a primary personality that can hold down a job and deals with the outside world. This is the original core self. It has no memory of past abuse and often experiences depression or physical symptoms without knowing why.
- one or more child personalities created to hold memories of abusive episodes so the primary personality can survive them. These selves are often frightened and confused.

- a "persecutor" personality created to absorb the tremendous rage the patient has against his or her abusers. The persecutor often turns the anger inward in the belief that the abuse is the fault of the primary personality and often tries to inflict punishment by, for example, taking drug overdoses or by slashing the wrists of the body that does not seem to be his or hers. And

- a "protector" personality created to shield the core self from the painful memories of the abuse, to protect the frightened child personalities and to keep the persecutor from harming the primary personality or from lashing out at other people.

Each personality has its own biological underpinning, a specific pattern of mental and biological states. Putnam has focused attention on how his patients make the switch from one personality to another. Typically, there is a period of seconds or minutes when physiological markers such as heart rate and breathing rate show disorganization. Following the disorganization, a new pattern emerges. The most visible changes are tension levels in facial muscles. Blood flow patterns in the brain are altered.

Over the course of a century, a great deal of evidence has accumulated from many studies that the various personalities in multiple personality disorder have their own distinctive biological patterns. A researcher at the conference described an individual named Timmy, one of whose dozen personalities is allergic to orange juice. If the allergic personality appears before Timmy finishes digesting orange juice, he will break out in hives. If Timmy reappears, the itching will cease immediately and the hives will begin to subside.

Treating multiple personality patients with any kind of medication is difficult because of the constant changes. Reactions to medication by different personalities can be radically different. In one woman, an alter ego had an almost lethal reaction to a test for tuberculosis, which the primary personality had taken earlier with no reaction.

Individuals with multiple personality disorder typically suffer from a variety of psychosomatic disorders, such as headaches, gastrointestinal pain and reproductive problems. These are symptoms that experts now recognize as common manifestations of early physical or sexual abuse.

One of the most recognizable symptoms of the disorder is an inability to maintain a consistent sense of time. Because different personalities keep emerging, the individual suffers from amnesia or blank spells and is likely to "wake up" in unfamiliar settings among unknown people. Most of the personalities are aware of lost periods of time or distortions in their experience of time and explain them away or cover them up in various ways.

Despite the turmoil in their minds, individuals with multiple personalities are adept at covering up. Dr. Richard Kluft, a psychiatrist at the Institute of Pennsylvania Hospital (also known as the Pennsylvania Hospital Clinical Institute) in Philadelphia, characterized many as smooth liars who appear to function well in the daily routine of life. Although strangers would not notice anything amiss, spouses and children are aware that something is wrong.

Once diagnosed, multiple personality disorder has an unusually high promise of successful treatment. Kluft, one of the most respected clinicians in the field, reported a 90% success rate among a sample of 52 patients.

Despite its good prognosis, the psychotherapeutic treatment is long and harrowing because it involves reliving and integrating the history of abuse and dealing with the emotional scars it has left. Once the overwhelming anger and horror are dealt with, the need for the split disappears.

(See also CHILD ABUSE AND NEGLECT; SEXUAL ABUSE OF CHILDREN.)

murder: U.S. profile   As defined by the U.S. Department of Justice Uniform Crime Reporting (UCR) criteria, murder and nonnegligent homicide are the willful killing of one human being by another. Not included in the definition are deaths caused by negligence, suicide or justifiable homicide or attempted murder by assault or other means, which are counted as aggravated assaults.

According to UCR tabulations, the total number of murders in the United States during 1990 was estimated to be 23,438, or 1% of the violent crimes reported. The most persons were killed in July and the fewest in February. The southern states, the region where most murders occurred, accounted for 43% of the total. The other regions had about half as many murders: the West accounted for 20%, the Midwest 19%, and the Northeast 18%. The murder rate rose 4% in 1989, from 8.4 per 100,000 population in 1988 to 8.7 per 100,000 in 1989, and another 8% in 1990, to 9.4 per 100,000.

Data based on incidents involving one victim and one offender showed that in 1990, 93.5% of black murder victims were slain by black offenders and 86% of white murder victims were killed by white offenders. In 85% of single victim/single offender murders, males were slain by males. The same data showed that nine out of every ten murdered females were killed by males.

Supplemental data provided by contributing agencies for 20,045 of the 23,438 murders in 1990 included the age, sex and race of both victims and offenders. Among victims, 78% were males, 90% were 18 years of age or older and the bulk, 49%, were between 20 and 34. Among victims whose race was reported, an average of 49 out of every 100 were black, 49 were white, and the remainder were persons of other races.

Over half of the victims were acquainted with (37.4%) or related to (13.6%) their assailants. Fourteen percent of assailants were strangers. For 34.7% of the victims the relationship with their assailant was unknown. Thirty percent of female victims were slain by husbands or boyfriends. Four percent of male victims were killed by wives or girlfriends.

Arguments resulted in 34.5% of the murders. Brawls while offenders were under the influence of alcohol resulted in 18.6%. Nineteen percent occurred during the commission of a felony (robbery, drug transaction, sex offense, arson, etc.), with another 2% suspected of having been related to a felony.

Firearms were used in three out of every five murders. Of the weapons reported, 50% were handguns, 6% were shotguns and 4% were rifles. Unknown types of firearms accounted for 5%.

Among other types of weapons, 17% were cutting or stabbing instruments, 5% were blunt objects (clubs, hammers, etc.), 8% were other dangerous weapons (poisons, explosives, etc.) and 3.6% were "personal" weapons" (hands, feet, fists, etc.).

A crime can be cleared in two ways: with a perpetrator arrested and prosecuted; or a perpetrator identified but not prosecuted for some reason. Thus clearance does not necessarily mean an arrest.

The clearance rate continues to be higher for murder than for any other Crime Index offense. Nationwide, law enforcement agencies cleared 67% of the murders occurring in their jurisdictions during 1990. In cities with populations under 10,000, the clearance rate was highest, 78%. By region, the South cleared 73%, the West 66%, and the Northeast 60%.

The largest category of those arrested was young black males. Persons under 18 years of age accounted for 7% of willful killings cleared. Nationwide, 52% of all murder arrestees were under age 25, and more than one-third, 38%, were 18 to 24. Ninety-one percent of those arrested were male and 9% were female. Blacks comprised 55% of arrestees, whites 44% and other races the rest.

The 1990 murder arrest total increased 9% above the 1989 total, was 9.3% higher than the 1986 level, but 4.1% lower than the 1981 total. While arrests of those over 18 went up 7.9%, arrests of those under 18 went up 15.5%. Male arrests went up 5% and female arrests went up 2%.

The *Uniform Crime Reports 1990*, in a table entitled "Murder Circumstances, 1986–1990," has a category called "Felony," which refers to murder in connection with a felony. A subcategory of felony is "Narcotics." In 1986 narcotics accounted for 3.9% of murders; in 1987, 4.9%; in 1988, 5.6%; in 1989, 7.4%; and in 1990, 6.5%. After doubling in four years, the number of felony murders related to drugs has dropped.

In an interview about the murder rate, for a December 31, 1989 *New York Times* article entitled "More Americans Are Killing Each Other," Jim Fyfe, a criminologist at American University, reported: "The high murder rate of many of our nation's cities can be traced to turf wars for such drugs as crack." His opinion was supported by police lieutenant David Kane of the homicide division in Milwaukee: "People are killing each other for the same old reasons: envy, greed, revenge. But the factors that lead to that are more varied with the drug situation."

Many law enforcement officials believe that there is a growing viciousness and disregard for life. Kane said, "People want to solve their problems right away and they don't worry about the consequences. It is instant gratification of anger. Years ago, guys would duke it out with their fists. Now they whip out their Magnum and start firing."

Commander William Booth of the Los Angeles Police Department said, "Most of these street gangsters are not mental giants. They can be offended by a whole lot of things, like the color red. Or they kill out of plain old boredom."

In 1990 Americans were killing each other at the rate of one murder every 22 minutes. Although the violent crime rate of 268.6 per 100,000 in the United States was similar to Canada's 269.4 per 100,000, in the United States murder represented 3.3% of the violent crimes while in Canada it represented only 0.9%.

While the 1990 total of 23,438 murders was an all-time high, the rate, based on the size of the population, was lower than in 1980, the nation's most murderous year, with 23,040 killings, a rate of 10.9 killings per 100,000 population. A slow, steady decline followed the 1980 high until 1984 and 1985, when the rate reached 7.9 per 100,000. The decline was due mostly to a drop in the number of people in their teens and 20s. In 1986 the rate went up to 8.6. In 1987 it was 8.3; 1988, 8.4; 1989, 8.7.

Experts attribute the increase in killing to a complex set of factors that is likely to continue to contribute to an increase in violence. Most often cited is the drug culture.

James Fox, a criminology professor at Northeastern University, told the *New York Times* that the arrival of the teenage years of baby-boomers' children was a contributing factor to the rise in the murder rate. He pointed out that beginning in 1986, the percentage of black victims increased each year. This, in his view, was due to heavy crack use in inner cities and the arrival at adolescence of black baby-boomers' babies. Typically, black parents have children at a younger age. The white boomers' children will start reaching their teens in the early 1990s, when their crime rate can be expected to grow.

While the more frequent murders that result from turf battles, fights on street corners and domestic violence receive relatively little media coverage, the relatively infrequent celebrity and family murders, serial murders and mass murders receive enormous publicity, arouse widespread fears and divert attention away from more prevalent problems.

(See also CAPITAL CRIME; FEAR OF CRIME; HOMICIDE; MAN-SLAUGHTER; MASS MURDERS; SERIAL KILLERS; STREET CRIMES.)

N

National Crime Information Center Operation (NCIC) A 24-hour, on-line information teleprocessing network, the NCIC of the Federal Bureau of Investigation provides information nationwide to the criminal justice system. Data are entered by police agencies throughout the nation.

Among other data, the NCIC records information on stolen property (vehicles, license plates, guns, securities, boats), persons for whom arrest warrants are outstanding, unidentified persons and missing persons who meet specific criteria. It also contains criminal histories of individuals arrested for serious crimes.

The NCIC Missing-Person File, Juvenile Category responds to inquiries within seconds. A missing-child record may be entered by a parent, legal guardian or next of kin who files a missing person report with any local or state law-enforcement agency.

The NCIC Foreign-Fugitive File contains both Canadian and other foreign warrants entered by the U.S. National Central Bureau (USNCB) of the International Police Organization (INTERPOL).

(See also ARREST: CONSTITUTIONAL RESTRICTIONS AND LEGAL PROCEDURES; CRIME STATISTICS; POLICE; STREET CHILDREN.)

National Rifle Association See GUN CONTROL: OP-PONENTS.

negligence See CRIMINAL LIABILITY.

O

outlaw motorcycle gangs Biker gangs resemble Mafia organizations in having a rite of initiation and in enforcing a code of silence. Once voted in, a member who has cheated another member, violated his rights or informed against him, can be expelled, beaten severely or killed. The gangs are all male. Although women may participate in gang activities and travel with the gangs, they are not members.

The public image of bikers as having grubby hair and full beards, dressed in boots and a World War II German army helmet remained essentially correct from the time of the various gangs' founding about 1947 through the mid-1970s. Although most outlaw gangs no longer permit their members to wear their original intimidating uniform, a substantial number of gangs are still recognizable.

Detective Sergeant Mark Loves of the New South Wales State Police Intelligence Group in Sydney, Australia spent four years studying outlaw biker gangs in the United States, Canada and Australia. In the winter 1991 issue of *Criminal Organizations,* newsletter of the International Association for the Study of Organized Crime, he described five stages in their development.

The first stage, in the late 1940s and 1950s, began when ex-servicemen in the United States and Canada sought to recapture the excitement and danger they had experienced during World War II. They were social rebels joined together by a common love of motorcycles. They organized as chapters, each with about ten or 15 members. These were the bikers whose image was made familiar by Marlon Brando in the movie *The Wild One*.

In the second stage, during the 1960s, hard-riding, hard-drinking gang members became known as "potborskis." They displayed tattoos and gang colors. Social alienation became even more manifest, to the extent that many stopped washing and indulged in gross public sexual behavior. Assaults and rapes were common.

Involvement in drug distribution began in the 1960s, but it was mostly within the gangs. Money taken in was spent mostly on bikes and parties. Little attempt was made to use the money in more sophisticated ways.

In the 1970s drug distribution began to take a more prominent role in gangs' activities, and they began to flaunt their wealth and flex their power. Turf wars broke out over drug distribution territories.

The potborski image lost favor and clubs became more selective in how they recruited. Money laundering became important. According to Cecil Kirby, a former biker gang member and later a member of a Canadian Mafia organization, and the author with Thomas Renner of *Mafia Enforcer: A True Story of Life and Death in the Mob* (1987), a typical gang is likely to have one or more legitimate businesses, including amusement arcades, bars and clubs, construction companies, motorcycle shops and trailer parks. Motorcycle shops provide a place to sell stolen motorcycle parts.

Although the gangs became more low-key during the third stage, members did not abandon public posturing, making their presence known. This stage, however, was waning in Canada and the United States by 1980.

In the fourth stage, the biker gangs became extremely quiet. Wild, antisocial activities were not evident. There was a general reassessment of the gangs' image, and potborskis began to be excluded from some gang activities. There was a recognition that members wearing colors attracted the attention of authorities. Although biker murders still occurred, the gangs avoided public confrontations; instead their enemies simply disappeared.

The gangs started developing outside criminal contacts. Accountants, real estate developers, lawyers and businesspeople who were not afraid to take a few criminal risks became gang associates. Money laundering became more sophisticated. Recruitment became increasingly selective and included only those who could

bring a needed skill. Drug distribution increased and criminal activities became more hidden. New chapters were started overseas.

Loves called the fifth and current stage "professionalization." Operations have gone further underground; members rarely involve themselves in overt criminal activity. With professional help, they have engaged in public relations (and even political lobbying) to improve their public image. They launder money through overseas property development. In short, they have come to resemble a good many other business enterprises.

There is no way of knowing what might have happened to the potborskis excluded from the professionalized outlaw biker gangs. They may have formed their own gangs, because first- and second-stage violent biker gang behavior has not disappeared in the United States. *USA Today* reported on August 13, 1990 the outcome of a biker rally in Sturgis, South Dakota over the previous weekend. The 300,000 bikers who congregated in the sleepy town were a boon for the merchants but a nightmare for the police.

Eleven people were killed, nine in traffic accidents, one from carbon-monoxide poisoning in his tent and one was shot by police as he charged them with a knife. There were 133 traffic accidents (78 involving injuries), 202 arrests for drunken driving and 73 arrests on drug charges, 1,060 traffic tickets and 2,143 warnings.

Because of biker attitudes and recklessness, Cecil Kirby, who in exchange for his testimony has been in witness protection programs, believes that bikers present a greater danger to informers in such programs than does even the Mafia.

Bikers take frequent pictures of one another, which circulate among the various clubs. The face of someone who has become an enemy becomes well known among gangs throughout the United States and Canada. Because they are frequently on the move, gang members have a significant potential for running into protected witnesses. Less concerned than the Mafia about their own safety and about killing bystanders, bikers have been known to ride their bikes up the stairs of courthouses and jails to get at a witness.

The activities of outlaw bikers overseas resembles the 1940–1960s model of behavior. The Hell's Angels motorcycle gang has been a particular problem in Germany, Switzerland and Great Britain.

In the late 1970s, Japanese citizens were shocked by the violent behavior of "bosozoku" (speed gangs), car-and-motorcycle riding youth. Relying on police data, Ronald Loftus, in the winter 1977 issue of *The Japan*

Interpreter, reported a correlation between low academic achievement and membership in the gangs. Since Japan has a highly competitive education system, he expected the behavior to persist among those who could not compete.

Despite their history of flamboyant behavior, outlaw motorcycle gangs have been virtually ignored by social scientists. Columbus Hooper and Johnny Moore of the University of Mississippi, who have studied them, pointed out in the summer 1983 issue of the *Journal of American Culture* that the gangs do not take kindly to those who wish to observe or question them.

A study by Hooper and Moore in the January 1990 *Journal of Contemporary Ethnography* supported Loves' portrait of the change in the motorcycle gangs' behavior. They found that the role of women had changed. In the 1960s women were partners in parties and hedonistic sexuality. In the 1980s the women were expected to engage in economic pursuits to support their individual men and benefit the gang. The change appeared to be related to the gangs' increased involvement in money-making criminal activities.

(See DRIVE-BY-SHOOTINGS; GANGS: STRUCTURED STREET.)

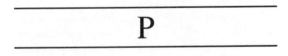

P

paraphilias   See SEX CRIMES RESEARCH.

parent accountability laws   There appears to be a growing consensus in the United States that parents ought to be held accountable for the actions of their children. The purpose of these so-called parent liability laws is to remind parents forcibly of their responsibilities and thereby ease the burden on law enforcement.

By June of 1990, 29 states had won federal waivers that permitted public housing authorities to evict families from projects if a child had been found to be using or selling drugs. Florida passed legislation that punished parents and other adults who let their guns fall into the hands of children. Laws in Hawaii and Wisconsin forced parents to support children borne by their unmarried teenage children, on the assumption that the potential penalty would encourage parents to teach their children sexual responsibility and thus lower the birth rate. Some cities have explored the possibility of forcing the parents

of delinquent juveniles to participate in counseling along with their offspring.

In 1988 California passed an anti-youth-gang law that permits parents to be arrested for failure to "exercise reasonable care, supervision, protection, and control over their minor child." California parents can be ordered into various types of treatment and counseling, and if they refuse penalties can be levied of up to a year in jail and a $2,500 fine. In Los Angeles, which regularly processes 30 or 40 such cases each month, the delinquency of parents has included toleration of guns and gang insignia in their homes, recruitment of their children into prostitution and drug addiction leading to complete neglect.

Los Angeles law enforcement officials were embarrassed the first time they tried to apply the anti-gang law. After arresting the mother of a 15-year-old boy who had participated in a gang rape, they learned that prior to the crime she had been taking parenting lessons.

Experts are skeptical that such laws can be effective. In an interview in *Scholastic Update* (April 5, 1991), Sanford Fox, professor of law at Boston College and co-author with F. M. Martin and Kathleen Murray of *Children Out of Court* (1981), said, "By the time children reach the age at which they become criminal problems, parents have less control over them." Some experts suspect that such laws might be declared unconstitutional if challenged.

Critics of such laws also point out a logical inconsistency. At the same time states are passing laws to make parents accountable for the behavior of juveniles, they are trying and sending to prison as adults more and more juveniles on the grounds that they are responsible enough to be punished as adults.

(See also JUVENILE JUSTICE: A SYSTEM OF CONTRADICTIONS.)

parole   See SENTENCING: A TREND TOWARD LONGER SENTENCES.

Payne v. Tennessee   See VICTIM IMPACT STATEMENTS: THEIR EFFECT ON DEATH SENTENCES.

pedophile   A person, almost always male, who is sexually attracted to children is called a pedophile. The *Diagnostic and Statistical Manual of Mental Disorders, 3rd Edition, Revised (DSM-III-R)* arbitrarily sets the age of the pedophile at 16 or older and stipulates that the pedophile must be at least five years older than the child.

Most definitions, including that of the *DSM-III-R*, focus on adult-to-child pedophilia. Particularly regarding incest, the emphasis seems to be on the adult who is a parent or in a quasi-parental relationship with a child and takes advantage of that relationship. This emphasis disregards pedophilic sexual tyranny by preteens or teenagers.

Generally, a pedophile's attraction is to children of a particular age range. The range may be quite specific. Those attracted to girls usually prefer eight- to ten-year-olds, while those attracted to boys usually prefer slightly older children. Many pedophiles are sexually aroused by both boys and girls.

Some pedophiles who act out their disorder with children may limit the activity to undressing the child and looking, exposing themselves, masturbating in the child's presence or gently touching or fondling the child. Others are more aggressive. They may perform fellatio (oral contact with the male genitals) or cunnilingus (oral contact with the female genitals) or penetrate the child's vagina, mouth or anus with their fingers, foreign objects or penis, using varying degrees of force.

A pedophile commonly explains his behavior as having an educational value for the child, providing the child with sexual pleasure or responding to the child's alleged sexual "provocativeness." Similar explanations are used to justify pedophilic pornography.

A pedophile may direct his sexual activities toward his own children or stepchildren, relatives or children outside his home. A pedophile who engages in pedophilia in the home often also engages in it elsewhere. Some pedophiles structure their activities in order to gain access to children. Frequently they work in occupations involving children, marry a woman with an attractive child or children (and often divorce her when the children grow beyond the pedophile's preferred age), trade children with other pedophiles, and, more rarely, abduct children, or bring foster children into their homes from third-world countries.

Pedophiles are often adept at gaining a child's affection and trust. With the exception of those cases in which the disorder is associated with sexual sadism, the pedophile is likely to be generous and attentive to the child's needs. However, he is likely to threaten the child to prevent him or her from reporting him.

(See also SEX CRIMES RESEARCH; SEXUAL ABUSE OF CHILDREN; STREET CHILDREN.)

plea bargaining   See PROSECUTORIAL DISCRETION IN THE DISPOSITION OF CASES.

police   The power to police in the United States is based on the right of state governments to promote order, safety, health, morals and the general welfare. Such power is not restricted to policing; it is inherent in the sovereignty of governments and includes the power to legislate any topic, subject to constitutional limitations.

The term police can be traced back to the Greek word *politeia*, which means all matters affecting the survival of the polis (city). In Latin, *politia* meant the state, which had the right to enforce limits on public and private behavior. Under the emperor's authority, the prefect of a Roman city could regulate public order, including fire regulations, religion, public assembly, public health, morality, construction of buildings, prostitution, begging and movement of foreigners. Regulations were enforced by magistrates, patrol officers and various other officials. The system disappeared with the fall of the Roman Empire. It was resurrected in the Middle Ages to justify the authority of princes and gradually took on the meaning of internal administration, welfare, protection and surveillance.

By the early 18th century in France, the word police had come to mean the administration of a city. By the middle of the 19th century, a group in London known as the Bow Street Magistrates began to use the term in a manner similar to the French use.

By the end of the 18th century, the concept of police had been narrowed down to a concept closer to the modern meaning of the term, a body of people organized to maintain and protect public order, safety, health, morals and the general welfare.

In 1801 Boston, Massachusetts was the first city in the United States to have a night watch, and in 1807 the first police districts were formed. In Britain in 1829, the government of Sir Robert Peel submitted the Metropolitan Police Bill to Parliament; after passage 1,000 men ("Peelers," later "Bobbies," after the prime minister) in six divisions were assigned to patrol the city of London. The Peel force became a model for many American police forces.

With financing from a wealthy philanthropist, Philadelphia, Pennsylvania created a centralized force of 24 day officers and 120 night watchmen in 1833, but disbanded it two years later. New York City organized a police force in 1844, followed by Cincinnati in 1855. In 1878 Washington, D.C. began using telephones in precincts. Cincinnati foot patrolmen in outlying districts were replaced by mounted officers in 1886. The first bicycle patrol was initiated by Detroit in 1897.

Eighteenth-, 19th- and 20th-century police have been analyzed and discussed from two widely different perspectives. One sees them as preservers of society from uncontrollable crime and mob violence—benevolent knights who give full-time attention to the community's welfare. The other sees them as a cadre of working-class toughs hired to establish discipline on the public streets and to hunt down minor criminals, vagrants, prostitutes, drunks and others who commit misdemeanors, in other words, instruments to maintain the well-being of the rich by keeping the poor in their place. Many American believe that both descriptions are true.

Clive Emsley asserts in his 1983 book *Policing and Its Context 1750–1870* that the evolution of modern police was much more complex than the two simplistic views so often proposed. In his view, the modern police grew out of almost two centuries of changing ideas and social structures, but also out of pragmatism, compromise, self-interest and local historical traditions.

One of the local historical distinctions among police forces around the world is the degree to which they are identified with the military and with their government. France's earliest gendarmes were expected to be army veterans. Moreover, Napoleon regularly siphoned off the best men for his army from the *garde municipal* formed in 1802 to patrol the streets and guard the gates and ports of Paris.

In England and the United States, a widespread recognition that the police could be used to put down civilian dissension aroused a strong public resistance to close identification of the police with the government. As a consequence, both the British and American police are local forces, organized and controlled by local jurisdictions.

Nevertheless, the British police was structured using a military style of organization, and American police adopted their model. Some American observers believe the military model to be inappropriate and point out that urban police function individually and without much direct supervision. They hardly qualify as small cogs in large organizational wheel. They are instead wheels unto themselves.

Although the function of American police officers is typically thought of as combatting crime and maintaining order, in practice it has evolved to include several other chores. A police officer quoted by Emsley said: "Cops aren't just crime fighters—we're in the aid business. Each time I answer an emergency, I have to think, 'What am I on this one—minister, psychiatrist, social worker, marriage counsellor or law-enforcement agent?' "

The multiple roles the police must play, without the resources or training for many of them, coupled with the suspicion among many people that their role is to hold down the lower classes, has the effect of isolating the police. Most officers socialize only with other police officers.

The belief that the role of the police is to keep the have-nots in their place is not held solely by outsiders. Anthony Bouza, who for nine years was the police chief in Minneapolis and before that spent 24 years divided between the New York City Police Department and the New York Transit Police, wrote in his 1990 book *The Police Mystique:*

> The problem arises from the hypocrisy in a society that insists that they [the police] control "them." *Them* refers to blacks, ghetto residents, the homeless, the poor, and all others who evoke a sense of fear or unease. These orders are implicit and indirect. The laws enabling control aren't there. The facilities to which "they" might be taken don't exist. The "offenses" of the group aren't crimes, but they do offend the overclass. . . . [police] are there to keep order. This means making unpleasantness invisible. The underclass must be kept in its place or the chief will lose his or her job."

Urban Police–Minority Group Tensions. Although tension between big-city police departments and minority communities continues at a high level, in many areas of the country it has eased somewhat since the late 1960s and early 1970s. As a consequence of better police training and court rulings that narrow the instances in which deadly force may be used, the number of police shootings of civilians has declined nationwide. In one police district in Boston known as Area B, police made 15,000 arrests in 1989 without killing anyone.

Despite a brief period of eased tension, tension flared up again in Boston over a murder case that received nationwide attention. Charles Stuart, a white man from the suburbs, apparently shot his pregnant wife, Carol, and then shot himself while they were seated in their car parked on an inner-city street. Charles then called police on his car phone to say his wife had been shot by a black man.

The police of Boston swept through black neighborhoods hunting for the killer until contradictory evidence emerged. The neighborhood sweeps created enormous ill will among black Bostonians. By 1992 calls for the resignation of the Boston police chief had become a persistent refrain.

The Stuart case was just the latest in two decades of heated rhetoric in Boston. In a February 21, 1991 *Boston*

Globe article entitled "Mixed Signals," author Daniel Golden said:

> Police and community are each frustrated over the same issue . . . Is it better to ravage gangs or to try to rehabilitate them? Within the department, advocates of establishing links with gang members fight to gain ground. Within the minority community, a swell of hard-line [fight crime at any cost] sentiment is challenging a longtime consensus [to criticize police and seek accountability for misconduct] . . . The result, sadly, may be the worst of both worlds: gangsters who are neither intimidated nor inspired to change."

One innovative Boston program called Adopt-a-Cop faded through lack of support. The program linked officers with youth groups.

On a national basis, one factor that has eased police-minority group tension is that the number of minority officers has risen steadily. Forty large U.S. police agencies operate under agreements with the U.S. Justice Department to increase minority hiring and promotion. In some cities the improvements have resulted in innovative cooperative efforts between police and the community. Former New York City Police Commissioner Lee Brown expanded patrols that worked with residents to force out prostitution and drug dealing and to intervene in gang rivalries likely to escalate into violence.

In Richmond, Virginia, the first black police commissioner started a drug-free block program. To achieve such a block, 80% of the residents have to agree that they want to be drug-free and are willing to testify in court against dealers. Given such an agreement, police give priority to that block.

Community Police. In reaction to the failure of standard approaches to street crime in America, more than 300 cities and towns nationwide—including San Francisco, Houston and Boston—have embraced the concept of Community Patrol Officer Programs (CPOPs). The goal of such programs is to develop a rapport between officers and the neighborhoods they patrol.

In March 1991 New York City's then-Police Commissioner Brown launched the nation's largest program to date. To explain the perceived value of community policing, during an interview for an April 1, 1991 *Time* article entitled "Back to the Beat," Herman Goldstein, professor of criminal law at the University of Wisconsin, said:

> Community policing is a deterrent to the improper use of force because it strengthens an officer's relationships with the community. The neighborhood support gives police a greater sense of confidence and authority, which reduces their need for using force. If police officers feel they don't have the authority, the power, to handle a situation, they're more likely to resort to brute force.

The once-familiar cop on the beat was reduced virtually to extinction by a series of reforms that created their own problems. In the early 20th century, a beat officer's task was to keep the peace, which included such chores as keeping street lamps filled with oil and securing housing for the homeless. However, during that period, many beat officers also gained a reputation for taking payoffs and for delivering their own brand of justice.

Reforms of the 1930s and 1940s narrowed the focus of police departments to the apprehension of criminals, particularly those who commit such serious crimes as murder, assault, robbery and rape. Other, "social work," functions were deemed more appropriate for city health and welfare departments, although those functions never disappeared entirely. Following World War II, police became a mobile force anonymously cruising through neighborhoods in patrol cars, linked to each other by two-way radios.

The most recent reform in the police delivery system was the virtually universal adoption of the 911 system for emergency calls. Being tied to the 911 system further reduced the role of police in neighborhoods, since the officers were busy rushing from one crime scene to another. A study of the New York City police found that they spent 90% of their time attending to emergency calls, which formerly had needed only 50% of their time. Little time was left for anything else.

Some observers view the 911-based style of policing, which has dominated urban departments for two decades, as a source of many of the forces' its current difficulties. The system requires that officers patrol such large areas that they are unable to learn any of their neighborhoods well. It forces them to spend all their time in their cruiser, where they can talk only to each other and not to residents or merchants of their communities. Worse, the system rarely stops crimes in progress; the police usually arrive after the commission of the crime is over.

Several cities, among them Houston, Newark, New York City and Richmond, have recognized the failures of the 911 system and are trying to revive the practice of having police walking the same streets every day. They are not finding the task easy. One difficulty with re-creating the earlier style of community policing is that centralized police departments, bound within rigid, military-like structures, find it difficult to reward police who walk the beat. To do so, police departments will have to find ways to evaluate success at preventing crimes rather than the usual method of counting crime and arrest records.

Many cities are trying to have patrol-car officers double as community police, but the frequency of 911 calls limits the time available. Some of the difficulties may be due to a lack of a clear-cut understanding by police and the public about what constitutes an emergency.

A study of 911 calls in Boston found that among 925,000 calls about half, 425,000, were inappropriate. People called to report lost dogs, ask for directions, report utility outages and ask the time.

Many departments are examining ways to reduce 911 calls. In Bouza's opinion, 911 has to be managed properly. One approach is "911 triage," redirection of the nonemergency calls and prioritization of calls. Not all calls should be responded to at the same speed, and some should not be responded to at all. Calls to report a theft for insurance purposes should be handled over the phone. Officers will take calls more seriously if they know that the most important ones are being dispatched on a first-priority basis.

The most urgent task is to establish a system that can respond to a real emergency within six minutes. The next most urgent is to educate the public that nonemergencies will not receive the same fast response time as emergencies. Studies have found that citizens are unperturbed if when reporting a nonemergency crime they are told that there will be a delay before officers arrive.

Many experts believe that the changes brought about by reforms such as 911 have fostered conditions that have contributed to the higher crime rates of recent decades. Several studies have found that the offenses to the quality of life that the police once attended to but now routinely overlook create conditions in which serious crime is more likely to occur.

The concept of a neighborhood atmosphere of deterioration is known as the "broken window syndrome," a term first used in a seminal March 1982 article in the *Atlantic Monthly* by James Q. Wilson and George Kelling. The authors held that unfixed broken windows, uncleared graffiti, overgrown weeded lots and other signs of decay demoralize residents. Petty disturbances such as loud radios frighten ordinary citizens out of proportion to their seriousness. Fear leads a neighbor-

hood's citizens to shun the streets. The abdication of responsibility encourages a cycle of deterioration, additional fear and more crime.

A goal of CPOP officers is to discourage crime by creating or maintaining stable neighborhoods. A community police officer in Houston had a bank of phones removed from outside a convenience store when drug dealers turned the phones into a business office.

In Washington, D.C. Chief of Police Isaac Fulwood established a community police program in two crime-wracked districts. In addition to access to the usual law books, the Washington's CPOP officers have access to a thick directory of governmental services to tap on behalf of their communities.

In Madison, Wisconsin Chief of Police David Couper assigned 310 officers to community police duties. Dealing with broken playground equipment is as much a part of the officers' daily routine as is dealing with crime. One officer passes out business cards with the phone number of the answering machine in his office. At the end of the day, he has a tape filled with requests for help, leads on crime and people who just want to chat with him. Arranging marital counseling for a chaotic household can be highly cost-effective. In many cities, more than 60% of emergency calls are generated by 10% of the households.

Research about how effective community policing is in reducing crime rates is still not conclusive. A 1981 study of the effectiveness of a foot-patrol experiment in Newark, New Jersey found that it did not lower the crime rate, but the visible presence of so many patrol officers made people feel safer and friendlier toward the police. More recent studies have shown lower crime rates. A west Houston neighborhood reported a 38% drop in serious crime over a six-month period in 1988. However, the neighboring Houston area reported increases in crime.

The daunting aspect of community police is that it calls for a radical expansion of what it means to be a police officer. It means moving beyond a few basic tools (handcuffs, billy club, gun). Some police academies have begun to restructure their curriculum to include social service skills. For many police, the move is long overdue.

However, some police administrators are suspicious of plans that would make patrol officers more independent, and some rank-and-file officers are suspicious of the idea of social work. In an interview with *Time*, Carolyn Robinson, a major with the Tulsa Police, explained their suspicion by saying "There's an unfounded fear that it detracts from the macho image and takes the fun out of putting the bad guys in jail."

Yet, according to Lieutenant Richard Kelly of the Massachusetts State Police, a psychologist who interviewed 600 police officers for his doctoral dissertation, most officers join the police force because they want to help people. Moreover, many become depressed by the relentless focus of their jobs on the damage left behind by violence, damage that they can do little to remedy.

More and more officers are patrolling permanent beats, going to community meetings and seeing to it that abandoned buildings are boarded up and broken traffic lights are fixed. Frank Hartman, a criminal justice specialist at Harvard University's Kennedy School of Government, told the *Boston Globe* that community policing reduces two kinds of fear: residents' fear of crime and police officers' fear of the neighborhoods they patrol. Nevertheless, criminologists are cautious about becoming overly optimistic.

While many officers are enthusiastic about community policing, opposition to it remains strong. Bouza questions the sincerity of the community police movement. He points out that there is notorious police antagonism to important symbolic groups such as the Guardian Angels and auxiliary police. These groups represent segments of the public that have been anxious and aggressive in engaging in partnership with the cops, yet it is these groups toward which the police have typically responded most coolly. Bouza adds, "The police penchant for secrecy and hostility toward the press could also be described as telltale signs of the cops' resistance to the notion of genuine collaboration."

The president of the Boston Police Patrolmen's Association (BPPA), Donald Murray, is strongly opposed to community policing. Two Boston police officers who had been working with gangs were wounded. When they subsequently reaffirmed their faith in the approach, Murray responded that he had no desire to become acquainted with the gang members known as the X-men, whom he described as "maggots."

BPPA attorney Frank McGee claims that the BPPA will remain opposed to community policing until the city is willing to add 500 officers to answer 911 calls. He told the *Boston Globe*, "The so-called manager doesn't take the heat. The officer takes the heat, whether it is a barking dog or a murder. Everyone who dials 911 thinks that his or her call is the most important call to be made to 911 that day."

McGee's view and those of others unhappy with the 911 systems is not shared by Bouza, who believes that 911 has become one of the givens of modern life, one that citizens in trouble automatically reach for when in trouble.

Police Presence as a Deterrent of Crime. The perception by the public of a rise in violent crime is usually followed by a demand for a greater police presence in the troubled area. Research data do not make a clear case for or against the idea.

An experiment in New York City in 1966 increased the level of police coverage in one of the city's high-crime precincts by more than 40%. A comparison with selected control precincts found a reduction of 33% in outside robberies.

In another experiment in New York City, between 1965 and 1971, the number of uniformed officers in the subway system was dramatically increased in order to cut down on robberies. The robberies did decrease as a consequence of the extra police presence.

In 1972 the Kansas City Police Department and the Police Foundation initiated an ambitious effort, the Kansas City Preventive Patrol Experiment, to determine the impact of additional police. The experiment systematically varied the level of preventive patrol across different areas of the city. In some areas, the number of preventive patrols was doubled. In other areas the patrols were eliminated. An evaluation after one year did not find that the level of patrol had any effect on crime rates or on citizen's perceptions of safety.

One of the questions that is inevitably raised about a focused police presence is whether a perceived drop in crime implies prevention, or whether crime is simply displaced to a less well-protected target nearby. In both of the New York studies, the level of displaced crime was found to be significant. However, in the Kansas City experiment, there was no displacement of crime from the heavily patrolled areas to the underpatrolled areas.

Bouza claims that the number of police available in a community is not nearly as important as how well they are managed. He said, "The usual debate centers on whether there ought to be more cops or not, yet no one can say what the right number is for a city. A very rough, seemingly sensible ratio is about two per thousand population, yet NYPD has about twice that total and Washington, D.C. has even more."

In Bouza's opinion most calls can be responded to by one officer. Studies in San Diego and Minneapolis revealed that police are more cautious, alert and careful when riding alone. Moreover, a greater number of calls can be answered.

Bouza explains his support of one-officer patrols:

Using two-officer patrols is a peculiar form of police featherbedding, yet large police agencies like New York and, before 1980, Minneapolis, have continued to waste tens of millions of dollars on the practice, while usually asking for more cops. However, reform means tangling with the unions. It should also be added that cops are fervid about backing each other up, and calls requiring a response in strength always result in large numbers arriving at the scene. One-officer patrols require additional training and encouragement of backup practices cops love to undertake, in any case.

In Bouza's opinion, the absence of an adequate answer to whether the presence of police makes a difference in the crime rate is the fault of police departments and city officials across the country, who appear to have little or no interest in doing adequate research to determine the best possible arrangements.

In the rare case that a department works out an arrangement to have police deployed where they are most needed, the arrangement is likely to be subverted by the political process. Minneapolis is an example. The police department there used a simple formula: assignment based on calls for service and on the incidence level of Part I Crimes of the Federal Bureau of Investigation's Uniformed Crime Reports (murder, rape, assault, robbery, burglary, theft, auto theft and arson). The arrangement meant that the city's trouble spots were assigned the most police. What Bouza calls the "overclass" resented the concentration of public services with the "underclass," and the system was gradually abandoned.

Another problem in determining the effect of the presence of police is the measurement of crime. Because an estimated 50% of crimes go unreported, no one really knows whether crime rates go up or down or fluctuate at all.

(See also POLICE BRUTALITY; POLICE STRESS; POLICE USE OF DEADLY FORCE.)

police brutality
The beating and torture of citizens by police is commonplace around the world. In some countries it is done with the connivance of the government, which has a vendetta or disdain for certain segments of the population. In most societies it is not acceptable when it is visible and therefore is usually hidden.

Citizens who are brutalized by the police and escape with their lives generally are afraid to testify against them. Particularly in countries that have a national police with intimate ties to the military, witnesses willing to testify about police brutality tend to disappear.

The United States does not have a national police. The U.S. Constitution reserves police power to the states. Most laws enforced on the streets are state statutes. The states confer their power on cities and towns, which have their own police departments. The result is a bewildering array of police departments, most with 10 or 20 members.

In his 1990 book *The Police Mystique,* police analyst Anthony Bouza, veteran of nine years as chief of the Minneapolis Police Department, described the nation's multiple police departments as a system that reflects "what our shapers treasured most: a government able to do minimal harm."

One of the reasons that American police departments do minimal harm when compared with forces in more repressive nations, according to Bouza, is that the police have some freedom to pick and choose which laws to emphasize and which to ignore. For the police officer, the law serves as a guide. Questions of conscience, ethics and morality become secondary because they are structured into the laws being enforced. Police agencies in which members do as they please without regard to the law become rogue departments.

Poor people are both perpetrators and victims of most street crime. Violence on streets and on television frightens the public, which creates pressure on police to magically erase it. Faced with this pressure and a seemingly endless daily fare of petty crimes, drug addicts, obstreperous drunks, sociopaths and the homeless, police may express their exasperation in acts of brutality.

Whether an inclination toward brutality is acted upon is a function of the police chief's view of the job. Bouza wrote, "Every police agency adopts an authoritarian and aggressive arrest approach or a watchman (lots of patrol and watching) model or a service posture [making sure every call is answered and there are not backlogs]. Usually the choice reflects the chief's philosophy."

From Bouza's perspective, explanations of the brutality visited on civil rights workers and demonstrators during the 1960s and on protesters at the 1968 Democratic convention in Chicago must take into account the philosophy of the police chiefs in charge and cannot be charged solely to the excitement generated by the events themselves. Nor can an instance of police brutality just after midnight on March 3, 1991 in Los Angeles, subsequently seen by the nation on videotape, be conceived of as an aberration.

The Los Angeles incident began at 12:47 A.M. on March 3, 1991 when the Los Angeles Police Department (LAPD) dispatcher notified nearby squad cars that the California Highway Patrol was pursuing a white Hyundai at high speed. Minutes later LAPD officers apprehended the driver, Rodney King, and two passengers. At 12:56 A.M. LAPD Sergeant Stacey Koon notified the nightwatch commander at the Foothills police station that one suspect had been beaten by the arresting officers.

Unknown to the police, an amateur photographer, sitting on his balcony overlooking the scene of the beating, captured the incident on videotape. The photographer turned his tape over to local and network news outlets, which showed it repeatedly across the nation over the next several days.

In the absence of the evidence of the videotape—despite the presence at the scene of the beating of 27 officers (21 from LAPD, four from the California Highway Patrol, and two from the Unified School District)—the officers involved in the beating could normally have expected their behavior to be ignored. Two of the Highway Patrol Officers did take down the names of the officers involved from their name tags and subsequently testified at their trial.

An April 1, 1991 *Time* article entitled "Law and Disorder" reported that tapes of radio calls and computer records of police communications on the night of the attack made evident the impunity the officers felt about their behavior. Although they knew their conversations were being recorded, they made racist jokes and boasted to other officers about the beating. Moreover, two nurses at the hospital where King was taken reported at a grand jury hearing that the officers who assaulted him showed up later at the hospital room to taunt him. King's doctor's reported that he had nine skull fractures, a broken cheekbone, a shattered eye socket and a broken leg.

Outraged Los Angeles citizens demanded the resignation of LAPD police chief Daryl Gates. When the chief refused, critics demanded that Mayor Tom Bradley, a former member of the LAPD, dismiss Gates. However, almost uniquely among police chiefs, the LAPD chief has civil service status and could not be dismissed by the mayor or the Police Commission,

except "for cause"—misconduct or willful neglect of duty. When he was relieved of his duties pending an investigation, Gates vowed to fight. Eventually, he did resign.

The glare of the Los Angeles beating raised questions about the prevalence of police brutality across the nation. Questions were asked repeatedly about whether the Los Angeles beating was an aberration, as Gates insisted, or further evidence that many police resort to violence when no threat to their own safety can justify it.

Some critics claim that racism is so pervasive within American police departments that the fight against crime has become a war waged against African-Americans. Others contend that so many criminals serve only token sentences or none at all that officers feel the need to play judge and jury at the crime scene. Many observers suggest that police work has become so dangerous that even well-meaning officers may snap under the pressure.

Police brutality is not confined to Los Angeles. An April 1, 1991 *Newsweek* article entitled "Los Angeles Aftershocks" reported three police brutality cases. In 1989 three off-duty Houston police officers, who had been drinking, tailgated a black woman on her way to work at 5 A.M. The chase ended when one officer shot and killed the woman. He was convicted of manslaughter and appealed his conviction. In Teaneck, New Jersey, after a grand jury exonerated an officer in the shooting death of a black teenager, the state's attorney ignored the finding and brought charges of manslaughter against him. For a beating they had received at a United Farm Workers demonstration in 1988, seven protesters in San Francisco won a settlement in a $424 million lawsuit.

Police brutality cases under investigation were described in a March 24, 1991 *New York Times* article entitled "In Officers' Murder Case, A Tangle of Contradictions." Five New York City officers were indicted for murder in the death of a 21-year-old Hispanic man suspected of car theft. Three teenagers, who were cruising the neighborhood while listening to a police scanner in order to chase squad cars, claimed that they saw officers hit, kick and choke the suspect as he lay facedown.

In Memphis a black county sheriff was convicted of violating civil service laws in the June 1989 choking death of a black drug suspect. The suspect's body was covered with bruises in the shape of shoe prints.

In Plainfield, New Jersey demonstrators charged that a police officer had beaten a 14-year-old black youngster. The boy and a friend were playing with a remote-controlled toy car on the sidewalk near his home. The toy caused a motorist to stop suddenly, and a police cruiser ran into the rear of the stopped car. The boy's parents contended that the officer jumped from the car, accused the youngster of obstructing traffic and at one point tried to choke him. The boy's parents were arrested when they tried to intervene.

Rodney King's beating was not the first on videotape. In 1989 viewers in Long Beach, California saw footage of a white patrol officer ramming a black man's head through a plate-glass window. The victim was Don Carlos Jackson who, since he retired from the Hawthorne, California police force in 1989, has devoted himself to exposing police racism. Jackson argues that for many officers the definition of a criminal suspect is virtually synonymous with a black male face.

A Variety of Explanations.   Police stress is often offered as a source of police brutality. Pressures have mounted in recent years as crack has poured into inner cities, bringing with it drug-dealing gangs armed with automatic weapons and hairtrigger temperaments.

In New York City, despite the city's highly restrictive guidelines for when an officer may fire a gun, between 1989 and 1991 the number of people shot by local police soared from 68 to 108. Throughout the 1980s the number of police fired upon has also increased each year. Nevertheless, the number of officers killed has fallen from 104 in 1980 to 66 in 1989, mainly as consequence of the use of bulletproof vests.

In an interview for the April 1, 1991 *Time,* article, Boston police officer John Meade, who heads the bureau of professional standards, said, "It used to be that arrested suspects got right into the patrol car. Now they put up a fight. Weapons suddenly turn up. Just like that, everything explodes."

Urban street crime happens most often in areas where there is poverty, inadequate education and lack of opportunity. Officers who tend to be recruited from quite different neighborhoods have little in common with those they are charged to patrol.

In an interview with *Time,* Ron DeLord, head of the Combined Law Enforcement Associations of Texas, said, "The bulk of police forces are white males of the middle class. Yet we send them into large urban centers that are black and Hispanic and poor, with no understanding of the cultural differences, to enforce white, middle-class moral laws. Doesn't that create a clash?"

Since law-abiding residents of inner-city neighborhoods are the most likely victims of muggers or drive-

by shooters, they are desperate for police protection. At the same time, in poor neighborhoods where everyone is treated like a suspect, the residents want the use of police force kept in check.

A segment on police brutality during a CBS *America Tonight* broadcast on March 28, 1991 included an interview with conservative white Republican Gerard Pompa who, while in the company of a black friend, was mistaken for a robbery suspect. Five New York City police officers dragged Pompa from his car, beat him, handcuffed him, threw him down and kicked him in the head over and over again. He said, "What I remember most was the savagery of it by the police."

In Pompa's opinion, police crime should be treated like any other crime and result in arrests. He said:

> When police engage in criminal behavior, we don't hear it called a crime. We hear it called a euphemism. We hear brutality, misconduct. We hear of police abuse . . . we have to start calling police crime what it is. It's attempted murder. It's assault. . . . arrest him, and . . . put him in jail . . . If you commit attempted murder, you don't go before a review board, you go before a district attorney who prosecutes you for attempted murder. Review boards are nice, but they are for minor infractions, the types of things that don't rise to the level of criminality.

The officers who beat Pompa were not prosecuted, but a civil court awarded Pompa and his friend $6,600,000.

Also interviewed were civil liberties attorney Burton Lowenstein and former New York City Police Commissioner Patrick Murphy. In response to a question of whether there was an epidemic of police brutality in the United States, Lowenstein said, "It is one that has been going on for some time. Everyone in the field, judges, prosecutors, and the vast majority of police officers, who are not bigots, psychopaths, or sadists, know that it is very widespread, especially in urban departments. Unfortunately, prosecutors have to work with the police, which is why there are so few prosecutions."

Former Commissioner Murphy felt that New York City police did a fine job of policing themselves and asserted that residents of the inner city were more frightened of criminals and drugs than they were of the police. He felt that substantial improvement had been made and cited the fact that police kill half as many people today as they did 15 or 16 years ago. He pointed out that an average of 60 police officers are killed annually nationwide.

In their 1983 book *The Badge and the Bullet: Police Use of Deadly Force,* Peter Scharf and Arnold Binder indirectly offer support for Murphy's assertion that the use of deadly force is limited among police officers. The actual occurrence of police fire hitting citizens is rare. In 1980 the New York Police Department had 21,000 officers, yet in 1979 only 80 police officers fired shots that hit human beings.

Research suggests that the average officer fires his or her gun once every nine years. If the average police officer works 200 days a year and handles eight assignments during a shift, then the chances of firing a shot on any particular assignment are 14,400 to 1. However, average statistics tend to conceal the fact that even in New York City there are "sleepy hollows," where police shootings are rare. They also blunt the fact that in many cities there are "violent scenes," where shooting may be a weekly or daily occurrence.

The violent scenes are the sites from which police brutality complaints arise. Lowenstein pointed out that among 15,000 complaints about the criminal justice system lodged with the Justice Department, 90% of them were against the police.

Lowenstein complained that there are no U.S. standards, federal, state or local, for handling police brutality problems. The system to handle police brutality crimes is designed to fail because all those who are supposed to enforce it have to rely on those who are committing the crimes. A mechanism outside the system is needed to pass judgment.

Complaints in Other Countries.   The United States is not the only democracy in which police brutality is a major issue. A surprising reversal in Great Britain of a conviction in the case of the "Birmingham Six" hinged on charges of police brutality. Six men were convicted of murdering 21 people in the bombings of two pubs in Birmingham in 1974.

The case was referred to the Court of Appeals in 1987 because of allegations of a former police officer who said that he had witnessed intimidation of five of the six men in custody. The appeal was denied.

In August 1990 the British government agreed to send the case again to the Court of Appeals. The decision was based on three factors: new evidence from witnesses who supported the men's claims about mistreatment while in custody; a police officer's testimony that disagreed with statements of the police about when the men were interrogated; and electrostatic document analyses, which revealed that alterations had been made in records.

Canada was also caught up in charges of police brutality. One of two articles on the police in the January 9, 1989 issue of *Macleans* began with an account of the 17-year-old black driver of a stolen car who died from a police bullet through the head, the latest in a series of controversial killings.

Despite the controversy, a Gallup Canada, Inc. poll of the general public found that 50% of Canadians considered the nation's 52,500 police officers to be very highly or highly trustworthy. Nevertheless, observers of community attitudes claimed that personal contacts between the public and the police were seldom welcomed or relaxed.

In interviews with *Macleans* reporters, police officers across Canada expressed frustration, a growing distrust of their fellow citizens and a deepening sense of isolation. Complaints of police brutality were far outweighed by police accounts of violence suffered at the hands of the public, ranging from a drunk's wildly thrown punch, to contact with an accident victim's AIDS-contaminated blood, to death by gunfire. Between 1978 and 1987, 35 Canadian police were killed.

The consequence for an officer of a decision made during a tense and explosive situation that may in retrospect appear wrong can result in a fine, a dismissal or a criminal charge. Decisions for Canadian officers became more complex in the 1980s. Growing Caribbean, Chinese and Vietnamese immigrant communities are targets for ethnic criminal organizations that for the still overwhelmingly white Canadian police are difficult to penetrate.

Statistics in Canada indicate that as many as 75% of police marriages end in divorce. During an interview with *Macleans*, Jaan Schaer, the coordinator of Toronto's employee's assistance program, asserted that the post-traumatic impact of a shooting incident can have a devastating effect on an officer's marriage.

Frederick Van Fleet, a consulting psychologist with the Justice Institute of Columbia University, supported Shaer's opinion. He said, "Of 21 police officers I counseled who were involved in shootings, 20 did not seek counseling until well after the fact. Those 20 had already divorced when I began counseling them."

Despite the charged emotions radiating from each controversial shooting, the statistics suggest that the Canadian police performed well when their workload was assessed against the number of complaints. Among the officers of the Royal Canadian Mounted Police (RCMP), a force of about 13,500 that enforces federal laws and provides rural police service in eight provinces and the North, there were 2,500 recorded complaints in

1987—fewer than 0.09% of 3 million contacts with the public.

The RCMP is one of the few police organizations willing to release such figures. Complaints against the RCMP were taken over by a civilian review board in 1988, and an increasing number of Canadian local governments were moving toward creating such bodies.

Troubled American Cities. The police of America's national capital, Washington, D.C., came under continuing criticism in the late 1980s and early 1990s about the use of deadly force. Discussions were widespread of a possible federal takeover of the department to combat the spread of drugs, which over a two-and-one-half-year period resulted in 46,000 arrests along with the loss of life of 300 dealers and users.

The April 4, 1989 *New York Times* described some of D.C.'s problems. The police chief and the mayor both attributed the crisis to the epidemic of crack. They argued that the drug trade in Washington is less structured than in other cities, a factor that spawns violence and makes detective work difficult.

Data from the D.C. Police Department's firearms and homicide branch revealed the disarray in which the department found itself. The firearms branch, which compiles evidence on guns used in crimes, had received so many cases that it had fallen two years behind in its investigations.

Similarly, the percentage of D.C. homicides solved by the homicide squad had fallen from roughly three of every four (a rate comparable to the national average) to one in three. Detectives attributed the drop to the fact that 70% of the slaying were drug related, crimes especially difficult to solve, because, as is not the case in most murders, assailants and victims are often virtual strangers.

On paper, the nation's capital appeared to be the best-policed city in the United States, with six officers to every 1,000 citizens, compared with two in most cities. However, police union officials pointed out that the size of the force had decreased. In 1989 there were 3,950 compared to 5,100 officers in 1972. Moreover, the police department's budget had been cut almost in half. One official pointed out that there was a surplus of officers in D.C. districts where there was political influence and a shortage in districts where they were needed.

In an interview with the *New York Times,* Edwin Delattre, a law enforcement expert with the American Enterprise Institute, a Washington think tank, claimed that it did little good to make 46,000 arrests when they led to only 1,400 incarcerations because of an understaffed court system and a too-small prison system.

Delattre traced most of the D.C. department's problems to the mayor's office. He said, "You tend to find troubled police departments in cities where there is trouble in City Hall—and that's Washington. Those troubles filter down. What's more, there's no overall planning in Washington, no coordination of courts and prisons, and rehabilitation and prevention programs."

The executive director of the National Association of Chiefs of Police described Washington's police chief as one of the best. He said, "The real problem is that the force is being tugged in all directions by a lot of things— the huge drug surge, politics, its budget, having to do a lot of extra assignments, such as helping to guard the president."

Chicago has been another scene of frequent of clashes between police and citizens. However, it was not until September 1989, when a group of black politicians asserted that brutality was increasing, that the city held hearings on police brutality. Similar complaints were heard in New York City, Los Angeles and other cities. And in September 1989 the United States Civil Rights Commission voted to ask the Justice Department to investigate city police departments.

Despite the complaints, most criminal justice experts believe that incidents of unnecessary force by officers have fallen during the last 30 years, largely because police forces are better trained and educated and more racially integrated. In an interview for an October 29, 1989 *New York Times* article entitled "Police Abuse Is Down, But Concern Has Risen," Daryl Borgquist, a spokesperson for the Justice Department's Community Relations Service, said, "Things are much, much better than they were 20 to 25 years ago. There are complaints about police behavior that wouldn't even have been considered misconduct 20 years ago."

At the same time, Borgquist and others were of the opinion that confrontations that ultimately lead to violence are rising. Moreover, they feared that as the nation becomes more intent on solving the drug problem, police may perceive that they have a broader mandate for violence.

In Chicago and most other cities, records of police brutality complaints go back only to the early 1970s, when complaints were investigated by the police. Today complaints are typically investigated by civilians who make recommendations to police superintendents.

David Fogel, who heads Chicago's Office of Professional Standards, contends that not all incidents of brutality are reported because people who have no faith in the system are unlikely to file complaints. Another barometer of police brutality is the number of civilians shot by police. In 1975 the Chicago police shot 136 civilians, killing 37 of them. In 1985 Chicago police shot 50 civilians, killing 19 of them. Most of the incidents involved armed civilians suspected of a crime.

Fogel's view was supported by a December 1, 1990 *U.S. News and World Report* article entitled "Cops Under Fire." The authors said, "Today's cops are under far more scrutiny than their predecessors were, thanks in part to governmental soul searching suggesting that police behavior had much to do with touching off the race riots of the late 1960's."

More than 75% of the major metropolitan police departments in the United States have some sort of civilian review agency. Police chiefs, conscious of the public's ambivalence, are keeping a close watch as well.

Sometimes officers find the scrutiny hard to take. Dallas police officer Jay James, who underwent a vigorous internal investigation in the spring of 1990 after he fired at and missed a man who pointed a gun at him, said, "I'm out there sweating bullets, my heart's going 95 miles per hour and some guy is sitting in an air-conditioned office telling me what I should have done."

The Effect of Litigation.   Some of the scrutiny of police is rooted in efforts to ward off lawsuits. The police present a tempting target for litigation.

A fear of being sued can make an officer vulnerable. In 1986 Federal Bureau of Investigation (FBI) agent Ed Mireles was involved in a Miami shootout in which two agents were killed and five were wounded. Prior to the shooting, the car in which Mireles was riding engaged in bumping the vehicle carrying two alleged bank robbers. Mireles was almost close enough to touch the driver. In an interview with *U.S. News and World Report,* Mireles said, "Knowing what I know now, I would have brought my 12-gauge shotgun to bear on those two . . . What flashed through my mind was the legal ramifications, the liability thing. But that would have ended the whole thing before it started." The outcome of the incident was that two of Mireles' fellow agents were killed before a wounded Mireles killed both assailants.

The cost of complaints keeps rising. In 1972 Los Angeles paid out $553,340 in judgments and settlements for police actions; in 1989 the city paid out $6.4 million, and in 1990 the sum was $10.5 million. It is difficult to assess whether the size of awards was getting larger or, each successive year more people chose to sue or

whether they had a lot more to sue about. In late March 1991 then-Chief Gates appeared before the city council to testify about the sums Los Angeles paid for successful complainants in police misconduct suits. In one suit, $265,000 was awarded to an 18-year-old youth who was dragged from his car and severely beaten by six officers. He sustained permanent ear damage. Although a civil court found the officers at fault, Gates told the council that a nine-month investigation was unable to specify which officer had done the beating. He said, "If you can't identify them, it's difficult to discipline them."

Spotty record keeping is an obstacle in determining the frequency of police misconduct. Many departments refuse to disclose the number of complaints they receive.

Even when accurate data is available, conclusions based on the number of complaints reported to local authorities about the police may not be accurate. Experts on police practices caution that a department with more complaints is not necessarily more tolerant of abuse among its officers than one with fewer complaints. In an interview for a March 24, 1991 *New York Times* article entitled "Attacks by the Police Are Hard to Uncover, Let Along Control," Jerome Skolnick, a professor of law at the University of California, Berkeley, said, "Paradoxically, the more confidence people have in their police force, the more reports they make about police misconduct."

San Francisco, which created a civilian Office of Citizen Complaints in 1982, received a total of 1,074 complaints in 1990, nearly twice the number received by the Los Angeles internal affairs division, although Los Angeles has a population and a police force nearly five times as large.

Many observers believe that the public remains reluctant to complain about police. The executive director of the New York Civil Liberties Union, Norman Siegel, has campaigned to have the entire New York City review board and its investigative arm made up of civilians. Of the 50-member investigative staff, 39 are police officers. He told the *New York Times,* "People don't have faith they are going to get a fair hearing because they are on the cop's turf, not on neutral turf."

Jury Verdict Spawns New Controversy.   Four LAPD officers were brought to trial in 1992 for the beating of Rodney King. The four were acquitted of assault and the jury could not agree about a charge of excessive force against one of the four. He was expected to be tried again later. The verdict shocked almost everyone in the nation who had seen the videotape. Within a few hours after the verdict was handed down, violence broke out and began to spread through a 46-square-mile area of south-central Los Angeles.

The Los Angeles Police Department seemed surprised by the violent response and was slow to respond. For a time, Chief Gates resisted Mayor Tom Bradley's call for National Guard assistance. The Los Angeles fire department had to let many fires burn unattended because there were not enough police officers to guard firefighters against snipers.

The violence went on for 48 hours. When it was over, 58 people were dead, 2,383 had been injured and $735 million in property damage had been sustained. The police chief promised to retire in June 1992. William Webster, former director of both the FBI and the Central Intelligence Agency (CIA), was appointed to head an inquiry into the preparation and activities of the 8,300-member LAPD, both before and after the violence broke out.

(See also ARREST: CONSTITUTIONAL RESTRICTIONS AND LEGAL PROCEDURES; ASSEMBLY-LINE JUSTICE; POLICE; POST-TRAUMATIC STRESS DISORDER; PROSECUTORIAL DISCRETION IN THE DISPOSITION OF CASES; STREET CHILDREN; STREET CRIMES.)

police stress William Kroes, Police Department psychologist in Los Angeles, said in his book *Society's Victims—The Police: An Analysis of Job Stress in Policing* (1985), "Part of the job of being a cop is getting involved in dangerous situations. But what of the psychological stress involved in these events, the fear or apprehension when one goes out on a dangerous call or the expectancy that danger may strike at any moment or the upset at having to witness human tragedy?"

One of the most dangerous calls an officer must answer is of a family disturbance. Approximately 22% of police deaths and 40% of police injuries on a nationwide basis are the result of interventions in domestic violence. Other high-risk activities are coping with drunks, robberies in progress, persons with knives or guns and high-speed chases.

The average officer does not face such high-risk events on a daily basis. However, officers on high-crime beats must remain in a constant state of heightened awareness. Thus these officers' bodies maintain a constant state of physiological reaction to crisis. A crisis reaction speeds up the heart rate and dumps adrenaline into the blood circulation and is likely to be accompanied by fear, uncertainty and anger. The excess adrenaline by itself can create trembling and a feeling of nausea. Research has found that anticipation before

danger can produce more stress than actual confrontation.

In his book *Police Passages* (1984), J. Stratton, departmental psychologist for the Los Angeles County Sheriff's Department, discussed what is probably the most stressful on-the-job crisis, an officer involved in a shooting incident. Two thirds of the officers who fire their weapons in the line of duty suffer psychological and physical problems. One third have moderate problems. The other third have severe difficulties that affect their family lives, sometimes resulting in separation and divorce. If the shooting leads to a loss of life, the consequences to the officer can be devastating, particularly if the shooting is based on a misperception, such as mistaking a toy gun for a real one.

In addition to the routine physical risk, there are psychological risks inherent in line-of-duty activities. These are tasks that involve tragic or loathsome duties. Among these are telling a parent of a child's death, accompanying a dead child to the morgue, dealing with a child abuse case, waiting for an ambulance with someone who is in great pain or dying, extricating a body after a traffic accident and dealing with the gruesome details in the aftermath of homicides and suicides.

Police work also carries a high potential for on-the-job injury. Many officers are injured, some quite seriously. For a variety of reasons, many officers do not report their injuries. In many departments, there prevails an attitude that injuries are just part of the job and are to be expected.

The psychological effects of an injury can be as traumatic as the physical ones. One type of effect may come when the injury arises as a consequence of a dangerous or potentially harmful situation. In this instance, the officer may for the first time recognize that he or she is vulnerable on the job to being severely hurt or permanent disabled and may develop a fear of being injured. Another type of effect may arise as a consequence of an injury that brings prolonged or intense pain or imposes stringent physical limitations. Officers tend to be fitness-oriented, and the experience of being disabled and not being able to do simple things such as go for a walk can be threatening to the officer's self-esteem.

Kroes describes a great many police stressors that are not inherent in the job. Instead they arise as a direct result of the way that police departments are organized, the level of funding of police departments and the public's attitude toward the police. The cumulative impact of these stressors leave police officers more vulnerable to the physical and psychological risks that are linked to the violence and tragedy-related aspects of their job. Among these stressors are the following:

- A sense of being overwhelmed by paperwork.
- A sense that decisions are made at the highest levels with little input from officers in the streets. The officers' feeling of powerlessness is a consequence of the fact that police departments are organized like military organizations. Like other professionals, highly trained officers who must make split-second decisions on the job resent being treated like children by their superiors.
- A sense that, when a street crisis results in the use of force, officers cannot be sure of support from their superiors.
- Conflicting expectations from superiors, from City Hall and from a range of police "audiences" (the officers' own families, judges, civil rights leaders, the media, the public).
- Job overload, experienced by as many as 70% of the police. This comes from the enormous range of services society expects from the police and is generally exacerbated by understaffing.
- The low esteem in which the police are held, which results in a consequent low level of pay and often requires officers to have second jobs, resulting in constant on-the-job fatigue.
- Frequent periods of inactivity (boredom on a stakeout, monitoring a radar unit, cruising alone in a police car), which can be so draining that the need for action may lead some officers to engage in marginal activities just for something to do.
- Shift work, which interferes with meal and sleep patterns and makes socializing with friends difficult.
- The officer's relationship with the courts, which is often adversarial. After having worked a full shift, officers are often kept waiting for hours to testify in order to suit the convenience of judges and attorneys. Officers who apprehend criminals, often at great risk, and who must deal with the victims of criminals' activities, frequently must stand by and watch the criminals walk away because of plea bargains. In time some officers wonder why they should bother to arrest anyone.
- Society's perceived negative attitude toward police. This is particularly painful. Officers may be called names, cornered at parties and baited, forced to explain to their children why other children make fun of their profession and assumed to be racist, either

when apprehending criminals in minority communities or when minority victims insist that officers are not trying as hard on their behalf to apprehend criminals.
- Physical or psychological trauma on the job. Officers so affected are often treated as malingerers and ordered back to work. After injuries on duty, accusations of malingering create great bitterness and probably impede recovery. If officers are able to return to their jobs, any sense of camaraderie they once felt within the department may be gone.

Joseph Hurrell and William Kroes performed a study published in 1976 under the auspices of the National Institute for Occupational Safety and Health in conjunction with the Police Foundation. Among 2,300 officers in 29 police departments, the study determined the following:

- 37% had serious marital problems.
- 23% had serious alcohol problems.
- 20% had emotionally disturbed children.
- 10% were taking prescribed drugs and street drugs, or were abusing drugs.
- 36% had serious health problems.
- Divorce was two to four times greater than in comparable nonpolice groups.
- Suicide was six times greater than in comparable nonpolice groups.

For police officers, alcohol appears to be a particular problem. A survey of occupations found that 8% of all "heavy drinkers" were police officers. In another study, 67% of officers sampled admitted drinking on duty. Mortality rates for alcohol-related cirrhosis of the liver is significantly higher among the police than among the general population.

The social culture of the police makes it easy for drinking to get out of hand. Gathering after work for a drink to unwind is an accepted custom. Alcohol eases the horror of the day and makes sleep possible. Officers who work vice or undercover are especially vulnerable. They must drink to maintain their cover, and alcohol helps to relieve the stress of the assignment.

Many spouses of police officers complain about a change over time in their personalities. Kroes calls this the development of the "working personality," a kind of hardening process that results in a more rigid, cynical attitude. Most distressing to families of officers is the deadening of their affect (emotionality). They seem to have lost most of their ability to feel and their zest for life is gone.

The personality changes evident in officers follow closely what Hans Selye, the father of stress research, calls the "general adaptation syndrome" (GAS). Selye found that the body's physiological response to prolonged stress develops in three stages. He defined the stages as follows:

- *Initial Alarm Reaction.* If stress continues, the body exhibits changes characteristic of the initial exposure to the stressor. Resistance to stress is diminished. If the stressor is strong enough, death may result.
- *Stage of Resistance.* If continued exposure is compatible with adaptation, the bodily signs characteristic of the alarm reaction virtually disappear and resistance rises above normal.
- *Stage of Exhaustion.* Following long-continued exposure to the same stressor, to which the body has become adjusted, adaptation energy is eventually exhausted. The signs of the alarm reaction reappear, but now they are irreversible, and the individual is likely to die.

The impact of stress on personality mirrors the biological stress syndrome. When an officer enters police work, he or she finds a world for which there has been no preparation and is thrown into the alarm reaction stage, sometimes referred to as the "Wyatt Earp" or "John Wayne" syndrome. Obviously the on-the-job exposure to stress continues. At this point, some officers quit or must be dismissed. Most officers show less overt evidence of strain, but they begin to have difficulty in their personal relations. In some departments, as many as 80% of the married officers are divorced within the first three years on the job. Other symptoms are evident, such as "edginess," psychosomatic complaints and health problems. During this stage the officer develops his or her working personality. In order to maintain this adaptation, the officer must become constricted in his or her personality.

If the stresses are chronic and/or great enough, the officer enters the last stage, breakdown or exhaustion. This stage is usually referred to as burnout syndrome, which has three prominent characteristics: emotional exhaustion, depersonalization (an unfeeling response to others) and a lack of a sense of accomplishment.

In the burnout stage, the officer can no longer maintain defenses against the stress. Physical ills, such as ulcers, diabetes and heart ailments, may develop. Depression is common and serious mental difficulties may lead to psychosis.

Kroes suggests that the stressors police must cope with are not going to disappear in the near future. Court dockets and prisons remain extremely overcrowded. Prison crowding has led to an increase in plea bargaining. In some states, such as Massachusetts, for every criminal admitted to a prison, one must be discharged. Corrections officials faced with the task of selecting among inmates to discharge shrug their shoulders and say, "The cream of the inmate crop is long gone as a consequence of earlier budget cuts. Those left in prison should stay there." Unfortunately, many of those who ought to remain in prison are set free to make room for more prisoners and quickly make more work for the police.

(See also BATTERED WOMEN: CONGRESSIONAL TESTIMONY; POLICE; POLICE USE OF DEADLY FORCE; PRISON OFFICERS' CODE OF SOLIDARITY: A SHIELD AGAINST VIOLENCE.)

police use of deadly force   For a constitutional democracy, the police use of deadly force raises difficult moral issues. The idea of a nation-state implies the concentration of the legitimate use of force in the hands of the state. However, the idea of a democratic society demands that the use of force be hedged in by firm rules.

Many communities have been torn apart by the perceived misuse of police deadly force. Of the 136 major urban riots during the 1960s, 84 were precipitated by perceived abuse by police, as were the Miami and Chattanooga riots of 1980 and 1982. It is estimated that in a given year at least 300, possibly as many as 600 people, are killed by police officers. In 1989 145 police officers lost their lives; 67 were killed by citizens, the other 78 were killed in accidents in the line of duty.

A police officer faced with a violent confrontation does not have much time for thought. The decision to shoot or not to shoot is the result of a complex matrix of social forces: department regulations, the legal context of the incident, the larger social culture.

In their 1982 book *The Badge and the Bullet,* Peter Scharf and Arnold Binder use Erving Goffman's concept of a "professional identity kit" to describe the role of the gun as a psychological tool of police self-identity. The gun, for many citizens, is the primary symbol of law enforcement. The possession of the means to kill other human beings, many police officers believe, creates a certain "presence" to which citizens respond.

Although some officers regard the gun as an unnecessary encumbrance, they are in the minority. Advertising directed at police extols the virtues of guns and their "software:" holsters, paper targets, gun sights and ammunition. Police humor often involves guns and the consequences of their use. The "macho" police officer is pictured as fearless in the face of guns.

In the view of Scharf and Binder, there is much cultural support for the blending of the idea of guns with the mythology of police work. Marshals of the Old West are pictured using guns to deal with gunfighters and G-men are pictured using guns to deal with mobsters during Prohibition.

The irony of the pervasiveness of the Old West image is that armed confrontations with desperadoes in the Old West were rare. Western states often had quite clear restrictions about gun use, both by citizens and by police officers. Moreover, the police in the East were largely unarmed until the latter part of the 19th century.

In the view of Scharf and Binder, at the intersection of art and police work, art shapes reality more than reality shapes art. The input of police consultants to films and TV movies is typically far less important to media producers than their own cultural images of police work.

Thus the police officer's role exists in a culture that puts great premium on the use of force. That emphasis feeds into the police officer's preoccupation with weapons.

Not all officers are obsessed with their guns. Some even admit their attitudes toward deadly force confrontations are far closer to terror than bravado. In private, many officers describe their fear of death and their abhorrence of the fake machismo of police work.

Although there is no evidence to support their conjecture, some observers believe there is an interactive effect between the "tool of the trade," the gun, and those who choose to be police officers. They suggest that the central role of the gun may be enhanced by the selection of militaristic personality types as police officers.

Others, including Lt. Richard Kelly of the Massachusetts State Police and Interpol believe that a powerful police socialization process supports the glorification of the gun. Most observers agree that two police traits are related to the use of deadly force: sensitivity to police status and suspiciousness. The use of force appears called for when a police officer feels he or she is being treated in a derogatory manner—pushed around or called a filthy name. Insolence in demeanor or the presence of such items as a black leather jacket and a motorcycle are likely to arouse a measure of police suspicion. The question of how possession of a gun interacts with those sensitivities and suspicion is little understood.

Actual firings of police weapons that hit citizens are rare. It has been estimated that the average police officer works 200 days a year and handles eight assignments per shift and fires his or her weapon on the average of once every nine years. Thus the chances of firing on any particular assignment are 14,400 to one.

According to the 1991 Statistical Abstract of the United States, between 1980 and 1989, the average number of officers killed annually was 152. The average number of officers assaulted was 60,396. Of those assaults, the average of firearms was 2,933 (4.8%), by knives or cutting instrument 1,596 (2.6%), by other dangerous weapons 5,378 (8.9%) and by hands, fists, and feet 50,487 (83%).

During 1989, the number of officers employed was 496,353. If those officers worked 200 days a year and had eight encounters per shift, there would be 794,164,800 encounters. From the perspective of the total number of annual encounters, the number of deaths of police officers and of civilians killed by police officers is extremely small. Even the number of violent encounters is 0.009%.

Nevertheless, an officer must always be prepared for a threat. The degree of threat depends on the type of unit to which an officer is assigned and the locale of the assignment. Some units and some locales carry a high risk of violent encounters.

Police officers think about using their guns far more often than they face situations in which they might possibly use them. Officers will occasionally draw their weapons to "motivate" a citizen to obey a particular command.

The premature drawing of a weapon can lead to an unnecessary escalation of a confrontation. Moreover, officers with guns unholstered have shot themselves while chasing felons or been shot with their own or their partners' weapons while engaged in physical altercations. Officers thus faced with physical contact with a citizen must remain highly conscious of the "safety of their guns."

Depending on the policy of the department, police sometimes use their weapons to fire warning shots. Often an officer will fire a warning shot rather than shoot a juvenile or a drunk with a weapon. On occasion, a warning shot will stop a brawl or a family fight in progress.

The use of deadly force is controlled on three levels: by state statute, by court decisions, and by departmental policy. Legal and administrative definitions are critical to the police officer who must establish early in an encounter what the options are.

Differences between jurisdictions can be significant. Scharf and Binder provide an anecdote:

There was this guy in Sparks [Nevada], where they can shoot you for running away with anything worth more than $100, who was running from one of their officers with his gun drawn. The guy ran across the street, which is the border to Reno where we don't do that kind of stuff. The guy turned to the officer and yelled out, "Too bad, sucker," and took off into a parking lot.

Even the rules for self-defense shootings are surprisingly varied. In some jurisdictions apparent possession of a weapon is sufficient to justify a self-defense shooting by an officer. In other jurisdictions the gun must have been pointed at the officer, while in others, the gun must have been fired. In some jurisdictions a physical attack or the use of a heavy object, such as a thrown typewriter, is sufficient justification to fire in self-defense.

Overall, police officers use their weapons far less than the various levels of authorization allow. The relatively few times that officers shoot in an inappropriate or out-of-policy manner are highlighted by the public attention they receive. The much greater restraint in the use of weapons, even where law and departmental policy permit, goes unnoticed.

Scharf and Binder conclude their book by saying,

The surprise of our observations over the last several years is not that there are unjustified and unnecessary shootings (as indeed there are) but that, given the number of citizens who are armed and the frequency of police-citizen armed confrontations, so relatively few shots are fired by the police and so relatively few people are killed by their bullets.

Introduction of Deadlier Weapons. The standard revolver used in about 4,000 police departments around the world is the Smith and Wesson Model 10, .38-caliber. Known as the ".38 special," the six-shot handgun is powerful enough to kill—or at least stop someone—but less likely to ricochet and hit bystanders than more powerful weapons. However, because of increasing firepower among American drug runners, police departments in the United States have started switching to more powerful weapons.

Despite there being no evidence that Canadian criminals were any more heavily armed than they had ever been, several Canadian police unions in 1989 began to urge that the standard .38 be replaced with the .357 Magnum, a similar-sized, more powerful gun that holds more cartridges. The .357 Magnum can increase muzzle velocity by as much as 30% and deliver twice the striking force of a .38.

In an interview for a January 9, 1989 *Macleans* article entitled "Furore Over Firearms," Detective Sergeant David Adamo, a 30-year veteran with the Montreal Police Department, claimed that most of his fellow officers would prefer the Magnum. He said, "Every force in every little jerk town around here has a better weapon. And we're in the centre of things, where the worst things happen."

But critics of the Canadian move to heavier weapons contend that the Canadian police did not have to deal with the heavily armed drug runners common in the United States. Darryl Raymaker, a Calgary lawyer and chairman of Calgary's Police Commission, said, "Calgary is not Los Angeles or Detroit. There are deep philosophical questions about raising the level of firepower. This is a pretty peaceful society."

Not everyone agreed that it was a good idea to give the U.S. police more powerful weapons. In an August 30, 1990 letter from Charles O. Lord, a former ordnance (military weapons) instructor, to the *New York Times* editor commented about a decision to give the New York City transit police powerful 9mm semiautomatic weapons. Lord said,

On firepower, my research indicates it took 10,000 rifle shots to wound one enemy in World War II and Korea, plus 50,000 more to kill a single enemy. The aimed shot by a trained shooter is still king. Only 25 percent to 33 percent of all of our soldiers in both those wars had the will to fire at an enemy in plain sight . . . A Federal Bureau of Investigation weapons report for 1987 concluded: "Except for hits to the central nervous system, reliable, reproducible instant incapacitation is not possible with any handgun bullet" . . . Thus the demand for high-speed bullets to increase stopping power is false. Better to take the cost of new guns and retrain officers to shoot well with the .38 special revolvers. Each shot in a vital zone will change the attitude of any criminal power. Firepower is not hit power.

A second letter to the *New York Times* editor from Lynn Zimmer, a sociologist at Queens College, New York, said about the proposed increase in firepower for the transit police:

I suspect that the upgrade is of symbolic importance rather than practical importance—that it bothers the police to be "outgunned by the criminals." Is this sufficient reason to give the police guns that pose a greater risk of bullets straying. We know why the criminals want these guns, and we know that many of them don't care if innocent bystanders are killed . . . I want to see evidence of specific cases where the lives of police officers or citizens would have been saved if only the police had had more powerful weapons

. . . Police officers should not be given 9-millimeter pistols just because the criminals have them.

Police experts who favor the .38 for its greater reliability point out that in the typical exchange of gunfire between a police officer and a criminal only three or four shots are exchanged. Hence, they see no need for greater firepower.

The shift toward more powerful weapons is likely to continue because the cost of making a change is often minimal. Arms manufacturers, anxious to introduce new weapons, frequently offer to exchange the new for the old. The manufacturers do not lose money on the exchange because they sell the old guns on the nation's huge second-hand gun market.

(See also ASSAULT WEAPONS; GUN CONTROL: ADVOCATES; GUN CONTROL: OPPONENTS; FELONY ARRESTS: SCREENING PROCEDURES; POLICE; POLICE STRESS; RIGHT TO BEAR ARMS: THE SECOND AMENDMENT.)

population density: implications for violence

The number of people per unit of space, that is, the population density, has an impact on the behavior of people in that unit. When densities become too high, the quality of life deteriorates and the length of individual lives may decrease.

The size of the world's human population is estimated to have been about 5 million people in 8000 B.C. By A.D. 1650, almost 10,000 years later, the population had grown to 500 million. A scant 200 years later, in A.D. 1850, the population had doubled to 1 billion. Eighty years later, in 1930, the population had reached 2 billion. By 1990, 60 years later, the world population had passed 5.3 billion and was growing at a rate of 95 million annually.

Not only is the world population doubling at shorter intervals, the human population is distributed in ways that intensify the impact of increasing size. Humans can be found throughout most of the world, but they tend to cluster in locations that offer geographic or economic advantages—rivers, seacoasts, valleys, cities.

Advantages of some locations are only imagined. All over the world, poor farmers are flocking from rural to urban areas in search of work that often does not exist. Once in a city, they live in squalid, substandard housing, with little or no sanitation. They suffer from malnutrition, low-birthweight babies, high infant mortality and a range of diseases associated with a lack of resources.

Some social scientists believe that the crowded poor may also suffer from what biologists call a "natural sink." Crowding increases the possibility of aggression

or accident and impinges on the biological functioning of organisms. High density alone can interrupt the successful completion of pregnancies and reduce life expectancy. The effects of density were explained by anthropologist Edward Hall in his classic 1966 book *Hidden Dimension.*

Hall pulled together research from many disciplines. Much of his book is devoted to analyzing the use by animals and humans of their senses—visual, auditory, kinesthetic, olfactory and thermal—in communicating and relating to one another. Overcrowding intrudes on and distorts those senses.

Hall theorized that humans and animals have a bubble of invisible space that constitutes their personal territory. Invasion of that territory, unless invited, is threatening.

One animal study Hall used to suggest the destructive effects of high density has been repeatedly cited over the years by other social scientists. In 1916 four or five Sika deer were released on James Island, 280 acres of uninhabited land in Chesapeake Bay. With no natural predators and a sufficient supply of food, the herd built up steadily until it numbered 280 to 300, a density of about one deer per acre.

In 1950 John Christian, an ethologist (a scientist who studies the behavior of animals) trained in medical pathology, advanced a thesis that increases and decreases in mammalian populations are controlled by physiological mechanisms that respond to density. He presented evidence showing that as numbers of animals in a given area increase, stress builds up until it triggers an endocrine reaction that kills off some of the population. Christian looked for an opportunity to study animals before, during and after population collapse. He found one in James Island.

In 1955 Christian shot five deer and made detailed studies of each animal's adrenal glands, thymus, spleen, thyroid, gonads, kidneys, liver, heart, lungs and other tissues. He noted the animal's general condition, the presence or absence of fat deposits and the contents of their stomachs.

Nothing happened during 1956 and 1957. But in the first three months of 1958, over half of the deer died. Christian and his colleagues recovered 161 carcasses for autopsy. The following year more deer died. The population eventually stabilized at about 80. Between March 1958 and March 1960 Christian collected an additional 12 deer for autopsy.

Size and weight of adrenal glands, which play an important part in the body's defenses, are not fixed. They respond to emergencies by releasing chemicals needed by the body to cope and under conditions of stress they enlarge. The size of the adrenal glands of the Sika deer remained constant from 1955 to 1958, the years of maximum population density and the period of natural sink when they died off.

Autopsies of the 12 deer that had lived in uncrowded conditions after the deaths of a large segment of the population revealed that the deer's adrenal glands had decreased in weight by 46%. Immature deer, which were a large proportion of casualties during the sink, showed the most dramatic post-sink changes. The weight of their adrenals dropped by 81%. Thus the enlarged adrenals of the animals under crowded conditions and their diminished size when crowding was relieved provided support for Christian's assumption that overcrowding has a profound impact on life itself.

A 25-year-long cause-of-death study at Philadelphia's Penrose Laboratory of 16,000 birds and mammals supported the idea that overstimulation and disruption of social relationships among animals leads to population collapse. Ethologists have been slow to suggest that their findings apply to humans, despite the fact that crowded, overstressed animals suffer from ailments that plague humans, among them circulatory disorders, heart attacks and lowered resistance to disease.

Flight reaction, keeping distance between one's self and an enemy, is one of the most basic and successful ways to cope with danger. However, for flight reaction to function there must be sufficient distance.

Distance Maintenance. Wild animals will allow any potential enemy to approach only up to a given distance before they flee. Birds and mammals not only have personal and social territories that they occupy and defend, they have customary distances that they maintain from each other. Some animals, walruses for example, favor contact and crowd together. Others, such as swans, avoid contact. Some species of birds seen resting on logs or in fields or along telephone wires are notable for the even separations between them.

Through experimentation, Hall determined that humans have four distances they maintain with others: intimate, personal, social and public. The way people feel about each other and the particular circumstances of an encounter are decisive factors in the distance maintained. People who are very angry or emphatic will move in close and "turn up the volume" by shouting. An amorous man will move closer to a woman, and if she does not reciprocate she will signal her lack of interest by moving out of range.

Each distance has a near and a far phase. Actual distances vary from culture to culture and vary somewhat depending on personality and environmental fac-

tors. A high noise level or low illumination will bring people closer together.

Crowding makes it difficult to maintain comfortable distances and increases the possibility that personal space will be invaded. Once invaded, an individual may react by fleeing or by fighting.

One of the chief differences between humans and animals is that humans have created screens, in such forms as private cars, separate apartments and private bedrooms, that shield the senses from intrusions and make it possible to pack more people into smaller spaces. But screens are not always effective. The buildup of density may become lethal. The constant stimulation of overcrowding may render populations vulnerable to disease. Disastrous plagues operated like a natural sink and reduced by one quarter the European population during the Middle Ages.

Screening that makes it possible to squeeze more people into smaller spaces is effective only so long as people feel safe and their aggressions are kept under control. If humans become fearful of one another, then fear resurrects the flight reaction, creating an explosive yearning for space.

Hall is not alone in his assumption that findings of animal research on population density are transferable to human overcrowding. A symposium on the use of space by animals and humans, held during the 1968 meeting of the American Association for the Advancement of Science, brought together scientists from a variety of disciplines who shared his opinion. The papers were published under the title *Behavior and Environment: The Use of Space by Animals and Men* (1971), edited by Aristide H. Esser.

A variety of conditions can produce stress, among them noise, smell, pain, extreme cold or heat and interruption of circadian (daily) rhythm. A stressor can have a greater or lesser impact depending on when it happens in the circadian chemical cycle. North Carolina State zoologist David Davis pointed out that stressors are probably additive in their impact. An organism subjected to loud noise might adapt, but if the organism is malnourished and crowded, the noise might result in failure of some vital biological system.

The main result of crowding in wild species is the elimination of low-ranking individuals. Seldom is there severe fighting, but sometimes there are injuries sufficient to lead to infections and death. Emigration from the group is often a choice.

Davis pointed out that emigration of large numbers of humans has been an important factor in the past to relieve overcrowding. However, now that there are no more uninhabited regions and the world may be fast approaching a maximum population, emigration has become less viable as an option.

Overcrowded animals, like the poor in the slums of large cities, suffer from overreaction to stimuli, low-birthweight babies, high infant mortality and early death. They present little direct threat to human populations, but slum populations around the world are potential powder kegs that can erupt in violent efforts to escape their fate. The fact that they seldom explode beyond the borders of their densely packed enclaves may be due to the fact that residents often kill each other over scarce resources or die an early death from injury or disease.

posses, Jamaican   According to law enforcement experts, across the United States, there are 30 to 40 Jamaican gangs, called posses, with a total membership of approximately 5,000. Their dispersion during the past several years has been astonishing.

Extraordinarily violent, clannish and cunning, the groups are usually based in Jamaican immigrant communities in large cities on the East Coast, among them New York, Miami, and Washington, D.C. They also are active in Dallas, Houston, several Midwestern cities, Anchorage, Alaska, and many smaller cities.

Their primary business is drugs, and they are more mobile than many other gangs. They have appeared suddenly in unlikely places such as small towns in the Midwest.

As do other American drug gangs, the Jamaicans hire local helpers when they open a crack house in a new area. The core of each operation remains Jamaican; no outsiders are permitted to reach the upper levels of the ring.

Many of the posses have their origins in the slums around Kingston, Jamaica, and some of their names reflect these roots. The Riverton City posse, the Maverly posse and the Waterhouse posse are named for Kingston neighborhoods. Two posses, the Shower and the Spangler gangs, claim vague affiliations with Jamaican political parties, although party leaders deny this. Some American law enforcement officials claim that the Showers and the Spanglers are the main groups and that all others are offshoots of those two. One group, the Jungle Lites, is alleged to be expert in guerrilla warfare tactics, skills in which police believe they were trained in Cuba.

Law enforcement officials are agreed that the Jamaican gangs are violent. They are well armed with automatic and semiautomatic weapons, and between 1985 and 1988 they had been linked to 800 murders, 350 in

1987 alone. The gangs don't hide their violence. A dispute between posse members in a Houston reggae club led to a fatal shooting in front of nearly 100 witnesses. Torture and maimings, such as kneecapping, are also common. Gang members are considered so dangerous that one city, Boston, has a special Jamaican entry squad.

The takeover of a small city by a Jamaican posse was described by a March 28, 1988 *Newsweek* article entitled "The Drug Gangs." Jamaicans descended on Martinsburg, West Virginia as migrant workers to harvest apples and peaches. It is not known whether they were posses originally or organized after they arrived. They stayed on to peddle cocaine. Hundreds squeezed into small apartments in a poor neighborhood called "the Hill" and turned a several-block area near the center of town into an open-air supermarket for drugs.

Martinsburg's 28-person police force was no match for the dealers. In an area where one or two murders per year were the maximum, there were 20 drug-related homicides in an 18-month period, as drug rivals struggled for control. Imported prostitutes worked the streets and local rates of venereal disease rose rapidly.

The local police asked for federal help. In the fall of 1986, 200 federal drug task force agents raided 26 drug dens, arrested 35 dealers and seized a cache of high-powered weapons. Police found a hit list of local judges and law enforcement officials. The arrested suspects claimed that the list was merely people targeted for a mystical Jamaican curse.

The raid prompted the most blatant dealers to move to Charles Town, 16 miles away—at least for a while. Nevertheless many dealers kept up a flourishing drug trade in Martinsburg and by 1988 could once again be seen congregating on some streets.

(See also ASIAN GANGS IN NEW YORK; GANGS: PICKUP OR
   TEMPORARY; GANGS: STRUCTURED STREET; OUTLAW MOTOR-
   CYCLE GANGS; VIETNAMESE GANG WARS WITH OTHER ASIAN
   GANGS.)

post-traumatic stress disorder (PTSD)   Scientific and clinical interest in traumatic stress has a long history, going back at least to the first Egyptian medical writings in 1900 B.C. Over the centuries, interest has waxed and waned.

The aftermath of the Vietnam War, which left a large number of people psychologically and emotionally damaged, helped to focus diagnostic, therapeutic and research attention on a collection of symptoms that arise in the wake of threats to an individual and/or loved ones. The threats may be natural disasters such as floods or earthquakes, personal disasters such as fires or automobile accidents, crimes such as mugging or murder, ongoing assaults such as physical or sexual abuse or continuing involvement with violence and its consequences such as that demanded of soldiers, police officers, emergency medics or firefighters. The threat-related symptoms that appear in the aftermath of trauma are called post-traumatic stress disorder (PTSD).

A high incidence of PTSD was not unique to the Vietnam War. After World War I, victims afflicted with similar symptoms were said to be suffering from shell shock. In World War II, the diagnosis was combat fatigue. Not surprisingly, some of those who endured shell shock or combat fatigue never fully recovered.

During America's longest war, the Vietnam War, more than a million young Americans, most of them between the ages of 19 and 21, engaged in combat in Southeast Asia. Fifty-eight thousand of them died there. Many committed suicide after returning home.

Vietnam was essentially a guerrilla war having few clearly identified fronts. An apparently peaceful countryside by day was often deadly at night. The enemy was likely not to wear uniforms and used women and children to kill Americans. For some soldiers, Vietnamese civilians came to be regarded as a part of the malevolent atmosphere and became targets for reprisals. Atrocities were committed on both sides of the conflict.

Upon returning home, especially at the height of the antiwar movement, some Vietnam veterans met outright hostility. Most were simply ignored by the civilian population. For some veterans, being ignored was as painful as overt hostility.

In the years following their return home, many Vietnam veterans experienced repeated nightmares about their experiences and intrusive images while awake. Some coped with the pain by a kind of psychic numbing.

By the latter half of the 1970s, some veterans with serious emotional difficulties stemming from their Vietnam War experience felt bitter about the war and alienated from the society that had sent them there. They remained aloof from traditional informal veterans' networks and mental health systems staffed by professionals, many of whom had opposed the war and were uninformed about the veterans' experiences and the effects the war had inflicted upon them. Clearly, there was need for a bridge between the veterans and those who might be able to help them.

A significant surge of scholarly interest in traumatic stress emerged during the 1980s. Many observers attribute the wave of new attention to the development of the concept of post-traumatic stress disorder, included as a new category in the third edition of the American Psychiatric Association's *Diagnostic and Statistical Manual of Mental Disorders (DSM-III),* published in 1980.

Following the development of a number of resources, including the publication in 1978 by Brunner/Mazel of the first volume, *Stress Disorders Among Vietnam Veterans,* dealing with the effects of extraordinary stressors, and the detailed *DSM-III*'s categorization of PTSD, mental health professionals and policymakers turned their attention to the complexity of the postwar adjustment of Vietnam veterans. In time, a national outreach program emerged with storefront veterans' centers and inpatient treatment programs in many VA Medical Centers across the nation.

Early PTSD Definitions.   The stress series volumes and the *DSM-III* clusters of symptoms enabled therapists to look with a more informed eye at cases that were not obviously connected with a trauma, either because the patient in therapy never mentioned the trauma or because a lengthy period had elapsed since the trauma.

The symptoms are characterized as a disorder separated into two subtypes: acute and delayed or chronic. Acute PTSD occurs when the onset of symptoms occurs within six months of the catastrophe and the duration of symptoms lasts less than six months. Delayed PTSD applies to cases in which six or more months elapse before a sudden onset of symptoms. Chronic PTSD refers to cases in which the symptoms endure for more than six months. The *DSM-III* suggested the following criteria for the diagnosis of PTSD:

A. The existence of a recognizable stressor in the life of the patient that would elicit significant symptoms of distress in almost anyone.
B. Reexperience of the trauma demonstrated by at least one of the following:
    1. Recurrent and intrusive recollections of the event.
    2. Recurrent dreams of the event.
    3. Acting or feeling as if the traumatic event were occurring at present.
C. A numbed responsiveness or reduced involvement with the external world beginning some time after the trauma, demonstrated by at least one of the following:
    1. Marked loss of interest in one or more significant activities.

2. A sense of detachment or estrangement from others.
3. Constricted affect (limited expression of emotion).

D.   The presence of at least two of the following symptoms that were not present before the trauma:

1. Hyperalertness or overreaction to being startled.
2. Sleep disturbance.
3. Feelings of guilt for having survived when others did not, or guilt about actions taken in order to survive.
4. Memory impairment and trouble in concentrating.
5. Avoidance of activities that bring back memories of the traumatic event.
6. Intensification of symptoms upon exposure to events that symbolize or resemble the traumatic event.

Therapeutic Intervention. A chapter by James Titchener on PTSD theory in *Trauma and Its Wake, Volume II* characterizes PTSD as "post-traumatic decline," which includes disruption of emotional responses resulting in self-imposed isolation, distrust of human relationships and dissociation (split in consciousness). "Psychic numbing" (a lack of sensitivity to stimuli) takes place when the trauma victim's mental system overloads and the victim is unable to handle intrusive memories of the catastrophe.

Titchener explains the decline in the aftermath of trauma by saying.

Most people believe that accidental horrors happen only to others. When they happen to the self, when the terror and losses of a catastrophic event strike, the infrastructure of the mind is wiped out, washed away, and crumpled. Reparative capacities often are not able to rise to the challenge. So, hollowed out, the victim falls back to a less complex, less stimuli-searching mode of existence, accepting less and trying less.

The course toward recovery involves an amount of time and effort almost always underestimated by the victim and the therapist. Titchener describes the therapeutic process by saying, "Together they must confront and come to terms with the patient's memories of helplessness, rage, losses sustained, guilt, and shame. We might summarize the recovery process as an internal negotiation in which the person arrives at a new and more realistic acceptance of these frightening memories."

The memories of helplessness must be verbalized and compared with the person's current situation to assess the probability of a repetition of the trauma. Many survivors live as if the fire, flood, attack, rape or other event will recur at any moment. Memories of the trauma and the events of the aftermath have to be repeated and processed (thought about, examined, compared, corrected) in detail in order to clarify thoughts and emotions that otherwise promote guilt and shame. The individual needs to learn to accept his or her behavior as reasonable, perhaps even moral and admirable, given the conditions surrounding the trauma and the period following it.

For those who succeed in overcoming the trauma, the perception of it and the role he or she played in it slowly approach the reality of the event. For those who fail at overcoming the trauma, life becomes a burden of weariness, isolation, inability to feel pleasure, disinterest in former pleasures and absence of ambition, lust or zest.

In the early phases of the aftermath of a trauma, denial through discounting the significance of the experience, minimizing the emotions aroused by the trauma and trying to control and manage the memories of the trauma seem essential. Soon the choice must be made to reduce denial. If the choice is made to maintain denial, then an increase in efforts to control thoughts, feelings and the conduct of life takes precedence over the processing of the memories. The dissociated memories remain unchanged in their meaning and they remain infused with their original emotion. Therapists frequently observe trauma victims in whom control over thoughts and feelings about the trauma takes so much effort that the individual has little left to expend on anything else.

Revised Definitions of PTSD. Many clinicians working with patients were not satisfied with the early formulations of PTSD symptoms. In September 1985 the Society for Traumatic Stress Studies was founded. Its goal was to develop research, policy, treatment, assessment and diagnosis criteria to serve a wide range of populations, among them rape victims and victims of other crimes, police officers and other emergency workers, combat veterans, surviving families of victims, and victims and families involved in intrafamilial abuse. The society joined in efforts that had been in progress since 1984 by the Work Group to Revise *DSM-III* of the American Psychiatric Association.

The efforts to revise the PTSD criteria were prompted, in part, by findings of researchers and clinicians that ran counter to accepted conceptualizations. An added spur to the efforts was the need of courts of law, insurance carriers and agencies disbursing disability benefits for more precise, reliable and valid criteria for diagnosis of PTSD than was available.

The Work Group's criteria for PTSD was substantially more elaborate and fit a broader population than prior efforts. With occasional points of clarification, the Work Group's revision as of April 1986 was as follows:

A. The catastrophic event precipitating PTSD is one that is outside the normal range of human experience and is psychologically damaging, such as a serious threat to one's life or physical integrity; serious threat to one's family or friends; destruction of one's home or community; or seeing another person who is mutilated, dying or dead or the victim of physical violence.

B. The traumatic event is repeatedly reexperienced in at least one of the following ways:
1. Recurrent and intrusive painful recollections of the event with no awareness of the stimuli that triggered the event.
2. Recurrent distressing dreams of the event.
3. Sudden acting or experiencing of the traumatic event as if it were occurring, including a sense of reliving the experience, hallucinations and flashbacks (disassociation), even if those reliving experiences occur upon awakening or when intoxicated (among children, themes or aspects of the trauma may be expressed in repetitive play).
4. Intense psychological distress upon exposure to events that symbolize or represent an aspect of the traumatic event, including anniversaries of the event.

C. Stimuli associated with the trauma are persistently avoided or there is a numbing of responsiveness not evident before the trauma, as indicated by at least two of the following:
1. Intentional efforts to avoid thoughts or feelings associated with the trauma.
2. Intentional efforts to shun activities or occasions that bring on memories of the trauma.
3. An inability to remember an important element of the trauma.
4. A marked reduction in interest in significant activities. (In small children developmental skills, such as language or toilet training, may be lost.)

5. A sense of detachment or estrangement from others.
6. A restricted range of emotion, a numbness to loving feelings.
7. A sense of a foreshortened future. (A child may not have expectations for an adult life).

D. Symptoms of increased arousal not present before the trauma persist, as indicated by at least two of the following:
1. Difficulty in falling or staying asleep.
2. Irritability or being given to outbursts.
3. Problems with concentration.
4. Hypervigilance (constant checking of environment).
5. Physical reactions to events that resemble some aspect of the traumatic event (for example, a woman who, after having been raped in an elevator, breaks into a cold sweat upon entering any elevator).

Societal Sealing Over. John Smith's chapter on PTSD theory in *Trauma and Its Wake, Volume II* introduces the concept of "sealing over." Sealing over allows the survivors of warfare to share responsibility for their extreme actions with the entire society of which they are a part. It allows a respite from the demands of making sense of and taking total responsibility for the events of war, and permits the painful experience to remain encapsulated or to be incorporated bit by bit into normal experience. Sealing over includes such ceremonies as ticker tape parades welcoming home the troops and expressions of support from families and from the society at large.

Vietnam veterans were denied opportunities for sealing over. They did not come home as a large group to welcoming ceremonies. They came home alone at the end of a tour of duty and were transported quickly from the horrors of war to the ordinariness of a civilian world uninterested in or hostile to their experiences. Unlike the veterans of previous wars, the Vietnam veterans were left without the option of the sealing-over stage. For them the medals, uniforms, parades, books and films had a hollow ring. Without a grand rationale for the war, the Vietnam veterans had to weave each strand of the experience into the overall fabric of their lives. They had to reach what Smith calls integration—that is, they had to accept personal responsibility for their actions and recognize the good and the bad aspects of the experience.

The intense examination of the strands of experience that has been taking place among Vietnam veterans has the potential to unravel the sealing over of other generations of veterans. The unraveling can lead older veterans to examine their reactions to wartime experiences frozen at age 19 or 20 without intense examination. Some of the antipathy to Vietnam veterans may reflect a personal and institutional response to the threat they pose to the sealing-over process of earlier veterans.

PTSD's Relationship to Criminal Behavior. The most significant feature of PTSD is that the survivor of trauma reexperiences the original trauma in one or more ways. The reexperience may come in dreams, uncontrollable and upsetting intrusive images, dissociative states of consciousness (periods of time about which the survivor or victim has no recall) and unconscious reenactments of the behavior that took place during the traumatic event. The unconscious reliving of the traumatic event may plunge the victim or survivor into criminal behavior.

Victims or survivors often exhibit approach-avoidance tendencies (are drawn toward and repelled by) situations associated with or reminiscent of the trauma. In the early phases of coping with the effects of the trauma (which may take many years), survivors or victims are likely to alternate between the approach and avoidance stages. This cyclical alternation can generate strong feelings of depression and anger, episodic rage and unconscious reenactments in an effort to master the unassimilated trauma.

John Wilson and Sheldon Zigelbaum's discussion of PTSD and its possible connection to criminal behavior in *Trauma and Its Wake, Volume II,* provides examples of unconscious reenactment of the traumatic episode(s). Among them are acting out in nightmare states or other unconscious thought in a dissociative or "flashback" state of mind; returning to the site of the trauma; risky and dangerous actions; aggression and adoption of a "survivor mode"; and the conscious or unconscious use of behaviors that were required for survival during the trauma.

Clinicians and researchers have observed survivors or victims enter into a survivor mode in response to a stimulus in their thoughts or in the environment. If an actual or perceived threat produces conflict with the survivor's or victim's self-concept, sense of morality or role obligations (for example as a parent, soldier, police officer), the survival mode of functioning may be precipitated and a dissociative reaction may occur. During such a reaction, the survivor or victim is likely to use the method of coping that was employed during the original trauma. If, for example, the survivor or victim is a former combat veteran, a dissociative reaction to situational stress or environmental stimuli could result in assaultive or violent actions.

In addition to assault or violence, another way in which the survival mode may precipitate a survivor or victim into criminal behavior is the "action addict" syndrome. Using the action addict syndrome, the survivor or victim maintains control over intrusive imagery by seeking out situations that provide a level of stimulation similar to that experienced during the original trauma. Individuals using this mode participate in events or seek out vocations that provide adventurous, dangerous, risky and challenging activity, such as parachute jumping, mountain climbing, gambling, smuggling, police work or firefighting.

Physiologically, an action-oriented activity generates a sense of "living on the edge," being fully alive, and may act as a natural antidepressant by generating endorphins in the brain. Endorphins are chemicals secreted by the pituitary gland that act on the nervous system and reduce pain, producing a kind of "natural high." The action-oriented activity confirms to the individual that he or she is still alive and may represent an effort to master the trauma with increased skills that lead to a successful outcome.

Another survival mode of functioning that may lead to criminal activity is seen in the depression-suicide syndrome of PTSD. In this syndrome, the person feels hopeless and trapped in the trauma, is flooded with intrusive imagery and reports that he or she feels like "a walking shell of his or her former self that should have died." Such an individual may demonstrate psychic numbing, survivor guilt, unexpressed grief, fear of repeating the trauma and desire for or fear of merger with those who died.

Persons caught up in the depression-suicide syndrome are likely to feel that they were victims of the events that exposed them to the trauma. Subjected to other stresses that cannot be easily managed, they may attempt suicide or unconsciously act out their depression and anger through actions that could result in death. The individual, for example, may engage in a pseudoassault by threatening or shooting at a police officer with no intention to kill, or may stage a robbery with the hope of being shot or verbally abuse someone prone to violence.

Separating PTSD-inspired Crimes from Other Crimes. To remedy a lack of a uniform procedure for organizing psychiatric/psychological documents for forensic purposes (as evidence in legal proceedings), Wilson and Zigelbaum offer an outline of useful material to be included in reports in cases in which defendants have been diagnosed as suffering from PTSD. The central forensic issue in such cases concerns a causal link between the defendant's mental state and the alleged crime. The professional's task is to establish as scientifically as possible the relation or nonrelation of PTSD to the criminal act.

For a comprehensive report, the authors advise gathering as complete a set of documents as possible for analysis. They suggest direct psychiatric investigations; results of biomedical and psychological tests; affidavits and statements made by significant others (loved ones, employers, close friends); records (medical, military, VA, school, organizational membership); legal documents, arrest records, police investigation reports, criminal indictments, laboratory tests; and any other documents that might aid in understanding the defendant.

The information brought together to prepare a final report should enable the examiner to gain a clear picture of the defendant's childhood and adolescence; family dynamics; academic and intellectual growth; adaptive skills and areas of vulnerability; motivational and career goals; sexual development and adjustment; personal health; work performance; and self-concept.

The question of whether a defendant with PTSD should be given treatment rather than be incarcerated is an issue that remains unanswered on a societal level.

The Struggle to Validate Treatment Techniques. The distance between Vietnam veterans and mental health professionals in the decade following the war's end is described in *Vietnam: A Casebook* (1988) by Jacob Lindy, the eighth book in the Brunner/Mazel series, as similar to other postdisaster environments in which estranged survivors are apt to shun traditional treatment.

To grapple with the problem, three groups came together in Cincinnati, Ohio. The Disabled American Veterans (DAV), an advocacy group, sought competent therapists to assist it in its efforts on behalf of Vietnam veterans. An analytic therapists' group with experience working with civilian disaster survivors agreed to develop a treatment strategy. And a research group, the University of Cincinnati Traumatic Stress Study Center, which had been studying disaster survivors, agreed to design a treatment outcome research study. Eventually, the VA Vet Center Program joined the efforts of the DAV in an outreach effort to bring veterans into treatment.

Individual treatments, once weekly for one year, were carried out by psychoanalysts at the Cincinnati Center for Psychoanalysis. Research evaluations of the efficacy of the treatment were administered at 18 months after the start of treatment. A major finding was that effective treatment was indeed possible, but it was more complex than anyone had envisioned.

Since 1980 when PTSD was first included in the *DSM-III*, research studies of the long-term effect of PTSD have increased in number and sophistication. What is perhaps the most extensive large-scale study of Vietnam veterans, by A. Egendorf and others published in 1981 by the Government Printing Office under the title *Legacies of Vietnam: Comparative Adjustment of Veterans and Their Peers,* identified involvement in combat as a critical variable in predicting the social and psychological problems of Vietnam veterans.

Those findings were supported by another large-scale study of Vietnam veterans conducted by J. Card and published by Lexington Books in 1983 under the title of *The Personal Impact of Military Service.* The study examined 1,500 men who had been first examined as ninth graders and then again 11 years after high school. The men were divided into Vietnam veterans, non-Vietnam veterans and nonveterans. The most significant finding of the study was that the occurrence and severity of post-traumatic stress disorder was not related to preservice characteristics or general adjustment to military life, but were strongly related to intensity of combat experience in Vietnam.

Research Not Confined to Vietnam Veterans. Clinicians recognized that PTSD was not confined to the person who was a victim of or participated in violence. Family and friends who had to learn to live with the maiming or loss of a loved one, or who witnessed violence, also developed PTSD. The organization Mothers Against Drunk Driving (MADD) insists that those killed by drunken drivers are victims of violent crimes and loved ones left behind are survivor-victims.

In all cultures, the death of a family member is traumatic for those who survive. Murder may be the most traumatic loss of all. Most murder victims leave behind friends and family, people who care for or depend on them. In 1990 there were 23,438 arrests for murder. If each victim killed left behind only three survivor-victims, then those forced during the year to cope with the pain and loss could number over 70,000.

In a chapter called "Contextual Influences on the Post-Traumatic Stress Adaptation of Homicide Survivor Victims" in *Trauma and Its Wake, Volume II,* researchers Morton Bard, Harriet Arnone and David Nemiroff described a retrospective study to measure the extent of trauma among those left behind. The researchers located the survivor-victims through the records of the Manhattan office the New York City Chief Medical Examiner. The homicides selected had occurred within two to five years of the study. For the purposes of comparison, a sample of the loved ones of suicide victims during the same period was included.

The researchers were critical of the fact that previous studies had focused only on the initial trauma and the survivor victim's immediate response. They sought to examine the survivor-victims' feelings and behaviors following a lapse of time.

In general, the study's subjects could relate in great detail events in connection with the death and the circumstances following. A striking feature about the affect (expression of emotion) of the survivor-victims of murder was the presence of strong feelings of anger and hatred. In this respect, their affect was quite similar to those found among survivor-victims of motor vehicle deaths. Both groups focused on the "intentionality" of the crime and felt anger at the person whom they viewed as responsible.

Moreover, many survivor-victims continued to have powerful feelings about their involvement with the criminal justice system, a relationship that frequently increased the traumatic stress of the homicide. Many remained angry at their treatment.

Although the criminal justice system appears to be a social-legal context that provides symbolic meanings for the whole society, in practice it focuses on the criminal rather than on victims and survivors. Ordinary citizens, who do not recognize the system's narrow focus, consider that one of its purposes is to acknowledge that a crime has been committed and that the affected individuals are victims. Moreover, an underlying assumption of citizens is that the criminal justice system's actions are intended to *set things right*.

A serious crime, particularly a homicide, is a breach in the rules that represent a society's shared values. For the law-abiding, disruption of the rules casts doubt on the assumption that others will not inflict harm. By apprehending and punishing criminals, the criminal justice system can restore confidence in the predictability of the social world.

Because the study's survivor-victims felt ignored by the criminal justice system, most did not feel that the system had set things right. To survivor-victims, pros-

ecutors entering into a plea bargain with the person or persons who killed their loved one seems tantamount to putting a price tag on their loved one's life.

Survivor-victims had other sources of fears. In some cases, particularly where there has been substantial media coverage, some feared that the murderer, upon release from prison, would seek revenge. Some families harbored the fear that one of their own members might seek revenge for the murder and, in so doing, become a murderer.

Following a homicide, survivor-victims feel isolated and stigmatized. They have a strong need to test the reliability of others and at the same time a strong urge to prove their own trustworthiness. The effort to stay involved in the legal process related to the crime represents an effort to reduce stress through self-repair and a struggle to rekindle social trust.

Added to the fact that many murderers are never apprehended and punished, exclusion from the legal process reinforces the survivor-victim's sense of disorder in the world and exacerbates the stress reaction. The world remains the unpredictable and unjust place it became at the time of the crime.

For all victims of violence, whether through participation in a war, a natural disaster or a crime, the world is forever changed, but with proper treatment it can become a place where a sense of well-being is possible.

prisoners: management of the persistently violent

The primary goal of prisons has not changed throughout their two centuries of operation: to confine criminals. An implicit corollary of that goal is to do so with a minimum of harm inflicted, on prisoners and officers.

There are essentially two reasons for isolating an inmate: first for safety, to protect the inmate from himself or herself, second as punishment for violent behavior.

Prisoners who are frequently and unpredictably violent present both logistical and ethical problems to prison officers and administration. It probably was easier when "social isolation" was an acceptable method of handling prisoners.

The earliest prisons were developed by Quakers, who believed that almost total isolation of prisoners would give them an opportunity to reflect on the inappropriateness of their behavior. The Philadelphia Society for Alleviating the Miseries of Public Prisons, founded in 1787, was dominated by Quakers.

The construction of the Eastern State Penitentiary, opened in 1829 at Cherry Hill in Philadelphia, reflected the Quaker premise. Cell blocks radiated out like spokes of a wheel from a central building. Prisoners lived alone in cells that had exercise yards attached. The yard walls were too high for prisoners to see each other.

Other states designed prisons in keeping with the Philadelphia model or at least adopted its philosophy. The effects of solitary confinement during 1822, the first year of its use at Auburn Prison in Auburn, New York cast doubt on its efficacy. Among prisoners kept in small cells without work or exercise, five died, one became insane and the others deteriorated.

Alarmed, Auburn officials changed the system. Instead of total isolation, they kept prisoners alone at night, but allowed them to eat and work together. However, they were required to maintain absolute silence.

Over the next 40 years, Americans debated the relative merits of the Philadelphia system of isolation versus the Auburn system of silence. The issue faded during the Civil War and after, but revived in 1876 when Zebulon Brockway, warden of Elmira Reformatory in upstate New York, proposed a rehabilitation model. He convinced state lawmakers to require that sentences be indeterminate, contingent on the behavior of inmates while in prison.

Following Brockway's example, rehabilitation became a goal of most U.S. prisons in subsequent years. However, for the most part, in actual practice rehabilitation has always been underemphasized and underfunded.

Regardless of the philosophy governing any given prison system, coping with persistently violent prisoners has never ceased to be a problem. For many years solitary confinement was the preferred solution, but reform efforts eventually made it less acceptable. The use of solitary confinement also dwindled as prisoners became more likely to sue prison officials who subjected them to unusual punishments.

Coping with New York's Worst.   An example of the dilemmas presented by a persistently violent prisoner is the case of Willie Bosket, a murderer considered by New York State officials as their most violent prisoner. Bosket became notorious in 1978 when, at age 15, he admitted killing two subway riders ''for fun.''

In April 1989, two weeks before he was scheduled to be sentenced for stabbing a prison officer in 1988, Bosket freed himself from a chain and beat another prison officer, leaving a six-inch gash in the man's head.

Bosket is normally kept behind a plastic wall in an isolation cell in the Woodbourne Correctional Facility in Woodbourne, New York. He is allowed out of the cell for one hour a day to receive visitors or for recreation.

Bosket appeared in court on June 5, 1989 to protest his treatment by prison officials, which he called humiliating. In leg irons and handcuffs that were bound to a belt around his waist, he challenged the methods prison authorities used to constrain him, claiming that they amounted to cruel and unusual punishment.

The judge watched a videotape of the procedure used by the prison officers to take Bosket out of his cell. He must turn his back to the plexiglas door and squeeze his hands out through a slot meant for a food tray. Officers shackle his hands and chain him to bars on the door. Then they apply leg irons through other slots. The door is swung open and Bosket shuffles backward with it.

Once the door is open, Bosket is unlatched and his hands are cuffed behind his back and padlocked to a wide belt so that he cannot move them to the front of his body. He is also chained by leg irons.

A regional administrator of the Virginia Corrections Department testified on Bosket's behalf that chaining was virtually never used in the United States. In his opinion the method of shackling Bosket to the cell door increased the opportunity for violence. He recommended that electronically controlled doors be installed so that correction officials could move Bosket without getting near him.

The judge ruled against Bosket. In his opinion, because Bosket had persistently assaulted officers, the prison authorities had logical justification for the measures they used. He said, ''Mr. Bosket has repeatedly demonstrated his incorrigible, violent nature.''

Bosket has often openly challenged the prison system and has said publicly that he laughs at prosecutors who try to control him. Prison officers are upset by his statements, claiming that he is virtually immune from the sanctions of the system.

Many consider Bosket to be a symbol of the failure to rehabilitate of the corrections system. He has been imprisoned almost continuously since he was 9. He once claimed that he had committed more than 2,000 crimes by the age of 15, including 25 stabbings and two murders.

Avoiding Legal Challenges.   In an era in which inmates are likely to challenge legally any decision to isolate them, prison systems, such as the Wisconsin Corrections System, use a highly codified approach to changing a prisoner's normal living arrangements. Moves may be made only by following a set procedure that requires due process hearings at every stage. The necessity for a move must be verified by an independent professional (social worker or psychologist) most often in person, but by phone in an emergency.

From her own experience working in cell blocks, Terry Landwehr, Wisconsin Corrections System Adult Division Administrator provided an example of an approach that protects officers who must move a prisoner against later claims of brutality. An inmate managed to get a pair of handcuffs, which he clasped on his wrists. He had them on so tight that his hands were turning blue. Nevertheless, he threatened to use the handcuffs as a weapon against anyone who came into his cell and tried to take them off.

Landwehr, a lieutenant at the time and in charge of the shift, called a designated psychologist with whom she had worked for six years, one who had also known the inmate for a comparable time and who was aware of the inmate's long history of violent behavior. The psychologist based his decision on the predictable damage to the inmate's hands that any delay would cause, on his experience of Landwehr's handling of other emergencies and on the inmate's history. He agreed that officers could go into the cell to subdue the inmate, remove the handcuffs and transfer him to a safer setting.

Whenever possible, in the process of gaining control of the violent prisoner, the officers wear protective clothing or carry shields. The procedures are documented each step of the way so they can be presented in court if need be.

Isolation is not a particularly effective method in terms of reducing an inmate's violence, and an isolated inmate is likely to deteriorate physically. In the Wisconsin system, isolation is generally limited to brief periods, typically no longer than five days and nights.

Solitary confinement is seldom used in modern U.S. prisons, for a variety of reasons. One is that space is too precious, particularly in older prisons.

Sometimes an inmate who screams or yells constantly will have to be isolated for the sake of the other inmates. More commonly inmates are segregated, moved to an isolation block of eight or ten cells. Most newer prisons include such blocks. At a given time, a few of these cells are likely to have inmates in them, so no inmate is completely isolated, and they generally are allowed to have magazines and books. Reminiscent of the Auburn Prison model, a few such units forbid talking among inmates.

Segregation in an isolation block generally is for incremental periods of time, 30, 60 or 90 days. If prison authorities want the time extended, due process hearings are required.

In the Wisconsin system, following a move that has involved any kind of force—which is common, since the move is usually the consequence of violence—the inmate is checked for physical damage by a nurse, a measure that protects the inmate who might need medical care and protects the prison officers from being charged with brutality.

Transfers Among Prisons.   Correctional facilities have learned to cooperate with one another to provide a different kind of isolation. Violence or instigation of violence is just one of many ways prisoners may distinguish themselves as leaders among other prisoners. Under the terms of an interstate compact, a method commonly used to isolate persistently violent prisoners who are leaders and who organize violence among their followers is to trade them with prisons or jails in other states.

In a new out-of-state facility, such inmates may take a year or two to build up new followings. About the time they get organized enough to make trouble in the new prisons, they may be traded again, to another state or back to the original state.

(See also CALIFORNIA CORRECTIONS SYSTEM; PRISON OFFICERS' CODE OF SOLIDARITY: A SHIELD AGAINST VIOLENCE.)

prison officers' code of solidarity: a shield against violence

Prisons are expected to punish, deter, isolate and rehabilitate offenders, while at the same time maintaining order and inmate productivity. Most prison staffs realize that they do little more than prevent escape and maintain internal order.

One factor that distinguishes a prison officer's job from that of other professionals who deal with violence is the ever-present risk of being the target of inmate violence or of being caught in its crossfire. The risk creates an officer subculture, which is described by Kelsey Kauffman, a former Connecticut prison officer, in *Prison Officers and Their World* (1988). While Kauffman's research was done on the most violent prisons in the Massachusetts prison system, it is reasonable to assume that many of her findings are applicable to other prisons.

Prison officers learn to live with a constant threat of violence. Unlike many other professionals—homicide detectives, traffic officers, social workers, paramedics, emergency room personnel—whose job it is to deal with the effects of violence, prison officers cope with violence done to an officer colleague or to an inmate whom he or she may have known for many years, adding grief to the customary psychic trauma left behind by violence.

Not only must the officer live with the psychological impact of violence, he or she must manage the physical horror left when the violence has run its course. In correspondence with Wisconsin Corrections System Administrator of the Division of Adult Institutions Terri Landwehr, she recalled her early experiences as an officer in a men's maximum security prison: "I have vivid memories of breaking up a fight and being soaked through to my skin with blood."

To the intimacy of prison violence is added the tension of dealing with the aftermath of violence in confined spaces in a locked facility. Landwehr wrote, "Another time I remember coagulated blood and chunks of flesh in a cell to which I was sent to investigate after an inmate in an 8 by 10 cell had tried to kill another inmate. My worst memory is of an inmate who committed suicide by diving headfirst off the walkway on the third tier onto the concrete below."

Outsiders find it hard to imagine the extent of violence in prisons. Landwehr mentioned a prison officer friend who had left a thriving law enforcement career in Chicago to take a job in a rural prison in order to move his family from the dangers of the city to the peace of the northern woods of Wisconsin. His home environment became more peaceful, but his change of profession proved to be anything but tranquil. He was shot twice on the job in the rural prison.

In her study of Massachusetts prison officers, Kauffman focused much of her attention on Walpole, the state's maximum security prison. In the introduction to the chapter "Prison Violence," she comments:

It was Walpole's violence more than anything else that seared the lives of the officers and inmates who worked and lived there . . . Walpole in the 1970s was characterized not merely by violence but also by sadism. Inmates did not just die at Walpole. They were mutilated, castrated, blinded, burned, stabbed dozens of times or more. Then they died . . . New officers expressed bewilderment at the sadism of inmate attacks on fellow inmates—the need, as one put it,

for "overkill." "Strangle a guy, castrate him fifty times while he's alive, stab him where it's not going to kill him . . . and then, after he's dead, stab him fifty more times." Only those officers who had fought in Vietnam found parallels in their own experience or imagination.

Some officers understood an inmate's need to arm himself and to demonstrate a willingness to meet violence with violence in order to survive, but most officers concluded from the violence that the inmates were not quite people but were more like animals. They felt supported in their assessment by the inmates' attitude of acceptance, almost indifference, toward violence. Even inmates hurt by violence adopted an attitude of nonchalance to convey that they had not been badly hurt.

Inmate self-inflicted violence—suicide, self-castration, self-mutilation—sometimes assumed the same bizarre qualities as violence directed at other inmates. The quest for drugs often precipitated self-inflicted harm. One inmate crushed his hand in a heavy metal door in order to get pain medication.

Many officers expressed frustration at their inability to protect inmates in their charge from death or serious injury. However, the level of violence at Walpole, the seeming indifference of the inmates to what happened to their fellow inmates and the officers' inability to stop the carnage inevitably led many officers to adopt at least a facade of indifference.

While officers may have affected indifference when inmates were the victims, they were passionate about inmate violence against officers. Data are scarce about how widespread violence against officers is, but a hint at its extent can be gleaned from a volatile period in 1979 when Walpole officers staged a walkout charging that over a three-month period 39 officers had been stabbed, blinded, severely beaten and scalded by inmates.

Every Walpole officer interviewed by Kauffman could cite dozens of cases where officers had been injured or had narrowly escaped injury at the hands of inmates. All reported repeated threats against them by inmates.

With an entire inmate population carrying a "shiv" (a knife or a razor), Walpole officers felt that they were at risk whenever they came in contact with inmates. Because inmates were allowed hot plates, and if denied them rigged makeshift substitutes, officers might be scalded rather than stabbed. Officers might also have their skulls broken with a large can of food or a mop handle.

The violence that most officers feared more than any other was spontaneous and unprovoked. Any officer, regardless of prior relationship with an inmate or inmates, could be hurt by these random, unpredictable attacks, most of which were brought on by the use of legal or illegal drugs. Legal drugs became a problem when prison doctors prescribed drugs for an inmate who hoarded them or was forced to turn them over to stronger inmates.

Officers particularly ran a risk of calculated, unprovoked violence from inmates who "would kill their mothers to get out of prison" or from those who just liked to kill and especially liked to kill officers.

Violence by Officers. Inmates were not the only ones implicated in the violence of the Massachusetts prison system, nor was all violence against officers unprovoked. Through ineptness, miscalculation or perversity, some officers triggered violence against themselves.

During the 1970s charges of Walpole officer brutality were constant. Although only one civil suit against Walpole officers in that decade was successful, officers Kauffman interviewed reported that physical force beyond the need for restraint or self-defense was used regularly as a means to maintain control and to deter assaults on officers. Officers occasionally discussed specific incidents of officer brutality that had been reported in the media or during public legislative hearings. With only one exception, the officers' accounts corroborated the allegations made by inmates.

Rarely did the brutality incidents involve a one-on-one incident between an officer and an inmate. More typically, the incidents involved five or six officers. Such incidents were dangerous for inmates not only because of the numerical disadvantage, but also because of the group psychology involved. Kauffman quoted one of her interviewees who analyzed the group effect by saying "Once one guy throws the first blow, they like all get their courage up and say 'Okay, it's accepted. Let's do a number on him.'"

Assaults by officers were usually a spontaneous response to some provocation by an inmate—such as throwing hot coffee or urine at an officer. (Throwing urine, according to Landwehr, is a common occurrence in prisons.) Once the violence had begun, the officers seemed to lose control. The interviewees said that the only reason that no one had been killed was simply luck.

From officers at the Massachusetts Treatment Center for Sexually Dangerous Persons housed at Bridgewater

State Mental Institution, Kauffman learned that spontaneous, unprovoked attacks against officers were common. Bridgewater officers were apparently prone to harsh retaliation. One officer told Kauffman, "It's a cardinal sin at Bridgewater for an inmate to hit an officer. If he hits an officer, whew! good night."

At Norfolk, the Massachusetts medium-security prison, and at Concord, the reformatory for young adult males, junior officers reported stories of violence past and present but said that they had never witnessed such events. The Concord officers asserted that whatever violence by officers did take place was done by a small clique who trusted each other to remain silent.

The Norfolk officers ascribed the lack of violence at their prison to the "laid-back" character of the officers and inmates and to the open access of inmates and officers to each other. One Norfolk officer explained, "You have 700 [inmates] . . . and you can't beat on one inmate and not expect 699 . . . to retaliate or to feel they have access to you."

The officers who instigated violence in any of the settings appeared to be few in number. As at other prisons where violence takes place in violation of official policy, the violence at Walpole and Bridgewater took place most often on the 3 P.M. to 11 P.M. shift, when administrators, psychiatric staff and other "outsiders" had gone for the day.

While the question of whether officers engage in violence has been discussed repeatedly in Massachusetts, in Kauffman's opinion there has been little discussion of why officers engage in violence. Based on her data, she reported that the most common justification is to control the inmates. However, an even more fundamental reason for violence by officers appeared to be deterrence. The officers believed that their violence prevented inmate violence against them.

Amid Walpole's random, unrelenting violence, officers felt that they had to anticipate it: "I have to get to knock this guy out before he knocks me out." Moreover, they felt that in order to survive, they had to establish and maintain a reputation for willingness to meet aggression with aggression. Demonstrations of such readiness were commonly considered matters of self-defense by both inmates and officers.

Even some officers who themselves rejected violence and declined to work on the 3 P.M. to 11 P.M. shift for that reason believed that the violence meted out by that shift was essential in the protection of all officers. Kauffman proposed that the source of their concern came from an administration that professed to oppose officer violence but did little to protect officers from attack. The officers felt justified in taking matters into their own hands.

In some instances, beatings by officers were not so much deterrence against tomorrow's attack as "payback" for a past attack. A Walpole officer explained the buildup of a need for revenge. He said:

It's not easy just to stand there and take it with an inmate pointing a razor blade at you and saying that he's going to get you or he is going to get your family when [he gets] out . . . you take it when what you'd like to do is swing at him and bury his head under concrete. But you just stand there and take it. You hear it day after day after day . . . you are waiting for the chance that he is going to take the first swing.

The ferociousness of some assaults by officers on inmates in response to seemingly minor provocations may be the end result of an accumulation of grievances. The minor provocation provides an excuse to get even.

A Relationship Between Crime and Punishment. Particularly at Walpole, Bridgewater and Concord, the officers interviewed by Kauffman recognized that just being in such prisons was punishment for the inmate's crimes. For the most part, their feelings of hostility toward inmates were connected to behavior inside prison and had little do with what the inmates had done outside to get themselves sentenced.

However, when Kauffman interviewed officers at Norfolk and at Bridgewater, institutions where the conditions of incarceration were relatively comfortable, she found that the officers felt the inmates were not paying sufficiently for their crimes.

On the value scale of crime, sex offenders rank the lowest and they often suffer the most at the hands of fellow inmates and officers. Officers' feelings were magnified at Bridgewater, where the inmates' crimes were among the most heinous and the behavior of the officers toward the inmates was most constrained.

Whatever acts of violence and lesser acts of vengeance Bridgewater officers committed against inmates stemmed in the main from their rage at the seeming discrepancy between the atrociousness of their crimes and their punishment. One officer fantasized about machine-gunning the inmate population, another about gassing them, a third about removing the officers from the institution and then flying over to drop a bomb on it. Despite the fact that Bridgewater was in many ways the safest and easiest prison to work in, the officers'

unresolved rage exacted a severe psychological toll from them.

Officers' Relations with Other Officers. Other explanations for the use of violence by officers were related to officer solidarity. Many officers who participated in violence against inmates were followers rather than instigators. Although they might have had serious reservations about their participation, they felt they had few other options. The pressure to conform was reinforced by genuine fears for survival, situations in which refusal to conform might result in their own deaths.

As an outgrowth of her research, Kauffman proposed that nine norms govern officer subculture. The details of the norms and the relative importance of each emerged from the answers to two questions: "What is the worst thing you could do in your own eyes as an officer?" and "What is the worst thing you could do in the eyes of other officers?"

The strongest and most stringently adhered to norm was "Always go to the aid of an officer in distress." The obligation to go to the aid of a fellow officer is viewed as the single most important responsibility of an officer. The strength of the norm lies in the recognition that an officer cannot survive on the job in prison for long if he or she cannot depend on the support of fellow officers when in trouble.

The ultimate sanction against an officer is to cast him or her adrift in an institution without the support of fellow officers. The chances of this happening are not great. Officers generally agreed that any officer should be helped, regardless of the officer's willingness to respond to the needs of other officers. So important is the norm of helping when there is trouble that once an officer has proven dependable in that respect, he or she is likely to be forgiven for violating other norms.

The second strongest norm was "Never lug drugs," that is, never bring in drugs to the inmates. Because alcohol or drug use by inmates is likely to precipitate violent confrontation, drugs and alcohol create a danger to fellow officers.

The third strongest norm was "Never rat," that is, never tell anything about an officer to an inmate, and never cooperate in an investigation or testify against a fellow officer in regard to the officer's treatment of inmates.

The prohibition against telling inmates anything about a fellow officer is directly related to officers' safety. If an inmate learns which officer has signed a report that resulted in a transfer to less comfortable quarters or if an inmate learns the identity of officers who beat him or who quelled a riot, he may vow to get even. Betrayal of information about a fellow officer to inmates could jeopardize the officer's life. Related to the prohibition against betrayal is an injunction against even discussing fellow officers and against revealing much about oneself to inmates.

The injunction against revelations is generally obeyed. When Kauffman asked the interviewees what they thought would happen in connection with an official inquiry in the event of an inmate's death due to an officer's brutality, most agreed that other officers would unanimously swear that the accused officer was being attacked.

Asked what they themselves would do, their answers were more varied. Some focused on the circumstances of the death and the identity of those involved. One officer said, "If it was this one particular person I think should be executed, or a few people in there that I think should be executed, I'd say I didn't see a thing . . . but there are some things that just cannot be tolerated. I think that I would probably step forward and tell them what happened and hopefully remain anonymous."

Some officers focused on their relationship to their fellow officers and their desire to remain employed. To testify against a fellow officer would mean betraying someone with whom the officer had suffered, to whom the officer owed past safety and about whom the officer cared.

For an officer opposed to violence, who felt loyalty to fellow officers and who wanted to remain employed, there were few more troubling dilemmas than the misbehavior of a fellow officer. To violate the central norms of the subculture was to violate one's fellow officers and the trust they had in you. For such a betrayal, the penalty was to be set apart from the officer community, a sanction that in a violent prison like Walpole could not be borne.

A principal factor that sustains prison violence lies in the unwillingness of both officers and inmates to testify against members of their own group. The resistance to testifying of both officers and inmates is based not on a conviction that the person who committed the violence was justified or that silence has an intrinsic value, but in the commitment to the group and in the fear of the consequences of violating the group's code.

The remaining six norms were not as stringently adhered to as the first three. They were: Never make a fellow officer look bad in front of inmates. Always support an officer in a dispute with an inmate. Always support officer sanctions against inmates. Don't be a white hat, that is, don't behave in any way that suggests sympathy or identification with the inmates. Maintain officer solidarity versus all outside groups. And show positive concern for fellow officers.

The degree of solidarity among an institution's officers is determined by the degree of threat the group perceives from outside itself and the degree to which it views itself as standing alone against that threat. At Walpole, the threat presented by inmates was constant and support from the administration was always in doubt. Therefore, the nine norms had substantial impact on the beliefs and behaviors of Walpole officers.

Kauffman's norms suggest that any efforts at prison reform must take into consideration the safety of officers and the impact that issue has on their behavior.

Officer Ambivalence About Violence.   Some officers in Kauffman's study viewed violence as an opportunity to gain prestige among fellow officers. Others had a predilection for violence. Although the popular image of the "brutal screw" did not apply to many officers, some described themselves and were described by fellow officers as "thriving on violence" and "enjoying the break in the routine." Despite a public deference given to such officers, fellow officers were frequently scathing in their assessments of them, making such comments as "A lot of them are scared deep down inside." The critics viewed the violence as intended to prove that the officers were not frightened.

One Walpole officer viewed violent officers as morally no different from the inmates. A Bridgewater officer described violent colleagues by saying "Some officers are banana heads. They look for trouble."

On the other hand, some officers interviewed by Kauffman saw no need to explain or justify their violence. She said about Walpole as an institution that there

> was the apparent acceptance by individuals on both sides— keeper and kept—that violence, at least in some forms, needs no justification: it is natural, a way of life, even a game if played within certain rules . . . Violence and retribution were understood and accepted by both sides . . . Officers who shared this perspective on violence viewed it as so routine a means of resolving difference that they often failed to consider other courses of action.

An inmate who spent years in Block 10 (for difficult-to-handle inmates) reminisced about pitched battles with officers: "I admit it. I threw shit at the guards, it got to be a game. They tried to dehumanize me and that's the one way they ended up succeeding. I threw the only things that was around to throw.'' The rules of the game—particularly what constituted fair violence—varied widely among officers and inmates.

Not surprisingly, officers most opposed to violence worked in those institutions where there was the least call for it. Despite the lesser amount of violence at Norfolk, one officer there felt that even at his institution officers were too prone to misread aggression for violence and to threaten force or some sanction. He viewed much aggression as a ritual—as a way of being somebody.

At Walpole, the institution where the officers had the least control and were the most regularly victimized, arguments in favor of violence seemed most compelling, a view that many saw society as acquiescing in. Nevertheless, even there, most officers had reservations about violence and a few categorically opposed and saw it as counterproductive. Such officers took the position that when fear spawns violence, that violence spawns more violence, which in turn spawns more fear.

A few Walpole officers viewed officer violence as wrong from both a societal and a personal perspective.

(See also CALIFORNIA CORRECTIONS SYSTEM; PRISONERS: MANAGEMENT OF THE PERSISTENTLY VIOLENT; PRISON OVERCROWDING: COPING WITH THE COSTS.)

prison overcrowding: coping with the costs

Between the years 1975 and 1985, the population behind bars grew faster than ever before, despite the fact that overall crime rates were not generally rising. The rate of growth continued to soar in subsequent years. In 1989 nearly 2% of all adults, approximately 3.5 million people, were in prison or jail or on parole or probation. Data reported in early 1991 found 1.05 million behind the bars of federal or state prisons or local jails.

Most jurisdictions meted out harsher sentences, whether or not they had mandated sentencing guidelines. From 1970 to 1985, the average sentence for persons convicted of federal crimes doubled, to 58 months. The most significant prison and jail population growth came from drug offenders.

In 1986 approximately 200 drug offenders entered Florida prisons each month. By December of 1988 approximately 900 drug offenders a month were entering Florida's prisons. The swelling numbers forced the state into a practice of releasing prisoners early. The average portion of their sentences served by released prisoners fell from a typical 50% to 35.4%.

New York State experienced a similar pattern. While the state's prison population more than doubled between 1980 and 1988, the number of drug offenders grew fivefold. The trend in the federal prison system was similar. An estimated 44% of federal prisoners are drug offenders, and the proportion is growing. Federal prisons are crowded to about 158% of their capacities.

In 1988 Florida added prison beds at a rate of 4,500 annually, but the system nevertheless was short by 30,000 to 40,000 beds. To solve the problem, experts calculated, would require 40 to 50 additional prisons. In Michigan, a prison building program was expected to add 28 new prisons by 1992. However, by 1989 prison officials predicted that overcrowding would increase tenfold by the time the buildings were completed.

Crowding and Violence. During an interview for an August 30, 1987 *New York Times* article entitled "Coping with Violence in Overcrowded Jails," Jere Krakoff, a Washington-based attorney for the American Civil Liberties Union's National Prison Project, said, "When you increase populations, almost inevitably there is an increase in violence."

The nation has 3,300 local jails. The problem of violence is acute in city jail systems, where many of the prisoners—in New York more than two-thirds—await trial. In an interview with the *New York Times,* Vincent Nathan, a court-appointed ''master'' of prisons that have come under federal jurisdiction, explained why the tension in jails is so high. "A pretrial prisoner is under stress that a sentenced prisoner is not." By that he meant that the uncertainty while waiting breeds dissension.

New York City's Corrections Commissioner Richard Koehler was of the opinion that about 2% of all inmates are prone to violence, regardless of prison conditions. He asserted that New York City's 150 cells set aside for dangerous prisoners ought to be doubled.

Prison-packing—doubling up in cells built for one prisoner, bunking dormitory-style, sleeping on mattresses on the floor in gymnasiums—increases the tensions that lead to violence and significantly increases the opportunities for it. In 1984, 107 inmates in the United States committed suicide. Another 89 were murdered by other inmates. And there were 8,871 reported assaults within prison walls, which many observers believes vastly underestimates the actual number.

In many states, city and county jails intended for short-term detention became overcrowded with convicts that the prisons could not squeeze in. By fall 1987 officials of the New York City Department of Corrections had to find room for 16,500 inmates packed into 11 city jails, an increase of more than 2,000 over 1986.

Jail tensions erupted into clashes between officers and prisoners, during which 65 inmates and five officers were injured.

Following those clashes, jail officers' behavior was scrutinized. In time the officers grew to resent the attention, pointing out that as the jails became more and more crowded, each officer—unarmed except in emergencies—was expected to oversee more and more inmates.

Not all inmates expressed their frustration at overcrowding through violence or rioting. During the last half of the 1970s and the first half of the 1980s, inmates filed hundreds of lawsuits to ask for better conditions. As a consequence, the federal courts ordered New York City and more than 40 other state and city penal systems to come under the supervision of the federal courts.

States under federal supervision are mandated to reduce overcrowding to free beds. In practice this means that escalation of "get-tough" sentencing creates a domino effect that increases the number of early releases. Although judges quadrupled the length of prison sentences between 1965 and 1985, the actual amount of time served remained constant.

The *New York Times* reported on November 26, 1989 that in Connecticut, where six out of 15 prisons were under court order, a law required that prisoners be released if the prison system operated at 119% of capacity for more than 30 consecutive days. In mid-November, when the system reached the 29th day of overcrowding, officials scrambled to reduce the inmate population by a variety of means, such as delaying transfers from local jails and releasing prisoners early.

Factors Responsible for the Growth in Incarceration.   Some observers contend that the current prison crunch is an outcome of the "baby boom," a period between 1946 and 1964 when birth rates in the United States (and in most industrial countries) soared. By the early 1970s, many of the "baby boomers" had reached their late teens or early 20s, ages at which people are most likely to commit crimes.

As the baby boomers reached "crime age," crime rates climbed rapidly. In 1960 only 1,887 crimes were committed for every 100,000 people. By 1975 the rate had reached 5,282 per 100,000.

A change in public attitudes toward crime contributed to the prison population growth. Rising crime rates fueled the public's fears, and in response to pressure elected officials pushed through laws that required more criminals to be put behind bars and to be sentenced to longer sentences. Not only were longer sentences man-

dated, minimum sentences for some crimes often became mandatory, and the use of probation was curtailed.

Legislation created new categories of felonies, such as sexual abuse, that carry lengthy sentences. Degrees of aggravation were added to such crimes as house burglary when a gun is carried. Drunken driving, formerly punished at the most by incarceration in county jails, in many states became a felony punishable by time spent in the state penitentiary. In several states convicts classified as habitual criminals could be given life terms. Prison bed capacity and budgets could not keep up with the added numbers.

The change in the public's attitude toward crime, according to Franklin Zimring, director of the Earl Warren Legal Institute at the University of California, Berkeley, who was interviewed for a November 26, 1989 *New York Times* article entitled "More and More, Prison Is America's Answer to Crime," was linked to television. Through it, the public has become more aware of specific crimes and the approach prosecutors and judges take toward offenders who commit them.

Zimring explained the response of politicians by saying "The increased visibility of the justice system makes the political risks of being visibly lenient on convicts substantially higher than the risks of being ostentatiously tough. In that sense the judges and the prosecutors may be in a tougher mood than the public."

Rehabilitation Ruled Out.   Overcrowding substantially interferes with any potential for rehabilitation programs. A letter to the editor of the *New York Times,* which appeared on December 28, 1989, written by Richard Ericson, president of the Minnesota Citizens Council on Crime and Justice, expressed the frustration of citizens who would like correction programs to become rehabilitative. He said:

> We send kids to college to learn to be responsible and productive citizens. When we send offenders to overcrowded prisons (at about the same cost as college), they simply learn to become better criminals.
>
> Obviously there are dangerous offenders who must be locked up. The answer is not to accelerate prison construction, but to reserve our prison space for those who are a real and present danger to society. For the others, alternatives to imprisonment have proved to be effective rehabilitation . . . And the savings can be invested by the states in programs that effectively attack the cause of crime—programs like Head Start, prenatal and neonatal care, improved schools, educational opportunities and family counseling.

Had adequate investment in such programs been started during the war on poverty in the mid-1960s, a generation would now have come to adulthood that was better equipped to be self-sufficient, peaceful, contributing citizens and parents.

Costs of Overcrowding.   Rioting as a consequence of overcrowding typically makes the problem worse by destroying available cell blocks. In the wake of rioting at Camp Hill Prison in Philadelphia in October 1989, federal prison officials agreed to accept as many as 800 prison inmates from Pennsylvania state prisons, which were operating at 38% over capacity. Federal officials reported that it was common practice for prisoners to be transferred from state prisons to federal prisons to relieve overcrowding or to protect inmates whose safety was threatened. As population of federal prisons continues to exceed their capacity, this safety valve can be expected to become less available.

Most experts believe that the known demand in most states does not reflect the true demand because judges, prosecutors and police are currently holding back on sending people to prison because of the overcrowding. While the high cost of imprisonment is a strong argument in favor of finding methods to rehabilitate prisoners, an even stronger argument is the fact that 98% of all prisoners will be freed eventually.

Escalation of Financial Costs.   The United States is estimated to spend about $22 billion annually on corrections (prisons, jails, parole and probation), with about $13.9 billion (64%) allocated to keep 673,559 people behind bars. Most states' per-inmate costs range from $15,000 to $40,000 a year. In many states, spending on corrections has become the fastest growing item in the budget.

The New York-based Criminal Justice Institute, whose figures did not include county jail inmates, reported that in 1989 prison spending ranged from a high of $30,535 in Alaska to a low of $9,066 in Arkansas.

The experience of escalating costs in Massachusetts was replicated in states across the nation. The price for housing 10,356 inmates in Massachusetts prisons amounted to $240 million in 1991, an average expense of $23,000 per inmate. The county jails housed an additional 6,858 inmates, at an average expense of $18,000 for each.

During the decade of the 1980s, Massachusetts, like many other states, had a massive building program. The state spent $1 billion to build new county jails and state prisons and to expand existing facilities, nearly doubling the number of existing county and state beds to 10,532. Unfortunately, the number of prisoners grew faster than

the building program, until the state prisons were housing on the average 73% above capacity.

Massachusetts citizens ruefully complained that $20,000 was enough to send to a youngster to the University of Massachusetts for a year, including room and board and modest summer living expenses. In response to complaints about the debt burden borne by the public to house prisoners, Suffolk County Sheriff Robert Rufo, during an interview for a April 1, 1991 *Boston Herald* article entitled "Prison Costs Running Mass $23G an Inmate," said, "Yes, it costs money to incarcerate criminals. But would you rather have a drug dealer in jail or on the street selling to your kid?"

Of course most taxpayers would rather have drug dealers in jail, but the crowding in Massachusetts prisons and jails is so acute that they are unlikely to spend much time there. Most corrections officials realize that the multiplication of prison beds cannot go on. States like Massachusetts faced with reduced revenues and across-the-board spending cuts must find ways to cut their corrections budget.

Privately Operated Corrections Facilities.   One cost-cutting approach has been to hire for-profit prison management companies. Three well-known for-profit companies are Corrections Corporation of America, the largest, U.S. Corrections and Wackenhut. A May 8, 1989 *Business Week* article entitled "The Search for Ways to Break Out of the Prison Crisis" reported that 3,000 inmates in 24 state and county institutions were being supervised in for-profit institutions, at a cost saving of 5% to 10%.

Some private firms develop programs to divert non-violent offenders from jail, typically those who are involved in such offenses as drug abuse, burglary or drunken driving. For example, a privately run halfway house in Hollywood, Florida allows offenders to have jobs. The offenders use their income to pay for their room and board. If the judge permits, they go home on weekends.

The nonprofit Vera Institute of Justice in New York City runs a program in which 1,200 people convicted of nonviolent crimes are sentenced to community service. The community service involves such tasks as housing construction for the homeless, nursing home repair and cleanup in poor areas of the city. The average two-week sentence costs taxpayers $900 compared to the typical cost of $3,000 for 30 days in jail.

In a February 9, 1987 *Scholastic Update* article entitled "The Struggle to Cap Sky-High Prison Costs," Robert Gangi, executive director of the Correctional

Association of New York, objected to privately run programs: "The authority to imprison a person puts you in a position to make life-and-death decisions. That should not be delegated to the private sector."

Boot Camps. Most corrections officials believe that methods other than turning corrections over to the private sector hold out more promise for long range cost. They favor new forms of incarceration and alternative sentencing.

Georgia, known as a law-and-order state, has been faced with such overcrowding for so long that its judges have become pioneers in alternative sentencing. Like several states, Georgia has developed a "boot camp" as an alternatives to prison for first offenders. Boot camps are modeled after military boot camps. The regimen includes pushups, hard physical labor, constant verbal abuse from officers and punishments such as scrubbing baseboards with toothbrushes and clearing the camp of rocks.

A February 1, 1988 *People* article entitled "Outside the Walls" described a Georgia boot camp program at the Al Burruss Correctional Training Center in Forsyth, where nonviolent offenders ages 17 to 25 are offered a choice of 90 days of a "shock incarceration program" or a longer stint in jail. Burruss inmates rise at 5 A.M. for cell inspection and must pass the next 13 hours of manual labor, meals, and exercise in virtual silence.

Boot camps are cheaper than longer prison terms, they relieve prison overcrowding and they are slightly more successful than traditional prison at reducing recidivism (repeat offenses). The boot camp emphasis tends to be on juvenile offenders, who are at an age at which rehabilitation works best.

Private-Public Business Programs. Some joint ventures between private industry and prisons seem to increase the chances of avoiding a return to prison. For example, a TWA (Trans World Airline) program trains some California inmates from the California Youth Authority to be reservation agents. At a Nevada prison, inmates split Cadillacs and Lincolns in half and reassemble them as stretch limousines.

By 1989 joint ventures had become a $600 million a year industry, employing 52,000 inmates in 50 states. Employers pay market wages—to the state and the inmates—but they save on compensation costs (health benefits, holidays and retirement), which typically add an additional 35% to the cost of wages. Moreover, employers can get a flexible work force that can be hired, laid off or fired as needed. On the negative side, the inmates tend to require more training and are often less productive than ordinary employees.

Not only does such work keep idle prisoners busy, it helps to pay for the cost of their upkeep. A Dover, New Hampshire program run jointly by the Strafford Jail and the GFS Manufacturing Company, an electronics firm, manufactures electronic chokes for power lines. The pay rate is $7 per hour. The jail deducts 60% of the income for room and board. From the remaining 40%, inmates pay taxes and save to pay off court-ordered fines. In some jurisdictions a percentage of the income goes into a victim assistance fund.

Historically, laws have restricted prison industries from competing with outside businesses or from making items that could be sold on the open market, thereby limiting their growth. Typically, prison labor has consisted of farming, road building and repair, and making such items as clothes, flags, filing cabinets and license plates, mostly goods sold by the state or used within the state's programs.

A growing number of experts believe that laws restricting prison industries are outdated. Former Chief Justice Warren Burger has said, "Whatever need there may have been to keep prison-made products off the market 100 years ago, there is no basis today if we really mean to try to make good, productive citizens out of these inmates." Burger describes prison industries as "factories with fences."

Not only are such programs often criticized for taking jobs away from other workers, they are often thought to give employers a cost advantage over others. Such critics fail to realize is that there are risks for employers in such programs.

Private industry managers often set up their businesses behind bars without recognizing some of the limitations imposed by such environments. Many prisons—particularly maximum-security facilities—are located in remote areas, adding time and cost to pickups and deliveries. Prison gates are typically electronically opened and shut on schedules related to the prison's need rather than those of the industry. A delivery truck carrying supplies that is delayed by traffic may not be able to make its delivery. Moreover, inmates are often called out during shifts for visits with attorneys or for therapy sessions.

A September 9, 1989 *Boston Globe* article entitled "Business Behind Bars" reported that New England's prisons have become strewn with failed industries, wiped out by too much expense and too little profit. A big stumbling block to private industry is a federal law dating back to the 1930s that prohibits the transportation of inmate-manufactured goods across state lines. A few states and counties have federal permission to sell across state lines, but with that permission comes a requirement to pay prevailing wages for comparable work in the area. Such wage requirements often eliminate the cost incentive for private companies to participate in prison programs.

Unicor, a sophisticated federal prison industry, makes electronic cabling for the Defense Department, among other products. Despite its sophistication and annual sales of $300 million, it lost money in 1988. Moreover, during a 12-day prison riot in Atlanta staged by Cuban detainees, a Unicor factory was burned to the ground.

Despite the failed ventures and the risks, many prison officials are committed to expanding their operations because of their rehabilitative potential and because a profit can be made. New Hampshire's prison operations in the fiscal year ending June 1989 earned $303,000 on $1.2 million in sales, a substantial 27% profit margin.

Alternative Sentencing. Many prison administrators, faced with a predicted doubling of their current populations by 1998, believe that it is not possible for society to build its way out of the overcrowding problem. Many support alternative sentences for prisoners convicted of nonviolent crimes.

Several states assign nonviolent offenders to intensive supervision. For example, in Georgia probationers meet with a probation officer five times a week and are expected to hold jobs. They perform community service work, have home curfew checks and submit to random drug tests. The cost of intensive supervision is about 20% of the cost of having the offenders in prison.

Some judges try to be creative in their sentencing. A judge in Albany, Oregon sentenced a demolition contractor who had been charged with theft and failure to appear in court to serve five years on probation and to advertise his crime and his punishment. The contractor bought space in two newspapers to publish his photo and a public apology. In his apology, the contractor urged voters to pass a bond measure to construct a new jail.

A Sarasota County, Florida judge, Becky Titus, known as a drunken-driving scourge, sentences first-time drunken-driving offenders to display a red-and-white glow-in-the-dark bumper sticker that reads: CONVICTED DUI, RESTRICTED LICENSE. Her husband, a public defender, asked the state's appellate court in 1985 to strike down his wife's orders. His appeal was denied.

After he had repeatedly failed to correct health and building code violations, a Los Angeles neurosurgeon who was one of the city's most notorious slumlords was sentenced to live 30 days in one of his own roach- and rat-infested tenements.

A Baton Rouge, Louisiana judge recognized soon after he won election to the district court bench that most of the defendants appearing before him were young school dropouts. He ordered defendants to earn high school equivalency diplomas.

Minnesota is considered by some prison reformers as a model of rehabilitation. Following guidelines based on an offender's crime and past record, a judge may sentence an offender to a community-based detention center, a halfway house or various forms of probation, leaving prison as a last resort. By preventing overcrowding, Minnesota can hold those who are sent to prison for longer periods.

Another more rigorous form of probation or parole than daily supervision is called "home handcuff" or "house arrest." Offenders leave their homes only for work, to job-hunt or for addiction treatment or other care. If they leave the house at an unscheduled time, an electronic bracelet triggers an alarm.

One device requires that the wearer touch the electronic wrist band to the phone. Another version has the capacity to check the offender's breath for alcohol and to forward the results. Nationwide, an estimated 14,000 men and women are supervised by an electronic home handcuff.

The Wisconsin Corrections System in the early 1990s took advantage of the potential of the home handcuff to institute a new concept of a prison, a prison without walls. The Wisconsin prison without walls has a warden and the array of officers typically found in an institution, but the prisoners live at home.

The job of the prison staff consists more of what is traditionally thought of as probation work. They attempt to keep prisoners gainfully employed, integrated into the community and away from criminal activity.

If the prisoners are not at work or at a treatment program, they are supposed to be at home. To enable the staff to keep track of their whereabouts, prisoners must regularly check in by touching their bracelets to a telephone receiver. At least for the time being, the Wisconsin program is limited to urban areas, where supervising the inmates is easier.

A Houston, Texas house arrest program seems to be less structured than the Wisconsin Prison Without Walls, but it uses more complex equipment. A February 1, 1988 *People* article, "Outside the Walls," described a 27-year-old housewife, Maria Arnford, who was sentenced to an electronically monitored house arrest program. Arrested first for drug possession and then for driving while intoxicated, she was given the choice of prison or house arrest.

When she chose house arrest, a Dallas-based firm called Program Monitor (PMI) installed a special phone equipped with a video screen, camera and transmitter in her living room. When PMI calls, day or night, Arnford must punch a button that sends her televised image to the company. The program costs the state of Texas about $8 a day, compared to the approximately $45 it would cost to maintain her in prison.

A runaway at 12, Arnford spent her teenage years drifting. Her husband of seven years spends half the year overseas working in offshore drilling. Subject to random drug and alcohol tests, Arnford may leave the house only at established times for therapy, community service or church.

Arnford described the discipline the regimen has provided in her life by saying "This program has been like a parent to me, the parent I never had."

Although inmates are uniformly in favor of alternative sentencing, not all victims are pleased when their offenders are allowed to escape prison time. In particular, the families of those killed by drunken drivers resent the designation of such offenders as nonviolent.

Since half of all U.S. inmates return to prison, most corrections officials look for ways to reduce recidivism as a key to trimming corrections budgets. The least expensive approach is to rehabilitate offenders and to find alternatives to sending people to prison.

(See also CALIFORNIA CORRECTIONS SYSTEM; CORRECTIONAL EDUCATION; JAILS; SENTENCING: A TREND TOWARD LONGER SENTENCES.)

prison reform   See CORRECTIONAL EDUCATION.

prison without walls   See PRISON OVERCROWDING: COPING WITH THE COSTS.

prison work programs   See PRISON OVERCROWDING: COPING WITH THE COSTS.

private security: the "rent-a-cop" movement
On busy weekends all over the United States, uniformed police officers can be seen patrolling malls, parking lots, arenas and stadiums. They are armed with pistols, police badges, radios and full official powers to stop, search, chase, arrest and summon reinforcements. However, most of them are not working for their regular public employer; they are working for stores, promoters, banks, even individuals who are having large parties at their homes.

The phenomenon of municipal police officers moonlighting as private security officers is spreading, often organized and arranged by their own departments or unions. While the municipalities, the police, the unions and the private employers sing the praises of this development for bringing additional income to the officers and improving security in anxious communities at no additional public cost, law enforcement experts have serious doubts. In particular, they wonder about the ethics, equity and liability of providing enhanced security only for those private interests that can afford it. They also worry about conflicts of interest of police officers who are hired privately.

Experts see the rent-a-cop movement as a continuation of the growing privatization of security in American society along with the development of private police forces, many of which employ former professionals, for malls, corporations, buildings, sometimes even whole neighborhoods.

Such private forces are not bound by all of the regulations and civil liberties concerns imposed on the public police to protect both complainants and defendants. By hiring off-duty municipal police, private employers gain access to the power of arrest and the weight of official authority that private security forces lack.

Some cities, such as Miami and St. Petersburg, Florida, enthusiastically arrange outside jobs, matching private employers with police officers and charging a fee to cover the expense of the program. In Florida some sheriff's departments and the state police have offered lowered rates in order to compete with local police.

A February 26, 1989 *New York Times* article entitled "When Private Employers Hire Public Police," pointed out that although the rent-a-cop movement involves thousands of officers and millions of dollars, there is no firm data on how many departments allow such off-duty work. William Cunningham, the president of Hallcrest Systems, whose company published a pioneer study on private security, estimated that 80% of American police departments allow such work, while 20% prohibit or severely restrict it.

New York City, for example, forbids an officer from performing off-duty security work in a police uniform or in the officer's regular precinct, to avoid conflict of interest. Until the late 1960s the New York City Police Department had a complete ban on moonlighting. When the policy was changed, officers were permitted such work, but not more than 20 hours per week.

Albert Reiss, a Yale University criminologist who examined the private hiring of public police for the U.S.

Justice Department, cited St. Petersburg as one of the best-run off-duty programs because the department oversees the program closely. Assignments are screened and do not include bars, credit or collection agencies or service as bodyguards.

The department also monitors performance. Officers on off-duty assignments are checked by radio or in person. For off-duty work, officers must check in and out of police headquarters and must change clothes there. Moreover, pay is processed by the department, which helps to keep down the number of off-duty hours worked. By contrast, in Seattle, where the police union matches private employers with officers, watch commanders faced with an emergency do not know where their moonlighting officers are.

A variety of economic and sociological factors are fueling the rent-a-cop movement, such as growing public concern with crime and municipal budget constraints. Many officers earn more from their sideline work than they do from their regular jobs. Off-duty police are subject to the same rules as on-duty officers and may work only in their own municipality. All must wear their guns.

In 1989 the Law Enforcement Policy Center of the International Association of Chiefs of Police in Arlington, Virginia distributed a policy paper and model administrative plan similar to St. Petersburg's to hundreds of police departments where off-duty work had been handled informally. The interest in the plan was sparked by mounting unease over legal and medical liability issues. The questions arose around such concerns as the public's responsibility for the cost of administrative overhead, the carryover effect of physical and emotional stress on the officer's primary duties and the conflicts of interest involved in serving a public agency and a private employer.

Although off-duty work may be inevitable, Mark Moore, a Harvard professor of criminal justice, told the *New York Times,* "At first it sounds great. More police out there at no more public cost. But in the long run, private financial relationships with public agencies undermines the notion of a public police force with equal protection for all."

Private security guards (distinct from rent-a-cops) outnumber America's half million police. In the opinion of Anthony Bouza, who was the chief of police in Minneapolis for nine years, following 24 years with the New York Police Department, private security standards are unfortunately not up to those of the police. In the main, private security guards are low level, unskilled, untrained and paid minimally for wearing a uniform.

Bouza believes that the growth of the private security industry stems from the desires of the rich to purchase their own security and from the gradual loss of confidence in the ability of the police to protect life and property.

(See also POLICE; POLICE STRESS; POLICE USE OF DEADLY FORCE; PRISON OFFICERS' CODE OF SOLIDARITY: A SHIELD AGAINST VIOLENCE.)

probable cause   See ARREST: CONSTITUTIONAL RESTRICTIONS AND LEGAL PROCEDURES.

probation   See SENTENCING: A TREND TOWARD LONGER SENTENCES.

prosecutorial discretion in the disposition of cases   The functions of the component parts of the criminal justice system appear to be clearly established: Police do the policing, prosecutors do the prosecuting and judges do the judging. Such a textbook ideal ignores the changing conditions and blurred roles that are the reality of the system today.

The role of the prosecutor has expanded over the past two centuries, as the Anglo-American criminal justice system has been transformed from a rural small-scale system of privately initiated prosecutions to a large-scale urban bureaucracy of paid professionals who initiate prosecutions on behalf of the state and dispose of large caseloads within the restrictions of an extensive and complicated body of legal procedure.

The system in which virtually all cases were disposed of by jury trials no longer exists. Today most justice is administered by prosecutors, who either terminate cases or negotiate plea bargains. This transformation was already well documented by the 1920s, but it has become complete only over the last quarter century. A primary reason for the change is the practice of plea bargaining, that is, making deals with defendants in return for guilty pleas, in lieu of trials.

In *The Prosecutor* (1979), William F. McDonald distinguishes three major types of plea bargains: explicit charge bargains, under the control of the prosecutors, which determine whether and what charges will be filed; explicit sentence bargains, under the control of judges, which determine what sentences will be imposed; and explicit exchange bargains, under the control of prosecutors, in which charges are dropped in return for something from the defendants, such as the return of property or payment of medical bills. There also are implicit sentence bargains in which lesser sentences are negotiated, without specific terms being promised. In some jurisdictions, prosecutors make sentence recommendations, which judges generally follow.

In a 1977 national survey of plea bargaining in 30 American jurisdictions conducted by the Georgetown University Institute of Criminal Law and Procedure, researchers found that the most common pattern of plea bargaining was one that involved both charge bargaining and sentence bargaining. The role of judges in the process appeared to be declining. The trend was toward more sentence recommendations by prosecutors, an encroachment on traditional judicial terrain.

When interviewed, judges in several cities said that they rarely questioned a prosecutor's recommendation, even when it did not appear to be appropriate for the crime. They simply assumed that the prosecutor's case was weak, and they preferred to see a serious criminal receive some sentence than to risk trial and the possibility of no sentence.

Habitual offender laws also increase the domain of prosecutors. Initiating a habitual offender proceeding is simply a particular kind of charging decision, but it has the automatic effect of lengthening the convicted criminal's sentence.

Over time, there has been a growing consensus that prosecutors should become involved earlier in the process, when defendants are charged. The President's Commission on Law Enforcement and Administration of Justice wrote in 1967:

> In some places, particularly when less serious offenses are involved, the decision to press charges is made by the police or a magistrate rather than by the prosecutor. The better practice is for the prosecutor to make this decision, for the choice involves such factors as the sentencing alternatives available under the various possible charges, the substantiality of the case for prosecution and limitations on prosecution resources—factors that the policemen often cannot consider and the magistrate cannot deal with fully while maintaining a judicial role.

The commission favored early elimination of as many cases as possible from the system without sacrificing the proper administration of justice. Gradually, in the 1970s, prosecutors in many jurisdictions did develop a broader view of their role and began to take real control over the screening process and to set systematic charging standards.

Aside from crowded court dockets, a major impetus for this was a heated public and scholarly debate over plea bargaining in the late 1960s. Although the American Bar Association and the U.S. Supreme Court had endorsed the practice, prosecutors were forced to defend it to the general public and to legal scholars.

As it had developed, plea bargaining had proven to provide benefits for all participants. Police came to rely on it to enlist the help of informants, whose cases would be reduced or dismissed in exchange. In 1972 the National Advisory Commission on Criminal Justice Standards and Goals, established by the Omnibus Crime Control and Safe Streets Act of 1968 and made up of 22 leading authorities in law enforcement and justice, recommended that by 1978 plea bargaining be abandoned.

In numerous jurisdictions it was partially or totally banned. Under the threat of no-plea-bargaining bans, prosecutors recognized the interdependency of initial screening and plea bargaining and learned to use their powers of dismissal to get something from defendants. Plea bargains assured prosecutors of high rates of conviction, helping cases that might otherwise be lost at trial because of weak evidence, sloppy police work, incompetent prosecution or unpredictable juries.

While there was general recognition that plea bargaining made it possible to deal with overwhelming caseloads, its propriety came under attack in the 1960s. Critics objected to the injustice of offenders escaping from the consequences of their crimes with little or no punishment; victims felt doubly wronged. An alternative solution was to reduce the flow of cases entering the system. Alaska's attorney general initiated a no-plea-bargaining policy in 1978. His intent was to force police to collect better evidence and prosecutors to better prepare their cases.

A major criticism of plea bargaining is the practice of "overcharging," an approach in which a defendant is charged with additional crimes and more serious charges than he or she could reasonably be expected to be convicted of. Overcharging gives police and prosecutors something with which to negotiate guilty pleas or enlist the services of informants. It permits prosecutors to reduce charges without giving anything away. Critics of overcharging view it as coercive, deceptive and corrupting.

One of the changes that new charging policies has brought is an increase in the threshold level of case acceptability. This means that a case has to be winnable at trial. For cases involving especially serious crimes or dangerous defendants, threshold standards can be lowered to traditional legal sufficiency.

In adopting a broadened screening function, prosecutors are in effect acting as quasi-legislators, raising political and philosophical issues of arbitrary power and legal responsibility that remain to be explored. Simply stated, the more immediate issues involve the question: Is it better to have a system in which a lot of criminals are given a little punishment or a system in which a few criminals are given a lot of punishment? This raises many other questions.

The encroachment of public prosecutors into the domains of the police and the judiciary have not gone without protest. When prosecutors has taken real control in initial screening decisions, police have typically reacted strongly. Following the institution of his no-plea-bargaining policy in Alaska, the attorney general was shocked at the protests by police, who had long been critical of prosecutors' use of plea bargaining.

Alaskan police were not objecting so much to the policy as they were to the new role played by the prosecutor in the screening process. They apparently felt that if a police officer believed a case was good enough to make an arrest, then it must have been good enough to go to trial. Every case rejected by a prosecutor was viewed as a criticism of the arresting officer.

Despite this, however, police often make arrests that they do not intend to have prosecuted. In some cases, they simply want to remind an offender to behave.

In some cases, an officer may make an arrest knowing that the charges will be dismissed, but wanting an offender to suffer the inconvenience of having to raise bail money, spend time in pretrial custody and pay substantial attorney's fees. However, the inconvenience does not amount to much if the defendant is released by a prosecutor a few hours after arrest.

The judiciary is unhappy with the encroachment of prosecutors because traditionally, judges have controlled the process and determined the sentence. In the current system of administrative justice, over 60% of incoming cases are disposed of by the prosecutor without a finding of guilt or innocence and 90% of convictions are obtained by plea bargaining.

Earlier in the century, judges protested vigorously the encroachment of prosecutors. More recently, only a few continue to buck the trend. In fact, some judges appear to be happy to have the prosecutors participate in the decision making; it diffuses responsibility.

In his book, *Police Mystique* (1990), Anthony Bouza, retired Minneapolis police chief and outspoken critic of the criminal justice system and the police especially, points out that the system could not survive without plea bargaining. Trials are expensive and time-consuming.

The real problem with plea bargaining, in Bouza's opinion, is that "too many DAs, in their haste to clear dockets and to improve their conviction batting average, have made bad bargains. Too many soft deals have been made with too much haste."

(See also ASSEMBLY-LINE JUSTICE; CASE STRIPPING; FELONY ARRESTS: SCREENING PROCEDURES; FELONY CONVICTION RATES; INFORMANTS; JURISDICTION IN CRIMINAL CASES; MASS MURDERS.)

prostitution   The definition of prostitution varies somewhat from one jurisdiction to another. A common definition is "a person who engages or agrees or offers to engage in sexual conduct with another person in return for a fee." *The Sourcebook of Criminal Justice Statistics 1990* of the U.S. Department of Justice, Bureau of Justice Statistics, defines prostitution and commercialized vice as "sex offenses of a commercialized nature, such as prostitution, keeping a bawdy house, procuring or transporting women for immoral purposes. Attempts are included."

In the United States during 1989, there were an estimated 107,400 arrests for prostitution and commercialized vice. There is no breakdown of how many of those arrests were of women who work in brothels, call girls who operate independently or as part of a ring in their own homes or other sites, or streetwalkers, who typically take their customers to "shady" hotels or motels, where they rent rooms for brief periods.

It is reasonable to assume that the bulk of the arrests is among streetwalkers. They are visible and hence more vulnerable to arrests and have little political clout.

"High-class" call-girl operations tend to be circumspect and/or to have some protection from law enforcement attention. Most owners of brothels also keep their activities hidden. A working-class suburban neighborhood of Boston recently was chagrined to learn that a brothel had been in operation for some time in its midst. Streetwalkers also are likely to constitute the largest group among the population of prostitutes, since it is possible to go into business without having political connections and without having to make a capital outlay.

Around the world wherever prostitution is defined as a criminal offense and regardless of whether the behavior of the male customer is defined as criminal, the bulk of enforcement efforts goes toward apprehending the woman. Whether prostitution should be a criminal offense and, if it is, who is subject to prosecution has been a hotly debated issue at times throughout the 20th century.

There was little in the way of organized opposition to prostitution in the United States until the early 20th century, when the progressive movement focused public attention on a number of social institutions. Populists and progressives, most of whom had small-town origins, pointed a finger at rapid industrialization, urbanization and immigration as the source of many evils.

Magazine articles outlined the horrors of prostitution. "White slavery" was a major theme. Prostitution was said to be perpetrated by "merchants in flesh," who recruited innocent, unsophisticated young immigrant girls, often minors, through coercion, lies and drugs. The most prominent organization in the antiprostitution crusade of that era was the American Social Hygiene Association, which used as its major reference work Jane Addams' 1912 book *A New Conscience and An Ancient Evil.*

World War I increased the concern of the "social hygienists" because of a growth in "camp followers" near military installations. The movement subsided during the depression years and revived again during World War II, only to subside once more once the war was over.

A More Recent Debate. The most obvious manifestation of a reawakened concern with prostitution was the formation of a prostitute union movement in Lyon, France in 1975. Prostitutes took over a church and publicized a list of grievances following a series of violent murders of prostitutes in the city. Although the murders provided the impetus, the strike was essentially aimed at police harassment and repression that had arisen from a revision in French prostitution laws, which prohibited trade in hotels, bars and cities. The law forced prostitutes to work on the streets and left them vulnerable to physical assault and repeated arrests.

The Lyon event set off similar protests in other large French cities and spawned other prostitute organizations in Europe and the United States. By calling their organizations unions, French prostitutes defined themselves as workers and attempted to separate prostitution from its historical association with criminal behavior. Their unions called for better working conditions, protested police harassment and sought social benefits such as pensions and unemployment.

In the United States, prostitutes' unions organized around the goal of eliminating criminal penalties against women. The first and best-known of the American unions was COYOTE (Call Off Your Old Tired Ethics), founded in San Francisco in 1973 by Margo St. James, a master strategist. St. James raised funds and secured media exposure by organizing "hookers balls," where the rich and famous mingled with prostitutes.

Having graduated from college and spent some time in law school, St. James was hardly typical of the overall U.S. population of prostitutes. In her arguments, she did not challenge the right of men to have access to prostitutes, nor did she suggest that prostitution was degrading work or harmful to women. Instead, she insisted that prostitution was merely a job for most women, one that was more lucrative than most women's work.

In her 1987 book *Uneasy Virtue: The Politics of Prostitution and the American Reform Tradition,* Barbara Meil Hobson pointed out that as interest in prostitution reform mushroomed, grass-roots union organizing declined. Instead of developing a network of local unions to cope with local problems, COYOTE evolved into a political lobbying and research organization, the National Prostitutes' Task Force, supported by civil liberties groups and the mainstream women's movement.

Activist prostitutes wove feminist arguments into their discussions of the causes and remedies for prostitution. They claimed that prostitution was a viable option for women to support themselves in a discriminatory labor market. One member of the Prostitute Union of Massachusetts (PUMA) asserted that prostitution was a mere extension of women's economic dependence on men. In her opinion, prostitutes were more open about the price of their services than were women who slept with men for the rent or for spending money.

Despite their attempts to merge their concerns with those of the feminist movement, the basic philosophy of prostitutes' unions was at odds with long-term goals of many feminists. At the same time that prostitutes were calling for prostitution to be viewed as a private matter between consenting adults free from state interference, feminist lawyers were attacking the failure of states to intervene in the private sphere in cases of marital rape and child and wife abuse.

Many feminists, while strongly supporting the unions' goal of decriminalization, were dismayed by the possibility that to institutionalize prostitution would suggest that women would always lack economic opportunities and be forced to serve as the sex objects of men.

For feminists the sexual exploitation involved in prostitution needed to be eliminated, not encouraged by legitimating it as work. The prostitutes' position was that they had freedom of choice to be prostitutes and make ten to 100 times more per hour than they could make as clerk-typists or waitresses.

The view of the prostitution reform campaigns earlier in the century had been that sexual freedom was the elimination of the male prerogative of controlling women's bodies in the home and in the marketplace. Late 20th-century women who identified themselves with the sexual liberation movement felt uncomfortable with the prostitutes' concept of their sexual service as therapy or recreation for men.

Although women still lacked political and social power, they had gained some measure of sexual freedom and wanted to break with a long tradition that dwelt on women's passivity and a portrayal of them as enslaved women. For them sexual liberation meant eliminating the power dynamics in sexual relations. But prostitutes in their trade must implicitly accept the power relationship and use it to their advantage, which is the essence of "turning a trick." The opposed perspectives have made it virtually impossible to mount an effective campaign around prostitution within the American feminist movement.

A challenge to the position of the prostitutes' union came in 1985 with the formation of a new prostitutes' collective called WHISPER (Women Hurt in Systems of Prostitution Engaged in Revolt). WHISPER attacked the idea that prostitution offers economic independence. The organization's newsletter offered graphic accounts of women in ropes and chains, branded by cigarettes and otherwise sexually degraded.

WHISPER's position refuted the picture presented by Arlene Carmen and Howard Moody's study of New York street prostitutes in *Working Women: The Subterranean World of Street Prostitution* (1985). The authors maintain that prostitutes freely choose their careers and pimps and can always find another man to pimp for them if they choose. WHISPER was disdainful of the notion that the prostitute-pimp relationship is voluntary.

WHISPER's portrayal of prostitution as sexual slavery, validated by prostitutes speaking for themselves, echoed feminist views of the 19th and early 20th century. One collective member advocated criminalizing the behavior of customers as a solution. Arresting customers, of course, would result in an immediate reduction in the number of middle-class customers and thus reduce the income of prostitutes.

In Sweden and Norway, feminists who have taken up the cause of the prostitutes mobilized the women's movement around prostitution politics. Internal conflicts were submerged in campaigns against rape, pornography and prostitution. Rape and prostitution were seen as different facets of male power and domination.

Scandinavian feminists analyzed pornography and prostitution as reflective of the weak economic status of women and social constructions of them as sexual commodities. They were able to build a consensus around remedies: greater penalties for profiteers in prostitution; no penalties against prostitutes or customers; social work support systems; more education about sexual relationships and equality.

Solutions Are Complex. Many of the abstract arguments about prostitution ignore the fact that prostitution is carried on in specific local communities. A survey of Boston residents, businesses and police in 1977 and 1978 found a majority in favor of some form of legalization through licensing or zoning. Some police favor legalization because they find enforcement of prostitution laws a futile and distasteful job.

The majority of those surveyed in Boston said they would find prostitution offensive in their neighborhood, in part because they associated prostitution with crime, venereal disease and neighborhood decay, associations that have existed for more than a century. They held such notions despite the fact that, throughout the 1970s, lawyers and social scientists had offered empirical evidence that venereal disease is spread more often by nonprofessionals, that only a small percentage of prostitutes commits other crimes and that prostitutes come into a neighborhood only after it is already in decline.

Advocates of legalization argued that the side effects of prostitution were brought about by its being illegal. West Germany and Holland were offered as models of the best approach to prostitution. The red-light district of Amsterdam was characterized as a clean, well-lighted place where three-story prostitution hotels exist side by side with family homes, shops, churches and restaurants.

Legalizing prostitution was not the intent when Boston instituted an experiment called the Combat Zone, an "adult entertainment" zone, where prostitutes were able to operate more or less without harassment so long as they stayed within the zone. The zone's next door neighbors, the residents of Chinatown, could not object effectively because at the time they had little political clout. Politicians saw the blighted zone as a first step in banning prostitution from the rest of the city. The short-lived experiment had no chance to evolve into anything resembling Amsterdam's peaceful coexistence.

The politicians failed to foresee a building boom in downtown Boston that would make the area attractive to investors. Nor did they anticipate that prostitutes from all over the country would be attracted to the area. Business lobbies laid the groundwork for dismantling the area, and its quick demise was speeded up by the murder there of a Harvard football star.

The idea of legalized prostitution began to seem less attractive. In Europe, peaceful coexistence began to deteriorate. Prostitution in Berlin became more brutal. Pimps became increasingly well organized, and it became virtually impossible for a woman to be an independent prostitute.

Amsterdam's red-light district became a part of a tightly controlled sex commerce industry. Increased heroin use increased the incidence of street prostitution and the number of juveniles in the trade. In Rotterdam, sex clubs began staying open 24 hours a day in the 1970s. When local residents complained, pimps retaliated by shooting at the leaders of the protest.

The worldwide threat of AIDS does not seem to have inspired many prostitutes to seek another line of work. The only adjustment made by some has been to carry their own supply of condoms.

Sexual Slavery.   The extent of the form of prostitution known as white slavery in the United States in the early part of the century is purported to be somewhat exaggerated. Yet according to Cecil Kirby, in his 1987 biography *Mafia Enforcer: A True Story of Life and Death in the Mob,* written with Thomas Renner, sexual slavery has survived and continues to be practiced by motorcycle gangs in the present-day United States and Canada.

In a chapter called "Girls for Sale," the authors wrote:

> Girls are as much a part of outlaw biker life as are drugs and violence, and they are probably our weakest link. They often carry our guns, hide our drugs, front for our businesses, gather information for us about cops and other bikers or places we want to rob, and act as our couriers in drug deals and other crimes. That gives them access to a lot of evidence that could put members of biker clubs in jail. . . . Bikers often kill some of the women to protect themselves. . . . A copper once said to me that there was no way of knowing how many women disappeared from Canada in white slavery and were killed. "It's like trying to document missing children," he said. "They're just swallowed up in the traffic and there's no one around to trace them."

According to Renner and Kirby, Canadian and U.S. biker clubs sold women to each other for $500 to $2,000 each. Anywhere from 50% to 100% of the women's earnings in prostitution were taken from her by the biker

who "owned" her. Renner and Kirby described the fate of many by saying:

> When the girls weren't making enough money for them, or when they said they wanted to go on a trip with their biker pimp-boyfriend, they'd be taken to the border and sold to some other biker gang member. The Outlaws or other gangs would use them for a while and either sell them again or kill them because they'd seen or heard too much.

During the 1970s a U.S. biker group called the Outlaws collected a lucrative income from white slavery. In so-called body rub parlors and topless bars they owned throughout the United States, a seemingly endless supply of women danced and worked as prostitutes.

Since the bulk of the women in sexual bondage around the world are not Caucasians, the term sexual slavery rather than white slavery better describes their plight. During the 1960s and 1970s, Japanese men took advantage of a strong currency and traveled abroad. Their travels inspired the yakuza, Japanese organized crime, to get into the "sex tour business." On a sex tour, as many as 200 Japanese men would take a jumbo jet on prearranged three-day junkets of drinking and sexual activity.

The yakuza expanded sexual slavery into Southeast Asia on an enormous scale. In their book *Yakuza: The Explosive Account of Japan's Criminal Underworld* (1986), David Kaplan and Alec Dubro estimate that as many as 80% of the one million Japanese men traveling abroad each year in Asia during the late 1970s had some contact with the sex trade.

In 1965 Japan normalized relations with Korea, and by the late 1970s more than 650,000 Japanese tourists were annually visiting Korea, where prostitution has been institutionalized as a work option for poor women. In every major Korean city, Kisaeng houses (brothels) were set up by the government. At the same time, hundreds of nongovernment brothels and tens of thousands of independent prostitutes joined the activities.

When asked by the Korean minister of tourism on a survey about their impressions of Korea, 80% of the male tourists cited "Kisaeng parties" as the most exciting feature in Korea.

The life of women in Kisaeng houses is grim. Generally, the women are impoverished migrants from the country, who are sold into a life of prostitution as minors, for as little as $200. The highly stratified society of Korea views prostitutes as permanently unpersons, comparable to India's untouchables. Managers confiscate most of the women's pay. Living conditions are inhumane. The women are kept functioning through the use of amphetamines and are subjected frequently to violence.

The money to be made from the tours encouraged the yakuza to engage in an international trade in sexual slavery that would eventually expand around the Pacific. In her book *Female Sexual Slavery* (1979), Kathleen Barry defined the international sex trade as including sex tourism, prostitution around military bases, traffic in women and children, "mail-order marriages" and pornography. In the poor countries of East Asia, with some help from local crime syndicates, the yakuza has participated in all aspects of the sex business, which affects hundred of thousands of mostly poor women and children, forcing them into prostitution at home and abroad.

The Japanese are not solely responsible for the sex trade in Asia. Sex tours from Western Europe, in particular West Germany and the Netherlands, while not as numerous as the Asian tours, have been prominent. With tourism as the third or fourth largest earner of foreign exchange in Asian countries, local government officials at the very least have condoned and, in many cases, promoted the sex trade.

Opposition in Japan to the sex tours was mounted in a well-orchestrated campaign by the 4,000-member Women's Christian Temperance Union, a skilled band of activists. The union played a major role in passage of Japanese antiprostitution laws during the 1950s. In June 1981 a series of carefully planned demonstrations followed Prime Minister Zenko Suzuki around on a heavily publicized tour of Southeast Asia. The protests were so effective that Thailand and the Philippines experienced a 25% drop in Japanese male tourists over the next few months.

As the protests staunched the flow of sex tours, the yakuza turned to luring tens of thousands of women throughout Asia to emigrate to Japan, with the promise of legitimate jobs and good pay. Once in Japan, the impoverished women found themselves at the mercy of hoodlums, who deprived them of their passports and pressed them into work as hostesses and dancers. Instead of finding a promising future, the women were thrust into a world of forged passports and Japanese brothels to work as poorly paid prostitutes. Unable to speak the language, they lived their new lives in tiny rooms, trapped in a life of slavery.

The traffic in immigrant women enraged Japanese critics even more than the sex tours had because, at the turn of the century, Japan itself was the victim of the same trade. However, the yakuza are making too much money for them to give it up.

Initial capital outlays are small. Women can be bought in the Philippines for as little as $1,000 and then "leased" to Japanese clubs for $1,000 a month. One Japanese hotel operator claimed that 70 Southeast Asian prostitutes that he controlled brought in more than $100,000 per month.

Given the nature of the trade, estimates of its size are rough, but all indicators suggest that it is massive. In the red-light district of Osaka alone, observers claim that as many as 10,000 women work as prostitutes.

Not all of the women in the sexual slavery trade view themselves as exploited. Despite the fact that they are likely to make half of what their Japanese counterparts make, for some women the money seems good compared with what they could make at home, particularly when they have a somewhat reasonable boss.

(See also APPENDIX 1E: THE YAKUZA; OUTLAW MOTORCYCLE GANGS.)

psychopaths See SOCIOPATHS.

pyromaniacs See ARSON.

R

rage, explosive The behavior that mental health experts refer to as explosive or neurological rage is characterized by instantaneous, unpredictable episodes of overwhelming fury triggered by trivial events. This rage is distinctly different from ordinary anger.

Classic symptoms of explosive or neurological rage are:

- Overreaction, far out of proportion to any provocation.
- Purposelessness. Unlike ordinary anger, it has no coherent or explicable psychological or social justification.
- Explosiveness. The rage arises in an instant and continues to build.
- It is out of character. It is inexplicable and does not typify that person's normal behavior.
- It feels "alien" to the person experiencing it. When the rage is past, he or she feels embarrassed and upset, as if he or she had not been himself or herself.

A significant number of people experience explosive rage. Many of the 4 million people in the United States afflicted with Alzheimer's disease have uncontrollable rages. Their inability to deal with these rages is one of several reasons that some families of Alzheimer's patients feel incapable of caring for them at home.

An estimated 1 million people suffer brain injuries each year from strokes, tumors or blows to the head. About 180,000 are injured in auto accidents. Researchers estimate that as many as 70% of those who suffer serious brain injury have some degree of constant irritability or explosive anger. A University of Pennsylvania study of 286 psychiatric patients found that 94% had such damage. Working with such patients can be risky and frightening.

Despite advances in understanding, researchers are of the opinion that too little attention is paid to people who suffer such attacks and that as a consequence they receive inadequate care. An August 7, 1990 New York Times article entitled "When Rage Explodes, Brain Damage May be the Cause," by Daniel Goleman described some of the research being done.

A scientist who at work screamed at his coworkers and at home punched holes in the walls when his four-year-old spilled food tried sedatives and psychothery for several years, to no avail. Finally he was referred to a neurologist who traced the onset of the violent episodes to an auto accident in which the scientist had sustained a severe head injury. The neurologist prescribed propanolol, a beta-blocker (a substance that interrupts sympathetic nervous system inhibitors) used to regulate his blood pressure, and the rages disappeared.

Dr. Stuart Yudofsky, chairman of the department of psychiatry at the University of Chicago Medical School, told the New York Times, "Explosive rage is very common, since it can be a symptom of any malady that destroys brain cells. And I suspect brain damage is, by far, the most frequent cause of these violent outbursts, though no one has exact numbers."

Violent criminals have been found to have a disproportionate share of brain injuries. Two studies whose subjects included 28 murderers on death row found that almost all had suffered serious brain injuries that could have triggered their violence. Causes of injury ranged from falls out of trees to regular beatings. However, Dr. Dorothy Otnow Lewis, a psychiatrist at New York University Medical School who conducted the death row studies, told the New York Times that brain injuries alone are not likely to provoke intense violence. "The most lethal combination is a history of neurological damage and abuse in childhood. When you have a kid who has some organic vulnerability, and you add being raised in a violent household, then you create a very, very violent person."

Lewis based her conclusions on a study of 95 boys who were in the Connecticut Correctional School in the late 1970s and whose subsequent arrests were tracked. Those who had shown no signs of neurological problems or childhood abuse did not commit violent crimes as adults. Those who had some brain injury or had been abused as children committed an average of two violent offenses. Those who had both a brain impairment and an abusive family history committed an average of five violent crimes. Nine in the last category had committed murder.

Injuries to certain parts of the brain such as the frontal areas of the cortex are most likely to result in rage attacks. One theory holds that such brain areas normally control aggressive impulses that originate in lower brain centers. Damage to these areas is thought to do away with inhibitions. Dementia of the "disinhibited type" has been proposed as a new diagnostic category in the next edition of the Diagnostic and Statistical Manual of Mental Disorders, 3rd Edition-Revised (DSM-III-R) the official diagnostic manual currently used by mental health professionals.

Dr. Gary Tucker, chairman of the psychiatry department at the University of Washington Medical School, who heads the DSM-III-R proposal committee, told the New York Times, "We see rage attacks as one example of a more general category of inappropriate emotional behavior due to brain trauma. It can take many forms, such as exposing oneself, or abrupt swings from crying to laughing."

Yudofsky and his supporters disagree. They argue that explosive rage is a unique psychiatric syndrome with a specific treatment available to control it.

A number of studies have reported propanolol to be a useful treatment. A study published in the spring 1990 issue of the Journal of Neuropsychiatry and Clinical Neurosciences reported the results of a study on white rats in which it was found that propanolol was highly effective in calming rage.

Another study, reported at the May 1990 meeting of the American Psychiatric Association, was led by Dr. Jonathan Silver, director of neuropsychiatry at Columbia Presbyterian Medical Center in New York City. The study involved a group of patients who had proven to be extremely difficult to treat. The 21 patients had all been kept in a psychiatric hospital for an average of 10 years. Using propanolol, the number of per-patient violent outbursts had been reduced from one a day to one every other day, a 50% reduction. In seven patients, the reduction was greater than 75%.

Propanolol is not the only medication that has shown promise in controlling violent rage. Other medications normally used for other maladies have been used with some success, such as lithium, normally used to treat manic depression, buspirone, used to treat anxiety, and carbamazepine, used to control seizures.

Many cases of explosive range cannot be explained by brain damage. Tucker said, "There are a large group of people with brain damage who do not have explosive rage and a sizable group of people with rage who have no brain injury."

Those who have episodes of rage without accompanying brain damage are classified in the current edition of the *DSM, (DSM-III-R)* in the category "Intermittent Explosive Disorder." The essential feature of this is several episodes in which control is lost of aggressive impulses, resulting in serious assaults or property destruction.

Experts in law and psychiatry doubt that new research on explosive rage will provide an avenue of escape from retribution for those who commit violent crimes. Nevertheless, explosive rage is being used increasingly as a defense in criminal trials, when there is no other sign of mental illness.

(See also ANGER; POST-TRAUMATIC STRESS DISORDER [PTSD].)

rape Forcible rape is defined by the *Uniform Crime Reports* of the Federal Bureau of Investigation (FBI) as the carnal (sexual) knowledge of a female forcibly and against her will. During 1990 there were an estimated 102,560 forcible rapes in the United States, comprising 6% of recorded violent crimes. The southern states, with the largest population, accounted for 88 victims per 100,000 females, followed by the West with 87, the Midwest with 83, and the Northeast with 56.

In the eyes of the law, a completed rape does not require emission, only a degree of penetration. The standard is one inch. Evidence of emission makes a stronger case in court, but sperm smears must be taken promptly as they tend to disappear in 24 to 48 hours.

An attempted rape is one that falls short of penetration.

Of all reported rapes during 1989, 83% were rapes by force. The remainder were attempts or assaults to commit forcible rape. The 1989 rate increased 2% over 1988, 7% over 1985 and 14% above 1980.

In the United States, the majority of rape victims are young, most frequently between 16 and 24, likely to be low income and usually white, although rapes of black females are disproportionate to their numbers.

Rapists in the United States are also young, 80% under 30 and 75% under 25. They are often poor and typically victimize someone of their own race.

Attempted rapes routinely occur on the street, in parks or playgrounds, or in parking lots or parking garages, during the daylight hours. Completed rapes more often occur in the victims' homes between 6 P.M. and midnight.

Statistics about rape are difficult to generalize from because rapes are known to be underreported. Some analysts believe that fewer than 10% of all rapes are reported.

The reasons for underreporting have remained the same for millennia: self-blame, psychological trauma and humiliation, the risk of not being believed and recognition by the victim that she will in future be perceived as tainted or "damaged goods" by others.

Despite massive efforts by feminist groups to help women understand that rape is not their fault, many victims still feel guilty. They wonder what they could have done to avoid it. In most cases, nothing.

Psychological trauma and humiliation overwhelm many victims, and they may try to cope by "crawling into a hole," pulling down the shades, locking the doors, taking repeated showers (to try to shed the feeling of being "dirty"), trying, alone, to regain their sense of personal integrity that was destroyed by the intrusion of rape.

This reaction may result in loss or destruction of evidence. Then, once a victim feels able to report a rape, she risks the suspicion of making a false accusation. Since rapes are usually committed out of the sight of others, it is her word against the rapist's.

Even among women who are able to avoid self-blame and are able to cope with the psychic trauma, the idea of reporting the crime is repugnant. They cringe at the idea of reliving the crime for strangers, first the police and then the courts.

Until massive efforts by feminists in the late 1960s and early 1970s brought about reform, treatment by the police and courts was almost as humiliating as the original rape. Many police departments now have officers, often women, trained to handle rape victims with sensitivity.

However, many courts are still brutal with rape victims. Until recently, in many states, those who steeled themselves to follow through on prosecution of a rapist could expect their rapist's defense attorney to look for some incident or incidents in their past lives to discredit their testimony. An examination of sexual history almost automatically prevented prostitutes from taking a rapist to court. After much lobbying by women's groups, the legislatures of many states passed so-called shield laws that exclude the introduction of the woman's previous sexual history.

Barred from examining her past sex life, instead of dwelling on the crime at hand, defense lawyers often suggest that a rape victim was a willing participant who changed her mind after putting herself in circumstances where she might expect sexual intercourse to take place. This defense ignores the element of force or threat involved in rape. Being a willing participant is far different from being forced to have sex by someone who is bigger or threatens mutilation or death.

Women are often reluctant to report being raped because they recognize that, like courts and defense lawyers, society is not always willing to view them as blameless. Women are thought somehow to have invited attack by flirting, wearing provocative clothing or simply being out after dark.

Especially if she lives in a small town, public knowledge of a rape can follow a victim for the rest of her life. Moreover, some husbands and fiances who view their wives or fiancees as property are apt to see them as damaged and forever changed.

Like prostitutes, married women raped by their husbands had no standing in the courts until recently. The law assumed that if the woman were married to the rapist, he had a right to have sex with her, even against her will. Again, after much lobbying, laws in most states were changed and now permit a woman raped by her husband to file charges against him. Researchers estimate that one husband in seven, at least on one occasion, forces his wife to submit to coitus or oral or anal sex.

Acquaintance Rape.   A rape by someone a woman knows is called acquaintance rape or (if circumstances fit) date rape. Acquaintance rape is a better term, since it covers all circumstances in which this type of assault can occur. It can just as easily be committed by a neighbor or a dormmate who offers a woman a ride home or asks to use the phone, as by a man on a date.

In 1989 the FBI Uniform Crime Reports tabulated 94,504 recorded rapes. Given all the factors that discourage women from reporting, particularly the reluc-

tance to report the behavior of someone they know, experts believe the actual number is much higher. They speculate that for every recorded rape, there are three to ten rapes that go unreported, which would mean that in 1989 the actual number of rapes could have been anywhere from 277,458 to 925,040. There are no data on how many of the rapes were acquaintance rapes.

A University of Arizona Medical School survey of working women and college students provided a base from which to estimate the number of acquaintance rapes. The survey found that four of five rape victims knew their attacker. If the survey findings can be applied across the nation and if the estimates of three to ten unreported rapes are accurate, then the number of acquaintance rapes committed annually may range from 221,966 to 740,032.

Sometimes a sexual assault may not fit the standard definitions of a rape but will still be a crime. For example, a 17-year-old slightly retarded Glen Ridge, New Jersey girl was coaxed into a basement with 13 male teenagers. Six of boys participated in inserting a lubricated broomstick, a miniature baseball bat and an unspecified elongated wooden object into the girl's vagina. Although the girl attended special education classes in a nearby town, she lived in Glen Ridge and played softball and basketball with the high school teams. Most of the boys involved in the incident had known her since she was six.

When the story of the rape became known, the residents of Glen Ridge split between those who blamed the boys for their behavior and those who blamed the girl, either for enticing the boys or for making their behavior publicly known. An October 5, 1989 *Rolling Stone* article, by Peter Wilkinson, entitled "Darkness at the Heart of Town," described the New Jersey town's response.

The residents responded in the ways a woman who has been raped, particularly by an acquaintance, can routinely expect. Friends of the 13 participants claimed that the retarded teenager was sexually provocative. One adult supporter of the boys said, "This is not a situation where any boy went out and did anything forcible to this girl. Some acts occurred, but unless I've misperceived, everything proven to have taken place will be shown to be voluntary. This case will be a tragedy for everybody."

One teenage supporter of the girl said, "It's a shame, because [she] just did it because she wanted to have friends. She just wanted to belong." In an interview, the girl told a reporter that she worried about the boys who were arrested. She said, "I do feel bad. Those were my friends. I thought I could trust them."

Wilkinson's research suggested that the behavior with the retarded teenager was consistent with other sexual activity among boys in the town. He interviewed a group of teenage boys who told him about a game common among the town's male teenagers, including those involved in the assault. Called voyeuring, it involves hiding under beds or in closets to watch others engage in sexual activity.

The boys who participate in voyeuring are so open about it that they include reminiscences of memorable voyeur experiences in the school yearbook. Much of the information available about the assault on the mildly retarded girl came from the boys' own accounts to friends.

A more typical acquaintance rape was described in a December 1990 *Ebony* article entitled "Date Rape," which recounted the experience of a southern California woman, Stacey Phillips. A male student Stacey had befriended at her junior college offered to come to her house to cook dinner. He was the best friend of a basketball player whom she had dated and viewed as a trusted friend.

After dinner, while looking at a photo album, the student started kissing Stacey. She told him to stop. He became more aggressive. She screamed at him and pushed him away. He pushed back, held her down and raped her.

Explaining the low incidence of reporting of such incidents, Phyllis Pennese, chairperson of the Women of Color Caucus of the National Coalition Against Sexual Assault, told *Ebony*, "We are still very much rooted in the myths around sexual assault. Our community buys into the notion that 'She went with him or she had on a tight leather miniskirt, so she must have wanted it.' "

Such arguments ignore the fact that rape has nothing to do with the way a woman is dressed, or that accepting a date or a ride or a cup of coffee is not agreeing to have sex. Women are repeatedly warned not to walk alone to their cars and not to open their doors to strangers, but they are rarely cautioned to beware of the rapist in their circle of acquaintances.

The question of consent is the issue around which acquaintance rape revolves. Women are so often unsure of their right to say no that they don't label the assaults they sustain as rape.

In an extensive study of 6,100 college students from 32 campuses, one in 12 women admitted that they had been forced to have sex, but only 27% of them labeled it rape. One in 12 men polled admitted that they had committed acts that legally qualify as rape or attempted rape, but only 1% of them called it rape.

In her book *Date Rape & Acquaintance Rape,* (1988) Dr. Andrea Parrot of Cornell University explored a number of societal myths about rape that place the blame on women. She pointed out that the police are more likely to believe that a rape took place if the woman is young, has bruises or injuries, did not know the rapist, did not do anything to "contribute" to the rape, reported the crime immediately, is hysterical and has medical evidence collected within hours of the rape.

The expectation that women will fight off a rapist goes against women's training, which is not to fight and not to hurt anyone, especially someone they trust or care about. Many women who are raped by acquaintances believe that any second they will come to their senses and stop forcing her to have sex.

Although society assigns to a man the responsibility for initiating dating and sexual encounters, a woman is expected to maintain control over him. Parrot pointed out the myth that a woman is responsible for a man's sexual excitement. She wrote: "We are all responsible for our own sexual excitement. The limbic system of the brain, which controls emotion, turns us off or on sexually. A partner may be the stimulus, but it is our own brain that turns us off and on."

To explain why the myths that lead society to blame women instead of their rapists are false, Parrot borrowed an analogy from Susan Estrich's 1987 book *Real Rape* about the theft of an owner's car from in front of his or her own home. The car theft is still grand larceny regardless of whether the owner might have left it unlocked, known the person or let the thief use the car six months before. The owner does not have to fight off the thief and come away with bruises or tell anyone who admires the car that they may not steal it. Logically the same standards should apply to rape.

Studies have borne out that many males operate on a set of self-serving assumptions. They believe that if they are out on a date and spend a certain amount of money, they are entitled to recompense in the form of sex. Moreover, men tell one another that when a woman says "no" she really means "yes."

A survey of 1,700 students ages 12 to 15, conducted by the Rhode Island Rape Crisis Center, had astonishing results. One fourth of the boys and one sixth of the girls thought a man had a right to "force" a woman to have sexual intercourse with him if he had spent money on her on the date.

Cassandra Thomas, director of a Houston rape crisis center, was shocked to hear women at a baby shower express the opinion that a women assaulted must have enticed the man, otherwise she would have screamed or fought. Thomas told *Ebony,* "What they don't understand is that you would expect a stranger to be crazy. But if it's someone you are out with, you don't expect this bizarre behavior. When it happens, you think, 'If he's crazy enough to do this, maybe he's crazy enough to kill me.' No one comprehends just how frightening that is."

Many of the misconceptions about date rape come from a societal view that male aggression is "normal" and that, regardless of that normal male aggressiveness, a woman is somehow responsible for his behavior as well as her own. Carra Sergeant, a Louisiana State University administrator and a sexual assault counselor, views that as a mindset that lets men off the hook. "That leads me to believe that men don't want to accept responsibility. Men are not uncontrollable animals. At the point a woman says 'no' it becomes rape, no matter what she consented to up to that point."

Bill Fisher, the head of the Philadelphia Rape Unit, reported that conviction rates for felony rapes average about 83%, but date rape prosecutions are much more likely to fail in court. Reports from other cities reflect a similar pattern.

The idea that there is a national epidemic of date rape has its critics. Murray Rothbard, in the February 25, 1991 *National Review* article entitled "Date Rape," wrote:

> For if the girl did not say no and did not physically resist, then sex did indeed take place by mutual consent. What do the feminists want? Will they only be satisfied if the two parties sign an express consent form before the act and have it notarized on the spot, with forms sent in triplicate to their respective attorneys and to the county clerk? If so the notary publics in college town are in for a thriving business.

Rothbard may not believe in a national epidemic of acquaintance rape in the United States, but the British police think they have one. Most British women believe that the likelihood of being raped by a stranger in a dark alley has increased considerably in recent years, but in reality they are more likely to be raped by men they know, in familiar places—frequently their own homes.

Only 39% of all British rape convictions involve strangers. Casual acquaintances account for 31%; typically the rapist is a neighbor who enters a single woman's home on a false pretext.

On American college campuses the percentages of rape victims who knew their assailants is considerably higher. The Third Annual Conference on Campus Violence held in January 1989 at Towson State University in Maryland was attended by 250 psychologists and law enforcement officers. Participants estimated that 13% to 25% of all college women become victims of rape or attempted rape.

Their estimates are consistent with those of a 1985 survey of 32 campuses conducted by *Ms.* magazine, the National Institute of Mental Health and Dr. Mary Koss, a professor of psychiatry at the University of Arizona School of Medicine, which calculated the ratio of rape victims to be one in six (16%) in a one-year period. Koss found that 84% of the women knew their assailants and that most of the rapes took place on campus. Sexual violence had surpassed theft as the most common crime on U.S. campuses.

What makes rape common on college campuses is male attitudes, in the view of Mark Stevens, a psychologist at the University of Southern California (USC), who conducts rape prevention courses. In an interview for a September 1989 *Good Housekeeping* article entitled "Rape on Campus," Stevens proposed that the attitude held by "nice, respectable" young men who think they have a right to force sex begins with the idea of "scoring." He said, "The attitude that women are objects and that treating them in a demeaning way makes a boy 'cool' and in control gets passed along from peers, older brothers, and media images—especially those in the pornographic magazines."

Young women take in similar confused messages about sexuality. Freshmen women, eager to be sophisticated, are particularly vulnerable targets. When rape does happen, the victim often blames herself for not having been more careful. Tragically, many drop out of school rather than live in close proximity to their rapist.

The *Good Housekeeping* article told the story of an 18-year-old woman who had planned to go to medical school, until she attended a dorm floor party. She had had a small amount to drink, but was not intoxicated, when a young man she knew slightly suggested that she accompany him to his room where, he said, "most of our buddies are.'' She had no reason to be wary of a "dorm brother.'' When she got into his room there was no one there. She pushed him away when he moved toward her, but he threw her on the bed and raped her.

The sound of loud pounding on his door by several of his friends, who were laughing, startled the rapist enough so the young woman could get away. Half dressed, she rushed screaming down the hall to her room. Witnesses who heard her screams could have helped substantiate her story when she went to the university dean the next day—but they did not. Instead, most of the rapist's friends were angry that she had "tried to get him into trouble.'' A short time later she dropped out of school and may never return.

A number of universities, such as the University of Southern California, the University of California at Los Angeles, Cornell and the University of Florida have rape prevention programs, but many universities have been unwilling to deal with the issue. They do not want to admit laxity in campus security. Increased security is expensive and bad publicity can hurt enrollment.

Gail Abarbanel, founder and director of the Rape Treatment Center at the Santa Monica, California Hospital Medical Center, has collected many college rape horror stories. One woman suffered through 14 interviews with college officials, but her attacker was never even called to answer her charges.

Another young woman felt she had no choice but to drop charges against a star college athlete when she was told that her rapist could bring a number of his teammates as character witnesses, but that she could not even bring her mother or a friend. In 60 cases, Abarbanel was aware of only one in which there was even a disciplinary hearing.

In the wake of four fraternity assaults in October 1989, the University of Missouri-Columbia temporarily suspended "little sister'' organizations operated by fraternities. The stated purpose of little sisters programs is to pair college women (little sisters) with fraternity men (big brothers) for social activities and to assist in fund raising for community service projects.

The little sisters programs had never been recognized or sanctioned by the university. Although only one victim was actually involved with the little sister program, the university's director of Greek life, Catherine Scroggs, said in an interview for an October 22, 1989 New York Times article entitled " 'Little Sister' Program Stopped After Assaults,'' "We finally said we're tired of hearing of women assaulted who were little sisters.''

Scroggs cited recurring problems. At the little sister rush parties, fraternity brothers select vulnerable female members. At "big brother'' hunt parties, women are sometimes forced to consume alcohol and read sexually explicit materials before meeting their big brothers.

One of the fraternity members involved with the little sister program described it as a great "recruiting tool.'' He said, "It's a great way for girls not in a sorority to get involved in the Greek system and for us to get guys [to join the fraternity].''

The University of Florida suspended the Beta Theta Pi fraternity for a year for publishing a chart that estimated the number of beers it took to seduce little sisters.

After seven rapes on or near the University of Syracuse campus in the summer of 1989, the university made plans to open an educational counseling program and to offer support services for victims. The university promised to develop an official policy that defined rapes and sexual assault, established disciplinary measures and encouraged students to report any sexual assault.

Gang Rape.   The data on gang rape are scant because most incidents go unreported, but it is estimated that one out of every four rape victims is raped by more than one assailant. Perhaps the most famous recent gang rape case occurred in the spring of 1989, that of the Central Park jogger, a woman raped by a marauding gang who beat her with a metal pipe and rock, slashed her with a knife and left her in a coma, bound and gagged. When she was found three hours later, she was near death.

In an interview about the Central Park jogger assault, for a May 8, 1989 Newsweek article entitled, "Going 'Wilding' in the City,'' James Comer of the Yale Child Study Center said, "No one really knows these kids or what was in their minds.'' The rapists may have had no coherent thought about the victim, but by their own accounts, they appeared to have been propelled by an accelerating frenzy, often seen in gang rapes. Momentum built as the assailants tried to outdo each other. The result was near death for the jogger.

Another well-known case of gang rape took place in 1983 at Big Dan's Tavern in New Bedford, Massachusetts where a 22-year-old woman was gang-raped on a pool table while bystanders cheered and clapped. A film about the incident called The Accused, starring Jodie Foster, was released in 1988. During at least one showing of the film, a group of male teenagers cheered at the rape scene.

In the extensive press coverage that followed the incident, the victim in this case was depicted as promiscuous, as if that somehow excused her rape by a gang of men for the amusement of another gang of men. Following the trial, the woman moved out of state and about five years later was killed in a one-car accident, which many of her friends were convinced was suicide.

While researching the background for the movie, the producers were startled to find that gang rapes in fraternity houses are almost epidemic in the United States. However, they are seldom reported, and when they are, it is usually by a third person and long after the fact.

Despite the lack of media coverage and police data on fraternity and athletic team gang rape, more may be known about the rituals connected with them than about gang rapes in other settings because the rapists are gathered in small communities that include students and faculty who are familiar with the methods for collecting social science data. Moreover, bragging about their exploits is a part of the ritualistic behavior associated with such rapes.

A typical fraternity gang rape is premeditated and almost always conforms to a script. A September/October 1990 *Ms.* article entitled "Fraternities of Fear: Gang Rape, Male Bonding, and the Silencing of Women" by Kathleen Hirsch described the typical scene, and a 1985 Association of American Colleges publication, "Campus Gang Rape: Party Games?" by Julie Ehrhart and Bernice Sandler, laid out the sequence of events.

Naive female students, new to a college or from a nearby college, are invited to their first fraternity party—usually early in the fall term. A victim is selected by a frat brother—either before the party starts or soon after she arrives—and she is "worked over" with a variety of ruses from flattery to subtle threats.

The woman may assume that the frat brother is seriously interested in her. In the words of Ehrhart and Sandler, she is "unaware that the 'friendly' persuasion of the [brother] is actually planned pursuit of easy prey."

Usually, drinking is a preliminary to entering the actual party. The goal is to have the woman become as inebriated as possible, without her becoming suspicious.

Under the impression that she will be with one man or will be left alone to "sleep off" the alcohol, the woman is led to one of the frat rooms. As soon as she enters the room, she is assaulted by the brothers waiting for her; or, more frequently, she goes to sleep and later regains consciousness to find that she is being raped successively by several men.

Dr. Chris O'Sullivan, a psychologist at Bucknell University in Lewisburg, Pennsylvania, studied 24 incidents of gang rape. Two were committed by male students in residence halls, nine by athletes and 13 by fraternities. The men involved seemed to think that what they were doing was okay, most often because they regarded the women as promiscuous. In virtually all the incidents, the raped woman was known by one or more of the men, a finding at odds with the pattern of selecting new, naive women described by Ehrhart and Sandler.

In O'Sullivan's sample, the women were distinguished in the rapists' minds from the women they dated in terms of respectability. One man involved in a gang rape told O'Sullivan that what happened to the woman was "not rape" because she had dated two of the men involved previously and had hurt the men's feelings by having sex with each of them.

Researchers have found that as a gang rape proceeds, that is, as each successive man takes his turn, the woman is viewed increasingly as a "whore" who deserves to be raped—even though, by their own words, the men do not consider what they are doing to be rape.

In an interview in the July 1990 issue of *College Security Report,* Daniel Keller, director of public safety at the University of Louisville, agreed with O'Sullivan's assessment that the men did not consider their behavior to be a rape. He thinks they may view their behavior as some kind of group sex.

O'Sullivan found evidence in the cases she studied that the group of men had committed group rape more than once. She told *College Security Report,* "In some cases, the men did it with women who consented. Then, they did it with women who probably didn't consent, but didn't protest. I think they don't even notice when a woman isn't consenting, once it becomes a habitual thing."

Among O'Sullivan's sample, the men typically formed a tight male group. She said, "The men tend to have grown up together. They have gone off to college together and maintained childhood friendships through adolescence and young adulthood." Moreover, O'Sullivan found that the rapists were apt to belong to the most esteemed groups on campus.

She found that more traditional fraternities and more traditional men were more likely to commit gang rape. "They stand when women enter. They buy into rigid sex roles. They are likely to believe you treat good women nicely and you can do anything to bad women.''

Fraternities appear to be incubators for sexual aggression aimed at women, ranging from verbal abuse to acquaintance rape to gang rape. A 1989 study by the dean's office of the University of Illinois at Urbana-Champaign found that frat men, who represented one quarter of the male student population, perpetrated 63% of student sexual assaults.

Unlike publicized gang rapes that conform to racial and class stereotypes and are viewed with outrage, fraternity gang rapes are seen almost as boyish pranks or rites of passage. Peggy Reeves Sanday, an anthropology professor at the University of Pennsylvania and the author of *Fraternity Gang Rape: Sex, Brotherhood, and Privilege on Campus* (1990), asserts that fraternities attract insecure males who have not yet broken their bonds to their parents.

In her opinion, the security offered by the fraternity is a powerful allure. The young men go through humiliating and often physically painful initiation rights that break family allegiances. Then they are inducted into a new set of highly masculinist norms.

Sanday wrote, ''Almost always male bonding turns against women. It is a matter of degree, not kind. The way in which men extract loyalty from one another almost always means that they elevate male bonding by making women the despised other and the scapegoat.'' During Sanday's interviews, the men characterized the women they slept with as ''beasts, bitches, cracks, gash, heifers, horsebags, life-support systems, scum, scumbags, scum buckets, scum doggies, swanks and swatches.''

Fraternities, with their characteristic degrading of women, unite men in a culture where they must compete intensely, at an age when their sexual identity is still a source of anxiety. In Sanday's opinion, fraternity men allay any insecurities they might have about same-sex attachments by having sex in front of each other and by dehumanizing women through gang rape.

Fraternity men spend inordinate amounts of time in planning, executing, documenting in frat logs and reminiscing about their bonding rituals. In her 1988 book *I Never Called It Rape,* Robin Warshaw provides a lexicon of the specialized words they use to describe their activities: baggings (a group of men corner a woman, drop their trousers, wriggle their penises and offer to gang rape her); land-sharking (kneeling on the floor behind a woman and biting her buttocks); rude-

hoggering (bedding the ''ugliest'' woman at a party); sharking (going up to a woman and suddenly biting her on the breast); and ledging (a practice that has driven some women to the verge of suicide through constant reminders of their observance of her seduction by one of their members).

The director of the Sexual Assault Recovery Services at the University of Florida, Claire Walsh, agreed with Sanday's assessment that gang rapists rape for each other's viewing. She said, ''Men rape for other men. It is a way of maintaining the myth of macho masculinity; a way to confirm their feelings of sexual adequacy. If a man in the room didn't participate, his sexual capacity could be called into question.'' Walsh thinks that men in tight male groups who gang-rape often feel a sense of isolation from the rest of society. She points to examples of gang rapes by rock groups, motorcycle gangs and youths such as those who raped the Central Park jogger.

The 1987 assault of Kristen Buxton at Colgate University in Hamilton, New York was a typical fraternity gang rape in its execution, but it had an atypical outcome. The events are described in the *Ms.* article on fraternities and were also reported in a December 17, 1990 *People* article entitled ''Silent No More.''

At emotional loose ends following the death of her grandmother and the end of a serious relationship, Buxton, a junior, accepted an invitation to a Sigma Chi end-of-summer party that promised ''safe lodging for all girls.'' Shortly after midnight, Buxton was shown to a second-floor bedroom of the Sigma Chi house, where the party was taking place. She had drunk a considerable amount and went to sleep. About 3 A.M., three men, freshman athletes, entered the bedroom.

According to statements later given by the men to police, Buxton did not become fully conscious until after the first man had raped her and gone back downstairs to brag about it. When she regained consciousness, the second man was on top of her and the third was waiting by the bed with his pants down. He climbed on her as she began screaming for help, which arrived moments later, when another woman rushed in.

Although Buxton's gang rape was typical, her response was not. She was clear in her mind about what had happened and she had support. Friends took her home to Marblehead, Massachusetts and her mother took her to a hospital. The hospital put her in touch with the Marblehead police officers who handle rape and they in turn called Colgate Security.

Concerned about the lack of responsiveness from college, Marblehead police officer Marion Conrad drove to Colgate three days later, where she found that little had been done to pursue the case. She next went to the Hamilton police, who opened a criminal investigation. The district attorney, Neal Rose, ultimately accepted plea bargains from the three men, Henry Lamarr Alston, Raymond Lee Hobson and Rodney Lamar Corbit, who received no jail time.

Buxton filed a $10 million lawsuit against Colgate, the fraternity, Sigma Chi, and Best Brands, a beer distributor. Buxton claimed that the district attorney urged her to drop charges because she would be "ruining the lives of three young men." The district attorney countered that his remarks were taken out of context. He claimed he was merely discussing her chances for success in court.

Many people believe that a young woman who drinks is somehow more responsible for putting herself at risk from rapists than the drunken rapists are for their actions. However, since the legal definition of rape hinges on the notion of consent, any sexual contact with a woman too drunk to be capable of giving permission is technically a crime.

Another premeditated fraternity gang rape happened to a young woman plied with liquor at Florida State University. She had some tequila to calm her nerves on her way to the stately Pi Kappa Alpha house, site of Florida State's most exclusive fraternity. She had a date with a handsome junior, Daniel Oltarsh.

When the young woman arrived, Oltarsh handed her a bottle of wine and left her in his room to finish it. The young woman does not remember what happened next, but according to police reports, Oltarsh forced her to have sex with him, then took her to the fraternity shower room, where he was joined by at least two other Pi Kappa Alpha brothers in a gang rape that included penetration of the victim with a toothpaste pump.

Police found the woman in the hallway of the Theta Chi house next door, where she had been dumped, with her skirt pulled up, her pants pulled down and the initials of a third fraternity scrawled on her thighs in ballpoint pen. In the months that followed, the campus was abuzz with rumors that depicted her as an accessory to her own rape. Dispirited and depressed, the victim was unable to assist the prosecution, and the state pursued it without her help. She eventually checked herself into a psychiatric hospital, where she tried to kill herself.

Oltarsh's fraternity brothers plea-bargained to lesser charges, and immediately following jury selection, Oltarsh pleaded no contest and was given a year's jail sentence, substantial for a rape case.

In *I Never Called It Rape,* Warshaw wrote, "In gang rape they experience a special bonding with each other . . . and prove their sexual ability to other group members." The special bonding extends beyond the gang rape incident. Following the assault, the close-knit all-male groups present a united, intimidating front to the victim, whether or not individual members participated in the rape.

After being raped by a popular football player at an exclusive West Coast liberal arts college, the victim did not press charges. She didn't know she could, because she thought rapists had to be strangers. However, she confided in her roommate and somehow the word spread. The victim found herself harassed by a "hate team" of men and women made up of her rapist's teammates and their friends.

As a consequence of the harassment, the victim asked for a leave of absence. After she explained her reasons, the dean granted the leave but took no further action. When the victim returned to school after five months, the harassment resumed and she dropped out of school permanently.

Buxton experienced episodes of the same kind of harassment. In a downtown Hamilton pub, a group of fraternity members surrounded her table and just stood there silently staring at her.

A 1985 study sponsored by the Association of American Colleges' Project found that close-knit all-male groups—such as fraternities and athletic teams—were involved in a disproportionate number of rapes, especially gang rapes. A 1987 National Institute of Health study of sexual assaults on campus, conducted by Dr. Mary Koss, found that athletes were involved in about a third of the rapes, both individual and gang.

According to Keller of the University of Louisville, the disproportionate involvement of athletes in gang rapes has not received much attention. In the view of sports sociologist Merrill Melnick, of the State University of New York at Brockport, the psychology of athletes involved in a gang rape is similar to the thinking patterns of the U.S. soldiers who, in 1969, massacred South Vietnamese civilians in My Lai. He told *College Security Report* that "groupthink," comes into play. "They are so caught up in the solidarity of the group and its activity that they choose not to speak out. I am sure one or more athletes understands this action is unacceptable, yet they choose not to speak out."

Melnick pointed out that athletes spend their lives following the orders of coaches and not making individual judgments. He believes such behavior can lead to a loss of personal initiative and will to think independently.

In most rape cases, whether single or gang rapes, the response of university officials has been to minimize what happened. In Sanday's view, what is at stake is brotherhood.

That's older males protecting younger males, protecting their lost youth, and protecting their actual fraternity brothers. Protecting the American dream. The dream in which the young man goes out with his buddies, works his way up, becomes head of everything, and makes a fortune. Along the way, if he has to rape a few people—competitors, women—that's sort of what we expect. The American dream is very misogynistic.

The problem of gang rape is not likely to go away any time in the near future. Therese Stanton of the National Anti-Pornography Civil Rights Organization discovered that 24-hour-a-day at-home access to 900-number "dial-a-porn," along with personal computer smut, have lowered the mean age of males accessing hard-core pornography down to about 15.

As the coordinator of the Brooklyn, New York Women's Anti-Rape Exchange, Stanton also documented that rapists are getting younger. One of the frightening trends reported to her was gang rapes of high school girls, who were thrown into a van, where a camcorder recorded the events. Such porn videotapes can be sold for about $5,000. Stanton theorizes that many of the serial killers of prostitutes are by trade "snuff" pornographers (people who commit actual murders while the cameras are filming).

Public indifference to gang rape can only contribute to its escalation. Syndicated columnist Mona Charen discussed the Central Park jogger case and that of the 17-year-old mildly retarded Glen Ridge, New Jersey girl:

People will ask: Why would such "nice" boys from such "good" homes do such terrible things? The answer is that they saw little to be ashamed of . . . Are these kids then committing rape just because they think they won't get caught? Not quite. Motives are always complex. But this much is sure—the absence of punishment is what sociologists call an "enabling condition." It doesn't cause the

behavior, but it permits it. In truly civilized societies, shame is the great enforcer. Shame is often feared more than the law. (*Boston Globe*, May 28, 1989)

Rape: Neither New Nor Rare. The meticulous tracing of the historical and factual evidence of rape by Susan Brownmiller in her 1975 book *Against Our Will* reveals rape to be a pervasive process of intimidation that affects all women, whether or not they have been actual victims of violence.

She said:

Man's structural capacity to rape and woman's corresponding structural vulnerability are as basic to the physiology of both our sexes as the primal act of sex itself . . . Man's discovery that his genitalia could serve as a weapon to generate fear must rank as one of the most important discoveries of prehistoric times, along with the use of fire and the first crude stone axe.

Over the centuries, distinctions about whether a rape was a crime or not often hinged on the class of the victim and the class of the rapist, class being defined as whether the man to whom the woman "belonged" was "high born." It was not until the 13th century, in the England of Edward I, that rape was declared a public wrong; however, the concept worked better in writing than it did in practice in the courts.

From the 13th to the 20th century, not much changed. "The later giants of jurisprudence, Hale, Blackstone, Wigmore and the rest," Brownmiller said, "continued to point a suspicious finger at the female victim and to worry about her motivations and 'good fame.' "

Brownmiller quoted Blackstone:

If she be of evil fame and stand unsupported by others, if she concealed the injury for any considerable time after she had the opportunity to complain, if the place where the act was alleged to be committed was where it was possible she might have been heard and made no outcry, these and the like circumstances carry a strong but not conclusive presumption that her testimony is false or feigned.

As the 20th century draws to a close, the opinion that Blackstone expressed is still widespread. A woman who does not report promptly, or who is too terrorized to scream or fight back, is at risk of not being believed.

Rape and War. That rape is an expression of power rather than of sexual desire becomes evident in Brownmiller's chapter on war. Those who marched in the First Crusade took time out for rape. During the American Revolution, one of George Washington's troops was sentenced to death for his second offense of rape. The Germans used rape as a weapon of power when they marched through Belgium during World War I, as did the Soviets on their march to Berlin during World War II. Although rape is punishable by death or imprisonment under Article 120 of the American Uniform Code of Military Justice, details of rapes by American soldiers in Vietnam emerged during exposés of the horrors of that war.

Brownmiller asserted that war offers a perfect psychological backdrop in which men can express their contempt for women. She said, "The very maleness of the military—the brute power of weaponry exclusive to their hands, the spiritual bonding of men at arms . . . confirms for men what they long suspected, that women are peripheral, irrelevant to the world that counts, passive spectators to the action in the center ring."

Rape becomes the victors' prerogative as the vanquished surrender yet another piece of property. Rape is committed by the conquerors on the bodies of the defeated enemies' women. Rape is a way to measure victory. Men of the defeated nation traditionally perceive the rape of "their women" as the ultimate humiliation. Frequently, fathers or husbands are forced to watch.

Despite its frequency, historians rarely discuss rape.

Rape Is Violent by Definition.   Most analysts agree with Brownmiller's assessment that rape is a crime of power and sex the weapon used. Menachem Amir would have added that the rapist is violent. In 1971 Amir, an Israeli sociologist and a student of Marvin Wolfgang, one of America's leading criminologists, published a landmark study of rape in Philadelphia entitled *Patterns in Forcible Rape,* a pragmatic, in-depth statistical study of the nature of rape and rapists.

Amir included such variables as methods of operation, gang rape versus individual rape, economic class, prior relationship between victims and offenders, racial and interracial factors. Amir's study overturned the stereotype that rapists are solitary and secretive; 43% of the sample operated in pairs. The most common characteristics of the rapists in Amir's study were that they were quite ordinary, and violence-prone.

In his 1989 book *Profiling Violent Crime,* Ronald Holmes, a professor of criminal justice at the University of Louisville, created sociopsychological profiles based on interviews and correspondence with murderers and rapists. He sorts them into four categories: Power Reassurance Rapists (also called Compensatory Rapists),

Anger Retaliation Rapists, Power Assertive Rapists and Sadistic Rapists.

The Power Reassurance Rapist is the least violent and aggressive among rapists and the least socially competent. He is likely to be single and to live alone or with his parents. He is likely to have a menial job and to be viewed as steady and reliable.

In Holmes' view, rape by the Power Reassurance Rapist is sexual, unlike those of other rapists. It is an enactment of his sexual fantasies. He is likely to ask his victim politely to remove her clothes and to use only enough force to keep her under control.

The Power Reassurance Rapist operates under the assumption that the victim enjoys the rape. He tends to rape within his own neighborhood and has a pattern of raping again within seven to 15 days. Although he begins his career as a rapist with little additional violence, violence tends to increase with subsequent assaults. He is likely to collect souvenirs from the victim's home and not infrequently to call to inquire about her health and possible ill effects of the rape. One rapist thought the victim enjoyed the rape so much that he promised to return, only to find the police waiting for him.

The Anger Retaliation Rapist's major purpose is to hurt women, for all the injustices, real or imagined, that he has suffered in his life at their hands. He views himself as athletic and masculine and is likely to be married. He is reported by friends to have a quick, violent temper. The rape tends to follow some precipitating incident with a woman significant in his life.

The Anger Retaliation Rapist rapes close to home. Once he gets the victim into his "comfort zone" (zone of control), he uses profanity to heighten his excitement and to instill terror into his victim.

The Power Assertive Rapist expresses his personal masculine dominance through rape. Simply because he perceives himself as superior he feels entitled to rape—it is what men do to women. Frequently he works in construction or is a police officer. A uniform is part of his masculine image. He tends to stalk his victim in places such as bars where there is an ample supply of females from which to choose.

If his victim resists, he will overpower her and he is likely to rip her clothes off. He is also likely to make multiple assaults on a particular victim. Although he is likely to have a regular sex partner, a wife or lover, the Power Assertive Rapist is likely to rape again within a 20- to 25-day cycle. The aggression used will escalate.

The Sadistic Rapist is the most dangerous. He has eroticized violence. His goal is to inflict physical and psychological pain. He is apt to be antisocial and aggressive in his everyday life if criticized or thwarted. Typically he is married, often living in a middle-class neighborhood and working at a white-collar occupation. He is compulsively neat about himself and his car and carefully plans his rapes to evade detection. He enjoys raising the level of fear in his victims by using gags, blindfolds, duct tape and handcuffs.

The rapes of the Sadistic Rapist may eventually result in death. The serial killer Ted Bundy said in an interview on death row, "A large number of serial killings are simply an attempt to silence the victims. A simple but effective means of elimination."

Rapes of Males. Holmes estimated that about 1% of all reported rape victims are men. Rapes of homosexuals are not likely to be taken seriously by the police. About the attitude of police toward homosexuals, Brownmiller said:

Here again, the parallels to the woman's experience are obvious. I have listened more than once to the story of a homosexual youth who tried without success to convince his local precinct that he was beaten up and raped by some strangers he met in a gay bar and thoughtlessly decided to entertain at home. To the cops in the precinct the raped youth was nothing more than a faggot who was "asking for it."

Brownmiller went on to talk about rape of males in prison.

Some modern sociologists have tried to downplay homosexual rape in American prisons by making use of that biased belief—this is a direct quote from an accepted source— "There is some question, as in heterosexual situations, as to whether the situation is really in fact rape or whether it is a seduction that has gone wrong."

Such sociologists have evidently not done adequate fieldwork or have chosen not to believe the results. Some sense of the scope of prison rape can be gotten from research done in 1968. After two rapes in Philadelphia prisons that were widely publicized, a joint study was conducted of the Philadelphia prison system by the police and the district attorney's office. Alan Davis, the prosecutor who was in charge of the investigation, concluded that rape in the Philadelphia prisons was "epidemic."

After 3,000 interviews by the task force with guards and inmates reluctant to talk, lie detector tests and scrutiny of prison records, 156 cases of rape over a two-year period were documented. Davis was of the opinion that he had only touched the tip of the iceberg. He speculated that the true number of rapes might have been closer to 2,000, in a constantly changing inmate population of 60,000 men.

Only 96 of the 156 documented cases had been reported to prison authorities by the victims; 64 had been written up in prison records; 40 had resulted in internal prison discipline; and 26 had been passed on for prosecution.

The task force developed a profile of the prison rapist. They found that men who raped other men were on the average three years older, one inch taller and 15 pounds heavier than their victims. Virtually every slightly built young man was approached sexually within a day or two of his admission to prison. Many were gang-raped. Some sought protection by entering into homosexual relationships with one individual. Davis learned that after a young man has been raped, he is marked as a victim and the designation follows him from one prison to another.

Davis and his investigators were startled to learn that the man who rapes another man in prison does not consider himself a homosexual. The prison view of such relations is that the aggressor is heterosexual and the passive victim is homosexual. This impression is supported by research done by anthropologist Mark Fleisher, who spent a year of research working as a correctional officer at the U.S. Penitentiary at Lompoc, California.

In his 1989 book *Warehousing Violence,* Fleisher estimated conservatively that about 10% of the Lompoc population was actively engaged in sexual activities. Compared with other prisons, Lompoc has a low rate of violence.

Fleisher asked inmates that he had come to know well why there were not more rapes at Lompoc. He was told, "Freelancing homosexuals [those not attached to one particular man], yeah fags, keep down the rapes. If there's enough homosexuals, he [new inmate] won't get turned out." One claimed, "Rapes are on cons who aren't homosexuals." Another said, "The feds will ship your ass [to a more restrictive prison] if they catch you."

Fleisher learned that in the prison hierarchy, there is a category of inmate who is even lower than the homosexual. He is called "the punk" and gets raped and beaten up because he is weak, lacks conviction and is easily manipulated. Since the prison officers share the inmates' low opinion of the punk, he probably would be wasting his time to report a rape.

Victim Precipitation. Amir describes rape as "ecologically bound." It is not so much that rapists prefer their own class and race (or sex in the case of prison rapes) as it is that rape is a crime of opportunity. Women who live in urban lower-class neighborhoods are at greatest risk of all kinds of crime, including rape. "Victim precipitation" is a notion in criminology that, without holding a victim responsible for a crime, asks if the victim could have done something differently to avoid it.

Amir concluded that 19% of the victims had precipitated their rapes. Many analysts subsequently concluded that Amir's definitions of precipitation were generous to the rapist. Giving a glass of water to someone who had raked the leaves in the yard or accepting a ride from a stranger might be considered unwise but they are not invitations to rape.

As a counter to Amir's conclusions, Brownmiller described the findings from a National Commission on the Causes and Prevention of Violence. The commission defined precipitating behavior as follows. In criminal homicide, whenever the victim was the first to use physical force against his subsequent slayer; in aggravated assault, when the victim was the first to use physical force or insinuating language, gestures and the like against his attacker; in armed or unarmed robbery, when the crime was preceded by "temptation-opportunity" situations in which the victim clearly had not acted with reasonable self-protection in handling money, jewelry or other valuables; in forcible rape, when the victim agreed to sexual relations but retracted her agreement before the actual act or when she clearly invited sexual relations through language, gestures and so on. The task force found that the rate of discernible precipitation was as follows:

Homicide	22.0%
Assault	14.4%
Armed robbery	10.7%
Unarmed robbery	6.1%
Rape	4.4%

The data suggest that Amir may have considerably overestimated the victims' precipitation.

The Victim's Chances of Being Believed. A mid-1960s FBI *Uniform Crime Report* noted that 20% of all accusations of rape reported to the police were determined to be unfounded (not accepted as valid). By 1973 the percentage of unfounded accusations had dropped to 15%. When New York City instituted a special sex crimes analysis squad and assigned policewomen instead of policemen to rape cases, the rate dropped to 2%, a figure that corresponded with the rate of false reports of other crimes.

A December 1968 *University of Pennsylvania Law Review* article entitled, "Police Discretion and the Judgement that a Crime Has Been Committed—Rape in Philadelphia" attempted to measure the yardsticks that police officers used to "found" a rape. They discovered that rapes reported "within hours" and cases involving strangers, weapons and "positive violence" had the best chances of being believed. Stranger rape in a car was less believable, and all date rapes in a car were deemed unfounded.

Although the law makes no distinction if the victim was intoxicated at the time of the rape, the police nevertheless "unfounded" 82% of such cases. The police were more likely to believe a complainant if she screamed than if she said she struggled silently. Black-on-black cases were held unfounded in 22% of cases and white-on-white in only 12%.

Although many police prior to the 1970s were convinced that charges of rape were made by prostitutes who did not get paid, in a 1973 Memphis study of police data, Brenda Brown, a department analyst, found that only 1.02% of all rape reports were filed by prostitutes. The largest number of those whose occupation was recorded, 27% of all victims, were students.

Brown determined that 73% of all founded rapes were committed by strangers. Existence of a previous relationship was the most frequently used reason for categorizing cases as unfounded.

In rape cases, defense lawyers are more likely to ask for a trial by jury than to take their chances with a judge. A University of Chicago Law School study by law professors Harry Kalven and Hans Zeisel, described in their 1966 book *The American Jury,* examined the jury bias in favor of rapists. The professors considered 106 cases of rape in order to compare the jury decisions to acquit with written statements by the judges telling how they would have voted.

Kalven and Zeisel found that juries rewrote the law. In the absence of overt evidence of force, the juries preferred to acquit on the grounds that they felt that actions did not carry the gravity of rape. The professors narrowed down the pool of cases by eliminating those in which there was evidence of "extrinsic violence," where the defendant and victim were total strangers and cases involving more than one assailant. In the remaining 42 cases of "simple rape," the judges would have convicted in 22 cases, but the jury actually convicted in only three.

Rape remains a crime that can be committed with a great deal of impunity.

(See also CAMPUS VIOLENCE; CLASSROOM VIOLENCE; SERIAL KILLERS; VIOLENCE AS FUN: THE CASE OF THE CENTRAL PARK JOGGER; VIOLENT CRIMES AGAINST WOMEN: THEIR CONNECTION TO GENDER BIAS.)

refugees Many of America's, and Western Europe's newest residents have been uprooted by violence in their countries of origin, and have had to suffer tremendous hardships in search of safety. Unfortunately, they have often found that they are not welcome in what they thought would be a haven.

Globally, there are an estimated 15 million people in need of resettlement. Prior to 1975 the United States annually received about 200 applications for asylum. By 1985 applications had grown to 16,000. Between 1975 and 1980 applications to West Germany rose from 9,494 to 107,818. Since the fall of communism and the new instability and nationalist activity in eastern Europe and the Balkans, these numbers have enormously increased.

To discourage spontaneous refugee arrivals, Western nations have set up orderly processing programs for resettlement. Specific quotas are established and refugees wait their turn. But only a fraction of the world's refugees are ever considered for resettlement.

Those who seek admittance into foreign countries are sorted into various categories, some of which overlap. Many fall into more than one category. They are defined as follows:

Immigrant: an alien who enters a foreign country legally and intends to establish himself or herself there permanently.

Migrant worker: an individual who travels to another country to secure gainful employment for a limited period.

Refugee: a person who has left his or her country and has good reason to fear persecution because of race, religion, nationality, membership in a social group or political affiliation should he or she return.

Political refugee: an individual who fears a threat to his or her life or freedom on account of a political belief, position or affiliation. This category may include deposed leaders as well as opponents of a current regime.

Illegal alien: a person who has entered a country illegally and who has no grounds to request asylum. An illegal alien cannot count on having full legal rights in the country in which he or she is living.

Detainee: an alien in the custody of authorities whose application for asylum is under consideration.

Internee: an alien who is placed in detention, for alleged security or other reasons.

Displaced person: an individual who because of war or natural disaster has had to leave his or her home, and who also may have been forced to leave his or her country.

Economic refugee: an individual whose desire for asylum is deemed by the host country to be motivated by the prospect of economic improvement. Such a person is not considered a refugee by most nations.

Environmental refugee: a person who has been forced to leave his or her home because of a disaster such as Chernobyl, prolonged drought, deforestation or the importation of Western agricultural practices unsuited to local conditions. Approximately 10 million people around the world fit this category. Environmental refugees are seldom counted in official tallies, although they have even less hope than most other refugees of ever being able to return home.

By their nature, refugees are inconvenient. In developing policy about refugees, governments must weigh a variety of issues: the control of immigration; the sanctity of borders; relations with neighboring countries; national values; and public opinion. To receive consideration, refugees must fit within the government's competing concerns. Otherwise, there is little incentive to bear the cost of accepting responsibility for them.

The delicate balance a government must achieve is explained by Bill Frelick in *Forced Out: The Agony of the Refugee in Our Time* (1989), edited by Carole Kismaric. Based on an image of themselves as good people, governments use humanitarian language to explain why they grant asylum in some cases. That image makes it difficult to explain why other refugees are rejected.

One approach to maintaining an acceptable self-image is to define those rejected as not being real refugees.

Officials refer to such people as economic migrants or illegal aliens not entitled to admission. Other rejections are explained by technicalities: Asylum seekers failed to wait their turns, have not obeyed the rules or have travel documents that are not in order. For example, West Germany passed a law that rejected asylum seekers who traveled to a safe country before applying for asylum in Germany.

A focus on formal documentation ignores the haphazard nature of refugee flight. Forced to flee his or her country, a refugee seldom has time to plan an escape, study immigration regulations or secure documentation. People who fear that their governments will persecute them for wanting to emigrate are unlikely to apply to that government for permission to leave.

Those who arrive haphazardly in a new country may enter or stay without permission or proper documentation, surviving on the fringes of society as illegal aliens, at the mercy of those who threaten to turn them in. Some take the risk of deportation by making application for asylum. A refugee's actions do not necessarily imply an effort to bypass the rules; they may simply reflect a lack of alternatives.

Despite the fact that most Western economies have coped well and even benefited from major European refugee movements in the past, the recent influx has sparked negative reactions. While the quantum leap in the numbers making application may have been a factor, some observers believe that resistance to the new immigrants lies more in the nature of the asylum seekers. Skin color has changed from white to yellow, brown or black, countries of origin have shifted from north to south, and reasons for fleeing no longer are to escape communism. Recent refugee flight is more likely to have been to escape deprivation, persecution and violence from left or right.

The motives for seeking asylum have always been a mix, a political push of persecution and an economic pull of opportunity. Yet the very existence of any economic motive in some cases has been used in the United States to deny hearings on the political merits of asylum claims.

Poverty-stricken Haitians fleeing a regime with a well-documented record of human rights abuse have been consistently denied refugee status in the United States. During years of civil war, poor Salvadorans fleeing a military that bombed and strafed their villages had an average of less than 4% of their claims approved. During the same years, equally poor Nicaraguans fleeing similar conditions inflicted by a "Communist" government had 84% of their claims granted.

Refugee Camps. Many refugees are forced to live in remote camps set up by the governments of the countries to which they have fled. The living conditions in many are horrendous.

The degree of freedom in refugee camps, that is, whether they are loosely organized communities or tightly controlled prisons, depends a great deal on how threatened the host country feels by those crossing its borders. The quality of living conditions in the camps is related to the numbers seeking refuge and the willingness of the host country to accept them.

Hong Kong's 11 refugee camps house 25,000 refugees who have fled Vietnam. Many of them live in compartments that are stacked and measure considerably less than the standard of 3.5 square meters (4.2 square yards) per person set by the World Health Organization as the minimum emergency living space. Almost 50% of Hong Kong camp residents have been in camp more than four years.

Hong Kong's camp populations keep rising. For the year 1987, 3,026 arrived by boat. During the first six months of 1988, more than 7,700 arrived.

Because refugee camps are often built in inaccessible locations, water sometimes has to be trucked in hundreds of miles. At the Makalle camp for famine victims in northern Ethiopia, water taps are turned on for a few hours a day. During dry seasons, water is rationed and falls short of the 15 liters (3.9 gallons) for one person for one day recommended by the United Nations High Commission for Refugees (UNHCR).

UNHCR also recommends a daily ration of over 2,000 calories a day for adults and children, but many refugees do not get enough to eat. Malnutrition is the major cause of death in refugee camps, followed by measles, diarrheal diseases, malaria and acute respiratory infections.

Camps are often located close to national borders, making refugees vulnerable to attack by the governments from which they are fleeing. Guerrillas frequently set up antipersonnel mines to terrorize camp inhabitants. As a protective device, some camps have daily air-raid drills.

Some refugees cling to the hope that in time they will be able to return home. Therefore, refugees who do not want to be taken any farther from home often resist being moved to a new site to reduce the risks attendant on being near a border or because water supplies are inadequate.

Statistics about life in refugee camps make grim reading. As of January 1, 1987, there were 5,600,488 refugees in camps. Seventy-five percent were women and children. The average length of stay in the camps was more than five years. Refugee children of school age numbered 2.5 million, but only 320,000 (less than 13%) were receiving primary education in UNHCR programs.

About 300,000 unregistered, unassisted, unprotected refugees, classified as displaced persons, were living along the border of Thailand and Cambodia. Approximately 793,000 of the 2.3 million Palestinians living in Jordan, Lebanon, the Gaza Strip, the West Bank and Syria were living in camps. The population density in the Gaza Strip was 4,500 people per square mile, and 80% of the people were refugees.

Some observers believe that camps may do more harm than good. For governments, a concentration of refugees in one place makes it easier to provide them with food, shelter, clean water, sanitation and health care. However, the concentration makes the refugees vulnerable to increased health risk and crime. Moreover, it makes them dependent on international aid.

In some cases, left to their own devices, refugees are assimilated into the local economy. In southern Sudan in the early 1980s, refugees from Uganda moved in among the Sudanese without having any discernibly greater problem than the local population. Renewed fighting led to camps being set up for a second wave of Ugandans. Before long the older group of refugees, drawn to the camps for the protection, food and medical care they offered, gave up their independence.

Segregation of refugees into camps also ignores the positive effect they can have on a local economy. East Africans who fled from Uganda and were accepted as refugees in Britain became a dynamic force. Vietnamese refugees have developed a retail business niche in the United States.

Refugees are less an immigration problem than they are a human rights issue. Blocking avenues of escape for victims of deprivation and mistreatment, whether through interception and turning back of boats or denial of entry at land border crossings, raises questions about the value the West places on human life and liberty.

rehabilitation   See CORRECTIONAL EDUCATION; PRISON OVERCROWDING: COPING WITH THE COSTS.

relapse prevention: treatment for sex offenders
Conventional wisdom among therapists has been that sex offenders cannot be treated successfully. New treatments suggest that, while there is no "cure," sex offenders can bring their behavior under control using the same kind of vigilance that alcoholics use to keep their problem behavior in check. The new approaches called relapse prevention help sex offenders interrupt a cycle of emotions, thinking patterns and fantasies that lead them to such crimes as rape, child molestation, exhibitionism or voyeurism.

Conservative estimates indicate that more than 75% of jailed sex offenders get no treatment. In 1990 there were 85,647 sex offenders in U.S. state and federal prisons—one out of every six prisoners. Their numbers are growing at a rate second only to drug offenders. While the general prison population increased by 20% between 1988 and 1990, the sex offender population grew by 48%.

A meeting of sex offender treatment specialists at Kent State University in Ohio was reported in the April 14, 1992 New York Times. Researchers at the meeting revealed the findings of a well-designed study of 110 men who completed an experimental program conducted by the California State office responsible for treatment and evaluation of sex offenders. The study participants, matched in age, background and the nature of their crime, were assigned to either a treatment group or a control group.

The most positive findings among those treated were among rapists, traditionally among the most difficult sex offenders to treat. During a period of almost three years following release, only one treated rapist was arrested for a new sex crime, while seven among the untreated control group were rearrested.

Among child molesters, the most common group in the California program, 5% of the treated committed a new offense within three years after release, compared with 9% of the untreated offenders. Moreover, the treated molesters who did commit new offenses took an average of 800 days compared with 400 days for those in the control group.

A Vermont treatment program had findings similar to those of the California program. In an evaluation of 473 sex offenders who had been out of prison for up to eight years, the average rate of sex crimes for the untreated control group was 38%, almost double that of the treated group.

In the Vermont treatment program, offenders read accounts and see videotapes that present the victim's perspective on the crime. Then they write accounts of what they imagine the victim in their own crime experienced. The offender reads his written account aloud to his therapy group and, playing the role of the victim, he answers questions posed to him by the group. Finally the offender re-creates the crime, taking the role of the victim.

The construction of empathy for the victim makes it difficult for the offender to continue to deny the victim's pain even in fantasy. Recognition of that pain strengthens the offender's resolve to resist his urges.

The program's focus is on day-to-day management of the offender's sexual urges. Offenders are at risk of committing new offenses when they are in high-risk situations, depressed or caught up in their fantasies. Relapse prevention treatment helps them develop strategies for handing moments of risk.

High risk might exist when, still angry over an argument, a rapist passes a woman hitchhiker on the road and is tempted. One way of preventing the cycle from escalating is to report his experience and how he handled it to his therapist or parole officer. If he handled it badly, the professionals explore with him other ways that he might have managed. Some programs have offenders set up teams of friends and family who keep an eye on his behavior and enable him to avoid situations of high risk (such as schoolyards for child molesters).

A technique called cognitive restructuring helps offenders learn to identify distorted stories they tell themselves. For example, child molesters often say "Some children are sexually seductive" or "I am showing the child love." Rapists often say "Any woman who resists is just playing hard to get." To offset this distorted thinking, some offenders carry cards with reminders such as "Two minutes of power is not worth 20 years in jail."

For sex offenders, sex fantasies are so powerful that they are returned to again and again. They become, in effect, planning stages on the way to commission of a crime. Strong emotions such as anger, loneliness or depression constitute the first stage. Sexual fantasies offer a measure of relief in the second stage. Rationalizations that justify the behavior are the third stage. Fantasies and rationalizations turn into a plan during the fourth stage. The crime is enacted in the fifth stage.

One behavior modification approach to interrupting the stages is to lessen the attractiveness of the sexual fantasies. This is done by pairing a favorite fantasy with an obnoxious one, such as a mental image of being confronted during the crime by three burly police officers or the crime being witnessed by one's parents.

Another behavioral approach is more direct. A therapist goes with an offender into a high-risk situation. When the offender experiences his urge, the therapist introduces an obnoxious stimulus such as smelling salts. Thus the arousing fantasy is coupled with a nauseating physical reaction.

For about 5% of the offender population, sexual urges are almost uncontrollable. For some of them, in order to make it possible to use other kinds of therapy, drugs are used. There are two types: One reduces male hormone levels and the other blocks the brain chemical serotonin. Drugs alone are ineffective.

The most successful candidates for treatment are those with no record of other kinds of offenses, who hold a job, have a network of family and friends and whose sex fantasies do not preoccupy them for hours each day.

Despite the effectiveness of relapse prevention techniques, the impression that sex offenders are impossible to treat persists. This gloomy viewpoint was reinforced by a widely read 1989 *Psychological Bulletin* article that reviewed treatment programs in use before 1985 and concluded that they were not effective. Relapse prevention techniques came into prominence after 1985 and were not included in the review.

The techniques are described in *Relapse Prevention with Sex Offenders* (1989) edited by D. Richard Laws and published by Guilford Press and in a chapter by William Pithers, director of the Vermont sex-offender program in *Handbook of Sexual Assault: Issues, Theories and Treatment* (1991) published by Plenum Press.

revenge   Many theorists, including Charles Darwin and Sigmund Freud, have assumed that revenge is instinctive and therefore inevitable. Based on their assumptions, they have argued about whether and when revenge is morally right and ignored the question of why there are those who do not seek revenge.

The behavior of those who do not aspire to retaliation suggests that revenge may be a cultural construct or learned response rather than a built-in reaction. A quarter of a century ago, Jack Hokanson, a psychologist at the University of Florida, designed a series of experiments to test conventional assumptions about revenge. He placed male students and partners at separate but electronically connected consoles, and attached each to a blood pressure measurement apparatus. The student and his partner were told to punish each other with electric shocks for failing to perform simple tasks.

As Hokanson expected, the students' blood pressures went up when they were attacked and went down much faster if they zapped back than if they did not. The experimental results seemed to support the standard explanation that rage and its physiological expression—the so-called fight-or-flight response—were aroused by an attack and were diffused by a counterattack.

But most angry episodes are social events. They assume meaning only in terms of the social assumptions shared by the participants. Beliefs about anger and the interpretations of experience are as important as the experience itself. To place the role of revenge in relation to these beliefs, Hokanson conducted a variation of the same experiment. He told each student that his partner was a teacher rather than another student. Instead of the student's blood pressure going down as expected following a return attack, it went up even more than it had from the initial attack. The supposedly instinctive biological revenge response seems to be complicated by social rules.

As did most scientists until the late 1980s, Hokanson initially performed his experiments with males only. Later, however, he ran out of males and had to use females. Like the males, the female students' blood pressures rose when they were attacked, but their blood pressures went up even more if they counterattacked, even though they thought they were attacking a guilty peer. When the female students felt insulted or attacked, they would calm themselves and lower their blood pressures by placating or rewarding their attackers, instead of by taking revenge.

Hokanson reasoned that the dissimilarity could be a consequence of hormonal differences—a higher level of testosterone in males and of estrogen in females. He designed his next experiment to rule out this intrinsic physiological variance as an explanation.

He designed the experiment so that women were rewarded for attacking and punished for rewarding. They very quickly learned to be as aggressive as the male students, and their blood pressures responded accordingly. Moreover, when male students were punished for attacking and rewarded for rewarding, they also quickly learned to reverse their typical response and their blood pressures corresponded. At the time, Hokanson's revolutionary findings were barely noticed—but they are revived periodically.

An April 16, 1989 *Boston Globe Magazine* article entitled "Is Vengeance Ours?: A New Look at the 'Instinctual' Need to Get Even," by Christina Robb,

cited many other studies besides those of Hokanson whose findings cast doubt on the widely accepted idea that the best cure for anger is revenge, and that there is a preordained link among attack, anger and revenge.

Among the places Hokanson's ideas were elaborated on was social psychologist Carol Tavris' 1989 book *Anger: The Misunderstood Emotion.* "The physiological rationales for ventilating anger," she wrote, "do not stand up under the experimental scrutiny. The weight of the evidence indicates precisely the opposite: Expressing anger makes you angrier, solidifies an angry attitude, and establishes a hostile habit."

In his many publications, Murray Straus, the director of the Family Research Laboratory at the University of New Hampshire in Durham has pointed out that everyone responds physiologically with a rush of adrenaline when attacked but what they do with that response is determined by the rules of their environment.

Robb cited the work of sociologist Richard Felson of the State University of New York at Albany, who specializes in the study of all kinds of attacks, including sibling squabbles, rapes and homicides by strangers. He has determined that not only is the desire for revenge governed by social rules of retaliation, so too is the initial attack.

In the perception of most attackers, the people they attack have wronged them in some way and made them lose face. Even though an attacker's perception may be wrong or may belong to the paranoid "I didn't like the way she looked at me" type of response, the significant issue is that the attacker felt attacked and sought revenge.

Murders and assaults, in Felson's view, are often "self-help" approaches to righting a perceived wrong. When social rules permit a third-party mediator, or if the victim receives an explanation or an apology, retaliation is rare.

Interruption of the Revenge Cycle. By establishing that vengeance is not inevitable, the findings of sociologists and psychologists like Hokanson over the last quarter of a century have suggested a need for a change in courtroom procedures. A few courts have begun ordering offenders to provide restitution to victims, a practice that often reduces vengeful feelings.

Massachusetts, in 1985, became one of the first states to enact a victim's bill of rights. The bill established a fund for victims that is paid for by offenders through fines. One of the main uses of the fund is to support a program of advocates for victims. The advocates help victims to write statements to let the court know at the time of sentencing the impact that the crime had on them.

The impact statements have turned out to be an unexpected therapeutic tool for the victims. The fact that victims have someone with whom they can air their revenge fantasies helps to dissipate them.

Historically, restitution in kind or cash prevented ancient human societies from having unending cycles of violence. The practice disappeared about A.D. 1400 and was not reconsidered until a British reformer, Margery Fry, raised the issue in the 1950s. In 1972 England passed the Criminal Justice Act, which provided for restitution. The idea soon crossed the ocean.

In 1987 Massachusetts victims collected $10.3 million in court-ordered restitution, and each year district and municipal court mediators facilitate thousands of agreements, apologies and voluntary restitutions. To their amazement, the mediators have found that vengeful feelings mostly evaporate in the alternative judicial process.

Albie Davis, director of community mediation in Massachusetts District Courts, has said, "The amazing thing is to see people who hated each other shaking hands, walking out and maybe even offering each other a ride home."

The meeting with the victims place the responsibility directly on the offenders. Moreover, the victims have a chance to see the offenders as something other than monsters.

Judith Herman, a psychiatrist and director of the Victims of Violence program at Cambridge Hospital in Cambridge, Massachusetts, supports the concept of revenge as a learned response in cycles of violence, in which offenders attack victims, who then seek revenge and attack the offenders, and so forth in a self-perpetuating ritual. However, the notion of a self-perpetuating, physiologically inspired cycle of violence fails to explain the one-way character of violence inflicted on women by men. Moreover, the intergenerational cycle of violence works differently for men than for women. Men who are abused as children typically grow up to become abusers, but women who were abused as children typically grow up to be victims of abuse again.

Not all men who are abused as children grow up to commit violent crimes nor do all women grow up to be victims of abuse. Psychologist Mary Koss believes that sex offenders are differentiated not by their history of abuse but by their social attitudes—the rules by which they think society operates. Men who abuse women view the relationship between men and women as highly adversarial, along rigid "I have to show her who is boss" lines.

If violence is a learned response, then there is hope for treatment to stop an ongoing cycle and hope for prevention to keep a cycle from starting. Professionals working with violent offenders and their victims hope that eventually the idea of vengeance will become obsolete.

Justice, Equity and Revenge. The concept of revenge involves more than just the relationship between criminals and their victims. In her 1976 book *Wild Justice: The Evolution of Revenge,* Susan Jacoby seems to accept the idea that revenge is learned, but she views the urge for revenge as a worthy goal of societies. Although Jacoby and Tavris share some common goals, Jacoby's perspective is quite different from that of Tavris, who focuses on the self-perpetuating cycle of violence and believes that a learned desire for revenge is destructive. Jacoby directs her attention toward the needs of the victims and of the society in which the victims live. She proposes that vengeance, in the form of justice and equity, is a legitimate concern.

The relationship between justice and revenge has been a major preoccupation throughout the recorded history of the West. To strike a balance between the restraints that enable people to live with one another and the impulses to retaliate when harmed is perceived as one of the essential tasks of civilization. The attainment of a balance in a society depends on the confidence of the victimized that someone will act on their behalf against offenders.

As a standard of public morality, justice is typically portrayed as an ideal that has replaced the concept of an eye for an eye. As a standard in private life, forgiveness is portrayed as the best alternative to revenge. Forgiveness is viewed as the most noble aspect of human nature and revenge as the most base.

The proper role of retribution, both inside and outside the courtroom, has become a source of institutional and individual confusion. Jacoby writes, "We see the tragicomic spectacle of victims (it makes little difference whether they are survivors of death camps or muggings) who must deny any animus if their testimony is to be considered credible."

Modern codes of justice consider personal vengeance unacceptable, even uncivilized. Bearing witness, as the survivors of the Holocaust and the families of Chile's "disappeareds" have done, is socially permissible as long as the witnesses display a concern for abstract justice and do not exhibit personal animosity. The witness who insists on accountability and retribution is terrifying to listeners because he or she wants to be heard and expects something to be done. The witness wants material satisfaction, not abstract "justice."

A victim wants an assailant punished not only to deter future assaults but to repair a damaged sense of civic order and personal identity. In the United States and to a lesser extent in Europe, there is a widespread perception that the judicial system has diminished as a deterrent to crime.

The concept of "just deserts" evokes a deep uneasiness in the modern world. The notion of "forgive and forget," however unrealistic, is more comfortable. To champion forgiving and forgetting avoids reminders of the fragility of human order.

Despite its unacceptability for real victims, revenge is a favored theme in books and dramas. The powerful appeal of the revenge theme suggests a wide gap between private feelings about revenge and the public pretense that justice and vengeance have nothing to do with each other.

The gap suggests failures not only in the criminal justice system but in the social justice system as well: for instance, minor punishments given to criminals in traditional positions of authority, such as bank officers, compared with punishments meted out to garden-variety burglars. Legal justice is tied up with questions of social equity.

The relationship between forgiveness and revenge is central to the resolution of private and public conflicts. However, the concept of forgiveness and revenge as polar opposites omits two crucial elements in the moral equation: the willingness to acknowledge culpability on the part of the offender and the degree of the offender's remorse. "I did it and I'm glad" as an admission of responsibility does little to inspire forgiveness.

Without contrition on the part of the offender, forgiveness is just a condition that may be meaningful for the one who forgives but does nothing to restore civilized relations between the victim and the offender. The friend or lover who says "I'm sorry you feel hurt" is quite different from one who says "You have every right to be upset. I'm sorry."

When the injury is a public matter, another factor in the moral equation is the pressure exerted by society to restore some equilibrium between victim and offender. This equilibrium is experienced as justice, and justice in public affairs is comparable to fairness in private ones. Forgiveness becomes impossible if a basic sense

of fairness is assaulted repeatedly. Moreover, the act of forgiveness is meaningless unless both parties realize there is something to forgive.

Forgiveness is a personal and private act that cannot be used as a standard for the resolution of public conflicts. For example, a peace treaty says in effect: "Forget that you bombed our cities and gunned down our people, sign the peace treaty and all will be forgiven."

True forgiveness is not the aim of a peace treaty. The aim is to halt a process of vendetta and destruction, to establish a zone in which collective and individual safety is possible. Since they are not based on forgiveness, international agreements need not break down because they are based on "fake forgiveness." When they do break down, it is because there is no international body that has sufficient authority to punish those who break such agreements.

Jacoby writes:

> One returns, inevitably, to the delicate balance between retribution and compassion that is required to achieve a just and viable social order. Unrestrained retribution destroys the noblest human hopes along with human bodies; the absence of measured retribution leaves vindictive force in the hands of those who are unable or unwilling to restrain themselves.

right to bear arms: the Second Amendment

Much of the furor surrounding the issue of gun control hinges on two opposed views of the meaning of the Second Amendment to the Constitution, which guarantees citizens the right to keep and bear arms. Article II of the Bill of Rights states, "A well regulated militia being necessary to the security of a free state, the rights of the people to keep and bear arms shall not be infringed."

To be understood, the amendment needs to be looked at in the context of the times in which it was adopted. The first ten amendments—the Bill of Rights—were not drafted until two years after the Constitution. Most of the individual states already had their own bills of rights, but several might have refused to sign the Constitution had there not been an understanding that a national bill of rights would also be adopted.

The second amendment grew out of a deep-seated fear of a national standing army that could be used to repress citizens. The First Congress, which approved the second amendment, also limited the national army to 840 members. During the debate in Congress on the Bill of Rights, Elbridge Gerry argued that "Whenever governments mean to invade the rights and liberties of the people, they always attempt to destroy the militia in order to raise an army upon their ruins.'' Thus state militias were viewed as a necessity to protect the states.

Many of the 3.5 million people who lived in the 13 colonies used their firearms to shoot wild game for food and to protect themselves against marauders. Every able-bodied male was expected to fight to protect his state if called upon and to bring his gun with him. When the Bill of Rights was ratified, citizens accepted the idea that each state would maintain its own military establishment.

In the two centuries that have elapsed since ratification of the Bill of Rights, a variety of wars have resulted in the establishment of a standing national army, one held firmly in check by safeguards. The remnants of state militias remain in the form of state National Guards. The need for citizens to have arms in order to be part of a militia is past.

In a January 14, 1990 *Parade Magazine* article entitled ''The Right to Bear Arms,'' former Chief Justice Warren Burger argued against the position that Americans have a right to bear arms. He said:

Americans . . . have a right to defend their homes, and we need not challenge that. Nor does anyone seriously question that the Constitution protects the right of hunters to own and keep sporting guns for hunting game any more than anyone would challenge the right to own and keep fishing rods and other equipment for fishing—or to own automobiles. To ''keep and bear arms'' for hunting today is essentially a recreational activity and not an imperative of survival, as it was 200 years ago. ''Saturday night specials'' and machine guns are not recreational weapons and surely are as much in need of regulation as motor vehicles . . . The Constitution does not mention automobiles or motorboats, but the right to keep and own an automobile is beyond question; equally beyond question is the powers of the state to regulate the purchase or the transfer of such a vehicle and the right to license the vehicle and the driver with reasonable standards. In some places, even a bicycle must be registered, as must some household dogs.

Opponents of gun control stress the second half of the Second Amendment, the right to bear arms. Gun control advocates stress the first half of the amendment, which indicated that the framers of the Constitution intended the right to bear arms to ensure the maintenance of organized militias, a need no longer pressing.

A different view on the two sides was proposed in the December 1989 issue of the *Yale Law Review,* by Sanford Levinson, a professor who described himself as a member of the American Civil Liberties Union (ACLU) and an advocate of gun control. Levinson argued that the Second Amendment offered neither the gun control advocates nor their opponents the refuge they sought.

The gun lobby, the National Rifle Association (NRA), argues that there should be no controls. However, there are times when even the right to free speech and the right to be safe from having one's home broken into without a warrant can be abridged. The right to bear arms is no exception.

The gun control advocates maintain that the Second Amendment was intended to apply to militias, not to individuals. However, at the time the Bill of Rights was framed, the militia was virtually synonymous with the idea of armed independent yeomen. The militia was each and every (male) citizen.

Levinson contended that many of his fellow liberals were inconsistent in their perspective on the constitutional right to bear arms. While they were willing to bear the social costs of free speech—speech insulting to minorities—and protection of the rights of criminal defendants—failure to convict even when guilty—they were unwilling to accept the social costs of the right to bear arms.

In the same issue of the *Yale Law Review* that contained Levinson's paper, feminist legal scholar Wendy Brown of the University of California, Santa Cruz, offered what for her were compelling reasons to oppose the right to bear arms. She proposed that the ''right'' to bear arms would typically go to the empowered members of society—the ''socially male''—and be used against the weak—women and minorities.

In an interview with the *New York Times,* Laurence Tribe, professor of constitutional law at Harvard University, argued that the courts have already decided against a universal right to bear arms. In his opinion, even if such a right existed, it would not preclude reasonable regulations. The Constitution protects ownership of private property, such as a car, yet it permits regulation in the form of speed laws.

Supporters of gun control contend that people using guns are responsible for most murders in the United States annually. Moreover, they note, guns kept for self-protection often end up being used by accident or intentionally against family members or friends.

Levinson argues that police departments have demonstrated an incapacity to protect citizens from criminals. Gun control would prevent innocent citizens from protecting themselves against criminals, who would get guns despite the law.

Ultimately, in Levinson's opinion, society will have to decide the issue of gun control on practical as well as on constitutional grounds. In his opinion, the decision on how society should regulate guns must go beyond constitutional interpretation.

(See also ASSAULT WEAPONS; CHILDREN AND YOUTHS WITH GUNS; GUN CONTROL: ADVOCATES; GUN CONTROL: OPPONENTS; GUN-FREE SCHOOL ZONES BILL; GUN OWNERSHIP.)

right to privacy See BILL OF RIGHTS: PROTECTION AGAINST GOVERNMENT TYRANNY.

riots In the sociological study of group behavior, mobs and riots are referred to as "acting crowds." In becoming active, a crowd gets caught up in an emotional atmosphere of hostility against an object. Crowd members have an unambiguous image of "we" versus "they." Rumor plays a significant role in the crowd by defining the situation and in encouraging the crowd to take action.

Ever since the Boston Tea Party, group violence has been a recurring theme in America's political and social history. To mention just a few incidents among many: the Revolution; the Whiskey Rebellion; skirmishes between supporters and opponents of slavery preceding the Civil War; the Ku Klux Klan's campaign of terrorism during Reconstruction; and violence by "Native Americans" against European Catholics, Jewish immigrants and Asians.

From the Civil War until the 1930s, labor strife in the United States often resulted in rioting. Weak labor organizations and their members were frequently pitted against superior armed forces and legal power wielded by employers. Frequently, confrontations resulted in violent actions, injuries and death—largely of strikers—and imprisonment for strike leaders.

Since World War I, the largest and most destructive riots in the United States have involved race: Chicago, 1919; Detroit, 1943; Rochester and Harlem, 1964; Watts, 1965; Detroit and Newark, 1967; Miami, 1982; Los Angeles, 1992.

After the fact, depending on the political perspective of the speaker, an acting crowd may be called a riot or a protest. In an effort to be neutral, speakers often call it a civil disturbance or civil disorder.

Between January and September 1967, 164 civil disturbances were recorded in which residents of black urban neighborhoods attacked white-owned businesses and harassed law enforcement officials. The police and the National Guard, who in Detroit and Newark in 1967 were mostly responsible for the 68 deaths and 1,049 injuries, described the incidents as riots. Many of the participants interviewed later described their behavior as protests, citing a host of grievances.

Aggression on the part of an undergroup, such as those living in inner-city communities, interpreted by those in power as riots rather than as protests is typically characterized as undemocratic, presumptuous and an explosion of impatience rather than the end product of a gathering storm.

America's sporadic group violence was explained partially by the Commission on the Causes and Prevention of Violence, which said:

America has always been a nation of rapid social change. We have proclaimed ourselves a modern promised land, and have brought millions of restless immigrants to our shores to partake in its fulfillment. Persistent demands by these groups . . . and resistance to those demands by other groups, have accounted for most of the offensive and defensive group violence that marks our history . . . Although we have an open political and social system, more dedicated than most to the dream of individual and group advancement, the majority are sometimes unwilling to hear or redress the just grievances of particular minorities until violent advocacy or repression call them to the forefront of our attention . . . And for all our rhetoric to the contrary, we have never been a fully law-abiding nation . . . Lack of respect for the law and at least tacit support for violence in one's own interest have helped to make the United States, in the past as at present, somewhat more tumultuous than we would like it to be.

Militant crowd political action, followed by forceful official reaction, is not peculiarly American. Europe has a long history of such political and social action. As in America, such activities have usually been issue-oriented and have taken place after official channels for handling conflict have been closed.

Official interpretations of protests persist long after the fact. Myths are still perpetuated about the 19th-century so-called Luddite movement in England, which arose during a severe economic depression. Efforts to relieve poverty brought about by the Industrial Revolution coexisted with an absolute belief in an employers' right to cut labor costs and maximize profits—a belief that sounds familiar in the United States in the late 20th century. Poverty-stricken workers were enjoined to be patient. After negotiations and peaceful protest had failed, the Luddites destroyed machinery in order to force concessions by manufacturers.

Officials and newspapers of the day called them "ignorant rabble" and "criminal mobs" who wanted to prevent progress. In fact, the Luddites enjoyed widespread popular support and were well organized and selective in their targets and the means they used against them.

European labor unions have been more associated with political parties of the left than have those in the United States. Protests have been about class inequality: working class against middle class; unpropertied versus propertied; the poor against the rich. Political street crowds have been standard fare in European politics since the French Revolution.

Political street crowds marching, shouting slogans and occasionally resorting to violence are also common in Asia, the Middle East and Latin America. They have often been a major factor in revolutionary movements. Youth, particularly university students, have tended to play a significant role in such demonstrations. American university students were active during protests in the 1960s and early 1970s.

Active Crowds in the United States in the 1960s. An analysis by the National Commission on the Causes and Prevention of Violence, published in 1983 by Chelsea House as *Violence in America,* volumes 1–16, reported that over the five-year period from mid-1963 to mid-1968, protests or counterprotests and ghetto riots involved more than 2 million persons. Civil rights demonstrations brought together 1.1 million, anti-Vietnam-War demonstrations 680,000 and ghetto riots 200,000.

Most casualties, including 191 deaths, took place during the ghetto riots. Another estimated 23 deaths mostly involved white actions taken against blacks and civil rights workers. Although group violence in the 1960s was at a higher level than in the decades immediately preceding, the numbers of casualties per 100,000 population did not match that reached during earlier decades of American history.

Official interpretations during the 1960s tended to focus on civil disturbances as irrational violence in which many were led by a few. An alternative interpretation of the behavior as political protests would have acknowledged some rationality to the incidents and raised the possibility of a need for change in the structure or distribution of power in society.

In an effort to understand the so-called race riots of the 1960s, the National Advisory Commission on Civil Disorders undertook a vast study. Its comprehensive findings (published by Bantam in 1968 under the title *Report*) described the commission's analysis of events in 23 cities, ten of which had suffered serious disturbances in 1967.

The commission found that there was no "typical" disorder. Riots did not always spring up from a single precipitating incident and the rioters were not all "hoodlums," criminals or the least educated. Although they tended to be high school dropouts, they were for the most part more knowledgeable than the average. They were young men proud to be black and hostile toward whites and middle-class blacks.

In most disorders, there were blacks who tried to prevent the disorder or cool it off. Negotiations were held between militant blacks and civic authorities in almost all the disorders, during which underlying grievances were discussed. The commission was unable to confirm any preconceived popular or even social-scientific pattern to the disorders, but from the large body of data collected the commission felt that it had identified a "chain." The chain's links were composed of "discrimination, prejudice, conditions of disadvantage, intense and pervasive grievances, and a series of tension-heightening incidents culminating in the eruption of disorder at the hands of youthful, politically aware activists."

Often the final incident that set off a disturbance was trivial, but it was the last in a series of exacerbating incidents. For example, in Newark during 1967, the incidents included the arrest of 15 blacks for picketing a grocery store, an unsuccessful effort by blacks to oppose the use of 150 acres in their neighborhood for a medical-dental center, an unsuccessful effort to get a black appointed as secretary of the Board of Education and resentment at the participation of Newark police officers in an East Orange, New Jersey racial incident.

On July 12, following a traffic accident in which a black taxi driver was injured, a crowd gathered outside the precinct police station. Later in the evening, as the crowd continued to grow, Molotov cocktails were thrown. The police dispersed the crowd. Window-breaking and looting followed, setting off one of America's most destructive riots.

The commission attributed the disorders to both long- and short-run factors. The long-range factors or "basic causes" were basically three: pervasive discrimination and segregation; black migration into and white exodus out of urban centers; the development of black ghettoes.

The short-range or "immediate" factors were unfulfilled expectations raised by judicial and legislative victories of the civil rights movement and a "legitimation of violence" by white state and local officials who had openly defied the law by resisting desegregation. A sense of powerlessness together with the preaching of violence by some black militants contributed to a feeling among inner-city residents that there was no way to change the system except through violence.

A riot in August 1965 in a Los Angeles neighborhood known as Watts matched the long-range and the short-range characteristics described by the commission. Watts was isolated from the rest of Los Angeles by the racial homogeneity of its population, by a lack of adequate public transportation and by poverty. Watts residents believed that the city administration and the police were racist. The police believed that Watts' black community was volatile.

On August 11, 1965 a crowd of Watts residents gathered to witness an arrest. Bystanders openly doubted whether the arrest was lawful. The police were slow in removing the prisoner from the scene and rumors spread that a police officer had kicked a pregnant woman. Looting and destruction of property followed and seemed to target sources of grievance. The property of black residents and black businesses was avoided.

Watts' rioters did not fit widely cherished stereotypes. Only 11% of those arrested had a criminal record; 58% were older than 25; 75% had lived in Los Angeles for more than five years; and as a group they had a median level of education comparable to the general population of Los Angeles, but tended to be poorer.

Watts Revisited. In 1992, more than a quarter of a century later, conditions of isolation and extreme poverty in south-central Los Angeles, which includes Watts, replicated long-term factors implicated in the 1965 riot. Poverty had in fact worsened. During the intervening years, major companies such as Bethlehem Steel, Goodyear, Firestone and others had closed down local operations. In 1991 alone almost 200,000 jobs were lost.

Other factors also had changed. South-central Los Angeles had become multiracial, and it suffered from the presence of violent gangs that were making vast sums of money from drug trade.

Unlike many earlier riots, the short-term spark that set off the civil disorder on Wednesday, April 29, 1992 was not a trivial incident and the circumstances were known to the rest of the nation. The story began at about midnight on March 3, 1991. An unemployed African-American construction worker named Rodney King, who was drunk, led police officers on a high-speed car chase. When the police caught up with King, he refused to get out of his car, although his two companions did so promptly.

Officers dragged King from the car and beat him repeatedly with batons. They later justified the beating on grounds that they mistakenly thought he was on PCP, a hallucinogenic drug known to make users behave violently, an impression that proved to be unfounded.

The beating of King by the police was videotaped by a man sitting on his apartment balcony overlooking the highway. He put his tape into the hands of a local TV station whose broadcast was picked up by other stations and aired across the nation.

Four officers were charged with the King beating and brought to trial. The four were acquitted of assault, and the mostly white suburban jury could not agree about a charge of excessive force against one of them. He was to be tried again later. Across the nation, the verdict shocked almost everyone who had seen the tape, in particular, residents of south-central Los Angeles.

Within a few hours after the verdict was handed down, violence broke out at the intersection of Florence Boulevard and Normandie Avenue and spread to Lake View Terrace, where Rodney King had been apprehended 14 months earlier. The rioters then moved on to headquarters of the Foothill Division of the Los Angeles Police Department (LAPD), the division to which three of the officers were assigned. The LAPD seemed surprised by the violent response.

In civil disorders, police face a dilemma. If they act quickly, they may later be accused of escalating the violence. If they respond too slowly, they may later be accused of abdicating control and letting the violence get out of hand.

LAPD may have chosen not to be accused of overreacting. Hours passed before the police entered many parts of the 46-square-mile south-central area of Los Angeles where stores were being looted and motorists were being dragged from their cars and beaten.

As late as 11 P.M. Wednesday night, at a time when at least two dozen fires were blazing out of control, Police Chief Daryl Gates, a target of much hostility among south-central residents, resisted the call of black Mayor Tom Bradley for National Guard assistance. The first contingent of military police did not arrive until Thursday afternoon.

The Los Angeles Fire Department had to let many fires burn unattended because there were not enough police officers to guard firefighters against snipers. By the following afternoon, police and firefighters were stretched to their limits. Residents, some enjoying the excitement and others saddened or appalled, milled about in the glass-strewn streets. The violence had spread well outside the south-central area, to Hollywood, the San Fernando Valley and Long Beach.

Although many Watts residents locked themselves and their children indoors and worried about being burned out of their homes or jobs, a number of ordinary citizens, in the absence of the police, went to the rescue of victims of the violence. Perhaps the most dramatic rescue was that of a white truck driver on his way to deliver sand to a cement plant. He was stopped, pulled from his truck and beaten. Barely conscious, he dragged himself back into his 18-wheel truck, but his eyes were too swollen for him to see. Two black men and two black women, all strangers, risked their lives to help him inch his massive truck away from the scene. They took him to a hospital, where he underwent four hours of brain surgery.

Unlike the riots in 1967, many black-owned stores were not spared, despite signs in the window identifying them. Korean-owned stores were a particular target, a reflection of tense relations between the area's blacks and Koreans.

Some of the looters seemed to enjoy the presence of circling helicopters carrying television cameras, but they objected to the presence of still photographers, several of whom were beaten as a consequence. The television tapes showed many looters, some parents accompanied by children, carrying great quantities of goods, including food, clothes, cameras, appliances and televisions. Unfortunately, gun and ammunition shops were also among those looted.

By midnight Thursday fires were breaking out in scattered areas all across Los Angeles. On Friday when the violence had largely abated, President Bush federalized National Guard troops and dispatched 4,500 to the area. In this respect, the 1992 Watts riot differed from ghetto riots of the 1960s, in which the National Guard units were called only when the situation seemed to be completely out of control and when their presence generally seemed to make matters worse.

An impressive call for peace and calm came from Rodney King who appeared on TV and said in a quavering voice, "Can't we get along? Can we stop making it horrible for the older people and the kids? It's just

not right. It's not going to change anything. We'll all get justice."

When the 48 hours of violence were over, 58 people were dead, 2,383 had been injured and $735 million in property damage had been sustained.

For several days, radio talk shows around the nation discussed the acquittal. The majority of the callers, both white and black, expressed shock and sadness at the exoneration of the officers. William Webster, former director of both the Federal Bureau of Investigation (FBI) and the Central Intelligence Agency (CIA), was appointed to head an inquiry into the preparation and activities of the 8,300-member LAPD, both before and after the violence broke out.

One of the surprising outcomes of the disorder was a truce among the city's two most deadly gangs, the Crips and the Bloods, both formed in 1968 and which between them have about 1,000 affiliated gangs. The truce made it possible for one gang member to visit relatives he had not seen for 20 years because they live in a rival gang neighborhood. Rumors circulated that the gangs had called a truce in order to turn their combined strength against their mutual foe, the LAPD.

Community social workers and police specialists on gang crime were skeptical of any organized behavior on the part of the gangs against the police, mainly because their loose structure makes it difficult for them to reach an agreement. Moreover, peace efforts had been underway with the gangs for months before the acquittal.

Gang experts denied that the gangs had played a major role in the rioting, pointing out that those who took to the streets were a mosaic of black, white and Hispanic people, including residents with 9-to-5 jobs.

The Aftermath. In mid-May the Reverend Jesse Jackson appeared before a congressional committee, where he accused the media of making the crowds in the street appear greater than they were. He said the number of individuals actually in the streets could not possibly have started the 5,000 fires that were ultimately set. In his opinion, many Los Angeles store owners were following examples of greed they had recently learned from corporate criminals and had set fire to their businesses to collect the insurance.

Jackson's negative opinion about television coverage of the riots was echoed in the May 11, 1992 issue of *Time* by Richard Schickel, who wrote:

> Television's mindless, endless search for the dramatic image—particularly on the worst night—created the impression that the entire city was about to fall into anarchy and go up

in flames. What was needed was a geography lesson showing that rioting was confined to a relatively small portion of a vast metropolis and the violent incidents outside that area were random.

Jackson came to the congressional committee armed with suggestions about how to rebuild deteriorating inner cities. He proposed that investment of one tenth of the nation's trillion-dollar pension fund could be used to set up development banks in America's inner cities. Such banks could offer loans for building and rebuilding of homes and businesses. He repeated his proposal at a massive rally in Washington, D.C. on May 16, 1992 held by the U.S. Conference of Mayors on behalf of America's cities.

The U.S. Justice Department promised to reopen an investigation of whether the four LAPD officers had violated Rodney King's civil rights. Although federal attorneys file several dozen brutality cases each year, only a few follow state acquittals. If the state prosecutors cannot get a conviction, federal attorneys are not likely to do better. Legal experts were skeptical that a federal suit in the King case could be won. They were wrong. Two of the officers were convicted. Juries in general are reluctant to convict police officers. Prosecutors had to prove that the police officers had intended to harm King.

Many middle-class African-Americans, who no longer live in the inner cities, were stunned by the 1992 civil disorder in Los Angeles. The violence may have been as much about class as about race: the have-nots versus the haves. But, as in many other riots, most of the damage was done to the residents' own neighborhoods rather than to more affluent areas.

One factor distinguished the Los Angeles riot of 1992 from earlier riots. The short-range injustice that precipitated the riot was clearly understood by many who lived outside the neighborhood. That understanding was evidenced by a large number of people who poured into the neighborhood to help with the cleanup, once the violence had subsided. Whether that understanding will have an effect on the long-range factors that brought on the disorder may not be evident for years. The riot seemed to impress the gangs. Gang leaders said that it did not make sense to be killing each other.

runaways See STREET CHILDREN.

rule of law See DEFENSE COUNSEL FOR INDIGENTS: DEVELOPMENT OF THE CONCEPT.

S

sanctuary movement The sanctuary movement was founded in Tucson, Arizona in 1982 by retired rancher Jim Corbett, a Quaker, and John Fife, a Presbyterian minister. In time 14 of Tucson's congregations participated. The movement spread until it included other churches and synagogues in several states as well as two cities, Cambridge, Massachusetts and Berkeley, California, a handful of university groups and for a brief time the state of New Mexico.

The impetus for the movement was the U.S. policy of refusing asylum to most Central American refugees. For example, during the period from June 1983 to September 1986, of 750,000 Salvadoran refugees who fled to the United States, only 528, or 2.6%, were granted political asylum.

Sanctuary leaders claimed that they were upholding the spirit of the U.S. refugee policy as it was restructured by Congress in 1980 to emphasize humanitarian considerations. Most sanctuary leaders were clergy or lay members of churches whose doctrines include an obligation to help those in need. They insisted that they helped oppressed people to escape from tyranny. The refugees' oppressors, in some cases governments, in others rebel forces, often were sponsored and aided by the United States government.

The U.S. government claimed that the sanctuary movement workers were breaking the law. The government's position was that those seeking asylum were not refugees but "economic migrants," who were simply trying to improve their standard of living. The designation of refugees as economic migrants is one of a number of ploys used by governments to turn away immigrants they would prefer not to keep.

Critics charged that the implementation of U.S. refugee policy aided those fleeing from Communist governments and turned back those fleeing from governments with which the United States had friendly relations. They supported their charges by pointing to the U.S. record of granting asylum. Of the 125,000 refugees admitted in fiscal year 1990, more than 90% were refugees from Communist countries. The minuscule quotas allotted to Africa and Latin America went mainly to exiles from leftist regimes in Ethiopia and Cuba. From 1981 through 1988, 103,355 Cuban immigrants were admitted as permanent residents under Refugee Acts. During the same period, 2,823 from Nicaragua and 940 from El Salvador were admitted.

Civil war erupted in El Salvador in 1980, when a small Marxist insurgency pitted itself against a corrupt military government allied with wealthy coffee-growers. With scant results to show for their efforts, during the 1980s, the Reagan administration channeled more than $1 billion to aid the El Salvador government, over the objections of the Democratic U.S. Congress. More than 60,000 civilians were killed in El Salvador between 1980 and 1989 by either government soldiers or rebels.

In January 1992, under heavy pressure from the U.S. government and the United Nations (UN), Salvadoran military officials reluctantly signed a peace pact with the rebels. The cease-fire went into effect February 1, 1992, when the army and the estimated 8,000 rebels began a staggered process of demobilization. The army agreed to disband five antisubversive battalions known for their brutality and to create a civilian police force with rebel participation.

Most observers expected clashes in El Salvador similar to those in neighboring Nicaragua, where, during 1991, the UN had supervised the demobilization process that followed the end of the war between the leftist Sandinista government and the U.S.-backed rebels known as the Contras. Expectations for Salvadoran violence were fulfilled.

In the two weeks following the Salvadoran peace agreement, right-wing anti-Communist groups issued death threats against church and labor organizations and bombed the empty cars of two journalists. In March 1992 a Jesuit priest was expelled for trying to prevent the Salvadoran National Police from tearing down the homes of peasant farmers to force them off a ranch they had occupied for some time.

The bias of U.S. asylum policy that failed to protect refugees from governments with which the United States had ties is revealed by the treatment of four applicants who won asylum in 1989. Three Nicaraguan Contra leaders were approved immediately. The fourth refugee, a Guatemalan man, had struggled for five years before he convinced the Justice Department that he had a legitimate fear of persecution if he were to be returned to Guatemala, where rightist government soldiers had killed his father and leftist guerrillas had killed his mother.

Prosecution of Sanctuary Workers. The membership of an estimated 435 U.S. churches and synagogues participated in helping illegal aliens from Central America to reach the United States, where they provided them with shelter and assisted them in obtaining legal status. Some of the sanctuary workers went to prison.

In 1984 Stacey Merkt, a volunteer at a shelter for Central American refugees in San Benito, Texas, was convicted and sentenced to 179 days in jail. When she began serving her sentence in January 1987, Amnesty International adopted her as a prisoner of conscience, which meant that the organization began a campaign to win her freedom. In April 1987 she was released to serve the remainder of her sentence under house arrest.

From the beginning, the participants in the Sanctuary Movement made no secret of their intent. They conducted open meetings and gave interviews to the media.

Although the ancient principle of sanctuary in churches and synagogues has little basis in modern law, government agents realized that they risked public outrage if they broke into churches to drag refugees away. Nevertheless, the U.S. Immigration and Naturalization Service (INS) sent undercover agents and informers to meetings to gather evidence. One informant had made a living smuggling aliens into Florida. When he was caught, the government made a deal with him to pose as a sanctuary movement volunteer.

On the basis of evidence gathered, the government brought 11 sanctuary workers to trial in October 1985 on 67 felony counts, each carrying a possible five-year prison sentence. The workers' strongest defense was to try to persuade the jury that international law, the Refugee Act of 1980 and the desperate plight of those trying to escape from Central America permitted them to help the refugees.

Although the motives of defendants are allowed in other kinds of felony trials, the U.S. District Court Judge Earl Carroll, known for harsh sentences, ruled that the defendants could not base their case on religious beliefs and referred to their trial as a "simple smuggling case." In what defense attorneys assumed was a move to lessen the chances that jurors would hear any comment about the movement's motives, the prosecution elected to forgo the use of about 100 hours of taped movement meetings.

Eight sanctuary workers were convicted. Following the trial, one juror reported that he and some other jurors were sympathetic to the defendants, but in the absence of a defense they thought they had to follow the law and their instructions.

In a subsequent trial in July 1988 of a Lutheran minister and a journalist/poet for smuggling two pregnant Salvadoran women across the Rio Grande in 1986, U.S. District Court Judge John Conway permitted inclusion of evidence about conditions in El Salvador and about a proclamation by Governor Toney Anaya that New Mexico was a sanctuary state. The defendants were acquitted.

In April 1989 the 9th U.S. Circuit Court of Appeals upheld the convictions of the eight Arizona sanctuary movement workers in a 3-to-0 decision. The court held that the sanctuary movement workers were not entitled to present evidence of their belief that immigrants are entitled to legal refugee status, which the court said would have "essentially put Reagan administration foreign policy on trial."

Following the 1986 convictions of the eight workers, the Tucson Southside Presbyterian Church, the Alzona Evangelical Lutheran Church, the Camelback United Presbyterian Church in Phoenix and the national organizations of the Presbyterian and Lutheran churches filed suit against the government, charging that the undercover investigation violated their First Amendment right to freedom of religion.

The suit was heard in U.S. District Court in San Francisco in December 1990. Judge Roger Strand ruled that the government does not have "unfettered discretion to infiltrate religious gatherings for criminal investigations." The government must have solid grounds for sending agents into religious gatherings.

A class-action suit brought by the American Baptist Churches against U.S. Attorney General Dick Thornburgh was also decided in U.S. District Court in San Francisco in December 1990. The suit challenged the routine INS denial of political asylum based on foreign policy decisions. In a landmark settlement, the INS agreed to stop the deportation of Salvadoran and Guatemalan refugees. The settlement required the readjudication of 150,000 denials and was expected to affect 500,000 Salvadoran and Guatemalan refugees in the United States.

INS Treatment of Haitians. For more than three decades, Haitian citizens have been victims of violence inflicted by their government or their military. The brutal dictatorship of the Duvaliers, "Papa Doc" and his son "Baby Doc," which lasted from 1957 to 1986, prompted many Haitians over the years to flee. Although the horrors of the Duvaliers' regime were well known, the United States Coast Guard, under orders, frequently turned back boatloads of Haitians intent on seeking asylum.

On September 30, 1991 a military coup ousted Haiti's first democratically elected president, Father Jean-Bertrand Aristide. Following the coup, 200 people were killed in a Port-au-Prince slum because they were supporters of Aristide. Two North American priests reported that the level of violence in the weeks and months after Aristide fled was greater than it had been during the worst years of the Duvaliers.

When the archdiocesan director of Catholic Charities in Boston met with Haitian refugees in Boston, many showed him their scars inflicted by "sectional chiefs," who would appear without warning in search of members of neighborhood improvement groups that had sprung up during the regime of Aristide. The refugees told of watching relatives garroted and dragged through their villages.

In February 1992 Florida's Catholic bishops urged the U.S. government to accept the many Haitian refugees who had fled the most recent violence. Most of the refugees were being housed temporarily at the U.S. naval base at Guantanamo Bay, Cuba.

Nevertheless, the Supreme Court twice rejected emergency requests by human rights lawyers to halt the repatriation of Haitians on the grounds that they would suffer irreparable harm and possible death if they were sent back. The deportations continued.

A Washington-sponsored peace accord signed in late February 1992 to end the Haitian crisis contained no more than vague language about the conditions necessary to permit the return of the exiled president. Despite the peace accord, a state of siege remained in Haiti. An American nun described conditions in the March 20, 1992 issue of *The Pilot:* "Families are telling their children to speak to no one. Of course the reason is the nightly cruising of the military through the neighborhoods, firing automatic weapons into the air."

The Impact of Immigration. Efforts by Americans like the participants in the sanctuary movement to rescue other refugees may be even more difficult in the future. Hostility toward immigrants legal or illegal appeared to increase in the early 1990s. The hostility seemed to be a response to the enormous number of immigrants who had come to the United States in the 1980s.

When the nation's largest wave of immigrants brought 8.8 million newcomers between 1900 and 1910, 90% of them were white Europeans. But when the second largest wave of immigrants, in the 1980s, brought more than 7.3 million immigrants; 80% of them came from Asia, Latin America and the Caribbean. Some white Americans fear that they will become a minority.

During his campaign to win the Republican nomination for president in 1992, Patrick Buchanan blamed many of the nation's problems on overlenient U.S. immigration policies. California governor Pete Wilson, playing on fears that the state had become a magnet for destitute immigrants, drafted and put on the ballot the "Taxpayer's Protection Act," which drastically cut benefits for new arrivals and other welfare recipients. Two thirds of the state's voters endorsed a three-year residency requirement for welfare recipients.

David Rosenberg, a former Massachusetts immigration official, believes the fears of people such as Buchanan and Wilson are misguided. During an interview for a February 23, 1992 *Boston Globe* article entitled "Open Doors: Closing Minds," he claimed that the drawbacks of immigration are more than overcome by its advantages. A vast body of research shows that there is little direct competition for jobs between new immigrants and native-born Americans. Yet the perception of competition posed by legal immigrants, illegal aliens and refugees is likely to keep the doors closed to those in desperate need of asylum.

satanic cult rituals   Data about satanic-related crimes are difficult to collect because by its nature "satanism" is secretive. Nevertheless, local and state police are becoming increasingly concerned about the effect satanic rituals can have on the behavior of people in their jurisdictions, particularly juveniles.

Sean Richard Sellers, a juvenile on death row in May 1991, practiced satanic rituals daily in the months prior to murdering his parents at the age of 16. He kept vials of blood in the refrigerator, some of which he drank, and he took drugs. During his childhood, Sean was humiliated and chastised by his uncle and stepfather for not participating in animal mutilation.

Concern over satanic cult sacrifices has led many police departments over the last decade to hold seminars and conferences, where they exchange data about satanism-related crimes. Such data is not otherwise available since routine local, state and federal crime statistics fail to reveal details of satanic rituals in connection with violent crimes.

Lieutenant Richard Kelly, now with Interpol and formerly director of the Massachusetts State Police Gang Squad, asserts that many officers suspect that some missing children may have become victims in satanic ritual sacrifices. Although the number of cults may be small, their influence seems to loom large among teenagers, and Kelly believes that police departments must make an effort to learn more about them.

Like most police officers who specialize in cults and satanic worship, Thomas Wedge, a former Ohio police officer, expert on satanism and the author of *Satan Hunters,* is careful to point out that satanism qualifies as a legitimate religion. It therefore enjoys the protections afforded more traditional religions, so long as no laws are broken. The estimated membership of the Church of Satan in the United States is about 20,000.

Many departments have assigned one or more of their force to specialize in cult crime. A Massachusetts state police cult specialist has a favorite story about charismatic cult leaders. He traveled to California to pick up an extradited prisoner who was an avid follower of satanic teaching. As the trooper and a colleague drove the prisoner out of town, he begged them to drive by the home of Anton LaVey, the founder of the Church of Satan, on the chance that the prisoner might catch a glimpse of the leader. They found LaVey watering his lawn. He stopped to chat with them. LaVey struck the troopers as gracious and they could glimpse the attraction he held for his following.

LaVey's two paperback books, *The Satanic Bible* (1969) and *The Satanic Ritual* (1972), provide the faithful with written dogma and liturgy, including rituals, rites, holy days and the nine "statements" of the devil. They also include chapters on the black mass and human sacrifice. The *Satanic Bible* offers a variety of invocations to the conjuration of lust, compassion and destruction.

The religion is based on the premise "the strong shall inherit the earth." Satanic teaching revolves around worship of the trinity of the devil: Lucifer, Satan and the Devil. Each church member is encouraged to "actualize" his or her own potential through magic, spells, rituals and incantations to the demonic trinity.

As with any religion, some members are more involved than others. There are three levels of participation. One resembles religious affiliation with other more traditional churches: regular attendance at church functions, observance of feast days and support through contributions. Children are born into the affiliation. Members may move from one satanic "denomination" to another. Membership requires only the completion of an application and the payment of a fee.

A more intense involvement might lead to affiliation with a satanic cult, with a charismatic leader, a less sophisticated system of beliefs and less formal ritual. The activity and longevity of a cult depends on the personal magnetism of the leader.

Serial killers Henry Lucas and Ottis Toole both admitted membership in devil cults. Lucas claimed that he was involved in the kidnapping of small children and was paid several thousand dollars to deliver them for human sacrifices.

Finally, a satanist might set himself up as an authority and worship the devil as he sees fit. If such a person forms a group, it is likely to have only a few members. Knowledge of formal liturgy and ritual practices will be limited. The group may frequently perform animal sacrifice, using mostly small dogs and cats.

Satanists believe there is "free agency" to choose between good and evil. People can choose to be good and after death go to heaven. If they choose evil, they will go to hell. Hell is like the heaven envisioned by Christians, where all wishes are granted and lusts satisfied. Faithful satanists will not only be granted all their wishes in hell, their servants will be Christians and fallen satanists.

Satanists believe in reincarnation, provided they have done what Lucifer, Satan and the Devil command. Their social class will never be lower than it was in a previous life.

Human sacrifice takes two forms, burning or blood. The burning sacrifice is considered to be a killing of vengeance or destruction, reserved for those who have done something against the coven or church and thus "deserve" to be killed. A blood sacrifice is reserved for those whose soul will be relinquished to Lucifer. The "martyred" soul will someday be reincarnated in the wasteland of the earth and later occupy a revered place in hell.

In the opinion of Ronald Holmes, who wrote *Profiling Violent Crimes* (1989), police officers who investigate satanic killings are apt to discover that the meticulous members of an organized satanic cult leave much less evidence than does a self-styled authority. Although many police officers view satanic practices as just another aberration with which they must deal, those who specialize in satanic cult behavior view the rituals as a particular threat to small children and animals.

(See also CULTS; MASS MURDERERS; SERIAL KILLERS; SOCIO-PATHS.)

search and seizure See BILL OF RIGHTS: PROTECTION AGAINST GOVERNMENT TYRANNY.

self-defense for women See MODEL MUGGING.

self-help groups Self-help groups are made up of people who feel a need for social support to accomplish a task, control an obsessive behavior or get through a particularly trying time. For example, parents of adolescent drug abusers often turn to self-help groups—also known as support groups—to share experiences and advice and avoid discouragement. Narcotics Anonymous helps drug addicts to share the burden of staying clean by helping and encouraging each other. Parents of Murdered Children was started by a couple whose daughter was murdered, to help them and other such families to overcome their grief.

Such groups do not do research. Their task is to help people manage their problems. There is therefore not much except anecdotal evidence to determine their rates of success.

Most mental health professionals agree that the most effective self-help organization is Alcoholics Anonymous (AA), founded in 1935. Less well-known is Narcotics Anonymous, founded in 1953, and other similar substance abuse self-help groups. Most are based on the model pioneered by AA, which uses a 12-step program.

The most basic tenet of AA is that one is an alcoholic (or drug user) and powerless over alcohol (or drugs) and that only a power greater than oneself can help. The primary task of the member is to maintain sobriety and help others to achieve it. Staying sober or clean is based on a 24-hour program, that is, staying sober or clean for one day at a time (the origin of that familiar phrase) and never promising to swear off the substance they abuse for the future or for life.

(See also ALCOHOL DEPENDENCE; DRUG ABUSE AND TRADE: PREVENTION AND EDUCATION.)

self-mutilation Based on reports from prisons, psychiatric hospitals and psychiatric wards in general hospitals, it is estimated that self-mutilation (self-inflicted wounds) is committed by 750 of every 100,000 people in the general population. This exceeds the estimates for suicide and attempted suicide. Self-mutilation is found in every nation and every social class.

In a March/April 1989 *The Sciences* article, "Little Murders," Armando Favazza, associate chairman of psychiatry at the University of Missouri in Columbia and the author of *Bodies Under Siege: Self-Mutilation in Culture and Psychiatry* (1992), pointed out that despite its widespread occurrence, self-mutilation receives too little public or medical attention. "In the bustle of the emergency room, where the medical establishment first encounters these patients, physicians find them unsettling in the extreme; the standard approach is to close their wounds quickly, dress their burns, and ignore their psyches.'' When attention is given to the underlying causes, the patient is often diagnosed as having a borderline personality disorder, a diagnosis for which there is no widely agreed-upon treatment.

With some exceptions, humankind is the only species that kills its own members or turns its destructive urges against itself. The rare instances in which animals inflict damage on themselves occur only under extraordinary physical and social conditions imposed by humans, involving confinement and deprivation.

This suggests possible explanations for self-destructive behavior in people, and indeed research has found that more than half of human self-mutilators have experienced physical and psychological abuse and a prolonged absence of love, nurturance and physical contact. However, environment is not sufficient to explain such behavior. Not everyone who was abused or neglected in childhood grows up to engage in self-mutilation.

A few self-mutilators have been found to be suffering from rare hereditary disorders associated with an imbalance in neurotransmitters, the chemicals that carry electrical signals between brain cells. Their symptoms—gnawing on their tongues, cheeks, lips and fingertips—can often be controlled by medication.

Although medication has not been found to help those who do not appear to suffer from neurological disease, the fact that some cases of such behavior are caused by biological disorders suggests that others may be as well. The chemicals suspected of being involved are endorphins, opiatelike substances that reduce sensitivity to pain.

A 1983 English study monitored an endorphin called metenkephalin in the blood of ten habitual self-mutilators. The researchers found that a patient who had mutilated him- or herself a week earlier had less metenkephalin in the bloodstream than a patient who had done so only a day earlier.

Unfortunately, the researchers could not rule out the possibility that elevated levels of metenkephalin might have been released in response to the injury. Another explanation might be that self-mutilators already have elevated levels of metenkephalin before they injure themselves. If so, they might have engaged in self-mutilation as a means of further elevating their meten-

kephalin levels in order to experience the endorphin's soothing effect.

Researchers also do not know whether the level of metenkephalin in the bloodstream is an accurate index of its level in the central nervous system, where the chemical has its effect. Levels of pain add still another complication. In a survey of 250 ''chronic cutters,'' as they are called by physicians, only 10% experienced great pain; 67% reported that they felt little or none. This finding suggests that self-mutilators would not have a great need for additional amounts of endorphins.

In Favazza's opinion, even if the role biochemistry plays in self-mutilation were clear, much about the behavior would remain unexplained. He feels that the behavior is often better explained in terms of the psychological and cultural context in which it is found.

Psychoanalysts paid little attention to self-mutilation until 1938, when the American psychiatrist Karl Menninger wrote *Man Against Himself,* a classic work on suicide. Menninger devoted a chapter to those who commit self-destructive acts without the intention of killing themselves. He viewed such acts as ''personal triumphs over the inclination toward death . . . While apparently a form of attenuated suicide, self-mutilation is actually a compromise formation to avert total annihilation, that is to say, suicide.''

While useful, in Favazza's opinion, Menninger's interpretation does not encompass all who self-mutilate. Only a fraction are severely psychotic. Most are calm, controlled and aware of how bizarre their actions seem to others.

Anthropological literature offers ample evidence of the long history of ritual self-mutilation, commonly as a form of atonement for sin. A study done by criminologist Hans Toch of the State University of New York at Albany of self-abusive prison inmates suggests that this sort of reasoning is not confined to ''primitive'' peoples. One inmate said, ''It made me feel that I had cut something out of myself.'' Common also is self-mutilation as a part of a ritual of passage from adolescence to adulthood.

The social significance of self-mutilation in industrialized nations can be seen most clearly in hospitals and prisons, where the incidence of self-cutting may be ten times higher than it is in the larger society. In one Canadian adolescent facility, 86% of the girls had carved letters on their skin. Such wounds for them signified not only bravery and unity with the other adolescents, they also aroused the sympathy of relatives, medical personnel and authority figures.

Favazza began his *Science* article on self-mutilation with a description of a typical self-mutilator. "Janet regularly . . . slices open her arms, legs, and abdomen. The best cuts, she says, are the one that require stitches, which she sometimes needs weekly. Janet has repeated this ritual for years, and has been hospitalized on a half-dozen occasions."

The majority of people like Janet hurt themselves superficially, in ways that can be treated at home or during a brief hospital stay. About a third of them interfere with the healing process, but most take pleasure in tending their wounds. They frequently report that their actions relieve anxiety and feelings of unreality. In Favazza's opinion, self-mutilators exert a small symbolic measure of control over the circumstances of their lives, which may otherwise seem overwhelming.

semiautomatic weapons See ASSAULT WEAPONS.

sentencing: a trend toward longer sentences
Once a defendant is found guilty in an American court, he or she must be sentenced within the specifications of the law. There is a federal criminal code, and each state has its own criminal code. The codes set out descriptions of behaviors considered to be crimes and attach to each a range of punishments. Regardless of whether a judge or a jury determines the form and details, a sentence is expected to accomplish four goals:

- Deterrence. The sentence should serve as a warning to others to refrain from similar acts.
- Incapacitation. The sentence should prevent the defendant's commission of additional criminal acts.
- Rehabilitation. The sentence should contain a suitable mixture of discipline and assistance that will prevent future criminal behavior.
- Retribution. The sentence should punish, in proportion to the crime.

The process of sentencing may include a hearing at which evidence is presented to influence the judge or jury. In most cases, the sentence hearing includes a presentence report from the probation department and other information that the prosecution and/or the defense chooses to submit. The defense sometimes hires an outsider to prepare a private presentence report containing evidence that the defendant has been accepted into a treatment program. Based on the defendant's past

record, the prosecutor may ask for leniency or for the maximum.

The court may pass sentence using any one or a combination of four basic dispositions: a fine, a suspended sentence, incarceration and probation.

In many instances, a fine involves restitution to the victim. A suspended sentence calls for a period of incarceration but suspends it contingent on proper behavior until the passage of a specified period. The suspended sentence is often coupled with probation. Probation is a form of controlled release under the supervision of a probation officer, requiring compliance with certain conditions and subject to revocation.

A typical public response to a sudden rise in violent crime rates is an outcry for longer prison terms. Advocates of deterrence say "We have to teach them a lesson." Advocates of incapacitation say "If we can keep them locked up, we can take back the streets."

Longer sentences, however, appear to have little relationship to the incidence of crime. In a March 17, 1991 *Washington Post* article entitled "Why Won't Crime Stop? Because We Cling to Our Favorite Social Myths," criminologist James Fyfe explained why.

> Consider the costs and benefits of convenience store stickups and the reasoning process of those who commit them. Robbers must run a 1-in-5 risk of being arrested; they may do long prison terms or get shot—all in return for hauls they know can be no more than $50 or $100. Does anyone seriously believe that people willing to bet these odds would be deterred by, say, increasing the maximum prison sentence for robbery from 25 to 30 years? Conversely, even if the penalty for armed robbery were reduced dramatically—to five years, perhaps—would any person who is rational in a middle-class sense commit a robbery to pick up pocket money?

The issue of appropriate sentence length is one of the most controversial policymaking areas associated with criminal justice. Although increased sentences may make the public feel better, they tie up resources needed elsewhere in criminal justice systems and in the larger society. Moreover, within the corrections system itself, increasing terms for some inmates means decreasing terms for others and reducing the numbers that can be sent to prison, in the absence of a massive building program.

An examination of average sentence length suggests that increasing it has only a limited effect on the average time served. For example, among prisoners released for the first time from federal prisons:

Year	Average Sentence (months)	Average Time Served (months)
1965	32.6	19.9
1975	39.8	18.5
1985	35.5	15.9

Although the number of prisoners charged with drug offenses increased during the mid-1980s, the average sentence hovered around 44 months, and the average time served remained about 15.9 months. Yet increasing prison sentences and making them mandatory for some crimes meant that some defendants went to jail in the 1970s and 1980s who might otherwise have received probation and had the effect of doubling the prison population during the 1980s. The odds of an arrest leading to a prison sentence went up 68% between 1970 and 1986.

For 50 years prior to the mid-1970s, indeterminate sentences dominated penal policy. A judge would set a minimum sentence; once the prisoner had served the minimum a parole board would determine if he or she were "ready" to be released.

In the 1970s and 1980s state legislatures adopted many approaches to modify or replace the indeterminate sentence. Maine required a judge to specify a fixed term and eliminated parole release and community supervision. California, at the other end of the spectrum, retained a parole period and permitted sentences to be modified according to circumstances. Arizona retained parole supervision that can last as long as 50% of the length of a sentence.

By itself, determinacy did not increase the prison population. But the major trend toward reliance on mandatory prison terms for repeat felonies or for specific crimes such as drug offenses or gun use did.

Rejection of the rehabilitative approach implied by indeterminate sentences fostered mandatory sentencing. In some states prosecutors and judges resist mandatory sentences by screening out or dismissing charges on a case-by-case basis; otherwise prisons would be even more crowded. But even without full compliance, mandatory sentencing has had a significant impact on both the likelihood of incarceration and on the length of sentences.

The state of Delaware illustrates the impact. In 1973 the legislature enacted a new criminal code which decreed that all multiple sentences would be served consecutively, one sentence following another, rather than concurrently, and prescribed longer sentences with mandatory minimums, ensuring that early parole could not undercut the longer terms. By 1985 one out of every seven prisoners in Delaware was serving a life sentence. Ninety percent of them had been sentenced under the new code.

If the trend continues, the U.S. prison and jail population of close to 1 million at the beginning of the 1990s could double again during the decade. At a prison construction cost of about $100,000 per inmate, the outlay for new prison space would be about $106 billion. Moreover, the yearly maintenance cost per inmate of about $25,000 would add an additional $26 billion each year. History has demonstrated that once new prison cells are built, they are kept filled.

Sentences for Career Criminals.   In 1972 criminologist Marvin Wolfgang and his colleagues found that of the almost 10,000 males born in Philadelphia in 1945, a small group (6%) was arrested for more than half of the offenses committed by their cohort. Subsequent research confirmed a similar pattern for adults: about 10% of those who dealt in drugs and committed robberies and assaults were responsible for hundreds of crimes a year.

Researchers warned that using such findings to shape sentencing policy might be premature because predictions of which offenders were high risk would be problematic. Despite the warning, career criminals have become a preferred target at all stages of the criminal justice process. While the pursuit of career criminals diverts attention and funds from other parts of the system, it does not appear to have convicted or incarcerated a much larger share of the most serious offenders than have conventional approaches.

The Impact of Crime and Punishment on Particular Neighborhoods.   Concern with crime during the Johnson and Nixon administrations led these presidents to impanel blue-ribbon commissions to examine the problem. The work of the commissions brought about improvements in the police and criminal justice systems and improved the conditions for the scientific study of crime.

The improved study of crime revealed that for decades crime has been clustered in certain neighborhoods. Such neighborhoods are mainly made up of African-Americans and Hispanics, replacements for former white residents who fled to the suburbs taking businesses and jobs with them. Since the 1960s, African-American and Hispanic neighborhoods have become densely populated, at the same time that their neighborhoods' reduced property tax bases have eroded municipal services. Clarence Lusane, in his 1991 book *Pipe Dream Blues:*

Racism and the War on Drugs, traces the imposition of drug- and alcohol-related criminal activities on impoverished African-American communities back to the days of slavery.

The threat of death or imprisonment has corroded and continues to corrode family and community life in many African-American neighborhoods. Beverly Coleman-Miller, special assistant to the commissioner of public health in Washington, D.C., pointed out in the March 10, 1990 *Washington Afro-American* that a young African-American male dies in such neighborhoods every 16 to 24 hours. Although African-Americans constitute about 12% of the total U.S. population, they make up about 47% of the U.S. prison population.

Statisticians from the U.S. Department of Justice estimated that at 1979 imprisonment levels, an American male born in 1985 had between a one in 30 and 48 (depending on which prison census was used) chance of serving a sentence in a state prison during his lifetime. An African-American male, however, had a one in five or nine chance of doing time.

The 1969 National Commission on the Causes and Prevention of Violence described the despair engendered by living in such communities.

To be young, poor, male; to be undereducated and without means of escape from an oppressive urban environment; to want what society claims is available (but mostly to others); to see around oneself illegitimate and often violent methods being used to achieve material success; and to observe others using these means with impunity—all this is to be burdened with an enormous set of influences that pull many toward crime and delinquency. To be also Black, Puerto Rican, or Mexican-American and subject to discrimination adds considerably to the pull.

In the mid-1960s President Lyndon Johnson told the nation that crime and violence were bred by "ignorance, discrimination, slums, poverty, disease, and not enough jobs."

During the 1970s Robert Martinson, author with Ted Palmer of *Rehabilitation, Recidivism and Research,* and his colleagues reviewed a great number of rigorous research reports on the effectiveness of correctional treatments. He located 231 studies around the world and found that no matter what the treatment, two thirds of prison inmates eventually return to prison. The universality of the recidivism rate suggests that new approaches such as rehabilitation of neighborhoods and the creation of economic opportunities are needed.

Expansion of Punishment. Former Minneapolis police chief Tony Bouza told an interviewer, "Not all poor people are street criminals, but almost all street criminals are poor people." Despite the beliefs of people like Bouza and President Johnson in rehabilitation and economic opportunities, the trend is toward increased punitiveness.

In her 1990 book *The Justice Juggernaut: Fighting Street Crime, Controlling Citizens,* political scientist Diana Gordon of New York's City College described a trend toward "community as prison." Although releases and suspended sentences have been common since the 17th century, probation as a movement did not begin in earnest until 1841 when John Augustus began bailing out public drunkards and petty thieves to reform them with kindness.

Augustus linked rehabilitation with surveillance for petty offenders. When early 20th-century progressives championed the idea of state responsibility for individual treatment of offenders, the idea of probation caught on. By 1970 when data began to be kept on a national basis, there were 1.3 million adults on probation, making it the most common form of official punishment.

Until the 1970s the declared justification for a non-prison sentence was rehabilitation. Since the 1970s new rationales have surfaced supporting the ancient theory of retribution with the aim of fitting the punishment to the crime by adding restitution, community service and intensive surveillance.

Through the 1970s and 1980s dozens of attempts were made to establish some type of custody that would permit inmates to leave prison for limited times in controlled circumstances. The only ones that appear to be surviving are those that Gordon calls "intermediate punishment," more stringent than probation but not as rigorous as prison.

For all but the most violent offenses, local custom determines who will go to prison. Some offenders in Massachusetts' intensive supervision program have been convicted of more serious crimes than have been offenders in Georgia's program, despite the fact that Georgia has the nation's largest program.

The popularity of intermediate punishment can be traced to the dilemma most states faced with the clamor for tougher punishment from the general public, the media and law enforcement on the one hand, and the fiscal crisis of the late 1970s (including the huge debt service generated by new prison construction) on the other.

Several studies in the 1960s and 1970s found that the outcomes were no better for those on probation than those who went to prison or had their cases dismissed.

Nevertheless, probation has continued to grow. In 1965, of those under correctional custody, 61% were on probation or parole. By 1985 the figure was 74%. In 1985 there were 1.9 million people on state or federal probation, four times as many as there were in prison; by 1987 there were 2.2 million people on probation.

Intensive supervision may turn out to be as costly as incarceration. Without factoring in the cost of electronic monitoring, it costs about six times as much as regular supervision, that is, meeting with the probationers at fixed intervals. Cost comparisons between prison and surveillance rest on two assumptions: that sentencing and release policies will not be affected by prison overcrowding and its fiscal implications, and that without intensive supervision prison space could still be found for most of the offenders, regardless of overcrowding.

If the trend toward more punitive approaches continues, intensive supervision ultimately may prove too costly and be abandoned for some other technique. However, in Gordon's opinion the precedent that makes it acceptable to keep citizens under surveillance will have been firmly established, a great loss in a democracy.

(See also JAILS; PRISON OVERCROWDING: COPING WITH THE COSTS.)

serial killers Multiple killings by the same person or persons committed serially over a period of weeks, months or years are called serial killings. Most analysts distinguish them from mass murders, that is, multiple killings in a single incident that takes place within a span of minutes, hours or days.

Most murders that are ever going to be solved are solved quickly because the culprit is obvious and/or is related to or acquainted with the victim. By definition, serial killers seldom have an obvious connection with their victims and hence are not easily apprehended. With rare exceptions, serial killers are male.

The *Uniform Crime Report* of the Federal Bureau of Investigation (FBI) aggregates separate murders and is not broken out to distinguish individual homicides from serial ones. In 1976 just 8.5% of all U.S. murders had unknown motives, a category that includes but is not exclusively composed of serial killings. By 1990 the percentages of unknown motives had risen to 27.7%.

During an April 1992 phone conversation, Jack Levin a professor at Northeastern University in Boston and

co-author with Professor James Alan Fox of *Mass Murder* (1985), reported that serial murders were rare prior to the 1960s. Any mention of them evoked an image of London in 1888–89 terrorized by Jack the Ripper, whose murders of prostitutes remain unsolved. In the 1960s serial killers became less rare. The number of their crimes rises annually. They seem to be confined mostly to the United States.

Data collected by Ronald Holmes, professor of criminal justice at the School of Justice Administration of the University of Louisville and an expert on criminal "profiling," revealed that between 1900 and 1970 there were 28 known serial killers with 742 victims among them. In the decade of the 1970s alone, there were 29 serial killers with 906 victims among them. In the 1980s there were 47 known serial killers with 670 victims.

The FBI's Behavioral Sciences Unit maintains a national register of serial killings that includes data on every known serial killing committed in the United States in the past half century. The unit has also set up a computer database for unsolved murders, the Violent Criminal Apprehension Program (VICAP).

VICAP's goal is to store standard data on the estimated 50,000 unsolved murders from the past decade, automatically search for new unsolved murders and generate up to 10 "best matches." Ideally, the system will link crimes committed by the same killer in different regions of the country, thereby allowing detectives to compare evidence and solve some of their most difficult cases.

Computer problems and a slow response by busy police departments to a 189-item VICAP report have delayed the system's becoming fully functional. But criminologists believe that such information-gathering is crucial to improve the ability of police to catch serial killers.

Despite great strides made in forensic science, the clearance rate for murders has fallen from 86% in 1970 to 67% in 1990. In part the reason is that more and more murders are "stranger homicides." Another reason is that serial killers are responsible for higher body counts. There are more cases like that of Randy Kraft, who is thought to have slain as many as 65 people in Los Angeles.

What is known about serial killers has been accumulated from interviews with those willing to talk. The majority of serial killers are white males, between 25 and 34, charming, charismatic and police "groupies" or interested in police work.

At the very least, serial killers are "street smart." But according to psychologist Robert Ressler, former FBI agent and a leading figure in the development of profiles of serial killers, who was quoted in an April 14, 1991 *Washington Post* article entitled "Serial Killers: Shattering the Myth: They're an American Phenomenon, and They're Not What You Think," serial killers are not nearly as intelligent as the book and movie *Silence of the Lambs* made them out to be. In Ressler's estimation, serial killers are invariably professional failures, even those like Ted Bundy, whose minor achievements were exaggerated by the press.

Vernon Geberth, a former New York City police officer and the author of a text on homicide investigations, agrees. In his opinion, serial killers appear smart because they kill strangers and keep moving, which is what makes them hard to catch.

There has been a tendency among psychologists and some law enforcement authorities to discount serial murders as acts of sex and focus on them as acts of power and dominance. Ressler disagrees with that perspective. "I have yet to see a serial killing that didn't have some sexual motivation. I have never seen a serial killer who is a happily married family man, or who had a long-term successful relationship with a woman."

In his book *Serial Murder: An Elusive Phenomenon* (1990), Steven Egger mentions that there appears to be a tendency in the academic literature to steer away from the fact that almost all serial killers are men. He views the tendency as a reluctance to see the behavior as an exaggeration of the kinds of behavior exhibited by the majority of males—predatory sexuality, the treatment of women as objects, desire for immediate gratification, narcissism and aggressiveness.

Types of Serial Killers.   Ronald Holmes, in his 1989 book *Profiling Violent Crimes,* discussed the category "lust offenders" originally developed by the FBI. Lust offenders are those whose crimes involve sex as a primary motive: rape, sexual assault, mutilation, necrophilia and picquerism (repeated stabbing or wounding, which results in sexual gratification).

The FBI classification of lust offenders makes a distinction between two types of serial killers, the "Disorganized Asocial" and the "Organized Nonsocial." The distinction between the two types can be useful in crime-scene analysis.

The Disorganized Asocial murderer is truly disorganized in his daily activities. His home, place of employment (if employed), car or truck, clothing and demeanor reflect his disorganization. His appearance, lifestyle and psychological state are disorganized.

The FBI's Behavioral Science Unit (BSU) has developed a list of personal characteristics and postoffense behavior of the two types of lust-offender serial killers. While the lists have not been tested by research, empirically they appear to hold up. The personal characteristics and social history of the Disorganized Asocial type include:

- below average intelligence
- social inadequacy
- unskilled work performance
- feelings of anxiety during the crime
- minimal use of alcohol
- lives alone
- lives or works near the crime scene
- has minimal interest in the news media
- nocturnal in habits
- has secret hiding places
- was a high school dropout
- low birth order status (not the firstborn of his family)
- father's work pattern was unstable
- family discipline was harsh or inconsistent

Behavior after the crime committed by the Disorganized Asocial may include the following:

- a return to the scene of the crime
- attendance at the funeral or gravesite
- placement of a commemorative notice in newspapers
- writing a diary or collecting news clips
- development of an interest in religion
- change in jobs
- significant behavioral change
- personality change

FBI analysts have developed interview techniques to use with the Disorganized Asocial serial killer. They advise

- an expression of empathy
- indirect introduction of evidence
- a counselor-type approach
- nighttime interviews

In Holmes' experience the Disorganized Asocial serial killer was often a victim during childhood of physical or emotional abuse. It is likely that he spent much of his childhood alone, not out of choice, but because he was different. Given his limited intelligence, low level of skill and absence of social skills, the Disorganized Asocial serial murderer lacks the ability to plan a crime. His crimes tend to be spontaneous.

Uncomfortable venturing far from home or work, the Disorganized Asocial serial murderer will commit his crimes in his own neighborhood. His lack of personal hygiene will be apparent from the evidence he leaves at the crime scene. As with all lust offenders, the Disorganized Asocial murderer will repeat the offense.

His return to the scene of the crime and attendance at the funeral stem from the desire to relive the crime. Diaries of the crime are commonplace, and probably over time videos of the crime will become more frequent mementos.

In stark contrast to the Disorganized Asocial type, the Organized Nonsocial personality is supremely well organized. His home, automobile and personality all reflect an insistence on order. His characteristics and history include:

- social adequacy
- sexual competence
- a marital or live-in partner
- high birth order
- harsh discipline in childhood
- controlled mood
- masculine image (his dress and car may be flashy)
- personal charm
- geographic mobility
- occupational mobility
- a strong interest in tracking his crimes in the media
- model behavior when incarcerated

The behavior of the Organized Nonsocial serial killer following the crime may include:

- moving the body
- disposal of the body in a manner to call attention to it
- return to the scene of the crime
- volunteering of information
- attempts to socialize with police

The FBI warns interviewers that the Organized Nonsocial serial killer will answer only what he has to and advises interviewers to use a direct strategy and to bring up only information they know to be accurate. He respects competence and any attempt to mislead him with false information may cause him to believe that there is no case, and he therefore will be uncooperative.

Unlike the Disorganized Asocial, the Organized Nonsocial is nonsocial out of choice. According to Holmes, "This offender is different from the disorganized aso-

cial; the latter is a loner because of his strange appearance. The organized nonsocial is a loner because there is no one good enough for him."

Ted Bundy, a college graduate and a part-time law student who killed an unknown number of young women, is classified somewhere between the two types. His presence was ultimately connected to the locales of his crimes because he charged his gasoline and signed receipts for his purchases. He found it difficult to deviate from his accustomed fashion of conducting his daily life.

Because he can make new friends, the Organized Nonsocial offender is able to venture far from home. The good impression he makes and his ability to appear more qualified than he is makes it possible to get employment in a new location. Many have held responsible jobs.

The Organized Nonsocial type feels comfortable cruising far afield for his victims. Bundy was suspected in the abduction of Roberta Kathy Parks from the campus of Oregon State University. He apparently drove her almost 300 miles to Seattle before he killed her.

The Organized Nonsocial offender is convinced he is always right and therefore perceives any criticism as destructive. He is often diagnosed as a sociopath, or as having an antisocial personality disorder, a so-called character disorder, which mean that he takes no responsibility, is unable to sustain a relationship for any length of time and feels no remorse for anything he does to others. Irritability and aggressiveness in everyday contacts are also common.

As an example of the combination of the irritability and lack of responsibility for his actions, Holmes described the comments of one organized nonsocial serial killer that he interviewed. The killer said, "One night I finally got a date with a young woman I had been trying to date for six months. We went out for a drink before dinner. We were sitting in a bar when a guy walked by. She watched him as he walked down the bar. I felt that she should not look at him while she was with me. So, what could I do? I killed her."

Although the Organized Nonsocial serial killer enjoys returning to the scene of the crime, many have learned from television that it is not a good idea. Often they will socialize in restaurants and bars frequented by police in order to hear them talk about cases that are special to them.

The crime becomes for the Organized Nonsocial—at least in part—a game played against others. When Holmes asked one serial killer, who was suspected of killing scores of young women, why only a few of the bodies had been found, he answered, "You only find the bodies they [the serial killers] want you to find." He explained that some are left where they can be found "to let you know he's still there."

The crime scene is quite different for the two types. The Disorganized Offender will attack or kill his victim in a sudden, violent frenzy, with little planning. The blitz will result in a crime scene with a great deal of physical evidence.

Although the Disorganized Asocial offender may know his victim, there is no personal relationship. He knows the victim only because she or he lives in the neighborhood. His is a blitz attack, there is no need for a relationship or conversation.

The Organized Nonsocial offender uses the language of intimidation to get his vulnerable victim into his "comfort zone." The victim is often rendered helpless with restraints. Prior to death, vicious attacks are used to inspire fear, which the offender relishes. Often death is prolonged to increase the killer's satisfaction.

Other qualities besides the Disorganized Asocial and Organized Nonsocial typology are used to make distinctions among serial killers. Some are characterized as "geographically stable" killers. They kill in the area where they live or in a nearby area. For example, Wayne Williams terrorized Atlanta with his murders of Atlanta children. Although police are not sure he killed all the children found, they are convinced he killed most.

"Geographically Transient" serial murderers, such as Ted Bundy, travel a great deal. They cruise not to find victims—several have told Holmes that victims could have been found down the block—but to avoid detection.

Most serial killers are not psychotic; they are in touch with reality. The few who are psychotic are likely to fit the category of "visionary" serial killers, that is, they are propelled to kill because of voices they hear or visions they see. The voices or the visions are apt to be attributed to God or the Devil.

Another category, the "mission" serial killer, is unlikely to be hearing voices or seeing visions. He is impelled by a need to eradicate a certain group of people. His self-imposed mission is to eradicate that group, such as Jews, blacks or foreigners.

The mission serial killer may be either an Organized Nonsocial personality or a Disorganized Asocial personality, but more often he is the former. Typically, upon his arrest, neighbors are amazed because he had seemed to be "such a fine young man." During his

interrogation, one serial killer who had set out to rid the world of prostitutes expressed pride at the service he had rendered the community.

The "hedonistic" serial killer obtains sexual satisfaction through homicide. Unlike the visionary or the mission murderer, who characteristically make a quick kill, the hedonistic killer savors the process. He receives sexual gratification from his interaction with the helpless victim. The killings are typified by fear-instilling activities, torture, dismemberment, necrophilia (intercourse with a dead body) and even anthropophagy (cannibalism). The hedonistic serial killer kills because he enjoys killing.

Still another type of serial killer is the "comfort-oriented" killer. The professional assassin is a comfort-oriented serial killer, who kills for material gain. Comfort-oriented serial killer H. W. Mudgett killed wives, fiances, and employees to collect money and property. The very few women serial killers are usually comfort-oriented killers.

The "power/control" serial killer receives gratification from the complete domination he has over his victim. One serial killer told Holmes, "What more power can one have than over life and death?" The power/control serial killer typically likes to prolong the killing scene and, when he does kill, he is likely to strangle his victim rather than use an "impersonal" weapon such as a gun or rifle.

Many victims are blindfolded. Observers often assume that blindfolds are intended to hide the identity of the killer, but since he usually intends to kill the victim, identification is not the point.

The blindfold is to generate fear. One serial killer explained that he blindfolded his victims—none of whom knew him personally or would recognize him—in order to confuse and terrorize them. Holmes believes that the blindfold has an added dimension; it further depersonalizes the victim.

As the killings go on, the serial killer's personality appears to disintegrate. He plans less, the time between killing episodes grows shorter and the killings become more vicious.

Victim Type.   In his report of an eight-hour interview with a serial killer, Holmes stated that he raised the question of the purported need for a particular type of victim. The killer responded:

> This assertion presupposes that, within the mind of each individual serial killer, there evolves a synthesis of preferred characteristics and, ultimately, a clear, specific picture of

his ideal victim—male or female, black or white, young or old, short or tall, large-busted or small, shy or forward, and so on. Then as the reasoning goes, when a typical serial killer begins an active search for a human prey, he will go to great lengths to capture and victimize only those individuals who closely fit the mold of his preferred "ideal" . . . however, I strongly believe that in the case of most serial killers, the physical and personal characteristics of those on their respective list of victim only infrequently coincide with the desired traits of their imagined "ideal" . . . none of my actual victims ever completely fit the mold of my "ideal."

In the opinion of the interviewee, there are two reasons for the discrepancy between the ideal victim and the real victim. The first has to do with the serial killer's caution. He is seldom able to find his preferred type of victim in a position for safe and easy capture.

The second is that the nature of the serial killer's compulsion precludes any prolonged or self-imposed delay. The respondent likened the serial killer to a hungry lion who might seek out a gazelle early in the hunt, but who will settle for a sickly hare when his hunger is too great.

(See MASS MURDERS; SOCIOPATHS.)

sex crimes research Referred to as paraphilias, sex crimes are sexual behaviors that are considered aberrant or socially undesirable. The term paraphilia is preferred because it emphasizes deviation (paraphilia means "love of the abnormal").

Mental health clinicians must diagnose the problems of people who come to see them before they can treat them. For diagnostic accuracy, recordkeeping standardization and to conform to guidelines that insurance companies will accept, many clinicians use the *Diagnostic and Statistical Manual of Mental Disorders (DSM)*, published by the American Psychiatric Association, to define paraphilia and its varieties.

The revised third edition *(DSM-III-R)* describes paraphilia in these terms:

The essential feature of disorder in this subclass is recurrent intense sexual urges and sexually arousing fantasies generally involving either (1) nonhuman objects, (2) the suffering or humiliation of oneself or one's partner (not merely simulated), or (3) children or other nonconsenting persons. The diagnosis is made only if the person has acted on these urges, or is markedly distressed by them.

For some paraphiliacs, the paraphilic fantasies or stimuli are always included in sexual activity. For others, the paraphilic inclinations occur episodically during periods of stress; at other times, they are able to function sexually without them. People with a paraphilia generally suffer from several forms, on the average three to four varieties.

With the exception of sexual masochism, which has a sex ratio of one female to every 20 males, the varieties of paraphilia are rarely diagnosed in females. The disorders are seldom seen in general mental health treatment settings. Despite the paucity of paraphilic patients presenting themselves for diagnosis and treatment, the presence of a large commercial market for paraphilic pornography and equipment suggests that the population who have paraphilias, but who are never seen by clinicians, is likely to be sizable.

The *DSM-III-R* provides a clue as to why paraphiliacs are seldom seen in clinics.

Because some of these disorders are associated with nonconsenting partners, they are of legal and social significance. People with these disorders tend not to consider themselves as ill, and usually come to the attention of mental health professionals only when their behavior has brought them into conflict with sexual partners or society.

Before a diagnosis can be assigned, the *DSM-III-R* requires that the behavior must have occurred over a period of at least six months. The specific paraphilias described in the *DSM-III-R* include:

- *Exhibitionism.* Sexual urges and sexually arousing fantasies involving the exposure of one's genitals to an unsuspecting stranger.
- *Fetishism.* Sexual urges and sexually arousing fantasies involving the use of nonliving objects by themselves (e.g., female undergarments).
- *Frotteurism.* Sexual urges and sexually arousing fantasies involving touching or rubbing against a nonconsenting person (the touching is sexually exciting, not the coercion).
- *Pedophilia.* Recurrent intense sexual urges and sexually arousing fantasies involving sexual activity with a preadolescent child or children (generally age 13 or younger).
- *Sexual masochism.* Recurrent intense sexual urges and sexually arousing fantasies involving a real, not simulated, act of being humiliated, beaten or bound, or otherwise made to suffer.
- *Sexual sadism.* Recurrent intense sexual urges and sexually arousing fantasies involving real, not simulated, acts of cruelty in which the psychological or

physical suffering, including humiliation, of a victim is sexually exciting.

- *Transvestic fetishism*. In a heterosexual male, recurrent intense sexual urges and sexually arousing fantasies involving cross-dressing (not to be confused with transsexualism, which involves a persistent sense of inappropriateness of one's own gender identity).
- *Voyeurism*. Recurrent intense sexual urges and sexually arousing fantasies involving the act of observing an unsuspecting person who is naked, in the process of disrobing or engaging in sexual activity.

Other paraphilias are mentioned in the *DSM-III-R* without being discussed in detail. Among these are telephone scatologia (lewdness on the phone), necrophilia (sexual preoccupation or intercourse with corpses) and zoophilia (sexual preoccupation or intercourse with animals).

A landmark study of sex crimes was completed by Gene Abel, with colleagues at Emory University School of Medicine, Columbia University and the University of Tennessee Center for Health Sciences. The results were reported in the March 1987 issue of the *Journal of Interpersonal Violence* under the title "Self-Reported Sex Crimes of Nonincarcerated Paraphiliacs." The study found that paraphiliacs who are not in institutions (prisons or mental hospitals), based on their own reports:

- are well educated and come from diverse socioeconomic levels.
- admit to having committed a substantially higher average number of crimes and higher number of crimes per victim than has previously been reported in the research literature.
- sexually molest young boys five times more than they do young girls.

Minimal attention has been given to the perpetrators of sexual crimes. Little is known about them and treatment programs are scarce. Until the study done by Abel and his colleagues, the only major studies had been done on incarcerated sex offenders. A study reported in 1965 carried out by the Kinsey Institute was done on sex offenders in prisons of the Midwest and California. The investigators gathered data from interviews with the offenders and from their arrest records, which suggested a low incidence of deviant sexual behavior.

Another study, done by L. V. Frisbie and E. H. Dondis, also reported in 1965, was published as a California Department of Mental Health monograph entitled "Recidivism Among Treated Sex Offenders."

The study focused on offenders incarcerated at Atascadero State Hospital in California and examined arrest records. Once again, the arrest records indicated a low incidence of sex offenses.

A major drawback to both studies was that they were done on offenders who were locked up and who presumably wanted to be paroled. Under those conditions, it would be unlikely that offenders would reveal information about sex crimes that they had committed that were unknown to authorities, for fear of being prosecuted for them. Such studies can be expected to reveal minimal rates of deviant behavior.

In an effort to obtain more reliable information, researchers in the late 1960s began using self-report measures as alternatives to official records. The two measures of crime complement one another, each having disadvantages offset by the other. The major disadvantage of self-reports has been that samples of nonincarcerated offenders have usually been small, and hence not a good basis for extrapolating to larger populations. Larger samples, better for generalizing, have been available only for incarcerated offenders, who can be expected to be reluctant to share information.

The Abel study took steps to circumvent the problems of both approaches. The study used only voluntary subjects who were not under court order to receive evaluation or treatment. Each participant signed a comprehensive consent form that instructed him to withhold the specifics of crimes that would tie him to a particular crime. Instead of crime details, the subjects were asked to describe the general characteristics of the age range of their preferred victim, the gender they preferred and the frequency of their various sex crimes.

To protect the data, each subject was assigned a confidential identification number (ID), and all information was kept in charts that were coded only by the ID numbers. The code matching the patient's name with his ID was kept outside of the United States, to prevent any possibility of the records being subpoenaed. In this manner, by keeping secret or revealing his code, the subject could maintain or surrender the confidentiality of his records.

For further protection, the research project obtained a Certificate of Confidentiality from the Secretary of Health, Education, and Welfare, which ensured that no city, county, state or federal agency could compel an investigator to reveal the identity of subjects participating in the research project. The final step taken to encourage cooperation of the subjects was to explain to the subjects that the study's goal was to help the subjects understand their behavior and how they might gain control of it.

A total of 561 subjects were recruited through contact with mental health, probation, forensic and criminal justice professionals and through ads in local media. The context in which the subjects were seen was comparable to any psychiatric setting in which sex offenders who voluntarily sought treatment or evaluation might be seen. At the Memphis, Tennessee site, the gamut of types of sexual offenders was seen. The New York City site, in the main, dealt with rapists and/or child molesters.

The data on each type of paraphilia were sufficient in the study to reflect characteristics of that category. However, the method of sample selection made it impossible to assume that the distribution in the sample actually reflected the numbers of people who practiced that kind of behavior in the general population. In other words, because child molesters were more plentiful in the study compared with other categories did not necessarily mean that they were more numerous in the general population.

Experienced clinicians interviewed the subjects for anywhere from one to five hours. In their tabulations, researchers counted only those instances admitted by the subject. If a client had been legally charged with five acts, but admitted to only two, the researcher counted only two.

Comparisons between available arrest records and the study's self-reported crimes were not of much use, because the frequency of self-reported crimes was vastly greater than the number of crimes for which the subject had been arrested. For example, among the more violent crimes such as rape and child molestation, the ratio was one arrest to 30 self-reported crimes. Among the less aggressive crimes, exhibitionism or window peeping, the ratio was one arrest to 150 episodes.

The subjects were predominantly young, with 67% between 20 to 39 years old. Their ages ranged from 13 to 76, with a mean age of 31.5. Half the subjects had participated in an adult relationship, that is, they were either married, had been married or were living with someone. Belying the idea that paraphiliacs are uneducated and unemployed, 66.9% of the sample had completed high school or more, 48.6% held full-time jobs and another 16% were students. The incomes of the households in which the subject resided were appropriate for their employment status. The subjects came from a broad spectrum of socioeconomic levels, with

53.9% residing in households in which the income was above $10,000.

The numbers of completed paraphilic acts ranged from an average of 7.3 rapes by paraphiliacs engaged in rape to an average of 1,139.2 acts for paraphiliacs engaged in masochism. Nonincestuous (outside the home or family) child molestation occurred an average of 281.7 times with male targets, and at a much lower rate of 23.2 times with female targets. Incestuous child molestation data revealed a reversal in the emphasis; 159 subjects targeted females within the home, while only 44 targeted boys within the home. (Incest here refers to a sexual relationship in which the adult or older child can be assumed to have the authority to play a parental role.)

The Abel study also obtained data on the number of victims. The number of paraphilic acts per victim by an offender was calculated in order to clarify the offender-victim relationship. The number of acts committed by incestuous paraphiliacs was far in excess of the number of victims, since, by definition, they involved themselves with the same victim or victims repeatedly. Since public masturbators often subject more than one victim to their behavior, their offender-victim ratio is less than one to one. Exhibitionists and voyeurs usually commit one act per victim. Pedophiles involved with children outside the home will occasionally return to the same victim, especially men who molest young boys.

To obtain a rough estimate of the impact of each diagnosis relative to the total number of completed acts, a percentage of total number of acts, by diagnostic category, was calculated. Exhibitionists and frotteurs were found to have committed the greatest number of paraphilic acts. Among 142 exhibitionists, there were 71,696 completed acts directed at 72,974 victims; among frotteurs, there were 52,669 acts directed against 55,887 victims.

Among the categories of pedophilia, 153 pedophiles committed 43,000 acts against 22,981 boys outside the home, while 224 pedophiles committed 5,197 acts against girls outside the home. In-the-home child molestation involved 159 pedophiles who committed 12,927 acts against 286 girls and 44 pedophiles who committed 2,741 acts against 75 boys.

The data in the Abel study on frequency of self-reported crimes bore little resemblance to the data on frequency attributed to incarcerated offenders. For example, a 1965 study reported the average number of pedophile paraphiliac offenses committed by an offender to be less than three. In the self-reported data the number of offenses ranged from 23.2 to 281.7 acts per offender.

The population of 561 subjects completed a total of 291,737 paraphilic acts against 195,407 victims. A surprising finding of the Abel study was a comparison of the percentage of the total number of specific paraphilic acts completed with the total number of all paraphilic acts. Only 0.3% involved rape against an adult, while 21.9% involved molestation of a child, suggesting how widespread the child molestation problem must be. Because treatment resources are limited in mental health and policy decisions must often be made about where to place the resources to maximize their effectiveness, the Abel research suggests that child molestation should have a high priority. Moreover, more attention needs to be given to the risks of molestation of small boys than has been given in the past.

(See also CHILD ABUSE AND NEGLECT; FROTTEUR; PEDOPHILE; RAPE; SEXUAL ABUSE OF CHILDREN; VIOLENT CRIMES AGAINST WOMEN: THEIR CONNECTION TO GENDER BIAS.)

sex offender, young   See SEXUAL ABUSE OF CHILDREN, INSIDE AND OUTSIDE THE FAMILY.

sexual abuse of children, inside and outside the family   Child sexual abuse within the family is defined as contact between a child and an adult member of the same household for the purpose of sexual stimulation of the adult or another person. The abuser, at least some of the time, shares a home with the child and fills a parental or quasi-parental role, but he or she need not be an adult. The abuser is often a preteen or older teenage relative. The abuser from outside the family may also be in a position of authority over the child, though not a relative or a quasi-parent, or the abuser may be a stranger.

A 1986 breakdown of Massachusetts Department of Social Services records of cases referred for prosecution found that among the perpetrators 27.5% were fathers, 11.6 were mother's male companion, 11.4% were stepfathers, 10.1% were male caretakers, 9.9% were uncles, 6.1% were brothers and 4.3% were mothers. Only 16.8% were strangers.

Incest is defined as a relationship in which a child is drawn or compelled to participate in sexual behavior by an adult or older child who can be assumed to have the authority of a parent, such as a parent, stepparent, fosterparent, grandparent, older sibling or parent's lover.

Estimates of the incidence of incest have climbed dramatically over the last several years. A study published in 1955 estimated the rate of incest at 1.9 cases per million, which, based on the size of the 1955 population, would have amounted to about 300 cases nationwide. The American Humane Association in 1969 estimated 40 cases per million, or about 8,000 cases nationwide. In 1979 sociologist David Finkelhor, an expert on domestic violence, estimated that 25% to 33% of American women and 16% of American men had been victimized as children, which would have meant that about 25 to 33 million women and 14 million men over the age of 15 had been sexually abused as children.

Despite the extreme variations in estimates, experts agree that the rate of child sexual abuse is much higher than earlier believed; that females are victimized more than males during childhood; and that a substantial portion of child sexual abuse takes place within the family, with the largest category of offenders being fathers, stepfathers and mothers' male companions.

A substantial number of fathers and father surrogates perceive children left in their care as property to be utilized as they see fit. Sexually abused children often carry into adulthood a feeling of being property to be sexually exploited. Experts estimate that 75% of teenage prostitutes were raped before the age of 12 by their fathers or father surrogates.

While elements such as geographic or social isolation, bedroom sharing, family stress and personality factors may have some effect on incidence, such elements are not sufficient to predict those who will fall into the pathological family patterns of sexual abuse. Fathers who abuse their daughters frequently have few other symptoms of disturbed behavior. Finkelhor characterizes the average incestuous father as a man with relatively normal sexual development, not stupid and not otherwise a criminal.

A question regularly raised in cases of incest is whether the mother knew what was taking place. The answer varies. Some daughters are convinced that their mothers know and passively comply in the daughter's replacement as sexual partner. Other daughters carefully keep the fact hidden from their mothers to prevent a family breakup.

During the 1960s and 1970s family violence—wife battering, child abuse and child sexual abuse—mobilized groups within different social movements with dissimilar philosophies around the separate issues. Help for battered wives emerged from feminists in the women's movement, who scraped together money to start shelters and lobbied to have laws changed. Aid for abused children arose among paid professionals, who sought government action and funding.

In the area of sexual abuse, the philosophy of traditional therapists has clashed with that of feminists. Traditional therapists are inclined to treat child sexual abuse as an aspect of family dysfunction, with the goal of keeping the family together, a position with which courts are inclined to agree. Feminist therapists, on the other hand, view sexual abuse as criminal behavior and advocate the removal of abused children from the home. They point out that social workers treat incest as a family illness when they would treat child molestation by a stranger as a crime.

Despite the inclination of social workers to treat sexual abuse within the family as a family illness, a substantial number of cases are referred for prosecution. Even when they are, many prosecutors are reluctant to pursue them because they are difficult to prove, a position with which Finkelhor finds fault, since, as he points out, many kinds of crimes that are difficult to prove are regularly brought to trial. Sexual abuse cases tend to be slow moving through courts because, in the view of some trial attorneys, judges do not like to handle them.

Judges also appear to be reluctant to send sexual abusers of children to jail. A study done by the *Boston Globe* of child molesters in the process of moving through the criminal justice system found that among 49 Massachusetts judges in 1987, almost half did not sentence sexual abusers of children to jail; the median sentence given by those who did was two years.

Criminal justice has not been equally kind to victims. Although there has been some recent movement to change state statutes, most states allow victims of childhood sexual abuse to file civil suits against their abusers for damages only within one to three years after reaching the state's majority age—18 or 21. In January 1991 California extended the statute of limitations to make it possible in some cases for victims to file suit no matter how old they are when they finally determine that an injury has taken place. Alaska, Colorado, Iowa, Maine, Montana and Washington have similar laws.

This change was considered necessary because some victims suppress their reaction to abuse; as a consequence many years may pass before they are able to recognize its lingering effects. The effects can take a variety of forms, including sexual promiscuity or avoidance, physical ailments, depression and often suicide.

Several factors contribute to the helplessness of children forced to cope with either a single incident or ongoing sexual abuse. Adults are in positions of power over them and in response to opposition can retaliate in brutal ways. Children fear, with good reason, that if they do tell about the behavior they will not be believed. Children's reports of abuse are often discounted as fantasy or reacted to with anger. When a child's report is accepted and criminal charges are filed, other family members often view the child as the one who broke up the family.

Many children do not speak out, and the effects of child sexual abuse linger throughout their lives. When battered women's hotlines became available in the late 1960s and early 1970s, many of the calls that came in were from women who had been sexually abused decades, in some cases as much as a half a century, before and who found in the hotline volunteers sympathetic listeners to whom they could speak of the horrors they had endured as children.

Prevention of Sexual Abuse of Children. Beginning in the mid-1980s, many social scientists and law enforcement experts leaned toward a theory that sex offenders ought to be given mental health treatment instead of simply being imprisoned. Many therapists adopted the view that abusers have sexual disorders called paraphilias. Such disorders lead to compulsive behavior that some offenders can learn to control through behavioral and chemical therapy and long-term supervision.

Nevertheless, treatment of offenders who sexually abuse children is done only on a limited basis in the United States. Andrew Vachss, an expert on sexual abuse of children, is an outspoken critic of the lack of attention to sex offenders and a supporter of rehabilitative programs, but he believes they should be conducted behind bars.

The experience gained by one of the most successful sex offender programs in the United States lends credence to Vachss' position. The program, located in Hennepin County, Minnesota, has determined that the most effective treatment is done in a locked facility and is offense-specific, that is, treatment is tailored to the offenders' crimes.

Formed in 1979, the program houses offenders in 24-bed cottages. Treatment, given by a treatment team that assumes the role of a surrogate family, is an around-the-clock task. The approach used is a mixture of confrontation and support.

A 1990 Justice Department report indicated that about 60% of untreated offenders repeat their offenses, compared with about 20% of those who are treated. However, despite such findings, sex offender treatment programs have fallen out of favor.

During an interview for a January 1, 1990 *New York Times* article entitled "Sex Crimes Against Children: Many Doubt There's a Cure," Dr. Janis Bremer, a therapist in the Hennepin program and a member of a national group set up to study treatment methods for sexual offenders, said, "It's only the last few years that people have started saying that certain sex offenders are incurable." The best hope, in her opinion, lies with treatment when the offenders are young before the behavior becomes ingrained.

Dr. Gail Ryan of the University of Colorado's National Center for the Prevention and Treatment of Child Abuse and Neglect qualified Bremer's comment by saying "I don't think we're prepared to say that anybody is incurable, but they may not be treatable with the current methods we have at our disposal."

There is wide agreement that sex offenders are difficult to treat, yet many experts believe that highly motivated offenders can benefit. But motivation is not always easy to determine.

A trend toward more punishment and less treatment was particularly evident in the state of Washington, once thought to be a national model for its treatment programs for rapists and child molesters. Following a series of crimes by individuals who had undergone years of state-sponsored counseling and therapy, a state panel called for life sentences for rape and child molestation and a requirement that sexual offenders register with the county in which they reside after leaving prison.

An April 22, 1990 *New York Times* entitled "Do Sex Offenders Belong in Treatment or in Jail?" reported that in response to a state-sponsored study that claimed treatment programs are ineffective, Massachusetts governor Michael Dukakis introduced a bill that would increase prison terms for sex crimes. He also called for an end to the practice of using civil commitments to send some sex offenders to a treatment center at Bridgewater State Hospital for the Criminally Insane.

According to Fay Honey Knopp, director of the Safer Society Program of the New York State Council of Churches, this shift in thinking also occurred in many other states. Some experts questioned whether rehabil-

itation could be carried out in prison. Others blamed failures on underfinanced, incomplete and poorly run state programs. Budget cuts are also likely to take a toll on such programs.

Children Who Sexually Abuse Other Children. If therapists are correct in their assessment that treatment that begins early is most effective, then children who sexually abuse other children should have first priority for treatment. Victimization by an older brother, a fairly common form of child sexual abuse, very often goes unreported and therefore untreated. Even when juvenile offenders are reported and charged, the juvenile system seldom punishes them severely or treats them. The offenders are most likely to be sent to a minimum security setting, with no treatment, or given probation, with treatment at a local clinic. The latter sentence gives them ample opportunity to inflict additional abuse on their former victims or to find new ones.

While 60% to 80% of child sexual abuse is done by relatives or quasi-relatives and 20% to 40% is done by nonrelatives or strangers, the only significant difference between the two types of abusers is the degree of opportunity available to them. The opportunities to abuse a child in one's own home or in one's care are much greater than the opportunities to abuse a stranger.

Deprived of access to a child in his care, the juvenile offender is likely to seek one elsewhere. Such patterns of behavior are well known because adult offenders in treatment typically reveal that their first sexual molestation occurred as early as age ten.

A conference on juvenile sex offenders held in Keystone, Colorado was reported in a May 30, 1989 *New York Times* article entitled "Children as Sexual Prey, and Predators." Dr. Judith Becker, a psychiatrist at Columbia University's New York State Psychiatric Center, told the conference, "I have been working with these kids for 15 years now. The age of the perpetrators has been decreasing and the age of the victims has been decreasing. When I first got involved, the average age of the victims was 12. Now it's 8."

The biggest increase in arrests for forcible rape has been among children 14 and younger, the biggest increase being among 13- to 14-year-olds. The 1990 *Uniform Crime Report* of the Federal Bureau of Investigation (FBI) revealed that boys age 15 and under accounted for 5.2% (1,605 arrests) of the 30,966 rape arrests made during the year in the United States.

In an interview for a January 14, 1991 *Boston Globe* article entitled "Children Who Molest Children," Hunter

Hurst, director of the National Center for Juvenile Justice, a private nonprofit agency in Pittsburgh, disclosed that rape arrests among 13- and 14-year-olds more than doubled in a decade. Hurst asserted that the statistics reflected an actual increase and were not just due to increased sensitivity and better reporting.

Many therapists believe that there is a strong correlation between the increase in child sexual abuse by adults and the increase in sexually abused children who themselves become abusers while still children. A Boston therapist who specializes in child abuse said, "No six-year-old is born with the knowledge of how to sexually abuse another person." Child perpetrators have acquired the notion that this is what adults do to children. Therapists refer to such children as "abuse reactive" instead of sex offenders because they are responding to what has been done to them.

(See also CHILD ABUSE AND NEGLECT; MULTIPLE PERSONALITY DISORDER; PEDOPHILE.)

sexual abuse prevention   See RELAPSE PREVENTION: TREATMENT FOR SEX OFFENDERS; SEX CRIMES RESEARCH.

sexual slavery   See PROSTITUTION.

skinheads   Human rights groups such as the Anti-Defamation League (ADL) and the National Institute Against Prejudice and Violence, which monitor hate groups, claim that skinheads are revitalizing the dwindling ranks of groups such as the Ku Klux Klan. An import from Great Britain, the skinhead phenomenon first attracted attention in the United States when a shaven-headed group from Chicago that called itself Romantic Violence took part in a national conference of white supremacists in Michigan.

The group attended the conference to promote a hoped-for American tour of a British white-power band, a tour that never took place. The group's members displayed the now-familiar shaven heads, neo-Nazi tattoos, steel-toed Doc Martens work boots and outspoken support of racism and violence.

Not everyone with a shaven head (a baldy) or partially shaven head (a two-tone) is a racist. In the opinion of the ADL, racist skinheads are considerably outnumbered by nonracist ones, but the number of racists is growing. As of fall 1990, racist skinheads were active in 31 states, compared with 21 a year earlier. Their membership had grown to 3,000.

Skinheads do not just talk about violence. Murders have been attributed to them, as well as scores of assaults on minority group members and vandalism of religious institutions, particularly synagogues. The most troubling trend, according to the ADL, is a growing pattern of recruitment in high schools and the acquisition of deadlier weaponry.

A typical series of high school-related incidents took place at Groves High School in Birmingham, Michigan, a suburb of Detroit. In late November 1988 three non-student skinheads entered the high school and were joined by three students . The six roamed the halls until they confronted two students, one black and one white. A brawl broke out. The skinhead students were expelled and transferred to another high school—where a small skinhead group already existed.

The problems at Groves were not over. On May 14, 1989 the outside of the high school was spray-painted with swastikas and the words "White Power" and "Skins." Sometime in mid-April 1989 racist flyers were found taped to a tree, a fence, a telephone pole and the outside of school doors. Two weeks later the word "nigger" was scrawled across the lockers of several black students. Other lockers were defaced with swastikas.

Another high school confronted with skinheads was Douglas High School in Castle Rock, Colorado, where about a dozen skinheads were responsible for several racial harassment incidents. Heavy drug users, the skinhead students were considered to exert a powerful presence on the school campus. During homecoming week in the fall of 1989, a noose was hung on a black student's locker with a sign that read "Wanted: Three Blacks, Reward."

Skinheads have tried with varying levels of success to recruit students directly on school campuses. In Waco, Texas they sent a mass mailing to parents of students at Waco High School. The letter, addressed to "proud parents," warned of the dangers posed by "minority gangs and drug pushers" and proposed that "it is time that common White Americans stood up and demanded that their children attend schools not polluted with drugs, gangs, and anti-Christian immorality." The letter offered additional information on request.

The favorite weapons of skinheads tend to be crude and simple: knives, bats, chains and Doc Martens boots. However, evidence has come to light of possession of more deadly weapons, including semiautomatic weapons, explosives and detonators. The skinheads have been helped by other organized hate groups. For example, Tom Metzger of the White Aryan Resistance (WAR) and his son John traveled to Phoenix in January of 1990 to lead skinheads in a commemorative march. Later the two men engaged in weapons training with the Arizona White Battalion in the desert.

The Chattanooga Confederate Hammer Skinheads and the Memphis group MASH are closely aligned with the Dallas-based Confederate Hammer Skins. The alliance has been the core of skinhead recruiting in other states and has maintained close ties with the Metzgers. One of the more active groups is the Old Glory Skins, based in Atlanta. It has a branch in Orlando, Florida. While the Confederate Hammer Skins and the Old Glory Skins have a level of organizational sophistication higher than most skinhead groups, it is not uncommon for skinheads to develop informal ties in other parts of the country.

Much of skinhead organizing has centered around several charismatic figures (most of whom are in their 20s, and therefore older than most rank-and-file members). Among the most successful leaders is John Metzger, who himself is not a skinhead. His WAR Youth Group works in tandem with his father Tom's White Aryan Resistance to organize skinheads throughout the country.

Another successful leader is Robert Heick of the San Francisco-based American Front. He has organized in California, Florida and Maryland. Still another is Michael Palasch, head of the National White Resistance in Metairie, Louisiana. He has formed chapters in Indianapolis, Cincinnati, Columbus and on Long Island, in New York.

Metzger, Heick and Palasch have gained "celebrity" status through numerous appearances on TV talk shows. The most notorious resulted in a brawl on the Geraldo Rivera program that injured the host. Following appearances on the Donahue and Oprah shows, John Metzger claimed that he received a thousand letters with money enclosed.

Given the membership's lack of discipline and antiorganizational impulses, the ADL does not believe that the separate groups will ever become a single national entity, but their recruiting power will probably contribute to the movement's long-term survival.

Although the ADL asserts that nonracist skinheads outnumber racist ones, the distinction between them often blurs. Some skinheads who claim that they are not racists avow a belief in "white pride." A good many skinheads eventually join a neo-Nazi gang. Some have been arrested for violently assaulting gays.

It is not unusual for blacks and Hispanics to belong to nonracist skinhead groups. They may be nonracist, but they are not nonviolent. On the contrary, they are likely to boast about how many fights they have been in with neo-Nazi skinheads. The entire skinhead milieu is a violent one. Skinheads have beaten, stomped and stabbed other skinheads, punk rockers, long-haired "hippies," gays and members of despised racial and religious groups.

In a civil suit filed by the Southern Poverty Law Center, on October 22, 1990, a jury in Portland, Oregon found Tom Metzger and his son John liable for the November 1988 slaying of Mulugeta Seraw, a 27-year-old Ethiopian student, at the hands of skinheads. The jury ordered a $12.5 million judgment against the Metzgers, concluding that they had incited the skinheads to violence against Jews and minorities.

In December 1990, in an effort to collect some of the money awarded in the judgment, lawyers for the family went back to court to seize Tom Metzger's assets. At the same time they obtained a court order against Wyatt Kaldenberg, former managing editor of Tom Metzger's white supremacist paper *War*.

James Elroy, an attorney for Seraw's family, claimed that Kaldenberg had opened a bank account to use as a front to collect money intended for Tom Metzger's use. Tom Metzger insisted that the account belonged to Kaldenberg and that he had opened it to raise money for the Metzgers' legal defense, appeal and trial transcripts.

In 1987 the Southern Poverty Law Center won a civil judgment of $7 million against Robert Shelton and the United Klans of America (UKA), effectively bankrupting that organization. The $12.5 million judgment against the Metzgers may have the same effect, but like the Klan they will likely find other outlets to express their hate.

(See also HATE CRIMES; HATE GROUPS, SOCIOPATHS.)

slumlords   See ARSON.

sociopaths   The characteristic behavior of the people referred to as sociopaths or psychopaths (the two terms are used interchangeably) is defined by the *Diagnostic and Statistical Manual, 3rd Edition, Revised* (DSM-III-

R) as antisocial personality disorder in adults and conduct disorder in children. The essential feature of this disorder is a pattern of irresponsible and antisocial behavior beginning in childhood.

In childhood, typical behaviors include lying, stealing, truancy, vandalism, starting fights, running away from home and physical cruelty. In adulthood, typical behavior includes shirking financial obligations, being an irresponsible parent, impulsivity, lack of planning for the future, disregard of social norms and illegal acts, such as destroying property, harassing others or stealing. Sociopaths are frequently in shady or criminal occupations.

Sociopaths tend to be irritable, aggressive and assaultive. They frequently beat their wives and children. They are often reckless and ignore their own safety and the safety of others; speeding and driving while intoxicated are common. They are promiscuous (defined as the failure to maintain a monogamous relationship for more than a year).

The most striking characteristic of sociopaths is their lack of remorse about the impact their behavior has on others. Frequently they feel justified in their mistreatment of others.

Although sociopaths evidence no signs of psychosis, they frequently are distressed by such symptoms as tension, an inability to tolerate boredom, depression and a belief that others feel hostile toward them, a belief that is likely to be valid given their behavior.

Sociopaths' more flagrant antisocial behavior tends to diminish after age 30. However, their interpersonal problems and dysphoria (persistent agitation and depression without an obvious cause) tend to continue. Lasting close, warm, responsible relationships with friends, family or sexual partners are rare.

The *DSM-III-R* asserts that some adults who exhibit several features of sociopathy but who manage to achieve power and financial success lack some aspects of the disorder, in particular the childhood onset of the symptoms, since these severely interfere with school achievement. For most the disorder is so incapacitating that they never become independent adults and are likely to spend many years in institutions. Moreover, they are likely to die at an early age.

The absence of consistent parental discipline appears to increase the likelihood of conduct disorder, which may later become antisocial personality disorder. Other contributing factors are child abuse, removal from the home and a childhood spent without parental figures of both sexes.

Much more common in males than females, incidence is estimated to be about 3% among American males and about 1% among American females. Compared to the general population, the risk is five times greater among first-degree biological relatives of males with the disorder and almost ten times greater for first-egree biological relatives of females with the disorder.

The disorder is more common among those living in poverty. There are several plausible reasons. The disorder results in a sporadic work history, frequent time spent in institutions as a consequence of criminal behavior and often an early death, all of which limit earnings. One result is that the children of sociopaths are likely to grow up in impoverished circumstances. Even when they do have money, sociopaths frequently ignore parental obligations. Their children often suffer from malnutrition, lack minimal hygiene or medical care and are forced to depend on neighbors or relatives who live elsewhere for food and shelter.

Adoption studies have revealed that both genetic and environmental factors contribute to the disorder. Both the adopted and biological children of parents with antisocial personality disorder have an increased risk of the same disorder or of psychoactive substance use disorder (drug abuse) or somatization disorder (a history of physical complaints or belief that one is sickly unrelated to any typical cause such as disease, injury, drugs or alcohol).

Robert Hare, a psychologist at the University of British Columbia in Vancouver, has spent more than two decades studying sociopaths. His research has led him to believe that sociopaths' faulty understanding of emotions may be due to an unusual neurological pattern. In normal right-handed people, the language center is always located in the left hemisphere of the brain. Among right-handed sociopaths, language is controlled as much by the right hemisphere as by the left. The pattern is rare and Dr. Hare believes it may signal a failure to develop during maturation. His theory is one of a long list of theories, none of which has thus far adequately explained the phenomenon.

Key traits Hare found among sociopaths were glibness and superficial charm. Some theorists do not accept the *DSM-III-R*'s position that successful adult sociopaths lack the early onset of the disorder. They suspect that the successful sociopaths were better able to use their glibness and charm to cover up childhood aberrations than unsuccessful ones, who wound up in institutions or were killed at an early age.

After decades of viewing sociopaths as psychotherapeutically untreatable because of their inability to form the emotional bonds necessary to therapy, several treatment centers in the late 1980s began reporting some success using behavioral methods. The most successful programs require sociopaths to remain in treatment for months or years under conditions in which the rules are firmly and strictly interpreted so patients cannot glibly "con" their way around them.

The initial reaction of a patient to an inability to manipulate the environment is to become depressed. Over time the sociopath becomes aware of an inner emptiness, and despair arises from recognition of his or her incapacity to make connections with others. Psychiatrist William Reid of the University Medical School in San Antonio, Texas, the author of *Unmasking the Psychopath* (1986), described the effect of treatment: "Despite his cool exterior, inside he is like a poor child on a cold night looking through a window at the warmth of a family gathered around the fire."

(See also MASS MURDERS; MENTAL ILLNESS: BEHAVIORS THAT ATTRACT NEGATIVE ATTENTION; SERIAL KILLERS.)

solitary confinement   See PRISONERS: MANAGEMENT OF THE PERSISTENTLY VIOLENT.

sports violence   Sports spectators throughout recorded history have been violent. The original Olympics were suspended due to the behavior of the crowds. In 1314 Edward II of England banned football because it touched off bloody brawls among fans. At a 1964 soccer match in Lima, Peru, 300 people were killed and 500 injured.

Security people in sports stadiums and arenas everywhere single out 20- to-30-year old males as the most likely fans to create disturbances. Although fan violence in the United States does not approach that found at soccer games in other parts of the world, there is consensus that fan violence over the last quarter century has escalated. One clear measure of the increase in violence is the rising cost of crowd control.

A January 31, 1983 *Sports Illustrated* article entitled "Violence Out of Hand in the Stands," by Bill Gilbert and Lisa Twyman provided a sample of some fan violence at sports events in the United States:

- At a Friday night of boxing in Madison Square Garden in 1978, two men were stabbed, another was shot by an off-duty corrections officer and a woman was treated for severe head lacerations after being struck by a bottle.
- In 1980 the Detroit Tigers temporarily closed the bleachers in their stadium to discourage chronically violent spectators.
- The Cincinnati Reds had their players and the players of the opposing team, the Pittsburgh Pirates, leave the field during a May 1981 game at Riverfront Stadium until control could be gained of the rowdy crowd.
- During a 1981 American League playoff game at Yankee Stadium, a fan equipped with a blackjack charged onto the field and knocked down the third-base umpire, who was saved from further injury by player intervention.
- Following a California State Lightweight Boxing Championship in Sacramento during the summer of 1982, a brawl broke out involving an estimated 75 to 100 fans and resulted in seven stabbings, four of which required hospitalization.

For a few years in the 1970s, Fenway Park in Boston was referred to as an open-air Animal House. Present-day security forces keep a tight rein on fan behavior. A July 8, 1991 *Boston Globe* article entitled "Fanning Fenway," described the differences between the current crowds and those of the 1970s:

> Gone since 1979 are the benches in the bleachers and their lounging pot-smokers and six-pack smugglers; long gone are the gamblers who used to congregate high in the right field corner, remarkable for betting large sums on the next pitch . . . also gone is the old security force of local college and semi-pro football players whose idea of a good deed was diving into a row of seats and tackling a miscreant.

In the opinion of Gilbert and Twyman, most sports executives perceive fan violence as a big problem and have called on the aid of experts. The experts generally agree that there are many sources of tension in sports crowds. Among them are close contact with strangers and competition for territory, services and information, all of which create a generalized irritability. Moreover, sports facilities are often inefficient, uncomfortable and unattractive, despite the fact that sports regularly draw larger crowds than many other recreational events.

Although sports events are exhibitions of skill and coordination, many contain elements of intrinsic violence. The games themselves stir up emotions. The language with which they are described is strikingly warlike—crush, demolish, trample, kill. Sports crowds are encouraged to respond to the game by cheering, booing, hissing, waving their fists and screaming criticisms.

Fans frequently forget that games are staged conflicts. Michael Smith, a Canadian sociologist and former football player, hockey player and hockey coach, believes that violence on the field contributes to violence among the spectators. By analyzing newspaper accounts of 68 episodes of collective violence among spectators during or after sporting events, Smith discredited the once-popular theory that sports act as a catharsis for spectators, draining away feelings of violence. In three quarters of the incidents, violence in the game precipitated spectator violence.

In an investigation of whether fights by athletes provoked violence by fans, Boston University education professor Dr. John Cheffers, a former Australian football player and track athlete, together with sociologist Dr. Jay Meehan and graduate students, used video equipment to observe sports spectators. The researchers found that violence among players triggered violence in the stands in 57% of the soccer games, 49% of football games, 34% of baseball games, but only 8.5% of hockey games. Cheffers speculated that hockey fans see so many fights that the fights lose their impact.

Contact sports provide most examples of fan violence, while golf, tennis and track provide few. Boxing crowds are not particularly disorderly, but when they do become aroused, the violence tends to be more lethal, often including guns or knives.

The Influence of Alcohol. Pat Sullivan, whose family operates the New England Patriots football team, finds the theories of the experts interesting, but he believes the main problem is that the fans are drunk. Many other sports officials agree with him. More than 90% of the home stadiums and arenas of professional teams serve beer and almost 40% serve hard liquor.

The sale of alcohol in professional sports stadiums is highly profitable and not likely to be discontinued. Invariably sports officials minimize the impact of alcohol sold in the stands and say the real problem is alcohol drunk earlier by fans or carried in coolers or brown bags.

There is general consensus that the reason college crowds present fewer security problems is that only a handful of colleges permit the sale of beer in their stadiums, which probably has the effect of reducing the amount of alcohol carried in and openly consumed. The same is probably true at a high school level where the amount of alcohol is even lower and the size of the crowds is smaller.

Bolstering the notion that many fans have already been drinking before they arrive, Joe McDermot, the executive in charge of security at Boston's Fenway Park, told Gilbert and Twyman that most of the trouble among the 35,000 people who cram Fenway Park on any given day tends to happen in the first few innings. He added that the beer served in the park is mostly froth and unlikely to account for the fans' behavior.

The assistant chief of security at Fenway Park, Stephen Corcoran, hires 50 to 60 college-age security assistants, who, dressed in blue blazers and carrying radios, keep in constant touch. When a security assistant identifies someone who is "incapacitated" and a police officer concurs, the person is escorted out, to the street if he behaves, or into custody if he does not (no arrest can be made unless he actually commits an offense).

Once fans become unruly, the preferred technique is to remove the three or four nearest to the aisle. This sends a message. Then as many as needed are removed one at a time as they go downstairs to get another beer or to relieve the pressure on their bladders.

Corcoran, who is also a middle-school administrator, views the problems at the ball park as similar to those at a junior high school. "It's the anonymity. I think fans are just like students, except here the clients are bigger . . . People do things here they would never do in their own community."

A particular problem at Fenway Park is busloads of out-of-town people. They pass the time on the trip to Boston emptying their beer coolers and often arrive on the edge of incapacitation.

A veteran Fenway Park usher said, "You know there's a problem when they walk in and you hear them talking about where they are going to meet after they get thrown out." Another said, "We watch for guys who aren't paying much attention to the game, just waiting around and hanging out."

Of those who hang out, Dr. Arnold Beisser, a Los Angeles psychiatrist with an interest in sports, has said, "We're seeing a new use of violence. It's being used not as a means to an end but for recreational purposes, for pleasure. It's an end in itself."

European Fans. The security cost for a single game at Fenway Park is about $10,000. Nevertheless, the security problems at American sporting events in no way compare with the difficulties faced by security forces at British football (soccer) games. The effort to keep the fans under control requires an enormous police presence. The cost per year is about $34 million in overtime, not including the expense of closed-circuit television systems within the stadiums, video scanners outside the stadiums, body scanners, metal detector gates in some stadiums and extra fencing. When the British police expect trouble, as many as 1,000 police may be on duty.

England was banned for four years from playing in other parts of Europe because of "football hooliganism" among fans. The ban stemmed from the May 1985 behavior of spectators from Liverpool at Heysel Stadium in Brussels, Belgium during the European Cup final between Liverpool and the Italian team, Juventus. Thirty-nine people, most of them Italians, were crushed to death in riots.

On April 11, 1989 executives of the governing Union of the European Football Association (AEFA) voted to permit English clubs to participate once again, subject to the good behavior of the fans. The approval came in the wake of a proposal by Prime Minister Margaret Thatcher's government of a law to require fans to carry photo identity cards to gain admittance to games. Those convicted of making trouble would be denied cards.

Making trouble is routine in England's old soccer stadiums (the newest one was built in 1923), which are laid out in separate standing-room terraces for rival fans, concrete areas where the police keep watch, and unsegregated stands where, for a higher price, fans are seated. (Presumably, seated fans who can pay more are better able to control their rivalry and thus don't need separation.)

Four days after its reinstatement by the AEFA, English soccer suffered a setback. Violence at a game in Sheffield left 94 fans dead and another 200 injured.

Several factors were implicated in the Sheffield tragedy. The allocation of stadium space into separate standing-room sloped terraces to keep fans apart resulted in overcrowding of the Liverpool terrace. To prevent deaths outside the stadium among 4,000 fans waiting for admission, the police opened the admission gates into the already crammed Liverpool terrace. The surge of newcomers at the top of the terrace created a wave of force that was transmitted down the slope. Fans at the bottom of the slope were suffocated or crushed against a steel-mesh antihooligan control fence meant to prevent violence.

The Sheffield incident was just one more in a string of violent events for Liverpool's fans. The ritual culture of a soccer game in North London is described by Lesley Hazelton in an excerpt from her book *England, Bloody England* (1990) which appeared on May 7, 1989 in the *New York Times Magazine*.

There were few families here at the Arsenal home ground. Not many women at all. Or young children. Or blacks. The 35,000-strong crowd, packed into a structure the size of a small spring-training stadium in Florida, consisted almost entirely of white men aged 15 to 30. All with lusty lungs for cursing and shouting, and lusty bellies filled with strong English ale.

At a critical moment in the game, according to Hazelton, the game on the field became of minor consequence.

Eyes glazed, fists punching in the air, they weren't . . . paying attention to the players. They were focused entirely on the Manchester United terrace . . . It was like some tribal dance . . . a combination war and fertility dance . . . Penned behind their fences, the Manchester supporters responded in kind, spurring the Arsenal fans to more contortions.

Fans entering the terraces are frisked by the police. A few of the items British police have confiscated from fans are sharpened coins, bricks, catapults, concrete, razor blades, spring-loaded spikes, plastic lemons filled with ammonia, tear-gas grenades, spiked balls and darts. While some of the violence is aimed at referees, linesmen and players, most of it is directed toward rival fans.

The typical terrace fan may or may not have a job, but he does have enough money to pay for the bus to the game, several pints of beer and the admission ticket. But he has no real chance of changing his economic status in England's rigid class society. Thus football becomes his only real interest.

There would appear also to be a psychic cost to the animosity that sours the experience. Emptying a soccer stadium is like a military operation. The wildly cheering, booing, singing mood of the game is erased by the presence of a solid line of police officers, police dogs and police horses, with a helicopter overhead. The fans become a silent crowd, slowly shuffling their feet along the pavement toward segregated trains that will whisk them promptly away from the temptations of violence.

Player Violence.   A level of violence on the playing field in the United States not called for by the rules of the game also appears to be escalating. An August 27,

1990 *Sports Illustrated* article entitled "Brawl Game," by Steve Wulf, described a brawl that began when Chicago White Sox pitcher Greg Hibbard hit Texas Rangers hitter Steve Buechele with a pitch. Buechele left the batter's box to charge the mound, precipitating a bench-clearing confrontation.

The fracas was the third such incident in a nine-day span and the tenth of the season. All of the incidents started when a batter objected to a pitch and went after the pitcher. Among the more gruesome scenes was Philadelphia Phillies catcher Darren Daulton repeatedly punching New York Mets pitcher Dwight Gooden in the back of the head and two Philadelphia players choking New York infielder Tom O'Malley. Philadelphia general manager Lee Thomas, whose team was involved in two bench clearances in a month, told Wulf, "It seems like a day doesn't go by anymore without a brawl, It's getting worse than hockey. What I'm afraid is going to happen is that one of these days a player is really going to get hurt in one of these fights."

A contributing factor to the violent pitcher-batter interaction is the fact that umpires have shifted the strike zone a bit to the outside and hitters are leaning more over the plate where they are less able to escape being hit by an inside pitch. Moreover, new major league pitchers are being taught to pitch inside. Young batters who have never experienced such a threat get angry.

To make matters more tense, some old-school pitching coaches pass along a code dictating that a pitcher should throw at a hitter who has homered off him or who has come up after one or more of his teammates have homered. There is general agreement that one way to keep fights between two players from involving the whole team is to punish severely the third man to join in the battle.

As players have gotten bigger and stronger, college basketball also seems to have become more violent. A February 11, 1991 *Sports Illustrated* article entitled "Bruise News" reported that a number of coaches are concerned that basketball is rougher than it was 20 or even ten years ago. Louisiana State University's Dale Brown put together a videotape of what he deemed was unnecessarily harsh treatment of one of his players that had gone unpenalized and sent it to the conference supervisor of officials. Oklahoma coach Billy Tubbs said, "The game has to be restructured. It's becoming block and tackle, push and shove."

In the view of free safety Jack Tatum, who played for the Oakland Raiders, football in the United States also needs restructuring to protect its players from vio-

lence. In his 1979 book *They Call Me Assassin*, written with Bill Kushner, Tatum proposed that rules are needed to cut down on injuries and to allow the game to be played with some degree of civilized behavior. He said:

> I could just make tackles without really trying to blast through the man, but I am expected to, and the rules are designed in my favor because people want the excitement of violent play . . . A receiver is looking for, and concentrating on, the ball . . . and the free safety acts like a missile homing in on the man's rib cage, head, or knees. It's got to hurt the receiver, and after a few hits, the man's will to win is warped.

Clearly, there are differences of opinion about the sources of sports violence. Some researchers believe violence on the field inspires violence in the fans. It is also possible that rowdy crowds precipitate violence on the field. American sports managers believe bootlegged alcohol prompts fan violence. In England working-class rivalries fueled by alcohol seem responsible.

Violence among players in football and hockey, which are perceived as America's most violent sports, seems to be related to how the games are structured and whether rules to protect players are developed and enforced. On both sides of the Atlantic, violence for its own sake has become a recreation for many.

street children   Some social critics make a distinction among runaway children, who presumably have a home they could return to, throwaway children, who have been pushed out of their homes, and street children, who travel in gangs in some of the world's large cities, such as Paris, Rio de Janeiro and Sao Paulo. Despite the differences in how they came to their plight, they face similar risks by having no permanent shelter, no secure means of support, no adult to turn to for help and no one who cares about their fate.

Children who are members of homeless families in the United States may sleep in the streets or in shelters. Shelters are typically overcrowded, rundown hotels in dangerous areas or barracks-type buildings such as armories or gyms. Both settings make children highly vulnerable to crime. Homeless children also are likely to be malnourished and undereducated. Many fear that such children are becoming an underclass that may never be brought into the mainstream of society.

A September 30, 1988 *Christian Science Monitor* story on troubled children included an interview with Molly Worthley, director of a private drop-in center in Portland, Oregon, who said, "It is difficult, when kids are 16 or 17, to find people who will take them into their homes [in foster care] . . . The year before last, we lost 17 kids. Kids die on the streets.''

Despite the risks, many runaways may be safer on the streets than they are in their homes. Mark David Janus, a Catholic priest who is a University of Connecticut psychologist, conducted a survey among 195 teenage runaways at a Toronto shelter.

Janus reported that 86% had been physically or sexually abused at home, while 67% had been abused on the streets. The contrast between home and the streets was more stark for girls: 94% had been abused at home and 64% on the streets. These teenagers had run away an average of 8.5 times before leaving for good, suggesting the hopelessness of conditions in their homes.

Based on differences in definition and counting methods, estimates of the number of youngsters who run away each year in the United States vary. There is general agreement that at least 300,000 live permanently on the streets, where many of them do not survive.

Parade Magazine, which has done periodic updates on runaways and throwaway children since 1978, estimated in July 1986 that the population of children on American streets had remained stable from 1982 to 1986 at about 1 million to 1.3 million, but that the proportion in the 12- to 14-year age range had increased.

A 1988 Department of Justice survey of 80 youth-serving agencies concluded that 450,000 juveniles annually leave home and stay away at least overnight. A narrower definition determined that approximately 13,500 juveniles were without a permanent or secure home or had run away from a juvenile facility. These findings were similar to those found in a 1975 Department of Justice study.

The Sourcebook of Criminal Justice Statistics—1990, published by the U.S. Department of Justice, reported that in 1989 there were 130,272 arrests of runaways. Analysis of data regarding 86,956 status offenders (those who commit acts that are crimes only if committed by persons under a specified age) from 14 states determined that 17,589 (21%) were runaways, and of that group 4,925 were 14 years of age or younger.

Most of the nation's approximately 500 shelters operate on minuscule budgets and have few beds to offer street children. The most extensive program in the United States is Covenant House, headquartered in New York, which cares for 18,000 youngsters annually in New York, Houston, Toronto and Fort Lauderdale. (The priest who founded and was the first director of Covenant House was accused of sexual abuse and resigned.

He was replaced by a nun. The negative publicity that followed threatened the continuing existence of the organization for a couple of years, but the new director and the board were able to keep it going.)

A profile of recipients who received help in the late 1980s from Covenant House revealed that 70% were white, 19% African-American, 7% Latino, and 4% other. Although most were in their middle teens, about one third of the boys had left home before the age of 12. Approximately 50% had been physically and/or sexually abused at home. The parents of 60% were alcoholic, drug abusers or had been in trouble with the law. Seventy percent admitted drug use and 25% had been born to mothers under age 17. Among the girls, 36% had been pregnant and 25% had been raped. Among the boys, almost 50% of those under 14 were sexually active, but only 23% used birth control.

Outside the United States, conditions for street children are even worse. Many of the children who steal and pick pockets on the streets of Paris and Rome were brought there from impoverished communities in other parts of Europe. After training by adults they were made a part of street gangs.

The January 25, 1991 issue of *Scholastic Update,* which was devoted to the question of why 40,000 of the world's children die each day, interviewed a spokesperson from the organization Save the Children, who said, ''The growing number of street children is one of the most serious problems facing the planet. An entire generation of children is being lost.''

Latin America is thought to have the highest number of street children, but millions also can be found in Asia and Africa. In Brazil an estimated 12 to 24 million children live on the streets. According to the Brazilian Health Ministry, the Brazilian Institute of Social and Economic Analysis and the Brazilian League of Human Rights, a war against the children was launched by death squads made up mostly of retired and off-duty police.

The death squads came into existence in the 1960s with the goal of getting rid of criminals not handled by Brazil's impotent courts and not incidentally getting rid of opponents of the military government in power at the time. Street children offered the death squads a new target, enhanced by rewards offered by some shopkeepers.

Since 1985 an estimated 1,500 children have been killed, not all by death squads. Children also have been killed in police stations and in secret police or military torture chambers.

Scholastic Update reported that almost 100,000 street children from across Brazil formed the National Movement of Street Boys and Girls of Brazil. Almost 800 of them marched on the capital city of Brasilia in September 1990, where they took over the speaker's podium of the Brazilian Senate to ask for basic rights such as health care, education and protection from violence. Legislation was introduced, but the killings and torture continued.

Trapped by abject poverty and indifferent societies, many street children turn to drugs to ease their physical and psychological pain. Unable to afford expensive drugs such as cocaine and heroin, they use substitutes such as nail-polish remover and glue. Drugs not only ease pain, they enable children to overcome their fear of the sort of activities they must engage in, such as prostitution and picking pockets, to earn a living.

An estimated 22,500 boys and girls—some as young as eight or nine—of Manila's 75,000 street children are prostitutes. Their market, mostly U.S. soldiers, may change or disappear with the closing of American bases in the Philippines.

Despite the fact that it is officially illegal in Thailand, prostitution is the nation's most lucrative tourist attraction. Commercial sex brings in visitors from Japan, Australia, Europe and the United States, who spend millions. In Thailand, young girls are sold into prostitution by their peasant parents for about $1,000 each, a significant amount for a family that may earn no more than $600 a year.

The sex business became a lucrative industry for Thailand during the Vietnam War, when Bangkok was a rest and recreation center for U.S. servicemen on leave. Current customers for Thailand's estimated 60,000 brothels and 800,000 prostitutes are middle-age businessmen.

Crippled children among Bombay, India's estimated 1.3 million street children are particularly vulnerable to men known as "uncles," who collect them in order to put them to work begging in exchange for a place to sleep and food.

(See also CHILD ABUSE AND NEGLECT; CHILDREN'S RIGHTS; EMOTIONAL ABUSE OF CHILDREN; GANGS: PICKUP OR TEMPORARY; JUVENILE JUSTICE: A SYSTEM OF CONTRADICTIONS; MULTIPLE PERSONALITY DISORDER; PEDOPHILE; SEXUAL ABUSE OF CHILDREN.)

street crimes   The term street crime is an umbrella category that includes murder, rape, robbery, assault, mugging, burglary, larceny, arson and auto theft. It is synonymous with sudden, often violent crimes that arouse fear or are experienced as intrusions into ordinary citizens' lives. Sometimes the idea is referred to as "neighborhood crime." Not all street crimes happen literally in the street or on the sidewalk.

Inclusions in the category of street crimes resemble those that make up the Federal Bureau of Investigation (FBI) Crime index, except that the index includes aggravated assault but not simple assault and it does not tabulate muggings separately. The National Commission on the Causes and Prevention of Violence in their 1969 report, published as *Violence in America,* volumes. 1–16 (1983), made an additional distinction by asserting that street crime is committed by strangers, while personal crime is committed by intimates.

Public perception of the most recent crime crisis began in the 1960s when crime rates began to rise. Some scholars question whether the current crime crisis is any different from ones that have gone before. In an address to the 28th Annual Judicial Conference of the Third Judicial Circuit of the United States, University of Michigan law professor Yale Kamisar asked, "When wasn't there a crime crisis?"

Other scholars suggest that the impact of drugs has made qualitative and quantitative differences to the current crime crisis. In his 1991 book *Pipe Dream Blues: Racism and the War on Drugs,* African-American journalist Clarence Lusane used the District of Columbia as a microcosm of the drug problem in America. Drug-related violence and shootouts became so common during the 1980s that a local band recorded a song to tell the world that D.C. did not stand for Dodge City.

Phencyclidine hydrochloride. (PCP), a hallucinogenic drug, followed by crack, a smokable form of cocaine, swept hundreds of local youth and adults into the drug culture and economy during the 1980s, and a bloody rivalry for control of drug traffic rocked many poor neighborhoods. The District's public hospital, D.C. General, reported injuries in children as young as eight years old who had been recruited into the traffic. Open-air drug markets serviced the District's estimated 20,000 cocaine addicts.

The District's criminal justice system aggressively pursued drug dealers and users. Of those charged with a drug offense between 1985 and 1987, 99% were African-Americans. The extent of the District's problem can be visualized from official figures. In 1986 the District, with 627,000 residents, reported 3,140 drug-trafficking convictions, while Manhattan (one borough of New York City), with 1.8 million residents, reported only 3,085.

One factor that may have distinguished the current crisis from earlier ones is the rate of increase in urbanization. In the 1960s alone, the population living in U.S. Standard Metropolitan Statistical Areas (central cities and their suburbs) climbed by 19%. Between 1930 and 1960 the rural population of the United States decreased by more than half. Another distinguishing factor may have been the high birth rate from 1946 to 1964, which beginning in 1961 introduced nearly 1 million people in the age range of 15 to 24 (the so-called crime-prone years for males) into the population each year.

The crime rate peaked in 1981 at 13,423,800 arrests and began to decline. However, in 1986 it once again began an upward trend and by 1990 had reached a total of 14,474,600 reported offenses. The 1990 Crime Index breakdown as an indicator of the level of U.S. street crime is as follows:

Murder and nonnegligent homicide	23,440
Forcible rape	102,560
Robbery	639,270
Aggravated assault	1,054,860
Burglary	3,073,900
Larceny-theft	7,945,700
Motor vehicle theft	1,635,900
Arson	data insufficient to estimate

If by definition street crimes are committed by strangers, then to make the crime index a more accurate estimate of street crimes, an estimated 51% of murders committed by relatives, friends and acquaintances (11,954) and an estimated 50% of rapes committed by acquaintances (51,280) must be subtracted. That leaves an estimated 14,411,366 street crimes in 1990.

Since the 1960s, crime levels have engendered widespread fear among residents of American cities. Much of the fear has been due to a rise in violent crime. Although the crime index increased by a modest 7.8% between 1981 and 1990, violent crimes increased by 33.7% during the same period. This may explain why in 1986 in a number of polls, Americans ranked crime as the most serious problem in their communities. Many claimed they were afraid to leave their homes after dark.

A seldom-mentioned factor in fueling public fears is the level of unreported crime. A representative national telephone survey by the Bureau of Justice Statistics (BJS) in 1987 found that only a little more than a third of victimizations (excluding murder) had been reported to police. The rates for reporting crimes varied: rape, 53%; robbery, 56%; larceny, 25%. Many respondents in the 1984 BJS survey said they had not reported a crime because they did not have sufficient evidence or because the injury was not important enough. Consequential or not, a street crime has a lingering psychological effect on the victim. People who have been burglarized often change their residence and if possible avoid the area in which the crime occurred.

Clearance of crimes by arrest has been low since the colonial era and thus has been a frequent target of public criticism. In 1990, 22% of FBI Crime Index offenses were cleared: 46% of violent crimes, 67% of murders, 57% of aggravated assaults, 53% of forcible rapes and 25% of robberies. The overall property crime clearance rate was 18%: 20% of larceny-thefts, 15% of motor vehicle thefts and 14% of burglaries.

Economic Impact. Street crime tends to have its greatest impact on poor people; street crimes are generally committed by poor people against other poor people who live in their neighborhoods. However, street crime sometimes moves out of the neighborhoods and into the central city, where tourists become favored targets.

This situation can have a severe economic effect on tourism, both in the United States and abroad. A U.S. State Department spokesperson issued a travel advisory in the spring of 1991 warning that street crime against travelers is a growing problem worldwide.

The State Department has been issuing travel advisories since 1978. These can have disastrous financial effects. In Jamaica, whose economy depends on more than 1 million tourists annually, 70% from the United States, officials were dismayed by an August 1991 State Department travel advisory warning Americans about crime in Kingston, the capital.

In September 1991 the value of the advisories came under attack by the Government Accounting Office (GAO). The GAO criticized the State Department for being inconsistent and misleading in its advisories, suggesting that political factors played a role in the department's failure to warn travelers that 139 American had been victims of violent crime in Mexico between June 1989 and February 1991.

Other analysts are frank in expressing their views that politics is used to manipulate the public's fear of crime. Political scientist Diana Gordon of the City College of New York begins her 1990 book *The Justice Juggernaut: Fighting Street Crime, Controlling Citizens* by saying "Even before the Democratic and Republican conventions of 1988, each of the potential presidential candidates was portraying himself as a relentless crime fighter and his opponent as more sympathetic to criminals than to victims."

According to Gordon, two decades of "get-tough" policy has dominated American criminal justice with no apparent reduction in street crime. Moreover, many more offenders are being punished more severely and the rights of criminal defendants have been narrowed. Get-tough programs may to some extent be responses to citizens' demands for protection but, in Gordon's opinion, they have more to do with criminal justice lobbies and ambitious politicians.

A factor almost never mentioned that may add to the public's overall feeling of danger is the annual number of traffic fatalities, which is more than double the annual homicide rate. The National Commission on the Causes and Prevention of Violence included violent behavior in connection with auto fatalities in their assessment of violence in America. The commission estimated that one in seven auto fatalities (14%) can be attributed to violent or reckless behavior by the driver, such as speeding or driving under the influence of alcohol or drugs. The behavior of the victim while under the influence is sometimes a factor too—a number of victims are killed each year because they are hit while sleeping in a street or highway.

In 1988 there were 47,093 traffic fatalities. If the commission's estimate is correct, then 6,593 fatalities that year were violence-related. Yet neither the FBI nor the BJS collects motor vehicle fatality data. It is left to the Highway Administration.

Prevention.   Many experts believe that one route to avoidance of street crime is the return of the neighborhood police officer. In an interview for a March 1986 *Scholastic Update* article entitled "New Weapons Against Street Crime," Robert Trojanowicz, head of the School of Criminal Justice at Michigan State University, said, "Community residents are the people who really control crime. The police officer intervenes when things get out of control. And, studies show, neighborhood residents feel safer knowing there's a familiar cop around."

A Police Foundation study suggested that fear of crime in crime-ridden areas contributes to a cycle of decay and disorder. James Stewart, director of the National Institute of Justice, the agency that commissioned the study, said, "Crime in a neighborhood blunts its vitality, withers its spirit, and infuses those law-abiding citizens unable to flee the neighborhood with a sense of futility and fear."

Since many people can't avoid high-crime areas because they live or work in them, a realistic tack is to work on changing individual communities. One such approach, called the Community Reclamation Project (CRP), tried to do just that in four communities of Los Angeles County. The strategies used by the CRP were described in a manual created by the project called *Rising Above Gangs and Drugs.*

In February 1989 the CRP, with funding from the federal Office of Juvenile Justice and Delinquency Prevention (OJJDP), set out to develop a model gang and drug prevention program for the target communities of Carson, Harbor City, Lomita and Wilmington. The CRP first identified existing resources and pinpointed gaps in services. Then by working with people in already existing programs, the staff helped design a plan with the goal of helping each community to take back its streets from gangs and drugs.

In keeping with the goal of disseminating information about how to reduce crime, the CRP's March 1991 newsletter described various Los Angeles law enforcement groups, including CRASH (Community Resources Against Street Hoodlums), OSS (Operation Safe Streets) and Computer Cops.

CRASH, a south Los Angeles, 80-officer criminal intelligence team of the Los Angeles Police Department (LAPD), handles roughly half of all the gang members in the city of Los Angeles. CRASH officers keep up-to-date books with photos and pertinent information about gang leaders, with the goal of getting leaders off the streets, since most members are followers. Deprived of their leaders, members may find something better to do.

The OSS, run by the L.A. County Sheriff's Department, was started in 1979 with the goal of vigorous arrest and prosecution of serious gang offenders. The head of Operation Safe Streets, Captain Raymond Gott, explained the need for community cooperation: "We could have 10,000 officers on the streets trying to take care of the gang problem, but unless the community becomes involved, there is very little we can do about the problem overall."

The Computer Cops, the LAPD's Support Division Gang Information Section, consists of 40 officers responsible for assimilating citywide data concerning the activities of street, motorcycle, ethnic and prison gangs. The section also monitors the gang files for the various CRASH units throughout the city.

Community programs take time to take effect. In the meantime, average frightened citizens need help in defending themselves. A supervisory agent in the FBI's Behavioral Science and Services Unit, Joe Harpold, advises that everyone should accept the possibility that a crime could happen to him or her. A mindset that accepts the possibility of crime is one that will accept the possibility of taking precautions.

Syndicated columnist Jack Anderson, after being mugged, offered a series of precautions he had garnered from experts in his April 17, 1991 column in *Parade Magazine*. He suggested that those who would avoid crime must:

- *Be aware of surroundings*. Muggers are most likely to select those who look most vulnerable. Being too preoccupied to look around suggests vulnerability.
- *Avoid predictable patterns*. Habitual patterns going to and from work make a criminal's planning easier.
- *Trust their instincts*. Many street crimes are done on the spur of the moment. When a small internal voice says to change direction, it should not be ignored.
- *Avoid traps*. Well-lit, populated areas, out of shadows and away from arm's reach of bushes, alleys or doorways, provide more safety.
- *Be aware that crimes don't happen just at night*. Activities such as jogging are better done with friends day or night.
- *Avoid clothes that serve as a trap*. Stylish shoes—men's or women's—tight skirts, flopping purses, tote bags or briefcases interfere with the ability to run. Also to be avoided are dangling jewelry or bulging wallets. The State Department advises travelers against wearing waist pouches, which advertise the location of valuables and can be cut or ripped off easily. To facilitate escape, packages in hand should be dropped. Things can always be replaced.
- *Be aware of distractions*. A mumbled question about change for a dollar or the location of the post office may be the prelude to a mugging.
- *Avoid gang territories, if possible*. Most gang violence is directed at other gangs, but a lot of bystanders get caught in the crossfire. For those who do not live in a gang's territory, it is best to stay out of them. For those who do, the best defense is knowledge of who

the gangs are and avoidance of them whenever possible.

(See also CRIME STATISTICS; FEAR OF CRIME; GANGS: PICKUP OR TEMPORARY; GANGS: STRUCTURED STREET; MODEL MUGGING; MURDER: U.S. PROFILE; PARENT ACCOUNTABILITY LAWS; POLICE; RAPE.)

suicide among youths   By 1989, over a period of three decades, the suicide rate for young Americans between the ages of 15 and 24 had almost tripled, making suicide the second leading cause of death for that group. The sharp increase in suicides for the 15- to 24-year-old population segment was in contrast to decreases in death rates for most other causes and thus considered a major public health problem in need of scrutiny.

To aid in understanding the sharp rise, the U.S. Department of Health and Human Services (HHS) organized a task force to investigate the problem. The task force published its findings in 1989 in a four-volume *Report of the Secretary's Task Force on Youth Suicide*.

In the past, suicide has traditionally been considered a mental health problem of older adults, particularly of white males over 35. Prevention efforts were based on the detection and treatment of psychological illnesses, mostly depression. However, beginning in 1980, more than half of all suicides occurred among those under age 40. Moreover, depression was less frequently implicated.

Almost 30,000 American take their own lives each year. This is greater than the annual 20,000 homicides. About 5,000 suicides a year occur among people ages 15 to 24. Although the suicide rate among the young continues to be lower than that of older age groups, its alarming increase at a time when suicide has been declining for older age groups is cause for concern.

At highest risk among the 15- to 24-year-olds were white males ages 20 to 24. Their risk per 100,000 in 1970 was 19.3; in 1980 it was 27.8; in 1986 28.4. The suicide risk for black males in the 20- to 24-year age group was lower and fluctuated. Per 100,000, in 1970 it was 18.7; in 1980 it was 20.0; and in 1986, 16.0. While much lower, the suicide rate for the 15- to 19-year-olds continued to rise, with the exception of black females, whose rate remained lower than any other group.

While suicide is often related to mental illness, only a portion of the young people who commit suicide have been diagnosed as mentally ill. Many, however, have had a history of a character disorder involving impulsive, aggressive, antisocial behavior, often complicated by substance abuse. Another large group comprises socially inhibited youngsters, who are perfectionists or prone to extreme anxiety when faced with social or academic challenges.

Certain risk factors are known to be associated with suicide. Among them are parental loss, family disruption, emotional stress, abuse and neglect, homosexuality, mental illness or drug use in a family member, a close relationship with a suicide victim, chronic or acute alcohol or drug abuse and access to firearms.

The breakup of a relationship, a recent arrest or the suffering of a rape, assault or beating are events that may trigger a suicide among the young. Moreover, researchers have found reduced levels of a serotonin metabolite (5-hydroxyindoleacetic acid) in the spinal fluid of young people who have committed suicide and other acts of violence.

A study reported in the November 10, 1990 *Science News* found that brain cells that mediate the perception of pleasure and pain in suicide victims differ from the same cells in people who die of natural causes. The study looked at opioid receptors that reside on the surface of some brain cells and sop up tiny amounts of opiumlike substances in the brain. The receptors play a critical role in an individual's sensations of well-being and suffering, physical and mental. Suicide victims and those who attempt suicide often say that they "can't take the pain" any more.

Access to lethal agents such as firearms, carbon monoxide or drugs makes successful suicide more likely. Guns are the most frequently used means of suicide for both males and females, followed by hanging, poisoning by drug overdoses and jumping from high places.

Five times as many males as females in the 15- to 24-year age group successfully commit suicide. Approximately three times as many females as males attempt suicide without succeeding. Information about suicide attempts is sketchy. There are an estimated eight to 20 attempts for every successful suicide. One out of ten who attempt suicide goes on to commit suicide successfully.

For many years suicide had been the third leading cause of death among young Americans 15 to 24, preceded by accidents and homicides. In 1984, because of a decline in the homicide rate, suicide moved up to second position.

Experts suggest that some other deaths, such as poisonings, single-car accident deaths and homicides, may actually be suicides. They observe that a number of deaths take place because potential suicides set up the conditions under which they will be killed, by driving recklessly or provoking someone with a short temper and a weapon.

However, recklessness is not clearly associated with suicidal impulses. One study examined recklessness using a new measure, the Sommerfeldt-Clark Adolescent Recklessness Scale (SCARS). They found that while some forms of recklessness appeared to be preceded by depressive illness and suicidal behavior, they were much more likely to be associated with substance abuse.

Many medical examiners and coroners believe that the number of reported suicides may represent only 50% to 85% of the actual number. A variety of factors contributes to underreporting. One is that different jurisdictions use different criteria to determine whether a death is a suicide. Some coroners require a signed suicide note. Personal biases, risk of the loss of insurance benefits, incomplete information and pressure from the family or community to avoid the stigma associated with suicide all contribute to underreporting.

The extent to which suicides are underreported makes it difficult to plan prevention strategies. The HHS task force recommended consulting behavioral scientists in the investigation of all youth suicides.

Information is also scarce about unusual patterns of suicide. Suicide clusters or "epidemics" sometimes occur in a community or school district within a short period of time. A number of youngsters of approximately the same age, usually known to one another—sometimes even best friends—commit suicide in separate instances. Sometimes as many as four have committed suicide together.

In March 1987, in Bergenfield, New Jersey, two boys and two girls, ages 16 to 19, killed themselves in a car by running the motor while parked in a closed garage. Only a day after the four were found, two girls died the same way in the Chicago suburb of Alsip, Illinois.

Unlike communicable diseases, suicide clusters or other unusual aspects of suicides are not reported to public health authorities. This makes it difficult to assess how often youth suicides occur in clusters, what proportion such suicides constitute of the total and whether their frequency is increasing.

One explanation for cluster suicides is the "contagion theory": the notion that the idea of suicide spreads among young people who are "exposed" either directly (when a friend or classmate commits suicide) or indirectly through television or radio reports, movies, books or discussions.

Some research suggests that indirect exposure through broadcast or print media might lead some susceptible individuals to commit suicide. Susceptible individuals may see themselves as similar in some way to the suicide victim or may imitate the suicide by choosing a similar method. If research determines that imitation is a real factor, then it could have a significant effect on the design of prevention measures.

One of the most troubling aspects for researchers of youth suicide is the lack of convincing data on the effectiveness of existing intervention programs. Evaluation is made difficult by a number of factors:

- the mobility of the young
- the absence of accurate data
- the lack of standard or comparable methods used in studies
- the difficulty of measuring the effectiveness of early intervention in preventing suicide later
- the difficulty of tracing anonymous hotline callers, particularly those who are mentally disturbed
- the difficulty of measuring the impact on suicide of programs not directly related to intervention or prevention
- the ethical issue of using a research control group that does not receive the designed intervention. Withholding effective treatment from a group at risk cannot be sanctioned. However, without a control group, it is virtually impossible to know how effective a treatment is
- the difficulty of isolating the effects of prevention programs from other variables
- the rarity of suicide, which makes it necessary to study large populations

Intervention Methods. Among the recommendations made by the HHS task force was the training of "gatekeepers," individuals most likely to come into contact with suicidal people. Gatekeepers include school personnel, counselors, coaches, parents and family members, friends, youth group and scout leaders, family physicians and members of the clergy.

Another recommendation was the development of an early screening device to identify those at risk. Ideally, such a device would be inexpensive, sensitive enough to distinguish high risks from low risks, quickly administrable by a variety of personnel, such as school or camp counselors or emergency room staffs, and easily scored and interpreted.

Another recommendation was the development of treatment strategies for the diverse population of suicide attempters. Innovative brief therapy is needed because

adolescents and their parents are resistant to long-term treatment. Moreover, because there is an increased risk of suicide among friends and families of those who succeed at suicide, support programs need to be developed and evaluated.

The task force also recommended the exploration and evaluation of means to limit the access of youth at high risk to lethal means of suicide, especially firearms. The United States is unique in the use of guns as the primary method to commit suicide. Over the past 15 years the methods of committing suicide changed dramatically. The proportion of suicides by firearms among both sexes increased while the proportion of suicides by poisons declined.

There is some evidence that controlling access to guns may reduce the overall frequency of firearm suicides. Some researchers suggest that if guns were unavailable, the impulse to commit suicide might pass before another method could be devised, or the potential suicide victim might switch to a less effective method. One study showed that teaching the principles of gun safety offered little hope of reducing the suicide toll.

In some institutions such as psychiatric hospitals and prisons, where suicides are more likely, special precautions are taken. Nevertheless, the suicide rate for juveniles in jail is five times higher than the national average. The most dangerous time is during the first hours of confinement.

Some communities have erected barriers on bridges to preclude suicide attempts, or put signs or telephones on popular bridges urging potential jumpers to call a local suicide prevention center before jumping.

The HHS task force recommended that suicide prevention programs be integrated into programs that address a wide range of self-destructive or problem behaviors, such as substance abuse, violence and unwanted teenage pregnancy.

The task force found that the state of knowledge about youth suicide was much less developed than about many other health problems. Acquisition of the needed knowledge, in the view of the task force, would take a carefully coordinated, sustained multidisciplinary approach to research. Moreover, prevention would demand commitment from health, mental health, education and social service institutions in both the public and the private sector.

The United States is not alone in its experience of a rise in youth suicide. In Norway, the richest country in Scandinavia, the suicide rate of 13.9 per 100,000 for age group 15 to 24 quadrupled in three decades. Over the course of eight days in early September 1990 nine people, eight of them under 30, committed suicide in the Bolzano region of northern Italy, an area that has a suicide rate six to seven times the national average. (Italy overall has one of the lowest suicide rates in the world, only 3.28 per 100,000.) Cluster suicides are apparently not exclusive to the United States.

(See also CHILDREN AND YOUTHS WITH GUNS; GUN CONTROL: ADVOCATES; GUN CONTROL: OPPONENTS.)

surveillance as a substitute for prison   See SENTENCING: A TREND TOWARD LONGER SENTENCES.

T

---

throwaway children   See STREET CHILDREN.

treatment programs in prison   Defendants convicted of violent offenses are more likely than those convicted of nonviolent offenses to be sentenced to prison and to serve longer terms, which raises the question of what happens to them in prison. In a study by J. Petersilia and colleagues entitled "The Prison Experience of Career Criminals," published by the Rand Corporation in 1980, information on a sample of prison inmates in three states was examined.

The researchers found that in-prison classification for security and participation in treatment programs was governed by the inmates' behavior in prison rather than by the nature of their convictions or past records. The study identified the most common kinds of programs as education and vocational training, and alcohol and drug abuse treatment. Inmates identified as having a great need for treatment in any of these areas typically had less than a ninth-grade education or a reading level below that of the ninth grade; no employment or schooling during the two years prior to the current prison term; and a self-reported serious drinking problem and/ or daily use of hard drugs in the two years prior to the current term.

Variation among the states in treatment needs and participation rates was considerable. The data revealed that a substantial portion of the inmate population with severe educational, vocational or drug-related problems were not in treatment.

The most frequently cited reason by high-need inmates for not participating in available programs was the belief that they did not need treatment. About 25% did not participate because of security reasons or due to discouragement by staff. For about 33%, drug programs were not available.

About half of the inmates claimed to have a work assignment that took up 30 to 40 hours each week. About 20% of those with no work assignment reported that there were no jobs available for them; however, most of those lacking work assignments appeared not to want them.

One highly successful educational treatment program entered its 20th year in 1991. The program was started by Elizabeth Barker, a former labor organizer and tenant activist who teaches English at Boston University. The original program began when a Boston University team needed practice for a television quiz program called the *GE College Bowl* and arrangements were made to compete against an inmate team at Massachusetts Correctional Institution (MCI)-Norfolk, a medium security prison.

On her first visit to MCI-Norfolk, the inmates who knew Barker was an English professor deluged her with their poetry. She became aware that some inmates longed for education for its own sake, and she soon proposed offering fully accredited courses, using unpaid faculty. While she waited for the Boston University administration to make its decision, Barker began a series of poetry readings.

By 1991, about 80 men had earned bachelor's degrees through the tuition-free program while in prison; others had completed their work after release. The first bachelor's degrees were awarded in 1977 and a master's program was begun in 1986.

During an interview for an April 7, 1991 *Boston Globe* article entitled "Poetry in Prison," Barker said,

> It isn't that no one ever gets arrested again. But it's usually something like a parole violation. The important thing is that none of our guys have hurt people after they have been released. This changes their heads. They want to help people not get into the trouble they got in. There is evidence everywhere that liberal arts education reduces recidivism to almost nothing.

In response to a question about why there are few programs like hers, Barker said, "So many politicians have taken a free ride on this 'get tough on crime' bit. They yowl that we're spoiling prisoners giving them a free education. But prisons that don't help people change their lives aren't tough on crime. They are tough on society."

(See also CALIFORNIA CORRECTIONS SYSTEM; CORRECTIONAL EDUCATION; ILLITERACY IN PRISONS; PRISON OVERCROWDING: COPING WITH THE COSTS.)

trial by jury   See BILL OF RIGHTS: PROTECTION AGAINST GOVERNMENT TYRANNY.

(See also REFUGEES; SANCTUARY MOVEMENT.)

Uniform Crime Reporting   See CRIME STATISTICS; INCIDENT-BASED CRIME DATA REPORTING SYSTEM.

U

underground railroad   The term underground railroad refers to the process by which refugees or fugitives are secretly, illegally transported out of areas in which their lives are threatened, usually across an international border. It is a complex support network of secret collaborators supplying food, transport, "safe houses," false documents or whatever may be needed to accomplish the goal. The term is familiar to Americans from its use to describe the widespread illegal practice in the pre-Civil War era of smuggling slaves from slave-holding states in the South to free states in the North and to Canada.

In current practice, the term refers to two quite different sets of conditions. To get around immigration laws, entrepreneurial "underground railroads" have been created. These smuggle illegal immigrants, usually from poor third-world countries, into the West. Those who use these networks are at the mercy of the smugglers, usually unscrupulous and vicious criminals, and risk their lives when they do so. They also are forced to pay enormous sums, sometimes obligating themselves to years of virtual indentured servitude after they have reached their destination, where they live in fear both of the authorities and their "benefactors."

A much smaller, humanitarian underground railroad is the sanctuary movement, made up of people who disagree on moral or religious grounds with U.S. policy that severely limits the immigration of Central American refugees fleeing civil strife by denying that they are endangered. The sanctuary movement is supported by approximately 435 North American churches and synagogues and many individuals. Sanctuary workers do not physically escort refugees across the border. They advise them on the best approaches to take to avoid apprehension. Once the refugees arrive in the U.S., movement workers shelter them in churches, synagogues or private homes, and later try to find housing and jobs for them.

V

vandalism   The term vandalism is derived from the Vandals, an east German tribe that invaded Western Europe in the fourth and fifth centuries and eventually sacked Rome in A.D. 455. Vandalism is malicious destruction or defacing of property. Whether a particular act is labeled vandalism often depends on the conditions under which it takes place and the socioeconomic class of both the vandal and those affected by the vandalism.

Some places, such as empty buildings, seem to invite vandalism. Construction companies have learned to forestall destruction by moving tenants into a building before completion or by keeping at least a few tenants in place during renovations.

Vandalism is sometimes an expression of the feelings of those forced to live in an area. Structures built without regard to aesthetics or the daily needs of those who use the structure are prime targets of vandalism. Troy West, an architect at the New Jersey Institute of Technology in Newark, in June 2, 1992 *New York Times* article entitled "Architects Rediscover the Best City Planners: Citizens" said, "It remains a radical idea to most architects in public projects to talk to the people who will use what they build."

The idea that people take care of property when they have a stake in it is not new. Colin Ward, a lecturer at Wandsworth Technological College in England, in his 1973 book *Vandalism,* asserted that architects understand that "public spaces are less prone to wanton destruction if they appear to be private places related to the adjoining building . . . and give the occupants a protective and surveillant attitude to them."

Dereliction and neglect evoke misuse and careless, if not willful, destruction of property by some, while good maintenance and materials of good quality inspire respect and pride. Vacant lots that have been turned into gardens or small parks in south-central Los Angeles were not touched during the 1992 riots. The gardens and parks were seen as community space. Similarly, small plots open to anyone who likes to garden have been tilled since World War II in The Fenway, a park in Boston, with little if any vandalism.

An example of the value in having a stake in a structure was revealed in a January 25, 1988 *Chicago Tribune* story about the Near North Health Service Corps' community health center. The center, a modernistic small building filled with plants, stands amid trash-strewn empty lots in the shadow of the gang-infested, crime-ridden Cabrini-Green housing project. Walls of crystal-clear glass brick enclose the center's lobby. Dark steel beams, the type that graffiti artists cherish, rise two stories high. Windows in the first-floor rear office, uncovered by grates or bars, are large enough to climb through. The center, which would appear to be a tempting target for vandalism, remains untouched.

The center's administrative director told the *Chicago Tribune,* "We wanted to build a facility that the whole community could feel part of. That's why we used glass brick. It gives a feeling of space and openness."

Most of the center's many programs are staffed by volunteers who live in the community. Many are unemployed, and the center encourages them to master certain job skills and then tries to help them find paying jobs.

According to police assigned to the public housing unit, two rival gangs rule many aspects of neighborhood residents' daily lives, dictating who can be where, both in the project's residential buildings and the surrounding area. But the health center is treated as a neutral zone, available to all.

Many architects have learned that ultimate destruction of a structural element, whether in a park, a residence or a public building, often begins with an almost negligible amount of damage produced intentionally or accidentally. If not repaired immediately, the damage is enlarged upon or replicated nearby until the element is so abused that it seems to be there for the purpose of destruction.

Damage of one feature spreads to others and begins what sociologists call the "broken window syndrome." As destroyed property is left unrepaired, a neighborhood's residents become demoralized and retreat behind locked doors, leaving the streets to the irresponsible and the criminal.

Certain areas within high-density structures can contribute to or retard the spread of vandalism. Intense use of lobbies, stairwells, elevators, laundries and trash collection sites guarantee that wear and tear will be out of proportion to that in the rest of the building. Yet the design and the materials used in such areas often do not reflect planning for heavy traffic and use. Deterioration begins early at these sites and spreads.

Architects are not the only professionals who escape accountability for professional misdeeds. Destruction of the insides of houses in East London was said to be the work of squatters, when in fact the damage was ordered by the area housing councils. The councils moved tenants out in accordance with plans to tear down the structures and vandalized them so the tenants could not move back in before the wreckers arrived.

Theories and Classifications of Vandalism. One theory known as the "law of diminishing vandalism" has many applications. Persistence in replanting and replacing destroyed plants until vandals get tired of destroying them is effective. A British Waterways Board rule states that when vandals smash up a site on a weekend, it is repaired Monday morning. If they come back the next weekend, it is repaired again. The third weekend they usually don't bother.

The U.S. National Park Service subscribes to the same rule but unfortunately does not have the money to keep up repairs. The February 24, 1990 *Washington Post* told of the plight of Meridian Hill Park, "the jewel of Washington's parks with its cascading fountain and majestic statues." Spray-paint artists have covered the park's walls and statues with political slogans and skateboarders have chipped the steps of the stone fountain, the centerpiece of the park.

Chief of the National Park Services Designing Service Darwina Neal, a landscape architect, told the *Washington Post* that the Park Service has a second rule: "The more people use a park legitimately, the less it will be used by those with illegitimate intentions." Meridian Hill Park is deteriorating because it has lost regular visitors and is left only with transients.

Although in the 1950s families in the Meridian Hill Park neighborhood often slept in the park on hot nights, present-day residents, fearful of drug dealers, avoid the park altogether. Unlike some less grand parks in residential Washington, Meridian Hill has no "friends" who call and complain about vandalism.

Psychologists theorize that vandals have destructive impulses. Sociologists propose that children and adolescents need outlets for play and adventure. Either notion implies that vandalism may be deflected or channeled into safer, harmless or constructive alternatives. "Scribbling walls" are often installed in playgrounds, youth centers and restrooms. Sometimes children in new housing developments are made "tree wardens" and given responsibility for trees named after them.

Vandalism often is linked to opportunity. The presence of a derelict house or large panes of glass and an absence of surveillance seem to invite vandalism. About children and the temptations of their environment, Colin Ward wrote:

Unruly and abusive he may be, but when he is striding down the up escalator, or pushing all the buttons on the animated museum exhibit, regardless of what is displayed . . . he is using the artefacts that the built environment provides in a way which, however selfish or inconsiderate, makes sense to him, even though it is the despair of his elders.

Perceptions of vandalism fall on a continuum from destruction that is invariably labeled vandalism and considered criminal and a social problem, to destruction that society tolerates without necessarily labelling it vandalism or taking punitive action. Sociologist Stanley Cohen refers to vandalism as "rule breaking" and proposes categories along a continuum based on the conditions under which vandalism is tolerated. He calls the categories ritual, protected, play, written-off, walled-in and licensed.

Property destruction in connection with Halloween, New Year's Eve and college homecomings are examples of ritualized vandalism. Acts by "protected groups," such as college students or military personnel on pass or leave, may be labeled pranks. The same acts if done by inner-city teenagers are likely to be perceived as vandalism.

In some areas competition among children to see who can break the most windows may be an institutionalized form of play. If an act takes place on a ritual occasion or is carried out by a protected group, then it is more likely to be defined as play.

Certain types of rule breaking are rarely reported or reflected in official statistics—for example, soaping windows or tipping over trash cans. This type of vandalism is particularly safe from prosecution. It is written off because each individual act is considered so trivial, although the overall cost may be considerable. Many advertising agencies supply contractors with extra copies of posters to replace those defaced.

A great deal of graffiti falls into the written-off category. The annual cost of graffiti is extremely high, in part because of its sheer quantity and in part because it often involves cleaning difficult-to-reach places such as trestles and highway overpasses. Nevertheless, graffiti is widely tolerated, even viewed with amusement. It has been dubbed "the last urban folk art."

The category "walled-in" resembles "written-off" except that the vandalism takes place in a closed setting such as a factory, a prison or a ship. A social scientist who spent several years at sea reported that expressions of hostility there may take such forms as throwing tools, dishes and equipment over the side. Sanctions against such activity are difficult to impose because direct evidence is difficult to obtain. Vandalism in schools and prisons usually falls into the walled-off category.

An example of licensed vandalism is the destruction sustained by hotels and bars that cater to professional athletic teams. Some establishments require a damage deposit before a team's arrival. Others add the cost to the bill.

Vandalism may be a means to an end. On April 15, 1988 three teenagers at Boston Technical High School planted a bomb in a school locker. Police and fire officials reported that at least one suspect wanted to create a fuss in order to start spring break a day early.

Vandalism may be ideologically motivated. A rule may be broken as a means to a particular end, or it may be broken as a challenge to the legitimacy of the rule. On occasion South African nationalists have committed acts of vandalism to protest an injustice done to a particular black South African. Sometimes they have done so to challenge their nation's apartheid laws.

Motivation and Meaning. There are common stereotypes of vandalism. They are sometimes treated as if they were equivalent, but most people can distinguish between a ten-year-old boy throwing rocks at street lights and sports fans tearing down the goalposts after a football game, or someone smashing a coin machine in a laundry.

Meanings become clearer if vandalism is classified into five types: acquisitive, tactical, vindictive, play and malicious. Acquisitive vandalism is committed in the course of or in order to acquire money or property. Such acts include stripping lead, copper or brass from buildings to sell; collecting such objects as street signs (often done by students); and looting parking meters, automatic vending machines and telephone coin boxes.

Tactical vandalism is done to call attention to some cause. Slogan painting fits this category. Tactical vandalism also may be a personal cry for help. Psychiatric committals are sometimes prompted by property destruction. Sometimes the homeless use window-smashing as a way to get arrested and be provided with food and shelter. Tactical vandalism also occurs in industrial settings to ensure regular rest periods or to break the monotony.

Vindictive vandalism may account for many cases that on the surface look meaningless. Vandalism offers a form of retaliation or rough justice. It is emotionally satisfying without carrying the risk of personal injury possible in a direct confrontation.

Play vandalism often involves endurance and skills testing. Children compete to break the greatest number of windows or street lamps or hit the largest number of moving targets. The fact that property is destroyed tends to be incidental to the activity. The point at which play become malice may be imperceptible.

Malicious vandalism is committed not just out of hatred but is enjoyed for its own sake. This kind of vandalism is often perceived as wanton.

There is no dearth of examples of malicious vandalism or what Cohen calls "the edge of impotent rage": ripping out flower beds; pouring acid on car paint; dumping sugar into gas tanks; slashing tires in a parking lot; defecating in the elevator of a high-rise; letting a slingload crash onto a wharf below; and throwing life jackets into the sea.

Cohen proposes that a substantial proportion of malicious vandalism can be characterized as "manufactured excitement" for those whose education and job opportunities doom them to a life of unemployment or menial jobs. Vandalism provides an opportunity to display toughness and offers stimulation and a sense of control without much risk.

victim impact statements: their effect on death sentences

During the last week in April 1991, the U.S. Supreme Court heard arguments in *Payne v. Tennessee*. This was a death penalty case in which the prosecution put on the stand a woman whose daughter and grandchild had been murdered and who had become the guardian of the surviving grandchild. The woman spoke about the continuing pain that she and her surviving grandchild suffered. The grandchild was also allowed to speak. At sentencing, the prosecutor made reference to the grandchild's statements. The prosecutor said something to the effect of "What kind of justice will this jury do for him when he grows up?" The defendant appealed.

To discuss the merits of impact statements, a Cable News Network (CNN) broadcast aired on April 27, 1991 brought together John Stein, deputy director of the National Organization of Victims' Assistance, who was in favor of such statements, and Ira Robbins, a professor of law at American University, who discussed their legal implications.

Robbins argued that the important issue in any case, but particularly in a death penalty case, is the moral blameworthiness of the defendant, not the character of the victim, or the eloquence of the victim's family in expressing their grief or the question of whether there is a surviving family. Those questions are fortuitous. The recent history of death penalty jurisprudence has been one of distinguishing the cases in which the death penalty is appropriate and those in which it is not. The search is for distinctions of principle, distinctions that focus on the defendant and not on the victim.

Those opposed to the inclusion of survivors' statements have been concerned that the Court might overturn earlier decisions. The first case was *Booth v. Maryland* in 1987, in which the court held by a 5-to-4 vote that so-called victim impact statements are unconstitutional and cannot be introduced at a death penalty proceeding. The majority opinion was written by Justice Lewis Powell. In 1989, after Justice Powell had retired, a different 5-to-4 majority, in *South Carolina v. Gathers,* reaffirmed the Court's position in the Booth case. Justice William Brennan wrote the majority opinion. Justice Brennan is also no longer on the Court. Only three justices are left who took the position that victim impact statements are unconstitutional. There therefore is a chance that the Court's position may be overturned.

The defense attorney in the *Payne* case claimed that the use of victim impact statements would lead to arbitrary convictions and arbitrary sentencing practices because they would be different in each case. John Stein's response to the idea that victim impact statements would lead to arbitrariness was that as a result of the *Booth* decision, many judges around the country extended the Court's reasoning to every criminal case by finding some sort of arbitrariness in the survivor's involvement at any stage of the proceedings.

In the view of those in the victims' assistance movement, the amount of blood on the floor, the amount of horror at the crime scene and the amount of pain inflicted on the victim are a part of what it is intentionally to commit a criminal act, and that horror extends beyond the crime scene. Stein recalled the statement of a victim who testified to the President's Task Force on Victims of Crime: "Why didn't anyone consult me . . . I was the one who was kidnapped, not the State of Maryland." The position of the victim's assistance movement is that by dint of the cruelty done to them, the victims ought to have a voice—though not a veto—in the sentencing decisions. A just system would listen to the victim as well as to the prosecutor.

Stein went on, "It is true that we are influenced by the people that we are allowed to listen to. The only question is are we allowed to listen to only the defendant and his ability to articulate or does the victim have a rightful place in those deliberations."

Robbins agreed with much of what Stein said and supported many of the changes that have been made on behalf of victims. However, he felt that the constitutional issue was whether the use of the victim's family's testimony in the sentencing phase of a death penalty proceeding was compatible with the defendant's constitutional rights or, as the Supreme Court has said on many occasions, that "Death is different."

"If we allow not only the question of the effect on the survivors to come into issue," said Robbins, "but also the character of the victim to come into issue, don't we start to get into some collateral questions?" A question asked of the Tennessee attorney general in the *Payne* case was whether the introduction by the prosecution of evidence about the victim's good character implied the right of the defense to rebut it. The result could be a minitrial not only of the defendant's character or blameworthiness, but also of the victim's.

The Supreme Court in the 1970s overturned the death penalties of many states because their application was arbitrary. The Court likened it to predicting where lightning would strike. Introduction of victim impact statements into decisions about the imposition of the death penalty could result in sentences based on whether there was a survivor or on a judgment of the victim's worth, which might revolve around whether he or she was a good person, was homeless or a pillar of the community.

According to Stein, there are already trials of the victim's character all the time in American courts—unconscionable trials, in his opinion. The introduction of victim impact statements could subject victims to more pain, but the choice would be theirs to make.

Moreover, Stein pointed out, the worth of victims is already being assessed, as evidenced by data demonstrating that the death penalty is more likely to be meted out if the victim is white. The Court has decided that those statistics alone cannot invalidate the death penalty. Those who work with victims are sensitive not only to the rights of the average victim but also to those of the average murderer. The typical murderer is likely to be poor, black and young (as is the victim). In Stein's view, no one is speaking on behalf of the murderers, who are often victims of brutal circumstances themselves.

In the *Gathers* case, Richard Haynes was a poor, undereducated black man, age 30 and evidently mentally retarded. He was a "street creature," who lived with his mother, a "poor benighted soul." A gang ridiculed him and stomped him to death. All this is known because of the victim impact statement made in court. Stein said, "Richard Haynes became a decent, worthy human being only because victim impact information was allowed in. I think the odds are that we will get closer to a classless justice system in the death penalty phase if we hear from the victims, who are overwhelmingly poor and black like Richard Haynes."

In the *Payne* case, the Supreme Court ruled in a 6–3 decision on June 27, 1991 that victim impact statements could be heard by juries in the sentencing phases of capital crimes.

(See also CAPITAL CRIME; DEATH PENALTY; GRIEF: EXPRESSIONS IN THE AFTERMATH OF VIOLENCE; REVENGE.)

victim retribution   See REVENGE.

Vietnamese gang wars with other Asian gangs

Unlike major organized crime rings—the Mafia in the United States and Canada, the Sicilian Mafia, the Medellin Cartel, the Japanese yakuza and the Chinese Triads—Vietnamese gangs in North America appear to be loosely organized and local. They are mobile, however, and frequently turn up far from their home city. When they do, they are usually on assignment from one of the more organized gangs.

There is a certain amount of attrition from the Vietnamese gangs to the more organized gangs. Because Vietnamese gang members work for and transfer into other gangs does not rule out violent expressions of bitter rivalry with other gangs.

One example took place in the fall of 1990, when New York City's lower Manhattan area was the scene of three apparent gang shootings. Investigators and others familiar with gang activities attributed the shootings to escalating feuds between Vietnamese and Chinese gangs.

One Vietnamese gang known as Born to Kill or B.T.K. (taken from a phrase worn on the helmets of some American soldiers in Vietnam) was under increasing pressure from police and the Federal Bureau of Investigation (FBI), as well as suffering from the loss of members to the better-paid and better-organized Chinese gangs. B.T.K. members appeared to be victims in at least one of the lower Manhattan shootings. Three men in their early 20s were shot in the head and their blood-soaked bodies were piled on top of one another. One man carried a note linking him to Born to Kill and another had a B.T.K. tattoo. The police said that there had been increasing tension between Born to Kill and a Chinese gang called Ghost Shadows.

Born to Kill is a loosely knit gang made up of mostly young Vietnamese-born immigrants, who specialize in extortion and robbery. The police characterize the gang as extremely mobile, ruthless and well armed.

A source of some of the friction surrounding B.T.K. was that its members crossed into territory claimed by more traditional and hierarchical Chinese gangs. A man believed to be the second-in-command of Born to Kill was killed by the Ghost Shadows in the summer of 1990. At the man's funeral, Chinese gang members opened fire at the crowd.

In an interview for a January 15, 1991 article entitled "New Immigrant Wave From Asia Gives Underworld New Faces," in the *New York Times*, Ko-lin Chin, a senior research analyst for the New York City Criminal Justice Agency and the author of *Chinese Subculture and Criminality: Nontraditional Crime Groups in America* (1990), said, "The Vietnamese and the Chinese are at war. There is more heroin trafficking, more and more immigrants, more money and therefore the stakes are higher. The gangs in the '90s, when they send a message, they kill people. Now the Chinese gangs are sending a message clearly and loudly: 'We want to be in power'"

Boston's Chinatown was the scene of a massacre of five men in a social club on January 12, 1991. Authorities feared that Asian gangs, brought by the new wave of immigrants, were transforming the city's small Chinatown. Neighborhood residents reported that ethnic Chinese from Myanmar, many of whom worked in nearby restaurants, stopped off regularly to play cards after work.

The killings came on the heels of the shooting death on January 8, 1991 of a part-time waiter in the lobby of his apartment building a few blocks from the social club murder scene. In an interview for a January 15, 1991 *New York Times* article entitled "Killing of 5 in Boston's Chinatown Raises Fears of Asian Gang Wars," Boston Police Department Chief of Detectives Joseph Saia said, "There has been no real organization of the criminal element in the Chinatown section of Boston since the mid-to-late 1980s, when the leader of the Ping On, the once dominant gang here, fled to Hong Kong

and his second-in-command was slain in his suburban restaurant"

Ping On was one of the triads, criminal societies that trace their roots back centuries and have access to the world's highest-quality heroin from the "golden triangle" region of southeast Asia. In August 1990 seven men with ties to Ping On were indicted on charges of running a $1.6 million money-laundering operation in Chinatown.

Before he fled to Hong Kong, Stephen Tse, the leader of Ping On, had spent more than a year in jail for refusing to speak to the President's Commission on Organized Crime. In addition, he had been arrested by Boston Police at one of his high-stakes gaming events.

Tse did not return for the funeral of his second-in-command, Michael Kwong. The absence of retribution for Kwong's murder apparently signified the demise of the Ping On.

Because of the style and severity of the attack on the five men, several neighbors speculated that the murders could have been part of a robbery perpetrated by Vietnamese gangs. Several times in recent years, Vietnamese gangs have targeted high-stakes card games run by Chinese immigrants, often shooting or stabbing the gamblers during the robbery. The gangsters are aware that the immigrants are unlikely to report thefts. However, Saia said that the card game was only a small one, so robbery did not seem a likely motive.

The Vietnamese gangs do not always need a rational motive. In an interview for the January 15, 1991 *New York Times* article entitled "New Immigrant Wave from Asia Gives the Underworld New Faces," Luke Rettler, head of the Manhattan District Attorney's Jade Squad, a unit that specializes in Asian crime, commented: "They are a kind of chaotic group. They seem to do things like deciding on a massage parlor to take off—on the spur of the moment."

A Boston television station reported that police were following a tip that four Asian men were seen in a car with California license plates near the club on the night of the murder. Law enforcement specialists familiar with Chinese-American gangs claim that several shootings in various cities have been committed by out-of-state Asian gangs.

Saia acknowledged that there were a lot of gangs and criminal elements vying for power in Chinatown. Ko-Lin Chin was of the opinion that the change in criminal activity in Boston's Chinatown mirrored changes in Chinatowns in New York, San Francisco, Toronto and Vancouver. "This new group of Chinese criminals has nothing to do with the traditional Chinese criminal organizations in Chinatown of triads, tongs, and street gangs.'' Some of the most violent new gang members are believed to be Vietnamese or ethnic Chinese from Vietnam.

The changes in Chinatowns across the country began with the immigration law of 1965, which removed barriers to Asian immigrants. During the 1980s the number of Asians in the Boston metropolitan area doubled to 100,000. Only about 8,000 of them live in Chinatown, an area of only a few square blocks.

A January 13, 1991 *Boston Globe* article entitled "Violence Fuels Fears in the Area," reported that in the mid-1980s, some members of New York's Chinese gang Ghost Shadows went to Boston to try to take control of the area. The result was a shootout in broad daylight.

Since the 1980s there has been an increasing number of attacks by roving Vietnamese gangs in Boston's Chinatown. In March 1986 the Quang Loi Company jewelry store was robbed by a Vietnamese gang that smashed the windows and took $200,000 in jewels.

Like traditional Chinese gangs, the Vietnamese gangs extort protection money from businesses. Many merchants migrated from Boston's Chinatown to smaller cities, such as Lowell, in order to avoid the Vietnamese gangs. The gangs followed and targeted the merchants' new locations for robberies.

Not everyone was surprised at the social club murders. Some experts who monitor Asian organized crime were surprised that something similar had not happened sooner. During an interview for a January 15, 1991 *Boston Globe* article entitled "Gangs Seen Vying for Chinatown Turf," James Goldman, a supervisory special agent for the U.S. Immigration and Naturalization Service and a specialist in Asian organized crime, said, "The Vietnamese have been coming and going and doing as they please. What you have now is a cottage industry. You have a potpourri of Asian criminals who lack any leadership. And whenever you have a situation like that, the potential for bloodshed is serious."

Discipline, a hallmark of triads, disappeared in Boston with Stephen Tse's departure. Such discipline and the fact that triads tend to victimize their own insular ethnic communities exclusively has made law enforcement inroads into organized Asian crime groups difficult.

A factor that has further hindered law enforcement efforts in Boston has been the lack of the clear demarcation as to who controls what typically found in much larger Chinatowns such as New York's or San Francisco's. Even gangs' names in Boston are not held to as fiercely as they are in other cities.

For example, Viet Ching members who migrate to Boston from Los Angeles do not use gang names, although they carry the symbols of gang membership— multiple tattoos and pierced nipples. With or without a name, Viet Ching members seem to be plentiful in Boston. Goldman said, "There are Viet Chings all over the place. I've seen at least a dozen recently."

(See also APPENDIX 1D, THE CHINESE TRIADS; ASIAN GANGS IN NEW YORK; GANGS: PICKUP OR TEMPORARY; GANGS: STRUCTURED STREET; OUTLAW MOTORCYCLE GANGS; POSSES, JAMAICAN; SKINHEADS.)

violence, aftermath See POST-TRAUMATIC STRESS DISORDER (PTSD).

violence as fun: the case of the Central Park jogger At about 9 P.M. on April 19, 1989, a band of approximately 33 young males set out to have a good time in Central Park, in New York City. As they roamed the northern regions of the park, the teenagers split into smaller groups. During their journey, they threw rocks at bicyclists and cars, assaulted an elderly homeless man and robbed a 52-year-old Hispanic man.

At approximately 10 P.M., one pack of six came upon the ninth victim of the evening's romp, a 28-year-old woman jogging alone. The pack chased the woman into a gully, raped her, beat her into unconsciousness with a rock and a metal pipe, carved her head and her thighs with a knife, bound and gagged her and left her for dead.

At about 11 P.M., police captured the first of the six boys who had participated in the attack on the woman jogger. In the interim, at least four more joggers had been assaulted. One of the boys arrested, a 14-year-old, told the arresting officers, "I know who did the murder."

Near death, the woman lay bound and gagged in a coma for more than three hours before passersby discovered her and called for help. By then she had lost two thirds of her blood and her body temperature had fallen to 80 degrees.

To describe the evening of marauding, the police and the media used the term wilding. While the public seemed to view the behavior as something new and out of the ordinary, to the police and some of the media the phenomenon had become increasingly familiar. They were later accused of coining the word, but there is evidence that it was already in existence. However, prior to the case of the Central Park jogger, bands of roaming youth had been typically referred to by the police and the media as "wolf packs."

Five years earlier, at a Diana Ross open-air concert in Central Park, wolf packs descended on concert-goers, robbing many and seriously injuring some. Earlier in 1989 several dozen teenage boys and girls ran through an uptown subway station at Broadway and 103d Street. Along the way, they robbed many commuters and pushed a derelict man onto the tracks.

A week after the attack on the jogger, six youths were indicted, and two others were indicted for a separate attack on a male jogger. The youngest defendant was 14. The oldest was 17. Only one had been in trouble with the law before. At least one had been sexually assaulted as a child.

A variety of explanations were forthcoming. Some theorists focused on class—the woman was an investment banker. However, the boys did not come from impoverished homes, they came from stable working-class families that provided them with such amenities as organized, adult-supervised sports and music lessons.

Some theorists focused on hatred of women, which seemed to have some validity since they had gang-raped the woman, but this was minimized since men also had been attacked during the rampage.

Many theorists focused on race; the victim was white and the assailants were black and Hispanic. The notion of race seemed to polarize New York City. A controversial black lawyer, Alton Maddox, suggested on radio that the rape was a hoax. Donald Trump paid $89,000 to take out full-page ads in four New York daily newspapers, declaring "I want to hate these muggers and murderers . . . BRING BACK THE DEATH PENALTY."

However, one of the boys dismissed race as an issue. He said, "She wasn't nothing."

One of the accused provided a rationale for the mayhem. He told a detective assigned to the case that the reason that they had embarked on the rampage was that "It was fun. It was something to do."

The game aspect of the behavior was reinforced by a New York youngster interviewed on a May 16, 1989 *ABC Nightline* television broadcast. The youngster said, "When we go wilding, we go beat up somebody."

The interviewer responded, "Anybody?"

The youngster answered, "Anybody."

Another youngster interjected, "They go around, they see something, all of a sudden, something pops in their head, they say, 'Yo, let's go beat this person up.' "

Still another youngster added, "And sometimes they do it for fun and sometimes they do it for money, you understand. They just do it just to do it."

The *Nightline* moderator, Ted Koppel, asked Rafael Flores, the director of Hotline Cares, if she was familiar with the term wilding. She told him that five months earlier a couple of youngsters on the hotline had described their previous night's activities and used the word. When she asked the callers to explain, they said, "Well, we were just doing what we wanted to get what we wanted."

Flores went on to say "There are those that actually go out there and wild for the purpose of committing crime, in order to support their habits. There are larger populations that are wilding for the 'fun' of it."

Also interviewed on the *Nightline* program was Terry Williams, a social scientist who has written several books on urban youth, including *Cocaine Kids* (1990). Williams asserted that the youngsters now use the term wilding as they formerly would have used "getting paid." He explained that getting paid was simply a way "kids used to go out into the streets, and . . . find a vic [victim] and take them off [rob them]."

Williams went on to say that what happened in the park seemed to him to be an initiation into a "crew" (a gang organized to make money). The initiation on that particular night involved a routine in which five or six youngsters would hit a vic while the others watched. The last vic happened to be a woman. In Williams' opinion, the leader of that group decided to do more than the other boys in the crew, to prove to himself that 'I'm the baddest, I'm the toughest.' The [gang] rape was a symbol of defilement."

Earlier in the broadcast, Brooklyn District Attorney Elizabeth Holtzman had tried to point out that the uniqueness of the attack on the woman jogger was that it was accompanied by rape. "This woman, of all the other events that took place that night, was the one who was most severely beaten, the most violated, and yet what seems to have gone unnoticed is that whether you're talking about Central Park or Golden Gate Park or Yellowstone Park, women in this country are subjected to an epidemic of violence."

After an interruption by Koppel, who failed to understand her point, Holtzman went on to say that she had seen little attention paid to the attitudes that exonerate sexual violence, dehumanize women and teach men that the way to show that they are true men is through sexual violence.

Holtzman's assessment was borne out in the media coverage of the case. Although there was great care to protect the woman's name because she was a rape victim, most of the coverage seemed to ignore the rape—perhaps because rape is so frequent—and to focus on the degree of violence.

In an interview for a May 8, 1989 *Time* article entitled "Wilding in the Night," sociologist Elijah Anderson of the University of Pennsylvania offered an explanation for how the violence could go to such an extreme. He said, "Kids who roam in groups gain a sense of power that they do not have individually. Caught up in the frenzy of the mob, each boy believes that he is the only one hesitant. He won't show remorse out of fear that the other group members will believe that he is a coward."

Anderson's view was supported by other social scientists. Franklin Zimring, director of the Earl Warren Legal Institute at the University of California, who conducted a 1984 study of youth homicide in New York, suggested in an interview for a May 8, 1989 *Newsweek* article entitled "Going 'Wilding' in the City," that the group may have been swayed by what he called "government by dare—you do it because you don't want to back out."

In the dynamics of the group, there is often at least one leader who can control the rest by manipulating their need to prove themselves. The initiator of a gang rape gains mastery not only over the victim but also over his cohorts, who feel obliged to equal his exploits.

In such a group, there is an element of anonymity and a loss of individual personality. Robert Panzarella, a professor of police science at New York's John Jay College of Criminal Justice, said, "Things he would never think of doing by himself he does in the group." Labor is divided so the end result is that "while the action of each individual can seem relatively minor, the action of the whole may be horrific."

Blacks who grieved for the jogger and attended a vigil on her behalf nevertheless wondered if a similar assault on a black woman would have aroused such an army of reporters and politicians. Their suspicion was borne out ten days later when a 19-year-old black woman was found strangled and possibly raped in another Manhattan park. Except for a headline that read "Another Woman Raped and Strangled to Death" in the *Amsterdam News,* a newspaper with a predominantly

black readership, the young woman's murder caused barely a ripple in the media.

Observers of all races across the nation also pointed out that extreme violence in their own neighborhoods seldom merited national attention either. Among the examples of horrendous crimes with little national attention was a 15-year-old girl, kidnapped at knifepoint at a Greyhound bus station in Los Angeles, held captive and sexually assaulted for five days. When she managed to escape, she flagged down a passing car with three teenagers inside. Instead of taking her to the police, the teenagers took her to a park and raped her again. Another example was two Denver students, who stabbed a man for his credit cards. They wanted to use the credit cards to buy camping equipment.

The Central Park jogger made a remarkable recovery. She regained consciousness in 13 days. A May 22, 1989 *Maclean's* article entitled "A City Transfixed by a Brutal Act," reported that when a nurse casually mentioned in her presence that she hoped to begin running again, the jogger said in a hoarse whisper, "Me too."

Although the jogger was expected to have permanent brain damage, she was able to return to work after a period of rehabilitation. Besides her recuperative abilities, the young woman was remarkable in other ways too. Having been born into a well-to-do family and educated at Wellesley College, she recognized that she was privileged and felt obliged to help others. To pursue an interest in helping third-world economies, she worked at the U.S. Embassy in Zimbabwe for three months before she entered graduate school. Her friends were of the opinion that she ignored warnings that she should not run at night because she could not imagine anyone being that vicious or coldhearted.

As the jogger did not fit easily into stereotypes, neither did the assailants. When the police began to sort out the facts of the case, they found that the boys' teachers characterized them as not the type to go looking for trouble. One boy was known for helping elderly neighbors in his middle-income Harlem apartment complex. Another was a born-again Christian, who had persuaded his mother to join his church.

Not everyone in the city became polarized. Marilyn Davis, a registered nurse and union official who lived in the same apartment complex as several of the defendants, organized a prayer vigil for the jogger's recovery. In an interview for a May 22, 1989 *People* magazine article entitled "Madness in the Heart of the City," Davis said:

The crime was horrendous and the perpetrators should be punished, but everyone is innocent until proven guilty. The media have lynched these boys. And we have gotten death threats, people saying they're coming to shoot Schomburg Plaza up. We're terrified to let out children to play on the sidewalk . . . I don't think that judging another person as less than human is a privilege any man walking the earth should have. Some of these boys committed a horrible crime, but they are not animals. They are *human* beings.

The question remained unanswered of how human beings could use violence as an initiation rite or could perceive violence as fun.

The idea that violence is fun is not unique to the United States. A May 22, 1989 *Maclean's* article entitled " 'Violence Is Nice. Honestly,' " by Paul Kaihla, described nightlife in the ganglands of the young in Toronto.

At Club Focus, a discotheque for young people, in the summer of 1987 about a dozen middle-class students fought off an attack by a larger group of skinheads. Proud of their prowess, the middle-class students dubbed themselves "The Untouchables" and went on to become the largest youth gang in the city, with a membership of about 200. Gangs of all types are proliferating in Toronto.

White gangs in Toronto are apt to emulate the Untouchables and black gangs are apt to emulate Jamaican drug-trafficking groups known as posses. In spite of their rivalry, black posses and white youth gangs share a hatred of Toronto's estimated 1,000 skinheads. Nevertheless most groups have adopted the skinheads' customary dress: black bomber jackets, white T-shirts, jeans with rolled cuffs and crewcut hair for whites and elaborate "flattop" haircuts for blacks.

According to police, Toronto gang members have used Club Focus as a meeting place to plan "swarmings," (mass attacks on fellow teenagers or adult victims), vandalism and lootings. Bouncers at Club Focus began using metal detectors to search teenagers for weapons after a 17-year-old was stabbed to death during a gang-related fight at another club owned by the same management.

Toronto's black teenagers began a practice of descending on the city on Tuesday nights when some movie theaters offer reduced prices. Among them were gang members who engaged in violence.

One security guard was swarmed by 60 youths in one incident and bitten on the chest in another incident. Sometimes the gang members focus on theft. Some stores have lost up to $80,000 in merchandise after marauding gangs invaded their premises.

In answer to a question from Kaihla, a 17-year-old said, "What motivates us? We like violence and all that. Violence is nice, man. Honestly."

The plague of gangs was not limited to Toronto. They stormed playgrounds in Montreal, exchanged gunfire in Vancouver and in Quebec a six-foot ten-inch, 225-pound skinhead and friends robbed, tortured and humiliated a five-foot-two, slightly retarded man after breaking into his apartment. A Quebec police officer, Detective Sergeant Michel Gagnon, described the skinhead incident as "a case of sheer gratuitous violence."

Nor was violent fun confined to North America. A May 22, 1989 *Maclean's* article entitled "Gang Warfare, Soviet Style," by Anthony Wilson-Smith, described the terror felt by parents in the Soviet city of Kazan, when the city's gangs declared May 1988 "love month" and adopted the slogan "Let us turn Kazan into a city without virgins."

Kazan's gangs were not an isolated aberration. Moscow police in 1989 reported that more than 4,000 youths took part in at least 30 clashes involving rival street gangs.

Since the mid-1980s, many young people who congregate on downtown Moscow's Arbat pedestrian mall have lived in fear of the "Lyuberi," a gang of ultraconservative teenagers from the suburb of Lyubertsy, who have staged intermittent raids on the Arbat.

In an encounter with another group, police arrested five teenagers who were caught boiling three human heads over a bonfire. The youths refused to say where they had acquired the skulls. They claimed they were making ashtrays.

In 1988 police in the town of Stepyanka, in the Republic of Byelorussia, broke up a gang of teenage youths after more than a year of vicious activities. Members boasted about and took videotapes of sessions involving robbery, torture and multiple rapes of teenage girls.

A Soviet parent lamented to the weekly newspaper *Moskovskiye Novosti* in 1989, "Where did such brutal intolerance among teenagers come from?" The parent's question is shared by parents around the world.

(See also CAMPUS VIOLENCE; CLASSROOM VIOLENCE; CRIMINAL THINKING: THEORIES AND TREATMENT MODELS; GANGS: PICKUP OR TEMPORARY; RAPE; VIOLENT CRIMES AGAINST WOMEN: THEIR CONNECTION TO GENDER BIAS.)

violence prevention: the evolution of a pilot program for adolescents Experts from a variety of disciplines believe that the best approach to curbing violence is to teach children how to avoid it. A February 1991 presentation to public health professionals entitled "Adolescent Violence and the Prevention of Violence," by Deborah Prothrow-Stith, M.D., an assistant dean in the Harvard School of Public Health, described a program she has introduced to some of the Boston schools.

Explaining why American adolescents are vulnerable to becoming involved in violence, Prothrow-Stith said, "Our children are killing each other because we teach them to do that. Firearms, urban settings, and poverty are part of the picture. Moreover, children who have witnessed a lot of violence or have been victims of violence are at risk. Also there is a national love of violence in America, which can be seen not only in the media but also in homes and classrooms."

Parents participate in the escalation of violence. Youngsters in classrooms have told Prothrow-Stith, "My momma would beat me up if I got beat up. I have to go back and beat the person so I don't get beaten."

Educators also contribute by setting up "good guy" versus "bad guy" dichotomies. In a discussion of a fight at a high school, Prothrow-Stith asked about the well-being of an adolescent who had been in a fight that he had started. The principal's response was "That guy deserves to be hurt."

Television and movies teach children that violence is the hero's first choice; that violence is always successful and always rewarded; that the hero is never hurt badly and is always around to appear in the next episode. Violence is the hero's way, the glamorous way, to solve a problem.

National leaders add to the mystique of violence. President Reagan in a press conference said, "Make my day," a phrase taken from a Clint Eastwood tough-cop movie, which means "Not only will I use violence, but I am going to enjoy it."

Adolescents are vulnerable to violence for a variety of developmental reasons. They are normally narcissistic (self-involved). The transition they must make from childhood to adulthood requires some self-centeredness. In Prothrow-Stith's words, "It means that the teenager feels pretty 'center-stage' as if all eyes were watching—very vulnerable to insults. Something that you and I might not consider important, for an adolescent in this developmental period occurred in television prime time with everybody watching."

Adolescents also are vulnerable to peer pressure, a normal characteristic of that developmental stage. They have a need to achieve independence from the family and to relate to each other. Thus peers and their opinions become highly valued.

To develop a prevention curriculum, Prothrow-Stith spent considerable time in classrooms. She described the scenario for a violent confrontation between adolescents. "It is very clear. Someone talks about someone else. It gets taken back to that person. By lunchtime it is brewing and escalating. Somebody says 'Three o'clock on the corner.' By three o'clock on the corner, you have a crowd of kids. They all won't fight, but they all have participated in making that fight. Claude Brown said it best in *Manchild in the Promised Land* (1965). He said, 'Of all the things that I was expected to do, it was clear that I was expected to fight and it was okay to be afraid to fight, but it was not okay to be so afraid that you didn't fight.' "

A Public Health Approach. Taking adolescent vulnerability to peer pressure into account, Prothrow-Stith and her colleagues based their tactics for violence prevention on public health strategies used for other health issues. Smoking prevention seemed to be the most appropriate model. Smoking, just three decades ago, was considered glamorous. Stars on television and in the movies smoked. Since then the public's positive attitude toward smoking has shifted to a negative one.

The tactics to bring about a change in smoking behavior involved labeling the product appropriately, health education, encouragement of the fitness movement and using the media to deglamorize smoking and to carry antismoking public service announcements.

Health education in the classroom was the first approach that Prothrow-Stith and her colleagues tried. They produced a curriculum geared toward tenth-grade students. The curriculum has also been used in middle schools and occasionally with younger students.

The curriculum says to the student "You are vulnerable." In the classroom, the students are questioned about whether they have personally seen someone get hurt badly, known someone in jail for an offense involving violence or seen someone killed. The number of positive responses is alarming. Similar questions asked in a Chicago survey found that 30% of the children had witnessed a murder.

The curriculum also says to the student "You don't have to accept violence." This is a difficult concept to convey because the youngsters live in a society that not only accepts violence, it glamorizes it.

While it is difficult to get youngsters to think about this differently, it is possible. To do so, the trainers ask the youngsters, "What do you get out of fighting and what do you lose?" The list of what you lose is much longer—including your job or your life or ruining your clothes or your face. These are concrete reasons for avoiding fighting.

The curriculum also provides students with an opportunity to role-play, to figure out how fights start, how they escalate and how they might be prevented. The major point is that it is easier to prevent a fight than it is to stop one, once it has begun to escalate. At three o'clock on the corner—unless the police are there to keep the combatants apart—the fight has become inevitable.

Some evaluations over time of the curriculum developed by Prothrow-Stith and her colleagues showed some change in attitudes and some reduction in suspensions from school. Perhaps the most reliable measure was the principal's impression that the number of fights had been reduced. Although evaluation measures were somewhat inconclusive it was clear that there was no increase in fighting as a consequence of the curriculum.

Beyond the Classroom.   Any curriculum can make only a small dent. The prevention curriculum may reduce the fights in the school, but the youngsters go home to the same families and the same television and the same larger society that reinforces violence. As a consequence, Prothrow-Stith and her colleagues felt they needed to find a community-based approach. They moved to the Boston City Hospital to institute a violence prevention program. The program was an attempt to use churches, boys' clubs, neighborhood health centers, parents' organizations and tenants' organizations in a concerted effort to communicate nonviolent methods to children.

Over the course of the effort, the program developers worked with Boston-based Hill, Holliday, one of the top advertising agencies in the nation, to develop a public service announcement. At the first meeting, one woman from Hill, Holliday underscored the foreignness of the violence prevention idea: "No one has asked us to advertise to poor teenagers before. We don't really know the market."

The first ad campaign the agency offered, which they called "Blow the Whistle," involved teenagers wearing whistles they were intended to blow when they witnessed violence. The ad agency staff's thinking grew out of the notion of strangers as bad guys and left out the idea of acquaintance and family involvement, which represents a great deal of violence.

A second, more appropriate campaign involved two 30-second spots. One spot begins with a teenage girl crying as she bends over a teenage boy lying on the ground. A voiceover says, "The second biggest killer of teenagers is guns and knives . . ." The girl says, "Oh, why did I tell you that guy was coming on to me?"

The voiceover continues, "and friends like these. When you try to make a friend jealous, you're forcing him to fight and fighting is a lousy way to lose a friend. Friends for life don't let friends fight."

The second spot is similar except that the girl is replaced with an anguished boy who says, "I didn't know he had a gun." The wording of the voiceover is changed slightly. "When you tell a friend to fight, you might as well be killing him yourself."

The campaign also included T-shirts. Groups from social agencies were involved in various ways. Some created rap songs. Some had theater events. Others involved themselves in mediation and conflict resolution activities at their schools or community agencies.

The program has become a citywide activity in Boston. An evaluation of the three-year effort was funded by Kaiser, at a cost greater than it took to produce the program. The evaluation revealed that the program had an unanticipated positive impact on the caregivers, the outreach workers, the counselors and the Sunday school teachers. The impact was smaller on children.

A telephone survey of attitudes and behaviors found very little change. A surprising factor was that attitudes toward prevention reported prior to the campaign were already quite positive, which may explain why there was so little change.

On a national scale, other activities are important to an overall strategy to change America's cultural acceptance of violence. Efforts to reduce the use of firearms are critical. Teaching nonviolent techniques and conflict resolution skills is also vitally needed.

One of the goals for Prothrow-Stith's work from the outset has been to determine what violence prevention strategies are appropriate for public health and what are appropriate for criminal justice. As a society, the United States has relied solely on criminal justice to deal with violence. The criminal justice system typically confines its attention to a victim and a perpetrator and seeks to punish the perpetrator.

However, the police in Boston have done some primary prevention in the areas of substance abuse and violence. Within the criminal justice system, some behavior modification programs have been quite successful at reducing recidivism rates.

A General Medicine Approach. General medicine ignores violence. Some of the successful criminal justice programs may be applicable to youngsters seen in emergency rooms, who obviously need more than just to be stitched up. After making repairs, emergency rooms typically send the wounded out without trying to prevent their return, as they often do with other behavior-related illnesses and traumas.

Improvement, recognition, and management of victims of violence deserves a lot of attention not only in emergency rooms but also in primary care physicians' offices. A federally funded program at Boston City Hospital is under way to look at protocols (standard methods for delivering treatment). Very little work has been done in the area of patients at risk of violence.

The only violence prevention protocol developed within health care was conceived by Boston pediatrician Peter Stringham, who based it on the concept of well-baby clinics (public health clinics where babies are brought for regular checkups and discussion of their progress). Continuing the idea of well-baby visits through adolescence, Stringham talked with families about disciplinary techniques, how they argued about their children and how much television-watching went on. He even wrote prescriptions for parents to read to their children.

Children in studies of violence are interviewed extensively to determine what sort of treatment would benefit them. However, outside of such studies few children who exhibit violent behavior receive a physical or psychological workup to determine appropriate treatment. Such children tend to be given a label such as attention-deficit disorder, conduct disorder or sociopath. Once labeled, a child's real problems are likely to be overlooked. Some are anxious. Some are depressed. Some have a lot of physical problems.

Interim Controls. Following Prothrow-Stith's presentation, Felton J. Earls, a member of the faculty of the Harvard School of Public Health's Department of Maternal and Child Health, told a story of a school principal he had met. In the interest of keeping weapons out of his school, the principal had introduced an unusual control measure.

Each morning he met the owners of weapons at the door, where they turned over their weapons to him for safe deposit in a barrel, to be retrieved at the end of the day. In addition to the return of their weapons, those

who turned them over also received free bus passes for transportation home.

The principal's logic was that he was getting to know the weapon owners, gaining the youngsters' trust by keeping his word and establishing the school as a violence-free zone.

(See also CENTERS FOR DISEASE CONTROL (CDC) VIOLENCE DIVISIONS: AN EPIDEMIOLOGIC APPROACH TO RESEARCH AND PREVENTION; CHILD EMERGENCY TRAUMA: A MODEL PREVENTION PROGRAM; CHILDREN AND YOUTHS WITH GUNS; GANGS: PICKUP OR TEMPORARY; VIOLENCE RESEARCH: A LONGITUDINAL STUDY OF VIOLENCE AMONG THE YOUNG; WEAPONS OF CELEBRATION.)

violence research: a longitudinal study of violence among the young Much is already known about the demographics of violence in the United States. America ranks first in violent crimes committed by the young. Males ages 14 to 24 in the United States commit 21.9 violent crimes per 100,000 population. The next highest rate is five violent crimes per 100,000 for that age group. American youngsters ages 13 through 24 account for 48.5% of the nation's homicide arrests and 52% of the violent crime arrests.

Violent crimes are officially defined as murder, forcible rape, robbery (stealing with the use or threat of violence) and aggravated assault (intentional, unlawful bodily injury with or without a weapon, or an attempt at or threat of such injury or death with a deadly weapon).

Among those countries that report their criminal justice data, the United States has the fifth highest homicide rate in the world. The only countries with higher rates are Guatemala, Thailand, Puerto Rico and Brazil.

U.S. data reported for 1989 by 10,503 law enforcement agencies, whose jurisdictions contain about 200 million people, revealed that there were 180,670 arrests for possession of or carrying a weapon. Firearms are intimately related to the homicide rate in the United States. In 1990, 64% of the homicides involved firearms. Of homicides among young men, an average of 75% are committed with firearms compared with 23% in other countries.

The association of homicides and firearms is consistent across the states. In those states with the highest homicide rates, Michigan, California, the District of Columbia, New York, Missouri and Florida, firearms-related homicides account for anywhere from about 50% to 90% of the total. Household surveys of crime have determined that armed victims of crime are twice as likely to be killed as unarmed victims.

The most overrepresented demographic group of homicide victims in the United States is young black males. Of all victims, 78% are young men and 48.6% are black.

Federal Bureau of Investigation (FBI) data on homicides reveals that most homicides occur in the context of an argument. Of the overall homicide totals, gang-related homicides represent only about 1%, those related to the commission of a felony about 15% and those associated with arguments 47%. About 20% of the homicides in the United States are committed by family members and another 30% by friends. Thus about half of the homicides occur among people who know each other.

Alcohol is implicated in about half of the homicides. The data on drugs such as cocaine is less dramatic, except in certain cities such as Washington, D.C., where the medical examiner's office has reported that approximately 80% of homicides are related to cocaine.

While a substantial amount is known about homicides, considerably less is known about the incidence and characteristics of nonfatal assaults. What is known comes from the Northeast Ohio Trauma Study of emergency room data, which reported an approximately 100-to-1 ratio of nonfatal assaults to homicides. Four times the number of assaults were recorded in the emergency room as those reported directly to the police.

Relatively little is known about the impact of socioeconomic factors on the demographics and epidemiology of homicide. Nevertheless, many observers believe that the high incidence of violent crime among young black males is related to socioeconomic factors. The lack of jobs engenders a sense of hopelessness and a feeling that life is not worth much. One Atlanta study looked at domestic homicides and found that when they were adjusted for socioeconomic status, the homicide rates in the black and white communities were the same; that is, poor whites were as likely as poor blacks to commit homicide.

While demographics are useful for defining the problem, they do not predict or prevent violence. For much of the 20th century, the vast amount of injury caused by violent behavior has been considered a social problem to be studied solely by social scientists. In February 1991 Felton J. Earls of the Harvard School of Public Health's Maternal and Child Health Department asserted that labeling violence a social problem had the effect of relieving medicine and education of responsibility for seeking to understand violence or prevent it.

A Complex Research Design.   Together with a group of other scientists at the Harvard School of Public Health, Earls' goal for the next one or two decades is to analyze the problem of violence in the United States as a public health problem in the same way that scientists in the late 19th century analyzed, and eventually solved, the public health problem of infectious diseases. The research group, which includes sociologists, criminologists, public health physicians, psychologists and lawyers, is engaged in a massive study to uncover the factors that generate violence, particularly in an urban context.

Social science is not funded as generously as the physical sciences, and the plan drawn up by Earls and his colleagues aims to build a funding infrastructure that will sustain a long-term study.

Their study is based on a theoretical framework developed in New Zealand. The New Zealand study proposed that there is a distinction between two kinds of developmental tasks (learning behaviors at various stages of life, such as learning to walk or to leave home to attend school).

Some behaviors under study are "adolescence-limited." Others are "life course-persistent." In the course of gaining some independence from their families, some youngsters engage in risky or delinquent behavior during a brief period in adolescence. Others begin such behavior early and persist in it past adolescence. A problem for understanding delinquent behavior is distinguishing between the two.

One widely held presumption is that otherwise good boys and girls suddenly become violent. Earls believes that explanation fits only rare cases. Instead, he believes that conditions for violence are set early in life, even as early as in utero during what he calls "staging phenomena." Moreover, he believes that as risk factors (poor health, an abusive family, loss of loved ones) accumulate, the probability increases that one of the various antisocial behaviors in which the child indulges will become violent.

In many populations that have been examined epidemiologically over the years beginning around age three and continuing to ages 25 and 30, the percentage of children who engage in seriously antisocial behavior varies between 5% and 10%, depending on the environment in which they live. In a rural environment, the rates in young children are about 5%. In an urban area such as Boston, inner London or New York City, the percentage of children who are seriously antisocial at various ages goes up to 10%. There are few environments where the rates are higher than 10%.

Serious antisocial behavior at the youngest ages among the life course-persistent children involves a great deal of physical behavior. The youngsters engage in a lot of fighting. They push their siblings and peers around— sometimes causing minor injuries. Typically, they are obstinate and stubborn and no one quite knows how to deal with them. Because the usual verbal techniques have little effect, they are often subjected to substantial physical punishment. The heavy-handed tactics teachers and parents use to control them only seems to fan the fire of their rebellion.

In persistently antisocial children between ages ten and 15, there is an early onset of sexual activity, cigarette smoking and alcohol use. By age 15, carrying weapons is added to the equation—often guns. In cities such as Boston, New York and Detroit, the weapons are likely to be knives, razor blades or sticks shaped into weapons.

Between the ages of 15 and 20 are found the highest rates of serious violent behavior among the life course-persistent youngsters. These are the years during which injury and death are clustered. By the time they reach about age 35, their participation in violent behavior appears to diminish. Some experts describe this age range as a period of "burnout."

By burnout, researchers mean that the antisocial individuals who account for high violence rates in their earlier years simply grow "tired" of the risks of their behavior or lose their physical agility and are no longer able to commit their antisocial acts. Some experts believe that such individuals merely switch to crimes that carry less risk of detection.

Earls suspects that the so-called burnouts can be found among those who beat their wives and children. There are other explanations. Many may be dead as a consequence of their behavior. Many may be serving long prison sentences.

At age 18, the adolescent-limited children are doing some of the same kinds of behavior done by the life course-persistent children. Because their data come from cross-sectional, short-term studies for periods of up to five years, researchers have difficulty in distinguishing between the two groups.

Official criminal justice statistics are often of little use to help researchers make the distinction because in some neighborhoods as many as half the boys have been arrested by age 18 to 20. It is very common in the United States to find some communities in which 50% to 60% of the boys have been arrested at least once.

Earls and his colleagues believe that the life course-persistent youngsters draw adolescent-limited youngsters into peer networks in which there is a lot of co-offending going on. Earls explained the researchers' thinking by saying "In other words, most of these adolescent-limited kids are basically good kids, sometimes experimenting, sometimes very curious about deviant behavior. And these more hard-core kids who are more experienced at lying and stealing and getting away with it are also good at recruiting gang members who are peers as associates and getting them involved in a very limited age way in such activities."

The goal of the long-term study is to determine whether the differences between the two groups can be identified. To do that, the researchers must do studies that cover a span from early childhood to adulthood, as much as 25 years.

One way the lengthy period is to be reduced is by using an accelerated design. Nine cohorts of youngsters will be recruited at different ages. Some will be enlisted when their mothers receive care at prenatal units. Others will be enrolled at ages three, six, nine and so forth up to age 24. The cohorts will be followed simultaneously for seven years.

Target date for starting the study was 1993. During the first three years, there will be no overlap of age group cohorts, but during years 4, 5, 6, and 7, the study will have participants who have passed from one age category into another, thereby providing considerable opportunity to make comparisons across cohorts.

At the end of three years, in 1996, the three-year-olds who have become six-year-olds can be compared on the basis of their earlier behavior and current behavior and their current behavior can be compared with that of the six-year-olds who have become nine-year-olds. From the collection of seven years of such observations, the researchers expect to be able to tell a "fabricated" story describing the passage of 27 years.

The sample size planned for all cohorts is about 11,000 people. In planning the study, the designers engaged in great debates about whether they should include males and females. The original intent was to study only males because they are far more violent than females, but there is evidence that violent behavior among females is increasing.

The reason that ultimately proved decisive for the inclusion of females was that their antisocial behavior tends to be in the area of sexual activity and early childbearing. As mothers they would be in a position to transmit to a new generation long-term perspectives that are reflected in behavior.

While the study's outcomes will focus on violence and delinquency for all groups, it will examine sexual activity as well as substance abuse for males and females. The study design also calls for measurement of biological and psychological variables and aspects of the child's family environment.

Perhaps the most important goal of the study is to link variations in the characteristics of the community in which an individual lives with variations in his or her personal characteristics. Earls explained why the link was important: "Sociologists have gone about their way studying community structures and psychologists, psychiatrists and pediatricians have gone about their way studying individuals and until now they haven't really put their strengths together to study both individual and community."

Another goal is to observe boys and girls growing up in different kinds of neighborhoods in the same geographical area. The geography of any large city reflects a variety of socioeconomic factors. It is obvious from looking at maps that, as poverty increases, so too does the birth of low weight babies, the incidence of infant mortality and rate of homicides and suicides.

Using similar maps for cities around the United States, the researchers will study children living in both high- and low-crime areas. By following them over time, the researchers expect to find links between the characteristics of neighborhoods and the characteristics of individual behavior.

(See also APPENDIX 2: LIMITS ON BEHAVIORAL SCIENCE IN STUDYING VIOLENCE; ASSAULT WEAPONS; CENTERS FOR DISEASE CONTROL (CDC) VIOLENCE DIVISIONS: AN EPIDEMIOLOGIC APPROACH TO RESEARCH AND PREVENTION; CHILD EMERGENCY TRAUMA: A MODEL PREVENTION PROGRAM; CHILDREN AND YOUTHS WITH GUNS; EMERGENCY MEDICAL CARE: THE IMPACT OF VIOLENCE; GANGS: PICKUP OR TEMPORARY; GUN-FREE SCHOOL ZONES BILL; STREET CRIMES; VIOLENCE PREVENTION: THE EVOLUTION OF A PILOT PROGRAM FOR ADOLESCENTS.)

violent crimes against women: their connection to gender bias

Gender Bias.   Every 15 seconds a woman in the United States is beaten by her husband or boyfriend.

Every six minutes a woman is forcibly raped. One fifth to one half of all American women were sexually abused as children, most often by an older male relative. Although there are male victims of such crimes, gender-bias crimes are directed overwhelmingly against women.

Gender bias has a long history. With rare exceptions, throughout history women have had little social power or authority. They have been the property of their husbands, fathers, brothers or lovers to do with as they wished. Why women have allowed themselves to be mistreated in centuries past is not clear.

One contributing factor that may have deterred women from demanding their rights is their size and muscular strength. Compared with men, on the whole, women are smaller and have less upper body strength, and are therefore less likely to win a physical struggle.

Although small size often can be compensated for by the use of weapons, women seem disinclined to use them. Police repeatedly advise women who have been attacked to stick their fingers in the attackers' eyes, but women find the advice difficult to follow.

Women's disinclination to use violent defenses perhaps better explains the subjugation of women than their size or their access to weapons. Women around the world are and have been over the centuries far less violent than men.

Eighty-five percent of all homicides are committed by men. Except in rare cases of self-defense, women do not kill strangers or even casual acquaintances. Among the 15% of murders committed by women, the vast majority are of family members, usually spouses or lovers who have abused the women for years.

Another factor in women's subjugation, perhaps as important as their disinclination to violence, has been their vulnerability to pregnancy. Bearing children, often dying in childbirth and being responsible for protection of children after birth has kept women economically dependent on men.

If throughout history women around the world have been abused, why, historians have asked, did they wait to raise objections on a large scale until the 1830s (when the feminist movement began), and what motivated them at that time?

The reasons for social change are often hard to determine. One explanation suggests that the change from home industries to factory labor brought about by the Industrial Revolution left some women idle and free to become introspective about their lives.

Another explanation argues that women were belatedly responding to the implications of the ideologies fostered by the French and American revolutions. They were demanding equal rights long denied to them by prejudice and superstition. This explanation raises the question of why American women waited for a half a century to notice that the Declaration of Independence did not apply to them.

One seldom-mentioned explanation of women's 19th-century rebellion is the spread of knowledge about contraception. Even though barrier methods of contraception, such as the condom and the diaphragm, had been in existence for thousands of years, knowledge about ways to avoid pregnancy remained limited among both men and women until books and travel spread the information. Even when women have had the necessary knowledge to avoid constant pregnancy, access to effective techniques has often been limited. In many parts of the world, knowledge about and access to contraception is still scarce.

Another explanation of why the stirring of revolt by women began in the 19th century is offered by William O'Neill, in his 1971 book *Everyone Was Brave*. He proposes that the transformation of the Victorian family from a loosely organized group into a strictly defined nuclear unit of father, mother and children at the center of social life laid an unbearable burden on women.

To make the burden more palatable, a mystique was developed that asserted that the moral purity and spiritual genius of women would find its highest expression in the home, safe from the morally corrupting effects of the man-made world.

The argument was self-defeating. If women's purity made them the guardians of the home and of public morality, then involvement with men was something to be avoided. Thus the Victorians taught women to think of themselves as a special class and thrust them into one another's company, where they speculated about how to improve the world.

A Victorian conception of women as wan, ethereal, spiritualized beings bore little resemblance to the real world in which women worked in fields, washed clothes by hand and toiled over great kitchen stoves. The daily labor of women somehow failed to prove to men that women were not delicate creatures in need of shelter from the harsh realities of life.

Victorian men believed that they had accorded women a higher and more honorable status than any previous generation. Men were mystified that so many women disagreed with their assessment and thereby threatened the whole system of values that revolved around the home. Feminism was a radical movement because it called into question the "cult of pure womanhood," whose central values were piety, purity, submissiveness and domesticity. Almost the only Victorian work considered suitable for women was connected with religion.

Nineteenth-century feminists repeatedly drew parallels between the slavery of African-Americans and their own conditions. One of the first tasks the earliest feminists undertook was to propagandize against the prevailing system of ideas. The first major work by an American feminist, Sarah Grimke, in 1838, was directed against clergymen who believed that God had ordained women's inferior state.

By the time women were given the vote in 1920, generations of women had spent lifetimes protesting, picketing, marching and going to jail with little to show for it. Despite decades of constant work, social changes in the lives of women were minor. Some women were allowed to work in business and/or go to college, but the ballot did not help women to advance their most urgent causes or improve their status. In William O'Neill's words: "The struggle for women's rights ended during the 1920s, leaving men in clear possession of commanding places in American life."

Four decades of quiescence followed, until the feminist movement came back to life in the early 1960s. Not much had changed in the interim. By the early 1990s, after three more decades of work, many more women were in the work force, but most still labored on the lowest rungs of the economic ladder.

The median earning for men in 1989 was $399 a week, or $20,748 a year. For women the amounts were $328 a week and $17,056 a year. For men who maintained families, the 1989 average weekly earnings were $425 or $22,100 a year. For women who maintained families, the amounts were $321 a week and $16,692 a year.

At the managerial and professional levels, differences were even greater. In 1989 men averaged $36,036 a year and women $25,376.

A blatant example of the continuing low status of women in the United States has been their absence from health care studies. Until the end of the 1980s, health studies focused primarily and often exclusively on men. Therefore, findings from studies on heart disease, cancer, sleep disorders and so forth conducted on men were extrapolated to women to whom in some areas, particularly heart diseases, they were not applicable. But compared to women elsewhere, American women in the 1990s seemed well off.

In some areas of the world, females are held in such low esteem that they never grow up to adulthood. Even though more boys are born than girls, population specialists have determined that under equal conditions, females are hardier than males, have a greater chance of survival at virtually every age and have a longer life expectancy. Therefore, the majority of the world's population should be female. But it is not.

The absence of tens of millions of women from the world's population, in the opinions of demographers, reflects a strong and continuing preference for males. In parts of Asia, including China and India, which have almost half the world's population, the preference for sons is so strong that daughters have a significantly lower chance of surviving.

Interviewed for a February 3, 1992 *Boston Globe* article entitled "The Grim Mystery of World's Missing Women," Joann Vanek, coordinator of the gender statistics program at the United Nations Statistical Office, said, "There are clearly cultural patterns operating and operating in very complicated ways to favor young boys rather than young girls." Some studies have shown that girls receive less food than boys. Other studies have found that parents are more likely to seek medical care for sons.

A study done in Bangladesh found that girls, no matter what their position is in the order of children born, are more likely to die before their fifth birthday. But girls with an older sister face what demographers Pradip Muhuri and Samuel Preston, who conducted the study, call an "excess risk of dying," six times higher than girls with no older sister.

Gender Bias as a Stimulus for Violence.   For women who manage to survive their early years, women's low status around the world means that a threat of violence remains throughout their lives. Moreover, when women are attacked, they are often blamed for bringing on the violence.

Awareness appears to be growing in the United States of the high volume of violence directed toward women. In connection with a bill introduced by Senator Joseph Biden (D.-Delaware) to combat violence and crimes against women on the streets and in their homes, the U.S. Senate Judiciary Committee held three hearings in 1990. A companion version was introduced in the House of Representatives; both bills bogged down in 1990, were reintroduced in 1991 and 1992 and once again did not make it through the system. They were reintroduced in January 1993 and Senator Biden's staff expected the

Senate version to be put on the Senate's agenda at some time during the year.

For the June 20, 1990 hearing, Biden's staff developed a fact sheet about violence directed toward women. The data indicated the following:

- During the 1980s, the rape rate rose four times faster than the national crime rate.
- From 1965 to 1990 assaults against women rose by 50%, while assaults against men declined.
- Less than half of all rapes are reported. Of those reported, fewer than 40% result in arrests.
- In 1988 there were 92,000 forcible rapes reported, which averages out to one rape every six minutes. Annually 3 to 4 million women are battered each year, which averages out to one every 18 seconds.
- Three out of four women will be victims of at least one violent crime during their lifetimes.
- The crime rate against women in the United States is significantly higher than in other countries. The U.S. rape rate is four times higher than Germany's, 13 times higher than England's, and 20 times higher than Japan's.

Violence against women was also addressed in the September/October 1990 issue of *Ms.*, which carried a section entitled "Violence Against Women: A *Ms.* Report on Life in Our Times." In an article entitled " 'Femicide': Speaking the Unspeakable," Canadian novelist Margaret Atwood was quoted as saying that she had once asked a male friend why men feel threatened by women. He replied: "They are afraid women will laugh at them." She then asked a group of women why they feel threatened by men. They answered, "We're afraid of being killed."

The authors of the femicide article, Jane Caputi of the University of New Mexico, Albuquerque, who also wrote *The Age of Sex Crime* (1987), and Diana Russell of Mills College in Oakland, California, author of several books on violence against women, discussed the massacre at the University of Montreal in which 14 female engineering students were killed and nine were wounded by a man armed with an assault rifle. They were dismayed at the media's failure to acknowledge the political nature of the crime. The media's failure came despite the killer's having left a suicide note blaming all his failures on women.

That the Montreal killings represented more than just one man's deranged thinking was evident when University of Alberta engineering student Celeste Brosseau participated in an engineering society skit night shortly after the massacre. Brosseau, who had complained about the sexism of the engineering faculty, was greeted by hundreds of her classmates chanting "Shoot the bitch."

Caputi and Russell said:

No one wonders whether individual perpetrators are crazy or have had bad personal experiences with African-Americans and Jews. Most people understand that lynchings and pogroms are motivated by political objectives: preserving white and gentile supremacy. Similarly, the aim of violence against women—conscious or not—is to preserve male supremacy . . . We think *femicide* best describes the murders of women by men motivated by hatred, contempt, pleasure, or a sense of ownership of women.

In the view of Caputi and Russell, femicide is the ultimate end of a continuum of terror that includes murder, rape, torture, mutilation, incestuous and extrafamilial child sexual abuse, physical and emotional battery, gratuitous hysterectomies, forced sterilization, criminalization of contraception and abortion, cosmetic mutilations, clitoridectomies (removal of the clitoris, the sensitive site of female sexual stimulation), infibulations (the closure of the vaginal opening with a clasp or surgical sutures to prevent intercourse, which can result in infection and death), historical immolation of witches in Europe, historical and contemporary immolation of brides and widows in India and "crimes of honor" in some Latin and Middle Eastern countries, where women believed to have lost their virginity sometimes are killed by male relatives.

Sexual harassment on the job is not always included in catalogs of violent crimes against women because it does not usually end in physical violence. However, by its nature sexual harassment keeps women anxious that it might. Moreover, sexual harassment often threatens a woman's livelihood.

Sexual harassment can take a variety of forms, including lewd conversation and/or display of lewd posters or pictures; sexual items left in a woman's locker or desk; remarks about her body; requests for sexual favors, sometimes coupled with the threat or promise of demotion or promotion; and touching a woman without her permission, particularly on the breasts or buttocks.

The issue of sexual harassment gained national attention in October 1991 during the U.S. Senate confirmation hearings on the nomination of Clarence Thomas to the Supreme Court. University of Oklahoma law professor Anita Hill alleged that she had been sexually harassed by Thomas when she had worked for him in government positions from 1981 to 1983. She claimed

that she did not lodge a complaint at the time because she feared she would be squeezed out of good assignments and possibly lose her job. Judith Resnick, a law professor at the University of Southern California Law Center, characterized Hill's testimony as a paradigm of a sexual harassment case.

During the hearings, it was implied that Hill had been scorned by Thomas and that she intended to get even by testifying against him, although under intense questioning, it became clear that Hill had not approached the Judiciary Committee staff to give testimony, the staff had approached her. She maintained public silence until her statement to the Federal Bureau of Investigation (FBI) fell into reporters' hands on October 5, at which point she felt she had no choice but to testify. Thomas denied her charges. Apparently the Senate either believed him or found no fault with his behavior since it voted to confirm his nomination.

The broadcast of the confirmation hearings stirred up debate about sexual harassment around the country, and over the next several weeks sexual harassment stories appeared frequently in the media. An October 21, 1991 *U.S. News and World Report* article entitled "Harassment: Men on Trial," reported that two female police officers in Long Beach, California had won a $3.1 million judgment after three years of sexual taunts from colleagues. The stress of the harassment led to the breakup of one woman's marriage, and both had left their careers in law enforcement. The New England Patriots football team and three of its members were fined nearly $50,000 for lewd remarks and gestures made to a female reporter in their locker room.

Aggressive male behavior toward women is not confined to harassment. A random sample survey done by Diana Russell of 930 San Francisco women revealed that they had been variously victimized: 44% by rape or attempted rape; 38% by child sexual abuse; 21% by marital violence; 16% by incestuous abuse; and 14% by wife rape. Russell's research on largely unreported rapes found a sharp increase in incidence over the last half century.

Virtually all experts agree that sex murders (murders in which sex plays some part) have risen substantially since the early 1960s. A surge in serial murders began in the 1950s, viewed by some experts as encouraged by the sensational media coverage they receive. The vast majority of serial killers are white males, and most of their victims are women.

Law enforcement officials have noted a growing viciousness in slayings. Justice Department official Robert

Heck told Caputi and Russell: "We've got people now killing 20 and 30 people and more, and some of them just don't kill. They torture their victims in terrible ways and mutilate them before they kill them."

In 1989 a California man, Curtis Adams, was sentenced to 32 years in prison because he tortured his wife for ten hours. After she refused to have anal sex, Adams handcuffed her, forced a bottle and then a broomstick into her anus and hung her naked out the window. He took breaks to read her Bible passages about women's obligations to obey their husbands.

A sense of entitlement is a major cause of sexual terrorism. Many men believe they have a right to do whatever they want to women and to get whatever they want from them. When female University of Iowa students complained about the loud stereos of male students on the floor above, the response was graffiti in the men's bathroom that was published in the university newspaper.

The graffiti was entitled "The Top 10 Things to Do to the Bitches Below." The list included calls to beat the women "into a bloody pulp with a sledgehammer and a laugh" and instructions on "how to mutilate female genitalia with an electric trimmer, pliers, and a red-hot soldering iron."

A plentiful source of gruesome ideas for violence that can be used against women is found in pornography and mass media "gorenography." An FBI study of 36 serial killers found that for 81% of the sample, pornography was ranked highest among their sexual interests. Ted Bundy maintained that pornography was central to the development of his violent behavior.

Atrocities perpetrated on women are rendered acceptable as humor and standard fantasy in a variety of formats from comic books to the best literature to box office favorites to snuff films. Femicidal atrocity is normalized by its omnipresence.

However, in the opinion of Caputi and Russell, if femicides were recognized for what they were and if nonlethal sexual assaults were taken into account; if incest and battery were recognized as torture; if the patriarchal home were seen as the prison it so often is; and if pornography and gorenography were recognized as hate literature; then the culture would have to acknowledge that there exists a reign of sexual terror comparable in magnitude, intensity and intent to the persecution, torture and annihilation of women as witches from the 14th to the 17th centuries.

Special Groups.   Although violence is directed against women in general, certain groups come in for particular attention. A homophobic killer, Stephen Roy Carr,

stalked two lesbians, Rebecca Wight and Claudia Brenner, on a hiking trip along the Appalachian trail in 1988. He opened fire on their campsite. Wight died at the site. Brenner, shot in the head, face, upper arm and neck, walked four miles for help. Carr's attack was one of 7,248 homophobic incidents in 1988. He was convicted of first-degree murder.

Cultural issues complicate recognition and remedies for violence toward women. The 1986 U.S. marriage fraud amendments to the U.S. immigration laws leave undocumented immigrant women at the mercy of their abusing husbands. Under the 1986 amendments, the U.S. Immigration and Naturalization Service requires that both partners file for residency—after they have lived together 21 months. Although the law allows for good-cause exemptions, many women believe that only their abusing husbands can file for their green card, the key to permanent U.S. residency status.

If the abused woman seeks medical help or police assistance, the abusing husband may threaten to have her deported. Representative Louise Slaughter of New York sponsored an amendment to clarify the language of the law, but even if the amendment passed, many women would not be helped because of their fear and because of language and cultural barriers.

Some crimes against women are being excused using the so-called cultural defense. After bludgeoning his wife to death in 1987, Dong Lu Chen was sentenced to five years' probation. At Chen's trial, an anthropologist testified that traditional Chinese values could account for his reaction to his wife's alleged infidelity.

Asian and feminist activists were outraged at the sentence because the cultural information was "inaccurate, archaic and irrelevant." Monona Yin of the New York-based Organization of Asian Women said, "How is wife-killing treated in China? It's treated as homicide."

In another cultural defense case, Lee Fong abducted a 16-year-old from her Denver home and assaulted her. He was acquitted in 1989 of kidnapping, sexual assault and menacing based on the cultural defense that "bride stealing" is a custom among the Hmong people of Laos.

After the acquittal, Maysee Moua, of the Asian/Pacific Center for Human Development in Denver, said, "Cultural practices, no matter how old, need to be discontinued in this country whenever they violate the civil rights of others."

While some of the cultural defense cases have been used for other crimes, most have involved violent crimes against women. Monona Yin said of the practice, "It's no coincidence that this stuff erupts around sexual customs. So many cultures are misogynist. Virtually any culture is going to provide justification for violence against women." American culture is no exception.

Constant Vigilance Required. During a presentation at one of the three 1990 Judiciary Committee hearings, Sally Goldfarb of the National Organization of Women (NOW)'s Legal Defense Fund told an anecdote that highlighted the selectivity of gender-biased violence. A law school professor began a section on rape in her criminal law course by asking each male student to tell the class what he did on a daily basis to protect himself from assault. The response was a puzzled silence.

The professor then asked the female students the same question. Each of them gave a prompt response: "I don't go to a certain mall because its parking lot is badly lit"; "I don't come to campus to use the library at times when there won't be many people around"; "I sleep with my windows locked no matter what the weather." One woman went so far as to carry a loaded gun.

Clearly, men fear crime in a variety of contexts, but women fear not only those same crimes, they also fear many other crimes aimed particularly at them because they are women. While a given situation may be threatening for a man, it may be perilous to a woman.

When a woman is attacked in a place where men are safe, it is a bias-related crime. Goldfarb cited as an example a case in New Bedford, Massachusetts in which a young woman was brutally gang-raped and then accused of having brought the attack on herself for having been in the bar.

Gender bias underlies the commission of crimes not thought of in that connection. A widely publicized case in Boston involved the fatal shooting of white, middle-class Carol Stuart, a pregnant woman on her way back from a birthing class. Her husband, Charles, who was also wounded, claimed that a black man had done the shooting.

When it was discovered that Charles had done the shooting himself, there were accusations of racial bias against the police for having looked for the assailant only in the black community where the crime had been committed. However, there was no discussion of gender bias in connection with the husband's decision to discard his pregnant wife by murdering her and collecting her insurance.

In Goldfarb's words, "Charles Stuart's heinous crime was not a unique aberration. It was actually part of a social pattern—a pattern that is founded on a deep-seated and widespread view that women's lives are worth less than men's."

Murder is a crime mostly committed by men. In the United States in 1989 males killed 16,603 males and 2,373 females for a total of 18,976. Females killed 1,171 males and 245 females for a total of 1,416. Husbands, including common-law husbands, were responsible for 33% of all murders of women between 1976 and 1987 in the United States. In 1989 almost 28% of all murder victims were killed by their husbands or boyfriends, while 5% of male victims were killed by their wives or girlfriends.

According to a 1991 Justice Department Bureau of Justice Statistics study, one in five women victimized by a husband or ex-husband reported that she had suffered at least three similar assaults in the previous six months. And almost a quarter of such women required medical care, compared with 13% of victims of other offenders.

The notorious beating and rape of a female jogger in New York's Central Park on April 19, 1989 was characterized by the media as a crime based on class and race bias. They failed to mention that it was also an expression of hostility based on gender.

Whatever progress women have made in recent years will count for nothing if women cannot take advantage of their opportunities for fear of jeopardizing their personal safety. When women are deprived of the ability to be safe in their own homes, to walk freely on the streets, to travel alone without fear of attack, privileges enjoyed routinely by men, their lives remain severely curtailed.

(See also BATTERED WOMEN: CONGRESSIONAL TESTIMONY; CAMPUS VIOLENCE; RAPE; SERIAL KILLERS; VIOLENCE AS FUN: THE CASE OF THE CENTRAL PARK JOGGER.)

W

warrants See ARREST: CONSTITUTIONAL RESTRICTIONS AND LEGAL PROCEDURES.

weapons of celebration In recent years throughout the United States, the blare of party horns and popping of champagne corks common to New Year's Eve celebrations, and the noise that characterizes other celebrations, such as those of victories in sports events, are accompanied by the sound of shots being fired into the air. As an expression of joy, guns are a lethal choice.

In an interview for a January 2, 1990 *New York Times* article entitled "Shots in Air, Death on the Ground," Captain James Phelan of the Chicago Police Department said, "It's like combat. It really sounds like a battle zone, with shots being fired all over the place."

In Los Angeles two teenage boys shot into the air to celebrate, then lowered their weapons and shot at police officers. The police returned their fire, wounding both.

In recent years bullets descending from such shootings have struck dozens of people as well as cars and other property. Ballistics experts warn that bullets are just as lethal when descending as they are when ascending.

A different kind of celebratory missile was used in Atlanta on New Year's Eve, 1990. Drunken revelers threw potted plants and fire extinguishers from upper-floor walkways into a hotel lobby below. Fifteen people were hurt; one required 17 stitches, another had a heart attack. Fifty people were arrested.

(See also CHILDREN AND YOUTHS WITH GUNS; GUN CONTROL: ADVOCATES; GUN CONTROL: OPPONENTS; GUN-FREE SCHOOL ZONES BILL.)

White Aryan Resistance (WAR)   See HATE GROUPS.

white-collar crime   See CORPORATE CRIME.

white slavery   See PROSTITUTION.

wife-beating   See BATTERED WOMEN: CONGRESSIONAL TESTIMONY.

wiseguy   A "wiseguy" is a midlevel member of a Mafia family. The term is used frequently in the media and by the wiseguys themselves.

Wiseguys embody not just an illegal occupation, but a way of life. According to Nicholas Pileggi in his 1987 book *Wiseguy: Life in a Mafia Family:*

> they lacked almost all the necessary talents that might have helped them satisfy the appetites of their dreams, except for one—their talent for violence. Violence was natural to them. It fueled them. Snapping a man's arm, cracking his ribs with an inch-and-a-half-diameter lead pipe, slamming his fingers in the door of a car, or casually taking his life was entirely acceptable. It was routine. . . . the common knowledge that they would unquestionably take a life ironically gave them life. It distinguished them from everyone else . . . If they were crossed, denied, offended, thwarted in any way, or even mildly annoyed, retribution was demanded, and violence was the answer.

Kevin Cullen in a February 4, 1990 article entitled "The Quiet Man," pointed out another common wiseguy quality: "Wiseguys are notoriously lazy."

A key element in most descriptions of wiseguys appears to be simmering, easily triggered violence. Ironically, neither Henry Hill, the principal mob member described in *Wiseguy,* nor Darin Nino Bufalino, an alleged murderer whom Cullen was writing about, seems to be easily provoked, even when circumstances might seem to warrant it. Moreover, neither could be described as lacking a work ethic. At age six, Bufalino began working at a racetrack picking up used programs and reselling them. At age 11, Hill began working at a cab stand across the street from his home. (The cab stand was the unofficial headquarters of a rising star in one of New York's organized-crime families.)

Obviously, wiseguys may differ in individual characteristics, but the one quality that Hill and Bufalino and other wiseguys seem to have in common is a willingness to use violence to achieve their ends.

(See also APPENDIX 1A: THE AMERICAN MAFIA AND OTHER ETHNIC CRIME ORGANIZATIONS; OUTLAW MOTORCYCLE GANGS.)

APPENDIXES

Appendix 1.   Organized Crime: Roots of America's Drug Traffic
   A.   The American Mafia and Other Ethnic Crime Organizations
   B.   The Sicilian Mafia
   C.   The Colombian Medellin Cartel
   D.   The Chinese Triads
   E.   The Japanese Yakuza
Appendix 2.   Limitations on Behavioral Science in Studying Violence
Appendix 3.   Resources
   A.   Prevention
   B.   Children
   C.   Domestic Violence
   D.   Substance Abuse
   E.   Civil Rights and Human Rights
   F.   Victims' Assistance
   G.   Criminal Justice
   H.   Corrections
   I.   Research and Scholarship

APPENDIX 1. ORGANIZED CRIME: ROOTS OF AMERICA'S DRUG TRAFFIC

INTRODUCTION

As with many other areas in the study of violence, there is a lack of agreement among scholars, law enforcement and the public about the definition of organized crime. For decades the Federal Bureau of Investigation (FBI), under the leadership of J. Edgar Hoover, denied the existence of nationwide crime networks. Hoover's denial puzzled many Americans who had been exposed to the efficient organizations of bootleggers during Prohibition.

Since the 1960s, U.S. law enforcement and Congressional committees have accepted the idea of crime organized on a national basis, but they have focused almost exclusively on the American Mafia, dominated by Italian-Americans, and to a lesser degree the Sicilian Mafia, dominated by Italians born in Sicily. In doing so, they have paid only limited attention to the growing impact of criminal organizations dominated by members of other ethnic groups, some native-born, others newly arrived.

Trying to stay even with crime in their own jurisdictions, law enforcement officials around the world have scant resources to cope with the growth of international criminal organizations, made possible by revenues from the worldwide distribution and sale of narcotics.

A. THE AMERICAN MAFIA AND OTHER ETHNIC CRIME ORGANIZATIONS

Among the better-known crime organizations doing business in the United States and Canada are the American Mafia, the Sicilian Mafia, the Medellin Cartel (Colombian drug "lords"), the Chinese Triads and Japan's yakuza. Mafia organizations have been known by a variety of names: the Outfit, the Clique, the Arm, the Syndicate and La Cosa Nostra (Our Thing). These various terms may refer to a national structure, a local branch or some other criminal group entirely, creating confusion about how organized crime is organized.

Despite the confusion, historian Stephen Fox wrote in his 1989 book *Blood and Power: Organized Crime in Twentieth-Century America,* "When the layers are peeled away, though, an essential core remains that may be called the Mafia." He based his assessment on manuscript collections, congressional hearings, and transcripts of wiretaps and interviews. Additional information about gang organization has recently become available in a flood of books written by defectors, such as *Quitting the Mob* (1992) by Michael Franzese and Dary Matera. The authors of such books tend to gloss over some of their own crimes, but they do provide a sense of the daily operation of organized crime.

Like many other modern institutions, organized crime has its roots in social upheaval. From about the mid-1880s on, American life was transformed by overlapping social revolutions. Capitalism turned a slowly-changing agrarian society into a rapidly changing industrial society based on ever more sophisticated technology and exploitation of natural resources. Immigration brought ethnic diversity to the United States, challenging the two-century-old domination of Protestants descended from the British, the so-called WASPs (white, Anglo-Saxon Protestants).

Unable to identify with the strains and enormous social changes of modernization and diversity, the WASPs dealt with the problems they could identify: crime, political corruption, saloons and foreigners. Sensing the beginning of a new political order in which their values would not be dominant, WASPs attempted to regain control. They devoted their attention to reforming corrupt politics and reducing the consumption of alcohol.

During the first two decades of the 20th century, as the level of immigration climbed to an average of a million a year, the idea of prohibition of alcohol gradually took hold through passage of statutes in 27 states. Prohibition finally became the law of the entire nation with the ratification of the 18th Amendment and the passage of the Volstead Act. This criminalization of alcohol brought into being an entire illegal industry devoted to supplying the enormous demand. This industry soon became nationally organized and provided invaluable training for criminal generations to come.

Fox reports that crime in the United States did not become organized until Prohibition provided the impetus in 1920. At the time, local gangs were dabbling with the idea of increasing their distribution of illegal drugs, but Prohibition made alcohol distribution more attractive.

Prior to 1920, groups of crooks with entrepreneurial aspirations paid off key police and politicians and in return controlled neighborhoods, sectors of cities or at most an entire urban area. The activities under the gangsters' protection, for the most part, were street crime, burglaries, prostitution and gambling confined to particular areas. The gangs did not operate on a regional or national scale.

Organized Crime's Ethnicity

An underlying theme of Fox's book is the ethnic aspect of organized crime in the United States.

Gangsters have always dealt in blood and power—blood in several senses of the word. Perhaps more so and longer so than in any other area of American life, ethnicity has mattered in the underworld, affecting methods, power, associations, and job specialities. For many observers of the American scene nowadays, ethnicity has become a touchily delicate topic . . . Gangsters have never felt bound by such discretion . . . "I'm not talking about Italians," Joe Valachi [a Mafia defector] said at his hearing in 1963. "I'm talking about criminals." A vital distinction.

The ethnic patterns of Prohibition endured for at least 40 years afterward. Gangsters remained mostly Irish, Jewish and Italian. "Blood ties" mattered.

From 1900 to 1920 more than 3 million Italian immigrants arrived in the United States. About 90% were from southern Italy and Sicily. Most came from peasant and working-class backgrounds. In Italy, their lives had

been bound by family, village and church, and by a suspicion of outside laws and law enforcement officials.

Italian bootleggers in the United States, isolated by internal pride and external hostility, generally lacked the ties to police and politicians enjoyed by Irish bootleggers. Compared with Jewish bootleggers, they had few ties to foreign sources and they lacked sophistication. What they lacked, however, they made up for with a reputation for unpredictable violence and an ability to scare people not otherwise easily frightened. The fear they generated gave them power.

The most powerful Italian bootlegging operations evolved in New York City. As elsewhere, murders and mergers consolidated independent operations. The winnowing process left five gangs, most of whose members were Sicilian-born.

Perhaps the most famous bootlegger of all was Chicago's Al Capone, who has been characterized as a buffoon avoided even by friends. Capone loved publicity and welcomed the company of journalists, who took his mumblings and shaped them into readable prose, thereby turning the gangster into a legend (and beginning an American tradition).

During Capone's era, Chicago was so disorganized and competitive that there was an average of one gang murder a week. The warfare brought the city constant national media attention. Before Prohibition, hoodlums never mixed with respectable people. After 13 years of Prohibition, proprietors of speakeasies mixed easily with the rest of the United States.

Most of the men who dominated organized crime from Prohibition until the 1960s began their careers as bootleggers. During Prohibition informal cooperation among bootleggers in different states became increasingly systematized. In May 1929 most of the major figures came together in Atlantic City for the first national convention of organized crime.

After the repeal of Prohibition, some bootleggers decided to remain in the legitimate liquor business. They purchased companies and bought distribution rights for various European liquors and wines, using relatives and stooges to act as fronts enabling them to secure legitimate licenses. Some former bootleggers became large-scale distributors. They knew how to push new brands into retail stores, bars and restaurants, and they retained contacts with old friends as former speakeasies were turned into cocktail lounges. Most bootleggers, however, left the liquor business to resume their pre-Prohibition activities, such as gambling and prostitution.

The Evolution of Mafia Organization

Sicilian immigrants to the United States brought the idea of the Mafia with them as a cultural norm, a customary way of doing business, rather than as a structured organization. Accustomed to unfriendly governments, Sicilian immigrants found the WASPs and the Irish equally unapproachable.

A transplanted Mafia provided the immigrants with a sense of order in their new communities. However, this was an illusion; the Mafia was essentially a secret criminal operation threatening Italian immigrants with robbery, murder, kidnapping and extortion.

The Mafia blossomed in unexpected places. Just after the Civil War, in the midst of the political disorder of the Reconstruction, the first Mafia family formed in New Orleans, where it flourished along the docks. The New Orleans Mafia became famous for its use of the "Mafia gun": a sawed-off shotgun that could be folded and concealed under a coat.

Another early Mafia family arose in the coal mining areas of northeastern Pennsylvania. In time, Mafia influence spread to the United Mine Workers Union and even to the mine owners. One family began when five brothers from New York named Morelli moved into Providence, Rhode Island, with its large Italian community. In time, they pillaged their way up into southeastern Massachusetts.

Cleveland immigrants had their own local gang, as did those in the steel mills and smelting plants of Pueblo, Colorado and the coal mines of central Illinois. These local mafiosi were content to dominate their own territories.

Two separate accidents of history changed the course of the American Mafia. About the time Prohibition was making American bootlegging an attractive enterprise, Benito Mussolini assumed power in Italy. To consolidate his power, he tried to subdue the Sicilian Mafia. A group of mafiosi who escaped Mussolini's clutches by moving to the United States settled in Buffalo, New York, where they started a principal Mafia family, eventually extending operations into Canada. Several other groups also settled in New York.

The new immigrants propelled the American Mafia toward a national structure by capturing and using as a foundation the Unione Siciliana, a mutual aid society started in Chicago in 1895. Created to provide life insurance, that is, funeral expenses, the Unione had done battle with various Italian outlaws. In the 1920s Sicilian gangsters took it over and transformed it into an operating front. Six different presidents of the Unione were murdered during the decade that followed the takeover.

From the early 1930s on, the Mafia was at the center of American organized crime. During 1930 and 1931 war broke out among New York's five Mafia gangs. Fighting extended to Chicago and the West Coast. By the time the killing stopped, Mafia families had been forced to broaden their membership beyond normal boundaries, in order to replace dead members. Allies and new non-Sicilian recruits had been drawn in.

Even more revolutionary than the inclusion of non-Sicilians was the formation of a new national Commission, an organizational invention without precedent in Sicily. The new governing body was formed to forestall future bloodshed.

The Commission met for the first time in the fall of 1931 and consisted of seven men, the five leaders of the New York families and one each from Chicago and Buffalo. The seven commissioners were expanded to nine in 1956. Decisions were reached by consensus and no one dominated. Each Mafia family remained autonomous on its turf. Mafia families not represented directly on the board nevertheless accepted its authority.

Meeting once every five years, the Commission gave the Mafia stability and an expansive new view. Commission operations went smoothly until a series of crises prompted an emergency meeting in 1957. That meeting, in the small western New York town of Apalachin, was interrupted by the police. Fifty-eight gangsters were arrested. Most were from the Northeast and Midwest, although some came from points as distant as Florida, Texas, Colorado, California and Cuba.

The publicity that ensued sparked congressional hearings the following summer. The Senate Select Committee on Improper Activities in the Labor and Management Field, chaired by Senator John L. McClellan (D.-Arkansas) with Robert Kennedy as chief counsel, convened hearings on the Mafia and its Apalachin conclave.

McClellan and Kennedy were zealous. The hearings stretched on until the summer of 1959 and included more than 100 attorneys, accountants and investigators; 15,000 witnesses; and 500 open meetings. Ninety-six of the witnesses before the committee were eventually convicted of various criminal offenses.

The professional interests of the men rounded up in Apalachin were concentrated in certain areas, some of them long associated in the public's mind with the Mafia. Twenty-two were in unions or labor-management relations; 17 in taverns, restaurants or hotels; 16 in the garment industry; 12 in real estate; 11 in import-export businesses; 11 in olive oil and cheese; ten in groceries; nine in vending machines; and nine in construction.

Fox believes that Robert Kennedy's role in the hearings was connected to the death of his brother John. Fox theorizes that the Mafia was responsible for John Kennedy's death. The alleged link between the president and the Mafia was Joseph Kennedy, the father of John and Robert.

Joseph Kennedy reputedly made his wealth as a bootlegger during Prohibition. Although he left active involvement in the underworld, Joe Kennedy was said to have maintained contacts with his former colleagues. Because he wanted his son to become president, Fox believes that Joe Kennedy called in favors from underworld friends, who helped round up votes that enabled John Kennedy to win the presidency in a very close election.

The underworld code expects favors to be returned. The new president insisted that his brother Robert become attorney general, hardly a favor in the eyes of the underworld. For 30 months, beginning at the end of 1956, Robert Kennedy had been the executive in charge of what was the most thorough investigation of organized crime that Congress had ever undertaken. As attorney general in his brother's administration, Robert continued his dogged pursuit of organized crime.

While the Mafia may not have instigated the president's death, there is evidence that they wanted him dead. During a recorded, wiretapped conversation, the boss of the Tampa Mafia said, "Kennedy's not going to make it to the next election. He is going to be hit." A member of the Buffalo Mafia answered, "They should kill the whole family, the mother and father too!" In the wake of his brother's assassination, Robert Kennedy appeared to lose interest in pursuing organized crime.

Changes Wrought by Drugs

In the late 1960s law enforcement officials believed that gambling and betting were the underworld's most productive activities, followed by loan sharking and narcotics. Initially they viewed a boom in drug distribution as just another lucrative mob scam, not much different from their other rackets. But narcotics quickly overtook other enterprises.

The Mafia Commission had long been opposed to drugs, on the grounds that they brought too much attention from the law, carried the risk of becoming addictive and increased the probability of killing outsiders. However, according to Claire Sterling, the author of *Octopus: The Long Reach of the International Mafia (1990),* the American Mafia permitted the Sicilian Mafia to bring drugs into their various families' territories for a percentage of the profits.

Despite the Comission's alleged no-drug-traffic or usage policy, younger members adopted drug trafficking as a quick way to get rich. Drug distribution crowded out more traditional Mafia activities. Loan sharks complained that people who borrowed money to pay for drugs were not able to pay the money back, no matter how much punishment was inflicted on them. Many younger members could not resist using some of the plentiful supply and array of drugs, and the organization became more and more violent and disorganized.

Large-scale Mafia pushers avoided bulky, low-profit marijuana in favor of lightweight, high-profit opium, heroin, morphine and cocaine. About the choice of drugs, Fox wrote:

> Different from any other gangster enterprise, these drugs were the wildest of wild cards, deranging for everyone involved, with peculiar, unpredictable powers of their own. From the 1960s on, as consumer demand in the United States for harder drugs kept building, the underworld got in ever deeper, both dealing and using. It was a fateful bargain, offering big money in the short run at the ultimate price of cohesion, security, and organization.

Narcotics contributed in an indirect way to opening the Mafia to public scrutiny. In 1962 Joe Valachi, a Mafia "soldier" for 30 years, was serving a sentence at the Atlanta federal penitentiary on a narcotics charge, when he become convinced that he had been marked for death as an informer. In response to his fear, Valachi killed a fellow prisoner, who he thought was his appointed murderer. To secure protection from the prison system, Valachi decided to talk to officials at length, on the record.

The Valachi Papers, by Peter Maas, written from oral interviews with Joe Valachi, brought Valachi's revelations to the attention of the public. The Valachi story was one of two books in 1969, both best sellers, that helped convince the public finally to believe in the existence of the Mafia. The other book, *The Godfather,* a novel by Mario Puzo, was based in part on stories that were part of the culture of Puzo's childhood. The son of illiterate Neapolitan immigrants, Puzo had grown up in New York's Hell's Kitchen, in profound isolation from those around him.

For a time enormous public interest was generated by the books, and by motion pictures based on them. Some defectors claim that some real mafiosi were entranced by their fictional counterparts and adopted some of their mannerisms.

Some social critics used the books and films to portray the Mafia as an alien intrusion imposed by criminal immigrants on a nation previously free of any organized crime, a position that ignored America's history of ethnic gangs. Others used the books and films to assert that the Mafia was a myth, a scapegoat for societal ills.

The Mafia-myth theory depended on two essential notions. It assumed that organized crime was a routine American enterprise designed to serve a need. The theory also assumed that crime operated on a principle of "ethnic succession," which holds that once adequately established in the United States, ethnic crime groups yield their position in the underworld to incoming immigrants farther down the social ladder.

Events in the 1970s made the Mafia-as-myth propositions untenable. Beginning early in the decade, a virtual flood of new information on organized crime became available. Many memoirs by mafiosi at various levels, from soldiers to bosses, were published. In addition, several high-level mafiosi flipped (gave evidence in exchange for protection). Moreover, Federal Bureau of Investigation (FBI) bugs and taps convicted mafiosi with their own words.

Given the extent of available information, there was no longer any doubt about the existence of the Mafia. The evidence made it clear that Mafia membership was a way of life, not simply a rung on the ladder of succession to middle-class respectability. Underworld businesses were not operated like other businesses. They were conducted in a context of cheating and violence. New immigrant groups did enter the underworld, but the predicted ethnic succession in which the Italians turned the underworld over to the new groups did not happen. Comfortably assimilated third- and fourth-generation mafiosi commuted from the suburbs to conduct their underworld business. Furthermore, it was clear that the underworld did not simply service needs, but created its own demand. Traditional underworld enterprises, such as gambling created a need to borrow from a loan shark to pay off the debts.

Beginning in the late 1960s, the American Mafia recruited Sicilians to augment their ranks. The new recruits were arrogant and intent on drug dealing. One American mafioso complained, "They hate the American people . . . They don't care who's boss. They got no respect. There's no family." Increased knowledge about the functioning of the Sicilian Mafia indicates that the loyalty of Sicilians in the United States lay not with their American Mafia colleagues but with their crime families in Palermo for whom drugs were and are a major source of income.

Newcomers Attracted by Drug Profits

While American Mafia families worked familiar turf, younger groups of organized criminals established new bases in narcotics trafficking. Many of the new gangsters were immigrants. But two of the new underworld groups, bikers (outlaw motorcycle gangs) and black gangs, were homegrown.

Biker gangs tend to have no fixed ethnic or geographic base. Their prototype, the Hell's Angels, was founded about 1950 in southern California. They served as a model for subsequent groups, such as the Pagans, begun in Prince Georges County, Maryland, the Outlaws, begun in Chicago, and the Bandidos, begun in Houston.

Attracted to violence, the bikers' initial criminal enterprises included tearing up bars, conducting small drug deals and stealing and fencing motorcycles. In time, they specialized in synthetic drugs, such as methamphetamines (speed), PCP and LSD (hallucinogens), which can be manufactured locally, avoiding importation.

The biker gangs emulated the structure of the Mafia and performed such chores for mafiosi as murder, arson, assault and loan-shark collections. Although efforts have been made in the late 1980s and early 1990s to clean up their image, bikers of the 1960s and 1970s, often heavy drug users, ignored traditional mob codes of avoiding confrontations with the legitimate world. Members indulged themselves in beating up or killing police officers and prosecutors.

The other homegrown criminals, black organized gangs, grew out of the social upheavals of the 1960s. Formerly Italian inner-city neighborhoods increasingly became black neighborhoods, where black hoodlums, with experience dealing in drugs or running numbers as low-level Mafia employees, took over. Along with the rest of organized crime, black gangs shifted from a concentration on gambling to a focus on narcotics.

In the early 1970s some observers predicted that black gangs would grow increasingly stable and displace the dominant Italians. By the late 1980s it was clear that the predicted succession was not going to happen. Black gangs tended to be short-lived and volatile. They held only black neighborhoods and never developed a national structure comparable to the Mafia and its Commission.

New immigrant crime groups proved to be more internally cohesive and durable, and more deadly. Before Castro's revolution, with the blessing of the Batista regime, American Mafia members ran lucrative casinos in Havana. Following the failed American Bay of Pigs invasion of Cuba in 1961, some Cuban hoodlums emigrated to the United States, where they resumed their friendships with the American Mafia. By 1985 a South Florida Cuban gang known as the Corporation, headed by Jose Miguel Battle, a former Havana vice cop, had enormous assets and a significant cash flow generated by 2,500 employees working in Miami, New York City and northern New Jersey.

The Colombian cocaine trade in the United States grew out of a partnership between Cuban and Colombian gangsters. In the beginning, Colombians sold cocaine to Cubans for distribution. But an explosion of American consumer demand for cocaine prompted the Colombians to establish their own distribution network. After violent turf battles, they shut out the Cubans and set up their own operations in Miami, New York, Los Angeles and Chicago.

The emergence of new Asian gangs coincided with liberalized immigration quotas between 1970 and 1980, which swelled the number of Chinese in the United States by 85%. Some of the new arrivals became members of Chinese tongs, traditional benevolent societies that historically have had criminal spinoffs and street gangs. Present in most Chinatowns around the country, the new gangs deal in gambling, prostitution, extortion, robbery and drugs, usually within Chinese-populated areas.

The new Chinese gangs often exploit tensions between FOB (fresh off the boat) and ABC (American-born Chinese) groups. When aroused, gang members resort to barrages of gunfire, often striking innocent bystanders. Faced with problems of multiple Chinese dialects and inconsistent transliteration of Chinese names into English, American law enforcement officers have great difficulty in identifying and tracking these new gangsters.

A wave of Vietnamese immigrants after the Vietnam War brought another new crop of gangsters. The Chinese and the Vietnamese had feuded in Asia for centuries, and to the consternation of local U.S. law enforcement officials, the new immigrants transferred their hostilities to the United States.

A former South Vietnamese leader, Nguyen Cao Ky, established in the United States an anti-Communist organization in exile, with generals of the former South Vietnamese army. Ky's group recruited recent Vietnamese immigrants and trained them to rob, kill, sell drugs and prey on Asian businesses and gambling dens. Victims are generally too frightened to cooperate with police. A former member of Ky's group has testified that the organization has a crime sector called the Dark or Black Side, with divisions in several cities, among them San Francisco, Chicago, Houston and Los Angeles.

Another new crime group, the Jamaican posses (named for the groups of vigilantes in Western movies), first appeared in the Jamaican election campaign of 1980 when they murdered hundreds of supporters of both parties. They emigrated to the United States and soon came to the attention of the law because they were dealing in drugs and killing people, particularly in New York and Miami. By 1988 authorities knew of 30 posses around the country with more than 3,000 members, thought to be responsible for as many as 800 murders.

The sheer numbers of outsiders in the underworld created tension and disorganization among the ranks of the Mafia. The newcomers' involvement with drugs made them so volatile that all the old organized crime rules were ignored. Gangsters on cocaine were likely to kill anyone, including police, women and children or bystanders. Their behavior increased the motivation of law enforcement officials to pursue organized crime; old mafiosi complained that their way of life was dead.

Beleaguered perhaps, but the Mafia was hardly dead. Many mafiosi offspring, despite their college educations, have continued to follow in their fathers' footsteps. Underworld life is too tempting. The pleasures of easy money and luxury continues to keep organized crime attractive to mafiosi despite the perils. For some, the perils only add spice to their lives.

The Era of RICO

Key portions of the Organized Crime Control Act of 1970, crafted by Robert Blakey, chief counsel to a Senate subcommittee and a former member of the Justice Department's organized crime section, reflected congressional sensitivity to public awareness of the Mafia as a consequence of *The Godfather* and *The Valachi Papers*. The new law mandated a federal witness protection program, expanded use of immunity for witnesses, increased money and staffing and instituted special Justice Department task forces against organized crime. The most important section of the new law, the Racketeer-Influenced and Corrupt Organizations (RICO)

Act, permitted prosecutors to pursue entire criminal enterprises.

Under RICO, any two of several dozen crimes committed during a ten-year period are sufficient to convict an individual of taking part in an ongoing rackets enterprise, since different crimes by different gangsters can point to the presence of a single underworld organization. Anyone planning or discussing a crime is as guilty as the actual perpetrator. This meant that bosses are no longer protected by having subordinates act on their orders. RICO also allows law enforcement officers to seize stolen loot as property forfeitures.

Federal prosecutors were initially reluctant to take advantage of RICO. Small easy cases lead to an impressive number of indictments and convictions that further a prosecutor's career, while RICO requires slow, complex investigations that might not succeed. More than a decade passed before federal law enforcement agencies shifted their attention toward RICO cases.

In a ruling referred to as the *Turkette* decision, the Supreme Court held in 1981 that RICO could be applied to criminal enterprises. Using RICO, Rudolph Giuliani, head of the Justice Department's criminal division from 1981 to 1983, and then as a highly visible U.S. attorney in New York City, became a prominent gangbuster. Less visible, but equally intent, federal prosecutors around the country mounted the most sustained assault on organized crime in American history.

By 1980 the Mafia had lost much of its influence in politics and labor unions. Nevertheless, gangsters retained their hold over a number of union locals and certain unions. Mafia families still controlled the Teamsters, the largest, strongest and richest American union. The Mafia used the Teamsters' bulging pension funds from 1.7 million dues-paying members to make loans on favored terms to chosen customers. But change was on the way.

A U.S. Justice Department report released on January 31, 1991 described the transformation of the American Mafia as a result of four law enforcement initiatives: RICO prosecutions, extensive electronic surveillance, civil racketeering suits (to sever the Mafia from the unions) and the witness protection program.

Over the course of a decade, after contributing information that led to convictions of Mafia leaders, more than 5,000 people made their way into the witness protection program. Federal prosecutors convicted 20 bosses of Mafia families and a long string of underbosses (seconds in command). In New York City, where the Mafia has been strongest, two of the five families are

thought to be out of business and a third is almost defunct. The other two are weakened but still potent.

Law enforcement loosened the Mafia's hold on labor unions using a model developed in a 1988 civil racketeering case against the Teamsters. Prosecutors convinced a judge that the Mafia had taken over the union. The court appointed an administrator and in time the membership elected a new non-Mafia-connected leader.

Second- and third-generation American Mafia family members facing long prison sentences have proven more willing than earlier generations to break the traditional *omertà* (code of silence). From 1982 to 1992, 16 "made" (sworn in during a secret ceremony) Mafia members agreed to testify for the government, compared with only two from 1963 to 1982.

Perhaps the most satisfying victory for federal prosecutors was the ten-count conviction on April 2, 1992 of John Gotti, reputed head of the Gambino family, the nation's largest and most powerful Mafia family. Among the charges on which Gotti was convicted were six murders, including that of his predecessor as head of the Gambino family.

Gotti had been dubbed the "Teflon Don" after being acquitted in separate trials for assault, racketeering and shooting a union official. After his conviction, he was renamed "Velcro Don," because all the charges stuck.

Even before Gotti's trial was over, an internal struggle began among those who aspired to take his place as boss. Many experts believe that Gotti has tried to retain his power and run the operation from prison, a not uncommon practice.

U.S. federal law enforcement agencies intend to continue their concentration on the Mafia. No one believes that any major Mafia family has been completely eradicated. Powerful families remain in New York City, New Jersey, Philadelphia, Chicago, Boston and south Florida. Nevertheless, Mafia operations in 20 cities, among them Cleveland, Denver, San Francisco, St. Louis and Tampa, have been so severely damaged that the Justice Department feels safe in shifting agents to focus attention on newer organized crime threats, among them Japanese and Chinese crime groups, the rival Los Angeles gangs known as the Crips and the Bloods, outlaw motorcycle gangs and Jamaican posses.

B.   THE SICILIAN MAFIA

The Sicilian Mafia's line of command finally was made clear in 1988. It rises in a pyramid from a base that covers every village in Sicily. At the base line of command are the capifamiglia, the family bosses. Three contiguous families are responsible to a *capo-mandamento,* who represent them on a provincial commission. The provincial commissions answer to the Cupola, the supreme governing body in Palermo. Islandwide decisions are made by an ultra secret Inter-Provinciale.

Two mafiosi made major contributions to understanding the hidden structure of the Mafia. The first, Joe Valachi, an American, was a foot soldier, an illiterate low-grade enforcer and hit man. The first ever to admit to being a member of an organized hierarchical secret criminal society known as the Mafia, Valachi appeared before U.S. Senator John McClellan's Subcommittee on Investigations in October 1963. He described a vertically structured, internationally connected, multibillion-dollar crime syndicate that has flourished in the United States since at least the 1930s.

Valachi explained the Mafia's blood oaths and the rules against disclosure; its lucrative operations in gambling, labor racketeering, usury, extortion and narcotics; and its methodical use of murder. At the time of Valachi's testimony, only seven of nearly 800 mob-initiated murders during and after Prohibition had been solved. Among those he could recall, Valachi had taken part in 33.

During his testimony, Valachi despaired of being understood by his listeners. He said, "What good is it, what I'm telling you? Nobody will listen. Nobody will believe. You know what I mean? This Cosa Nostra, it's like a second government. It's too big." Valachi was correct in his assessment of the impact he was making. No one was arrested after his testimony. Law enforcement officials dismissed him as either a liar or as mentally ill.

Two decades later, another mafioso, Tommaso Buscetta, received a different reception. He was no foot soldier. Thick police dossiers established him as a ranking Mafia leader. Fluent in three languages, Buscetta had traveled everywhere. While Valachi's view was from the bottom up, Buscetta had seen the Mafia from the top down. The two men had come to share a common purpose, however: to destroy the Mafia.

Of the two, Valachi was more open in his testimony. Buscetta left enormous gaps in his revelations designed to protect his vanity and his former inner circle from prosecution. Nevertheless, he revealed enough in court to change worldwide perceptions of the Cosa Nostra. Buscetta was a key figure in the American government's prosecution of the enormous New York "Pizza Connection" drug trial, and in Italy during a week on the witness stand in Palermo at the Mafia's maxitrial, Buscetta testified against 264 Sicilian mafiosi.

In her 1990 book *Octopus: The Long Reach of the International Sicilian Mafia,* Claire Sterling lays out a thesis that the Sicilian Mafia, an organization distinct from the American Mafia, has extended its reach throughout most of the Western world and is mainly responsible for the drugging of the United States. Heroin trafficking has made local chieftains into international economic giants.

About their rise to power, Sterling wrote:

> Starting in 1957, a small band of criminals presumed to be operating within the confines of a small Mediterranean island grew into a multinational heroin cartel operating around the planet. Today, they are brokers for much of the world's cocaine as well. Indeed the Sicilian Mafia is the only organized crime syndicate capable of moving both heroin and cocaine across the oceans and continents in massive quantities.

The scope of the Sicilian Mafia's activities did not become evident to law enforcement authorities anywhere until the early 1980s. By then they had strategic operations in Bangkok, London, Munich, Marseilles, Montreal, Caracas, Sao Paulo and some 25 cities in the United States. Scarcely a country in Europe, Asia, Africa and North and South America had not been penetrated and corrupted.

The rise of the Sicilian Mafia is due in part to support from corrupt Italian financiers. Their continued growth can be attributed to inept coordination between Italian and American police agencies, the naivete of most American investigative agencies and collusion with Italian politicians who court Mafia campaign contributions and the half-million votes Mafia bosses are thought to control.

Until the 1950s, Sicilian Mafia activities were confined mostly to Italy. Change came when American Mafia boss Lucky Luciano was deported to Italy in 1946. He used his considerable talents to organize the first heroin "pipeline" from Italy to other parts of the world. After his death in 1962, his Sicilian heirs modernized the system by creating a vertical industry. They imported opium from Turkey, Lebanon and other countries, refined it in Italy, exported it to the United States and laundered their vast incomes in Europe.

For two decades law enforcement agencies in both Italy and the United States underestimated the power of the Sicilian Mafia. Whenever American investigators stumbled across Sicilians, they assumed they were replacements in the dwindling ranks of the American Mafia. They failed to recognize that the Sicilians represented a separate organization controlled from Palermo. The Sicilians looked down on their American counterparts who controlled only local drug traffic, while they controlled it worldwide.

Italian and American researchers estimate that the Sicilian and American gangs may make as much as $250 billion annually, an amount that would make their income equivalent to the gross national product of the 20th wealthiest nation in the world.

The Pizza Connection

In the mid-1980s American investigators were finally in a position to comprehend the independence of the Sicilians from the American Mafia through their investigation of the so-called pizza connection heroin ring. The result at the time was the most extensive drug case to ever come before an American judge and jury.

Federal Bureau of Investigation (FBI) investigations of the activities of the New York Mafia family of Joseph Bonanno uncovered a Sicilian faction headed by Salvatore Catalano, a Queens, New York banker and businessman. Investigators learned that couriers for Catalano's group routinely transferred enormous amounts of cash through investment houses and banks in New York, Italy and Switzerland. Eventually they understood that Catalano had been sent to New York for the express purpose of managing the heroin business for his Sicilian family.

Court-approved wiretaps uncovered other names, including that of Sicilian-born Pietro Alfana, the owner of a pizzeria in Oregon, Illinois, whose uncle, Gaetano Badalamenti, was suspected of smuggling heroin into the United States from Brazil.

The case broke in April 1984, when Spanish authorities, alerted by the Americans, arrested Alfano, Badalamenti and his son in Madrid. Within a month, U.S. indictments had grown to 38. U.S. officials estimated that over the previous five years, the pizza connection had smuggled 1,650 pounds of heroin into the United States with an estimated street value of $1.65 billion.

The Sicilian Mafia made inventive use of America's love for pizza. From 1963 onward, nearly all Cosa Nostra troops in the United States went into the pizza business. They used their businesses as shelters, washed drug money through them, skimmed the cash taken in, pulled scams on their customers and passed narcotics from one shop to another. Some took over businesses peacefully, others threatened to bomb owners reluctant to sell.

The Mafia-pizza linkage created a monopoly on all the necessary supplies for the pizza industry—ovens, oils, tomato sauce, meat, mushrooms and mozzarella cheese. The Sicilian-born owner of Roma Foods did business with 650 U.S. pizzerias. The U.S. Immigration and Naturalization Service found it curious that nine out of every ten Sicilian aliens they deported had been working in a pizzeria when located.

In the mid-1980s the Sicilian Mafia, in collusion with several American Mafia families, imported as much as five tons of heroin a year through many intersecting rings, employed thousands of people and delivered heroin to every corner of the country. After six years of arduous and often brilliant investigation, the FBI and the Drug Enforcement Administration (DEA) succeeded in exposing only a single faction of an American Mafia family that worked with about 30 men in a single Sicilian heroin ring bringing in only about 330 pounds (150 kilos) of heroin a year. No U.S. agency was equipped or prepared or imaginative enough to investigate the entire system.

Sending the traffickers to prison in the Pizza Connection case did not make much of dent in the problem, but it did mark the first time that recognition was made in a court of law of the existence of an organized international conspiracy, encompassing raw material acquisition, drug refining, transport, marketing and money laundering. Every bit of information that would stand up in court uncovered in the five years of investigation required dogged perseverance. The Sicilians were working in a country unaware of their criminal history; they spoke in code, had multiple passports and faded into America's huge immigrant population.

The FBI was hampered for half a century by its longtime director J. Edgar Hoover's dogged disbelief in the existence of organized crime. The DEA had an enormous data bank, but its agents were not looking for links among drug traffickers.

The value of cooperation between Italian and U.S. law enforcement was demonstrated in 1981 when an FBI snapshot of a stranger talking to two known traffickers was shown to Italian police. They identified him as Giuseppe Bono, a top-level international trafficker whose Milan company laundered millions of drug-traffic dollars.

Investigation of Bono alerted agents to the marriage of one of his associates at New York's St. Patrick's Cathedral in November 1980, where pictures of the 500 guests had been taken. DEA agents carried around pictures of the guests for several years until they matched the photos with names. All turned out to be Sicilian mafiosi.

A significant reason that neither the United States nor Italy could make a dent in the two Mafias was that, despite membership restrictions on both sides, they each used the other's country to dodge arrest warrants and avoid jail.

The Cherry Hill Ring

A law enforcement operation dubbed Iron Tower was assumed by many to mark the end of the Sicilian Mafia in the United States. Shortly before Christmas 1988 American and Italian agents working together broke the Cherry Hill (New Jersey) heroin ring of the American Mafia's Gambino family. In various regions of Italy, 133 traffickers were arrested. Another 75 were arrested in New Jersey, Pennsylvania, California, Illinois, Florida and New York. In reality, this operation hardly caused a ripple in heroin traffic in the United States.

The operation did provide a glimpse of the magnitude of the subterranean enterprise. Moreover, it uncovered the continuing existence of Sicilian Mafia families thought to be extinct.

American law enforcement incorrectly assumed that the huge number of arrests in Italy and the United States resulted in shrinking the Mafia share of the heroin trade to less than the Chinese Triads' 40% share. What they did not know was that the Chinese were turning over their heroin to the Sicilians for distribution.

Even as the FBI was announcing the end of the Sicilian Mafia connection, the Sicilians were entering a phase of enormous expansion by including cocaine in their distribution. Due to saturation, by 1988 the price of cocaine on the American market had dropped by two thirds. At the same time, cocaine was selling for four times as much in Europe, the Sicilian Mafia's exclusive narcotics distribution territory. To increase sales, particularly in Europe, the drug lords of Medellin, Colombia, who control most of the world's production of cocaine, stepped up their trade with the Sicilian Mafia.

A History of Power Competitions

Until the 1980s, almost no one in Italy would inform on the Mafia. Fear and terror held people back, as did pride and strong ethnic loyalty. Even as the Mafia robbed, kidnapped, extorted, murdered, bribed government officials, terrorized judges and juries and rifled the public till, many experts insisted that the organization did not exist. In Sterling's words, ''Men of Honor are bound by oath to swear Cosa Nostra is a fiction, on pain of death. Thus, it is probably the only structured criminal organization extant that has operated without leaving a material trace for over a hundred years.''

Since the Mafia's inception, it has contained old and new generations in every era. Each new set, more violent than the previous one, has challenged the ruling incumbents. At the turn of the century, the Mafia's average murder rate was one a day. By the 1920s it had risen to two a day. In the 1940s with the advent of the submachine gun, it went up to three a day.

Despite its violence, the Sicilian Mafia cultivates a Robin Hood-like image. The Mafia grew out of the needs of the poor for order and representation. Except for collecting taxes, the state had little interest in or concern for them. Landholding barons exploited the poor and the Catholic Church aligned itself with the barons. Although in league with the state, the barons and the church, the Mafia appeared to administer a degree of even-handed justice to the poor. For some peasants justice meant gaining satisfaction from the efforts of their *capo-costra* (head of the clan), while for others it meant a blast from the *lupara,* the sawed-off shotgun. The folk image of the mafiosi was of men brave, manly, contemptuous of the law and even on occasion generous and wise.

The most-feared-ever *capo di tutti capi* (head of all heads of the clans), Luciano Leggio began serving a life sentence for murder in 1974. From his cell in Italy, he plotted the strategy that won the Great Mafia War of 1981–83 between the Sicilian clans. The war spread to Western Europe, Canada, South America and the United States. When the war was over, thousands of Leggio's opponents or potential opponents had been shot, strangled, poisoned, bombed or stabbed to death, and as many as another thousand had disappeared.

Lulled into believing that the Sicilian Mafia was dead or at least dying, killed off by internal warfare, the Italian police were astounded when the Great Mafia War erupted. At stake was the enormous potential of the worldwide heroin market. An average of one corpse a day was produced by the Mafia in Palermo, Sicily's capital. Not all the corpses were members of rival Mafia clans; many were eminent public figures gunned down in daylight or blown up by car bombs. For his efforts, Leggio gained control of the Mafia's global heroin network.

Conservative estimates place the annual turnover in income of the Sicilian and American mafias at about a quarter of a trillion dollars. The main beneficiaries, the "made" mafiosi (those sworn in during a ritual ceremony) are few. There are thought to be fewer than 2,000 in the United States and about 15,000 in Sicily. For every made mafioso, there are about ten "associates" and "earners," plus legions of "protectors" (attorneys, politicians, judges, police and businesspeople).

Venezuelan, British, Turkish and Bulgarian Connections

In the late 1950s, Sicilian Mafia clans in a fever to gain primacy in the heroin trade engaged in the worst shooting war in memory. Following the bombing death of seven officers of the carabinieri (paramilitary police), Italian law enforcement cracked down on the Mafia. A committee of six Mafia "wise men" decreed suspension of all criminal activities that might suggest organized crime. Known mafiosi scattered to new locations around the world. The most able went to Montreal, Caracas, Sao Paulo, Mexico City and New York.

Conditions were ideal in Venezuela, where citizenship is easily acquired and from which Venezuelan citizens cannot be extradited. Officials in Venezuela claim that the Mafia does not exist in their country. Nevertheless, Venezuela's Sicilian Mafia branch, accountable only to Palermo, assures a copious flow of narcotics to the United States and Europe. The organization revolves around the three Cunteras brothers and an assortment of relatives, including several cousins named Caruna. Singly or in pairs, the relatives have been positioned strategically in London, Geneva, Montreal and Miami, where in the process of moving drugs they have become international financiers.

Britain proved to be almost as comfortable for the Cunterases and Carunas as Venezuela. Cargoes in transit from one British commonwealth country to another do not have to clear customs. The Venezuelans supplied the British drug market, laundered money, financed international transactions and used Britain as a free port for transshipments of drugs from Asia's Golden Crescent to North America. Like Venezuela, Britain has also been reluctant to acknowledge the presence of the Mafia.

Shortly after Leggio entered prison, pieces of the pipeline were put together to solidify the Sicilian Mafia's power in the heroin business. The Palermo bosses linked up with the *babas,* the leaders of the Turkish arms-drugs crime ring, who are brokers for morphine base

from all over Southwest Asia's Golden Crescent, the world's largest opium-producing region, which includes Iran, Pakistan and Afghanistan. They also linked up with the Camorra of Naples, an 18th-century secret society resurrected in the 1950s. The Camorra had developed the world's most extensive smuggling routes.

In the wake of the Sicilians' agreement with the *babas* and the Camorra, well-equipped and well-staffed heroin refineries sprouted in Italy virtually overnight. Addiction rates in Europe skyrocketed.

The Communist republic of Bulgaria also had a part to play. Bulgaria is uniquely placed for smuggling between Asia and Europe. The nation shares a long, porous land border with Turkey. Half of the 50,000 trucks that cross Bulgaria's border each year are Transport International Routier (TIR) trucks, which by international agreement can be customs-sealed and travel freely.

Using a state corporation called Kintex (later renamed Globus), the Bulgarians became active in the passage of arms through Europe to the Middle East. For a cut of 15% to 30%, Bulgaria not only permitted drugs to flow through their nation, Kintex also swapped arms for drugs.

Sofia, Bulgaria's capital, became a drug traffickers' haven, a place they could run to when law enforcement was on their heels. While they rested from their labors, Kintex took charge of their cargoes. Within a short time after the agreement between the babas and the Sicilian Mafia went into effect, nearly three quarters of the morphine base arriving in the West was coming through Bulgaria. The drugs were financing a huge illicit traffic in arms. When the military took over in Turkey in 1980, Turkish right- and left-wing terrorists were found to have nearly a million weapons between them.

From the summer of 1977 forward, independent heroin dealers had three choices: to use the Sicilian distribution system, broker their deals through Palermo or go out of business. Thus the Sicilians had a virtual monopoly.

Italy's Maxitrial

The importance of the arms-drug linkage to the Sicilian Mafia was obvious to Italian Judge Carlo Palermo when he stumbled across evidence of the pact in 1980. He was targeted to be killed by a radio-controlled bomb, but the bomb missed him and killed a woman and her children.

The reality of the Mafia emerged from several million pages of courtroom transcript in a series of dramatic trials in Palermo and New York. The most dramatic was the maxitrial of the Mafia in Italy.

Five investigating magistrates in Sicily's anti-Mafia force drafted indictments against the Mafia as a unit. As the date for the maxitrial drew near, these investigators were forced to live under siege, cut off from their families and protected by guards.

The trial got under way in a bunker courtroom built into a wall of Ucciardone prison. Thirty steel cages held 464 defendants, who were defended by 200 attorneys. Fifty additional lawyers represented friends of the court: relatives of the dead, the city of Palermo and the Sicilian region.

To prevent death, natural or otherwise, from interrupting the proceedings, two full sets of judges presided. The indictment ran to 8,687 pages, together with 250,000 pages of documentation, with 400 pages devoted to the defendants' names and the charges against them. The charges covered only the decade 1975 to 1985, when the Sicilian Mafia became an international cartel.

For the first time since the Sicilian Mafia's birth about 1865, Mafia defectors, the *pentiti* (penitents), stripped away the fiction that the Mafia did not exist. Although the *pentiti* risked their lives and made an invaluable contribution, many Italians perceived them as traitors. They were offered no leniency by the courts, no reduced sentences and no government protection for themselves of their families.

Buscetta, transported from the United States to Palermo to testify, confirmed the structure of the Sicilian Mafia and emphasized that the chain of command had to consent to murders, particularly those of important people.

Luciano Leggio was brought from his prison cell to the witness stand, where he reminded the court that no one who had ever accused him was still alive. He concluded his testimony by saying "To all these charges, I have one answer: I was in jail. I'm still in jail. Excuse me, but how could I be running around the country, walk the streets, return to my cell, unless all this was done with permission . . . I don't see any sergeants or prison guards or prison directors in a cage. If such people helped me, why haven't they been charged?''

No one in the prison system has ever been charged. No one in the prison system has ever been foolhardy enough to oppose Leggio.

After nearly two years of hearing the evidence, a verdict handed down in December 1987 supported the

key points of the indictment: the *unicita* or "oneness" of the Mafia; the heroin network built under its direction; responsibility for murders; and the collective guilt of its governing body. All the members of the Cupola were convicted, along with 323 others. No Mafia boss of any consequence was acquitted, except Leggio. No one could prove he ran the Mafia from jail.

Few outside Palermo could imagine the courage of the judges, jurors and the police, who put their lives on the line and whose chances for surviving before, during and after the trial were not good. The achievements of the heroes began to come undone soon after the trial was over.

In the autumn of 1988 the Italian Supreme Court disallowed the concept of *unicita,* the only principle by which the justice system could nail down the Mafia. By the end of 1988 judges, police officers and *pentiti* who had risked their lives were disavowed. Palermo's anti-Mafia force was disbanded and its police team was dispersed. By early 1989 only 60 of the 342 defendants were still in custody. Even Luciano Leggio, thought to be tucked away in prison permanently, expected to be released soon. In May 1989 an appellate court in Rome ruled that the Mafia never existed.

The Mafia appeared to have anesthetized Italy's governing class. As long as they saw the Mafia as a peculiarly Sicilian phenomenon, arrogant political leaders thought they could handle it by ignoring it.

Faint winds of change began to appear in Italy in late 1989. The Mafia became a direct threat to the governing class. Northern Italy's financial centers make the nation the world's fifth richest industrial country. Using its billions in narcotics funds, the Sicilian Mafia moved north to set up banks, invade the stock market, buy legitimate industries and become an enormous supplier of foreign exchange. But even as anti-Mafia forces gathered, the Mafia pitted them against each other by sending anonymous letters to individuals and by planting rumors in the media.

Nevertheless, in the spring of 1989, Italy's Guardia di Finanza issued a red alert (a warning of imminent danger) concerning the implications of the continuing presence of the Mafia in Italy once the European Common Market eliminated barriers such as customs, passport controls and police roadblocks within the member nations in 1992.

Arrogant as ever, the Mafia of Calabria in the spring of 1990 sent death threats to a Catholic bishop who dared to speak out against Calabria's organized crime.

C. THE COLOMBIAN MEDELLIN CARTEL

Colombian drug traffickers are a study in power and control through unabashed, unremitting violence. After eliminating competition through murder, four men from the city of Medellin gained mastery of Colombia's cocaine traffic. In time, the four came to be known as the Medellin Cartel, or Colombia's druglords. The four were: Pablo Escobar Gavira, known as El Padrino (the Godfather); Jorge Luis Ochoa Vasquez, known as El Gordo (the Fat Man); Carlos Lehder Rivas, known as Joe Lehder; and Jose Gonzalo Rodriguez Gacha, known as the Mexican. By the middle of the 1980s, they controlled more than 50% of the cocaine coming into the United States, as much as 50 metric tons (110,231 pounds), worth an estimated $2 billion, per year.

In their book, *Kings of Cocaine: Inside the Medellin Cartel—An Astonishing True Story of Murder, Money, and International Corruption* (1989), Guy Gugliotta and Jeff Leen document two decades in the bloody struggle for supremacy over production and distribution of cocaine. The authors characterized the four kingpins as "utterly single-minded, and willing to do absolutely anything to get what they wanted."

Collectively, the four druglords employed hundreds, possibly thousands, including campesinos (peasant farmers) to grow and process coca crops, airplane pilots to transport the drug, distributors to market the drug in the United States, attorneys to handle legal problems, bagmen (money handlers) to offer bribes and launder money and hired assassins to eliminate competition and enemies. They kept each of their organizations separate but came together to cooperate on large deals and to make policy.

The hometown claimed by the four Colombia drug traffickers, Medellin, earned a reputation in the 19th century as a smuggling center by virtue of its *paisa* peddlers who sold notions to rural households. Present-day men and women of Medellin call themselves *paisas,* in honor of the tough, resourceful, adventurous people of Antiochia (an area of northwestern Colombia), who in the 19th century were considered crude by other Colombians.

By the middle of the 20th century, the nature of the goods smuggled and the methods of transport had changed, but the inclination to smuggle had not. Respectable people made a living smuggling liquor and cigarettes by ship from the United States and airlifting television sets, stereos and radios from the duty-free ports of the Panama Canal Zone. Colombia's cocaine industry flourished and took root in Medellin.

Before 1973 the criminal cocaine trade was a cottage industry in Chile, controlled by a few refiners, who bought coca leaf and paste from Bolivia and Peru and transported it to Chilean laboratories. Once processed into cocaine, the drug was sent north to the United States, often using Colombian smugglers. Demand was limited to the rich and sophisticated. Though lucrative, the market remained small.

When Chilean army General Augusto Pinochet Ugarte overthrew the constitutionally elected government in September 1973, his police jailed or deported dozens of drug traffickers. The Chileans transported their technology north to Colombia and resumed business, but not for long. Within two years the Colombians had squeezed virtually all foreigners out of the cocaine business.

A few years later the Colombians brought their philosophy of not sharing to Miami. A clue that a major change in U.S. cocaine traffic had taken place came in July 1979 in a suburban Miami shopping center called Dadeland Mall. Two men, who arrived in a white truck, followed a Colombian who was a top cocaine dealer in Miami into a liquor store. One man opened fire with a silenced .380 Beretta automatic handgun. The second man joined him with an Ingram MAC-10 machine pistol. To cover their getaway, the men sprayed the mall parking lot with their weapons.

By 1979 Miami had become a boom town, its banks filled with laundered cash. The *Miami Herald* reported a series of bizarre drug executions, and Colombians referred to the Dade County morgue as The Dead County Morgue. Less than three months before the Dadeland Mall murders, there had been a daylight shootout on the Florida Turnpike, involving a ten-mile pursuit of a black Audi 5000 by a white Pontiac Grand Prix. Police found the body of a Colombian in the trunk of the abandoned Audi.

Colombians had been turning up dead in Miami and Dade County for months. The Dadeland murders and the turnpike shootout signaled the onset of an unexpectedly savage cocaine war. The Colombians transformed Miami and Metropolitan Dade County into a war zone.

The reason was soaring cocaine profits. For years the Colombians had purchased coca leaf in Bolivia and Peru, processed it in Colombia and shipped it north to the Cubans in Miami for distribution. Demand surged in the late 1970s, sparking a rapid rise in cocaine prices.

In one year the price in Miami rose from $34,000 to $51,000 per kilogram (2.2 pounds), the standard measure of cocaine. The Colombians eliminated Miami's Cuban intermediaries and took over distribution.

Longtime Colombian traffickers came south in force from a traditional stronghold in New York City's Jackson Heights, Queens. They were joined by an estimated 20,000 illegal aliens who poured in from Colombia. Within three years, four or five Colombian groups controlled Miami's cocaine trade.

A New Breed of Trafficker

The Columbian druglords of the mid-1970s were older men who simply added drugs to the other items in their portfolios of smuggled goods. They were supplanted in the 1980s by younger traffickers who focused on cocaine and who forced them out by reducing their power or by murdering them.

Of the four who would become kings, one of the first to move into cocaine trafficking was Pablo Escobar. After being picked up in 1976 by the DAS (the Colombian equivalent of the Federal Bureau of Investigation [FBI]) for transporting cocaine through downtown Medellin in the spare tire of a pickup truck, Escobar's prosecution dragged on for years. His case was handled by nine separate judges, one of whom reported being threatened. The matter ended when the case documents disappeared. Death threats against the arresting officer were carried out five years after the arrest, when the officer was gunned down.

One of the last of the four cartel linchpins to enter the cocaine trade was Jorge Luis Ochoa Vasquez. The Ochoa brothers were introduced to trafficking by their uncle Fabio Restrepo Ochoa, an old-time *paisa* smuggler. Although all three brothers became heavily involved in the cocaine business, Jorge dominated the Ochoa clan. In 1978 it was rumored that Jorge ordered the murder of his uncle in order to install himself as the undisputed head of the organization.

By the mid-1970s Escobar, Ochoa and other young Medellin traffickers had become the leaders of Colombia's escalating cocaine trade. However, the growth of the business remained limited because cocaine was being transported to the United States a few kilos at a time hidden in luggage or on the bodies of the smugglers. What the leaders needed was a dependable method of shipping large quantities and a reliable distribution method. Of equal importance, they required someone who understood how everyday life worked in the United States, someone who could manipulate Americans.

The person who met the traffickers' need to transform cocaine transportation and distribution was Carlos Enrique Lehder Rivas. Because he had lived in the United States, Lehder understood the country better than the other traffickers. Lehder's parents had divorced when he was four, and he moved with his mother to the United States when he was 15. While there, Lehder fantasized a revolution in which he would gain power and one day rule Colombia. He greatly admired Adolf Hitler and Che Guevara, idol of the revolutionary left.

Lehder had a knack for attracting others to do his bidding. One of those Lehder used was an American named George Jung, whom Lehder met while serving time in the Federal Correctional Institution at Danbury, Connecticut. Jung had been involved in moving thousands of pounds of marijuana by airplane. After he was caught, he jumped bond and returned home, where he began selling marijuana out of his parents' house. His mother turned him in and he was sent to Danbury.

To while away the time in prison, Lehder and Jung dreamed of smuggling cocaine. They were the first to recognize that methods developed for smuggling marijuana could be adapted to cocaine. They foresaw that they could make millions by providing air transport service for cocaine producers, who could be encouraged to pool small loads into big ones.

After they were released from prison, Lehder and Jung began by smuggling shipments of cocaine to gain a stake, with Jung and some of his friends acting as carriers. On one trip Jung turned over 50 kilos (110 pounds) of cocaine to a hairdresser, an old marijuana contact, in Manhattan Beach, California. Within two weeks the hairdresser had sold all 50 kilos and given Jung $2.2 million. This sale was the turning point for Lehder.

In time, Lehder and Jung went shopping for planes and for an island to set up a sanctuary for drug smugglers. Within a month of launching their air transport, Jung suspected Lehder of cutting him out. Although the accusation was true, Lehder denied it and turned his attention to construction on Norman's Cay in the Bahamas, chosen for its small number of residents.

During a stay in prison in Medellin for smuggling Chevrolet station wagons into Colombia, Lehder had met another American marijuana smuggler, Steve Yakovac. After Yakovac was released from prison, he began flying shotgun on Lehder's monthly cocaine runs from Norman's Cay. In seven trips, Yakovac helped to smuggle into the United States 1,358 kilos (2,987.6

pounds) of cocaine. From each trip, he brought back $1.3 million to Lehder.

Like Jung before him, Yakovac was eventually forced out of Lehder's organization, as was later a Norman's Cay neighbor, Ed Ward, a marijuana smuggler who for a time participated in Lehder's operation. In January 1981 Ward was arrested by a Drug Enforcement Agency (DEA) agent who had pursued him for three years. As part of a plea-bargain agreement, Ward testified about Lehder before a grand jury.

Before Lehder forced Yakovac out of his organization, the American had had an opportunity to meet other members of the cartel. The largest load of cocaine ever handled on the island, 314 kilos (690.8 pounds), was flown into Norman's Cay on August 16, 1978, accompanied by its owner, Jorge Ochoa. On other occasions Ochoa's occasional smuggling partner, Pablo Escobar, also visited the island.

On a day when both Ochoa and Escobar were on the island at the same time, Yakovac escorted the two men and their wives to a Bahamian bank to open accounts. With Yakovac translating, the Colombians asked that the banks serve as a channel to their accounts in Panama. The arrangement called for Lehder to deposit cash in the Bahamas and the banks to send it by wire to Panama. In effect, the Bahamian banks agreed to launder the money.

Remarking on the Bahamian involvement, Gugliotta and Leen said, "A lot of Lehder's money ended up in the pockets of Bahamian officials. The Bahamas in 1979 was a nation for sale, and Carlos Lehder wasn't the only one buying. More than a dozen marijuana and cocaine entrepreneurs independent of Lehder had set up pipelines of their own on seventeen Bahamian islands."

The transport of large shipments to Lehder's island and the establishment of a money-laundering arrangement symbolized the closeness of the working arrangement among Ochoa, Escobar and Lehder. This relationship formed the nucleus of the coalition that ruled the cocaine trade during its period of great expansion.

Miami Under Siege

While Lehder was working out the details of his growing distribution system, conditions in Miami continued to worsen. The Mariel boatlift of 1980 added 125,000 Cuban refugees to South Florida's population. To the ordinary citizens who wanted to leave, Fidel Castro had added thousands of criminals from Cuba's prisons. This population, in conjunction with Miami's

trigger-happy cocaine dealers, helped raise the city's murder total from 349 in 1979 to 621 in 1981.

Money laundering in Miami reached such heights that the Federal Reserve Bank of Miami in 1979 reported a $5.5 billion cash surplus in 1979, an amount greater than the combined surpluses of all other Federal Reserve Bank branches in the country.

President Reagan in January 1982 announced the formation of a cabinet-level task force to coordinate a federal offensive against drugs in South Florida. More than 200 federal law enforcement people headed south. The Bureau of Alcohol, Tobacco and Firearms cracked down on automatic weapons. Internal Revenue Service agents focused on money laundering. Army helicopters chased drug planes. Navy radar surveillance planes searched for smuggling flights. Navy ships boarded boats suspected of carrying illegal drugs.

Unfortunately, the organization with the best chance of making a difference in the drug war, the U.S. Attorney's Office, continued to face severe obstacles. Woefully understaffed, with a high employee turnover, the office had no one with the time to follow evidence trails up the pyramid of the cocaine business. The powerful Racketeer Influenced Corrupt Organizations Act (RICO), which made it possible to seize a criminal organization's assets and which had been employed successfully in the fight against the Mafia, was seldom used. No one had yet tried to put the overall cocaine picture together.

A glimpse of the size of the problem came during a routine cargo inspection of a Transportes Aereos Mercantiles Panamericanos (TAMPA) flight on March 9, 1982 by Customs agents at Miami International Airport. The inspectors had constantly heard that cocaine was coming in on TAMPA. But they had heard the same rumor about every other airline flying between Miami and Colombia.

The inspectors noticed a sharp medicinal smell in the air and found a number of haphazardly labeled and unnumbered bound boxes. Most boxes had yellow plastic banding, but some had white. One of the inspectors pushed a screwdriver into a white-banded box labeled "JEANS." When he pulled out the screwdriver, white powder poured out. On seeing the powder, one inspector had a vision of being killed by drug traffickers right on the spot.

The TAMPA cargo seizure amounted to 3,906 pounds of pure cocaine, with a wholesale value of $100 million, an amount four times larger than any previous cocaine confiscation. The size of the seizure indicated a level of cooperation among traffickers vastly beyond what U.S. law enforcement officials had previously thought possible. The haul represented the cargos of 15 separate trafficking organizations, including those of Jorge Ochoa and Pablo Escobar.

The ever-increasing amounts of cocaine coming into the United States reflected improvements in the cartel's operations. In 1980 Ochoa brought an American engineer to Colombia to establish a long-range navigational and communications system at Acandi in northwest Colombia, a few miles from Panama. The new system permitted the Ochoas to route and track all of their flights in the United States. The family kept four or five strictly compartmentalized groups of pilots operating at the same time, each with its own routes and distributors.

Despite the tracking system, by 1981 the Ochoas had so much cocaine backlogged that they needed to find more and better ways to move it to the United States. The Ochoa family and Escobar's group, Los Pablos, proposed bringing greater control into the business by sharing loads and dividing up jobs. A summit meeting at the Ochoa ranch brought together brokers, including one of Escobar's lieutenants, and some of the Ochoas' stateside distributors. Jorge Ochoa outlined plans for expansion.

Jorge Ochoa became the boss of cocaine transportation. In the months following the summit, results were apparent in an enormously increased volume of cocaine transported to the United States.

Having restructured the drug scene in Miami and the Bahamas, the cartel druglords turned their attention to Colombia. In their usual style, restructuring in Colombia was marked by kidnappings, torture and murder. Most of the furor centered in Medellin. The police were helpless to stop it. By 1982 the city was in the hands of the young cocaine traffickers. If police or politicians did not take bribes to remain silent, they were killed. Old-time smugglers were pushed into retirement or were murdered.

Violence: A Colombian National Norm

Gugliotta and Leen believe the four tough, smart, deadly drug criminals, Escobar, Ochoa, Lehder and Gacha, were able to survive in Colombia because their behavior did not disturb the national conscience. Violence has been a hallmark of Colombian public life. During an era known as La Violencia, from 1948 through 1950, rival militias from the country's two traditional political parties killed an estimated 300,000 people before a truce was struck that permitted the parties to share power in an arrangement called the National Front.

Many Colombians view the National Front compromise as an old-boy network. Therefore, political outsiders of the left and the right, including six guerrilla groups, frequently have resorted to violence to solve their differences.

Secure as a wealthy druglord, Escobar and his Los Pablos bought property all over Medellin as well as elsewhere in Colombia and in Miami. Conspicuous consumption took over the city and development spilled into the surrounding hills.

Lehder elected to spend his money to transform the Colombian city of his birth, Armenia. In the face of so much obvious wealth, and with customs that made kidnapping among traffickers commonplace, it eventually occurred to someone in November 1981 to kidnap Lehder. However, he managed to escape.

During Lehder's recuperation in the hospital, publicists were bent on turning him into a hero. At the same time, his pistoleros were out looking for his abductors. The kidnappers turned out to be an urban guerrilla group with about 2,500 members called M-19 (the April 19 Movement).

A month after the kidnappings, in December 1981, a small plane flying over a major soccer match dropped a load of leaflets. The leaflets, dated December 3, 1981, bluntly stated that 223 top-level "businessmen" had met in a general assembly and had decided that they would no longer tolerate ransom kidnappings by guerrilla groups seeking to finance their revolutions.

The signatories of the leaflet's message were Colombia's 223 top drug traffickers. The new organization's name was Muerte a Secuestradores (MAS), "Death to Kidnappers." Its stated objective was the public and immediate execution of all those involved in kidnappings, beginning from the date of the message. The statement offered 20 million pesos ($330,000) for information leading to the capture of a kidnapper and promised that the kidnappers would be hanged from a tree, shot and marked with the MAS's sign. Kidnappers in jail could expect to be murdered; if that was impossible, retribution would fall on friends in jail and on close family members.

MAS signaled another crossroad for the cocaine lords. Although they had cooperated in business and socialized together, they had never taken a joint public position together. By mid-January deeds ascribed to MAS had been blown to enormous proportions.

Carlos Lehder boasted that he was a member of MAS and that he had contributed generously to the Liberal Party and its presidential candidate. This indiscretion publicly linked him and his cartel colleagues to both the vigilante murders and the Colombian political establishment.

Pablo Escobar viewed Lehder with distaste because of his use of cocaine and his tendency to say stupid things. Yet in his own way, Escobar's behavior brought even more limelight to the cartel. In 1982 Escobar won election to the Colombian Congress as an alternate representative for Jairo Ortega, from the community of Envigado. The election meant that when Jairo Ortega was sick or absent, Escobar would substitute for him. Thus the wealthiest drug trafficker in Colombia had become a congressman. The position provided him with immunity from prosecution.

Escobar took up good works. He even had a radio program called "Civics on the March" and a social works program called "Medellin Without Slums." For about two years a bevy of journalists and public relations experts managed to portray him as a humble man of the people intent on returning good back to the poor but proud neighborhoods from whence he had sprung. But the police were not taken in. They knew him as a killer, an enforcer who never forgot an insult, held grudges and took revenge.

Law Enforcement Attempts to Control the Cartel

In mid-1981, the year that Jorge Ochoa took over cocaine transportation, John Phelps arrived in Bogota to take over as U.S. DEA special agent-in-charge for all of Colombia. Phelps instructed his staff to devote its full time to cocaine intelligence. Phelps was convinced that cocaine was more of a threat to the United States than marijuana. By the end of his first year in Colombia, Phelps had a list of the top ten traffickers, among them Escobar and Ochoa.

Phelps' resident agent in Medellin, Errol Chavez, categorized the Medellin traffickers as falling into two groups, "brokers" and "others." The brokers constituted perhaps a dozen crime families, including those led by Ochoa and Escobar. The brokers were capable of putting together a large load of cocaine, financing it, and arranging for transportation and insurance.

The brokers' method of organization involved a meeting in a Medellin hotel or restaurant at which "others" were invited to piggyback on brokers' loads, in amounts anywhere from one to 100 kilos. Each trafficker packed

his or her cocaine and coded it with a personal combination of symbols and colors.

Agent Chavez's analysis came at a high price. During his two-year tour in Medellin, six drug ring informants that he had cultivated were murdered. As a warning to Chavez, a human tongue was left in the backyard of his home.

In 1982, at the same time that Escobar became a congressman, Belisario Betancur won election as president of Colombia. Betancur's first priority was to make peace with Colombia's myriad guerrilla groups and to launch a program of economic and social reforms. Drug traffickers were of little interest to him.

Betancur's election was good news for the cartel because he had pronounced himself to be philosophically opposed to extradition of Colombian nationals to the United States. By 1982 extradition led the agenda of drug traffickers' concerns. Lehder topped the list of extraditable drug fugitives.

Gugliotta and Leen explained why the traffickers were so opposed to extradition:

> Extradition . . . took traffickers out of the familiar, malleable Colombian ambience . . . The whole legal system in the United States was different and, most Colombians thought, merciless. Put a Colombian in a gringo court on drug charges, and he would be sent away forever. In Colombia nobody wanted to try drug cases; in the United States it seemed as though the courts were competing for the opportunity . . . from the time the bilateral extradition treaty took hold in 1982, the cartel had lobbied furiously to have it either ignored, declared unconstitutional, or abrogated, preferably all three.

Betancur's opposition to extradition was related to his views on national sovereignty and did not reflect his views on drug trafficking. In December 1982 his new attorney general, Carlos Jimenez Gomez, appointed National Police Colonel Jaime Ramirez Gomez to take over an anti-narcotics unit. Ramirez had a passion for information-gathering. He "collected" people and learned what they knew, and his knowledge of crime was encyclopedic.

Ramirez got along well with the U.S. Embassy and the DEA and welcomed their help. His unit tripled in size. When bribes did not interest Ramirez, the cartel began to threaten him, making as many as ten threats a week. Despite the threats, Ramirez had trouble considering the traffickers as anything other than neighborhood punks.

Two important events took place in the spring of 1983. One was a drop in cocaine prices to below $5,000 per kilo, an indicator that the quantity being produced had taken a quantum leap. By lowering the price, the Medellin cartel opened up a new mass market for their produce. The other event was the appointment of Lewis Tambs to be U.S. ambassador to Colombia. An avid anti-Communist, Tambs was instructed to work on the drug problem in Colombia.

Although Ambassador Tambs and Betancur were on opposite sides of the fence politically, they liked each other. Betancur ignored Tambs' promotion of the idea that drug traffickers and guerrillas were allied in a joint venture to tear down Colombia.

By mid-1983 Tambs had allied himself with DEA's Phelps and Colombia's National Police Colonel Ramirez to do battle against the Medellin cartel. What the allies needed was a political spokesperson to put narcotics on Colombia's national agenda. Since Betancur would not, they needed someone else who was prominent.

The key political issue at the time was "hot money," contributions to Colombian politicians from drug traffickers. Two principal targets were Envigado congressmen Jairo Ortega and his cartel alternate, Pablo Escobar. Accusations about hot money were made principally by New Liberals, the reformist wing of the Liberal Party.

As part of the New Front sharing of powers, Colombian presidents are obliged to allocate a certain number of cabinet posts to the opposition. When Betancur assigned the justice ministry to the New Liberals in August 1983 and appointed Senator Rodrigo Lara Bonilla to the post, he presumably did so in the knowledge of Lara Bonilla's opposition to hot money. However, he never openly supported his appointee.

When Phelps and Tambs visited Lara Bonilla after his appointment, Lara Bonilla confirmed that he did not feel that he had the president's backing. Nevertheless, he did not intend to turn away from the drug problem.

Two weeks after Lara Bonilla's appointment, on the floor of Congress, Jairo Ortega accused him of having accepted a million-peso campaign contribution from a contributor who had served time in a Peruvian jail for drug trafficking. Ortega waved a photocopy of the check in the air. Lara Bonilla flung the accusation back at his accusers, and went on to raise questions about Pablo Escobar and the Death to Kidnappers movement. With one speech, he had foregone any chance of getting along with the Medellin cartel.

By 1983 the druglords were feeling vulnerable. Escobar's carefully crafted public image began to crumble. A Bogota paper published a front-page story on his 1976 drug bust. Minister of Justice Lara Bonilla opened an investigation of several private transport and charter firms believed to be controlled by drug traffickers. Colombia's Civil Aeronautics Board canceled flying permits for 57 small aircraft. On the same day an investigative judge outside Medellin formally reopened the 1976 case against Escobar and 12 days later ordered him arrested.

Betancur's refusal to sign papers to permit the extradition to the United States of Lehder and two marijuana traffickers limited Lara Bonilla's ability to make inroads into drug trafficking. Nevertheless, he pushed on. In mid-October 1983 the Colombian Congress agreed to consider the possibility of revoking Escobar's immunity. In late October Lara announced that six of the nine teams in Colombia's professional soccer league were partially owned or controlled by drug traffickers. In November Colombia's National Institute of Renewable Resources fined Escobar for bringing 85 zoo animals into the country illegally in 1981. In January 1984 Escobar announced his withdrawal from public life.

Tracking the Production Process

Public embarrassments, however, did not curtail the cartel's activities. In February 1984 the cartel met in summit to discuss market expansion. More and better transportation had become a necessity because they had amassed more cocaine than ever. A vast complex of laboratories had come on line in September 1983 and was producing almost 4,000 kilos (8,818 pounds) a month. Ochoa planned a set of integrated factories capable of producing more than half of the 70 tons (140,000 pounds) of cocaine that entered the United States each year.

Making cocaine is a complicated, multistep process that requires tons of chemicals, most importantly acetone and ether. Processing a kilo of cocaine requires 17 liters of ether. In the early 1980s the entire U.S. annual production of ether amounted to only 60 million pounds from five producers, and there were only seven foreign producers worldwide.

Phelps realized that Colombian cocaine traffickers had to import chemicals, including ether. He launched his agents on a year-long effort to track chemicals using informants, court-ordered wiretaps and undercover visits to Colombian chemical firms. Agents examined records of imports from January 1, 1978 to June 30, 1981. During that period, the importers had brought in a total of 4,000 metric tons (8,818,480 pounds) of ether, enough to produce 300 tons (600,000 pounds) of cocaine. The agents' final report said, "While acetone has fairly wide industrial application in Colombia, ether does not, with perhaps as much as 98 percent of the latter destined for illicit users."

The study determined that the largest supplier of ether to the narcotics industry was J. T. Baker Chemical Supply Company of Phillipsburg, New Jersey, and concluded that the DEA could damage the cocaine industry by interfering with the supply of ether.

Phelps presented his findings in mid-1982 to Colombian Attorney General Carlos Jimenez Gomez, who immediately restricted ether and acetone imports. In response to the survey results, J. T. Baker Chemical Supply Company changed its export practices.

On November 22, 1983 Frank Torres walked into J. T. Baker with a request to buy 1,300 55-gallon drums of high-grade ethyl ether for cash, approximately $400,000. He asked to have the drums unlabeled and offered to take delivery anywhere in the United States. The salesman stalled Torres, telling him he could not fill the order immediately. After Torres left, the salesman called the DEA.

A week later Torres received a call from DEA agent Mel Schabilion, who claimed to work for North Central Industrial Chemicals (NCIC) in Chicago. The NCIC was a DEA sting operation. Schabilion said that he had heard about the delays and offered to help. A week and a half later, hidden cameras filmed Torres making a $15,000 down payment on an ether delivery.

At Torres' instruction, the NCIC sent 76 drums of ether to the Port of New Orleans. Two were equipped with radio transponders. On March 4, 1984 the transponders' coordinates were tracked to a ranch owned by the Ochoa family. By March 6, 1984 the beeper signals had moved to Colombia's eastern llanos, a vast area of savannah and tropical forest.

Production Strike Force

When the ether did not move by March 7, Phelps informed Jaime Ramirez. On March 10 a crew of 42 men that included antinarcotics veterans, a Colombian SWAT team (called GOES) and one DEA agent took off in two helicopters and an airplane on a search mission. The mission required rapid action because once the aircraft appeared in the air over rural Colombia, people on the ground, traffickers and/or informants, would know that a military maneuver was in progress and take defensive measures. Finding the first airstrip

was not easy. By the time one was finally spotted, the aircraft were almost out of fuel.

A processing operation adjacent to the airstrip, an area called Tranquilandia, contained a major fully integrated laboratory that employed, fed and housed 100 people. The aircraft, once refueled, returned to the air to fly reconnaissance and soon found other airstrips.

The aircraft was not large enough to allow seizures of material. Therefore, over the course of a little more than two weeks, the officers set fire to 14 labs and encampments, seven airplanes, 11,800 drums of chemicals and 13.8 metric tons (30,424 pounds) of cocaine.

By now law enforcement officials recognized that the cartel no longer depended on the output of tiny backyard labs. A major revelation of the operation was that Bogota cocaine boss Jose Gonzalo Rodriguez Gacha, who had been regarded as a second-level trafficker, had a huge financial stake in the jungle operation. Law enforcement officers began to think of him as a partner in the Medellin cartel.

In the wake of the Tranquilandia operation, the wholesale price of cocaine in Miami rose for the first time in three years. The cartel had been hurt.

Exacting Revenge

Besides possible retaliation for the destruction of their means of production, law enforcement officials feared what the cartel might do to Justice Minister Rodrigo Lara Bonilla. From the time the cartel had tried to smear him with the hot money accusation, Lara Bonilla had gone after them with extreme vigor. Due to his efforts, 300 small airplanes, most belonging to the Ochoa family, had had their licenses revoked. Ochoa's Hacienda Veracruz remained under investigation, as a consequence of transmissions from the ether drum transponders during a stopover there. Moreover, with information supplied by Ramirez and the antinarcotics police, Lara Bonilla had publicly denounced 30 politicians for taking hot money and had attacked the cartel's involvement in professional soccer.

Lara Bonilla and his family lived under constant threat. Despite the risks he and his family faced, an extradition order for Lehder signed by Lara Bonilla lay unsigned on President Betancur's desk. Los Quesitos, one of several Medellin murder gangs closely identified with the cartel, picked up a contract put out on Lara Bonilla.

On the morning of April 30, 1984, Ambassador Tambs received a phone call from a pleased Lara Bonilla. The threats against him and his family had been getting progressively worse. The Foreign Ministry had decided to send him and his family out of the country to Czechoslovakia, where he would serve as ambassador. On the evening of the same day, a Yamaha motorcycle swooped down on the limousine carrying Lara Bonilla and emptied the magazine of a MAC-10 into the minister of justice.

Within hours of Lara Bonilla's assassination, Betancur's cabinet agreed to implement extradition. Six days later the extradition order for Carlos Lehder was signed.

The Cartel's Fluctuating Fortunes

In the wake of the crackdown in Colombia following Lara Bonilla's death, the cartel built a large lab in the Darien jungle of southern Panama, 50 miles from the Colombian border. For a price, General Manuel Noriega, a friend of Fidel Castro and for a long time on the payroll of the Central Intelligence Agency (CIA), took the cartel under his wing. The cost of sanctuary for Escobar alone came to $1 million annually, payable to the general.

Uncomfortable away from home, cartel members sought ways to return to Colombia. They enlisted the help of former Colombian president Alfonso Lopez Michelsen, who was in Panama then as an outside observer of Panama's election. The cartel asked the former president to carry back to President Betancur a message of conciliation and a promise by the cartel to become involved in legitimate business.

Another effort to get at the cartel began a month after the destruction of Tranquilandia when a pilot named Adler Berriman (Barry) Seal was introduced to the cartel. Bored by legitimate flying, Seal had become an "all-purpose smuggler." Faced with 61 years in prison in the United States in two separate court cases, Seal signed an agreement on March 28, 1984 to plead guilty to remaining charges against him with a proviso that sentencing would be withheld to see what he could accomplish on behalf of the government as an undercover informant.

Although he had never met the cartel leaders, Seal had already flown for an Ochoa distributor in Miami, beginning in 1981. At the same time the cartel was asking for forgiveness from the Colombian government, it continued to operate the Panama lab, set up other labs in Nicaragua and arranged for Barry Seal to transport a 1,500-kilo (33,069-pound) shipment of cocaine.

A second meeting to negotiate the cartel's return to Colombia was set up with Attorney General Carlos Jimenez Gomez. The cartel gave Jimenez a six-page letter addressed to Betancur declaring their "frank and honest position on narcotics trafficking."

The letter outlined a deal the cartel was offering. They promised to bring home their money, stay out of politics, turn over to the government their laboratories and clandestine airstrips, aid in developing substitute crops to replace marijuana and cocaine and collaborate in campaigns aimed at the eradication of domestic consumption of drugs and the rehabilitation of addicts.

In return for their concessions, the cartel asked Betancur to end the state of siege, reframe extradition procedures and refrain from applying the extradition treaty for offenses committed before the date of the letter. Betancur ignored the messages and appointed another drug opponent to succeed Lara Bonilla, to whom he gave support. By the end of the summer, the United States had initiated extradition proceedings on more than 60 Colombians, and Colombian authorities had jailed 13.

Over the course of several risky weeks, Seal obtained films of Nicaraguan government involvement in drug trafficking. The mission was nearing completion when Ron Caffrey, chief of the DEA's cocaine desk in Washington, briefed National Security Council aide Oliver North and CIA official Dewey Clarridge about Seal's flights into Nicaragua. North asked if the story could be leaked to the press. Caffrey stated that a leak would ruin the mission and end Seal's usefulness to the DEA.

Nevertheless, when Seal returned from Nicaragua on July 8, 1984, he learned that the *Washington Times* was about to break the story of his infiltration. The case had to be wrapped up quickly. Law enforcement officials were able to take into custody dealers in the United States, but Escobar, Ochoa, Lehder and Rodriguez Gacha all escaped arrest.

The cartel's fortunes continued to go wrong in Panama. On October 19, 1984 a Bogota Superior Court judge indicted Escobar for the murder of Rodrigo Lara Bonilla and named the Ochoas and Rodriguez Gacha as material witnesses. The case against Escobar rested primarily on the testimony of Jaime Ramirez.

Ramirez felt somewhat guilty about not forewarning Lara Bonilla about the risks involved in making the cartel's secrets public. Frustrated at not being able to lay hands on the cartel members, he made Lehder a special project. Of the whole group, Lehder was the only one whose extradition had been signed, whose appeals had been exhausted and who could be put right on a plane and sent to the United States immediately upon capture. By the end of 1984 Ramirez tracked Lehder to a small house three blocks from the Panama Canal. Informants said that Lehder had been in Medellin the week before.

Although 1984 appeared to be filled with successes against the Medellin cartel, those on the front lines did not notice much difference. Security at the U.S. embassy had deteriorated throughout Tambs' tenure until, by October 1984, Tambs felt the embassy was under siege. The State Department told Tambs to reduce the U.S. delegation to a bare minimum. Johnny Phelps spent his final months before his midyear departure carrying a Swedish machine pistol as he traveled to work in an armored van. Gun battles took place every night in his neighborhood.

By August 1984 Escobar and Rodriguez Gacha were back in Medellin. The cartel's presence was felt everywhere. An attempt was made to bribe and threaten the judge who had indicted the cartel in the Lara Bonilla assassination into dismissing the indictment. As the year wore on, it became clear that the crackdown had not succeeded. The flow of cocaine had continued uninterrupted to the United States, and the traffickers had not been intimidated, extradited or arrested in meaningful numbers. Weary of the tension, Colombian public opinion wavered between outrage and resignation, between crackdown and appeasement. The public's wild mood swings have occurred over the years with increasing frequency and more intensity.

In November 1984 information that a kidnapping contract had been put out on the Medellin DEA resident agent, corroborated by Colombian DAS agents, prompted the closing of the Medellin DEA office. Information that one of Tambs' security guards had been bribed to kill him led the State Department to send Tambs home for Christmas and refuse him permission to return. With his allies gone, Jaime Ramirez was left to pursue the Medellin cartel alone.

Unlike his cartel colleagues, Jorge Ochoa had not returned to Colombia quickly. With their wives, Ochoa and Cali cocaine boss Gilberto Rodriguez Orejuela had settled in Spain. Alerted by an informant as to their identity, the Spanish police watched the traffickers for two and a half months. Increasingly nervous about the Colombians' intentions, the police arrested the two men when they learned of their plans to buy 10,000 acres of ranchland in southern Spain.

When Ochoa was taken into custody, both the United States and Colombia asked to extradite him. The defense lawyers capitalized on the Spanish public's anti-U.S.

sentiment. One of Ochoa's lawyers portrayed his client as a pawn in a dirty war waged by the United States against Nicaragua. Ultimately the decision was made to extradite Ochoa to Colombia. The prosecution appealed. The decision was reversed on January 21, 1986. Ochoa was to be extradited to the United States. The defense appealed and the matter dragged on.

The Questionable Handling of Barry Seal

Informant Barry Seal was the major witness in the United States able to testify against Ochoa, if and when he was extradited. But Seal had run into legal problems. Federal law enforcement jurisdiction is broken into districts, which critics often refer to as fiefdoms. Seal's difficulties revolved around crimes he had allegedly committed in the Middle District of Louisiana, before he became an informant in the Southern District of Florida. In the eyes of federal officials in Louisiana, despite his participation in one of the biggest cocaine cases in the history of the DEA, Seal remained an arrogant manipulator.

The cartel was anxious to get Seal out of the way before the first four Colombians ever extradited from Colombia landed in Florida in January 1985. First he had to be found.

While his murder was being arranged, Barry Seal continued to polish his image as a DEA informant by working undercover. In January 1985 he engineered the seizure of 90 kilos (198 pounds) of cocaine, along with the arrests of nine Colombians, in Las Vegas. In February he paid a $20,000 bribe to the chief minister of the Turks and Caicos Islands, a British colony south of the Bahamas. The scene was taped by a hidden DEA video camera.

Confirmation of the contract on Seal's life came on June 5, 1985 when Max Mermelstein, an "all-purpose gringo" cartel employee who coordinated cocaine flights in Miami was picked up by a drug task force. Mermelstein lived in constant fear of his immediate employer, Rafa Cardona, a trafficker who free-based cocaine. To arresting officers, Mermelstein seemed relieved to be in custody, although he faced the potent charge of operating a "continuing criminal enterprise." Mermelstein had a choice between cooperating with law enforcement officials or spending his life behind bars. He decided to cooperate.

On October 24, 1985 Seal appeared before a federal judge in a sentence review proceeding. Because Seal had put his life in peril on behalf of the government, the judge reduced his sentence to time already served.

U.S. District Judge Frank Polozola in Baton Rouge, whose hands were tied by the Florida sentence, was furious. At a hearing on December 20, 1985, he laid out conditions for Seal's probation. If Seal broke any one of the conditions, he would serve five years in prison. Except with the judge's permission, Seal was not to travel outside Louisiana, even to be a government witness, and he was to pay a fine of $35,000.

The judge added two additional conditions that insured Seal's assassination. Seal would no longer be allowed to have armed bodyguards, and he was required to reside at a Salvation Army Community Treatment Center for a period of six months. Seal's lawyer pointed out that the plea bargain had called for no incarceration. The judge countered that the treatment center was not incarceration.

When the risk to Seal's life was pointed out, Judge Polozola said Seal should go into the Witness Protection Program. Because of his earlier experiences with the program, Seal refused. Polozola was unwilling to grant a gag order preventing all parties from talking to the press. Seal was taken directly to the halfway house from court.

Preoccupied with money worries when he drove into the Salvation Army lot on February 19, 1986, Seal failed to notice a parked car. Before he could get out of his car, the driver of the parked car placed the muzzle of a silenced MAC-10 less than two feet from Seal's head and fired 12 times.

The Massacre at the Palace of Justice

Daily life in Colombia continued to deteriorate. The Medellin cartel had concluded that the extradition process agreed to by the United States and Colombia could not be deterred by either public opinion or threats to political officials. The only course was to do away with the extradition treaty itself. The cartel turned its sights on the Colombian Supreme Court.

During the summer of 1985, the individual members of the Supreme Court were besieged by death threats to themselves and their families. Gugliotta and Leen quoted one of the letters addressed to the wife of one of the justices. "You must convince your husband to abrogate the treaty. Remember, we are the same people who dealt with Rodrigo Lara Bonilla. Your bodyguards won't save you, no matter how many you have."

At 11:40 A.M. on the November 6, 1985, 35 M-19 guerrillas carrying machine guns, automatic rifles and grenades flowed into the Colombian Palace of Justice. They took 250 hostages. For the next 26 hours hundreds of soldiers, police and commandoes tried to subdue the guerrillas to no avail. When the seige finally ended, at least 95 people were dead, including the Supreme Court chief justice, 11 of the court's 24 associate justices and all the guerrillas.

In the aftermath of the tragedy, the only top-level official to express the opinion that the seizure was sponsored by the cartel was Justice Minister Enrique Parejo Gonzalez. Gradually over the course of the following year, other Colombians came to share his conviction.

Betancur's presidency never recovered from the carnage at the Palace of Justice; 1986 was a year of unremitting violence. Murder became the leading cause of death among males 15 to 40. Medellin averaged ten murders a day. The cartel engaged in direct confrontation with the Colombian government and, in the process, systematically destroyed every national institution. The courts, the political parties, the Congress, the police, even the soccer teams and the bullfights had been compromised. Despite the chaos, however, extradition of drug traffickers to the United States continued.

On May 25, 1986 Virgilio Barco Vargas replaced Betancur as president. Like Betancur before him, Barco ignored drug enforcement. The murders continued.

In Spain, on July 13, 1986, after 20 months and six separate court findings, Ochoa was ordered returned to Colombia, where he was sentenced to 20 months in jail. Two days prior to the start of Ochoa's sentence, the same judge who passed sentence released him on parole upon payment of a 2.3 million peso ($11,500) bond. Ochoa served only 30 days in jail in Colombia.

After three years as Colombia's anti-narcotics police chief, Jaime Ramirez was relieved of his duty in December 1985. Slated for promotion, he was scheduled to spend most of 1986 at Colombia's Superior War College. No one had cost Escobar more money than Ramirez. During his final year, Ramirez had hounded Lehder. After repeated unsuccessful attempts on the police officer's life, the cartel's assassins caught up with Jaime Ramirez on November 17, 1986 on a highway bridge. A gunman emptied the magazine of a MAC-10 into him as his wife and children looked on.

The Concept of the Colombian Drug Lords as a Cartel

For a long time U.S. law enforcement officials resisted the idea that a single group of Colombian cocaine traffickers could control such a large segment of the trade. Although every list of traffickers always included

Escobar, Ochoa and Lehder at the top, they were considered independent. It was not until 1983 that the term cartel was accepted. Despite massive arrests and adaptations of U.S. laws to cope with the reality of the cartel, cocaine continued to pour into the United States.

The idea of treating the cartel as a cartel occurred in the stairwell of the U.S. Attorney's Office in Miami, when two assistant U.S. attorneys, Bob Dunlap and Bob Martinez, conversed about their respective cases and recognized that they were working on different parts of the same, bigger case, a conspiracy involving the Ochoas, Escobar, Lehder and others. Martinez proposed to Dick Gregorie, chief of the Major Narcotics Section, that they stop trying all the cases separately and try them as one big RICO case. RICO, the Racketeer-Influenced and Corrupt Organizations Act, was a tool that had been used effectively for two decades against the American Mafia.

In their spare time, Martinez and DEA Special Agent Carol Cooper worked on the case for several months until August 1986, when Jorge Ochoa was released in Colombia after serving only 30 days. Outraged by the release, less than a week later Gregorie, Martinez, Cooper and another assistant U.S. attorney, Mark Schnapp, gathered to construct a case from the files and documents crammed into what they called the Ochoa War Room. For a week the four attorneys worked 14-hour days until they built an indictment based on the collected evidence.

The indictment named Pablo Escobar, Carlos Lehder, Gonzalo Rodriguez Gacha and the three Ochoa brothers as the cartel's leaders and called the cartel the world's largest cocaine-smuggling organization. On the morning of August 16, 1986, the day that the indictment was to be returned by the grand jury, a press conference scheduled to announce it was canceled. Word had leaked to the Colombian government, which had put pressure on the State Department, which had put pressure on the Justice Department. Washington called and ordered that the indictment be sealed. The cartel indictment was not released in the United States until November 18, 1986, the day after Jaime Ramirez's murder.

In Colombia, the indictment caused a sensation. With the exception of the newspaper *El Espectador,* the Colombian press normally protected itself from the cartel's wrath by avoiding mention of its activities, except for occasionally using information aired in American newspapers or television. However, reporting even secondhand news about the cartel with any regularity could be dangerous.

Although the U.S. press treated the cartel indictment story as just another large drug indictment, *El Espectador* carried the indictment story as a two-part special report. Editor-in-chief Guillermo Cano Isaza led anti-cartel crusades, by writing frequent editorials calling for stiffer drug laws and supporting extradition. Cano, a distinguished member of the Liberal Party, fought a lonely battle.

On December 17, 1986, as Cano was returning home from work in a station wagon filled with Christmas presents, he stopped to make a turn. A young man climbed down from a motorcycle nearby, unhurriedly opened a musical instrument case, removed a snub-nosed MAC-10, walked to the driver's window of Cano's car and pulled the trigger.

Cano's murder resulted in outrage. Journalists, frightened and infuriated, fanned the flames. Humiliated, President Barco turned law enforcement loose in a full-scale crackdown. Barco, unlike Betancur before him, refused to ignore guerrilla dealings with drug traffickers. Two major guerrilla groups, seeing public opinion turning against them, publicly denounced the traffickers.

The crackdown's modest success lifted the mood in Colombia. Gugliotta and Leen explain the short-lived national euphoria:

> By now the traumas of Colombia's drug wars were capable of transforming even small triumphs or failures into earth-shaking events. After the horrors of 1986, the country was on a giddy upswing again. Bad guys were getting arrested; the police were seizing drugs; things looked pretty good for a change, even if it didn't last. And it didn't. On January 13, 1987, word reached Bogota that Colombian Ambassador to Hungary Enrique Parejo Gonzalez, the former justice minister, who had successfully challenged the cartel for two hard years, had been accosted in a Budapest blizzard and shot five times in the face.

Miraculously, Parejo survived the attempt on his life.

National success against the cartel was desperately needed. Success finally came when a campesino caretaker complained about the behavior of tenants in a rented house to National Police Major William Lemus, who in December 1986 had taken over as chief of police of a town about 30 miles east of Medellin. Lemus felt that it was important to check out the tenants. In doing so, he captured Lehder after an all-night stakeout.

The paperwork had been completed on Carlos Lehder in 1984, so the police could extradite him immediately. Lehder arrived in the United States at 1:15 A.M. on February 5, 1987, less than two days after the campesino had murmured his complaint.

More successes came with the trial of Barry Seal's accused killers, which opened on April 6, 1987. Max Mermelstein, as a prosecution witness, mesmerized the jury as he told of arranging 38 flights, each carrying 450 kilos (992 pounds) of cocaine. The jury found the defendants guilty and voted to give them life imprisonment. Several weeks later the rumor was out that a seven-figure contract had been put out on Max Mermelstein.

Unraveling the Government

For five years the cartel had battled the bilateral treaty and in the course of doing so had murdered more than 30 judges, including half of the Supreme Court, had put dozens of politicians on its payroll and had bought publicity to depict the treaty as a violation of national sovereignty. Nothing worked until December 12, 1986 when the Colombian Supreme Court, in the course of reviewing several dozen challenges to the treaty, ruled that the enabling legislation supporting the treaty was unconstitutional, because it had been signed by an interim president. The court suggested that the current president might want to sign the enabling legislation in his own name.

Barco re-signed, but the action marked the first round in the battle to come. As 1987 progressed, the Supreme Court issued a series of findings that hemmed in the government. On May 28, 1987 the justices tied 12–12 on the issue of whether Barco had a right to re-sign the enabling legislation. A temporary justice brought in to break the deadlock voted that the re-signing had been unconstitutional. The treaty was dead.

With characteristic efficiency, Pablo Escobar set out to wipe out charges pending against him. In short order, all cases against him were dismissed. The only cases left stemmed from the mid-1970s, cases for which all witnesses were dead.

In the late afternoon of November 21, 1987, a traffic officer stopped Jorge Ochoa's car. To no avail, Ochoa tried to bribe the officer. By 9 P.M. Ochoa was tucked away in a maximum security military prison. A six-person legal team from the U.S. Departments of Justice and State went to Colombia to help look for a mechanism to extradite Ochoa. The team considered Attorney General Carlos Hoyas Jimenez and President Barco as helpful, but felt that others were blocking any initiatives.

By the end of the first week, Ochoa had six attorneys working for him, three of them former Colombian Supreme Court justices. On December 30 the defense team leader met with a Bogota Criminal Court judge.

He pointed out that Ochoa had already served 21 months in Spain while waiting for charges against him to be settled. The judge signed his release and Ochoa left the same night on a charter flight out of the country. On January 18, 1988 Attorney General Hoyas Jimenez's car was ambushed and sprayed with machine gun bullets.

By the time Carlos Lehder's trial finally opened on November 17, 1987, U.S. Attorney Robert Merkle of the Middle District of Florida had assembled a massive case that spanned the period from Lehder's prison time in Danbury in 1974 to his presence in Medellin in 1985. Merkle laid out Lehder's career as a huge conspiracy to flood the United States with cocaine. The multiple facets of the Medellin cartel emerged as Merkle presented the testimony of 115 prosecution witnesses. The most vivid testimony came from Lehder himself, in the form of taped radio and television interviews he gave in Colombia to explain himself.

After 42 hours of deliberations, the jury found Lehder guilty on all counts. The judge sentenced him to life without parole plus 135 years.

Drug traffic-related slaughter continued in Colombia. In September 1989 presidential candidate Luis Carlos Galan, who was committed to fighting drugs, was assassinated. The government once again declared war on the traffickers. The cartel struck back. On December 15, 1989 cartel leader Jose Gonzalo Rodriguez Gacha was killed. Between August 18, 1989 and January 17, 1990, when an apparent truce was declared, the cartel was alleged to have set off 263 bombs, killing 209 people and wounding hundreds more. The January 17, 1990 truce coincided with the release of hostages, one a member of President Barco's extended family and the other the son of a close aide.

On March 22, 1990 a minor party leftist candidate for president, Bernardo Jaramillo, was assassinated. After Barco was accused by critics of negotiating with the traffickers, extraditions were reinstated on March 28, 1990.

The political heir to the assassinated Luis Carlos Galan, Cesar Gaviria, who swept 51% of the primary vote, advocated a hard line against traffickers. Although he was under constant threat, observers did not believe that Gaviria would be assassinated because the crackdowns that follow such an act cause expensive disruptions in the cocaine business. Instead, the traffickers were expected to resort to bombings, kidnappings and murders to make it clear to the public that a crackdown exacts a price.

At the start of a new decade, the cartel appeared to be winning once again. On April 13, 1990 the Colombian Supreme Court decided that the government did not have the right to confiscate the assets of druglords, a highly successful technique used in the United States. Moreover, assets already seized had to be returned. On its emotional roller coaster with the druglords, the Colombian public appeared to have tired of the war and once again be in favor of negotiating with them.

In September 1990 President Gaviria offered reduced sentences and no extradition if druglords surrendered and confessed to a crime. After negotiating further concessions, Jorge Ochoa and his two brothers turned themselves in. Police were not allowed inside the custom-built prison where the brothers were held in their hometown of Itaqui, a community long controlled by the Ochoas. The municipality of Itaqui supplies the Ochoas' guards.

Colombian and foreign drug experts objected to the concessions on the grounds that there was no evidence that the Ochoa trafficking operation was being dismantled or scaled down. By May 1991 angry law enforcement officials insisted that the Ochoas were operating their business from the prison. They claimed that a 12-ton shipment of cocaine seized three months after the Ochoas entered prison belonged to the brothers.

Using an elderly priest as his negotiator, Pablo Escobar also set the terms of his surrender. He demanded and was given a guarantee that he would not be extradited. Colombian police claim that he put together an infrastructure that enables him to continue to run his operation from his custom-built prison in his hometown of Envigado, a community where he holds tremendous power.

Demoralized by the loss of hundreds of their comrades in battles against the cartel, Colombian police characterized the concessions as imbecilic. Cocaine continues to flow out of Colombia and into the United States.

On July 22, 1992 Pablo Escobar, his brother Robert, and eight associates escaped from their hillside prison compound known as The Cathedral when government officials tried to move them to a military prison. On August 13, 1992 Escobar was indicted in New York on federal charges of conspiracy to plant the bomb that destroyed an Avienea Airline jet in the sky over Colombia in 1989, killing 110 people, including two Americans.

On January 22, 1993, three days after Escobar sent a letter to Colombia's attorney general threatening to launch a new terrorist campaign, a car bomb exploded, injuring 15.

D. THE CHINESE TRIADS

A worldwide heroin trade is organized by Chinese secret societies called Triads based in Hong Kong. The Triads make billions from all the usual businesses of organized crime—gambling, prostitution, extortion, loan sharking, protection rackets, murder-for-hire and political and civic corruption—but they make most of their money from heroin. The world's population of heroin addicts doubled during the 1980s. Their addictions bring in an estimated $200 billion in illegal profits annually.

The Triads control the Golden Triangle, a mist-covered, 4,500-mile stretch of rugged mountains where annually about 1,500 tons (approximately 70%) of the world's opium and heroin are produced. The area includes the four northern provinces of Thailand, the western fringe of Laos and a broad stretch of northeast Burma.

Gerald Posner, in his 1988 book *Warlords of Crime: Chinese Secret Societies—The New Mafia,* asserts that the Chinese Triads are the most powerful criminal syndicates in existence and pose the most serious and growing threat to law enforcement worldwide. Hong Kong police officials claim that law enforcement in the United States, Canada and Europe is at least 30 years behind in its understanding of the Triads.

The Hong Kong Superintendent of Police told Posner, "I can assure you that these criminal Triads based out of Hong Kong make the Mafia look like child's play. No one else comes close—not Sicilians, not Corsicans, not Colombians, no one."

Triad societies have been in existence for centuries. A factor that makes it difficult for law enforcement to acquire knowledge about the Triads is that they are closed to outsiders, particularly to Caucasians. Hong Kong police believe there are at least 50 secret Triad societies in the British colony. One of the largest is the 14K Triad, whose membership is estimated to be about 30,000. (The 14K's name incorporates both the symbol for gold and the street address of their headquarters.)

While the Triads are based in Hong Kong, they have ties around the world rooted in elaborate ritual, kinship and mutual commercial interests. The Triads' underground banking system moves billions of dollars each year without leaving a paper trail.

Posner believes the Triads control the heroin trade in the United States. But Claire Sterling, the author of *The*

Octopus: The Long Reach of the International Sicilian Mafia (1990), believes that the Sicilians control heroin in the United States. There is no question that they are both heavily involved.

The flow of heroin begins with the harvest of poppies each year by indigenous Southeast Asian peoples. The chain of events from the growth of the poppy to the cultivation of opium to the refinement of heroin has not changed since the discoveries of the narcotic uses of these drugs.

Poppies are first transformed into opium in fieldside chemical laboratories. In nearby, more sophisticated, laboratories the opium is refined into morphine or heroin by Chinese chemists employed by private armies. The various chemical processes that change poppies into heroin reduce its volume to 10% of its original bulk, making transport easier, a major reason for setting up labs near the poppy fields.

From the labs, the heroin is hauled by mule and horseback to the borders of several Asian countries, where it is transferred to trucks, ships and planes and sent for distribution to Triads located on five continents. The amount of Southeast Asian heroin confiscated each year is thought to be less than 3% of the area's total output.

The opium-producing areas of the world not only produce narcotics, they also consume them. Southeast Asia has achieved the unhappy distinction of being the capital of illegal drug production because Southeast Asia has had a pervasive, deep-rooted opium problem for centuries. Posner attributes much of the blame to policies of European colonial powers and modern Western intelligence agencies.

After being processed into morphine or heroin, approximately half of the production, 750 or more tons, remains in Southeast Asia; the rest is exported. The world's second largest opium producers, the Central Asian countries of Afghanistan, Pakistan and Iran (often called the Golden Crescent), produce about 600 tons, of which only about 15% (about 90 tons) is exported.

Triad Origins

Chinese history reveals that secret societies have existed since 1,500 years before Christ. The modern-day Triad societies were founded in the late 17th century, 30 years after the Manchus swept into China. As a result of their repressive control in the northern two thirds of the country, an anti-Manchu rebellion was organized in the south around 128 militant Buddhist monks in the Foochow monastery.

In 1674 the Manchus sent a large contingent of armed forces to the monastery where, after a fierce battle, the monks were slaughtered. Five monks who escaped are credited with founding the first Triad society with the goal of overthrowing the Manchus and restoring a Chinese imperial government.

Hundreds of additional Triads formed to accommodate the alienated. They spread throughout China and became the arbiters of social and political grievances. Rather than report their disputes and crimes to the local police, citizens turned to the Triads to settle differences and to mete out punishment.

The Triads thus became unofficial local governments. The philosophy of many broadened from opposition to just the Manchus to opposition to the presence of "white devils," particularly the British, who forced China to engage in opium trade.

In response to various Triad-sponsored rebellions, the Manchus embarked on a campaign of vengeful suppression, during which they killed 1 million people. During the campaign, many Triads fled from China to Hong Kong and to the United States. By 1847 British officials estimated that in Hong Kong, behind the cover of artisans' guilds, workers' associations and sports clubs, almost three quarters of the colony's population were Triad members.

By the mid-1800s the Manchus' campaign to eradicate the secret societies threatened the Triads' existence. To stave off extinction, some segments of the largest secret societies engaged in an assortment of illegal activities, including piracy, smuggling and extortion. Mainland Triads sent members to Chinese communities in other countries to organize and protect various kinds of vice and crime that thrived among homeless settlers. By the late 1880s the bulk of the income of many Triads came from illegal sources.

By the time a successful revolution overthrew the Manchus and established a republic in 1911, Triad membership had grown to an estimated 35 million. The first new government of the Republic of China was formed by Dr. Sun Yat-sen, a senior Triad member. He was joined by Charlie Soong, member of a Shanghai Triad called the Green Gang and an international financier, and by General Chiang Kai-shek, the warlord who lost control of China in 1949 to the Communist revolution. In exchange for their support, the new government allowed the Triads to become a powerful lobby in the affairs of the new China.

Chiang Kai-shek's ambition to lead a unified China, as the military chief of a new imperial dynasty, prompted him to use the Triads as a coercive arm of his political party, the Kuomintang (KMT). In exchange for control over most criminal activities and prominent positions in Chiang's government, the Triads carried out a KMT campaign to abolish labor unions, arrest left-wing and Communist leaders and close newspapers that were critical of the government.

For his help, Tu Yueh Sheng, leader of the Green Gang, was made a general in the KMT, and his position as the "Opium King" was fortified. The nation disintegrated into autonomous regions controlled by powerful military warlords. Chinese poppy cultivation, along with opium export, increased.

With Chiang Kai-shek's aid, China became the first modern country in which secret criminal societies played a fundamental role in legitimate government. The police and the military were infiltrated and often controlled by Triad members, guaranteeing noninterference in their criminal activities. Indeed, few criminal enterprises in China could be conducted without Triad oversight or involvement.

Hong Kong Triads

Held in check by British authorities, the Hong Kong Triads were not able to achieve the level of governmental dominance of their counterparts in mainland China. The 1941 Japanese occupation of Hong Kong presented the Triads with an opportunity to consolidate their power. Some of the larger Triads reached agreements with the Japanese that permitted them to run their illegal businesses. In exchange for information and help in maintaining order, the Japanese allowed the Triads to destroy the police files on their secret societies dating back to 1842.

When the British regained control of Hong Kong in 1945, they were at a formidable disadvantage. Understaffed and barely able to keep up with the daily volume of serious crime, the police were no match for the postwar Triads. Not only were their files gone, police force ranks had been decimated by wartime deaths and injuries. Postwar police recruitment drives to rebuild their ranks brought swarms of Triad members into the Hong Kong police force, where they promoted raids on competitors' gambling and opium dens.

During the months immediately preceding the fall of Nationalist China, Britain adopted an open-door policy for Chinese seeking refuge in Hong Kong. More than three quarters of a million people fled to the British colony. Among the refugees were many Triad members.

British authorities were unable to provide effective services in areas into which the squatters crammed. Most squatters distrusted outsiders. Perceiving an apparently lucrative target for vices, the established Hong Kong Triads attempted to take over control, only to be repulsed. The squatters had brought their own secret societies with them and resisted penetration.

The mainland Triads brought with them the heroin trade. By 1950 Tu Yueh Sheng, the Green Gang leader, had established large-scale heroin refineries. French colonialists were also responsible for enormous numbers of addicts in Indochina. Narcotics operations accounted for 25% of French Indochina's revenues during World War II.

Not only did British and French policies create gigantic populations of addicts, they contributed to the development of a highly organized smuggling network. Colonial administrations, interested solely in huge profits, granted distribution licenses to Chinese merchants. The Chinese traffickers, interrelated by kinship and shared business interests with the Triads, monopolized the opium trade in Southeast Asia and played a major role in the post-World War II heroin boom. Drug trade successes in China and Indochina were replicated in Thailand and Burma.

Posner traces the long and complex involvement of the Central Intelligence Agency (CIA) in the politics of Southeast Asia and the agency's contribution to the growth of the heroin trade. Americans handpicked Ngo Dinh Diem to take control of Saigon's political machinery. Diem also controlled Saigon's extensive underworld.

Over the next 15 years, between 1955 and 1970, the United States permitted the South Vietnamese to become enmeshed in the narcotics trade. Many South Vietnamese government leaders spent more time dealing narcotics than they did fighting Communists. The CIA was also active in abetting drug trafficking in neighboring Burma, Thailand and Laos.

By 1971, 15% of the U.S. Army in the area, 40,000 soldiers, had become addicted and another 60,000 had become occasional users. When the soldiers went home and the Vietnam market collapsed, the Triads' solution was to ship more heroin to the United States as well as to other nations around the world.

Posner interviewed a retired CIA agent, who had spent 15 years in various Southeast Asian assignments, about the U.S. role in drug trafficking. The former agent told him:

Nobody in Washington ever made a conscious decision to move opium around Asia. The French did make that conscious decision . . . they actually used it to pay for operations the government wouldn't fund. For us it was different. We had all the money we needed. For us, helping a little in the opium business just ensured loyalty from people we needed to rely on. In retrospect, I don't know if it was worth it . . . We just helped a lot of people get wealthy there.

Transshipment Through Hong Kong

Hong Kong is an open door through which heroin flows undetected. The Customs and Excise Service has 2,700 agents to deal with one of the most congested cities in the world.

Hong Kong has three avenues of entry. All have their special customs service horrors. The airport brings in 30,000 passengers a day, 5,300 an hour at peak hours—all potential drug couriers. The air cargo complex handles 670,000 tons of cargo a year, approximately 1,835 tons a day, including unknown quantities of drugs.

An average of 28,600 people cross the border from mainland China each day, each a potential courier. Each day cars bring almost 4,110 tons of cargo across the border, and trains almost 4,300 tons of cargo.

The Hong Kong government has gone to great lengths to encourage the movement of trade and commercial cargo through its free port, where almost nothing is taxed. The Hong Kong chief of customs admitted to Posner that he did not have sufficient personnel to concern himself about shipments of heroin that stopped in transit on their way to another destination.

The Triads alter shipping invoices so that commercial goods in which heroin is hidden do not appear to have originated in a drug-producing country. They also change the papers of legitimate shipments from non-drug-producing countries to read as if they were from drug-producing countries in order to use up the limited time of the police.

Surpassed only by Rotterdam, Hong Kong is the second busiest port in the world, handling 56 million tons of cargo each year. On an average day, there are 5,000 vessels in the harbor. Some 27,000 oceangoing vessels and 16,000 river ships come and go each year. An estimated 140,000 small boats and junks (flat-bottomed boats with battened sails) constantly travel in and out of the harbor. The junks are the key links to fishing trawlers carrying drugs up the coast from Thailand.

The Dutch Connection

If Hong Kong is a major heroin exit gateway out of Asia, then Rotterdam, the world's largest and busiest seaport, is the major entry gateway to Europe. With a population of only between 14 and 15 million, the Netherlands has more than 20,000 regular heroin users. Yet in the spring of 1987, when other countries were upset about their citizens' use of drugs, the Dutch capital of Amsterdam dedicated a museum to the lore and enjoyment of marijuana.

The Netherlands' relaxed attitude about drugs has created not only a domestic addiction problem, it has encouraged foreign narcotics merchants, particularly the Chinese, to move into the country. Dutch law makes it extremely difficult for the police to cope with narcotics traffic. A trafficker must be in physical possession of illegal drugs to be prosecuted. Sting operations and plea bargains are forbidden. Wiretaps cannot be used in direct evidence. Sentences are short and jails are as comfortable as college campuses.

The Triads moved into the Netherlands before World War II. The 14K was the first Triad in Amsterdam's Chinatown, where it set up two illegal gambling dens and a prostitution service. In the 1950s the 14K operation was taken over by a young gangster named Chung Mon, nicknamed "the Unicorn." He reorganized the gambling and opium trade and, by 1960, had made Amsterdam's Chinatown the site of one of the most profitable 14K operations outside the Orient.

By 1970 Chung Mon oversaw a distribution network that brought dozens of couriers into Amsterdam and conveyed heroin loads through Rotterdam hidden in cargo shipments. Not only did he tailor a smokable form of heroin for Dutch and Chinese addicts, he developed an injectable form for the large U.S. soldier population stationed in Germany as well as for French and British addict populations. By 1973 Chung Mon was distributing large loads of street-level heroin to organized crime groups in the United States, England, France, Germany, Italy and Spain.

The lure of easy money brought other Hong Kong Triads, along with an ambitious Triad from Singapore, into Amsterdam. The quiet Chinese community erupted in a savage series of gunfights as rival gangs lined up on opposite sides of the narrow streets and opened fire on one another with shotguns. The Dutch police went to the Unicorn for help. He gave them a list of most of his competitors. By 1980 the business had grown so large that most of the major Hong Kong Triads were represented.

Tongs: American Structures Open to Triads

Chinatowns in cities all over the United States are the product of a history of discrimination and segregation. In 1851 tens of thousands of Chinese fled the bloodshed of the Taiping Rebellion against the Manchu dynasty. The United States was hardly welcoming. The Chinese were exploited for their labor but regarded as unfit for U.S. citizenship. U.S. immigration laws prevented laborers from bringing any women with them and prevented them from marrying white women. Chinese immigrants were subject to large surcharges on business transactions, banned from working for corporations, forced to live only within the confines of their own communities and not allowed to testify in court.

The wave of immigrants in the 1880s included Triad members. When Chinese immigrants were faced with campaigns of hatred and vilification in major American cities, Triad members seized the opportunity to establish American Triad branches, called tongs (town halls).

The tongs handled everything, including food, rent and the enforcement of local laws. They became, in effect, unofficial local governments. In addition, the tongs controlled local Chinatowns' vice operations, including the opium trade, prostitution and gambling. By the turn of the century, Chinatowns had reputations as places of depravity and attracted whites interested in gambling halls, opium dens and brothels. White patronage allowed Chinese vice to expand faster than if it had been confined solely to Chinese customers.

By the 1930s an influx of Chinese women changed the sex ratio in American Chinatowns and began a shift toward husband-wife family patterns that dampened the enthusiasm of Chinatowns for vice. World War II shifted the American public's racial bias against Asians from Chinese to Japanese, and the war reduced the numbers of young white males attracted to Chinatown vices.

In 1965 the U.S. government opened up Chinese immigration. Fleeing Hong Kong's slums, thousands crushed into overcrowded American Chinatowns. The 1960 New York City population of 20,000 Chinese climbed to 300,000 in 1985, with 1,400 more arriving each day. With new recruits, the tongs expanded their vice rackets to meet the needs of the incoming residents.

By the last decade of the 20th century, five major tongs extended across the United States. In order of size, the largest was located in New York City, the second largest in San Francisco, the third largest in the Southwest and Los Angeles. The other two were located on the Pacific Coast, with branches in the East.

Because tongs are involved in many useful and charitable enterprises in the Chinese community, membership in a tong is legal in the United States. The Hong Kong police superintendent told Posner that he believes the legal status of U.S. tongs gives the Triads a tre-

mendous advantage. The San Francisco police think it is unfair to automatically equate tongs with criminal enterprises and assume that only some tong members are criminals.

A 1985 Federal Bureau of Investigation (FBI) report on organized crime observed that, while most members of the various U.S. tongs were law-abiding citizens, Triad influence was evident in certain tongs in major cities. The Triads perceived as exerting influence were many of Hong Kong's major Triads, including the 14K.

Mike Yamaguchi, an assistant United States attorney in San Francisco who is an expert on Chinese organized crime, speculates that there may be a Triad commission in New York that oversees Chinese crime nationwide. When pressed for details by Posner, Yamaguchi said, "It's silly to think the Chinese syndicates are so formally organized in the Orient that they wouldn't take the structure with them here to the U.S. You underestimate criminal societies that have operated for hundreds of years . . . they have already clearly established extensive operations in Europe."

Further complicating an already complex pattern, the tongs in recent years have employed newly organized Vietnamese gangs for some of their more violent work. Some of the brutal youth gangs that have sprouted across the United States include former members of the Special Forces soldiers from the South Vietnamese military who were trained in assassination and the use of explosives.

The advantage of using such gangs is that they direct attention away from the Chinese community and focus it on Vietnamese immigrants. For the Vietnamese, the employment means getting cut into the larger crime picture.

The FBI has reported that many tongs also use youth gangs as "street muscle." But the tongs don't find it easy to control unruly gangs of 14- and 15-year-olds, newly arrived from Hong Kong, who have no respect for their elders.

In the fall of 1977 three teenage gunmen, intent upon assassinating the leader of the Wah Ching boys, California's largest Chinese youth gang, entered a San Francisco landmark, the Golden Dragon restaurant, and opened fire. They killed five and wounded 11, none of them Wah Ching gang members. This was the first violent Chinatown explosion that had extensive coverage in the American press.

The public assumed something had gone wrong with the normally peaceful Chinatown. They blamed tough gangs. Few understood that the visible youth gangs were the bottom-rung, low-level foot soldiers for powerful criminal syndicates. At the time, the existence of

Triads was unknown to U.S. law enforcement. What was commonplace in Hong Kong and Bangkok appeared strange and inexplicable in the United States.

Many tongs get support from the Chinese Nationalist government in Taiwan. In October 1984 a San Francisco journalist, Henry Liu, a vocal critic of the Taiwan government, was gunned down in front of his suburban home by killers dispatched from Taiwan by the United Bamboo.

During the course of the investigation into the Liu murder, a massive heroin network was uncovered. Thirteen Triad members, who were in the midst of preparations to import billions of dollars' worth of Golden Triangle heroin, were arrested.

Leaving Hong Kong

The Triads are searching for new locations because the British have agreed to turn over political control of Hong Kong to China in 1997 and the Triads do not believe they will be able to function under the Communists. They plan to move their operations to another democracy, where they will have all the privileges of ordinary citizens.

The United States is high on the Triad list of desirable locations. Yamaguchi believes that the astonishing surge in San Francisco banking activity and a giant growth in cash in an increasing number of independent Chinese banks is evidence that the Hong Kong Triads are already in the process of picking up their operations and moving them to San Francisco.

Jon Elder, police chief of Monterey Park, California, a community that Chinese Triads invaded, told Posner, "Asian organized crime will end up being the number one organized crime in North America in the next five years. In my humble opinion, they'll make the Mafia look like a bunch of Sunday-school kids."

Not everyone thinks that the Triads will find it easy to establish themselves in North America. One DEA agent told Posner, "Some of the Triads may be coming here in 1997, but they aren't going to find it all that easy to take over here. They are going to have a lot of trouble with the tongs and with the Young Turks who think this is their country. They aren't going to take kindly to new syndicates trying to run the businesses."

Global Law Enforcement Is Not Prepared

The European Economic Community, with its decreasing vigilance over international borders, may become one big marketplace for the Chinese Triads. Despite a burgeoning European addict population and a doubling or tripling of the amount of heroin entering into Europe during the 1980s, few European countries have budgets specifically allocated to fight the Triads.

The war against the Triads cannot be fought effectively by any one country. Yet international police cooperation is scarce. The International Criminal Police Organization (Interpol), the sole worldwide police organization, serves mainly as a data bank. The United Nations invests only $20 million a year in combating drug abuse and makes little effort to encourage eradication or suppression.

The DEA has mounted the largest law enforcement effort. However, in almost every country except Thailand and Mexico, the DEA serves in a liaison and advisory capacity and is prohibited from becoming operational.

Legal measures to thwart drug traffickers are lacking in many countries. Most prohibit seizure of a criminal's assets, a crucial measure in fighting money-laden drug traffickers. Many of the major drug-producing and transshipment countries do not have effective criminal conspiracy laws. The United States is alone in having the Racketeer-Influenced and Corrupt Organizations (RICO) Act.

Extradition treaties need to be universal for drug trafficking. There are currently no international sanctions against countries such as Taiwan that provide sanctuary for drug and crime lords. Law enforcement agencies worldwide need agents who understand Chinese criminals and their long history and tradition and who can speak one or more Chinese dialects.

E. THE JAPANESE YAKUZA

Japan's organized crime rings, the yakuza, came to the attention of U.S. authorities in the spring of 1976 through the efforts of Michael Sterrett, a young federal prosecutor. During Sterrett's successful investigation and prosecution of Hawaiian gambling kingpins and their ties to Las Vegas mobsters, he uncovered involvement in Hawaiian crime of Japanese nationals.

Hawaii's ethnic groups, one quarter of them ethnic Japanese, one third white and the rest mainly an assortment of other Asians, have kinship ties throughout the Pacific Basin. Besides offering personal ties to Asian nations, Sterrett recognized that Hawaii offers a number of elements attractive to organized crime: machine party politics; an active labor movement; widespread acceptance of prostitution, gambling and drugs; a massive tourist industry that brings in millions of visitors from around the world; and a geographic location that makes it a convenient stopping-off place between Asia and North America.

Like the Sicilian Mafia, the yakuza has a long tradition and deep cultural roots. David Kaplan and Alec Dubro's 1986 book *Yakuza: The Explosive Account of Japan's Criminal Underworld* traces the criminal gangs' history, impact on Japan and national and international operations.

A booming trade among Pacific Rim nations, rapidly expanding economies in East Asia, the steady growth of Japan and California and increasing participation of China in the world economy offered enormous growth potential in the 1970s for legitimate and illegitimate businesses. That potential made Sterrett wonder what impact a "yakuza connection" might have on the $85 billion worth of goods being shipped between Japan and the United States.

Japanese police appeared reluctant to answer Sterrett's questions. Given Japan's low reported crime rate, the little they were willing to share was startling. Official figures revealed that 100,000 gangsters organized into 2,500 crime families live and work in Japan. Yakuza syndicates, like Japan's efficient legitimate corporations, appeared to be well financed and highly organized.

The yakuza control an estimated 26,000 legitimate businesses and an unknown number of illegal ones. Like the American Mafia, the yakuza syndicates are involved in prostitution, pornography, gambling, loan-sharking, trucking, smuggling and extortion. For a fee, the yakuza break strikes and silence dissenters. Like the American mobs, the yakuza control large areas of the construction and entertainment industries, including movie studios, nightclubs and professional sports. About half of the Japanese mobs' income comes from drug traffic.

Unlike the American Mafia, the yakuza are accepted into Japanese society. Yakuza groups maintain offices that display the gangs' emblems on the front doors. Some yakuza members wear lapel pins similar to those worn by Rotarians and American fraternity brothers. Several large gangs publish their own newspapers and magazines. After a recent gang war, feuding leaders called a press conference to announce that the war was over and to apologize for any inconvenience to the public. The syndicates' stable social position is made even stronger by their alliance with Japan's nationalistic political right.

Yakuza Acceptance Rooted in Japanese Custom

The yakuza portray themselves as guardians of the nation's traditional values, moral descendants of Japan's noble warriors, the samurai. The public seems to accept the self-portrait as valid and see the gangsters as patriots and Robin Hoods rather than as gangsters.

The yakuza connection with the samurai begins in the 17th century when after centuries of civil strife, Ieyasu Tokugawa, the first great shogun (military ruler), unified the islands into a nation. A period of peace and isolation began for Japan, depriving 500,000 samurai of employment. Some samurai became merchants, some became civil servants and philosophers and some became bandits and organized themselves into groups called *hatamoto-yakko*.

To fend off attacks by *hatamoto-yakko,* young townsmen formed into opposing bands called *machi-yakko*. Many bands were brought together by shopkeepers, innkeepers or artisans. Others were rounded up by local construction bosses. All bands included homeless wanderers and some stray samurai.

The *machi-yakko* became folk heroes. Like most folk heroes, they owe most of their reputation to legend rather than deed. The modern-day yakuza, who see themselves as "honorable outlaws," consider the *machi-yakko* as spiritual ancestors.

Many observers believe that less illustrious members of the medieval underworld are the true ancestors of present-day yakuza. They are the *bakuto*, traditional gamblers, and the *tekiya,* street peddlers. In ancient Japan, the *bakuto* controlled vice in towns and along busy highways and the *tekiya* controlled it within the nation's markets and fairs. The Japanese police classify most yakuza members as either *bakuto* or *tekiya*. A third group, the *gurentai,* hoodlums, was added after World War II. The generic name yakuza is thought to have evolved from a losing combination, 8-9-3 (in Japanese, ya-ku-sa), in a gamblers' card game called *hanafuda* (flower cards).

The early *bakuto* groups dealt severely with those who broke the gangs' rules. Short of death, the heaviest punishment was expulsion. For serious violations that did not merit death or expulsion, the *bakuto* introduced the custom of *yubitsume,* a practice in which the top joint of the little finger was ceremoniously severed to make the sword hand weaker and hence more vulnerable. The custom spread to other crime groups and has increased in modern times. Sometimes the severed joint is amputated and presented by way of an apology. A

1971 governmental survey found that 42% of modern *bakuto* members have one severed finger joint and 10% have more than one.

The original *tekiyama* gained a well-deserved reputation for shoddy goods and deceptive sales techniques. Made up of the same types of marginal people as the *bakuto,* they attracted members of Japan's ancestral class of outcasts, the *burakumin,* who formed a class similar to the untouchables of India. In 1867 the *burakumin* numbered about 400,000 of Japan's 33 million people. The *tekiya* gangs offered the *burakumin* a path out of a life of abject poverty and disgrace.

Unlike the *bakuto,* the *tekiya* operations were by and large operated under legal status. Despite their legitimacy, the gangs nurtured crime, and since they were constantly on the move, they carried their various rackets into new territories, along with a network of wanted criminals.

The tattoo, another visible trademark of the modern yakuza, has a long history that stems from two customs. Japan has a noble tradition of tattooing remarkable designs that goes back as early as the 3rd century. A less gracious tradition was a practice by authorities of tattooing a black ring around the arm of an outlaw to distinguish him from the rest of society. Extensive tattooing that might take up to 100 hours came to be a symbol of strength and endurance.

Like other organized crime groups around the world, the early yakuza developed elaborate ceremonies to initiate new recruits into the organization. The ceremonies focused on a new member's prescribed duties within the group and demanded that the member pledge unswerving loyalty to the group for life.

Like the Italian Mafia, the yakuza organized in families with a boss at the top. New members were adopted to fill the roles of older brothers, younger brothers and children. Kaplan and Dubro discuss in detail the importance to the yakuza of a unique, widespread Japanese relationship known as *oyabun-kobun,* which means father role/child role. The *oyabun* is the provider of advice, protection and aid. In return, the *kobun* offers unswerving loyalty and service. Within the early yakuza gangs, the *oyabun-kobun* relationship created strength and cohesion, sometimes even fanatical devotion. Despite encroaching modernization, the *oyabun-kobun* relationship continues to foster a high level of loyalty, obedience and trust within the yakuza.

The *bakuto* in general and the traveling *bakuto* in particular became the basis of leading characters in a genre of Japanese literature, *matabi-mono* (stories of wandering gamblers), that has had great acceptance from the public since the turn of the century. The yakuza has capitalized on two virtues embodied in the *matabi-mono* stories, the virtue of *giri,* loyalty, duty, gratitude and debt, and the virtue of *ninjo,* human emotion or feeling. In the words of Kakuji Inagawa, perhaps the most powerful *oyabun* in Japan, ''The yakuza are trying to pursue the road to chivalry and patriotism. That's our biggest difference with the American Mafia, it's our sense of *giri* and *ninjo.* The yakuza try to take care of all society if possible, even if it takes one million yen to help a single person.''

Gangster Patriots

The yakuza has a long intricate relationship with Japan's political far right. Modern ultranationalism, Japan's reactionary, conservative political tradition, can be traced to the 1880s in Kyushu, the southernmost of the four major islands. Kyushu was the home of a large number of disgruntled ex-samurai, many of whom had taken part in rebellions against the new social order that began in 1867 when the shogun of the Tokugawa family was replaced by the young Emperor Meiji.

The Meiji Restoration transformed Japan from a feudal state into an industrial power. The era between 1890 and 1914 brought not only a doubling of the nation's industrial production but also the birth and growth of the first parliament and political parties and the growth of a powerful, autonomous military that invaded China, annexed Korea and in 1905 defeated Russia.

Discontent among ex-samurai in Kyushu was exploited by patriots and politicians critical of the new regime's corruption and disregard for tradition. The city of Fukuoka became a breeding ground for antigovernment thought. Out of Fukuoka emerged Misuru Toyama, a leader who joined the forces of crime and politics in a manner that persists to the present.

To control labor unrest, Toyama organized hoodlums into a disciplined work group and a fighting force. By handing out money to followers on the street, Toyama fostered a reputation as a local Robin Hood. Toyama's rise to national power in 1881 came with his founding of the Genyosha, the Dark Ocean Society, a forerunner of Japan's modern secret societies and patriotic groups. Under the guise of goals to defend the emperor, respect the nation and defend the people's rights, Toyama tapped into the sentiment of the ex-samurai for expansion abroad and authoritarian rule at home. Almost single-handedly, Toyama formed a patriotic social order to use as a paramilitary force within Japanese politics. Using terror, blackmail and assassination, the Dark Ocean Society influenced the military officer corps and the government bureaucracy and played a key role in sweeping Japan into East Asia and ultimately into war with the United States.

In the first large-scale cooperation between the rightists and the underworld, Toyama and his followers participated in 1892 in a new Japanese phenomenon, a national election, resulting in the bloodiest election in Japanese history. Genyosha's next successful operation was the creation of an incident in Korea that would serve as a pretext for Japanese troops to move in and stay for 50 years.

Following the Korean invasion, ultranationalism became a permanent part of Japanese politics. The Dark Ocean Society served as a model for the formation of hundreds of Japanese secret societies, which continue to blur distinctions between gangsters and ultranationalists.

The traditional yakuza groups had in common with the Genyosha and its successors a mystical world view that worshipped power, resented foreigners and foreign ideas (such as liberalism and socialism), revered a romanticized past, observed Shinto (the state religion) as the core of their belief systems and deified the emperor as a living Shinto god. Both groups were organized in a *oyabun-kobun* structure.

The bases of authority among the rightists and the gangsters have always been threatened by liberal and left-wing attacks on traditional society. With the emergence of a noticeable left and a labor movement at the turn of the 20th century, fear among the yakuza *oyabun* made them converts to ultranationalism.

In 1919, setting up a structure resembling his Dark Ocean Society of almost four decades earlier, Toyama, together with Takejiro Tokunami, minister of home affairs, created the Dai Nippon Kokusui-kai, a federation of 60,000 gangsters, laborers and ultranationalists. Under a vague banner of ancient Japanese values, the Kokusui-kai served as a massive, violent strikebreaking force comparable to Mussolini's Blackshirts in Italy.

Kokusui-kai evolved into the paramilitary arm of the Seiyu-kai, one of the two dominant parties of the day. The Seiyu-kai's principal opposition, the Minseito party, organized its own gangster force, the Yamato Minrokai, filled with yakuza drawn from construction gangs. The gangs became so well integrated with the parties that a few of the gangs' bosses ran successfully for seats in the Diet, Japan's parliament.

The 1920s represented the peak of Japan's prewar liberalism. In spite of a political climate fraught with assassinations, police repression and a renegade military, Japan prospered. The middle class expanded, labor

unions grew and universal suffrage was introduced. At the same time, Toyama's political power continued to expand.

By the 1930s rightist groups had multiplied. During the period from 1930 until the end of World War II, Japanese police recorded 29 rightist "incidents," including repeated attacks on leading politicians, resulting in the assassinations of two prime ministers and two finance ministers, and attempted coups by military officers and ultranationalists. As moderate politicians fell to assassination or withdrew from political life, the nation became destabilized and the practice of democracy virtually disappeared from Japan.

In 1937, before a crowd of 18,000, Toyama introduced the Japanese to their new prime minister, Prince Konoe. With many of Toyama's allies in power, Japan slid into a decade of repression known to many Japanese as the Dark Valley. A ruthless militarism organized every segment of society for the purpose of political regimentation and indoctrination. A Japanese sweep over the European colonies of Asia seemed to be at hand.

Yakuza groups aided the military by traveling to occupied Manchuria or China to take part in "land development" programs. Resource-rich Manchuria provided a windfall for the yakuza. A money-making scheme attractive to the gangs was participation in the Japanese government's Opium Monopoly Bureaus (modeled after the British colonial pattern of a century earlier) that fostered addiction as a highly lucrative method of weakening Manchurian public resistance.

For yakuza gangs that stayed at home, military expansion brought more money into Japan. After battles over contracts and territories among various yakuza gangs in the port city of Kobe, the Yamaguchi-gumi, under the leadership of Kazuo Taoka, emerged victorious. Over the next quarter century, Taoka transformed his waterfront gang into the largest yakuza syndicate in Japan, reaching a peak of 13,000 members in 36 of Japan's 47 prefectures (administrative subdivisions; provinces). Taoka became the godfather of Japanese crime.

About the same time Taoka was taking over the Japanese docks, the Lucky Luciano mob was taking over the Manhattan and Brooklyn waterfronts in New York City. While the American gangs went on to use the huge cash reserves generated by liquor sales during Prohibition to grow into national syndicates, the Japanese gangs tended to remain city or neighborhood gangs.

The bombing of Pearl Harbor changed life dramatically for the yakuza. The war had moved big business and the army as far to the right as they wished to go, and they no longer needed the rightists or gangsters as an independent force. Kazuo Taoka spent the war years in prison.

American Occupation Aids Resurgence of the Rightists

Kaplan and Dubro track America's complex role in bringing ultranationalists back to political power in Japan. While the assistant chief of the occupation's Government Section, Colonel Charles Kades, the principal architect of Japan's constitution, worried about the yakuza, American policy in regard to food rationing fostered a black market. The Americans disarmed the civilian police, allowing gangs to roam freely. However, an even more serious threat to Japanese democracy came from the active support by some occupation officials of gangs and their leaders.

Just below General Douglas MacArthur in the chain of command reigned General Courtney Whitney, who believed that the comprehensive plan for the occupation meant strengthening the Japanese left and inhibiting Japan's warmaking inclinations. By left he meant unions, liberals, socialists and Communists.

Opposed to Whitney was General Charles Willoughby, head of intelligence (G-2). Willoughby distrusted the Japanese left, Chinese and Soviet Communists and American liberals. He used G-2 to give aid, comfort, money and position to the Japanese ultranationalist right, the people Whitney and Kades were bent on removing from public life.

Whitney and Willoughby mirrored two factions represented in the U.S. Government in planning for the end of the war. The Roosevelt administration favored elimination of the emperor and a general suppression of Japanese nationalism. Opposed were American conservative business interests, which feared a leftist Japan and lobbied to keep Japan's socioeconomic structure more or less intact.

Although the occupation police failed to notice them, a new and far more ruthless type of *oyabun-kobun* group, the *gurentai*, was being formed, one that would serve as a model for most of the yakuza gangs to follow. One of the most visible *gurentai*, Akira Ando, received money, work and friendship from many high-ranking occupation officials, despite a conviction by a military court for possession of black market items.

American policy was not the only contributing factor in Japan's return to the right. As the April 1952 signing of a peace treaty with the United States to end the occupation drew near, the powerful Japanese minister of justice, Tokutaro Kimura, anticipated a leftist move toward power. He called together a group of influential rightists to discuss his fears. Worried that the Communists had infiltrated the Reserve Corps (the forerunner of the army), Kimura is alleged to have said, "Can't you call together men with common beliefs to fight desperately against the Communist Party, to preserve the national policy?"

Kimura's plea was alleged to have been answered by his henchman Nobu Tsuji: "Justice Minister, there is nobody who would risk their lives but gamblers, racketeers, and hoodlums . . . those who talk about theories are not useful when it actually comes to a fight. There are none but those fellows, who risk their lives for their bosses."

Though the details of the scene may have been exaggerated, a variety of historical sources have confirmed that such an event took place and that preparations to launch a 200,000-man force were made. While the effort by a government official to bring together ultranationalists was in itself remarkable, it was even more remarkable that Japan's highest-ranking law enforcement official would support bringing together scattered yakuza bands to form a single cohesive underworld force.

Kimura was only one of several ultranationalists in positions to wield great political influence in postwar Japan. Nobuake Kishi, held by the Americans as a Class A war criminal in Sugamo Prison, was mysteriously released from prison in December 1948 and entered politics in 1952. In 1955, with funds from the ultranationalists, the conservatives merged the Liberal Party with the Democratic Party to form the Liberal Democratic Party (LPD), which effectively held the Japanese Communist Party in check. Kishi became deputy prime minister of the LDP in 1955 and prime minister when the incumbent was forced to resign for health reasons after only three months.

In spite of substantial disorder, Japan's governments in the postoccupation years were essentially middle-of-the-road conservative. While the nation's archconservatives were unable to find strong grass-roots voter support for their causes in the postwar era, they maintained their power through old-line political bosses in the countryside and gangsters in the city.

New Yakuza Directions

In the early 1950s millions of people participated in the black markets and the *oyabun-kobun* rackets that flourished in the war's aftermath. Emerging rapidly from the ruins of World War II, Japan by 1968 had become the world's third largest economy. As economic conditions improved, many participants drifted away from the postwar rackets to less precarious occupations. Those who remained formed the core of a new yakuza empire.

As Japan made its economic recovery, gangs shifted from black market control of necessities to control of luxuries. During the war, Japan kept weary soldiers going on amphetamines, typically referred to as speed or uppers. During the occupation, amphetamines were stolen from military stores and sold to the general population. A lucrative market that over the years has fluctuated but persisted, amphetamines became a yakuza monopoly.

Before the war, many forms of prostitution were traditionally viewed as respectable in Japan and not the domain of gangsters. After the war ended, economic desperation prompted many families to sell women to the yakuza, who used them as prostitutes in the cities. When public solicitation and the management of prostitutes were outlawed in 1958, prostitution and nearly all organized vice fell into the hands of the yakuza and their associates. Sexual slavery became a high-profit source of income.

When the government legalized most forms of gambling to gain a source of revenue, the *bakuto* lost exclusive control of public gambling and turned their attention to vice, drugs and other businesses. As money and leisure made entertainment popular, the yakuza forced their way into theaters, cabarets, bars, restaurants and the burgeoning movie industry. They also exerted influence in professional sports ranging from sumo wrestling to baseball.

The Japanese Police

The Japanese police force prides itself on being the world's best, yet it has never satisfactorily explained how 100,000 gangsters can continue to thrive on the islands. Anthropologist Walter Ames, who spent 18 months doing field research with the Japanese police, reported that the gangs usually receive warnings before huge raids. To permit the police to save face, the gangsters usually leave behind a few guns to be confiscated.

An easy rapport exists between the local police and the local gangsters, who know each other by name. Like their criminal counterparts, the police have at best a high school education and come from families of modest means. Most Japanese police officers sympathize with the conservative views of the yakuza. Rigorous initial investigation of police recruits screens out anyone with left leanings. Like the yakuza, the police view themselves as latter-day samurai.

The amiable relationship between the police and the yakuza provides a bridge for police corruption. The Japanese political left has long accused the police of being easy on the yakuza's political activities on the right. The gangs respect the police and understand their duty to enforce the law. After a gangland murder, the guilty yakuza will usually turn himself in and confess, fully prepared to suffer the consequences.

Criminologist Eric Von Hurst, a longtime resident of Japan, described the yakuza as an alternative police force. He believes that the Japanese police are terrified of unorganized crime. There is little street crime because the gangsters control their turf and provide security.

Since the early 1970s an increasing number of journalists, lawyers and social scientists have raised questions about the continued existence of a 100,000-person underworld and the accuracy of police data. Kenji Ino, the author of 12 books on the yakuza and Japan's right wing, believes the police count of yakuza is wildly inaccurate. Their count includes only "registered yakuza" and leaves out rightist gangs, young thugs employed by the yakuza and other associates.

Despite the unwillingness of the Japanese police to believe that the yakuza might become a problem in the United States, in 1982 the Tokyo Metropolitan Police assigned Masanori Kita, a 20-year veteran, to the Japanese Consulate in Honolulu to serve as a liaison to local and federal police. Kita concluded that the yakuza in Hawaii are more of a problem for the Japanese than the Americans, because a great deal of the yakuza international activity involves smuggling guns and pornography back to Japan.

Briefly in the early 1980s U.S. official attitudes stiffened toward the yakuza in an effort to forestall their entrenchment in the United States. Customs officers in Hawaii were joined by Immigration and Naturalization Service (INS) agents and the Federal Bureau of Investigation (FBI) in a campaign to identify, prosecute and deport yakuza. However, by the spring of 1985 the crackdown petered out, a victim of budget cutbacks.

At the same time that budgets to combat the yakuza were being reduced, the U.S. House Committee on Foreign Affairs released a staff study entitled *U.S. Narcotics Control Programs Overseas: An Assessment.* The section on Japan said:

1. Japan is a likely transshipment point for narcotics: It is one of the commercial hubs of the region, has a huge organized crime network (the yakuza), and such a clean international image that U.S. Customs does no incoming cargo checks on shipments coming in from Japan.

2. It is impossible to know Japan's significance as a transit point for narcotics, due to lack of cooperation from the Japanese. The Japanese share very little narcotics intelligence with the United States, refuse to permit "controlled deliveries" through their territory, will not provide conviction records or their list of names of 100,000 known yakuza members, or other important information.

Expansion into Hawaii

Before and since World War II, the Japanese have found Hawaii a congenial spot for a vacation. In 1984 alone 814,000 Japanese spent $1 billion in the islands. Faced with the same problem of what to do with huge profits that plagues any highly successful criminal organization, the yakuza has invested heavily in Hawaii. Many Hawaiians are willing to sell whatever they have to sell to the yakuza for cash without asking any questions. By the mid-1980s the yakuza had invested over $100 million in the islands.

Japanese tourists tend to leave their inhibitions behind and indulge themselves while in Hawaii. Police estimate that at least 500 prostitutes are working in Honolulu at any one time. The Japanese tourists also provide a ready market for home-grown marijuana, a massive cottage industry generating as much as $600 million a year.

The yakuza has linked up with Hawaii's powerful crime figures, and the Hawaiian police believe that the Japanese gangs have become the second most powerful criminal syndicate in the state, right behind the native Hawaiians.

The major barriers that have blocked agreements between the yakuza and the American Mafia, which would have made it easier for the yakuza to operate on the U.S. mainland, have been cultural and linguistic. In order to do organized crime business, a level of trust must be established between the gangs that permits the exchange of several million dollars without a written contract. Since the 1970s Japanese mobsters have been visiting Las Vegas, a place where the two mobs have been able get together to eat, drink, gamble and have access to sex, as preliminaries to trust.

A possible consequence of a working alliance between the American Mafia and the yakuza would be an increase in international theft. One of the American Mafia's most substantial money sources is organized theft from New York's Kennedy International Airport and from the New York docks. Mob-controlled theft from cargoes between the United States and Japan could bring in billions.

In the view of Kaplan and Dubro, the yakuza do represent a threat to the United States. To succeed in the American market, the yakuza do not have to take over the country. They simply have to proceed with caution and ally themselves with the right people. In the authors' words, "By the time they succeed, the gangs will come to be regarded as part of the cost of doing business here, as they are in Japan."

APPENDIX 2. LIMITATIONS ON BEHAVIORAL SCIENCE IN STUDYING VIOLENCE

Scientific studies of human social behavior are sometimes referred to as behavioral sciences in order to include those areas, such as biology, that overlap the social sciences. The social sciences are often compared unfavorably with physical sciences such as chemistry and physics because they are necessarily less precise, dealing with human behavior, judgment and relations rather than with physical structures, physical laws or quantifiable measurements. Moreover, laboratory experiments tend to play a limited role in social science research.

There are other reasons, less obvious, for these unfavorable comparisons. Physical scientists, like social scientists and everyone else, participate in everyday social life in a community. They therefore are likely to feel that they already know everything there is to know about how daily life operates, and feel able to dismiss social science findings as "just common sense." Findings that disagree with prevailing common sense are dismissed as flawed, or not "real" science.

Because social scientists are immersed in social life and therefore affect it and are affected by it, experimental psychologist Julian Simon, in his classic 1969 text *Basic Research Methods in Social Science: The Art of Empirical Investigation*, asserted that social scientists struggle with problems not faced by other scientists. "A physicist rarely has to worry about his experiment being contaminated by his own bad mood on the day of the experiment, by the occurrence of a newspaper strike or a war that day or because of his having inadvertently given his subjects too much information."

Social science research tends to raise more questions than it answers. Results are seldom all-or-nothing. A new treatment method for sex offenders may work better than an old one 60% of the time, but such a finding raises the questions of why the new method does not work in 40% of the cases and whether the old method might be better in some cases.

Because of this inconclusiveness, which promotes dismissive attitudes toward social sciences as not "real" science, funding, both public and private, is only a fraction of what it is for physical (or "hard") sciences. As a consequence, a great deal of social science is done using what physical scientists call a "benchtop approach," that is, using whatever resources can be mobilized inexpensively: graduate students, friends, family or captive populations such as students or prisoners all become objects of study.

It is not possible for social scientists to propose hypotheses about most behaviors, particularly violent behaviors, and then set up laboratory conditions in order to systematically manipulate selected variables and thereby determine the accuracy of their hypotheses. With the exception of some who work with animals, social scientists interested in aggression in humans do not have the options available to biologists interested in aggression in animals. There are no laboratory humans, as there are rats.

Biologists can establish and manipulate a wide range of conditions. To mention only a few of the options, they can selectively breed rat litters for characteristics such as temperament; vary amounts of food supplies, affection or companionship; change environmental temperatures or amounts of light; inflict disease or trauma; or create "natural disasters," such as floods or cave-ins. Biologists can then compare the outcomes for the experimental animals with a matched control group that shares all the characteristics and conditions of the experimental group except for the manipulated variables.

The brief lifespan of rats means that biologists can know results within a relatively short time. Moreover, they can have multiple groups running at the same time under different experimental conditions. Short lifespan also makes it possible for biologists to do longitudinal studies over many generations. Social scientists seldom have the option of following individuals from birth to death or even for significant periods of time. One exception is an ongoing research project begun in the 1940s with 99 members of Harvard University's classes from 1939 to 1944 called the Study of Adult Development, which has followed the men's health and psychological status.

Even when it is possible, and ethical, to set up experimental conditions, it is not easy to find control groups that exactly match experimental groups. Social science problems usually involve more than one important variable, and they may be difficult, sometimes impossible, to separate. For example, juveniles without records of crime are usually found to come from families with more resources than those of juvenile offenders.

What will not be clear in such comparisons is what difference such environmental factors make to the behavior the researcher is examining. Perhaps the nonoffenders have committed offenses but have been shielded from police attention by their families' influence. Or perhaps the nonoffenders have not committed offenses because they had no need, or no opportunity, or their families have imparted to them a different set of values. (And under what conditions do such values take root?) The researcher has to minimize as many differences as possible between an experimental group and a control group; otherwise differences in results might be attributable to differences between groups rather than to experimental conditions.

Controversial Experiments

Research into human behavior is fraught not only with practical problems but also with ethical ones. For example, a social scientist interested in the study of violence associated with riots is not free to treat a crowd as a laboratory and start a riot to observe the sequence of events. Aside from the ethics of an act that might result in participants being maimed or killed, a social scientist as participant observer would have difficulty keeping an accurate record of events and might be harmed or face criminal charges.

Without the option of starting one, a social scientist interested in riots has to reconstruct the events of a real, spontaneous one after the fact, through news accounts, interviews with participants, police records and/or historical records, all of which are inadequate surrogates for the real thing. Accounts may be biased in various ways. By using multiple sources, a social scientist may be able to construct a balanced account—with luck.

On occasion, social scientists join gangs as participant observers to examine group behavior. The researchers often tell the gang their purpose, but such knowledge introduces the risk of the subjects' changing their behavior through self-consciousness, or by minimizing or exaggerating their deviance. Such research carries the risk of having the gang turn on the researcher. Moreover, it is open to criticism for participation in illegal behavior.

Besides such issues as ethics, social science research is often controversial because experiments with human subjects carry potential for long-range damage to the subjects. Most biomedical and social scientists have to explain the procedures and implications of their research to their subjects and have them sign consent forms. They also have to have their research plans reviewed and approved. Approval is made by designated groups known as either the "human subjects" or "ethics" committee of the medical school or university by which a researcher is employed. Many of these protective procedures came into use in the 1970s.

Some classic pre-1970s studies in aggression, if proposed now, would probably not be approved. Among such studies were those conducted by Muzafer and Carolyn Sherif, University of Oklahoma social psychologists.

The Sherifs began their work in 1949 at a time when it was widely believed that the principal sources of intergroup aggression were race or religious differences. They thought that cultural values, particularly beliefs in competition and self-advancement, were equally likely sources and set out to test whether the achievement of goals by one group at the expense of the other engenders hostilities, even though both groups are composed of similar socially and emotionally adjusted individuals.

The researchers established summer camps for children to which they brought 11- and 12-year-old boys from stable white Protestant families. During the first experiment, the campers were given several days to form friendships. Then they were separated from their new friends and sorted into two groups of about a dozen each called the Red Devils and the Bull Dogs. The two groups ate and slept separately and participated in activities designed to foster intragroup solidarity.

A series of contests brought the two groups into competition for prizes. A camping knife was promised to each member of whichever team won the overall competition. As the Red Devils fell behind in the competition, frustration and tempers mounted on both sides.

To add to frustrations, the experimenters staged a party with refreshments. They battered half of the cake and ice cream and made sure the losing Red Devils arrived first at the party to claim the unbattered treats. The late-arriving Bull Dogs were upset with the food left behind and insults were exchanged.

At lunch the following day, further insults were followed by the hurling of food and cutlery. Throughout the rest of the day the teams engaged in sporadic warfare using green apples as weapons. None of the researchers' attempts to restore cooperation had any effect until they arranged a competition with a team from a neighboring camp to provide the teams with a common enemy. In effect, to solve the problem of localized aggression, the researchers had to create a potential for hostilities on a larger scale—the whole camp against an external enemy.

Five years later, with two other groups in whom they had engendered hostility, the Sherifs tested the hypothesis that working together on a common endeavor promotes harmony. They created disasters in living conditions. The camp water supply broke down requiring the efforts of both groups to track down the problem and fix it, and the food truck got stuck, requiring both groups to haul it out with a rope. At the end of their stay, the two groups voted to go home together on the same bus.

Another classic but controversial investigation that probably would not meet the criteria of university human subjects or ethics committees today is Yale University psychologist Stanley Milgram's famous 1965 "Eichmann Experiment." Milgram set out to measure the obedience of subjects who were ordered by a legitimate authority to harm another human being.

Milgram told his volunteer subjects that they were testing the effects of punishment on learning. They were told to administer potentially injurious doses of electric shock to ostensible victims, who exhibited symptoms of distress and pain in response to the increases of the nonexistent shock.

Prior to the experiments, behavioral scientists had predicted that no more than 1 or 2 percent of the subjects, who were from a range of backgrounds—teachers, laborers, salespeople, clerks—would administer the highest level of shock. They were wrong. An astonishing 65% of the subjects did so. The basic experiment has been repeated in several countries with similar, usually even higher levels of conformity.

Nonlaboratory Methods

To cope with the obstacles presented by working with human subjects, social scientists have developed an array of techniques, each of which has its own limitations. Most empirical research in the social sciences can be characterized either as comparison problems or measurement problems. If a psychologist compares a treatment for prison inmates against a commonly accepted standard, then it is a measurement problem. If two treatment techniques are measured against each other, that is a comparison problem.

Comparison problems are often described as hypothesis-testing research, an approach that has dominated discussion of research in social science and has emphasized the use of statistics. But despite its dominance, it is only one of many possible approaches.

Patricia Kendall and Paul Lazarsfeld, masters of the art and science of conducting surveys, suggested that wariness of hypothesis-testing is often called for. They wrote in "Problems of Survey Analysis," a chapter in Robert Merton and Paul Lazarsfeld's 1950 text *Continuities in Social Research*, "Our thinking is rarely far enough progressed to enable us to start with a sharply formulated hypothesis; most studies are exploratory, directed toward the general examination of the field in order to develop theoretical formulations."

Documents, particularly public documents, provide a rich source of data for social scientists. For example, a social scientist might investigate the role domestic violence plays in divorce by examining divorce records. Such a search would be labor-intensive because of the many steps involved in obtaining the records and because of the time required to read them.

Many records might not mention domestic violence because there were no incidents or because the issue had been settled in negotiations prior to reaching court. To clarify the information, a researcher might follow up the document study by contacting those involved.

Documents also can be used to assess the cost/benefit ratio of social policy decisions. To assess the value of a mandatory five-year term imposed on every adult convicted of a violent crime, researchers collected data on a sample of offenders, including dates, types of offenses and prison time served. Then they determined whether each sample member would have been free at the time of his or her most recent crime if his or her sentence had been lengthened for a previous crime. The percentage of offenses that would have been thus prevented was calculated. Analysis of the findings suggested that if every defendant convicted of a violent felony in the United States were given a five year-sentence, the prison population would increase by 150% to produce an average reduction of 6% in adult violent crime.

Questionnaires are widely used, and have been under intense development since World War II. They can be administered in person, by mail or by telephone.

To conduct its National Crime Survey (NCS), the Bureau of Justice Statistics of the U.S. Department of Justice draws a representative sample of U.S. households in a complex multistage process. Each housing unit is in the sample for three years, during which seven interviews take place at six-month intervals. The first and fifth interviews are in person. The other five are by telephone. About 62,700 housing units were included in the 1986 sample and about 97,000 people were interviewed.

The use of telephones can save money but introduces a bias against low-income households. In suburban areas where about 95% of households have phones, the bias would be small, but in some rural areas, as many as 40% to 50% of households might be without telephones. Telephone surveys, of course, also leave out the homeless.

An interviewer has to avoid leading a respondent toward an answer by her manner or voice inflection, and the designer of the questionnaire has to avoid leading the respondent by the words and phrasing of questions. A respondent does not have to be able to read a written questionnaire. It can be read aloud.

A substantial amount of what is known about criminal behavior has come from surveys of inmates using questionnaires. Such surveys have revealed that sex offenders generally have committed many more offenses than the crimes for which they have been arrested or incarcerated. The limitation of such surveys is that some respondents lie, either by denying crimes or by exaggerating them, and some have faulty memories.

The development of a questionnaire requires that a social scientist already know something about the target population in order to ask appropriate questions. Sometimes a social scientist may have to spend time with a group, simply observing, before creating a questionnaire. Formal or informal interviews are a time-honored method used by social scientists, particularly when little is known about an area under scrutiny. Interviews may provide a basis to develop a questionnaire or they may be used in conjunction with a questionnaire.

Descriptive Research

Descriptive research is usually the starting point of new areas of study. Sigmund Freud's case history "Miss Anna O" and similar histories of patients laid a foundation for many modern clinical practices in psychiatry and psychology. Much anthropological research sets out to create a rounded description of a culture.

Ronald Holmes, professor of criminal justice at the University of Louisville, created descriptive profiles of violent crimes by examining more than 100 homicide and rape cases submitted to him by police agencies. To go beyond the submitted cases and to create a training aid for law enforcement personnel, he interviewed and corresponded with many murderers, rapists and others who had committed violent personal crimes, asking them questions about their crimes, motivations and methods.

Path-breaking descriptive research begins with no guidelines, no standards and no intellectual framework. The researcher must use concepts borrowed from other fields and frame them using ordinary language. He or she must decide what to look at, what is important or valueless, what to record or leave out and what to follow up on.

Classification

Once descriptive research provides some data, it may be possible to begin classification. Classification sorts out collections of people, behaviors or characteristics and makes it possible to coin names that researchers can use to talk about such phenomena. Sometimes the sorting comes first followed by classifications called taxonomies, and sometimes the order is reversed. An 18th-century achievement that demonstrates the value of classification is the work of Swedish botanist Carolus Linnaeus, who developed a scheme that sorts the entire plant world and reveals family relationships of various species.

Although considerable research has been done on violence and aggression, there is a lack of agreement about terms and definitions. The field lacks a widely accepted basic theory to help organize research.

Although criminal violence includes a heterogeneous array of behaviors, it is a subcategory of a larger general category, aggression. The taxonomic problems presented by the study of violence are discussed by Florida

State University correctional psychologist Edwin Margargee in "Psychological Determinants and Correlates of Criminal Behavior" included in *Criminal Violence* (1982), edited by sociologist Marvin Wolfgang and criminologist Neil Alan Weiner, both of the University of Pennsylvania.

About a definition of violence, Margargee wrote, "Most of us think we know exactly what it means; the problem is that our definitions may not agree with anyone else's."

Many issues intrude on the development of a precise definition of aggression. The issue of "intentionality" focuses on whether aggressors have a reasonable expectation that their behavior would hurt the victims and whether injury was desired by the aggressors. Another issue is whether the victims were actually injured, despite the intent of the aggressors to inflict injury.

Psychological injury is a particularly controversial issue. It raises questions about whether verbal disparagement, scolding, coercion and sexual harassment should be considered aggression. Few researchers in criminal violence study the impact of obscene phone calls, blackmail, extortion and sexual coercion, although they undoubtedly do inflict injury on their victims.

Another issue is whether acts of omission such as the failure of neighbors to telephone the police when a victim is calling for help should be considered violence. Omission is often a factor in corporate crime. Omission was central in the criminal prosecution of the Ford Motor Company's failure to correct design flaws in the placement of the Ford Pinto fuel tank that resulted in many deaths. A jury in February 1978 ordered Ford to pay $125 million in punitive damages, later reduced by a judge to $3.5 million.

The term violence usually is reserved for more extreme forms of aggressive behavior that are likely to cause substantial or critical injury to the victim. The National Commission on the Causes and Prevention of Violence defined violence as the "overtly threatened or overtly accomplished application of force which results in the injury or destruction of persons or property or reputation, or the illegal appropriation of property. Inclusion of the word threatened permits classification as violent behavior that fails in an attempt to injure the victim."

Aggression is often classified into two categories, instrumental and emotional. Instrumental aggression seeks a goal or a reward and is not necessarily accompanied by anger. Instrumental aggression is a street gang's call for action or a nation's mobilization for war or a paid assassin's cool planning of a murder.

Emotional aggression is a response to pain, threat, frustration or provocation, imagined or real. It is accompanied by physical reactions, which are the result of stimulation by hormones that cause the heart to pump faster, bringing additional blood to the face and oxygen to the muscles, cause the palms to sweat and, if not controlled, result in an aggressive act.

Generalizability

A problem faced by social scientists who study human behavior is whether their findings from small samples are generalizable to larger populations. For example, Milgram's experiments in the laboratory are seemingly milder forms of aggression. Thus they raise the question of whether they can be generalized to more extreme forms of aggressive behavior thought of as violent.

Studies of inmates raise questions about whether they accurately represent the larger population of criminals. They may represent a segment of the total population not bright enough to avoid being caught. On the other hand, they may represent a segment of the population bright enough to have escaped being killed in the practice of their profession.

Convictions in a court or jurisdiction may reflect the prejudices of the local police, prosecutors or judges, and not the particular behavior of the criminals. Highly sophisticated mathematical procedures have helped social scientists to sort out many of these distinctions, but the original research has to be well designed and well executed, or it succumbs to the fatal flaw known as GIGO (garbage in, garbage out).

Choices of Subjects

Any researcher has to focus on a given area in the vast range of behavior available to be studied. Much of the work done on violence has been connected with research into crime, in which the emphasis has been on crime, mostly street crime, rather than on violence.

With rare exceptions, such as attorney Russell Mokhiber's descriptive work *Corporate Crime and Violence: Big Business Power and the Abuse of the Public Trust* (1988), corporate crime is seldom studied. The reasons are varied. Corporate crime is seldom prosecuted. The connection between such a crime and the violence it inflicts is more indirect. A corporation is made up of individual managers, creating complexities in criminal law about who can be charged with intent. Prosecutors, judges, researchers and corporate criminals are likely to belong to the upper-middle socioeconomic class and have similar lifestyles. The dearth of corporate criminals to be studied, their absence from prison even when convicted and a researcher's identification with them may generate a belief that violence lies elsewhere.

The Role of Theories

Theories provide a framework for research and suggest avenues to be explored. Because violence is so pervasive and includes such diverse behaviors as assaults, domestic violence, infanticide, street gang activities, self-mutilation, ritualized violence, violent sports and wars, to name a few, theories that encompass all behaviors have to be broad. Theories about the origins of violence have abounded over the centuries. Aggression has been attributed to witches, demons, the position of the stars and physical defects, including mental disorders, faulty genes and brain trauma.

Some theories have been more persuasive than others. Darwin's 19th-century theory of evolution proposed that violence served a useful purpose by enabling the fittest to survive. The idea that aggression was biologically necessary was embraced not only by early psychologists but also by policymakers in support of war. Early in the 20th century, at a time when Asians were assumed to be more peaceful than Europeans, British psychologist William McDougall proposed that white Europeans were biologically more aggressive than Asians—and hence presumably more fit to survive.

Acceptance of a theory of innate aggression received a boost from Austrian zoologist Konrad Lorenz's 1971 book *On Aggression.* Lorenz proposed that the strongest male overpowers other males to get the most desirable female and to pass on his genes. He also proposed that animals fight over territory to ensure an ample food supply and also fight to establish a dominance structure.

Lorenz likened aggression to steam rising in a kettle that has to be drained off lest it explode, a theory known as the hydraulic model of aggression. A great number of animal studies have suggested that while a capacity for violence may be inborn, its overt expression tends to depend on situations in the environment.

Evidence that males are more violent than female suggests that aggression is partly innate. But apart from the sex difference, there is little evidence that aggressiveness is genetically determined. Nevertheless, the pendulum swings back and forth between the two viewpoints. Social scientists lean toward the idea that violence is learned because there are striking differences

among cultures about whether violence is encouraged or suppressed.

Theories inspire research. In their 1977 book *Violence and Aggression,* Ronald Bailey and the editors of Time-Life Books proposed that four ingredients generally are present in most acts of human aggression—arousal, trigger, weapon and target.

Arousal refers to physical changes such as increased heart rate, flushed face, accelerated breathing, clammy hands and feelings that occur in consequence of pain or frustration, or in response to expressions of aggression. The trigger may be a chance remark by a bystander or a stop in the flow of traffic, an occurrence completely removed from the source of the arousal, but serving to convert emotional arousal into an act of aggression. The weapon used may be a sharp tongue, a fist, a gun, a club or even a car. Targets are the recipients of aggression and sometimes trigger it merely by exhibiting attributes such as gender or socioeconomic status. A substantial body of social science research has examined various aspects of these four ingredients.

Collective behavior theories suggest that violence is more likely to happen in groups and violence between groups tends to be more volatile than between individuals. Participation in a group seems to intensify feelings, which are more likely to be translated into action. Group membership also confers a measure of anonymity.

Theories also have an impact on social policy. The idea that inmates could be rehabilitated inspired the growth of prisons (''correctional'' institutions) throughout most of the 20th century. In the 1970s a public notion that crime had gotten out of hand and that criminals were being coddled inspired a movement toward a retributive model of imprisonment which in turn led to the overcrowding of prisons. High costs and overcrowding are leading toward a community surveillance model, keeping criminals out of prison but under intense supervision.

There are two major theories about how to deal with aggression. One stems from the view that aggression is innate and is linked to the catharsis theory of Freud or the hydraulic theory of Lorenz. This view holds that aggressive feelings have to be let out in some form, through direct aggression or through socially accepted outlets such as violent sports or entertainment. A need for catharsis is a premise that underlies much psychotherapy.

The other view holds that aggression can be prevented and controlled. A great deal of research suggests that verbal aggression does not reduce hostility. Some experiments suggest that it may even have the opposite effect. One prevention and control approach involves changing the conditions that arouse anger. The other identifies techniques that nullify anger before it can be expressed. These include allowing the aggressor time to cool off, offering recompense and a willingness to share the aggression in a manner that shames the aggressor into repressing his or her anger. The techniques developed by Mohandas Gandhi and Martin Luther King, Jr. support the notion that nonviolence, like violence, can be learned. Much remains to be learned.

APPENDIX 3. RESOURCES

A. PREVENTION

ACTION
The Federal Domestic Volunteer Agency
Washington DC. 20525
(202) 606-5108

Primary federal volunteer organization. ACTION provides a variety of volunteer opportunities for people of all backgrounds. Is the umbrella agency for ACTION Drug Prevention Program; Foster Grandparent Program; National Center for Service Learning; Office for Voluntarism Initiatives; Retired Senior Volunteer Program; Senior Companion Program; Volunteers in Service to America (VISTA); Young Volunteers in Action.

Alliance of Guardian Angels, Inc.
982 East 89th Street
Brooklyn NY 11236
(718) 649-2607

Founded in 1979. A nonprofit, all-volunteer organization whose purpose is to prevent crime and to provide role models for young people. Has chapters in 67 American, Canadian and Mexican cities. Minimum age is 16. Oldest member is 80. In red berets and T-shirts, unarmed members patrol mass transit systems, shopping mall parking lots, rock concerts and drug-infested public parks and streets. Provides self-defense demonstrations and speakers for a no-weapons, no-drug policy.

Big Brothers/Big Sisters of America
230 North 13th Street
Philadelphia PA 19107
(215) 567-0394

The movement began at the turn of the century, when concerned citizens organized to stem the tide of juvenile delinquency. Over time, the approach shifted to prevention. The first national Big Brothers and Big Sisters Federation organized in 1917 and disbanded in 1937, a victim of the Great Depression. A national Big Brothers

Federation organized in 1945, followed in 1970 by an international Big Sisters Federation. The two organizations merged in 1977. Approximately 15 million children grow up in single-parent families, most of which are female-headed. An estimated one fifth have no relative to provide emotional support. One benefit of Big Brothers or Big Sisters is that they are non-relatives who value the child. For them Big Brothers/Big Sisters fills the gap with volunteers matched to their needs. There are not enough volunteers; nearly 40,000 children wait to be matched. Minority volunteers are especially needed.

Center on Human Policy
Syracuse University
200 Huntington Hall, 2nd floor
Syracuse NY 13244-2340
(315) 443-3851

Founded in 1971. A university-based policy, research and advocacy organization involved in the movement to ensure the rights of people with disabilities. Studies and promotes open integrated settings for the disabled. Uses a wide range of advocacy strategies: legislation, letter-writing, community education and monitoring. Fosters and implements model programs. Publishes a variety of books and pamphlets. Has an independent press, the Human Policy Press. Developed material for national television show *Feeling Free*. Provides technical assistance.

Center for Nonviolent Communication
3326 East Overlook Road
Cleveland Heights OH 44118
(216) 371-1123

Founded by psychologist Marshall Rosenberg, who presents workshops around the world to demonstrate the choices available in communication. Puppets are often used to illustrate. A "jackal" models disagreeable, demanding or difficult communication. The vulnerable giraffe "sticks his neck out" to get what he wants. Emphasizes compassion as motivation for action rather than blame, guilt, shame, fear or coercion. Workshop participants learn how to make clear requests and to avoid taking critical messages personally. Workshops emphasize personal responsibility.

Center to Prevent Handgun Violence
1225 I Street NW, Suite 1100
Washington DC 20005
(202) 289–7319

Founded in 1983. Works to prevent handgun violence through education, legal action and research. Formed a coalition with the nation's top law enforcement officials, medical/health leaders, educators, attorneys, entertainers and the news media to promote prevention. The coalition examines how handgun violence happens, determines which groups are most at risk and develops programs to reduce the risk.

Coalition to Stop Gun Violence
100 Maryland Avenue NE
Washington DC 20002-5625
(202) 544-7190

Coalition of 34 national, religious, professional and civic organizations concerned about gun violence, including such groups as the American Association of Suicidology, the Pan American Trauma Association, the Central Conference of Rabbis and the U.S. Conference of Mayors. Gathers and disseminates facts about guns. Tracks legislation. Brings witnesses and experts to Washington for hearings and press conferences. Goal is to ban the manufacture and sale of guns to private individuals, with exceptions.

Educational Information and Resource Center (EIRC)
700 Hollydell Court
Sewall NJ 08080
(609) 582-7000

Originated in the 1970s with the Federal Bureau of Investigation concept, "crime resistance," later "crime prevention." Developed TIPS, "Teaching Individual Protective Strategies," or "Teaching Individual Positive Solutions." Goals are to help students meet responsibilities to assist in ensuring their own safety and that of others and to promote and maintain positive student attitudes and behavior. Encourages students to reduce conflict and crime and to find positive solutions to conflict. Program begins in kindergarten and continues through eighth grade with systematic and sequential teaching units.

Fortune Society
39 West 19 Street
New York NY 10011
(212) 206-7070

Founded in 1967 by ex-offenders and concerned citizens to educate the public about prisons and criminal justice issues; to provide ex-offenders with support and services necessary to break the cycle of crime and incarceration. Educates the public through its speaker's bureau. Mails free of charge *The Fortune News* to inmates and sponsors throughout the country. Free services include counseling, career development and tutoring. More than 100 volunteers from all walks of life participate. Often functions as an extended family. Views itself on the cutting edge of society's most challenging problems— race and class, substance abuse, hard-core unemployment, crime and the ability to live peaceably in a free society.

Foster Grandparent Program (FGP)
c/o ACTION
Washington DC 20525
(202) 606-4849

Began in 1965 as 21 demonstration projects. Volunteers were initially assigned to work with young children in different types of institutions: pediatric hospital wards and publicly supported homes for orphans, the mentally retarded or the emotionally disturbed. The premise was that older Americans had love and experience to share with children in need of it. The program now includes disabled and chronically ill children; teen parents in need of parenting; boarder babies; preschool intervention; substance abuse; homeless children; abused children; and illiteracy. To serve in FGP, a volunteer must be at least age 60, have a low income, no longer be in the regular work force and be capable of serving children with exceptional or special needs 20 hours a week, usually spread over five days. Volunteers are paid a stipend. In addition, transportation, a meal, liability insurance and an annual physical are provided. Some volunteers have worked in the program as long as 25 years. There are more than 270 FGP projects, with approximately 20,000 Foster Grandparents.

Habitat for Humanity, International, Inc.
121 Habitat Street
Americus GA 31709-3498
(912) 924-6935

Builds houses for the poor using volunteer labor. Purpose is to further the goal of eliminating inadequate and poverty housing as a witness to the gospel of Jesus Christ and to raise awareness of this work. Has 15 centers in the United States, two in Canada and one in Australia. Has sponsored projects in 29 countries. Premise is that building a better habitat is working for justice and eventual peace in the world. Has individual and group members. Has campus chapters. Thousands of students from 100 schools spend their spring breaks working with affiliates.

Illusion Theater Prevention Program
528 Hennepin Avenue, Suite 704
Minneapolis MN 55403
(612) 339-4944

Begun in 1977 as a collaboration with the Hennepin County Attorney's Child Sexual Abuse Prevention Program, it creates plays for children, adolescents and adults around difficult, controversial social issues. Tours nationally. Among its productions are *Touch,* about acceptable and unacceptable ways for adults to touch children; *No Easy Answers,* about adolescent sexuality and sexual abuse; *For Adults Only,* about sexuality and violence; and *Family,* a musical about family and interpersonal violence.

Institute to Reduce Human Violence Through
   Religious Studies
499 National Press Building
Washington DC 20045
(202) 783-6553

Founded by Jules Bernfield of Alexandria, Virginia. Dedicated to the idea that violence offends God. Defines violence as nations at war with one another, neighbors in conflict and clashes among ethnic, social and racial group values that erupt into bloodshed. Principles: clergy should have the option to not minister to those prone to violence; members cannot do violence to one another; clergy should not accept rank or pay from the military.

Laubach Literacy of Canada
P.O. Box 6548
Station A
Saint John NB E2L 4R9
Canada
(506) 634-1980

Incorporated in 1981, is the Canadian affiliate of Laubach Literacy International. Runs literacy programs teaching adults to read and write on a one-to-one basis.

American affiliate is Laubach Literacy Action, 1320 Jamesville Avenue, Box 131, Syracuse NY 13210.

Literacy Volunteers of America, Inc. (LVA)
5795 Widewaters Parkway
Syracuse NY 13214
(315) 445-8000

Founded 1962. Developed a program for tutoring adults and teenagers in basic reading and writing. In 1974 began developing English as a Second Language program. Has developed the *Tutoring Small Groups Handbook.* In collaboration with Head Start, provides literacy instruction for Head Start parents. Also works with older adults. Number of affiliates exceeds 350.

Milton S. Eisenhower Foundation
17251 I Street NW, Suite 504
Washington DC 20006
(202) 429-0440

Based on the idea that the "reconstruction" tradition represented by the Kerner Commission (the President's National Advisory Commission on Civil Disorders) and the Eisenhower Commission (National Commission on the Causes and Prevention of Violence) were even more relevant for the 1980s than they had been for the 1960s. A private sector version of the Eisenhower Commission, the foundation has worked since 1981 to reduce urban violence through youth empowerment programs, community revitalization, and grass-roots action. Has financially supported, technically assisted and carefully evaluated more than 30 local programs nationwide. Particularly successful in assisting neighborhood organizations in continuing crime prevention after initial funding. Creates local ownership of programs, through a "bubble-up," grass-roots approach. Converts street-level program outcomes into national level policy recommendations. Began a Social Development Corporation to provide technical assistance to governments, community organizations and the private sector.

National Assault Prevention Center
P.O. Box 02005
Columbus OH 43202
(614) 291-2540

Two divisions, the Child Assault Prevention Project (CAP) for children and the Assault Prevention Training Project (APT) for adults, work to prevent interpersonal violence through curriculum development, research and evaluation, public education and training. More than 220 CAP projects nationwide provide service to more than a million children, parents and teachers. CAP published *Strategies for Free Children: A Leader's Guide to Child Assault Prevention.* Offers prevention services, does research and provides workshops for persons with disabilities and in-service training for staffs, significant others and community people.

National Association of Town Watch, Inc. (NATW)
P.O. Box 303
Wynnewood PA 19096
(215) 649-7055

Founded in 1981. Dedicated to the development of organized, law enforcement-affiliated crime and drug prevention activities. Members include neighborhood, community, town, block and crime watch groups; law enforcement agencies; state and regional crime prevention associations; and a variety of interested individuals, civic groups and businesses. Sponsors annual "National Night Out" each year on an evening in August to promote crime and drug prevention activities, strengthen police relations and encourage neighborhood camaraderie. Publishes quarterly newsletter, *New Spirit.* Alerts national media to local community crime prevention strategies.

National Coalition on Television Violence (NCTV)
Monitoring and Newsletter Office
P.O. Box 2157
Champaign IL 61825-2157
(217) 384-1920

Founded in 1980. Primary goal to reduce glamorized violence on TV. Over 3,300 members and associated endorsers. Focus has been on prime time and Saturday mornings. Activities include contacting, monitoring and boycotting advertisers and TV stations. Also studies violence in other entertainment media such as films and video games, and the glamorization of alcohol, tobacco, illicit drug use and degrading sexual portrayals. Offers members a monthly newsletter, *NCTV NEWS,* and guidance on protesting glamorized violence.

National Committee for Prevention of Child Abuse
  (NCPCA)
332 S. Michigan Avenue, Suite 1600
Chicago IL 60604-4357
(312) 663-3520

Founded in 1972. Committed to reducing child abuse; informing concerned citizens; making child abuse prevention services available to all parents and children. Has done an annual nationwide public service media campaign, including public service announcements on television and radio, in newspapers, consumer magazines, business and trade journals and transit and outdoor advertising displays. Observes April as Child Abuse Prevention month. Dedicated to cost-effective prevention programs. Community-based programs include support programs for new parents; parent support and self-help groups; prevention education and life skills training for children and young adults; programs for abused children and young adults to minimize the longer-term effects of abuse and reduce the likelihood of their becoming abusive parents. Does advocacy and engages in research and evaluation. Works in 50 states and the District of Columbia.

National Crime Prevention Council (NCPC)
Information and Referral Services
1700 K Street NW, 2nd floor
Washington DC 20006
(202) 466-6272

Best known for McGruff, a gravel-voiced cartoon dog detective wearing a rumpled raincoat, who says "Take a bite out of crime." Funded by a variety of federal and private sources. Handles thousands of requests for information each year from law enforcement officers, teachers and community organizers about how to start up and maintain a crime prevention program. Maintains the computerized Information Center, the most comprehensive data base of crime prevention activities in the United States, and the Resource Center, which contains 1,000 books and reports, along with an extensive collection of brochures, articles and promotional materials gathered from local crime prevention programs across the country.

National Trust for the Development of African Men
908 Pennsylvania Avenue SE
Washington DC 20003
(202) 543-2407

Goal is to enfranchise African-American men, using the perspective of the rich African-American history and culture that predates modern history and the settling of the New World. Focus is on young people, but recognizes the need to maintain a cadre of African-American adults to serve as teachers and mentors. Operates three training institutes—Leadership Development, Teacher Training and Youth Entrepreneurs.

Network of Educators on Central America (NECA)
1118 22 Street NW

Washington DC 20037
(202) 429-0137

Provides classroom resources for grades K–12. Provides teacher training in the history, economy and cultural traditions of Central America, including strategies for teaching Central American students and for teaching about the region. Offers educators tours to Central America. Develops programs to build relationships and to promote cross-cultural understanding between North and Central America. Publishes quarterly *Central America in the Classroom*. Promotes the *Human Rights Emergency Response Network* on behalf of teachers because organizing and teaching are considered subversive in many places and teachers have been killed or have disappeared.

People Organized to Stop Rape of Imprisoned Persons
P.O. Box 632
Ft. Bragg CA 95437
(707) 964-0820

Monitors prison rape and acts as a support group for survivors. Advocates the separation of vulnerable prisoners from violent ones, as is done in the San Francisco Jail; penalties for prison officers who rape prisoners; greater vigilance on the part of prison officers to prevent rape.

POSITIVE, INC.
11125 SW 156th Terrace
Miami FL 33157
(305) 252-1249

Founded in 1988 by Miami Mayor Xavier Suarez with the aim of developing real alternatives and solutions to the growing problem of street gangs. Offers education, counseling and career training. Focus is on intervention, prevention and rehabilitation. To participate, a youth must be in school or employed. Provides leisure activities including sports, culture and the arts. Gang members are referred to alternative schools and to POSITIVE, INC.'s meetings.

Quest for Peace (a program of the Quixote Center)
P.O. Box 5206
Hyattsville MD 20782-0206
(301) 699-0042
Bulk shipments to:
Quest for Peace
c/o Condor Warehouse
44880 Falcon Place, Unit 113
Sterling VA 22170

Begun in 1984 to provide humanitarian aid to the rural poor of Nicaragua, working with the independent Institute of John XXIII on the Campus of the University of Central America. Aid is now in the form of thousands of developmental projects, in which communities set their own priorities, such as feeding programs, vegetable growing, potable water and medical supplies. Founded in the spring of 1986, Project Clean Your Desk enlisted the aid of 100 schools. By 1990 more than 200 schools and other groups had joined and the project was renamed School Supplies for Nicaragua. The austerity program of the new government imposed "user fees" on books and school supplies, threatening to prevent tens of thousands of rural children from attending school. Nicaragua is a country of children; the average age is 15 (in the United States it is 31).

Quixote Center
P.O. Box 5206
Hyattsville MD 20782-0206
(301) 699-0042

Sponsors: Quest for Peace, sending supplies and development funds to Nicaragua each month, and supports the Mothers of Matagalpa development model. Potters for Peace, supporting potters' cooperatives in Nicaragua. Priests for Equality, working toward gender equality in language and symbol. Search for Justice, working to cut off war-related aid to El Salvador. Equal Justice, U.S.A., monitoring human rights violations in the United States.

Sex Addicts Anonymous (S.A.A.)
P.O. Box 3038
Minneapolis MN 55403
(612) 339-0217

A fellowship of men and women who share their experience, strength and hope with others in order to recover from sexual addiction or dependency. Common goal is to become sexually healthy and to help others do the same. Modeled after the 12-step program of Alcoholics Anonymous but is not affiliated with any other 12-step program. Has a variety of tapes, books and pamphlets, including a brochure that offers a self-assessment, a reading list and a brief explanation of the cycle of sexual addiction.

VISTA
c/o ACTION
Washington DC 20525
(202) 606-4849

Established in 1964, Volunteers In Service to America (VISTA) is the oldest ACTION program. Goal is to alleviate the impact of poverty. Volunteers live and work among the poor, serving in urban and rural areas and on Indian reservations. More than half of VISTA's programs are youth-oriented and address such problems as child abuse, drug use prevention, runaways, illiteracy and lack of job skills.

Volunteer House
University of Puget Sound
1500 North Warner
Tacoma WA 98416
(206) 756-4044

Six students formed Volunteer House. The students, who live together in campus-owned housing, are committed to serving as volunteers and encouraging other students to do the same. They work in a mentoring program for at-risk students, a literacy program and a kitchen for homeless people. They promote volunteerism through a newsletter, speeches in dormitories, public meetings and posters.

B. CHILDREN

American Bar Association Center on Children and the
    Law
1800 M Street NW, Suite 200S
Washington DC 20036-5886
(202) 331-2250

Founded in 1979. Is a project of the ABA Young Lawyer's Division. Mission is to improve the quality of life for children through advancements in law, justice and public policy. Services include publications on liability, child abuse and neglect, child support, foster care, adoption, drugs, children and family issues and education; consultation to attorneys and other professionals; training of attorneys and child welfare workers; reduction of delays in case terminations; improved attorney/caseworker coordination; curriculum for Child Protective Service workers; policy analysis; conferences. Publishes monthly *ABA Juvenile and Child Welfare Reporter*.

ACLU's Children's Rights Project
132 West 43rd Street
New York NY 10036
(212) 944-9800

A national program of litigation, advocacy and education designed to insure that when governments intervene in the lives of troubled families and children that appropriate services and treatment are provided. Project also seeks to ensure that when the state must remove a child from its biological parents, an alternative, permanent placement be arranged as soon as possible. Has filed suits against several states and the District of Columbia to remedy inadequate child welfare systems, particularly troubled foster care systems.

Adam Walsh Child Resource Center
319 Clematis Street, Suite 409
West Palm Beach FL 33401
(407) 833-9080

Dedicated to the prevention of child abuse, abduction and exploitation. Provides direct assistance to families of missing and exploited children. Ensures that families' legal rights are protected and that public exposure is given to cases as needed. Has identified ten model child protection statutes. Develops programs to prevent crimes against children.

American Association for Protecting Children
(A Division of The American Humane Association)
63 Inverness Drive East
Englewood CO 80112-5117
(303) 792-9900

(800) 227-5242

Purpose is to improve the capability of public and private agencies to respond effectively to child abuse and neglect. Offers consultation and technical assistance to public sector child protective services nationwide. Does not work directly with children and families. Publishes books and a quarterly magazine, *Protecting Children*. Responds to requests for information on child abuse and neglect through toll-free access 1-800-2 ASK AHA.

American Counseling Association (ACA)
Affiliate of the International Association of Addictions
    and Offender Counselors (IAAOC)
5999 Stevenson Avenue
Alexandria VA 22304
(703) 823-9800

Founded in 1974. Membership is interdisciplinary and includes counseling professionals in the related fields of addictions treatment and public offender rehabilitation. Involved in such areas as drug/alcohol abuse, codependency, gambling, relationships/sexual dependencies, adult and juvenile offender rehabilitation, vocational rehabilitation and school settings. Publishes IAAOC Newsletter six times a year, ACA newspaper 18 times a year, *Journal of Addictions and Offender Counseling* biannually. Offers a legal defense counsel service. Holds an annual convention. Lobbies on counseling issues.

Canadian Society for the Prevention of Cruelty to
   Children
356 First Street, Box 700
Midland ONT L4R 9Z9
Canada
(705) 534-4350

Publishes the quarterly journal *Empathic Parenting* for professionals, parents and others concerned about the emotional abuse of children. Supports strengthening the emotional bond between parent and child. Creates and distributes booklets and videotapes for use in schools to give boys and girls an appreciation of the issues related to parenting, before they are physically able to conceive children. Speaks to groups about the rights of children.

Center on War and the Child
P.O. Box 487
35 Benton Street
Eureka Springs AR 72632
(501) 253-8900

Founded in 1987 to inform, educate and involve the public concerning the militarization of children and their victimization by war. Promotes nonviolent social change by challenging social factors and institutions that condition children to accept violence and militaristic solutions to conflict. Publications include *WarChild Monitor* (newsletter), *Networks,* Associates newsletter, Center Updates, Action Alerts, and Summary Reports.

Child Find Canada
3150 5th Avenue NW
Calgary ALTA T2N 4S3
Canada
(403) 270-3463
(800) 387-7962

Founded 1983. Not-for-profit organization funded through private and corporate donations. Volunteers run programs. Services are free to parents. Purpose: to aid in the location of missing and/or abducted children and to help reunite them with their legal guardians; to prevent through education the abduction of children and situations in which children run away. Has affiliates in eight provinces of Canada.

Child Find (Ontario) Inc.
345 Lakeshore Road East
Oakville ONT L6J 1J5
Canada
(416) 842-5353

Has eight active support chapters throughout Ontario, each of which works on the local level primarily addressing the issues of public awareness and prevention. Programs include: Kid Check/All About Me, fingerprinting and photographing of children and providing a description booklet for parents; public awareness, talks to groups; Streetproofing Program, workshops for children in preventive skills to avoid abduction and molestation; fundraising; distribution of posters and fliers with descriptions and pictures of missing children.

Childhelp USA
6463 Independence Avenue
Woodlands CA 91367
(818) 347-7280

Founded in 1959 to care for hurt, abused and neglected children. Offers national crisis hotline for child abuse, which handles 170,000 calls each year from across the nation. More than half the calls are for immediate intervention. State-of-the-art technology permits a professional counselor to stay on the line while a local agency is contacted. Another program, the Village of Childhelp, is a residential treatment program for severely abused and neglected children ages 2 through 12. Offers family services including the Specialized Foster Family Program.

Children's Creative Response to Conflict Program
   (CCRC)
Fellowship of Reconciliation
Box 271
Nyack NY 10960
(914) 358-4601

Founded in 1972 by the New York Quaker Project on Community Conflict. After years of nonviolence training with adults, the staff began weekly workshops in New York City public schools. Tens of thousands of workshops have been conducted throughout the United States, Canada, Europe and Asia. Offers a variety of workshops. Teachers learn how to train children in mediation. Also offered are skills in group problem solving. Publications. Fourteen branches in ten states and the District of Columbia as well as one related program in Ontario. CCRC's handbook *The Friendly*

Classroom for a Small Planet is used by 20,000 teachers.

Child Welfare League
440 First Street NW, Suite 310
Washington DC 20001-2085
(202) 638-2985

Founded in 1920. Member agencies work with more than 2 million children annually. Oldest and largest voluntary organization in North America devoted to the well-being of children, youth and families. Develops internationally recognized child welfare standards. Provides training and consultation. Lobbies for child-oriented public policy. Maintains an advocacy network of tens of thousands. Largest publisher of child welfare materials.

Children's Defense Fund (CDF)
122 C Street NW
Washington DC 20001
(202) 628-8787

Founded in 1968 under the name Washington Research Project by Marian Wright Edelman, who has been dubbed the "101st senator for children's issues," the name was changed in 1973. Goal is to educate the nation about the needs of children and to encourage preventive investment in children. Organizes, lobbies, gathers data and publishes a lengthy catalog of titles related to children and teenagers.

Children's Healthcare Is a Legal Duty (CHILD)
Box 2604
Sioux City IA 51106
(712) 948-3500

Purpose is to prevent and oppose religion-based child abuse and neglect. Best known for work against religion-based medical neglect of children. Opposes all exemptions from parental duties of care, including religious exemptions for child abuse, child endangerment, immunization and metabolic screening. Provides insight into parenting in its newsletters. Has approximately 300 members in 44 states and three foreign countries.

Children's Rights of America, Inc.
12551 Indian Rocks Road, Suite 9
Largo FL 34644
(404) 432-9404

Provides specific case-by-case location assistance and counseling for families of missing children, including coordination of donated investigative services; dissemination of photographs, catalogs, and confirmation of sightings; a Prayer Watch; and technical assistance. Provides advocacy and support for child victims, 24-hour hotline and street outreach.

Covenant House
346 West 17th Street
New York NY 10011-5002
(212) 727-4000
(800) 999-9999

Daily serves 1,400 throwaway, runaway, homeless children off the streets in 15 locations. Is the largest program of its kind. Spends $40 million annually in direct care, more than the federal government in all its programs for homeless youngsters. Has 1,500 staff and 1,400 volunteers. When all beds and sleeping areas fill up, youngsters sleep on the floor. Has an in-house medical clinic that treats a wide range of ailments, including head lice, frostbite and venereal diseases. New York workers focus on the Port Authority Bus Terminal, where thousands of youngsters arrive each year to escape from homes where they have been abused, and the extended Times Square district, a major sex-and-drugs-for-sale location. An outreach van cruises the streets each night with food and offers to help.

Defense for Children International-USA (DCI-USA)
210 Forsyth Street
New York NY 10002
(212) 353-0951 and 353-0952

Founded in 1983, this is the U.S. section of the worldwide DCI movement. DCI is a nongovernmental human rights organization headquartered in Geneva, created during the International Year of the Child (1979) with a mandate to promote and protect the rights of the child through collection and dissemination of information; monitoring and investigation of violations; organization of advocacy campaigns to respond to children's rights abuses; development and advocacy of improved national and international standards regarding the rights of children; and implementation and support of direct-service programs at points of greatest need. Provides a variety of publications, such as *Children's Rights in America: Convention on the Rights of the Child Compared with United States Law.*

End Violence Against the Next Generation, Inc.
   (EVAN-G)
977 Keeler
Berkeley CA 94708
(415) 527-0454

State law, school board regulations or court decisions in 29 states permit hitting of children in school. Corporal punishment has been ruled out for many groups, including the military and prisoners; only children may be hit. Goals are to collect and disseminate information about corporal punishment; to promote alternate methods of education and disciplining children; to conduct and promote research into the relationship of physical punishment to behavior problems; to reduce the amount of violence against the next generation in order to promote a peaceful, creative society.

Girls Incorporated (formerly Girls Clubs of America)
30 East 33d Street
New York NY 10016
(212) 689-3700

Founded in 1945 by joining 19 affiliated clubs; by 1991 had grown into a national network of over 200 centers in 122 cities. Twenty-five hundred professionals and 8,000 volunteers run local centers, providing an average of 30 hours of activities per week after school, on weekends and in the summer. Programs encourage careers in science, math, and technology; inform and encourage postponement of sexual activity, pregnancy and parenthood; provide leadership and peer instruction skills to teach others to avoid addictive substances; increase girls' interest in sports and fitness. Among the girls served, 46% are from racial or ethnic minorities and 53% are from single-parent homes, most of which are headed by women.

Institute for the Community as Extended Family
    (ICEF)
Child Sexual Abuse Treatment and Professional
    Training Program
P.O. Box 952
San Jose CA 95108-0952
(408) 453-7616

Founded in 1971 as the Child Sexual Abuse Treatment Program (CSATP). Provides professional and self-help services to sexual abuse victims and their families. Began professional training program in 1977. Spawned independent self-help groups Parents United, Daughters and Sons United and Adults Molested as Children United. Has an extensive catalog of booklets, articles and audio- and videotapes.

Legal Services for Children (LSC)
1254 Market Street, 3d floor
San Francisco CA 94102
(415) 863-3762

Founded in 1975 as a comprehensive law firm providing services free to young people. Clients include children who are alone, hurt, abandoned, molested, sexually assaulted, victims of crime or accused of crime or both. LSC helps youngsters restore or create a normal life. Each young person is helped by an attorney and a social worker, who is a community resource specialist. The attorney deals with legal issues and the social worker finds resources, such as housing, guardians, counseling, school placement and job training.

National Alliance for Safe Schools (NASS)
6931 Arlington Road, Suite 400
Bethesda MD 20814
(301) 907-7888

Founded in 1977 to provide technical assistance, training and research in crime prevention and discipline improvement in public schools. Technical assistance is provided in three formats: the SMART Program (School Management and Resource Teams); the conduct of security audits; and help in forming interagency working groups. The SMART Program involves entire school districts. Student referrals are computerized and used to devise intervention plans. Security audits provide profiles of a school district's policies and practices in handling crime and discipline; interagency work groups bring educators together with criminal justice professionals to address the needs of at-risk youth. Has worked since 1983 with the U.S. Departments of Justice and Education to develop and implement the SMART Program.

National Association of Child Advocates
1625 K Street NW Suite 510
Washington DC 20006
(202) 828-6950

A national association of child advocacy organizations with 94 members in 43 states as of 1990. Goals: to reform state and local systems to effect better public policy and outcomes for children; to raise visibility of child advocacy efforts; and to heighten credibility of child advocates. Provides technical assistance. Sponsors an annual conference. Develops techniques to disseminate information. Publishes *The Child Advocates Information Exchange,* 10 E. Main Street #100, Victor NY 14564.

The National Association of Counsel for Children
    (NACC)
1205 Oneida Street

Denver CO 80220
(303) 321-3963

Founded in 1977 to improve legal protection for children. Goals: to provide training and information to child advocates and to establish a strong foundation of member practitioners to work with children affected by legal proceedings. Issues a quarterly newsletter, *The Guardian,* to share recent court decisions, strategies and resources. Holds one or more seminars annually on children's law issues. Provides guidelines for a maltreated child's guardian ad litem (guardian appointed by a court to protect a minor's interests). Works cooperatively on amicus curiae (friend of the court) briefs presented before state supreme courts and the U.S. Supreme Court.

National Center for Prosecution of Child Abuse
American Prosecutors Research Institute
1033 North Fairfax Street, Suite 200
Alexandria VA 22314
(703) 739-0321

Founded in 1985 by the American Prosecutors Research Institute in response to dramatic increases in reported child abuse cases. Mission is to improve investigation and prosecution of child abuse cases through court reform, professional specialization and interagency coordination. Committed to full accountability for child abuse, along with comprehensive support services for children. Serves prosecutors' needs by providing training and technical assistance; a clearinghouse on court reforms, case law, legislative initiatives and trial strategies; research on reducing trauma in court for child sexual abuse victims and, in cases of drug-affected children, child fatalities; parental abduction; a nationwide network of child abuse prosecutors. Specialized publications, guides and resource manuals include *Investigation and Prosecution of Child Abuse;* publishes a monthly newsletter, *Update.*

National Center for Youth Law (NCYL)
114 Sansome Street, Suite 900
San Francisco CA 94104-3820
(415) 543-3307

Founded in 1970. Dedicated to improving the lives of poor children in the United States. NCYL attorneys are experts in law that affects children and are available to assist child advocates nationwide to increase the effectiveness of legal services delivered to poor children. Among other cases, NCYL attorneys were responsible for court actions that set a standard for safe and humane treatment of juveniles in institutions, stopped the practice of trying juveniles twice for the same offense and recognized the rights of non-English-speaking students in public schools. Played a major role in implementation of the Adoption Assistance and Child Welfare Act of 1980. NCYL was instrumental in passage of federal law to prohibit housing discrimination against families with children. Center has an ongoing involvement with health professionals to insure health care availability to children. Has helped to develop case law that makes it possible to go into federal court on behalf of children. Publishes *Youth Law News* bimonthly to subscribers.

National CASA (Court Appointed Special Advocate) Association
2722 Eastlake Avenue E, Suite 220
Seattle WA 98102
(206) 328-8588

Founded in 1976 when Judge David Soukup of Seattle recognized that he often did not have enough information to make proper decisions in cases involving children. He obtained funding to recruit and train community volunteers to come into the court and argue in the children's interests. In 1978 the National Center of State Courts selected the Seattle program as the "best national example of citizen participation in the juvenile justice system." By 1991 there were more than 13,000 volunteers in 434 CASA programs in 47 states, with new programs starting up at a rate of four each month. Programs are known by a variety of names, such as Volunteer Guardians Ad Litem, Child Advocates and Voices for Children. The National CASA Association will help start a local program with funding, training, support and resource materials. Holds an annual national conference.

Orphan Foundation of America
1500 Massachusetts Avenue NW, Suite 448
Washington DC 20005
(202) 861-0762

Founded in 1981. A national nonprofit serving interests and needs of older orphans and foster care youth. More than 350,000 children are wards of the nation's foster system, and two thirds are too old for adoption. Offers scholarships to youths who are in or have aged out of the foster care system.

Pearl S. Buck Foundation, Inc.
P.O. Box 181

Perkasie PA 18944-0181
(215) 249-0100
(800) 220-BUCK

Founded in 1964. Mission reflects the lifelong interest of its founder in fostering cross-cultural understanding and helping displaced children around the world. A particular mission is thousands of Amerasian children fathered by Americans who have lived, worked or served in Asia. Such children are outcasts in their own societies and often denied citizenship, health care or education.

PTAVE-Parents and Teachers Against Violence in
   Education
560 S. Hartz #408
Danville CA 94526
(415) 831-1661

Promotes a school climate that enhances the dignity of teachers and students. Views corporal punishment as hindering that mission. Considers collective punishment (the punishment of the group for the misbehavior of a few) as alarming, since it assumes that well-behaved students could apply pressure to the misbehaving ones. Such punishment embitters those unjustly punished and alienates them from those in authority and from those who misbehave.

Society for Young Victims
54 Broadway
Newport RI 02840

Founded in 1975. Goals: to make Americans aware of the number of child disappearances in their communities and in the nation each year; to return lost children to their rightful custodians; to seek legislation and promote social attitudes that will benefit children and deter the criminals who kidnap and harm them; to give aid and solace to the families of missing children and aid their searches. Offers a variety of services, such as child fingerprinting, photographs of children for the media, attorney referrals, expert witnesses in custody cases and training. No cost to searching parents. Three staff members and 3,000 volunteers nationwide. Supported by a mixture of corporate and nonprofit sponsors.

UNICEF (United Nation's Children's Fund)
3 United Nations Plaza
New York NY 10017
(212) 326-7000

Committed to serving the needs of children around the world and changing public attitudes toward children. A particular concern is refugee children. Just prior to the Persian Gulf War, 1.4 million refugees poured into Jordan alone in desperate need of food, water, shelter, clothing and blankets. UNICEF provided a wide range of supplies, including blankets, water purification and sanitation equipment, medical kits, vaccines, midwifery kits and vehicles.

C.   DOMESTIC VIOLENCE

AMEND (Abusive Men Explore New Directions)
777 Grant Street, Suite 600
Denver CO 80203
(302) 832-6263

Founded in 1977; a program of the Arapahoe Psychotherapy Collective. A nonprofit group of six private practice offices with an overall board of directors. By 1991 had treated 7,500 men. Offers a treatment program to help abusive partners change their lives. Trains and supervises therapists. Makes educational presentations to the community. Provides resources for the treatment of children and adolescents. Enables volunteers to learn to serve the community, particularly in their "Save-a-Life" campaign, a ten-year effort to inform the public about the impact of domestic violence.

B.A. Press
1269 North E Street
San Bernadino CA 92405
(714) 884-6809

Publishes counseling programs that use the self-help approach. Offers manuals for sponsors and group leaders and handbooks for participants for a Batterers Anonymous program and for a Molesters Anonymous program. Also offers *National Directory: Domestic Violence* and mailing list.

Emerge: A Men's Counseling Service on Domestic
   Violence
18 Hurley Street, Suite 23
Cambridge MA 02141
(617) 547-9870

Founded in 1977 to counsel abusive men who wanted to change their behavior. Operates on the premise that violence is learned. Has also worked with battered women's advocates to change social institutions that reinforce sexist violence. Views wife beating as only one of a range of abusive and controlling behaviors. Is involved in a community education project aimed at dating violence among high school teenagers. Offers training for peer counseling, criminal justice personnel and mental health professionals. Does research and disseminates written materials.

National Coalition Against Domestic Violence
  (NCADV)
P.O. Box 34103
Washington DC 20043-4103
(202) 638-6388

Founded in 1978, it is the only national organization of shelters and support services for battered women and their children. In 1970 there were no shelters; by 1991 there were over 1,200 nationwide. Represented in both rural and urban areas; works with women from all backgrounds. Holds a national meeting three times a year, a national conference every two years and regional training sessions on a regular basis. Publishes a quarterly newsletter, the *NCADV Voice,* and a monthly Public Policy Alert. Coordinates lobbying and testimony before Congress and state legislatures.

Pennsylvania Coalition Against Domestic Violence
(also known as Alianza Contra La Violencia
  Domestica Del Estado de Pensilvania)
2505 North Front Street
Harrisburg PA 17110-1111
(717) 234-7353
(800) 932-4632

Founded in 1976 by representatives from nine community-based domestic violence groups, who met at a state legislative hearing on the Protection from Abuse Act. Principal goals: development of a statewide network of services for domestic violence victims; advocacy for improvement of systems and institutions that deal directly with victims; provision of education and prevention programs. By 1980, 28 domestic violence programs were operating within the state; of those, 16 had shelters. In 1982 Pennsylvania passed the Domestic Violence and Rape Crisis Services Act; in 1984, the Spousal Sexual Assault Statute; and in 1986, the Domestic Violence Misdemeanor Probable Cause Arrest Law, which mandates that responding law enforcement agencies must inform victims about local domestic violence programs. Following passage of the Probable Cause statute, police referrals increased by 50%. In some local areas, requests for help in filing for protection orders increased anywhere from 100% to 700%.

D.   SUBSTANCE ABUSE

Al-Anon Family Group Headquarters, Inc.
P.O. Box 862 Midtown Station
New York NY 10018-0862
(800) 356-9996 (general information and free
  literature)
(800) 344-2666 (meeting information in United States)
(800) 4434525 (meeting information in Canada)

Every alcoholic deeply affects the people close to him or her. Understanding alcoholism is the best defense against the emotional impact it can have. Family members who are otherwise mature and capable may become confused and contribute to an alcoholic's problem. Al-Anon Family Groups are fellowships of relatives and friends of alcoholics who share their experiences and offer each other support. Anonymity is stressed to protect the members against the stigma attached to drinking and to help them learn to trust each other. Members follow the 12-step program developed by Alcoholics Anonymous. As of January 1990 there were groups in 101 countries. Alateen is a fellowship of young Al-Anon members, usually teenagers, whose lives have been affected by someone else's drinking.

Alcoholics Anonymous World Services, Inc.
P.O. Box 459 Grand Central Station
New York NY 10163
(212) 686-1100

Begun in 1935 by a New York businessman and an Akron, Ohio physician. The two found that they were able to stay sober by helping others to get sober. The program they evolved is a fellowship of men and women who share their experiences of the impact alcohol has had on their lives. The only membership requirement is a desire to stop drinking. A key to the program is regular attendance at meetings. Has a catalog of books and pamphlets that can be used at meetings.

Narcotics Anonymous (NA)
World Service Office, Inc.
P.O. Box 9999
Van Nuys CA 91409
(818) 780-3951

Founded in 1953 in southern California by several drug addicts seeking recovery and a better way of life. Philosophy is summed up in the First Step: "We admitted that we were powerless over our addiction." The focus is on addiction rather than any specific drug. To start a group takes only a place to meet and two or more addicts. The World Service Office will supply a complimentary startup kit upon request.

National Clearing House for Alcohol and Drug
   Information (NCADI)
P.O. Box 2345
Rockville MD 20852
(301) 468-2600
(800) 729-6686
TDD (800) 487-4889 or (301) 230-2867

NCADI is supported by the federal Office of Substance Abuse Prevention (OSAP), created by the Anti-Drug Abuse Act of 1986 to reduce the demand for illicit drugs and prevent alcohol and other drug problems in the United States. NCADI services include: a free videotape loan program; dissemination of bimonthly information service *Prevention Pipeline* and of grant announcements and application kits; free data base searches on alcohol and other drug-related topics; referrals made based on the nation's most comprehensive set of alcohol and drug resources. Offers a regularly updated publication catalog. Works in partnership with the Regional Alcohol and Drug Awareness Resource (RADAR), which consists of state clearinghouses, specialized information centers of national organizations, the Department of Education Regional Training Centers and others. Each RADAR network member offers a variety of information services.

National Council on Alcoholism and Drug
   Dependence (NCADD)
12 West 21st Street
New York NY 10010
(212) 206-6770

Founded in 1944. Until January 1, 1990 known as the National Council on Alcoholism. Aims to reduce the incidence of alcoholism and other drug addictions and their related problems. Carries out its mission through its staff and board and through a network of 37 state and 196 local affiliate organizations and volunteers. Nation's ninth largest voluntary health organization. Sponsors conferences and develops education materials for special groups such as adolescents and minorities. Sponsors National Alcohol Awareness Month in April and National Alcohol-Related Birth Defects Awareness week beginning on Mother's Day. Runs 24-hour toll-free hotline (1-800-NCA-CALL), which provides information and referral.

Parents Against Drugs (P.A.D.)
70 Maxome Avenue
Willowdale ONT M2M 2K1
Canada
(416) 225-6604
(416) 225-6601 (support line)

Founded in 1983. Devised strategies and programs aimed at prevention and support of and education about drug and alcohol abuse. Offers workshops and a help line for distressed parents. Works with parents, offers teachers training and practical strategies and provides youth with speakers, pamphlets, films and training in peer education. Conducts awareness campaigns.

E.   CIVIL RIGHTS AND HUMAN RIGHTS

American Bar Association's Commission on the
   Mentally Disabled
1800 M Street NW
Washington DC 20036

In operation since 1976. Offers disability legal research services for an agreed-upon fee. Publishes the nonprofit *Mental and Physical Disability Law Reporter.* Information covers such areas as civil commitment, mental health, criminal justice issues, rights of the developmentally disabled, sexual rights, remedies, liability and professional standards, federal programs and statutes, jurisdictional issues, state programs and statutes, disability categories and AIDS/public health concerns.

American Immigration Lawyers Association (AILA)
1400 I Street NW, Suite 1200
Washington DC 20005
(202) 371-9377

Founded in 1946, it is the national bar association for immigration attorneys. Provides more than 3,100 members with information and services through 33 local chapters and numerous national committees. The *Monthly Mailing* publishes information from individual members. The *Immigration Journal,* geared to the practicing attorney, provides analysis of trends and recent cases. Lawyers Inquiry/Network Exchange (ALINE) enables members to contact each other for advice and guidance. Holds an annual conference in June. Regularly meets with government agencies. Formed as the American Immigration Law Foundation (AILF) in 1987, which seeks to create and support a variety of law-related programs and services. AILF opened a Legal Action

Center in Washington, D.C., in 1991 as a clearinghouse for those concerned with high-impact litigation.

Amnesty International, USA (AIUSA)
322 Eighth Avenue
New York NY 10001
(212) 807-8400

Founded in 1962. Works impartially to free prisoners of conscience, those jailed solely for their beliefs or ethnic origins, provided they have neither used nor advocated violence. Works to ensure fair trials for all political prisoners. Strives to abolish torture and execution. Focuses attention on the suffering of ordinary citizens. Organizes members to write letters on behalf of prisoners. Investigates and reports human rights violations all over the world. Does not hesitate to report violations in democracies as well as repressive regimes. Pursues long-term agendas, such as refugee rights, women's rights and the ratification of major human rights conventions to outlaw torture and the death penalty. Offers a wide range of publications, including *Amnesty Action,* a member newsletter and alert. Has approximately 375,000 members. Urgent Action Office: P.O. Box 1220, Nederland CO 80466; (303) 440-0913.

Association of American Indian Affairs, Inc.
245 Fifth Avenue
New York NY 10016
(212) 689-8720

Founded in 1923. Purpose is advocacy for American Indians and Alaskan Natives. Does not advocate assimilation into the white culture. Champions a multicultural system of nations within the nation. Supports the preservation of Native American tribal ceremonies and religious rites. Provides technical assistance, small grants, legal assistance, amicus curiae (friend of the court) briefs in U.S. Supreme Court cases and public education. Publishes research, drafts legislation, advises agencies working with tribes, cooperates with Indian organizations, offers scholarship programs and testimony at congressional hearings.

Center for Democratic Renewal (CDR)
P.O. Box 50469
Atlanta GA 30302-0469
(404) 221-0025

A multiracial, multiethnic, interfaith nonprofit organization dedicated to promoting constructive, nonviolent responses to hate violence and the white supremacist movement. Publishes *The Monitor,* a bimonthly newsletter on the activities of far-right groups such as skinheads, neo-Nazis, Klansmen and others devoted to the perpetuation of institutionalized bigotry and racism.

Center for Social Justice (CSJ)
Order of the Sons of Italy in America
291 E Street NE
Washington, DC 20002
(202) 547-2900

An antidefamation organization, CSJ offers regional training sessions to other groups in the struggle to eliminate bias and bigotry. Cosponsored (with the American Jewish Committee) distribution of a film documenting Italian efforts to save Jews during the Holocaust. Strives to end the use of ethnic terms such as Mafia and Cosa Nostra instead of organized crime. Has sponsored public image research on the public's perception of Italian-Americans. Publishes *Capital Notes,* a newsletter.

Chinese for Affirmative Action (CAA)
17 Walter U. Lum Place
The Kuo Building
San Francisco CA 94108
(415) 274-6790

Founded in 1969. Opposes any form of bigotry, police brutality, overt and subtle racism, discrimination or harassment in the workplace. The average client has a low income and limited English proficiency. From 1985 to 1990 caseload rose from 69 complaints to 253. Besides directly helping clients, also supports appointment of Asian-Americans to public boards and commissions, use of bilingual services by tax-supported agencies and fair distribution of public resources; conducts research.

Commission for Racial Justice (CRJ)
700 Prospect Avenue
Cleveland OH 44115-1110
(216) 736-2100

Established in 1963 by the General Synod of the United Church of Christ, in response to the assassination of Medgar Evers. Focus is wide and includes: African-American family life; capital punishment and penal reform; battered wives; teenage pregnancy; racially motivated violence; minority church empowerment; homelessness; increasing the number of minority students in colleges; voter registration. Responsible for the first national study documenting the disproportionate impact of hazardous waste disposal on minority communities.

Publishes the *Civil Rights Journal,* carried weekly in approximately 250 newspapers and six national networks. Has offices in New York City, Washington, D.C. and Endfield, North Carolina, where it has a major program.

Committee Against Anti-Asian Violence (CAAAV)
121 6th Avenue, 6th floor
P.O. Box 20756 Tompkins Square Station
New York NY 10009
(718) 857-7419

Founded in 1986 to give a voice to Asian-American concerns about racism, racist violence and police brutality in the New York area and to work with other communities under attack. Work includes victim advocacy, community mobilization, documentation of anti-Asian violence, public education, lobbying and coalition building. Publishes a newsletter, *The CAAAV Voice.*

Committee of Concerned Scientists, Inc.
53-34 208th Street
Bayside NY 11364
(718) 229-2813

Founded in 1973 to assist foreign colleagues whose human rights and scientific freedom have been violated. Appeals to Congress to put restrictions on foreign aid appropriations and to the president to speak directly on behalf of those who are prevented from leaving their countries, those under house arrest and those who have been jailed and tortured. Generates media coverage.

Cultural Survival, Inc.
53-A Church Street
Cambridge MA 02138
(617) 495-2562

Founded in 1972 by a group of social scientists at Harvard concerned with the fate of tribal people and ethnic minorities around the world. Operates on the premise that small traditional societies are not extinguished by historical processes but by greed and incomprehension. Publishes a quarterly magazine, books, occasional papers and special publications. Also has a slide show to document abuses. Serves as a center for distributing the publications of other groups. Has supported projects on five continents. Considers cultural survival to mean a people's having a say in its future. Assistance programs help to assure a land base for a particular society; to protect it from assault and disease; and to strengthen its own organizations. Seeks ways for human beings to live together in plural societies.

Family Resource Coalition
200 South Michigan Avenue, Suite 1520
Chicago IL 60604
(312) 341-0900

National coalition of nonprofit organizations representing 2,500 professionals who work with family resource programs and related issues across the United States and Canada. Provides technical assistance to those in the field, including practitioners, policymakers, educators and journalists. Family resource programs have their roots in settlement house work, parent education efforts (particularly Head Start) and self-help groups. Lobbies Congress for preventive, community-based resources. Has a network of state affiliates and "affinity groups." Publishes *The FRC Report.* Serves as clearinghouse.

Human Rights Watch
485 Fifth Avenue
New York NY 10017
(212) 972-8400
(also has offices in Washington, D.C., Los Angeles and London)

Founded in 1975. Links the five Watch Committees—Africa Watch, Americas Watch, Asia Watch, Helsinki Watch and Middle East Watch—and coordinates and supports their efforts. Began with the establishment of the Helsinki Watch, prompted by the persecution of Soviet and Czechoslovak citizens for attempts to establish Helsinki monitoring groups. Expanded to include all 35 countries that signed the 1975 Helsinki Accords. Americas Watch began in 1981 to monitor the Reagan administration's selective approach to "totalitarian" governments and "authoritarian" governments. Collects data on and publicizes the human rights policies of governments, and in armed conflicts, on both sides. Monitors murders, "disappearances," kidnappings, torture, reprisals for nonviolent expression or association, exile, psychiatric abuse, censorship, denial of the right to assembly, denial of right to travel or relocate, denial of political freedom, violation of due process and discrimination.

International Alert
379-381 Brixton Road
London SW9 7DE
England
(071) 978-9480

International Alert, the Standing International Forum on Ethnic Conflict, Genocide and Human Rights, is registered in the United Kingdom and the Netherlands. Objectives are to provide nongovernmental initiatives in conflict resolution; to identify root causes of violent group conflict and to facilitate remedies; to alert the public about conflict that may escalate into mass killing and genocide; to stimulate political dialogue; to promote protection of minorities and respect for human rights. Works with all parties to a conflict. Organizes conferences and seminars. Publishes conclusions and monitors implementation. Promotes cooperation among scholars, researchers and activists. Collaborates with the United Nations at all levels.

International Association of Official Human Rights
  Agencies
Hall of the States
444 North Capitol Street NW
Washington DC 20001
(202) 624-5410

Founded in 1949 at the annual meeting of the human rights agencies of four states. Now includes approximately 160 human rights agencies in the United States and Canada. Goals are to foster human relations, enhance human rights practices under law and promote civil and human rights around the world. Provides leadership in development and enforcement of statutes. Offers staff and management training, seminars, a clearinghouse exchange, federal and state liaison, technical assistance and a quarterly newsletter.

International Association on the Political Use of
  Psychiatry (IAPUP)
General Secretary
Dr. Robert van Voren
Postbus 3754
1001 AN Amsterdam
Netherlands
(020) 27 94 91

IAPUP is an independent confederation of national groups opposed to the political use of psychiatry wherever it occurs. Seeks the release of direct and indirect victims of this practice. Publishes the *IAPUP Information Bulletin,* which includes such information as lists of victims whose present whereabouts are not known and summaries of research carried out by the Independent Psychiatric Association. Has published *A Biographical Dictionary on the Political Abuse of Psychiatry in the USSR,* which contains entries on those in the former Soviet Union who are known to have abused psychiatry

for political reasons. Some entries include dialogue from interrogations provided by the victims who survived.

Leadership Conference on Civil Rights (LCCR)
2027 Massachusetts Avenue NW
Washington DC 20036
(202) 667-1780

Founded in 1950 by A. Philip Randolph, Roy Wilkins and Arnold Aronson to promote the goals recommended in the historic report of President Truman's Committee on Civil Rights entitled *To Secure These Rights.* Began with 30 organizations, now includes 185 representing minorities, labor, women, religious groups, disabled persons and older Americans. Member organizations differ in size, structure and broad objectives, but share a common commitment to an integrated plural society, with equal rights, equal opportunities and justice for all. Expanded perspective beyond civil rights in law to social and economic conditions that promote equal rights. Publishes *Civil Rights Monitor.*

MADD (Mothers Against Drunk Driving)
National Office
511 E. John Carpenter Freeway, Suite 700
Irving TX 75062

Founded in 1980. Has state and local chapters all over the United States. Goal is to get drunken drivers off the road. By 1990 drunken driving deaths had been cut by 20% and more than 1,000 new antidrunken driving laws had been passed. Aims to cut such fatalities by another 20% by the year 2000.

NAACP Legal Defense and Educational Fund, Inc.
  (LDF)
99 Hudson Street
New York, NY 10013
(212) 219-1900

Founded by the National Association for the Advancement of Colored People (NAACP), has been a separate organization for three decades, with a separate board, staff, office and program. Cases are handled by LDF staff and cooperating attorneys at the Federal District, Appellate and Supreme Court levels. Cases typically have government policy implications that can affect large numbers of people. In 1989–90, LDF attorneys were involved in almost 24 death row cases and in more than 100 others.

National Center for Law and the Deaf (NCLD)
800 Florida Avenue NE
Washington DC 20002

Provides a variety of legal services to the deaf community, including representation, counseling, information and education. Works to end injustice and discrimination against deaf people nationwide and to establish and enforce their legal rights. Assists groups concerned with local or national legislation, such as interpreter laws.

National Council for Civil Rights (Liberty)
21 Taybard Street
London SE1 4LA
England
(071) 403-3888

Formed in 1934 by Ronald Kidd as a consequence of watching agents provocateurs arrest hunger-striking demonstrators whom they had previously incited to act. Functions as an independent, nonpartisan political campaign organization. Goal is to secure the equal rights and liberties of individuals and groups, as long as they do not infringe on the rights of others. Serves as a pressure group to persuade those in authority to protect and extend human rights and civil liberties that are essential to individual quality of life and to the health of democracy. Campaigns to create a popular ''culture of rights.'' Lobbies Parliament. Brings test cases before the British courts and the European Court of Human Rights.

National Emergency Civil Liberties Committee
175 Fifth Avenue
New York NY 10010
(212) 673-2040

A nonpartisan organization that initiates and supports court cases to safeguard existing civil and political freedoms and to extend the boundaries of justice and equity in American life. Is represented in its efforts by law firms in New York, Philadelphia and Miami. Annually publishes the *Bill of Rights Journal* to coincide with Bill of Rights Day (December 15). Won a suit against the Federal Bureau of Investigation on behalf of Freedom Riders in 1961. Won a 1981 suit on behalf of a ''whistleblower'' child welfare worker. Fought and won a ten-year battle to get a visa for the wife of the assassinated President Allende of Chile.

National Institute Against Prejudice and Violence
31 South Green Street
Baltimore MD 21201
(301) 328-5170

Founded in 1984. The only national center dedicated exclusively to the study of and response to ethnoviolence, defined as attacks against people because of their race, religion, ethnicity or sexual orientation. Ethnoviolence includes vandalism, arson, verbal harassment, physical assaults and murder. Serves as a clearinghouse for information. Researches effects of ethnoviolence on victims and communities, with goal of building effective programs of education, prevention and response. Provides education and consultation. Sponsors conferences and has published several books. Publishes the *National Institute Against Prejudice and Violence Forum,* a newsletter.

National Urban League
500 East 62d Street
New York NY 10021
(212) 310-9000

Founded in 1910 to promote the full participation of African-Americans and other disadvantaged citizens in the economic and social life of the community. Is the seventh largest social service agency in the United States. Serves 1.5 million people in areas such as job placement, job training, housing assistance and health care from a national office and 113 affiliates. Conducts research. Advocates to the public and to Congress. Annually publishes *The State of Black America.*

People for the American Way
2000 M Street NW, Suite 400
Washington DC 20036
(202) 467-4999

Founded in 1980 to counteract bigotry and intolerance. Particular focus is anticensorship campaigns, battles against the religious right and lobbying efforts related to Supreme Court nominations. Has 290,000 members. Goal is a free marketplace of ideas and a true appreciation of the diversity of America.

Physicians for Human Rights (PHR)
58 Day Street, Suite 202
Somerville MA 02144
(617) 623-1930
Founded in 1986 to bring medical, psychiatric and public health skills to protect human rights around the world. Works to prevent participation of doctors in torture, other serious abuses and the death penalty; to defend imprisoned health professionals; to stop physical and psychological abuse of citizens by governments; and to provide medical and humanitarian aid to victims

of repression. By 1991 had conducted 30 missions in 19 countries. Once each month PHR tries to help an imprisoned health professional who has been tortured or is seriously ill by sending a *Medical Action Alert* to all members, who in turn contact members of Congress and foreign ambassadors. Voted in 1989 to work toward the creation of an international movement of physicians for human rights. Produced a handbook on the conduct of medical evaluations for political asylum applicants. Provides a quarterly newsletter *Physicians for Human Rights Record.*

Prisoners' Rights Union
1909 Sixth Street
Sacramento CA 95814
(916) 441-4214

Founded in 1971 after a lengthy strike to improve conditions at Folsom Prison failed. Goals are to educate California prisoners about their civil rights, to advocate human rights for all prisoners and to aid in maintaining a free flow of information among the various organizations that work in prison advocacy. Operates Inside/Out, a press that disseminates information for attorneys, advocates and jailhouse lawyers. Directs prisoners to information and programs. Publishes *The California Prisoner Resource Guide,* which includes information on public and private advocacy groups, and *The California State Prisoners' Handbook.*

Project Equality
1020 East 63rd Street, Suite 102
Kansas City MO 64110
(816) 361-9222

Founded in 1965. A Catholic, Protestant and Jewish interfaith program to promote racial equality by attacking lack of economic and employment opportunity and encouraging the religious community to use its substantial spending power to reverse these conditions. Newsletter, *Update,* informs members of companies that participate in Project Equality so they can lobby non-participants and channel their business to participants.

Southern Poverty Law Center (SPLC)
400 Washington Avenue
Montgomery AL 36195-5101
(205) 264-0286

Incorporated in 1971 on the assumption that a few important legal cases could change the South and that well-conceived mailings would generate contributions to support the effort. Julian Bond was the first president.

Earliest cases included the reapportionment of the Alabama Legislature and the desegregation of the Montgomery YMCA. In 1980 focused attention on the Ku Klux Klan through the Klanwatch Project. Secured a $7 million judgment against the United Klans of America and six UKA members for their role in the death of a black youth. Operates without government funds. Produces several publications, including the *Law Report.* Founder Morris Dees described the development of the center in *A Season for Justice* (1991), written with Steve Fiffer.

F.   VICTIMS' ASSISTANCE

Canadian Centre for Victims of Torture
193 Yonge Street, Suite 501
Toronto ONT M5B 1M8
Canada
(416) 362-5266

Founded in 1977 with help from the Canadian medical group of Amnesty International to address the needs of torture victims claiming refugee status in Canada. Approximately 20% of all new immigrants to Canada are refugees, the great majority of whom are victims of violent oppression. Originated from the need of Toronto physicians to have patients counseled in urgent legal and social problems as refugees and from the demands of attorneys and others to have clients and families treated physically and emotionally. Acts as an advocate on the clients' behalf. Operates an intensive program of information to raise public awareness at local, national and international levels to support its work and to contribute to the body of knowledge about the social and medical treatment of torture victims. Supported the establishment of the El Salvador Human Rights Commission's founding of the Dr. Jose Roberto Rivera Martelli Children's Clinic in San Salvador for children who have witnessed torture and/or been orphaned. Offers a Job Readiness Training Project and English as a Second Language program. A volunteer program provides escorts, interpreters and befrienders.

Compassionate Friends
P.O. Box 3696
Oak Brook IL 60522-3696
(312) 990-0010

A self-help organization offering friendship and understanding to bereaved parents. Purpose is to aid parents grieving over the death of their children and to foster the physical and emotional health of parents and siblings. Publishes a national newsletter. Holds an annual conference. Has a catalog of books, pamphlets and audio and videocassettes that address parental and general bereavement.

Cult Awareness Network (CAN)
2421 W. Pratt Boulevard, Suite 1173
Chicago IL 60645
(312) 267-7777

A coalition of volunteer affiliate groups throughout the United States. Founded to educate the public about the harmful effects of "coercive persuasion," mind control techniques used by destructive cults. Members are former cult members and friends and families of past and present cult members. Represents the estimated 5 million people who have been seriously affected by more than 2,500 destructive cults. Maintains communication with similar organizations throughout the world. Focus is a support group for former cult members.

Disabled Living Foundation (DLF)
380-384 Harrow Road
London W9 2HU
England
(071) 289-6111

A charitable trust that studies those aspects of daily living that present special problems to disabled people. Produces publications for those who work with disabled people, in a voluntary or professional capacity, and for disabled people and their families. Provides a telephone/letter inquiry service staffed by professional advisors. Has the most comprehensive data base on equipment for daily living—17,000 items are listed. Offers a clothing and footgear advisory service, including telephone and letter inquiries, regular courses, resource papers and publications. Has an equipment display center that also offers courses on the use of equipment. Has a reference library and publishes a catalog of its many publications. Provides a brochure of the many locations of Disabled Living Centres, which are demonstration and information resource centers concerned with the practical aspects of daily living.

National Victim Center
307 W. Seventh Street, Suite 1001
Ft. Worth TX 76102
(817) 877-3355

Founded in 1985 in honor of Sunny von Bulow to fight for the rights of victims of violent crimes. Connects victims with providers of care, service and assistance, and helps grass-roots organizations to develop programs. Conducts seminars to train victim advocates, criminal justice and law enforcement officials and others. Serves as a clearinghouse and resource center. Has an extensive library and library resource program and a speakers' bureau. Offers a newsletter, *NetWorks*. Sponsors the national Coalition of Victims' Attorneys and Consultants.

Oxfam America
115 Broadway
Boston MA 02116
(617) 482-1211

Offshoot of the organization founded in 1942 in England as the Oxford Committee for Famine Relief. One of seven autonomous Oxfams (others are in the United Kingdom, Ireland, Belgium, Quebec, Australia and Hong Kong), Oxfam America is an international nonprofit that accepts no government funds. Committed to funding self-help development and disaster relief projects in poor countries in Africa, Asia, Latin America and the Caribbean. Usually works with local organizations that have identified community needs and are developing practical ways to meet them. Provides funding for the resettlement and repatriation of more than 40,000 refugees returning to Namibia from exile in neighboring countries. Sponsors the annual "Fast for a World Harvest."

Parents of Murdered Children (POMC)
100 East 8 Street B-41
Cincinnati OH 45202
(513) 721-5683

Provides emotional support to parents and other survivors and promotes a healthy resolution of their grief. Offers help in coping with the criminal justice system. Office staff helps people who call to link up with others in their vicinity and will also help parents and family members to form a local chapter.

Rape Treatment Center (RTC)
Santa Monica Hospital Medical Center
1250 Sixteenth Street
Santa Monica CA 90404
(310) 319-4000

Founded in 1974. Has provided free professional treatment for more than 12,000 victims and their families. Offers 24-hour emergency care, evidence collection, legal assistance and professional counseling. Has several programs, including Stuart House, an innovative facility for sexually abused children, and the School Prevention Program for Teenagers, which reaches 20,000 high school students each year. Offers a variety of publications. Has served as a model program for hospitals and other agencies across the country.

Samaritans
500 Commonwealth Avenue
Boston MA 02215
(617) 247-0220

Founded in 1974 to help the suicidal and despairing 24 hours a day, seven days a week. Has a staff of six who train volunteers. Volunteers, who donate 24 hours of their time each month (one four-hour shift per week and one eight-hour overnight shift each month), befriend those who call on the phone or come in to the center. Annually volunteers contribute approximately 20,000 hours. Samaritans also do preventive education with teens, college students and the elderly and spend time with inmates at the Charles Street Jail. Trains teens to provide peer counseling. Contacts with the homeless and mentally ill continue to rise.

Survivors of Incest Anonymous, Inc. (SIA)
P.O. Box 21817
Baltimore MD 21111-6817
(301) 282-3400

Founded in 1982. SIA is a 12-step self-help recovery program for women and men 18 years and older. There are no dues or fees. Incest is defined broadly. Goal is to help members recognize that recovery may be painful but that they are no longer alone. Offers pamphlets and booklets at nominal fees, international support groups, pen pals and speakers.

TASH Inc. (Technical Aids and Systems for the Handicapped, Inc.)
70 Gibson Drive, Unit 12
Markham ONT L3R 4C2
Canada
(416) 475-2212

Established in 1978 as a marketing corporation by the Canadian Rehabilitation Council (CRC) in conjunction with the National Research Council (NRC). CRC is an association of more than 80 nonprofit organizations at national, provincial and regional levels whose objectives are the provision of comprehensive rehabilitation services for physically disabled children and adults. TASH's purpose is to provide technical aids that are not readily available from other suppliers. Technical aids, used appropriately, enhance the independence and living conditions of many disabled persons.

Victims of Crime and Leniency (VOCAL)
P.O. Box 4449
Montgomery AL 36103
(205) 262-7197

Founded in 1982. Members are crime victims, criminal justice professionals and advocates. Provides crisis intervention and support, information and referral to resources, assistance and information during the course of victims' involvement with the criminal justice system, referral for legal assistance, representation at parole hearings and advocacy. Successfully lobbied on behalf of the Courtroom Attendance Act, Restitution Withholding Act, Alabama Crime Victim's Compensation Commission Act and Parole Notification Act. Provides a quarterly newsletter.

Volunteers for Medical Engineering (VME)
c/o UMBC
5202 Westland Boulevard
Baltimore MD 21227
(301) 455-6395

Provides technical services and devices for elderly and disabled persons through the volunteer efforts of engineers, scientists and medical personnel. VME serves as an incubator for innovative ideas vital to improvement of the lives of those with disabilities. VME programs include customization of devices, basic research and development, market-ready prototypes from volunteer ideas, leases of previously owned computer and communication devices and equipment at nominal rates. The VME Future Home demonstrates home automation and communications technology for independent living. VME Employability includes computer skills training, remote classroom access and work site modification.

G.   CRIMINAL JUSTICE

American Restitution Association (ARA)
c/o Horton Hall
Shippensburg PA 17257
(803) 744-3381

Promotes the development of formal restitution programs for both juvenile and adult offenders. Made up of juvenile justice and criminal justice professionals and others committed to the belief that the needs of offenders, victims and the public are best served in a system of justice with accountability as a central principle. Provides a newsletter, notices of workshops and conferences, a directory of restitution programs, access to publications and videotapes by leading authorities.

Crime Stoppers International (CSI)
3736 Eubank Boulevard NE, Suite B-4
Albuquerque NM 87111
(505) 294-2300
(800) 245-0009

Founded in 1976 by the New Mexico State Police Department, based on the assumption that public apathy and fear of reprisals can be overcome by rewards and guaranteed anonymity. Began with a reenactment of "the crime of the week" on television. By 1980 had spread to 416 programs in 46 states, plus four in Canada. In 1983 a program began in England. Is most effective at solving dead-end crimes, which otherwise cannot be solved without reliable information from a witness. CSI serves as an umbrella organization and as a clearinghouse for information and as a problem solver for local programs.

Foundation for the Establishment of An International Criminal Court and International Law Commission
1493 Tunnel Road
Santa Barbara CA 93105
(805) 682-1449

Founded in 1970. Goals are to hold individuals accountable for their actions under international law. Believes in enforcing international law and order. To ensure civilized international behavior, upholds four "C's": codes of conduct to deter would-be aggressors and oppressors; commissions of inquiry, impartially constituted from among nations, to determine the facts of disputes; courts or international tribunals to judge cases, either permanent courts or ad hoc as at Nuremberg; and corrections, enforcement mechanisms including international policing and sanctions. Sponsors working conferences in different part of the world.

Helsinki Institute of Crime Prevention and Control (HEUNI)
(affiliated with the United Nations)
P.O. Box 34
SF-00931 Helsinki
Finland
(358-0) 343 2077

Established in 1981 to assist the countries of Europe to respond to challenges posed by crimes, many of which are national and international in scope. Despite the differences in legal, economic, social and cultural conditions, the manifestations of crime tend to be similar. Primary objective is to promote the international exchange of information on crime and criminal justice. Organizes seminars and meetings, collects information, conducts research and provides scholarships. Part of the United Nations' global network of regional and interregional institutes. Includes a research and training center in Rome, regional institutes in Asia and the Pacific, Latin America and the Caribbean, Africa and the Arab countries.

International Association of Airport and Seaport Police (IAASP)
580-2755 Lougheed Highway
Port Coquitlam, BC V3B 5Y9
Canada
(604) 942-2132

Founded in 1969 to pool experience, exchange ideas and provide professional approaches on a worldwide basis for policing airports and seaports. Although cargo theft has been reduced, drugs and terrorism have become a major concern, as has the movement of hazardous materials. Co-sponsored in 1990 with the U.S. Department of Transportation the Working Conference on Maritime and Port Security. Goal is to ensure the safety of persons and cargo. Published *Security Recommendations and Standards for Cargo Security at Airports and Seaports,* available at a nominal cost.

International Association of Campus Law Enforcement Administrators
638 Prospect Avenue
Hartford CT 06105
(203) 233-4531

Founded in 1958. Includes colleges and universities throughout the United States, Canada, Mexico and other countries; membership is open to organizations and individuals involved or interested in campus law enforcement administration. Holds annual training conference. Publishes *Campus Law Enforcement Journal.* Monitors and interprets legislation that affects law enforcement. Serves as a forum to exchange ideas.

International Association of Chiefs of Police
1110 N. Glebe Road, Suite 200
Arlington VA 22201
(703) 243-6500

Founded in 1893. Membership of more than 12,500 in 71 nations. Works to facilitate exchange of information and foster police professionalism. Established worldwide training programs in 1970s. Has many sections, such as Indian Country Law Enforcement, Police Information Officers, Psychological Services, Railroad Police, University Police, and Police Physicians.

International Association of Justice Volunteerism (IAJV)
University of Wisconsin-Milwaukee
Criminal Justice Institute
P.O. Box 786
Milwaukee WI 53201

Committed to the improvement of the juvenile and criminal justice systems through citizen participation. There are 300,000 volunteers nationwide. Membership is open to organizations and individuals. Sponsors a national forum. Publishes quarterly newsletter, *IAJV in Action*.

International Centre for Comparative Criminology
University of Montreal
C.P. 6128, succursale A
Montreal PQ H3C 3J7
Canada
(514) 343-7065

Founded in 1969 for the purpose of establishing regular exchanges between European and North American criminologists. Interacts with organizations such as UNESCO, the United Nations, the Council of Europe and the World Health Organization (WHO). Contributes to the dissemination of criminological knowledge through symposia, conferences, seminars and study sessions. Uses the combined methods and data of law, sociology and psychology. Continues and complements research carried out at the University of Montreal's School of Criminology.

International Criminal Police Organization—Interpol
50, Quai Achille Lignon
69006 Lyon France

First Congress held 1914. By 1988 had 146 member states. Goal is to promote international cooperation and coordination among criminal law enforcement authorities, within the limits of the laws of the different countries and the Universal Declaration of Human Rights. Is forbidden to undertake activities of a political, military or religious nature. Police officers are assigned to the General Secretariat by their own countries. Each member state has one permanent police force that serves as the country's Interpol National Central Bureau.

Legal Services Corporation (LSC)
400 Virginia Avenue SW
Washington DC 20024
(202) 863-1820

Created by federal statute in 1974, replacing the Office of Legal Services, established in 1965 as part of the Office of Economic Opportunity. Its employees are not federal employees; it is a nonprofit corporation funded by Congress. It provides grants to approximately 325 local, independent legal service agencies throughout the country, which provide legal assistance in civil matters to those eligible. The local agencies also receive funding from other sources, such as state and local governments and foundations. LSC also provides special grants for law school clinics, legal assistance to migrant workers and Native Americans, computer-assisted legal research and alternative dispute resolution projects.

National Association of Criminal Defense Lawyers (NACDL)
1110 Vermont Avenue NW, Suite 1150
Washington DC 20005
(202) 872-8688

Membership of over 6,400 attorneys. Affiliated with 48 state and local criminal defense organizations with 20,000 members. Mission is to preserve the adversary system of justice, to maintain and foster independent and able criminal defense lawyers and to ensure justice and due process for persons accused of crime. Publishes *The Champion* monthly and the *Washington Digest*, a summary of legislation and activities in Washington critical to members. Offers Hotline Panel of Legal Experts to members. Quarterly meetings provide continuing education seminars. Ethics Committee issues advisory opinions in thorny issues. Offers a collection of briefs. Defends member attorneys being attacked or harassed.

Restitution Education, Specialized Training, and Technical Assistance Program (RESTTA)
Pacific Institute for Research and Evaluation
7315 Wisconsin Avenue, Suite 900 East
Bethesda MD 20814
(301) 951-4233

Founded in 1984. A joint project of the Pacific Institute for Research and Evaluation and the Office of Juvenile Justice and Delinquency Prevention of the U.S. Department of Justice. Major activities are subcontracted to the Institute for Court Management of the National Center for State Courts and the Policy Sciences Group at Oklahoma State University. RESTTA offers training and technical assistance to jurisdictions that want to implement or refine juvenile restitution programs. Offers model programs. Faculty and technical assistance providers include experienced judges, restitution program administrators and legal experts. Allows local jurisdictions to decide what kind of information and support they need and then provides it in the most appropriate manner. RESTTA resources include the National Restitution Resources Center, which is part of the Juvenile Justice Clearinghouse (NCJRS); the *Guide to Juvenile Restitution;* the *National Directory of Juvenile Restitution Programs,* which includes basic information on 378 U.S. restitution programs; *Restitution Improvement Curriculum;* video training tapes; the RESTTA monograph series; and a *Policy and Procedures Manual,* which provides administrative guidelines for a formal restitution program.

Safe Streets Bureau
Office of the Sheriff
County of Los Angeles
Hall of Justice
Los Angeles CA 90012
(213) 617-7392

Gang suppression agency. Has separate operations aimed at prevention, prosecution, intelligence, resource coordination and the like.

Vera Institute of Justice
377 Broadway, 11th floor
New York NY 10013
(212) 334-1300
Founded in 1961. Conducts action-research projects in criminal justice reform. Develops new approaches to move ex-prisoners considered unemployable into the regular labor market. Has spawned several independent programs including the Manhattan Bail Project, now the New York City Criminal Justice Agency, which makes recommendations to the court concerning release on recognizance, and the Manhattan Bowery Corporation, which develops nonpenal approaches to public drunkenness. Current projects include the New York City Community Service Sentencing project, which provides work and supervision for community service sentences; Neighborhood Work, which provides immediate part-time, short-term employment to individuals recently released from prison; Vocational Development, which

develops methods of channeling persons at risk of involvement with crime into employment. Operates Easy Ride, which employs mentally retarded and visually impaired graduates of a special training program accomplishing a variety of non-driving tasks, as well as ex-offenders in a transportation program for the elderly and disabled. Research department evaluates projects and conducts studies of felony dispositions, women on parole, crime and employment, fines in sentencing and family court dispositions.

Volunteers in Prevention, Probation, & Prisons, Inc.
  (VIP)
521 N. Main
Royal Oak MI 48067
(313) 398-8550

In 1959 a Royal Oak Michigan Juvenile Court Judge, Keith Leenhouts, convinced eight friends to become volunteers working with juveniles. Eventually 500 citizens joined the effort. A similar program began in Boulder, Colorado in 1961. One of two national organizations of volunteers assisting juvenile offenders (the other is the National Information Center on Volunteers in Court). Convened the first annual national conference in 1970. Publishes the *VIP Examiner* and established a national academic center at the University of Alabama, where training materials were developed. Offers technical assistance to new programs and helps to revamp already existing programs.

H.   CORRECTIONS

American Correctional Chaplains Association (ACCA)
c/o Sr. Betty Bender
ACCA Secretary
P.O. Box 731
Stayton OR 97383-0731
(503) 769-7613

Provides spiritual and professional fellowship among persons in correctional chaplaincy; promotes professional approach that respects different religious beliefs; provides and supports religious programs and services; stimulates support of correctional chaplaincy by various faith groups.

American Association for Correctional Psychology
c/o Robert Smith
College of Graduate Studies
West Virginia University

Institute WV 25112
(304) 766-1929

Members hold doctorates or master's degrees in behavioral science and are engaged in administration, practice, teaching and research related to correctional psychology. Goals are to bring together behavioral scientists interested in the psychology of crime and the criminal justice system; to promote professional practices in criminal justice and law enforcement settings; to teach the psychology of crime, delinquency and criminal justice; to support effective treatment approaches; and to stimulate research into criminal behavior. Affiliated with the American Correctional Association. Official publication is *Criminal Justice and Behavior*.

Center for Alternative Sentencing and Employment
    Services (CASES)
377 Broadway 11th Floor
New York NY 10013
(212) 334-1300

Formed in 1989 by the consolidation of two demonstration projects of the Vera Institute of Justice. The Court Employment Project (CEP) administers alternative-to-incarceration programs for felony offenders and provides counseling and support programs. The Community Service Sentencing Project (CSSP) administers similar programs for persistent nonviolent misdemeanor offenders and also provides support services to participants, most of whom are unskilled, unemployed substance abusers. CASES also operates a Parental Support Unit and a Drug Relapse Prevention Unit. In fiscal year 1990, provided services to almost 2,200 men and women.

Correctional Education Association (CEA)
8025 Laurel Lakes Court
Laurel MD 20707
(301) 490-1440

Founded in 1946, CEA is the only professional association of educators and administrators who provide services in correctional settings. Publishes *The Journal of Correctional Education*.

Human Kindness Foundation
Sponsors Prison-Ashram Project
Route 1, Box 201-N
Durham NC 27705
(917) 942-2138

Founded in 1973. Nonprofit organization whose goal is to encourage kindness as an active force in the world.

Major project is the Prison-Ashram Project, which offers friendship and free resources (books, tapes, correspondence, newsletters, workshops) to prisoners throughout the world. Believes that merely receiving help can perpetuate a sense of helplessness. Teaches the helped to give help.

International Association of Correctional Officers
    (IACO)
P.O. Box 7051
Marquette MI 49855
(906) 227-1689

Founded in 1977. Has members from 50 states, 10 Canadian provinces and overseas. Goal is to promote professionalism, professional solidarity and greater training opportunities. Offers captivity insurance and has lobbied for increased death benefits for those killed on the job.

International Association of Residential Community
    Alternatives (IARCA)
P.O. Box 1987
LaCrosse WI 54602
(608) 785-0200

Incorporated in 1964 as a nonprofit service organization. Represents residential and other alternative community-based correctional programs. Purpose is to provide information, training and other services. Membership includes individuals, agencies and affiliates. Promulgates a code of ethics. Offers annual and regional conferences and training, liability insurance and technical assistance. Publishes both the *IARCA Journal* and *Canadian News* bimonthly.

National Association of Juvenile Correctional
    Agencies (NAJCA)
55 Albin Road
Bow NH 03304-3703
(603) 271-5945

Founded in 1903. Members include agency heads and other individuals in each state responsible for juvenile delinquency programs. Implements and disseminates ideas, experiences and techniques to prevent, control and understand juvenile delinquency. Publishes *NAJCA News*.

National Constables Association (NCA)
16 Stonybrook Drive
Levittown PA 19055

(215) 547-6400
(800) 272-1776

The office of constable, predecessor of the modern police officer, dates to the Middle Ages in Britain, where it still exists. Duties vary by state. Constables are elected or appointed; some are self-employed independent contractors who carry out non-crime-prevention duties under the direction of police chiefs, county commissioners and other local officials. Most have power of arrest and can carry a weapon. The office has been abolished in 13 states. The NCA was founded in 1973, in part to resist the erosion of the role of the constable. Its objective is to upgrade quality of performance and the status of the position. Provides members access to liability insurance; offers technical assistance to state associations; holds a yearly convention, which includes training seminars.

Osborne Association and The Correctional Association
   of New York
135 East 15th Street
New York NY 10003
(212) 673-6633

The Correctional Association of New York was founded in 1844 as a citizens' organization devoted to difficult policy issues not addressed by professional or by criminal justice organizations. The Osborne Associates was founded in 1913 by Thomas Mott Osborne, dedicated to the development of services for imprisoned or newly released clients and their families. Both associations are served by a single board, but each has its own executive director, staff and programs. Correctional Association operates AIDS in Prison, Latino Prisoners, Public Policy, Community Outreach, Pen Pals and Prisoners' Projects. The Osborne Associates operates the Bureau of Vocational Placement, the Assigned Counsel Alternatives Advocacy Project, Family Works (model parenting for incarcerated fathers), El Rio (for crack users) and Living Well (for those with HIV at risk of seroconversion, and their families). It awards the Osborne Medal for distinguished service by an ex-offender.

Prison Fellowship
P.O. Box 17500
Washington DC 20041-0500
(703) 478-0100

Some 40,000 trained volunteers teach Christian principles seminars and follow-up Bible studies in prisons. Community service projects link nonviolent offenders with churches. Aftercare programs work with ex-prisoners. Volunteers also minister to crime victims. Offers marriage and prerelease Life-Plan seminars. Works for legal reforms that hold offenders accountable, restore victims' losses and protect the public.

Vocational Foundation, Inc. (VFI)
902 Broadway
New York NY 10010
(212) 777-0700

Founded in 1936 to provide jobs, training, education and counseling for high school dropouts, teen parents, youth released from prison and other unemployed young adults from New York City's poorest neighborhoods. Each year places 1,500 youths in the building or engineering trades, clerical jobs and the food and apparel industries. Seventy percent of the troubled youth the program takes in become wage earners within a few months. Offers educational programs in conjunction with the New York City Board of Education. Teen fathers program, in addition to vocational counseling and jobs, provides training in parenting and family planning. Can keep youth out of expensive correctional institutions for about $4,000 each annually, including an average $100 weekly stipend.

I.   RESEARCH AND SCHOLARSHIP

Assassination Archives and Research Center (AARC)
918 F St. NW, Suite 510
Washington DC 20004
(202) 393-1917

Established in 1984, AARC is a permanent center for the study of assassinations. A major goal is to collect and preserve materials of value to scholars that might otherwise be lost. The scope includes all assassinations, national and international, historic or current, but is limited to political murders and attempted murders and not to the broad field of homicides. Since assassination is a technique of terrorism, AARC collects materials on terrorism worldwide. Has been the recipient of a number of large private collections.

Canadian Section of the International Association of
   Penal Law
P.O. Box 6446 Station "A"
Saint John NB E2L 4R8
Canada
(613) 996-2348

Founded in 1924. Made up of individuals and groups interested in penal law. Holds congresses throughout the world. Is world's principal scholarly organization devoted to criminal law and procedure. Approximately 3,000 members in 68 countries, with 37 national groups. Brings an interdisciplinary perspective to the analysis of crime. Publishes the *Revue Internationale du Droit*.

Criminal Justice Statistics Association (CJSA)
444 North Capitol Street NW, Suite 445
Washington DC 20001
(202) 624-8560

National organization of criminal justice professionals in government agencies, academia and other settings, who conduct research and provide information to policy and program decision makers at all levels of government. Serves as a clearinghouse, convenes conferences and seminars and provides consultation and training to criminal justice specialists. Offers several publications, access to a network of analysts and promotes dissemination of information on computer hardware and software.

International Association for the Study of Organized Crime (IASOC)
Department of Criminal Justice
C.W. Post Campus
Long Island University
Brookville NY 11548
(516) 299-2594 and 299-2468

Founded in 1984 to promote the communication and dissemination of information among members, other associations and criminal justice agencies; to encourage research into organized crime; to provide research and evaluative services to public and private agencies; and to establish a center for information on organized crime and related subjects. Publishes a newsletter, *Criminal Organizations*.

International Society for Social Defense
Società Nazionale di Prevenzione e Difesa Sociale (SIDS)
Palazzo Communale delle Scienze Sociale
Piazza Castello, 3
I-20121 Milano
Italy
(2) 871627

Founded in 1947. Has a multinational membership of administrators, magistrates and professors. Purpose is to fight crime through preventive and responsive meth-

ods. Publishes a semiannual directory and workbooks. Corresponds in English. Publishes in French and English.

International Third World Legal Studies Association (INTWORLSA)
c/o International Center for Law in Development
777 United Nations Plaza Suite 7E
New York NY 10017
(212) 687-0036

An international association whose goal is to aid understanding of maldevelopment and underdevelopment, dependency and impoverishment, exclusion and oppression, and how the law contributes to these problems. Publishes an annual journal, *Third World Legal Studies*.

International Penal and Penitentiary Foundation
Secretary-General: Dr. Konrad Hobe
Bundesministerium der Justiz
Postfach 200365
D-5300 Bonn 2
Germany
(0228)584226

Founded in 1951. Promotes studies in crime prevention and treatment of offenders through scientific research, publications and teaching. Holds an annual meeting each year in a different part of the world. Has 22 member countries and five corresponding member countries. Publishes in English and French.

Institute for the Study of Genocide
John Jay College of Criminal Justice
899 10th Ave
Room 623
New York NY 10019
(212) 237-8631

Founded in 1982 to promote and disseminate scholarship on the causes, consequences and prevention of genocide. Conducts surveys, sponsors research and monitors violations of human rights. Sponsors conferences and meetings to advance research, study patterns of recognition and denial, assess effects of genocide and consider how to detect and stop crime. Publishes a newsletter and compiles teaching guides. Supports implementation of domestic and international legislation that outlaws genocide and provides for sanctions.

National Commissioners on Uniform State Laws (ULC)
676 N. St. Clair Street

Chicago IL 60611
(312) 915-0195

Founded in 1892 for the improvement of state criminal laws. Represents both state governments and the legal profession and operates as a confederation of state interests. More than 300 practicing attorneys, judges, law professors and government officials serve as Uniform Law Commissioners, without compensation. Appointed by the states, they are selected for legal expertise and experience. Focus is problems created by differences in state laws. Areas addressed have included the elimination of jurisdictional child custody disputes, crime victims' reparations, rules of criminal procedure and electronic transfer of stock ownership. Develops Uniform Acts, which legislatures are urged to adopt as written, and Model Acts, which serve as guidelines.

Pacific Institute for Research and Evaluation
7315 Wisconsin Avenue, Suite 900 East
Bethesda MD 20814
(301) 951-4233

Founded in the mid-1970s in California to do research and programming in the prevention and resolution of social, health and justice problems. Primary focus is on drug abuse prevention, alcoholism and juvenile delinquency. Services include basic research, on-site evaluation, model demonstration development, program development and implementation, training and technical assistance. Draws on disciplines of sociology, psychology, political science and criminal justice. Has divisions in Maryland, Virginia and California.

Sellin Center for Studies in Criminology and Criminal Law
437 Vance Hall
3788 Spruce Street
Philadelphia PA 19104-6301
(215) 898-7411

Has an interdisciplinary approach to the study of criminology. Emphasizes behavioral sciences, but also includes physical science and management disciplines: risk analyses, legal studies, psychiatry, neurology, endocrinology, biology, individual personality and the criminal justice system. Has produced numerous government reports, books, articles, monographs and presentations. Supplies information, analysis and testimony frequently to government bodies, including Congress.

University Research Corporation/Center for Human Services (URC/CHS)
7200 Wisconsin Avenue, Suite 600
Bethesda MD 20814-4820
(301) 654-8338

URC was founded in 1965 and CHS (a nonprofit affiliate) in 1967 to address such problems as the high school dropout rate, teen pregnancy and drug and alcohol abuse. Helped shape the standards for the Head Start program. Trains executives to cope with the global economy, supervisors to improve productivity, workers with low job-readiness skills, managers coping with multicultural work forces and villagers in less-developed countries (LDCs) to protect the lives of their children.

BIBLIOGRAPHY

ABC. "Jail for the Mentally Ill. Why Are They Here?" *20/20*, April 19, 1991.

ABC. "A National Town Meeting: The Legalization of Drugs." *The Koppel Report*, September 13, 1988.

ABC Nightline. "Wilding." May 16, 1989.

Abel, Gene, et al. "Self-Reported Sex Crimes of Nonincarcerated Paraphiliacs." *Journal of Interpersonal Violence*, March 1987.

Achenbach, Joel. "Serial Killers: Shattering the Myth; They're an American Phenomenon, and They're Not What You Think." *Washington Post*, April 14, 1991.

Adams, James Ring. *The Big Fix: Inside the S & L Scandal.* New York: John Wiley & Sons, 1990.

Adams, Ronald D. "Comparison of Drug and Alcohol Use by Sex and Black/White Student Groupings." *Technical Report #34*, Atlanta, GA: V.P. Research, Pride, Inc., December 15, 1989.

"Addressing School Violence." *Boston Globe*, December 13, 1990.

Alpert, Geoffrey. *The American System of Criminal Justice.* Beverly Hills, CA: Sage Publications, 1985.

Altman, Daryl. "To Treat Child Abuse, Let Pediatricians Identify High-Risk Cases." Letter to editor, *New York Times*, January 24, 1989.

American Psychiatric Association. *Diagnostic and Statistical Manual of Mental Disorder, 3rd Edition—Revised.* Washington, D.C.: American Psychiatric Association, 1987.

American Society of Journalists and Authors. "He/She Who Gets Slapped." *ASJA Newsletter*, June 1990.

Amnesty International U.S.A. *United States of America: The Death Penalty and Juvenile Offenders.* New York: Amnesty International, 1991.

Anderson, Jack. "How Not to Be a Target." *Parade Magazine*, April 7, 1991.

"Another AK-47 Massacre." *Time*, September 25, 1989.

Anti-Defamation League. "Skinheads Target the Schools, An ADL Special Report." New York: Anti-Defamation League, undated (circulated spring 1991).

"Apparent Drug Deal Ends in NU Student's Death." *Northeastern University Alumini News*, June 1990.

Ardiff, Martha Burns. "Model Mugging." *North Shore Weekly*, August 23, 1989.

Artenstein, Jeffrey. *Runaways: In Their Own Words: Kids Talking About Living on the Streets.* New York: Tor, 1990.

Ashcraft, Michael. "Social Security: Campus Police Carry New Powers and Sometimes Guns." *New York Times*, August 5, 1990.

Associated Press. "Judge Curbs U.S. Spying on Religious Units." *Boston Globe*, December 12, 1990.

———. "Imprisoned Racist Admits to 2 Killings in '80." *New York Times*, August 21, 1990.

———. "Shots in Air, Death on the Ground." *New York Times*, January 2, 1990.

———. "TA Settles Bosket Suit." *Newsday*, September 26, 1989.

Ayres, Drummond, Jr. "Slaying of Vietnamese Exiles in Washington Renews Refugee Fear." *New York Times*, September 25, 1990.

Bair, Karen. "A 196-Year Push to Make Prisons Work," *Scholastic Update*, February 9, 1987.

Baker, James, et al. "Los Angeles Aftershocks." *Newsweek*, April 1, 1991.

Baker, Kimberly. "Youths Agree to Truce in Bid to End Rivalries in Boston." *Boston Globe*, April 29, 1991.

Bailey, Ronald. *Violence and Aggression.* New York: Time-Life Books, 1976.

Bane, Vicki, et al. "Silent No More." *People,* December 17, 1990.

Bard, Morton, Harriet Arnone, and David Nemiroff. "Contextual Influences on the Post-Traumatic Stress Adaptation of Homicide Survivor-Victims." In *Trauma and Its Wake, Volume 2, Traumatic Stress: Theory, Research, and Intervention,* ed. Charles R. Figley. New York: Brunner/Mazel, 1986.

Barnicle, Mike. "A Beacon Made Dark." *Boston Globe,* December 10, 1989.

Barrett, Laurence. "Have Weapons, Will Shoot." *Time,* February 27, 1989.

Bass, Allison. "A Mind Divided: Experts Probe Split Identities." *Boston Globe,* November 6, 1989.

———. "Women Far Less Likely to Kill Than Men; No One Sure Why." *Boston Globe,* February 24, 1992.

Battersby John. "Decision to Reinstate Hangings Angers S. African Rights Activists." *Christian Science Monitor,* March 5, 1991.

Bayh, Birch. "Let's Tear Off Their Hoods." *Newsweek,* April 17, 1989.

Beaty, Jonathan, and Richard Hornik. "A Torrent of Dirty Dollars." *Time,* December 18, 1989.

Beaty, Jonathan, et al. "The Other Arms Race." *Time,* February 6, 1989.

Belcher, John, and Frederick DiBlasio, *Helping the Homeless.* Lexington, MA: Lexington Books, 1990.

Bell, Alison. "Campus Showdown: The School Battlefield." *Teen,* November 1988.

Bennett, Georgette. *Crimewarps: The Future of Crime in America.* Garden City, NY: Anchor Books, 1987.

Berger, Gilda. *Violence and Sports.* New York: Franklin Watts, 1990.

Berlow, Alan. "Ballots and Bullets." *The New Republic,* June 4, 1990.

Bern, Christopher, and Robert Parry. "A Drug Crackdown in the Alps." *Newsweek,* April 10, 1989.

Bernstein, Richard. "The Right to Bear Arms: A Working Definition." *New York Times,* January 28, 1990.

Biddle, Frederic. "Business Behind Bars." *Boston Globe,* September 3, 1989.

Bierman, John, and Alan Berlow. "A 'Fascist Disneyland.' " *Maclean's,* May 28, 1990.

Binder, David "Violence by Bands of Racist Skinheads Stalks East Germany." *New York Times,* August 21, 1990.

Bird, Caroline, and Sara Welles Briller. *Born Female: The High Cost of Keeping Women Down.* New York: David McKay Company, 1970.

"Blackboard." *New York Times,* January 6, 1991.

"Blackboard Jungle." *U.S. News and World Report,* February 13, 1989.

Blake, Andrew. "INS to Revamp Rules on Salvadoran, Guatemalan Asylum." *Boston Globe,* December 20, 1990.

Blake, Patricia. "Blood, Business, 'Honor.' " *Time,* October 15, 1984.

Blumenthal, Ralph, et al. "In Officers' Murder Case, A Tangle of Contradictions." *New York Times,* March 24, 1991.

"Boarding Schools' Hard Balancing on Drug Tests." *New York Times,* June 6, 1986.

Booth, Cathy, et al. "Law and Disorder." *Time,* April 1, 1991.

Borger, Gloria, et al. "Judging Thomas." *U.S. News & World Report,* October 21, 1991.

Bouza, Anthony. *The Police Mystique.* New York: Plenum Press, 1990.

Bredemeir, Brenda Jo. "Values and Violence." *Psychology Today,* October 1985.

Broner, Ethan. "Societal Anxieties." *Boston Globe Magazine,* April 7, 1991.

Brooke, James. "Peru Suggests U.S. Rethink Eradication in Land Where Coca Is King." *New York Times,* November 18, 1990.

Brown, Mark Malloch. "The Refugee Camp: Solution or Problem?" In *Forced Out: The Agony of the Refugee in Our Time,* ed. Carole Kismaric. New York: Human Rights Watch and J. M. Kaplan Fund, in conjunction with William Morrow, W. W. Norton, Penguin Books, and Random House, no date (approx. 1989).

Brownmiller, Susan. *Against Our Will.* New York: Simon and Schuster, 1975.

"Bruise News." *Sports Illustrated,* February 11, 1991.

Bruning, Fred. "A City Transfixed by a Brutal Act." *Maclean's,* May 22, 1989.

———. "Countdown to the Electric Chair." *Maclean's,* October 26, 1987.

Buermeyer, Nancy. "Hate Crimes—Attack on Community." *National NOW Times,* March/April 1991.

Burgess, Anthony. "Circus Maximus, British-Style." *New York Times,* April 23, 1989.

Burger, Warren. "The Right to Bear Arms." *Parade,* January 14, 1990.

Burden, Ordway. "Book Review of *Inside the Criminal Mind*." *Journal of Political Science and Administration*, vol. 13, 1985.

"Burglaries Bring 7-Year Suspension for a Fraternity." *New York Times*, December 23, 1990.

Burke, Dan. "A Study in Fear: Violence in the School of Hard Knocks." *Maclean's*, May 22, 1989.

"Burma's Shave with Freedom." *U.S. News and World Report*, June 11, 1990.

Bush, John. "Criminality and Psychopathology: Treatment for the Guilty." *Federal Probation*, vol. 43, 1983.

Bussard, Rick. "E.D.I.T." Newsletter, Colorado Department of Corrections Substance Abuse Involvement Programs, July 1991.

Butterfield, Fox. "An Army with Its Own Grievances." *New York Times*, June 6, 1989.

———. "Killing of 5 in Boston's Chinatown Raises Fears of Asian Gang War." *New York Times*, January 15, 1991.

Cambridge, Massachusetts Police Department. "Search and Seizure Training Memo." Undated, in effect March 1991.

Came, Barry, et al. "A Difficult Job to Take Home." *Maclean's*, January 9, 1989.

Campus Law Enforcement Association. "IACLEA Position Statements." *Campus Law Enforcement Journal*, March–April 1991.

"Campus Police Dust Off Old Ideas: Bicycle Officers." *New York Times*, July 15, 1990.

"Campuses No Longer a Safe Haven." *USA Today*, November 29, 1990.

"Can Whistle Help Prevent Campus Rape?" *New York Times*, October 8, 1989.

Caputi, Jane. "The New Founding Fathers: The Lore and Lure of the Serial Killer in Contemporary Culture." *Journal of American Culture*, fall. 1990.

Caputi, Jane, and Diana Russell. " 'Femicide': Speaking the Unspeakable." *Ms.*, September/October 1990.

Carmen, Arlene, and Howard Moody. *Working Women: The Subterranean World of Street Prostitution*. New York: Harper & Row, 1985.

Caruso, Michelle. "Prison Costs Running Mass. $23G an Inmate." *Boston Herald*, April 1, 1991.

Castelli, Jim. "Campus Crime 101." *New York Times*, November 4, 1990.

CBS *America Tonight*. "Police Brutality." March 28, 1991.

Celis, William III. "Date Rape and a List at Brown." *New York Times*, November 18, 1990.

Charen, Mona. "What Ever Happened to Shame." *Boston Globe*, May 28, 1989.

"Charting the Aftermath of Child Abuse." *Science News*, January 12, 1991.

Chin, Ko-lin. *Chinese Subculture and Criminality: Nontraditional Crime Group in America*. Westport, CT: Greenwood Press, 1990.

Clinard, Marshall, and Peter Yeager, *Corporate Crime*. New York: Free Press, 1980.

CNN. "Discussion of Case Before the Supreme Court, *Payne v. Tennessee:* Propriety of Use of Victim's Survivors Statements in Determining the Imposition of the Death Penalty." Broadcast April 27, 1991.

Cohen, Duffie. "The Struggle to Cap Sky-High Prison Costs." *Scholastic Update*, February 9, 1987.

Cohen, Stanley. "Property Destruction: Motives and Meanings." In *Vandalism*, ed. Colin Ward. New York: Van Nostrand Reinhold Co., 1973.

"College Considers Punishment for 4 in New York Theft." *New York Times*, December 9, 1990.

"Colleges Must Report Crimes on Campus." *USA Today*, December 10, 1990.

Conteras, Joseph. "Reporters as Targets." *Newsweek*, October 2, 1989.

Convey, Kevin. "The Great Scare." *Boston Magazine*, February 1990.

Cook, P., and D. Nagin. *Does the Weapon Matter?* (PROMIS Research Project Publication 8). Washington, DC: INSLAW, December 1979.

Cooke, Patrick. "They Cried Until They Could Not See." *New York Times*, June 10, 1991.

Coplon, Jeff. "Skinheads." *Rolling Stone*, December 1, 1988.

Cullen, Kevin. "Gangs Seen Vying for Chinatown Turf." *Boston Globe*, January 15, 1991.

———. "Law Enforcement, Huge Profits, Inadequate Remedies." *Boston Globe Magazine*, November 9, 1986.

———. "Mob Death May Mean Mafia in N.E. Will Realign." *Boston Globe*, June 18, 1989.

———. "Mob's Slip: Loose Lips: Recorded Boasts Are Mafia's Undoing." *Boston Globe,* November 19, 1989.

———. "Piercing a Perfect Cover." *Boston Globe,* June 16, 1989.

———. "Uncovering the Godfathers of Chinatown Crime." *Boston Globe,* August 19, 1990.

Cullen, Kevin, et al. "Glut of Guns a Menacing Sign." *Boston Globe,* April 29, 1990.

Cummings, Judith. "On Congested Highways, California Motorists Turn to Violence." *New York Times,* July 28, 1987.

Curtiss, Aaron, and Carol Watson. "Driver Hurt, Officer Escapes Injury in Separate Shootings." *Los Angeles Times,* February 3, 1992.

Daley, Suzanne. "Doctor-Sleuth Teams Fight Child Abuse." *New York Times,* June 7, 1988.

Daley, Yvonne. "Beating of Gay Man Raises Stakes for Vt. Hate Crimes Bill." *Boston Globe,* April 22, 1990

"Dangerous Lessons: Campus Crime Series." *USA Today,* November 29–December 7, 1990.

Daly, Martin, and Margo Wilson. *Homicide.* Hawthorne, NY: Aldine de Gruyter, 1988.

Debner, Claudia. *Crime and Criminal: Opposing Viewpoints.* St. Paul, MN: Greenhaven Press, 1984.

"Deng's Great Leap Backward." *Newsweek,* June 19, 1989.

DePalma, Anthony. "New Jersey Reviews Care for Neglected Children." *New York Times,* May 28, 1989.

DiCanio, Margaret. *The Encyclopedia of Marriage, Divorce, and the Family.* New York: Facts On File, 1989.

———. "Forensic Medicine." In *The Facts On File Scientific Yearbook 1988,* ed. Margaret DiCanio. New York: Facts On File, 1988.

———. "Mental Illness: Emerging Clues About Normal and Aberrant Behavior." In *The Facts On File Scientific Yearbook 1989,* ed. Margaret DiCanio. New York: Facts On File, 1989.

———. "Why Deinstitutionalization? The About-Face in Mental Health." *Berkshire Eagle,* September 27, 1980.

Dillin, John. "Drug Crisis Burdens Prison System: Illegal Narcotics Pouring Across U.S. Border Fuels State Prison Population Problem in Georgia." *Christian Science Monitor,* November 6, 1989.

Dionne, E. J. "Prison Spending Rises Fastest in State Budgets, Legislators Report." *New York Times,* August 8, 1989.

Dirks, Raymond, and Leonard Gross. *The Great Wall Street Scandal.* New York: McGraw-Hill, 1974.

Doerner, William. "The Face of Repression." *Time,* July 3, 1989.

Doherty, Shawn. "Teaching Kids How to Grieve." *Newsweek,* November 13, 1989.

Dolphin, Ric. "Furore Over Firearms: The Push for Deadlier Weapons." *Maclean's,* January 9, 1989.

Dowd, Maureen. "N.R.A. Is Set for Offensive Over Gun Ban." *New York Times,* March 19, 1989.

"Drug Arrests and the Courts' Pleas for Help." *New York Times,* April 9, 1989.

"A Drug Program Focuses on Talk." *New York Times,* December 7, 1986.

Duffy, Brian, et al. "Days of Rage." *U.S. News and World Report,* May 11, 1992.

Duffy, James E. "Literacy: New Alliances." Address presented at the Annual Conference of the Correctional Association, San Francisco, CA, July 27, 1987.

Dumaine, Brian. "New Weapons in the Crime War." *Fortune,* June 3, 1991.

Egger, Steven. *Serial Murder: An Elusive Phenomenon.* Greenwood Press, Westport, CT. 1990.

Ellement, John. "Reports of Hate Crimes in Boston Up 20% in '90, Police Report Says." *Boston Globe,* January 24, 1991.

Elliott, Dorinda. "We Have Enthusiasm and Daring." *Newsweek,* May 8, 1989.

Emmerman, Lynn. "Clinic Keeps Its Sparkle Amid a Battered Neighborhood." *Chicago Tribune,* January 25, 1989.

Ericson, Richard. "Reserve Prisons for the Dangerous Offenders." *New York Times,* letter to the editor, December 28, 1989.

Erlanger, Steven. "Once Again, Vietnamese Are Turned Out to Sea." *New York Times,* November 19, 1989.

Escobar, Gabriel, and Rene Sanchez. "5 Children Wounded in NW Attack." *Washington Post,* December 21, 1990.

Esser, Aristide. *Behavior & Environment: The Use of Space by Animals and Men.* New York: Plenum Press, 1971.

Evans, Leonard. *Traffic Safety and the Driver.* New York: Van Nostrand, 1991.

Farah, Douglas. "Medellin Cartel Vows Renewed Terrorism." *Boston Sunday Globe,* April 1, 1990.

Farber, M. A. "For Out-of-Towners, New York City Is a Drug Mart." *New York Times,* December 3, 1989.

Farnham, Alan. "Inside the U.S. Gun Business." *Fortune,* June 3, 1991.

Farnsworth, Clyde. "Bush Presents Plan to Help Andean Nations Grow Non-Coca Crops." *New York Times,* July 24, 1990.

Farrell, John Aloysius. "Open Doors: Closing Minds." *Boston Globe,* February 23, 1992.

Fasteau, Marc Feigen. *The Male Machine.* New York: McGraw-Hill, 1974.

Favazza, Armando. "Little Murders." *The Sciences,* March/April 1989.

Fennell, Tom, et al. "Rich and Powerful." *Maclean's,* August 17, 1987.

Field, Garry. "The Psychological Deficits and Treatment Needs of Chronic Criminality." *Federal Probation,* December 1986.

Figley, Charles R. *Trauma and Its Wake, Volume II, Traumatic Stress: Theory, Research, and Intervention.* New York: Brunner/Mazel, 1986.

Finlayson, Ann. "The Criminal Element." *Maclean's,* August 17, 1987.

Fitzgerald, Francis. *America Revised.* New York: Random House, 1979.

Fletcher, Connie. "What Cops Could Tell You About Crimes Against Women." *Glamour.* January 1991.

Flint, Anthony. "Lawsuits New Weapon Against Campus Rape." *Boston Globe,* September 25, 1989.

———. "Youths at Congress Talk of Urban Violence." *Boston Globe,* April 29, 1991.

Ford, Beverly. "Arrests Don't Ease Students' Fears." *Boston Herald,* January 22, 1990.

Ford, Royal. "Vermont Rape Victims Kept Waiting for Justice." *Boston Globe,* September 2, 1990.

Ford, Peter. "Respect Stays Out of Reach." *Christian Science Monitor,* December 20, 1988.

Foreman, Judy. "An Epidemic of Maternal Deaths." *Boston Globe,* July 15, 1991.

Forestier, Katharine. "The Revolt of the Intellectuals." *New Scientist,* June 3, 1989.

Fox, Stephen. *Blood and Power: Organized Crime in Twentieth-Century America.* New York: William Morrow, 1989.

Franzese, Michael, and Dary Matera. *Quitting the Mob.* New York: HarperCollins, 1992.

Friedman, Leon (ed.). *Violence in America: Final Report of the National Commission on the Causes and Prevention of Violence,* vols. 1–16. New York: Chelsea House, 1983. (Originally published 1969.)

Fyfe, James. "Why Won't Crime Stop? Because We Cling to Our Favorite Social Myths." *Washington Post,* March 17, 1991.

Gabor, Andrea. "Cocaine Countries Try to Grow Straight." *U.S. News & World Report,* October 23, 1989.

Gehring, Thom. "The History of Correctional Education." Paper circulated by the Correction Association, Laurel, MD, no city, no date.

Gelman, David, and Peter McKillop. "Going 'Wilding' in the City." *Newsweek,* May 8, 1989.

Gerard, Jeremy. "Jennings Creates a Gun-Control Special." *New York Times,* January 23, 1990.

Gergen, David, et al. "Secrets Behind the Gun Lobby's Staying Power." *U.S. News and World Report,* May 8, 1989.

Germani, Christian. "Serial Killings Are Rare." *Christian Science Monitor,* August 2, 1991.

Gerzon, Marc. *A Choice of Heroes: The Changing Faces of American Manhood.* Boston: Houghton Mifflin, 1982.

Gest, Ted. "Convicted by Their Own Genes." *U.S. News and World Report,* October 31, 1988.

Gest, Ted, and Amy Slatzman et al. "Harassment: Men on Trial." *U.S. News & World Report,* October 21, 1991.

Gest, Ted, et al. "Guns." *U.S. News and World Report,* May 8, 1989.

Gibbs, Nancy. "Bigot in the Ivory Tower." *Time,* May 7, 1990.

———. "Wilding in the Night." *Time,* May 8, 1989.

Gilbert, Bill, and Lisa Twyman. "Violence Out of Hand in the Stands." *Sports Illustrated,* January 31, 1983.

Gillespie, Cynthia. *Justifiable Homicide: Battered Women, Self-Defense and the Law,* Athens, OH: Ohio State University Press, 1989.

Gillespie, Marcia Ann. "Delusions of Safety." *Ms.,* September/October 1990.

Gillies, Laurie, et al. "Gang Terror." *Maclean's,* May 22, 1989.

Goffman, Erving. *Behavior in Everyday Places.* Garden City, NY: Anchor Books, 1962.

Goldberg, Debbie. "Use of Drugs, Alcohol Plays Role in Campus Crime, Study Shows." *Boston Globe,* February 4, 1990.

Golden, Daniel. "The Arming of America." *Boston Globe Magazine,* April 23, 1989.

———. "Mixed Signals." *Boston Globe Magazine,* February 17, 1991.

Goldfarb, Sally. "Violence Against Women: The Need for a Federal Response." *National NOW Times,* March/April 1991.

Goleman, Daniel. "Architects Rediscover the Best City Planners: Citizens." *New York Times,* June 2, 1992.

———. "As Bias Crime Seems to Rise, Scientists Study Roots of Racism." *New York Times,* May 29, 1990.

———. "Black Scientists Study the 'Pose' of the Inner City." *New York Times,* April 21, 1992.

———. "Probe Into the Enigma of Multiple Personality." *New York Times,* June 28, 1988.

———. "A Sad Legacy of Abuse: The Search for Remedies." *New York Times,* January 24, 1989.

———. "Sexual Harassment: It's About Power, Not Sex." *New York Times,* December 22, 1991.

———. "Therapies Offer Hope for Sex Offenders." *New York Times,* April 14, 1992.

———. "When Rage Explodes, Brain Damage May Be the Cause." *New York Times,* August 7, 1990

———. "When the Rapist Is Not a Stranger." *New York Times,* August 29, 1989.

Gomez, James. " '91 Seen as Year Gang Wars in County Took Turn for Worse." *Los Angeles Times,* December 22, 1991.

Goodman, Ellen. "Live from New York, It's the Bigot in a Comic Mask." *Boston Globe,* May 17, 1990.

Gordon, Diana. *The Justice Juggernaut: Fighting Street Crime, Controlling Citizens.* New Brunswick, NJ: Rutgers University Press, 1990.

Gordon, Suzanne. "Women Finally Emerging from Male Shadow." *Boston Globe,* June 24, 1991.

Green, Dorothy. "Patterns of Violence Over a 28-Year Span in a Woman's Correctional Institution." Interview, May 17, 1991.

Gosselin, Peter G., and Peter Mancusi. " 'Blip' in Records Led U.S. Investigators to Boston Banks." *Boston Globe,* March 17, 1985.

Gottlieb, Alan M. *Gun Rights Fact Book.* Bellevue, WA: Merril Press, 1988.

Greenwood, Peter. "The Violent Offender in the Criminal Justice System." In *Criminal Violence,* Marvin Wolfgang and Neil Weiner, eds. Beverly Hills, CA: Sage Publications, 1982.

Greer, Colin. " 'We Must Take a Stand.' " *Parade Magazine,* April 28, 1991.

Gross, Jane. "Epidemic in Urban Hospitals: Wounds from Assault Rifles." *New York Times,* February 21, 1989.

Gugliotta, Guy, and Jeff Leen. *Kings of Cocaine: Inside the Medellin Cartel.* New York: Simon and Schuster, 1989.

Hall, Edward. *The Hidden Dimension.* New York: Anchor Books, 1990.

———. *The Silent Language.* New York: Anchor Books, 1973.

Hallock, David. "College Nightmare." *U.S. News & World Report,* April 8, 1991.

Hand, Douglas. "Morality Lessons? Hear! Hear!" *New York Times,* April 9, 1989.

Handgun Control, Inc. "Handgun Control Semi-Annual Progress Report." Washington, DC: Handgun Control, Inc., January 1991.

Hardy, James Earl. "A World of Pain." *Scholastic Update,* January 25, 1991.

Harrington-Lueker, Donna. "Protecting Schools from Outside Violence." *Education Digest,* December 1990.

Harrison, Eric. " 'Murder Epidemic' Alarms Chicago." *Los Angeles Times,* June 23, 1990.

Hazelton, Lesley. "British Soccer: The Deadly Game" *New York Times Magazine,* May 7, 1989.

———. *England Bloody England,* New York: Atlantic Monthly, 1990.

Heilbroner, David. *Rough Justice.* New York: Pantheon Books, 1990.

———. "Trials and Errors." *Northeastern University Alumni Magazine,* September 1990.

Henry, William III. "Upside Down in the Groves of Academe." *Time,* April 1, 1991.

Hirsch, Kathleen. "Fraternities of Fear." *Ms.,* September/October 1990.

Hobson, Barbara Meil. *Uneasy Virtue: The Politics of Prostitution and the American Reform Tradition.* New York: Basic Books, 1987.

Hofmann, Paul. "Italy Gets Tough with the Mafia." *New York Times Magazine,* November 13, 1983.

Holbrooke, Richard. "A Dilemma for Washington." *Newsweek,* June 12, 1989.

Holmes, Ronald. *Profiling Violent Crime: An Investigative Tool.* Newbury Park, CA: Sage Publications, 1989.

————. *Serial Murder*. Newbury Park, CA: Sage Publications, 1988.

————. *Sex Crimes*. Newbury Park, CA: Sage Publications, 1991.

Hook, Donald. *Death in the Balance: The Debate over Capital Punishment*. Lexington, MA: Lexington Books, 1989.

Howe, Peter. "Dukakis OK's Ban on Assault Weapons." *Boston Globe,* December 10, 1989.

————. "Killings in Chinatown: Clubs Part of Neighborhood Fabric." *Boston Globe,* January 13, 1991.

————. "6 Gunned Down at Chinatown Club; 5 Are Dead." *Boston Globe,* January 13, 1991.

Hughes, Robert. "The N.R.A. in a Hunter's Sight." *Time,* April 3, 1989.

Hyer, Marjorie. "Activists Lose on Appeal." *Washington Post,* April 1, 1989.

Ingersol, Sandra, and Susan Patton. *Treating Perpetrators of Sexual Abuse*. Lexington, MA: Lexington Books, 1990.

Ingram, Carl. "No Pattern Seen in Road Shootings." *Los Angeles Times,* August 19, 1987.

Jackson, Lisa. "Society Loves a Good Victim." *Newsweek,* July 24, 1989.

Jacobbi, Marianne. "The Woman Who Had to Speak Out." *Good Housekeeping,* August 1990.

Jacobs, Sally. "Gang Rivalry on the Rise in Boston." *Boston Globe,* March 26, 1989.

Jacoby, Susan. *Wild Justice: The Evolution of Revenge*. New York: Harper & Row, 1976.

Johnson, Brian. "The Reality of Rape." *Maclean's,* October 24, 1988.

Johnson, Dirk. "Police Abuse Is Down, But Concern Has Risen." *New York Times,* October 29, 1989.

Johnson, Holly. "Homicide in Canada." *Canadian Social Trends,* Winter 1987.

Johnson, Joan. *The Cult Movement*. New York: Franklin Watts, 1984.

Johnson, Kirk. "Long Drug Sentences Run into a Barrier." *New York Times,* July 25, 1989.

Kahn, Joseph. "Testing Individual Rights: Two Cases." *Boston Globe Magazine,* April 7, 1991.

Kaihla, Paul. " 'Violence Is Nice. Honestly.' " *Maclean's,* May 22, 1989.

Kandell, Jonathan. "Prosperity Born of Pain." *New York Times,* July 7, 1991.

Kantrowitz, Barbara. "Growing Up Under Fire." *Newsweek,* June 10, 1991.

Kaplan, David. "Violence in Our Culture." *Newsweek,* April 1, 1991.

Kaplan, David and Alec Dubro. *Yakuza: The Explosive Account of Japan's Criminal Underworld*. Reading, MA: Addison-Wesley Publishing Company, 1986.

Kaslow, Amy. "Furor Over BCCI Scandal Draws In More Agencies." *Christian Science Monitor,* August 5, 1991.

————. "Rogue Bank Casts Its Net Worldwide." *Christian Science Monitor,* November 12, 1991.

————. "Unraveling of BCCI's Secret Tapestry Begins." *Christian Science Monitor,* August 16, 1991.

Kaufman, Irving. "The Battle Over Drug Testing." *New York Times,* October 19, 1986.

Kaufman, Jonathan. "The Collective Good." *Boston Globe Magazine,* April 7, 1991.

Kauffman, Kelsey. *Prison Officers and Their World,* Cambridge, MA: Harvard University Press, 1988.

Keller, Oliver. "The Criminal Personality or Lomborso Revisisted." *Federal Probation,* March 1980.

Kelly, Richard. "Post-Traumatic Stress Syndrome in Police Officers." Interview, March 19, 1991.

Kendall, John, and Jack Jones. "Law Agencies Forming Task Force: 4 Men, Women Held in Highway Shooting Death." *Los Angeles Times,* July 29, 1987.

Kendall, Patricia, and Paul Lazarsfeld. "Problems of Survey Analysis." In *Continuities in Social Research,* ed. Robert Merton and Paul Lazarsfeld. New York: Free Press, 1950.

Kessler, Daniel, Irwin Redlener, and Maria New. "Why Reports of Child Abuse Are 'Unfounded.' " Letter to the editor, *New York Times,* December 27, 1988.

Kifner, John. "New Immigrant Wave from Asia Gives the Underworld New Faces." *New York Times* January 6, 1991.

Kismaric, Carole (ed.). *Forced Out: The Agony of the Refugee in Our Time*. New York: Human Rights Watch and J. M. Kaplan Fund, in association with William Morrow, W. W. Norton, Penguin Books, and Random House, no date (c. 1989).

King, Wayne. "Police Departments Try to Pick Up on Satanism." *New York Times,* July 16, 1989.

————. "Sarah and James Brady Target the Gun Lobby." *New York Times Magazine,* December 9, 1990.

Kleiman, Dena. "Stopping Child Abuse Before It Happens." *New York Times,* January 8, 1989.

Kopstein, Andrea, and Patrice Roth, "Drug Abuse Among Race/Ethnic Minorities." Rockville, MD: National Institute on Drug Abuse, Division of Epipdemiology and Prevention Research, November 1990.

Koretz, Gene. "Crime May Not be as Bad as the Numbers Make It Look." *Business Week,* March 18, 1991.

Kozol, Jonathan. *Rachel and Her Children,* New York: Crown, 1988.

Kravitz, Lee. "Our Crowded Prisons: Do They Cause Crime or Cure It?" *Scholastic Update,* February 9, 1987.

"Kracking Down on Crack." *Time,* January 8, 1990.

Kroes, Wiliam. *Society's Victims—The Police: An Analysis of Job Stress in Policing,* 2d ed. Springfield, IL: Charles C Thomas, 1985.

"Ku Klux Klan Stages Parade Through Palm Beach." *New York Times,* July 29, 1990.

Kunen, James. "Madness in the Heart of the City." *People,* May 22, 1989.

Lacayo, Richard. "Anatomy of an Acquittal." *Time,* May 11, 1992.

———. "Back to the Beat." *Time,* April 1, 1991.

———. "Law and Disorder." *Time,* April 1, 1991.

———. "Noriega on Ice." *Time,* January 15, 1990.

———. "Under Fire." *Time,* January 29, 1990.

LaFraniere, Sharon. "Court Upholds Drug Testing of Justice Department Applicants." *Washington Post,* March 30, 1991.

Landau, Elaine. *On the Streets: The Lives of Adolescent Prostitutes.* New York: Julian Messner, 1987.

Landwehr, Terri. "Coping with Violence in a Maximum Security Prison." Interview, February 9, 1991.

Langreth, Robert. "Pediatric Pain." *Science News,* February 2, 1991.

Laquer, Walter. *The Age of Terrorism.* Boston: Little, Brown, 1987.

LaVey, Anton Szandor. *The Satanic Bible.* New York: Avon, 1969.

———. *The Satanic Rituals.* New York: Avon, 1972.

Law-Yone, Wendy. "Life in the Hills." *Atlantic,* December 1989.

Lawson, Carol. "Hawaii to Screen for Potential Child Abusers." *New York Times,* December 17, 1989.

Lee, Felicia. "Police Consider Gangs of Youth Hard to Combat." *New York Times,* December 11, 1990.

———. "When Violence and Terror Strike Outside the Schools," *New York Times,* November 14, 1989.

Lehr, Dick, and Kevin Cullen. "Hampden DA's Actions Aid Reputed Mafia Figures." *Boston Globe,* January 21, 1990.

Leo, John. "A Criminal Lack of Common Sense." *U.S. News & World Report,* August 21, 1989.

Leslie, Connie. "Pencils, Papers and Guns." *Newsweek,* December 5, 1988.

"Lessons in Violence." *U.S. News & World Report,* February 13, 1989.

Levin, Jack. "The Boomerang Effect." *Bostonia,* September/October, 1989.

———. "Hate Crimes Against Women." *Bostonia,* January/February 1991.

Levin, Jack, and James Alan Fox. *Mass Murder: America's Growing Menace.* New York: Plenum Press, 1985.

Lewin, Tamar. "In Crime, Some Gender-Related Inequities." *New York Times,* January 20, 1991.

———. "Gunshots Cost Hospital $429 Million." *New York Times,* November 29, 1988.

Lewis, Ricki. "DNA Fingerprints: Witness for the Prosecution." *Discover,* June 1988.

Lindy, Jacob. *Vietnam: A Casebook.* New York: Brunner/Mazel, 1988.

Lineberry, William (ed.). *The Struggle Against Terrorism.* New York: W. H. W. Wilson, 1977.

" 'Little Sister' Program Stopped by Assaults." *New York Times,* October 22, 1989.

Lombardo, Robert. "Civil Forfeiture: A Powerful Tool Against Commercial Gambling," *Criminal Organizations,* vol. 5, no. 1, 1990 (Newsletter of the International Association for the Study of Organized Crime).

Lorch, Donatella. "3 Are Found Slain Execution Style Near City Hall." *New York Times,* October 16, 1990.

Lord, Charles O. "Retrain New York Transit Officers to Use the Guns They Have." Letter to the editor, *New York Times,* August 30, 1990.

"Lost Children." *World Press Review,* June 1990.

Lupo, Alan. "The New Mobsters." *Boston Globe Magazine,* May 14, 1989.

Lusane, Clarence. *Pipe Dream Blues: Racism and the War on Drugs.* Boston: South End Press, 1991.

McCall, George, and J.L. Simmons. *Issues in Participant Observation: A Text and a Reader*. Reading, MA: Addison-Wesley, 1969.

Maccoby, Eleanor, and Carol Jacklin, *The Psychology of Sex Differences*, vol. 1. Stanford, CA: Stanford University Press, 1974.

McCombs, Phil. "Unlocking the Criminal Mind." *Washington Post*, March 5, 1984.

McDonald, William (ed.). *The Prosecutor*. Beverly Hills, CA: Sage Publications, 1979.

———. *The Defense Counsel*. Beverly Hills, CA: Sage Publications, 1983.

Mc Fadden, Robert D. "Reliability of DNA Testing Challenged by Judge's Ruling." *New York Times*, August 15, 1989.

McKibben, Gordon. "93 Crushed to Death in Stadium." *Boston Globe*, April 16, 1989.

———. "Soccer Deaths Wound English." *Boston Globe*, April 23, 1989.

McKee, James. "Collective Behavior and Population." *Introduction to Sociology*, New York: Holt, Rinehart, 1969.

Madison, Arnold. *Arson*. New York: Franklin Watts, 1978.

Magid, Ken, and Carole, McKelvey. *High Risk: Children Without a Conscience*. New York: Bantam Books, 1987.

Magnuson, Ed, et al. "Do Guns Save Lives?" *Time*, August 21, 1989.

Magnuson, Ed, et al. "Suicides: The Gun Factor." *Time*, July 17, 1989.

Mahara, Davan, and Len Hall. "2 Are Arrested in Drive-By Shooting of Teen at Home." *Los Angeles Times*, December 31, 1991.

Maio, Kathi. "Hooked on Hate?" *Ms.*, September/October 1990.

Maiuro, Roland, and Jane Eberle. "New Developments in Research on Aggression." *Violence and Victims*, Spring 1989.

Malcolm, Andrew. "More Americans Are Killing Each Other." *New York Times*, December 31, 1989.

———. "More and More, Prison Is America's Answer to Crime." *New York Times*, November 26, 1989.

———. "When Private Employers Hire Public Police." *New York Times*, February 26, 1989.

Marcus, Ruth. "Energized Conservatism Rules High Court Solid Majority Starting to Reverse Decades of Liberal Precedents." *Washington Post*, June 30, 1991.

Martin, Douglas. "Coping with Violence in Overcrowded Jails." *New York Times*, August 30, 1987.

Martz, Larry. "Revolution by Information." *Newsweek*, June 19, 1989.

Martz, Larry, and Peter McKillop. "The Copycat Suicides." *Newsweek*, March 23, 1987.

Marx, Jean L. "DNA Fingerprinting Takes the Witness Stand." *Science*, June 17, 1988.

Massing, Michael. "In the Cocaine War . . . The Jungle Is Winning." *New York Times Magazine*, March 4, 1990.

Mathews, Jay. "Juror Voices Distress Over Sanctuary Defense Failure to Present Witnesses Criticized." *Washington Post*, May 3, 1986.

———. "Reporter, Cleric on Trial in Aliens Case; Pair Accused of Helping to Smuggle Salvadoran Women into U.S." *Washington Post*, July 15, 1986.

———. "On Trial in Tucson: Law vs. Consience Jury Being Picked for 11 Sanctuary Workers." *Washington Post*, October 25, 1985.

———. "Sanctuary Workers Acquitted of Smuggling Illegal Aliens; Albuquerque Verdict Gives Movement Big Legal Victory." *Washington Post*, August 3, 1988.

Mathews, Tom, et al. "The Siege of L.A." *Newsweek*, May 11, 1992.

Mauss, Armand. *Social Problems as Social Movements*. Philadelphia: J.B. Lippincott Co., 1975.

Meggessey, Dave. *Out of Their League*. Berkeley, CA: Ramparts Press, 1970.

Meltz, Barbara F. "Abuse of Another Kind." *Boston Globe*, April 17, 1989.

"Message from the Executive Director . . . The State of the Project." *Community Reclamation Project News*, March 1, 1990.

Meyer, Karl. "Homeless Legion of the Lost." *New York Times Book Review*, April 9, 1989.

Michaud, Stephen G., and Hugh Aynesworth. *Ted Bundy: Conversations with a Killer*. New York: New American Library, 1989.

Micheels, Peter. *Heat: The Fire Investigators and Their War on Arson and Murder.* New York: St. Martin's Press, 1991.

Miedzian, Myriam. *Boys Will Be Boys: Breaking the Link Between Masculinity and Violence.* New York: Doubleday, 1991.

Milgram, Stanley. *Obedience to Authority: An Experimental View.* New York: Harper & Row, 1974.

Miller, Mark. "A Jamaican Invasion in West Virginia." *Newsweek,* March 28, 1988.

Milton S. Eisenhower Foundation. *Youth Investment and Community Reconstruction: Street Lessons on Drugs and Crime in the Nineties, An Executive Summary,* Washington, DC: Milton S. Eisenhower Foundation, 1990.

Milton S. Eisenhower Foundation. "Progress Report," Washington, DC: Milton S. Eisenhower Foundation, undated (1990 or 1991).

Ming Pao News. *A Chronicle of the Chiense Democractic Uprising,* trans. Zi Jin and Qin Zhou. Fayetteville: University of Arkansas Press, 1989.

Moffett, George III. "Bank Failure Robs Needy Children." *Christian Science Monitor,* July 23, 1991.

Mokhiber, Russell. *Corporate Crime and Violence: Big Business Power and the Abuse of the Public Trust.* San Francisco: Sierra Club Books, 1988.

Money, John, and Anke Ehrhardt. *Man and Woman, Boy and Girl.* Baltimore: Johns Hopkins University Press, 1972.

Monroe, Sylvester. "The Fire This Time." *Time,* May 11, 1992.

Montgomery, M. R. "Fanning Fenway." *Boston Globe,* July 8, 1991.

Moorehead, Caroline (ed.). *Betrayal: A Report on Violence Toward Children in Today's World.* New York: Doubleday, 1990.

Morganthau, Tom, et al. "The Drug Gangs." *Newsweek,* March 28, 1988.

Morrow, Lance "Evil." *Time,* June 10, 1991.

———. "Rough Justice." *Time,* April 1, 1991.

Moses, Paul. "Judge Keeps Bosket in His Chains." *Newsday,* June 6, 1989.

"Moving Target." *Time,* May 1, 1989.

Moynahan, James M., and Earle K. Stewart. *The American Jail.* Chicago: Nelson-Hall, 1980.

Murphy, Sean. "Families of Slain Montreal Students Gather for Funeral Ceremonies." *Boston Globe,* December 10, 1989.

Musto, David. *The American Disease.* New York: Oxford University Press, 1988.

Mydans, Seth. "On Guard Against Gangs at a Los Angeles School." *New York Times,* November 19, 1989.

National Advisory Commission on Civil Disorders (Kerner Commission). *Supplemental Studies for The National Advisory Commission on Civil Disorders.* New York: Frederick A. Praeger, 1970.

National Advisory Commission on Civil Disorders (Kerner Commission). *Report.* New York: Bantam, 1968.

National Commission on The Causes and Prevention of Violence. *Violence in America,* Volumes 1–16. New York: Chelsea House, 1983.

Naylor, Robin Thomas. *Hot Money and the Politics of Debt.* New York: Linden Press/Simon and Schuster, 1987.

Neuberger, Maurine. *Smoke Screen: Tobacco and the Public Welfare,* Englewood Cliffs, NJ: Prentice-Hall, 1963.

Neuffer, Elizabeth. "Borderless Europe Beckons to Drug Traffickers." *Boston Globe,* July 15, 1990.

"New Dorm Locks to Foil Intruders? Students Object." *New York Times,* October 14, 1990.

"New Law Ends Parents' Tragic Battle." *USA Today* November 12, 1990.

"The New Refugees." *U.S. News and World Report,* October 23, 1989.

"The Newsletter of Public Safety, Crime Prevention, Asset Protection, Liability Avoidance." *Campus Security Report,* July 1990.

"The Newsletter of Public Safety, Crime Prevention, Asset Protection, Liability Avoidance." *Campus Security Report,* February 1991.

"News Tips." *Office of Media Relations Bulletin,* Washington, DC: Rush-Presbyterian-St. Luke's Medical Center, October 1990.

"New Strategies Appear to Reduce Student Behavior Problems with Neighbors." *Northeastern University Alumni Magazine,* December 1989.

"New Weapons Against Street Crime." *Scholastic Update,* March 21, 1986.

Nichols, John. "A Program for the Predatory Anti-Social." *The Advocate* (American Mental Health Counselors Association) June/July 1991.

Norris, Joel. *Serial Killers: The Growing Menace.* New York: Doubleday, 1989.

O'Ballance, Edgar. *Language of Violence.* San Rafael, CA: Presidio Press, 1979.

O'Brien, Nancy Frazier. "Catholics Work to Ease Plight of Haitians." *The Pilot,* February 28, 1992.

O'Neill, William. *Everyone Was Brave: A History of Feminism in America.* Chicago: Quadrangle Books, 1971.

Oriard, Michael. *The End of Autumn.* Garden City, NY: Doubleday, 1982.

"Outside the Walls." *People,* February 1, 1988.

Pantridge, Margaret. "Rx for Fear." *Boston Magazine,* February 1990.

Parmley, Suzette. "Children Who Molest Children." *Boston Globe,* January 14, 1991.

Parrot, Andrea. *Date Rape & Acquaintance Rape.* New York: Rosen Publishing Group, 1988.

Patnoe, Jerry. "Book Review of *Inside the Criminal Mind.*" *Journal of Criminal Law and Criminology,* vol. 76, 1985.

Peirson, Gwynne. *Police Operations.* Chicago: Nelson-Hall, 1976.

Petersilia, J., and P. Honig, with C. Hubay. *The Prison Experience of Career Criminals* (R-2511-DOJ). Santa Monica, CA: Rand Corporation, 1971.

Phillips, Andrew. "Death in the Stands." *Maclean's,* April 24, 1989.

Pileggi, Nicholas. *Wiseguy: Life in the Mafia Family.* New York: Pocket Books, 1985.

"Policing the Police." *Time,* September, 10, 1990.

Pomice, Eva. "From Organized Crime to Organization Men." *U.S. News and World Report,* May 16, 1988.

Posner, Gerald. *Warlords of Crime: Chinese Secret Societies—The New Maifa.* New York: McGraw-Hill, 1988.

Postman, Neil. *The Disappearance of Childhood,* New York: Delacorte Press, 1982.

"President Urges Changes in Policy on Sex Assaults." *New York Times,* December 2, 1990.

Prothrow-Stith, Deborah. "The Epidemic of Violence and Its Impact on the Health Care System." *Henry Ford Hospital Medical Journal,* vol. 38, nos. 2, & 3, 1990.

Prothrow-Stith, Deborah, and Felton J. Earls. "Adolescent Violence and the Prevention of Violence." Lecture, Harvard School of Public Health, February 28, 1991.

Prothrow-Stith, Deborah, and Howard Spivak. "Three Ways to Ease Adolescent Violence." *Boston Globe,* April 29, 1991.

Pruett, Kyle. *The Nurturing Father.* New York: Warner Books, 1987.

Pummer, Christopher. "Teen-agers Arrested Over Shots at Cars." *Los Angeles Times,* December 21, 1991.

Purdum, Todd. "The Reality of Crime on Campus." *New York Times,* April 10, 1988.

Raab, Selwyn. "Getting the Drop on the Mob." *New York Times,* December 2, 1984.

Radin, Charles. "Poetry in Prison." *Boston Globe,* April 7, 1991.

———. "Tufts Students Find a World of Subject Matter." *Boston Globe,* March 21, 1991.

"Rape: Not by Strangers." *Economist,* February 25, 1989.

Raposa, Laura. "Airlines Cut Fares to Battle Gulf War Jitters." *Boston Herald,* February 12, 1991.

Reid, Paul. "Action Must Come from Within the Community." *Boston Globe,* April 29, 1991.

Relin, David Oliver. "Lost to the Streets." *Scholastic Update,* January 25, 1991.

Renner, Thomas C. *Mafia Enforcer: A True Story of Life and Death in the Mob.* New York: Bantam Books, 1987.

Ressler, Robert, and Tom Shachtman. *Whoever Fights Monsters . . . . : A Brilliant FBI Detective's Career-Long War Against Serial Killers.* New York: St. Martin's Press, 1992.

Reuters. "Drive-By Gunfire Kills 7 in Colombia Drug City." *Boston Globe,* October 15, 1990.

Euters. "19 Girls Reported Killed in Kenya Dorm Attack." *Boston Globe,* July 15, 1991.

Ribadeneira, Diego. "Weapons Are an Ominous Part of a School Day in Boston." *Boston Globe,* November 18, 1990.

Riley, Michael. "Corridors of Agony." *Time,* January 27, 1992.

Robb, Christina. "Are We Hooked on Media Violence?" *Boston Globe,* July 8, 1991.

———. "Is Vengeance Ours?" *Boston Globe Magazine,"* April 16, 1989.

Robert Wood Johnson Foundation. "Urban Hospitals Tackle Tough Public Health Problems with Innovative Programs." *Advances* (national newsletter of the Robert Wood Johnson Foundation), Fall 1990.

Roberts, Steven, et al. "The New Refugees." *U.S. News and World Report,* October 23, 1989.

Ropby, Pamela. "Prostitution and Politics." In *Social Problems and Public Policy: Deviance and Liberty,* ed. Lee Rainwater. New York: Aldine Publishing Co., 1974.

Rodman, F. Robert. "Shattered Children." *New York Times Book Review,* December 17, 1989.

Rule, Sheila. "British Debate Entry of Hong Kong Refugees." *New York Times,* July 23, 1989.

———. "British Homosexuals Report Rise in Attacks." *New York Times,* August 19, 1990.

Rule, Ann. "Rape on Campus." *Good Housekeeping,* September 1989.

———. *The Stranger Beside Me.* New York: Norton, 1980.

Russell, Thomas. "Repatriated Haitians Being Harassed, Says U.S. Nun." *The Pilot,* March 20, 1992.

Salholz, Eloise. "Short Lives, Bloody Deaths." *Newsweek,* December 17, 1990.

Samenow, Stanton. *Inside the Criminal Mind.* New York: Time Books, 1984.

Sandza, Richard. "The NRA Comes Under the Gun." *Newsweek,* March 27, 1989.

Scharf, Peter, and Arnold Binder. *The Badge and the Bullet.* Westport, CT: Prager Publishers, 1983.

Schmalz, Jeffrey. "Children Shooting Children: Move Is on for Gun Control." *New York Times,* June 18, 1989.

Schmeck, Harold, Jr. "DNA and Crime: Identification from a Single Hair." *New York Time,* April 12, 1988.

"School for Hard Knocks." *Time,* June 13, 1988.

Sege, Irene. "The Grim Mystery of World's Missing Women: In Asia, The Ratio of Boys to Girls Is Way Out of Line." *Boston Globe,* February 3, 1992.

"7 Deadly Days." *Time,* July 17, 1989.

Shannon, Elaine. "Back to the Beat." *Time,* April 1, 1991.

Shearer, Lloyd. "Does Beating Deter Delinquency?" *Parade Magazine,* December 3, 1989.

Sherman, L. W., and R. H. Langworthy. "Measuring Homicide by Police Officers." *Journal of Criminal Law and Criminology,* Winter 1979.

Shengold, Leonard. *Soul Murder: The Effects of Childhood Abuse and Deprivation.* New Haven, CT: Yale University Press, 1989.

"Should You Own a Gun for Protection?" *U.S. News and World Report,* May 8, 1989.

Shover, Neal. *Aging Criminals.* Beverly Hills, CA: Sage Publications, 1974.

"The Sicilian Connection." *Time,* October 15, 1984.

Simon, Julian. *Basic Research Methods in Social Science: The Art of Empirical Investigation.* New York: Random House, 1969.

Simpson, Peggy. "Conflict in Academia: Why Was Bunny Sandler Sacked?" *Ms.,* November/December, 1990.

"Small Turnout at White Supremacist Rally in Atlanta." *New York Times,* January 7, 1990.

Smith, Michael. *Violence and Sport.* Toronto: Butterworth, 1983.

Smith, Vern, et al. "Children of the Underclass." *Newsweek,* September 11, 1989.

Smolowe, Jill. "Closing the Doors: With Millions of People in Search of Asylum, Compassion Is Drying Up." *Time,* July 3, 1989.

"A Snitch's Story: In L.A., An Informer Blows the Whistle on Himself." *Time,* December 12, 1988.

"Special Report: Colleges and Student Safety." *USA Today,* September 28, 1990.

Stanger, Ted. "New Mandate: Shoot to Kill." *Newsweek,* April 8, 1991.

"Stages of Post-Trauma Reactions." *MADD, Massachusetts Newsletter,* Winter 1989/1990.

Stanley, Alessandra. "Child Warriors." *Time,* June 18, 1990.

Statman, Jan Berliner. *The Battered Woman's Survival Guide.* Dallas, TX: Taylor Publishing Company, 1990.

Steinway, Susan. "The Fear Index." *Boston Magazine,* February 1990.

Sterling, Claire. *Octopus: The Long Reach of the International Sicilian Mafia.* New York: W.W. Norton, 1990.

———. *The Terror Network, The Secret War of International Terrorism.* New York: Reader's Digest Press, 1981.

Stewart, James. *Den of Thieves.* New York: Simon & Schuster, 1991.

Strahinich, John. "Snitch." *Boston,* March 1991.

"Students' Fears Prompt New Steps on Campus Safety." *New York Times,* November 25, 1990.

"Studies Link TV to Early Suicide." *New York Times,* September 14, 1986.

"Study Cites a Vulnerability to Suicide." *New York Times,* November 21, 1989.

"Suicide Brains: Naturally Prone to Pain." *Science News,* November 10, 1990.

"Suicide Rise." *World Press Review,* December 1990.

Sullivan, Mercer. *"Getting Paid: Youth, Crime, and Work in the Inner City.* Ithaca, NY: Cornell University Press, 1989.

"Suspect Arrested in Razor Attacks." *New York Times,* January 21, 1990.

Sutherland, Edwin, and Donald Cressey. *The Principles of Criminology.* Philadelphia: Lippincott, 1974.

Tarshis, Lauren. "The World's Shame." *Scholastic Update,* January 25, 1991.

Tatum, Jack, and Bill Kushner. *They Call Me Assassin.* New York: Everest House, 1979.

Tavris, Carol. *Anger: The Misunderstood Emotion.* New York: Simon and Schuster, 1989.

Thomas, Charles, and Donna Bishop. *Criminal Law: Understanding Basic Principles.* Newburg Park, California: Sage Publications, 1987.

Ticer, Scott. "The Search for Ways to Break Out of the Prison Crisis." *Business Week,* May 8, 1989.

Timerman, Jacobo. *Prisoner Without a Name, Cell Without a Number.* New York: Alfred A. Knopf, 1981.

Toufexis, Anastasia. "Report Cards Can Hurt You." *Time,* May 1, 1989.

Tomasson, Robert. "21 States Imposing Drug Tax and Then Fining the Evaders." *New York Times,* December 23, 1990.

Torrey, E. Fuller. *Nowhere to Go.* New York: Harper & Row, 1988.

"To Stem the Violence." *Boston Globe,* April 29, 1991.

Traynor, Bernard. "Civil War for Army?" *New York Times,* June 6, 1989.

Treaster, Joseph. "Trench Battle Routs Drugs in the Bronx." *New York Times,* February 12, 1991.

Treen, Joseph. "For Some Chinese, Life in US Entails Slavery." *Boston Globe,* January 7, 1991.

Turner, Renee. "Date Rape." *Ebony,* December 1990.

Tye, Larry. "Hate Crimes on Rise in US." *Boston Globe,* July 29, 1990.

————. "Louisiana Case Galvanizes Death Penalty Debate." *Boston Globe,* May 17, 1990.

Ubell, Earl. "Whodunit? Quick, Check the Genes!" *Parade Magazine,* March 31, 1991.

"U.N. Assembly Adopts Doctrine Outlining Children's Basic Rights." *New York Times,* November 21, 1989.

Underwood, Nora, and David Lindorff. "Dangerous Times: Teenagers Brutally Assault a New York City Woman." *Maclean's,* May 8, 1989.

U.S. Congress, Office of Technology Assessment. *Criminal Justice, New Technologies, and the Constitution,* OTA-CIT-366. Washington, DC: U.S. Government Printing Office, May 1988.

U.S. Department of Defense. *Terrorist Group Profiles.* Washington, DC: Government Printing Office, 1988.

U.S. Department of Health and Human Services. *Report of the Secretary's Task Force on Youth Suicide,* vols. 1–4. Washington, DC: U.S. Department of Health and Human Services, January 1989.

U.S. Department of Justice. *Uniform Crime Reports: Crime in the United States, 1989.* Washington, DC: U.S. Department of Justice, 1990.

————. *Uniform Crime Reports: Crime in the United States, 1990.* Washington, DC: U.S. Department of Justice, 1991.

————. *Sourcebook of Criminal Justice Statistics, 1990.* Washington, DC: U.S. Department of Justice, 1991.

U.S. Senate. "Hearing Before the Committee on the Judiciary, United States Senate, 101st Congress, 2d Session, On Legislation to Reduce the Growing Problem of Violent Crime Against Women, Part 1." Washington, DC: Government Printing Office, June 20, 1990.

U.S. Senate. "Hearing Before the Committee on the Judiciary, United States Senate, 101st Congress, 2d Session, On Legislation to Reduce the Growing Problem of Violent Crime Against Women, Part 2." Washington, DC: Government Printing Office, August 29, 1990 and December 11, 1990.

Vachss, Andrew. "How We Can Fight Child Abuse." *Parade Magazine,* August 20, 1989.

van den Haag, Ernest, and John Conrad. *The Death Penalty: A Debate.* New York: Plenum Press, 1983.

Vann Woodward, C. *The Strange Career of Jim Crow,* 2d rev. ed. London: Oxford University Press, 1966.

"Violent Crime in US Rose 10% in 1990, FBI Reports." *Boston Globe,* April 29, 1991, reprinted from Washington Post.

Volk, Patricia. "Being Safe." *New York Times Magazine,* February 11, 1990.

Walker, Lenore. "Terrifying Love." *New York Times,* December 31, 1989.

Waller, Douglas. "A World Awash in Refugees." *Newsweek,* October 9, 1989.

Wambaugh, Joseph. *The Blooding.* New York: Bantam, 1989.

Ward, Colin. *Vandalism.* New York: Van Nostrand Reinhold, 1973.

Warren, Roland. *Politics and the Ghettos.* New York: Atherton Press, 1969.

Warrior, Betsy. *Battered Women's Directory,* 8th ed., Cambridge, MA: Author, 1982.

Warshaw, Robin. *I Never Called It Rape.* New York: Harper & Row, 1988.

Watson, Russell, et al. "Reign of Terror." *Newsweek,* June 19, 1989.

WCVB-TV (ABC Affiliate). "Early Release." Segment of nightly program *Chronicle,* January 6, 1991.

Webb, Eugene, et al. *Unobtrusive Measures.* Chicago: Rand McNally, 1966.

Wedge, Thomas. *Satan Hunters.* Canton, OH: Daring Books, 1988.

Wen, Patricia, and Paul Feeney. "Three Students Held After Bomb Explodes in Locker." *Boston Globe,* April 16, 1988.

Weisburd, Stefi. "Fingerprinting DNA from a Single Hair." *Science News,* April 23, 1988.

Weiss, Joan. "Prejudice, Conflict, and Ethnoviolence." *USA Today,* May 1989.

Weissmann, Gerald. *The Woods Hole Cantata.* Boston: Houghton-Mifflin, 1985.

"What Readers Say." *Parade Magazine,* April 8, 1990.

Wheeler, Linda. "Washington's Jewel of a Park Losing Its Luster to Vandalism" *Washington Post,* February 24, 1990.

Whitney, Craig. "The Rage That Is Unleashed in Soccer Stadiums." *New York Times,* April 23, 1989.

———. "Stamping Out the Fire of Religious Violence Is as Hopeless as Ever." *New York Times,* May 21, 1989.

Wilkinson, Peter. "Darkness at the Heart of Town." *Rolling Stone,* October 5, 1989.

Will, George. "Playing with Guns." *Newsweek,* March 27, 1989.

Wilson, Colin, and Donald Seaman. *The Encyclopedia of Modern Murder.* New York: Arlington House, 1988.

Wilson, Edward O. *Sociobiology: The New Synthesis.* Cambridge, MA: Harvard University Press, 1975.

Wilson-Smith, A. "Gang Warfare, Soviet-Style." *Maclean's,* May 22, 1989.

Winslow, Robert. *Society in Transition: A Social Approach to Deviancy.* New York: Free Press, 1970.

Wisconsin Correctional System, Thompson Correctional Center. Wisconsin Training Packet, June 1989.

Witkin, Gordon, Ted Gest, and Dorian Friedman. "Cops Under Fire." *U.S. News and World Report,* December 3, 1990.

Witkin, Gordon, et al. "Kids Who Kill." *U.S. News and World Report,* April 8, 1991.

Wolff, Craig. "Flatbush Youths Harass Strollers in the Village." *New York Times,* May 28, 1989.

Wolfgang, Marvin, and Neil Alan Weiner (eds.). *Criminal Violence.* Beverly Hills, CA: Sage, 1982.

"Women and Hate Crimes." *National NOW Times,* March/April 1991.

Wood, Chris, et al. "Police Under Fire." *Maclean's,* January 9, 1989.

Woodward, Whitney. "When You Run: The Problems That Follow." *Teen,* October, 1989.

Wright, C. E. "Child Abuse: A Vicious Cycle." Letter to the editor, *Science News,* March 2, 1991.

Wulach, James. "The Criminal Personality as a DSM-III-R Antisocial, Narcissistic, Borderline, and Histrionic Personality Disorder." *International Journal of Offender Therapy and Comparitive Criminology,* December 1988.

Wulf, Steve. "Brawl Game." *Sports Illustrated,* August 27, 1990.

Wyman, Anne. "Sexually Abused as Children, 2 Talk of Rage." *Boston Globe,* April 23, 1989.

Yochelson, Samuel, and Stanton Samenow. *The Criminal Personality, Volume I: A Profile for Change.* New York: Jason Aronson, 1976.

———. *The Criminal Personality, Volume II: The Change Process.* New York: Jason Aronson, 1977.

Young, Leotine. *Wednesday's Children: A Study of Child Neglect and Abuse.* New York: McGraw-Hill, 1964.

Zia, Helen. "Women in Hate Groups." *Ms.*, March/April, 1991.
Zimmer, Lynn. "Risk Is Too Great." Letter to the editor, *New York Times,* August 30, 1990.
Zimring, Franklin E., and Gordon Hawkins. *The Citizens Guide to Gun Control,* New York: Macmillan, 1987.
Zinmeister, Karl. "Growing Up Scared." *Atlantic Monthly,* June 1990.
Zobel, Hiller. "Calling It 'Date Rape' Doesn't Change a Thing." *Boston Globe,* December 10, 1989.

INDEX

Boldface locators indicate main headings.